Innovation, Strategy, and Transformation Frameworks for the Modern Enterprise

Anacleto Correia
Portuguese Naval Academy, Portugal

Pedro B. Agua
Portuguese Naval Academy, Portugal

A volume in the Advances in Business Strategy and Competitive Advantage (ABSCA) Book Series

IGI Global
PUBLISHER of TIMELY KNOWLEDGE

Published in the United States of America by
IGI Global
Business Science Reference (an imprint of IGI Global)
701 E. Chocolate Avenue
Hershey PA, USA 17033
Tel: 717-533-8845
Fax: 717-533-8661
E-mail: cust@igi-global.com
Web site: http://www.igi-global.com

Library of Congress Cataloging-in-Publication Data

Names: Correia, Anacleto, 1961- editor. | Água, Pedro B., 1968- editor.
Title: Innovation, strategy, and transformation frameworks for the modern enterprise / edited by Anacleto Correia, and Pedro B. Água.
Description: Hershey, PA : Business Science Reference, 2023. | Includes bibliographical references and index. | Summary: "The book provides a quick introduction to the topic by exploring frameworks in contemporary businesses. Frameworks are the organized and methodical techniques that businesses use to solve particular difficulties, manage processes, and make choices based on accurate information. They offer a shared understanding of best practices in numerous domains, including enterprise architecture, IT service management, business process management, project management, IT governance, agile methodologies, and innovation. Organizations can build a strong foundation and adapt to a rapidly changing business environment by incorporating these frameworks"-- Provided by publisher.
Identifiers: LCCN 2023029650 (print) | LCCN 2023029651 (ebook) | ISBN 9798369304587 (hardcover) | ISBN 9798369304624 (paperback) | ISBN 9798369304594 (ebook)
Subjects: LCSH: Business enterprises--Technological innovations.
Classification: LCC HD45 .I53785 2023 (print) | LCC HD45 (ebook) | DDC 658.4/063--dc23/eng/20230719
LC record available at https://lccn.loc.gov/2023029650
LC ebook record available at https://lccn.loc.gov/2023029651

This book is published in the IGI Global book series Advances in Business Strategy and Competitive Advantage (ABSCA) (ISSN: 2327-3429; eISSN: 2327-3437)

British Cataloguing in Publication Data
A Cataloguing in Publication record for this book is available from the British Library.

For electronic access to this publication, please contact: eresources@igi-global.com.

Advances in Business Strategy and Competitive Advantage (ABSCA) Book Series

Patricia Ordóñez de Pablos
Universidad de Oviedo, Spain

ISSN:2327-3429
EISSN:2327-3437

Mission

Business entities are constantly seeking new ways through which to gain advantage over their competitors and strengthen their position within the business environment. With competition at an all-time high due to technological advancements allowing for competition on a global scale, firms continue to seek new ways through which to improve and strengthen their business processes, procedures, and profitability.

The **Advances in Business Strategy and Competitive Advantage (ABSCA) Book Series** is a timely series responding to the high demand for state-of-the-art research on how business strategies are created, implemented and re-designed to meet the demands of globalized competitive markets. With a focus on local and global challenges, business opportunities and the needs of society, the **ABSCA** encourages scientific discourse on doing business and managing information technologies for the creation of sustainable competitive advantage.

Coverage

- Strategic Alliances
- Core Competencies
- Differentiation Strategy
- Strategy Performance Management
- Small and Medium Enterprises
- Resource-Based Competition
- Outsourcing
- Ethics and Business Strategy
- Value Creation
- Co-operative Strategies

IGI Global is currently accepting manuscripts for publication within this series. To submit a proposal for a volume in this series, please contact our Acquisition Editors at Acquisitions@igi-global.com or visit: http://www.igi-global.com/publish/.

The Advances in Business Strategy and Competitive Advantage (ABSCA) Book Series (ISSN 2327-3429) is published by IGI Global, 701 E. Chocolate Avenue, Hershey, PA 17033-1240, USA, www.igi-global.com. This series is composed of titles available for purchase individually; each title is edited to be contextually exclusive from any other title within the series. For pricing and ordering information please visit http://www.igi-global.com/book-series/advances-business-strategy-competitive-advantage/73672. Postmaster: Send all address changes to above address.

Titles in this Series

For a list of additional titles in this series, please visit: www.igi-global.com/book-series

Transformational Interventions for Business, Technology, and Healthcare
Darrell Norman Burrell (Marymount University USA)
Business Science Reference • © 2023 • 440pp • H/C (ISBN: 9798369316344) • US $295.00

Handbook of Research on Designing Sustainable Strategies to Develop Entrepreneurial Intention
Ramakrishna Yanamandra (Skyline University College, UAE) and Logaiswari Indiran (Universiti Teknologi Malaysia, Malysia)
Business Science Reference • © 2023 • 642pp • H/C (ISBN: 9781668487815) • US $295.00

Strategic Management and International Business Policies for Maintaining Competitive Advantage
Ailson J. De Moraes (Royal Holloway University of London, UK)
Business Science Reference • © 2023 • 411pp • H/C (ISBN: 9781668468456) • US $295.00

Digital Natives as a Disruptive Force in Asian Businesses and Societies
Omkar Dastane (UCSI Graduate Business School, UCSI University, Malaysia) Aini Aman (Universiti Kebangsaan Malaysia, Malaysia) and Nurhizam Safie Bin Mohd Satar (Universiti Kebangsaan Malaysia, Malaysia)
Business Science Reference • © 2023 • 322pp • H/C (ISBN: 9781668467824) • US $250.00

Handbook of Research on Sustainable Consumption and Production for Greener Economies
Richa Goel (Symbiosis International University, India) and Sukanta Kumar Baral (Indira Gandhi National Tribal University, India)
Business Science Reference • © 2023 • 481pp • H/C (ISBN: 9781668489697) • US $295.00

Cases on the Resurgence of Emerging Businesses
Shefali Saluja (Chitkara Business School, Chitkara University, India) Dhiresh Kulshrestha (Chitkara Business School, Chitkara University, India) and Sandhir Sharma (Chitkara Business School, Chitkara University, India)
Business Science Reference • © 2023 • 316pp • H/C (ISBN: 9781668484883) • US $265.00

Handbook of Research on Sustainability Challenges in the Wine Industry
Bartolomé Marco-Lajara (University of Alicante, Spain) Armand Gilinsky (Sonoma State University, USA) Javier Martínez-Falcó (University of Alicante, Spain & Stellenbosch University, South Africa) and Eduardo Sánchez-García (University of Alicante, Spain)
Business Science Reference • © 2023 • 435pp • H/C (ISBN: 9781668469422) • US $295.00

IGI Global
PUBLISHER of TIMELY KNOWLEDGE

701 East Chocolate Avenue, Hershey, PA 17033, USA
Tel: 717-533-8845 x100 • Fax: 717-533-8661
E-Mail: cust@igi-global.com • www.igi-global.com

Table of Contents

Detailed Table of Contents

In this work, the authors design a combined system of blockchain and value stream mapping (BVSM) to monitor and improve production processes. The proposed blockchain value stream mapping (BVSM) system not only captures real-time performance but also helps to improve the performance of the manufacturing process. The transparent, immutable, decentralized, and accurate blockchain information is transferred to the value stream mapping (VSM) system to reflect dynamically the status of the manufacturing process. All changes in the production process are continuously monitored to help managers quickly make appropriate improvement decisions. Two case studies of a garment company in Vietnam and a JCB factory in India from a reference are used to illustrate the implementation of the proposed BVSM system.

This chapter focuses on the process-oriented model for software development using the PRINCE2 method, and it is divided into two primary parts. The first part offers a theoretical overview of project management, encompassing project definition, the definition and classification of project management, including the characteristics of both traditional and agile project management. Additionally, within this part, the process of software development and the key characteristics of PRINCE2 are presented, including the description of the processes defined by the mentioned method. The second part of the chapter is dedicated to integrating the software development process with the PRINCE2 processes. The constructed process-oriented model includes the nine phases with both the PRINCE2 processes and software development processes intertwined. Based on a critical review of the usefulness of the integration model, the advantages and disadvantages are presented. This well-structured model can significantly contribute to the successful management of software projects.

Toyota Motor's success as a global brand automobile manufacturer has inspired manufacturing organizations worldwide to pursue lean transformation. However, a lack of understanding of lean sustainability hampers their progress towards achieving true lean organization status like Toyota. Without proper measurement, the gains from lean improvements remain unknown, leading to inaccuracies in strategy deployment. This chapter aims to define sustainable lean transformation gains and propose indicators to measure them. Extensive literature review reveals the importance of tangible and intangible indicators. To validate the proposed measurements, a survey involving 7 lean experts and 92 practitioners was conducted. Data analysis utilized content validity index, inter-rater agreement, and measurement model analysis. The chapter concludes by suggesting research opportunities to enhance lean management knowledge.

This chapter presents a method, applicable to the program and project portfolio prioritization procedures, named RAB2/E matrix (rapidity, autonomy and benefit / extended), where the letter "E" means "extended," since this new approach is derived from another original matrix (RADAR DE PROJETOS 2015) with new features. After performing these procedures related to portfolio prioritization, any project management methodology—such as PMBoK©, PRINCE2®, and ZOPP—can be applied to control the tasks which have to be done. The already mentioned new features were implemented in the prior matrix according to the aspects of internal and external influences perceived. In order to get better comprehension of how this new method was planned, and which were its foundations, this chapter also describes some techniques that can be used as tools for program and project portfolio prioritization. A statistic sample about the implementation of this method RAB2/E matrix are in its conclusions.

This research chapter outlines an improvement process for software development and requirements management in small to medium-sized software companies with teams up to 25 members. It integrates elements from the Waterfall Model and Agile to address challenges in developing software for home loan services in Thai commercial banks. The study aims to achieve Capability Level 3 in the CMMI model, analyzing projects in the Thai software industry. Specific practices SP1.1 – SP1.5 and generic goals GP1.1 – GP3.2 of the requirements management process group are considered, referencing IEEE 12207-2008 and IEEE 1074-2006 standards. The outcomes include developed processes, guidelines, and tested tools. SCAMPI assessment by three experts shows improved benefits realization (avg. score: 4.373), work performance (avg. improvement: 34.34%), and process capability (avg. score: 88.22%), affirming Capability Level 3.

observed that some characteristics of good governance are evident across the majority of the countries examined in this chapter; however, the level of maturity remains relatively weak.

This chapter explores how strategic management systems drive sustainable business models. It discusses the link between sustainability and financial success, leveraging frameworks like RBV and Triple Bottom Line. Practical insights from cases like Unilever and Patagonia are examined, emphasizing stakeholder engagement and performance metrics. The role of emerging trends like circular economy and digitalization is highlighted. The chapter underscores the need for integrating sustainability systematically and offers a roadmap for organizations to achieve lasting impact.

The chapter aims to understand customer perception after the introduction of robots in the robotic mobile fulfillment system (RMFS) storage areas for Amazon. Based on a netnographic analysis focused on the use of RMFS by the American company Amazon, the work is mainly aimed at improving our understanding of the performance of RMFS and the perception of this technology by customers of service companies in general and retail companies in particular. Improved productivity, reduced operation time, agility and flexibility, improved picking accuracy, optimal space utilization, cost of capital, and work ergonomics are the main motivations perceived and discussed by the virtual community behind the introduction of RMFS in Amazon's storage areas. Several risks of RMFS robotization are discussed based on the qualitative study conducted. Finally, a classification of the customers' perception of this new technology is made by distinguishing the variables of perceived usefulness and ease of use.

There is an overreliance on initiating change in the form of projects. This denies potential strategy, increases risk, and generally disrupts operational flow. With the introduction and recognition of more types of change comes the possibility to strategically harness the right type of change that is fit for purpose, and this is just a start to the potential cost saving that organisations can realise. Operational flow is the life blood of an organisation and the way it delivers value to customers. Too many interruptions will not only slow down flow but can stop it all together. This is not a sustainable possibility for an organisation or the smaller units that form it. Strategically using different types of change to increase flow brings a return on investment at the project level and a cumulative ROI overall as flow brought by ChangeOps increases across the organisation in an interlinked system of influence and output.

Much like other governments in the world, the South African government through the Department of Public Service and Administration (DPSA) in collaboration with Government Information Technology Officer Council (GITOC) and the Auditor General (AG) has developed Corporate Governance of Information and Communication Technology Policy Framework (CGICTPF). CGICTPF is based on King III Code of Good Governance, ISO 38500 Standard for the Corporate Governance of ICT, and COBIT as a comprehensive Governance ICT Process Framework and is applicable to all spheres of government. The department of transport was also mandated to implement and use this framework as a government entity to improve the status of ICT government. The chapter is about how CGICTPF was implemented in the public sector using the Department of Transport as a case. Semi-structured open ended interviews data were collected with institutional theory as a lens. It is concluded that management support and proper organizational structures create positive outcomes in environments with high regulatory requirements.

Every day, the business environment is changing rapidly and becoming complex, so organizations must develop new and out of the box strategies and implement such frameworks that can transform the business to another level in this competitive market. In this era, customer preference is the main differentiator, so organizations need to shift their focus to customer experience. Customer experience has become an emerging way of creating a competitive advantage. A customer experience boosts the business growth and drives the revenue for organization by making happy and loyal customers.

The research carried out in the chapter aims to analyze the importance of innovation and ICT as key factors of successful business, that is, to what extent innovation and ICT influence the competitiveness and development of the digital economy in Serbia compared to other countries of the Western Balkans. The research covered the period from 2020 to 2022, while the methodological concept is based on descriptive analysis of secondary data from the World Economic Forum. The results obtained through the research explicitly show that the countries of the Western Balkans do not invest enough funds in the ICT sector, which has a negative impact on their further development and growth of macro-competitiveness. Compared to other countries of the Western Balkans, Serbia is progressing significantly faster in the field of digital transformation. Despite this, it still lags behind the EU countries when it comes to the adoption of ICT, infrastructure, and innovation systems.

Preface

In today's fast-paced and ever-evolving business landscape, enterprises are confronted with unprecedented challenges. The complexities of a rapidly changing world demand that organizations not only adapt but also thrive in the face of uncertainty. To achieve this, enterprises must be equipped with innovative strategies and transformative frameworks that enable them to remain competitive and responsive to market needs. This edited reference book, *Innovation, Strategy, and Transformation Frameworks for the Modern Enterprise*, delves deep into the core frameworks that empower organizations to foster innovation, implement effective strategies, and successfully navigate the digital transformation journey.

Frameworks are the organized and methodical techniques that businesses use to tackle specific challenges, streamline processes, and make informed decisions based on reliable information. They serve as a shared repository of best practices across various domains, including IT service management, business process management, project management, IT governance, agile methodologies, and innovation. Incorporating these frameworks into their operations equips organizations with a sturdy foundation that enables them to adapt to the rapidly changing business environment.

This comprehensive reference book explores a wide range of pertinent and widely adopted frameworks, providing valuable insights into their applications, benefits, and potential synergies. Each chapter of the book is dedicated to a distinct aspect of innovation, strategy, or transformation. Real-world scenarios are illuminated through theoretical discussions, case studies, and practical examples, demonstrating how these frameworks can drive organizational performance and impact business outcomes.

Some authors explore governance models and IT service management. These frameworks give businesses the tools they need to set up efficient methods for managing IT resources and services, improving service effectiveness, efficiency, and regulatory compliance.

A few chapters go into different business process management frameworks, providing information on how businesses can streamline operations, make the most use of their resources, adjust to shifting market conditions, and develop ground-breaking process improvements.

Agile methodologies and project management are also highlighted, with a focus on PRINCE2 and Scrum approaches. With the help of these strategies, businesses can manage challenging projects, foster innovation, lead strategic initiatives, and satisfy stakeholder expectations.

Innovation, Strategy, and Transformation Frameworks for the Modern Enterprise provides a comprehensive understanding of these frameworks and their practical applications across diverse domains. It's a valuable resource for a broad audience, including teachers, instructional designers, curriculum developers, program administrators, educational software developers, policymakers, researchers, education and training professionals, privacy practitioners, government officials, consultants, IT researchers, academicians, and students.

The book's aim is to bridge the gaps between these seemingly disparate subjects, often isolated within their own areas of expertise. By bringing them together within the pages of this book, we hope to create a synergistic effect that promotes increased awareness, iteration, and recursion among the chapters. In doing so, we aspire to highlight the potential interconnections and relationships among ideas from diverse fields, all of which contribute to the ongoing paradigm transformation in business, government, and academia.

The chapters in this book encompass a wide spectrum of topics, from IT service management to sustainability and corporate social responsibility frameworks, reflecting the multifaceted nature of modern enterprise management. As we navigate a world marked by unprecedented changes driven by AI and global dynamics, it is crucial for business, government, and academic leaders to engage in thoughtful reflection about the future of society. This book serves as a platform for such reflection, offering insights that transcend traditional boundaries and foster holistic thinking.

We invite you to embark on this journey through the realms of innovation, strategy, and transformation frameworks. As you delve into the pages of this book, we hope you will discover new perspectives, practical guidance, and the inspiration to explore the potential of these frameworks to drive innovation, implement effective strategies, and navigate the complexities of digital transformation in today's ever-evolving business environment.

CHAPTER OVERVIEW

Chapter 1: "Combining Blockchain With Value Stream Mapping for Production Process Improvement" by Hop Nguyen and Lam Nguyen

This chapter introduces an innovative approach, the Blockchain Value Stream Mapping (BVSM) system, which combines blockchain technology with Value Stream Mapping to monitor and enhance production processes. BVSM not only provides real-time performance insights but also facilitates improvements in manufacturing processes. Through two case studies, one involving a garment company in Vietnam and another at a JCB factory in India, the authors illustrate how BVSM can be implemented to monitor and dynamically reflect the status of manufacturing processes. The BVSM system ensures transparency, immutability, decentralization, and accuracy of information, aiding managers in making rapid, informed decisions for process enhancement.

Chapter 2: "Process-Oriented Model for Managing Software Development Projects Using the PRINCE2 Method" by Katja Kous

This chapter presents a process-oriented model for software development projects, incorporating the PRINCE2 method. The chapter is divided into two main parts. First, it provides a theoretical overview of project management, emphasizing project definition, project management classifications, and characteristics of both traditional and agile project management. It also delves into the software development process and key features of PRINCE2. The second part focuses on integrating software development processes with PRINCE2 processes, creating a well-structured model comprising nine phases. The chapter examines the advantages and disadvantages of this integration model, demonstrating its potential to significantly improve software project management.

Chapter 3: "Towards Achieving a Sustainable Lean Transformation: Measuring Tangible and Intangible Gains" by Azim Osman, Ahmad Noor Kamar, and Syed Rahamadulla

Toyota's success has inspired global manufacturing organizations to pursue lean transformation. However, achieving lean sustainability remains a challenge. This chapter aims to define Sustainable Lean Transformation Gains and proposes indicators to measure them, bridging the gap between lean improvements and strategy deployment. By incorporating both tangible and intangible indicators, the chapter validates the proposed measurements through a survey involving lean experts and practitioners. The chapter concludes by suggesting research opportunities to enhance lean management knowledge and practices.

Chapter 4: "The Method RAB2/E Matrix: An Approach for Effective Program and Project Portfolio Prioritization Procedures" by Altino Moraes

In this chapter, the Method RAB2/E Matrix (Rapidity, Autonomy, Benefit / Extended) is introduced for Program and Project Portfolio Prioritization procedures. Derived from a previous Matrix, this method offers new features that consider internal and external influences that can impact and raise risks in solution development. The chapter explains the planning and foundations of this new method and describes techniques that can be used as tools for prioritization. The chapter also presents a statistical sample illustrating the implementation of the Method RAB2/E Matrix in its conclusions.

Chapter 5: "Attaining CMMI Level 3 With Agile Development in Small-Medium Firms" by Pitiphat Joembunthanaphong

This research chapter outlines an improvement process for software development and requirements management in small to medium-sized software companies. The study integrates elements from the Waterfall Model and Agile to address challenges in developing software for home loan services in Thai commercial banks. The chapter aims to achieve Capability Level 3 in the CMMI model by referencing specific practices and generic goals. The outcomes include developed processes, guidelines, and tested tools, validated through SCAMPI assessment, which affirms Capability Level 3 achievement.

Chapter 6: "Digital Transformation Risks and Uncertainties in European Union and Indian Industry" by Anitha Kumari

The chapter examines the risks and uncertainties of digital transformation in the European Union and Indian industry. It explores the impact of the fourth industrial revolution and digitalization on businesses and presents a digital strategy model and a digital transformation risks and uncertainties framework. Using secondary data and statistics, the chapter offers insights into mitigating risks and uncertainties associated with digital transformation and provides direction for digitalization in businesses.

Chapter 7: "Optimizing Patient Flow in Emergency Care Units Through SMED and Lean Healthcare" by Andrei Bonamigo, Patricia Bernardes, Luiz Conrado, and Robisom Calado

This chapter addresses the challenges in delivering high-quality healthcare with limited resources by applying Lean Healthcare principles. It suggests solutions for implementing Lean in healthcare, focusing on a patient-centered approach, process efficiency through patient pathways, employee feedback, data-driven decision-making, and maximizing human resources. The chapter emphasizes the importance of clear communication, employee motivation, and continuous improvement efforts to improve healthcare efficiency, patient satisfaction, and quality.

Chapter 8: "A Review of Governance Frameworks for National Spatial Data Infrastructure" by Munir Ahmad and Asmat Ali

This chapter examines the governance framework of National Spatial Data Infrastructures (NSDIs) in five South Asian countries. It analyzes six key components underpinning NSDI programs and explores the strategies and structures employed by these countries. The chapter provides insights into how each country approaches NSDI governance, shedding light on the strengths and weaknesses of their respective frameworks.

Chapter 9: "Promoting Strategic Management Systems for Sustainable Business Models: Ideas and Guidance" by Chukwuemeka Azinge

This chapter explores how strategic management systems drive sustainable business models. It discusses the link between sustainability and financial success, leveraging frameworks like RBV and Triple Bottom Line. The chapter offers practical insights from case studies of organizations like Unilever and Patagonia, emphasizing stakeholder engagement and performance metrics. It also highlights emerging trends such as the circular economy and digitalization and provides a roadmap for organizations to integrate sustainability systematically into their core strategies.

Chapter 10: "Consumer Perception of Robotic Mobile Fulfillment Systems: A Netnographic Case Study of Amazon" by Badr Bentalha

This chapter investigates customer perception following the introduction of robots in the Robotic Mobile Fulfillment System (RMFS) storage areas for Amazon. Utilizing a netnographic analysis, the study explores the performance of RMFS and customer perceptions regarding its technology. The chapter delves into the motivations and risks associated with RMFS robotization, offering insights into customer classification based on perceived usefulness and ease of use.

Chapter 11: "ChangeOps: Strategically Harnessing All Types of Change to Create Increased Effectiveness and Operational Flow" by Isolde Kanikani

This chapter challenges the conventional reliance on project-based change initiatives and introduces the concept of ChangeOps. ChangeOps strategically leverages various types of change to enhance operational flow, emphasizing the importance of maintaining a consistent flow of operations in organizations. The chapter highlights the potential cost savings and cumulative return on investment (ROI) associated with implementing ChangeOps across the organization.

Chapter 12: "An Institutional Perspective of CGICTPF Implementation in the Public Sector" by Mampilo Phahlane

This chapter examines the implementation of the Corporate Governance of Information and Communication Technology Policy Framework (CGICTPF) in the public sector, using the Department of Transport as a case study. Through semi-structured interviews and an institutional theory lens, the chapter explores the impact of management support and organizational structures on the success of CGICTPF implementation. It concludes by highlighting the positive outcomes and improved regulatory compliance resulting from effective implementation.

Chapter 13: "Role of Customer Experience-Driven Business Innovation Framework for the Modern Enterprises" by Deepa Sharma, Vinod Kumar, and Sadhna Chauhan

This chapter explores the role of customer experience-driven business innovation in modern enterprises. It emphasizes the significance of customer experience as a competitive differentiator and discusses how it drives business growth and revenue by creating happy and loyal customers. The chapter explores emerging trends and offers practical guidance for organizations to integrate customer experience systematically into their strategies.

Chapter 14: "Innovation and ICT: Key Factors of Successful Business" by Ivana Domazet, Darko Marjanović, Deniz Ahmetagić, and Jadranka Stantić

This research chapter analyzes the importance of innovation and information and communication technology (ICT) as key factors in successful businesses. The study examines their impact on competitiveness and the development of the digital economy in Serbia and the Western Balkans. It highlights the need for increased investment in the ICT sector and compares the progress of Serbia to other countries in the region.

Chapter 15: "Driving Social and Environmental Impact: Exploring Sustainability and Corporate Social Responsibility Frameworks" by Filiz Mızrak

This chapter explores how sustainability and corporate social responsibility (CSR) frameworks drive positive social and environmental impacts for businesses. It analyzes the origins, key principles, and practical applications of these frameworks and examines the societal expectations and regulatory landscape that demand responsible and sustainable business practices. The chapter offers insights into the benefits and challenges of adopting sustainability and CSR and provides case studies of organizations that have successfully integrated these principles into their strategies.

Chapter 16: "Agile and IoT Methodologies in Managing IoT Projects: A Comparative Study" by Soukaina Merzouk, Abdelaziz Marzak, and Nawal Sael

This chapter presents a comparative study of agile and IoT methodologies in managing IoT projects. It evaluates existing methodologies, such as DSDM, DAD, Less, and ELDAMeth, considering their capabilities, characteristics, and behaviors. The chapter aims to assist in selecting the most suitable methodology for IoT projects by identifying their respective advantages and limitations. Additionally, the chapter suggests the potential for a new, approved IoT management methodology.

IN SUMMARY

In conclusion, this edited reference book, *Innovation, Strategy, and Transformation Frameworks for the Modern Enterprise*, represents a comprehensive and invaluable resource for a wide range of professionals and academics navigating the complexities of the modern business landscape. We have embarked on a journey through a diverse set of chapters, each offering unique insights into the critical frameworks that underpin innovation, strategy, and transformation in today's enterprises.

From the pioneering combination of Blockchain and Value Stream Mapping for production process enhancement to the strategic integration of software development with the PRINCE2 method, and from the pursuit of Sustainable Lean Transformation to the implementation of digital strategies in healthcare, this book presents a rich tapestry of ideas and methodologies.

Furthermore, our exploration extends into the realms of governance frameworks for spatial data infrastructure, the role of customer experience-driven business innovation, the impact of innovation and ICT on business success, and the significance of sustainability and corporate social responsibility. Additionally, we delve into the management of IoT projects and the strategic harnessing of change through ChangeOps.

By uniting these diverse topics under one cover, we promote a holistic understanding of the interconnectedness of ideas across various fields. In an era characterized by unprecedented paradigm shifts driven by AI and global dynamics, it is crucial for business, government, and academic leaders to reflect on the future of society within these dimensions.

We believe that the juxtaposition of these chapters within this book offers a unique opportunity for readers to identify potential relations and interconnectedness of ideas across diverse fields, all contributing to the ongoing transformation of business, government, and academia.

This book is designed to serve as a guiding light for those who seek to leverage these frameworks to drive innovation, implement effective strategies, and successfully navigate the complexities of digital transformation in today's fast-paced business environment.

As editors, we hope that this compilation inspires our readers to explore, innovate, and adapt in an ever-changing world. We encourage you to delve into the chapters that resonate most with your interests and challenges, and to use the knowledge within to drive positive change and advancement in your respective domains.

The collective wisdom and expertise within these pages reflect the collaborative efforts of numerous authors who have generously shared their knowledge and experiences. We extend our heartfelt gratitude to all contributors who have made this book possible.

In closing, we invite you to embark on this intellectual journey, explore the diverse frameworks presented herein, and join us in shaping the future of innovation, strategy, and transformation in the modern enterprise.

Warm regards,

Anacleto Correia
Portuguese Naval Academy, Portugal

Pedro B. Água
Portuguese Naval Academy, Portugal

Chapter 1
Combining Blockchain With Value Stream Mapping for Production Process Improvement

Van Nguyen Hop
https://orcid.org/0000-0002-4209-1321
International University, Vietnam National University, Ho Chi Minh City, Vietnam

Hoang Nguyen Lam
International University, Vietnam National University, Ho Chi Minh City, Vietnam

ABSTRACT

In this work, the authors design a combined system of blockchain and value stream mapping (BVSM) to monitor and improve production processes. The proposed blockchain value stream mapping (BVSM) system not only captures real-time performance but also helps to improve the performance of the manufacturing process. The transparent, immutable, decentralized, and accurate blockchain information is transferred to the value stream mapping (VSM) system to reflect dynamically the status of the manufacturing process. All changes in the production process are continuously monitored to help managers quickly make appropriate improvement decisions. Two case studies of a garment company in Vietnam and a JCB factory in India from a reference are used to illustrate the implementation of the proposed BVSM system.

INTRODUCTION

Blockchain technology is a serviceable tool that can provide a lot of positive value to manufacturing systems. Blockchain solutions can seamlessly connect all production stations with secured, real-time, and transparency information that could help to significantly monitor and keep track production process. The blockchain solution could provide some remarkable benefits for manufacturing systems such as:

DOI: 10.4018/979-8-3693-0458-7.ch001

- Operations management: status of raw materials, product movement, production rate, and other process parameters are known exactly for any type of item, at any location, and at any time. Blockchain provides the real-time status of all manufacturing stations with accurate and authentic data. Distributed ledger technology creates an ideal platform for managing every aspect of manufacturing operations.
- Traceability solution: It is difficult for a large company to keep track of every transaction. Blockchain-based solutions can help to record everything in the process chain. With the help of RFID sensors and tags, the blockchain tool could allow the manager to trace back all product's origins and from any transaction point of the manufacturing process such as materials traceability, counterfeit detection, historical versions of engineering designs, property tracking.
- Product management: companies are often difficult to keep track of all items. It could create the chance for scams or low quality statistical data. A distributed ledger function of the blockchain would be the ideal environment for managing products in multiple locations. Data is shared safely and quickly to all participants for different purposes such as quality checking, production control, inventory management, etc.
- Real-time management: the key power function of the blockchain is traceability and authentication. It means that blockchain can provide a real-time tracking solution for not only identifying product location but also updating the current status of the production process. Therefore, human errors and the process performance are continuously monitored for appropriate adjustments, if any.

Besides the benefits of blockchain implementation, the organization also faces some significant challenges such as scalability, user experience, energy efficiency, etc. Specifically, the application of blockchain in production system may include the following key challenges:

- Scalability: one of the most significant challenges for blockchain is scalability. Traditional blockchains like Bitcoin and Ethereum can handle only a limited number of transactions per second. As more participants join the network, the transaction throughput can decrease, leading to slower transaction confirmation times and higher fees.
- User experience: many blockchain applications struggle with user experience issues. Complex wallet management, long confirmation times, and the need for technical expertise can deter mainstream adoption.
- Energy consumption: proof of work consensus mechanisms, as used in Bitcoin, can require substantial energy consumption. This raises concerns about environmental impact and sustainability. Transitioning to more energy-efficient mechanisms, like Proof of Stake, introduces its own set of challenges.
- Adoption and education: blockchain technology is relatively new, and there's a lack of awareness and understanding among the general public. Achieving mass adoption requires not only technological solutions but also educational efforts to help users understand the benefits and risks.
- Lack of standardization: the lack of industry-wide standards can lead to fragmentation and hinder interoperability between different blockchain implementations.

Based on the aforementioned characteristics, two fundamental questions naturally arise: how can we harness the advantages of blockchain to enhance the performance of the manufacturing system? And how can we effectively address the challenges to successfully implement a blockchain-based production system? In response to these inquiries, our research introduces the concept of a Blockchain Value Stream Mapping (BVSM) system. This system not only captures the real-time statuses but also contributes to the enhancement of the production process across multiple dimensions. Furthermore, our study also conducts comprehensive managerial analyses of organizational changes necessary to tackle the challenges associated with blockchain implementation. Derived from these analyses, specific digital transformation strategies and practical guidelines are proposed to facilitate a successful adoption of blockchain technology.

Our contributions in this work are threefold. Firstly, we design a blockchain system to capture all production process information in real-time, immutable, and transparent manner. This enables constant monitoring of any alterations within the production process, empowering managers to promptly make appropriate decisions. With such timely adjustments, manufacturing systems can seamlessly adapt to environmental fluctuations. Secondly, the blockchain-generated information is integrated into the VSM system to recommend improvements across various facets. Moreover, blockchain technology addresses certain limitations of traditional VSM tools, such as unreliable information and sequential processing. Lastly, we conduct a thorough managerial analysis of the organizational changes necessitated by blockchain implementation. This analysis yields specific transformation strategies and practical guidelines that pave the way for effective blockchain adoption.

For a better understanding of the benefits of the combination of a blockchain with the VSM tool, the following Table 1 summarizes the differences between the traditional VSM and the proposed blockchain VSM.

The rest of this chapter will be organized as follows: a thorough literature review is conducted to encompass the up-to-date developments and/or applications of both blockchain and Value Stream Mapping (VSM) within manufacturing systems. The subsequent section describes the proposed system structure and elucidates the implementation process of BVSM for enhancing manufacturing systems. Subsequently, managerial analyses are conducted to identify organization changes, delineate implementation strategies, and provide practical guidelines for the successful integration of blockchain technology into manufacturing environment. In the next section, some results are presented for two real cases of a garment company in Vietnam and a JCB factory in India. The final section summarizes the main research contributions and provides directions for future research.

Table 1. Traditional VSM vs. blockchain VSM

	Blockchain VSM	**Traditional VSM**
Method	Data are collected automatically with real-time confirmation.	Data is not automatically updated.
Data Security	Data is confidential and accurate.	The data is collected from many sources. It leads to deviation and error.
Time	The data collection time is almost instant	It takes a lot of time and manpower to collect data to improve a big-scale system.
Improvement Solution	It is possible to propose various improvement options for different parameters at the same time.	The improvement solution(s) is limited because the data is discrete and inconsistent. It also takes a lot of time to search, analyze and get confirmation from different departments.

LITERATURE REVIEW

Recently, some autonomous tools such as radio frequency identification (RFID), value stream mapping (VSM), and blockchain are often used to visualize and improve complex and dynamic systems such as warehousing systems, transportation systems, and manufacturing systems. In this section, we review the current study and implementation of such advanced technologies to show the need for a combination of these tools for monitoring and enhancing the manufacturing system performance. Furthermore, we also explore the existing literature concerning change management and digital transformation. This investigation aids us in comprehending the challenges, tactical recommendations, and implementation guidelines crucial for the successful adoption of blockchain.

Radio Frequency Identification (RFID)

RFID is a wireless system for storing identification and location information of items or assets. The RFID system includes three components: tags, readers, and software. The tag is a microchip to store information about the items. The reader is a tool to read or write data on the tags. The software is used to receive, process, and transfer the data linked from the reader to the database or the Enterprise Resources Planning (ERP) system. The popular applications of RFID systems are in transportation (Martinus et al., 2021), in supply chain (Zhang et al., 2018), and in production systems (Cao et al., 2018; Ding and Jiang, 2018; Zhang and Wang 2019). In manufacturing systems, the main application of the RFID is to monitor the production flow by its traceability function. Cao et al. (2018) emphasized real-time data collection for processing RFID data of production logistics. Different clusters of multi-attribute RFID information are formed by a similarity model and a clustering solution to detect any issue of the material supply process. Besides the advantages of using RFID systems for ease of production control and tracking production process, Ding and Jiang (2018) also analyzed the RFID production data and revealed that the generated RFID data are increasing and sometimes discrete, uncorrelated, and hard-to-use. A data analytic approach is proposed to extract hidden information and insights to utilize valuable data. In another aspect, Zhang and Wang (2019) focused on determining the optimal location to install RFID devices and developing a heuristic algorithm to control the production system. The objective of these solutions is to reduce both production costs and the negative impact of inventory inaccuracy. Furthermore, Huang et al. (2019) also pointed out that the main shortcomings of using RFID are the burden of manipulating the tags and the burden in the calculation when it is used for real-time or near-real-time data collection. This fact reduces the efficiency of the production process. Occhiuzzi et al. (2019) also summarized the common structures and challenges for RIFD applications in the industry. All these challenges of using RFID in manufacturing systems such as inaccurate data and lack of trust are also recognized in our case study of a garment company in Vietnam.

Blockchain

Blockchain is a recent advanced technology that allows data securely transferred based on encryption protocols. On the blockchain, all of the data will be stored in a series of the block as an accounting notebook where all transactions are closely monitored. The most outstanding difference of blockchain is that no need for any middle process to censor information for data transmission. The records stored in the blockchain are transparent, reliable, and accessible to all members. Each block in the chain includes three elements: data, a hash of the previous block, a hash of the current block. Data will be protected by an encryption algorithm. The hash codes are randomly generated sequences to control the transactions and to detect changes in blocks. In literature, blockchain is widely studied in the last decade for handling issues of the supply chain and manufacturing systems.

For supply chain systems, various research works have addressed from high-level application frameworks (Azzi et al., 2019; Helo and Hao, 2019; Schmidt and Wagner, 2019) to detailed solutions for different challenges in the supply chain operations such as tracking the flow of goods (Song et al., 2019; Wang et al., 2020; Liu and Li, 2020), players coordination (Longo et al., 2019; Giovanni, 2020), reliable, protected and real-time data (Yang et al., 2019), inventory management (Casino et al., 2019). Specifically, the strongest points that the blockchain could help to improve the performance of the supply chains could be the ability of product traceability all over the process and gaining trust among channel members for enhancing supply chain coordination. On one hand, tracking and tracing material flows throughout the supply chain are studied by Song et al. (2019). The impact of the blockchain on traceability is analyzed to improve the performance of the supply chain. Wang et al. (2020) designed a blockchain-based system to enhance real-time information sharing and improve the efficiency of the supply chain in terms of product traceability. The solution algorithm for smart contracts is to support transactions in blockchain by updating the block of the logical traceability tag. Liu and Li (2020) addressed the traceability issue in supply chain management. A blockchain framework is introduced and some solution algorithms are developed to handle traceability issues in a cross-border e-supply chain system. On the other hand, accurate and reliable information and trust sharing are the decisive factors to coordinate the whole supply chain. However, many supply chain members in practice are not willing to share information (Longo et al.,2019). Therefore, it is often difficult to implement coordination contracts for the supply chain. Longo et al. (2019) investigated the transparency and reliable, protected, and real-time data sharing ability of the blockchain to enhance the trust among parties in the supply chain by a simulation model. In another interesting work, Giovanni (2020) studied two coordination frameworks of a traditional online platform and a blockchain for a two-stage supply chain including a supplier and a retailer. They showed that the blockchain platform can remove all risks and save the transaction costs of the traditional online system due to delivery and service and also pay high transaction costs. Besides, their obtained results also reveal that visibility, transparency, and security are also improved for the whole chain's operations. The burden of investment and variable costs for setting up a blockchain is also pointed out. To enhance the ease of blockchain implementation in operational and economical aspects, some conditions for using smart contracts in blockchain systems are recommended. For more blockchain applications in the supply chain, interesting readers could find some recent comprehensive reviews in the works of Dutta et al. (2020) or Lim et al. (2021).

Besides the supply chain systems, recent developments in blockchain implementations paid increasing attention to improving the performance of the manufacturing systems (Barenji et al., 2019; Zhang et al., 2019; Zhang et al., 2020; Leng et al., 2020; Westerkamp et al., 2020; Yu et al., 2020; Rozman et al., 2021; Wang et al., 2021; Tao et al., 2021; Teng et al., 2021). The most advantageous functions of blockchain in terms of trustable, transparency, secured transactions are usually applied in two main areas of cloud/shared manufacturing and smart manufacturing. Cloud manufacturing systems share and collaborate with different parties that face security, trustfulness, and flexibility issues due to centralized coordination mechanisms. A blockchain-based cloud manufacturing system could be a good solution for these issues (Barenji et al., 2020; Yu et al., 2020; Wang et al., 2021; Tao et al., 2021; Rozman et al., 2021). For instance, Barenji et al. (2020) introduced a blockchain cloud-based ubiquitous manufacturing platform for integrating 3D printing SMEs in a secure, reliable, and trustable network. Similarly, both Yu et al. (2020) and Rozman et al. (2021) implemented blockchain-based shared manufacturing frameworks to control distributed and trustable methods for sharing manufacturing resources. On one hand, Yu et al. (2020) constructed a resource operation blockchain with a smart contract to perform the resource sharing mechanism of the Blockchain-based Shared Manufacturing system. On the other hand, Rozman et al. (2021) also designed a so-called cross-chain solution that integrates a blockchain with a shared manufacturing platform for scalable, transparency, and immutability, trustable transactions between entities. Recently, Tao et al. (2021) also considered the trustfulness among members in the manufacturing service networks. The process transactions typically relies on static information, which could lead to data inaccuracies due to the uncertainties present i the working environment. A combined framework of digital twin and blockchain is proposed to improve the trustful collaboration between the members of the network. However, Wang et al. (2021) addressed the still opened third-party trust issue of the blockchain cloud manufacturing systems. They proposed a blockchain cloud manufacturing platform incorporated with a voting mechanism to reduce the "dirty" data effect. In another direction, some research works focused on studying the application of blockchain in smart manufacturing systems (Zhang et al., 2019; Zhang et al., 2020; Leng et al., 2020; Westerkamp et al., 2020; Teng et al., 2021). The advantage of trustful communications is still explored in the study of Zhang et al., (2019). The blockchain-based security and trust mechanism are implemented in the smart manufacturing system to securely store, integrate, and communicate quality data among entities of the system. Besides, Teng et al. (2021) also exploited the trustless feature of blockchain to construct a configurable blockchain-enabled smart manufacturing system. The optimization formulation of block size, task scheduling, and supply-demand matching is solved to share the manufacturing resources for more flexible manufacturing plans that maximize the customers' net profit. Other blockchain benefits of transparency, immutable, security, distributed, and efficient transactions are also utilized in the research of Westerkamp et al. (2020) for product traceability solutions in the manufacturing process. A method using product tokens on a blockchain helps to keep track and complete traceability of manufactured products. Some other studies such as Leng et al. (2020) and Zhang et al. (2020) combined blockchain with the Industrial Internet of Things (IIoTs) to handle manufacturing disturbances and support security solutions. Many comprehensive reviews for blockchain applications in manufacturing systems could also be found in Kasten (2020), Lohmer and Lasch (2020), Javaid et al. (2021), Leng et al. (2021).

Managerial Aspects of Blockchain Implementation

Numerous studies have concentrated on the development of blockchain-based systems in manufacturing applications. However, numerous challenges and technical complexities hinder the practical implementation of these developed blockchain-based systems. Recently, several research works have addressed the issues related to blockchain implementation. Tseng et al. (2023) conducted a study investigating the impacts of adopting blockchain technology in production processes on the operational performance of large enterprises. This study investigated whether the adoption of blockchain technology is influenced by a company's size and its level of investment in innovation. The research also examined the effects of adopting new technologies and investing in research and development (R&D) on overall business performance enhancement. The results indicate that both size of company and level of R&D investments are significant driving factors behind the adoption of blockchain technology. Larger companies in the

United States tend to adopt blockchain technology, and enterprises' investments in innovation contribute to the improvement of business performance and operational efficiency

In addtion to the impact on company performance, other studies by Lohmer and Lasch (2020) and Su et al. (2023) focus on the challenges and barriers that companies face when implementing blockchain technology in their operations and manufacturing systems. On one hand, Lohmer and Lasch (2020) studied the digital transformation process to facilitate blockchain applications in operations management and manufacturing. They pointed out that the scientific contributions and successful industrial applications in blockchain-based systems are still limited and mostly in the pilot phase (proof-of-concept stage). The authors conducted interviews with experts to find out the potential and barriers to the adoption of blockchain technology in operations management and manufacturing. On the other hand, Su et al. (2023) addressed a number of technical challenges that manufacturing companies may face when implementing blockchain technology.

Furthermore, Jovanovic et al. (2022) also discussed the conditions that contribute to the successful deployment of blockchain-based platform ecosystem. This study investigated the factors influencing the adoption across industries among global supply chain participants by analyzing the platform value drivers and platform governance mechanisms within a blockchain platform system. The platform's value is derived from the digitalization of workflows and ecosystem leverage, while platform governance encompasses strategic (off-chain), technological (on-chain), and interoperability (on- and off-chain) governance – serving as mechanisms for effectively managing a blockchain-based platform ecosystem.

Moreover, Munim et al. (2022) also recognized that the blockchain technology is still not widely adopted across industries despite its various benefits. They proposed a multi-criteria decision-making (MCDM) framework for assessing blockchain adoption strategies. The framework is built upon critical factors for blockchain adoption and encompasses four adoption strategies: single use, localization, substitution, and transformation. The analysis utilized the Bayesian Best Worst Method (BWM), a probabilistic Multi-Criteria Decision Making (MCDM) method. This proposed framework provides companies with the groundwork to comprehend the essential elements that require enhancement in order to expedite the process of adopting blockchain technology.

In summary, while there are various benefits that could be achieved through the adoption of blockchain-based systems in manufacturing, such as enhancing efficiency, transparency, immutability, cost savings, and traceability, the successful implementation of this technology is still limited. The reasons have not been fully investigated in different aspects such as challenges, barriers, and implementation strategies. So far, there is no work that covers a comprehensive analysis of all these aspects to provide practical guidelines and strategies for the successful implementation of blockchain -based systems. The need for such a general framework could help reduce the failure rates in blockchain technology adoption in the manufacturing environment.

The Value Stream Mapping

Value Stream Mapping (VSM) is a Lean manufacturing tool that helps to visualize the production process for detecting non-value added activities. From the drawn VSM, the manager could remove wastes and arrange reasonable manpower, increase value-added activities, eliminate bottlenecks, etc. VSM applications in manufacturing systems have been extensively discussed in the literature (see the review of Romero and Arce, 2017). In some recent works, the trend of using standalone VSM (Busert and Fay, 2019; Masuti and Dabade, 2019) is gradually replaced by the combination of the VSM or the Dynamic

VSM with other tools (Knoll et al., 2019; Huang et al., 2019; Stadnicka and Litwin, 2019; and Sultan et al., 2021). On one hand, Busert and Fay (2019) extended the value stream mapping approach to analyze manufacturing processes by synchronizing and enhancing the quality of data flows. Masuti and Dabade (2019) also utilized the VSM to record the current status of the manufacturing process for removing wastes and bottlenecks such as setup time at the welding station, excess inventory, underutilized press station, etc. On the other hand, Knoll et al. (2019) integrated the multidimensional process mining (MDPM) techniques with the VSM to improve the performance of a mixed-model assembly line. The system has continuously recorded the performance, evaluated and analyzed any possible waste at all stations of the production process. Besides, Stadnicka and Litwin (2019) pointed out the VSM shortcomings of only performing static analysis. The integrated system of a VSM and a system dynamics analysis (SDA) tool is designed to show that not only wastes are identified and removed, but also the impact of the WIP and the production volume issues are recognized. In another interesting case, Huang et al. (2019) explored the advantage of IoTs devices to provide real-time/near-real-time information to the dynamic value stream mapping (DVSM). The material flow status is analyzed and visualized for improvement. Recently, Sultan et al. (2021) integrated Value Stream Mapping (VSM) with the discrete event simulation model to identify and remove wastes along the Indian surimi supply chain. The VSM monitors the downstream operations to analyze what integration framework could coordinate better the supply chain. It reveals that the complete vertical integration is superior to other settings of no vertical integration and partial vertical integration.

In short, the VSM should receive accurate and on-time data to reflect dynamically the status of the manufacturing process. However, no system so far could provide traceability, reliability, and transparency transaction data for the VSM. Therefore, there is a need for an appropriate integration framework that could combine the VSM with other tools to efficiently monitor the manufacturing system.

Summary

Based on the aforementioned reviews, it is observed that although a certain level of improvement could be achieved by some system settings, there is still a need for secured, transparent, instant status to send to the VSM for visualizing and enhancing the performance of the manufacturing process. The use of RFID, Blockchain, and VSM together could meet that requirements. RFID just plays the role of collecting and storing data. The blockchain updates instant status and performs transparent, secured, decentralized, and efficient transactions. The VSM visualizes automatically the system. The combination of these tools could bring significant benefits for the manager to monitor, quickly adjust, and improve the efficiency of the production system. Furthermore, the implementation of blockchain-based systems often encounters numerous challenges arising from technical and managerial complexities. As a result, clear and practical guidelines and strategies for the successful integration of such systems are currently lacking. Therefore, a comprehensive analysis is imperative to establish a general framework for the adoption of blockchain-based systems within the manufacturing context.

BLOCKCHAIN VALUE STREAM MAPPING (BVMS) SYSTEM

To improve the perform ance of the manufacturing system, we need not only to collect a large amount of data but also real-time and reliable information from the production process. To this end, we proposed a system that not only collects correctly, quickly, and reliably the production process parameters but also automatically updates the status. That could help the manager have the right decision right away. The proposed Blockchain Value Stream Mapping System (Figure 1) can automatically monitor and track the production flow. The timestamp is recorded automatically when there is a change at any stage of the production process. The process parameters from the Kanban cards such as order batch size, …., will be collected via the RFID system. The role of the blockchain in our system is to keep track of the production process. The VSM tool helps to visualize the production workflow and performance. It helps the managers to improve the performance of the system.

Figure 1. The blockchain value stream mapping system

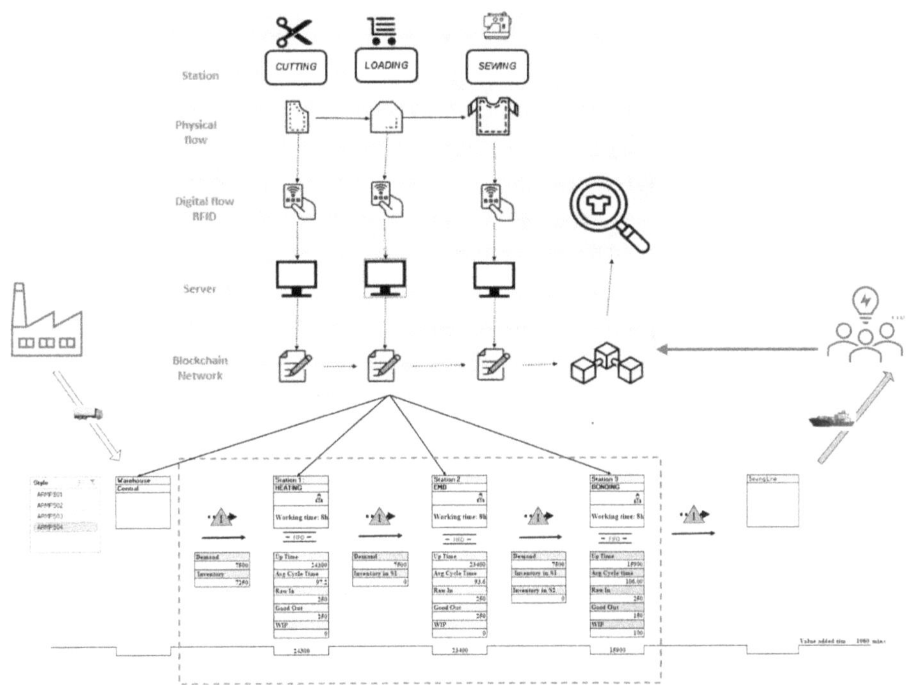

The Production Blockchain

Our blockchain system is built under the Flash framework of Python. It is a web framework that allows to building of web applications. All production and blockchain information is stored in the MySQL database management tool. The following Figure 2 presents the structure of the proposed blockchain. In this system, the production data at the end of each process is encrypted (hash function) and posted on the blockchain network, the computers (nodes) will be responsible for decrypting those cryptos (called mining). When one node transmits the decoding signal, the other nodes accept or do not accept the result (proof of work). If that block's information is accepted by over 50% of the nodes then the data will be added to the chain and at the same time, the data will be on the ledger. From there, all of the data will be saved on the server (database) which works as the data storage to visualize productivity on Dashboard.

Figure 2. The blockchain structure

The users can communicate with the Blockchain system via a UI (user interface). It is constructed by the popular API client Postman. With the UI, the users can read the Blockchain's responses and create, save, and send the HTTP/s requests. The process is illustrated in Figure 3.

Figure 3. The API operation flow of the blockchain

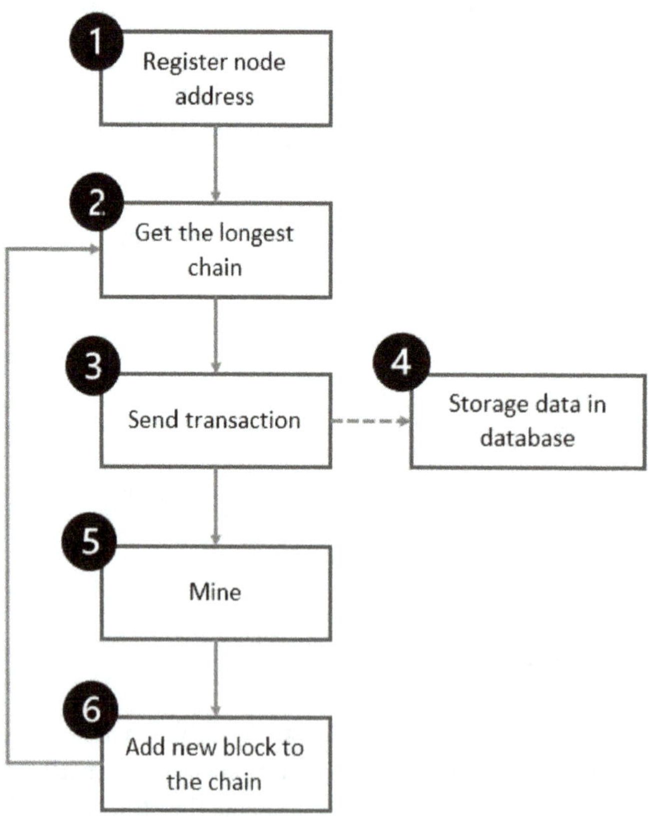

In this flow, the users use two basic HTTP methods of GET and POST to work with the blockchain system in the following six stages:

Stage 1: A set of participants in the network is registered in every node to form a consensus or reach a peer-to-peer community. For example, we register the HEATING (Station 1) into the Blockchain by running the client network registration (Figure 4): http://127.0.0.1:7001/nodes.register.

Figure 4. The client network registration


```
{
    "message": "New nodes have been added - Station 1",
    "total_nodes": [
        "127.0.0.1:7001",
        "127.0.0.1:7002"
    ]
}
```


Stage 2: Before sending a specific transaction or adding a new block at each station, the active node needs to update the current longest chain by running: http://127.0.0.1:7000/nodes/resolve.

Stage 3: A transaction containing the following production data is created:

Sender: Station which sends transaction (production data).

Recipient: Station which will receive a transaction (production data).

Style: The code of current PO (purchasing order).

Amount: The quantity of WIPs or finished goods.

Stage 4 and 5: Sever will automatically calculate and start mining a transaction block. If mining successfully, a new valid block will be created. Besides that, all contents of the block are saved in MySQL production database.

Stage 6: The newly mined block is added into the current chain.

The process is repeated from Stage 2 to Stage 6 until all station blocks are added to the Blockchain.

The Proposed BVSM System

The proposed model includes a User Interface (UI) at each station, a Blockchain, and a Value Stream Mapping (VSM). The IU at each station activates the blockchain, display, and update production data from production plan and process status. Then, the provided data will be used to keep track of the status of the process and visualize the workflow by the VSM. The managers will analyze the system to improve productivity, processing time, WIP level, and line balancing (see Figure 5).

Here, we describe operations at all stations to show how the blockchain captures the real-time status of the production process. Then, the VSM also illustrates how to visualize the system for improvement. The input of the system is the production plan sent from the planning department with the following basic information.

Style ordered: ARMPS20.
Station 1: 5000 pcs.
Station 2: 5000 pcs.
Station 3: 5000 pcs.
Inline (starting date): 16/2/2021.
Offline (shipment date): 28/2/2021.

Figure 5. The proposed BVSM model

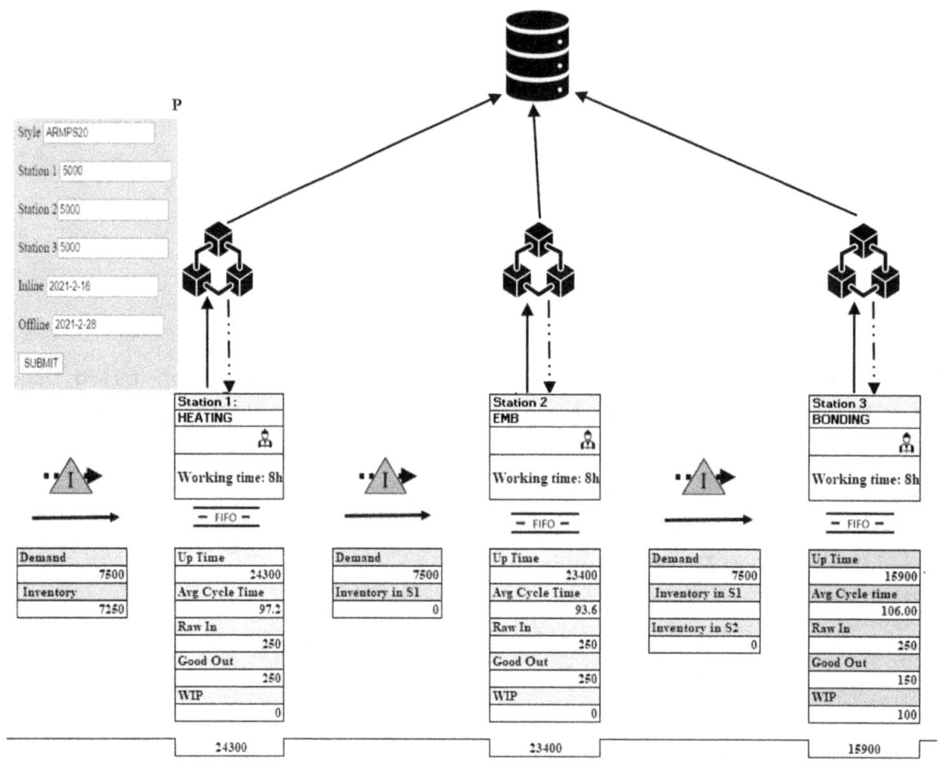

At each station, an UI (User Interface) will allow the operator to get and update the production data from the production plan, from/to the blockchain, and to the process status, respectively. At Station 1, the first block called Genesis Block is created without any transaction to initialize the Blockchain. Then, the operator updates the production plan information (station, order style, quantity) to the database and carries out the job at Station 1. When the job is completed and physically transferred to the next station. The blockchain will capture processing data (sender, recipient, style, amount of finished goods) in real-time to send the transaction to the next block. The system will validate the transaction. It means that the transaction is mined to post to the blockchain. If the mining process successes, the system will get one coin as a reward. This corresponds to append a new block to the blockchain. Each updated block has its hash code and proof to protect the content inside the block. Now, the transaction has the right to be added to the new block. The current blockchain has 2 blocks which means the length of the chain is 2. This process is illustrated in the following Figure 6.

Figure 6. Transaction mining process at Station 1

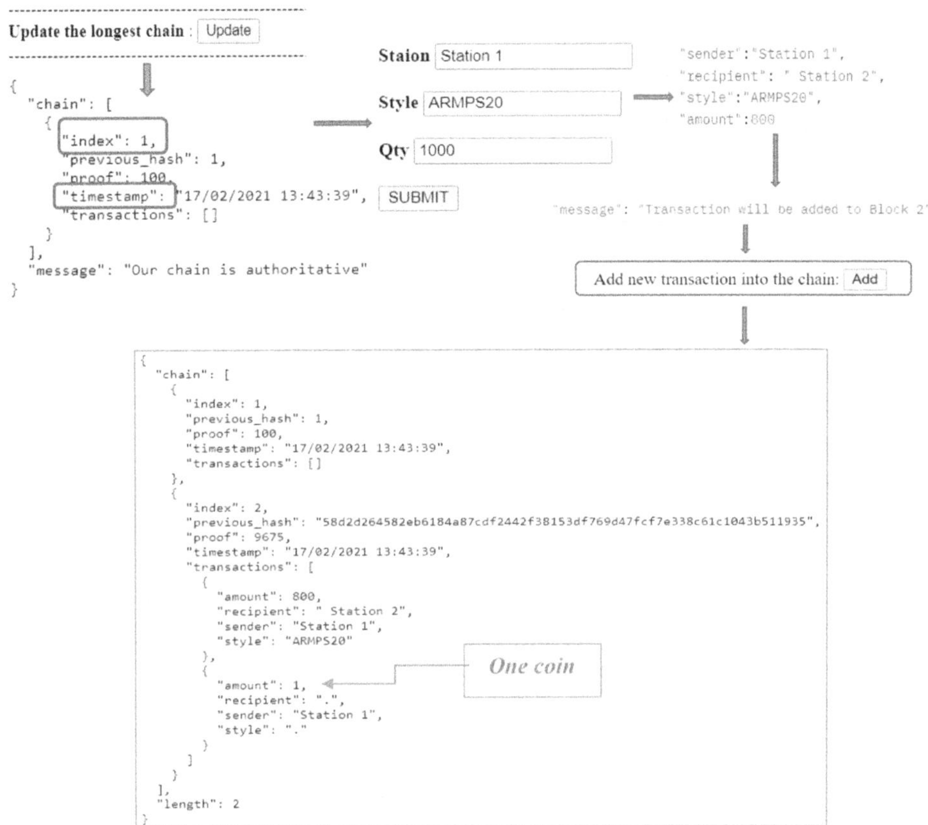

At Station 2, the longest chain is updated to Station 2 with the received transaction from Station 1. The operator physically starts working for the job at Station 2 and updates the production data to the system. Station 2 sends a transaction to the next block of Station 3 when the job is completed. The new transaction is validated and be ready to add to the new block. The system mines a block for getting validation of new transactions to post on the blockchain. If the mining process successes, the system will add Block 3 to the blockchain. The transaction is updated to the new block of the current chain. The length of the chain now includes 3 blocks (see Figure 7). A similar process is repeated for Station 3 and so on. The system mines a new block to update the chain. All transactions are kept for every station. Obviously, data on the blockchain cannot be changed or adjusted. All outgoing transactions at the destination stage are confirmed in real-time with reliable data. Each block of data is identified by a hash. The hash code of the block is generated relative to the hash of the previous block, and that helps to link blocks together, forming a chain of blocks. These features are especially useful for production managers. It can help them to understand the production process status as well as come up with the production plan to suit the real situation.

To improve the performance of the current system, the secured information from the blockchain is visualized in real-time by Value Stream Mapping (VSM) tool. The VSM is a typical lean diagram to show product flow and the process status at each workstation. The value chain diagram reflects what is actually going on to identify non-value-added activities for improvement.

Figure 7. Transaction mining process at Station 2

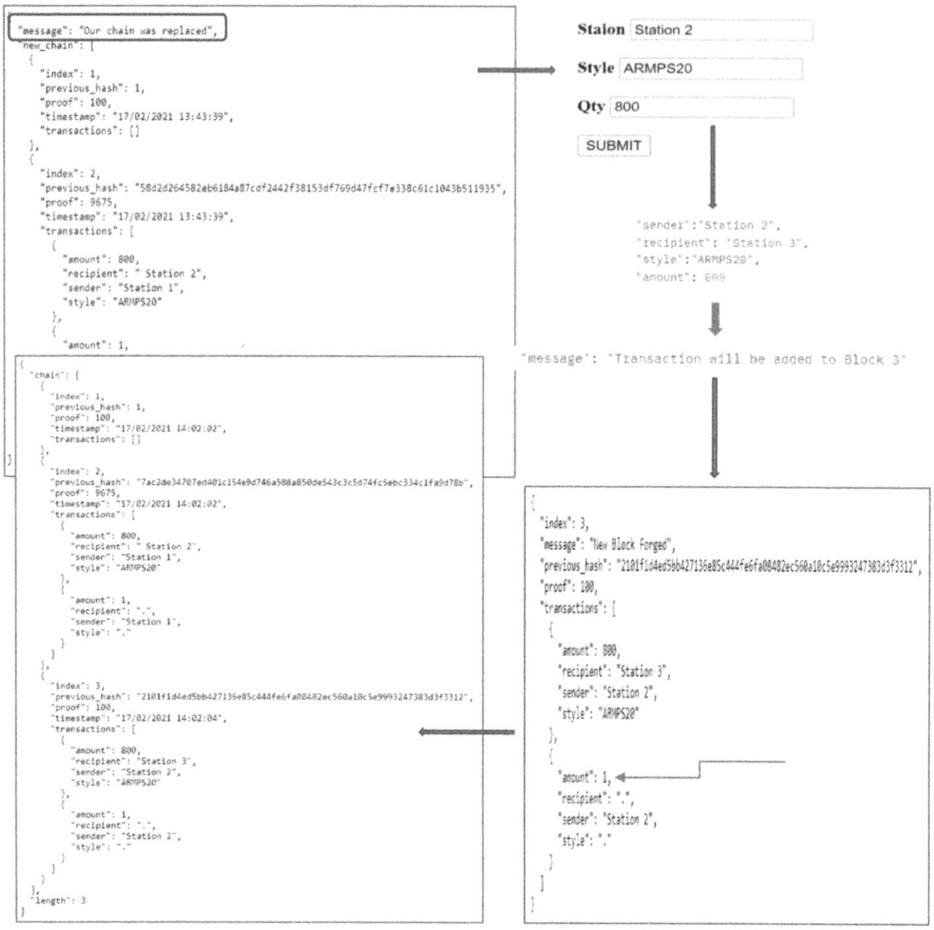

The bottom section of Figure 3 illustrates an example of a VSM diagram of the code AMRPS04 obtained from the data of the blockchain. This VSM contains full process information such as customer orders, inventory levels, shipment quantity, etc. Several key performance indices (KPIs) are also collected from the workstations such as total processing time (Uptime), average cycle time (seconds/pcs), the quantity of semi-finished products (Raw In – pcs), the quantity of finished goods (Good Out – pcs), work-in-progress (WIP), value-added time (VA – seconds or minutes), etc. From this information, the potential wastes or the bottlenecks of the system can be easily identified.

MANAGERIAL ANALYSIS

Organizational Changes

Implementing a blockchain-based system in manufacturing process as the proposed BVSM could lead to various organizational changes. These changes can be both positive and challenging, affecting diffferent aspects of the organization. The positive changes could bring benefits for the production system. The changes create challenges could help us to pave the way to define the appropriate implementation strategy for the proposed BVSM system. Therefore, we focus on investigating the stucture and the operational process flow of the proposed BVSM system to identify some potential organizational changes that creates challenges. In such regards, the structure of the proposed BVSM system presented in Figures 1 and 2 could create the following changes:

- Process redesign: implementing blockchain might require reengineering existing manufacturing processes to integrate with the decentralized and transparent nature of the technology. As per Figure 1, the managerial flow of information has changed from the traditional records at each station in the form of production cards to the auto-collection devices of RFID and processing and transfering by blockchain system. This could lead to more efficient, reducing errors, and streamlined workflows.
- Cross-Functional Collaboration: blockchain implementation often involves different departments, including IT, operations, quality control, and finance/accounting, working closely together to ensure successful integration. The data collected from production processes could be used and processed by the related departments and returning back to the BVSM system. Cross-functional collaboration becomes essential.
- Change in Data Handling: blockchain relies on accurate data, which might necessitate changes in how data is collected, validated, and shared across the organization. In our BVSM system, the real-time and accurate data is updated production flow. This could helps to manage the production process in more reliable manner.
- Trust and Accountability: The transparent and tamper-proof nature of blockchain can influence a culture of increased trust and accountability among stations, as actions and transactions become more traceable. In the BVSM system, accurate and reliable data could help planning and controlling process to be more efficient.
- Training and Education: operators, technicians, and engineers will need training on how to use the new system effectively. This could involve understanding how to interact with the blockchain and manage troubleshoot issues.
- Resistance to Change: some employees might be resistant to adopting blockchain due to unfamiliarity or fear of job displacement. Change management strategies will be crucial to address these concerns.
- Monitoring and Analytics: the transparency of blockchain data can lead to improved real-time monitoring and analytics. The organization might need to adapt its analytics practices to leverage this new data source effectively.
- Investment and Budget: blockchain implementation requires investment in technology, personnel, and ongoing maintenance. Budget allocation and resource planning will need to be adjusted accordingly.

Overall, implementing a blockchain-based system in manufacturing processes can lead to a significant transformation of the organization's structure, processes, and culture. These changes also create some challenges as mentioned previouslly. Addressing these challenges requires collaboration among developers, employees, and managers across different departments of the company. Overcoming these hurdles can lead to more robust and widely adopted blockchain solutions. To navigate these changes successfully, a well-thought-out change management strategy, clear communication, and collaboration among various departments will be essential.

Digital Transformation Strategies

As per aforementioned analysis of changes, the adoption of the BVSM system in a production process requires careful planning and execution. Here are specific strategies to consider for successful adoption of the BVSM system in manufacturing environment:

- Identify Use Cases: analyze the manufacturing processes to identify suitable use cases where blockchain can add value, such as process tracking, quality assurance, status updates, performance monitoring, and compliance verification.
- Start Small: begin with a pilot project focused on a specific process or product. This minimizes risks and allows you to test the technology's feasibility before scaling up.
- Collaboration and Ecosystem Building: collaborate with different departments ans stakeholders of the process such as planners, quality controllers, production operators/managers, and IT engineers to build a blockchain-based ecosystem that spans the entire value chain. This enhances transparency and collaboration.
- Technology Evaluation: choose a suitable blockchain platform or protocol (public, private, consortium) based on the production process requirements. Consider factors like scalability, consensus mechanism, and interoperability.
- Change Management: develop a comprehensive change management plan that includes stakeholder engagement, training, and communication to ensure smooth adoption across the organization.
- Data Architecture and Integration: plan how the existing data systems will integrate with the blockchain. Plan in details the transition plan to upgrade current data/records into the digital storage system of the BVSM. Decide what data will be stored on-chain and off-chain, ensuring efficient data flow.
- Privacy and Security: implement privacy features to protect sensitive data while maintaining transparency. Employ strong security measures to safeguard the blockchain network and associated data.
- Smart Contracts Development: design and develop smart contracts that automate processes like order updates, transaction verification, parameter monitoring, and performance measures. Ensure contracts are secure and audited.
- Scalability Planning: consider potential scalability challenges as expanding the BVSM system for similar manufacturing processes. Explore solutions to accommodate increased transaction volumes.
- Performance Testing: thoroughly test the BVSM solution's performance under different loads to ensure it meets the expectations.
- User-Friendly Interfaces: develop intuitive user interfaces that simplify interactions with the blockchain for both internal users and external partners.
- Monitoring and Analytics: implement tools for monitoring the blockchain network's health and performance. Leverage blockchain data for advanced analytics to gain insights into manufacturing processes.

- Continuous Improvement: after implementation, gather feedback and continually optimize the system based on user experiences and evolving business needs.
- Educational Initiatives: educate employees and stakeholders about the BVSM system, blockchain technology, its benefits, and how it integrates into manufacturing processes. This reduces resistance and increases adoption.
- Partnership with Technology Providers: collaborate with technology providers, consultants, and blockchain experts who have experience in manufacturing to ensure successful implementation.
- Long-Term Strategy: develop a roadmap for the long-term evolution of the BVSM solution. Consider how it will adapt to changing technologies and market demands.
- Measurable Goals: set clear and measurable goals for the blockchain adoption, such as reduced operational costs, improved traceability, and enhanced collaboration.
- Patience and Flexibility: understand that blockchain, sepecifically, the BVSM adoption is a journey, and challenges may arise. Maintain a patient and adaptable mindset to overcome obstacles.

Successful adoption of the BVSM system in manufacturing requires a holistic approach that addresses technology, processes, people, and regulatory considerations. By following these strategies, the benefits of the BVSM system is maximized. It also drives innovation in the manufacturing system.

Implementation Guidelines

With the strategy mentioned earlier, the next steps involve developing a well-structured approach for successfully implementing the BVSM system in manufacturing processes. Here are comprehensive guidelines to follow when adopting the BVSM solution in a manufacturing environment:

- Define Clear Objectives: identify the specific goals to achieve through the BVSM adoption. It is important to note that the integration of blockchain and VSM could provide managers with a tool to monitor, adjust in real-time, and enhance the efficiency of the production system, allowing it to adapt to fluctuation in the environment.
- Conduct Feasibility Analysis: assess the suitability of blockchain for manufacturing processes in terms of providing traceability, reliability, and transparency of transaction data for the VSM. Determine whether the benefits outweigh the costs and potential challenges.
- Select Appropriate Use Cases: identify specific processes or areas within manufacturing where BVSM can provide the most value. Examples include monitoring production process, tracking transactions, and ensuring quality.
- Engage Stakeholders: involve key stakeholders from different departments, including operations, IT, warehousing, planning and finance/accounting. Ensure their buy-in and gather input throughout the process.
- Collaborate with Partners: work closely with different departments such as warehouse, quality, planning, and IT to establish a collaborative BVSM ecosystem that enhances transparency and efficiency.
- Choose the Right Blockchain Platform: select a suitable blockchain platform (public, private, or consortium) based on the requirements for scalability, tracibility, and data analytics.

- Design the Blockchain Network: define the architecture, nodes, consensus mechanisms, and permissions for blockchain network to integrate with the VSM. Determine which parties will have access and control.
- Develop Smart Contracts: design and develop smart contracts that automate predefined processes, ensuring accuracy and reducing manual intervention.
- Integrate Data Sources: integrate existing data systems with the blockchain, deciding which data will be stored on-chain and off-chain for optimal efficiency. Define what data flow to integrate with the VSM for process improvement.
- Establish Governance Framework: develop rules, protocols, and governance mechanisms for managing the BVSM system, including decision-making and dispute resolution.
- User-Friendly Interfaces: design intuitive user interfaces that simplify interactions with the BVSM for both technical and non-technical users.
- Training and Education: provide comprehensive training for employees, partners, and stakeholders to ensure they understand how to use the BVSM system effectively.
- Test and Quality Assurance: thoroughly test the BVSM solution in a controlled environment to identify and rectify any issues before deployment.
- Pilot Testing: conduct a pilot implementation with a small-scale project to validate the feasibility and benefits of the BVSM solution such as the pilot project for three-station in the illustrative example .
- Iterative Implementation: implement the BVSM in phases, starting with less critical processes and gradually expanding to more complex areas.
- Change Management: develop and execute a change management plan that addresses employee concerns, communicates benefits, and ensures smooth adoption.
- Monitor and Evaluate: continuously monitor the BVSM system's performance, gather feedback, and evaluate its impact on processes and outcomes.
- Continuous Improvement: iterate and refine the BVSM system based on user feedback, evolving technologies, and changing business needs.
- Document and Share Learnings: document the implementation process, challenges faced, and lessons learned to facilitate future improvements and knowledge sharing.
- Long-Term Strategy: develop a roadmap for the ongoing development and evolution of the BVSM system to keep it aligned with your manufacturing objectives.

By following these guidelines, we can navigate the complex process of the BVSM adoption in a manufacturing system and maximize the benefits of this transformative technology.

ILLUSTRATIVE RESULTS

In this work, we investigate a garment company in Vietnam to illustrate the proposed BVSM system. The complete production process of the case study is presented in Figure 7. To control this production process, the company has implemented a Kanban-and-RFID system to capture all process data that could help to run the product flow smoothly. However, due to human errors and lack of trust, the data is not automatically updated, slowly collected from many sources, and sequentially transferred which leads to a lot of information deviation. The proposed BVSM system could help to capture and transfer transparent, reliable, and authentic data to keep track efficiently the overall productivity and production activities. In this case, we only study three sample stations of Heating (Station 1), Embroidery (EMB, Station 2), and Bonding (Station 3) for production orders of three SKUs: ARMPS01, ARMPS02 and ARMPS03.

Current Status

A common problem at the company is unstable productivity in the first few days of the new batch of a production order after the changeover. Among some reasons for this problem such as unstable processing parameters, inappropriate machine setups, and conditions, waiting for raw materials, poor line balancing is a key issue. Unsuitable worker assignment significantly affects the production and delivery plan of the company. Managers currently evaluate the previous performance of the operators to allocate them to the stations for new production orders. Sometimes, some new orders require high skills. The experience justification may lead to an inappropriate assignment. In consequence, production output can not meet the expected demand. To correct this problem, the managers measure the production quantity in the first two days of the new orders at the three considered stations. If the average output of finished products does not meet the daily demand, the managers will adjust the previous assignment to rebalance the line by calculating the number of operators to support each station. The number of additional workers to be assigned to a station depends on the range of the required production rate (Table 2). The required production rate is:

$$R = \frac{D}{A} \tag{1}$$

Where D: Demand per day (pcs/day).
A: Average output (pcs/day).

Table 2. Range of required product rate

Rate	Assignment Rule	Number of Suppoters
[0, 1]	0	No Supporter
(1, 1.25]	Overtime	Overtime Works
(1.25, 2]	1	Add 01 Supporter
(2, 3]	2	Add 02 Supporters

Improvement Solution

However, unbalancing worker arrangement issue still happens due to delay and inaccurate information of the production process status. To help the managers arranging properly workers to stations in faster and more accurate decisions, the proposed BVSM system is implemented to provide real-time and reliable data of the production process.

Figure 8. The current production control system of the investigated garment company

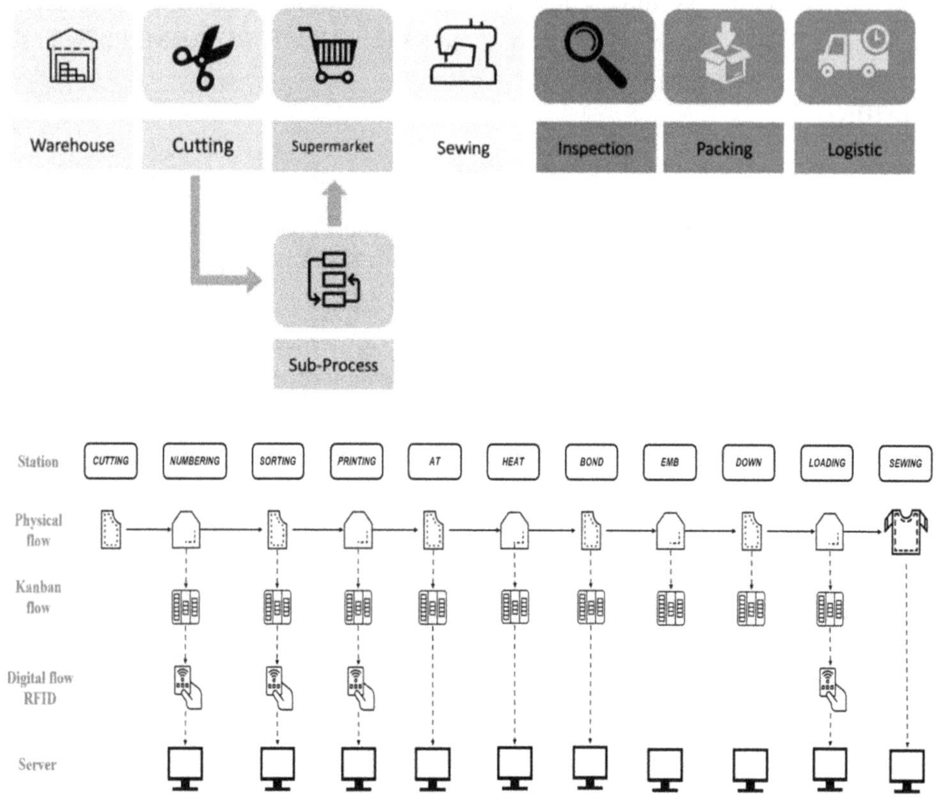

From the obtained data, the dashboard of working progress is established to monitor the current performance of the stations with many advantages of time-saving of gathering data, real-time analytics, inventory control. The dashboard is a well-built productivity graph to track important measures of the stations such as Work-In-Process (WIP), Efficiency (Eff), Finished Goods (FGs), and other KPIs. The following Figure 8 illustrates an example of a dashboard for the production order of the ARMPS04. There are three charts for each station. The first chart shows the number of finished goods (orange bar) compared to the order quantity (blue bar) for the item. The second chart continuously updates the production status of the ordered item at each station such as inventory level, input semi-finished goods, output finished goods, and products in the process. The third chart reports the productivity of the considered station. It is the ratio between the actual output over the production capacity in a period. The dashboard is continuously monitored which could help production managers easily managing the process, controlling materials flow, and making some adjustments or improvements.

Besides the dashboard, the blockchain also provides real-time production data for the VSM system. For item code ARMPS01, the production plan is automatically updated with the following information (Table 3a).

- Demand: Number of products to be completed
- Total working day: production Lead-time
- Daily demand: daily standard output per station

- Working time: total working time.
- Takt time

Then, the first 2-day average output and efficiency for ARMPS01 item are continuously updated as in Table 3b. It is observed that the productivities at all three stations are at a low level of production output. This performance cannot meet the expected demand. Therefore, the managers have to make some adjustments by arranging additional supporting operators for all three stations. The calculation results show that we need one more operator for Stations 1 and 2, two more operators for Station 3 (see Table 3c). The improvement production outputs at Stations 1, 2, and 3 are 107 pcs, 168 pcs, and 248 pcs, respectively.

Figure 9. Performance dashboard of the ARMPS04 order

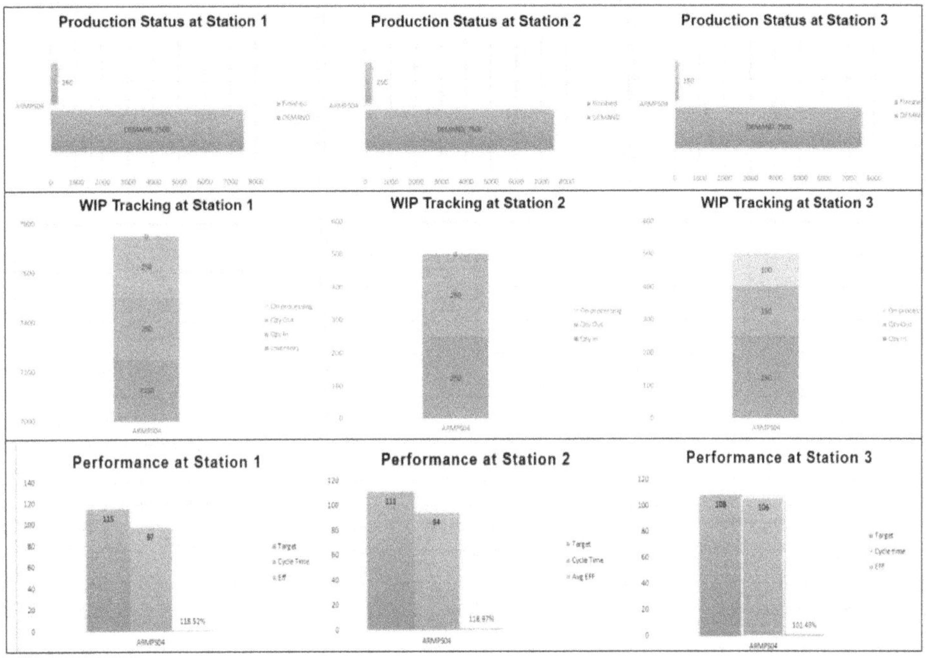

Similar processes are also applied for the productions orders of ARMPS02 and ARMPS03 items that are illustrated in Tables 4 and 5, respectively. The obtained improvement results for the ARMPS02 item at Stations 1, 2, and 3 are 82 pcs, 214 pcs, and 410 pcs, respectively. The obtained production outputs for the ARMPS03 item at Stations 1, 2, and 3 are 88 pcs, 39 pcs, and 110 pcs, respectively.

From the above results, we summarize the performance of all three stations for 03 items before and after improvement as in the following Table 6. It is observed that if we do not adjust the initial worker assignment as in the first 2 days, the total lead-time of three production orders will be prolonged. The higher lead-time, the more delayed the delivery time. After adjustment, the efficiency at all three stations is improved to 100% with more supporting manpower. It is just an example of the worker assignment. In general, the other KPIs of the process such as WIP rates, productivity, or efficiency can be improved in the same way by other production process parameters such as status of raw materials, the status of semi-finished products, inventory level, etc. All these process parameters can be obtained in real-time from the blockchain to supply for the VSM that helps the managers to make the decision quickly for necessary adjustments. To this end, the performance at all three stations will be improved the line balancing in terms of the better takt time level.

Table 3. Detailed information of the VSM for the ARMPS01 item

STATION 1					
Style	Demand	Total working day	Demand per day	Total Working time (s)	Takt time
ARMPS01	13000	31	419	892800	68.68
STATION 2					
Style	Demand	Total working day	Demand per day	Total Working time (s)	Takt time
ARMPS01	13000	30	433	864000	66.46
STATION 3					
Style	Demand	Total working day	Demand per day	Total Working time (s)	Takt time
ARMPS01	13000	29	448	835200	64.25

(a) Production Plan of the ARMPS01 Item

STATION	WORKER	PROCESSING TIME	HUMAN TIME	OUT PUT	AVG OUT PUT/ WORKER	AVG CYCLE TIME	EFF
Station 1	1	28800	28800	312	312	92.31	74%
Station 2	1	28800	28800	265	265	108.68	61%
Station 3	1	28800	28800	200	200	144.00	46%
	3						21%

(b) Productivity Status of the ARMPS01 Item

STATION	Total workers	Supporter	Demand of Over time	Supporter 1	Supporter 2	Supporting time (s)	Supporting time (Hr)	Deman Target / Day
Station 1	2	1	0	107	0	9910	2.753	419
Station 2	2	1	0	168	0	18294	5.082	433
Station 3	3	2	0	[illegible]	48	35752	9.931	448

(c) Improvement Worker Arrangement for the ARMPS01 Item

Additional Case Study

Another case is investigated to show the advantages of the proposed BVSM system in tracking and controlling the production process. We compare our proposed BVSM system with the Traditional Value Stream Mapping (TVSM) for the case of JCB factory in India (Masuti and Dabade, 2019). The results are justified in terms of value-added time, non-value-added time, and production lead time, respectively. The current state map and the future state map for the JCB factory are presented in Appendices A and B. After implementation of the TVSM, the total value-added time (VAT), the non-value added time

Table 4. Detailed information of the VSM for the ARMPS02 item

STATION 1					
Style	Demand	Total working day	Demand per day	Total Working time (s)	Takt time (Target)
ARMPS02	15000	22	682	633600	42.24
STATION 2					
Style	Demand	Total working day	Demand per day	Total Working time (s)	Takt time (Target)
ARMPS02	15000	21	714	604800	40.32
STATION 3					
Style	Demand	Total working day	Demand per day	Total Working time (s)	Takt time (Target)
ARMPS02	15000	20	750	576000	38.40

(a) Production Plan of the ARMPS02 Item

STATION	WORKER	PROCESSING TIME	HUMAN TIME	OUT PUT	AVG OUT PUT/ WORKER	AVG CYCLE TIME	EFF
Station 1	1	28800	28800	600	600	48.00	88%
Station 2	1	28800	28800	500	500	57.60	70%
Station 3	1	28800	28800	340	340	84.71	48%
	3						29%

(b) Productivity Status of the ARMPS02 Item

STATION	Total workers	Supporter	Demand of Over time	Deman worker 1	Deman worker 2	Supporting time (s)	Supporting time (Hr)	Deman Target / Day
Station 1	1	Overtime	82	0	0	3927	1.091	682
Station 2	2	1	0	[illegible]14	0	12343	3.429	714
Station 3	3	2	0	340	70	34729	9.647	750

(c) Improvement Worker Arrangement for the ARMPS02 Item

(NVAT), and the production lead time (PLT) are reduced by about 156 minutes, 430.3 minutes, and 586.3 minutes, respectively (see Table 7). To this end, Masuti and Dabade (2019) also reported some improvement actions such as tackle implementation for center section robot welding station, providing new fixtures at the press operation station, inventory control at the tacking station, and provision of pallets resulting Rs.1542104.94 total cost saving.

However, the waiting time and inventory control are key problems to extend the production lead time. It significantly impacts the company's production capacity, especially since the production outputs cannot meet daily demand and delivery of products as planned in the high season. Therefore, the revenue in peak season is not much better than in the low season. To handle these obstacles, the proposed BVSM could help to reduce NVATs that are inventory time and waiting time at each workstation. The advantage of the BVSM to capture real-time and reliable information could help to improve the production rate of all stations. The updated production plan adapts with the current conditions of the production process to meet the required demand on time. As result, the total NVAT was cut off by about 1143.3 mins. The total lead-time is also reduced by about 1299.3 minutes by implementing the BVSM (see Table 7).

Table 5. Detailed information of the VSM for the ARMPS03 item

STATION 1					
Style	Demand	Total working day	Demand per day	Total Working time (s)	Takt time
ARMPS03	6000	32	188	921600	153.60
STATION 2					
Style	Demand	Total working day	Demand per day	Total Working time (s)	Takt time
ARMPS03	6000	31	194	892800	148.80
STATION 3					
Style	Demand	Total working day	Demand per day	Total Working time (s)	Takt time
ARMPS03	6000	30	200	864000	144.00

(a) Production Plan of the ARMPS03 Item

STATION	WORKER	PROCESSING TIME	HUMAN TIME	OUT PUT	AVG OUT PUT/ WORKER	AVG CYCLE TIME	EFF
Station 1	1	28800	28800	100	100	288.00	53%
Station 2	1	28800	28800	155	155	185.81	80%
Station 3	1	28800	28800	90	90	320.00	47%
	3						20%

(b) Productivity Status of the ARMPS03 Item

STATION	Total workers	Supporter	Demand of Over time	Deman worker 1	Deman worker 2	Supporting time (s)	Supporting time (Hr)	Deman Target / Day
Station 1	2	1	0	88	0	25200	7.000	188
Station 2	1	Overtime	39	0	0	7163	1.990	194
Station 3	3	2	0	90	[illegible]	35200	9.778	200

(c) Improvement Worker Arrangement for the ARMPS03 Item

Table 6. Comparison performance

	Current Assignment						Improvement Solution					
	Number of Workers			Efficiency			Number of Workers			Efficiency		
ARMPS	01	02	03	01	02	03	01	02	03	01	02	03
Station 1	1	1	1	74%	88%	53%	2	OT	2	100%	100%	100%
Station 2	1	1	1	61%	70%	80%	2	2	OT	100%	100%	100%
Station 3	1	1	1	46%	48%	47%	3	3	3	100%	100%	100%

Table 7. The case of JCB factory in India

	Current State Map	Future State Map of TVSM	Time Saved by TVSM	Future State Map of BVSM	Time Saved by BVSM
Value Added Time (mins)	2298.3	2142.2	156	2142.3	156
Non-value Added Time (mins)	18209.5	17779.2	430.3	17066.2	1143.3
Production Lead Time (mins)	20507.8	**19921.5**	**586.3**	**19208.5**	**1299.3**

CONCLUSION

In this chapter, we presented the proposed Blockchain Value Stream Mapping for monitoring and improving the manufacturing process. In this system, the RFIDs will collect production data for the Blockchain. The role of the blockchain in our system is to keep track of the production process. The VSM visualizes automatically the production workflow and performance. With this integration, the blockchain could provide traceability, reliability, and transparency of transaction data for the VSM. The combination of these tools could bring significant benefits for the manager to monitor, quickly adjust, and improve the efficiency of the production system. With these on-time adjustments, the manufacturing systems could run smoothly to adapt to any fluctuation of the environment. Furthermore, a thorough analysis of the challenges and barriers associated with the adoption of a blockchain-based system has been meticulously undertaken. This analysis aims to offer clear and practical implementation strategies and guidelines for the proposed BVSM system. Subsequently, a prototype of the BVSM system has been developed and implemented for three workstations within a production line at a garment company located in Vietnam. An illustrative experiment is conducted to show the improved performance of the manufacturing system by rearrangement worker assignment. Furthermore, another case of the JCB factory in India from a reference is also tested to illustrate the advantage of the proposed BVSM system over the traditional VSM method. In the future, the BVSM could be extended to integrate with other tools which could help to control automatically and efficiently the manufacturing system.

REFERENCES

Azzi, R., Chamoun, R. K., & Sokhn, M. (2019). The power of a blockchain-based supply chain. *Computers & Industrial Engineering*, *135*, 582–592. doi:10.1016/j.cie.2019.06.042

Barenji, A. V., Li, Z., Wang, W. M., Huang, G. Q., & Guerra-Zubiaga, D. A. (2020). Blockchain-based ubiquitous manufacturing: A secure and reliable cyber-physical system. *International Journal of Production Research*, *58*(7), 2200–2221. doi:10.1080/00207543.2019.1680899

Busert, T., & Fay, A. (2019). Extended Value Stream Mapping Method for Information Based Improvement of Production Logistics Processes. *IEEE Engineering Management Review*, *47*(4), 119–127. doi:10.1109/EMR.2019.2934953

Cao, X., Li, T., & Wang, Q. (2018). RFID-based multi-attribute logistics information processing and anomaly mining in production logistics. *International Journal of Production Research*, *57*(17), 5453–5466. doi:10.1080/00207543.2018.1526421

Ding, K., & Jiang, P. Y. (2018). RFID-based production data analysis in an IoT-enabled smart job-shop. *IEEE/CAA Journal of Automatica Sinica*, *5*(1), 128 – 138. doi:10.1109/JAS.2017.7510418

Dutta, P., Choi, T. M., Somani, S., & Butala, R. (2020). Blockchain technology in supply chain operations: Applications, challenges and research opportunities. *Transportation Research Part E, Logistics and Transportation Review*, *142*, 102067. doi:10.1016/j.tre.2020.102067 PMID:33013183

Giovanni, P. D. (2020). Blockchain and smart contracts in supply chain management: A game theoretic model. *International Journal of Production Economics*, *228*(107855), 1–18. doi:10.1016/j.ijpe.2020.107855

Helo, P., & Hao, Y. (2019). Blockchains in operation and supply chains: A model and reference implementation. *Computers & Industrial Engineering*, *136*, 242–251. doi:10.1016/j.cie.2019.07.023

Huang, Z., Kim, J., Sadri, A., Dowey, S., & Dargusch, M. S. (2019). Industry 4.0: Development of a multi-agent system for dynamic value stream mapping in SMEs. *Journal of Manufacturing Systems*, *52*, 1–12. doi:10.1016/j.jmsy.2019.05.001

Javaid, M., Haleem, A., Singh, R. P., Khan, S., & Suman, R. (2021). Blockchain technology applications for Industry 4.0: A literature-based review. *Blockchain: Research and Applications*, *2*(4), 1-11. doi:10.1016/j.bcra.2021.100027

Jovanovic, M., Kostic, N., Sebastian, I. M., & Sedej, T. (2022). Managing a blockchain-based platform ecosystem for industry-wide adoption: The case of TradeLens. *Technological Forecasting and Social Change*, *184*(121981), 1–15. doi:10.1016/j.techfore.2022.121981

Kasten, J. E. (2020). Engineering and Manufacturing on the Blockchain: A Systematic Review. *IEEE Engineering Management Review*, *48*(1), 31–47. doi:10.1109/EMR.2020.2964224

Knoll, D., Reinhart, G., & Prüglmeier, M. (2019). Enabling value stream mapping for internal logistics using multidimensional process mining. *Expert Systems with Applications*, *124*, 130–142. doi:10.1016/j.eswa.2019.01.026

Leng, J., Yan, D., Liu, Q., Xu, K., Zhao, J. L., Shi, R., Wei, L., Zhang, D., & Chen, X. (2020). ManuChain: Combining Permissioned Blockchain with a Holistic Optimization Model as Bi-Level Intelligence for Smart Manufacturing. *IEEE Transactions on Systems, Man, and Cybernetics. Systems*, *50*(1), 182–192. doi:10.1109/TSMC.2019.2930418

Leng, J., Ye, S., Zhou, M., Zhao, J. L., Liu, Q., Guo, W., Cao, W., & Fu, L. (2021). Blockchain-Secured Smart Manufacturing in Industry 4.0: A Survey. *IEEE Transactions on Systems, Man, and Cybernetics. Systems*, *51*(1), 237–252. doi:10.1109/TSMC.2020.3040789

Lim, M. K., Li, Y., Wang, C., & Tseng, M. L. (2021). A literature review of blockchain technology applications in supply chains: A comprehensive analysis of themes, methodologies and industries. *Computers & Industrial Engineering*, *154*(107133), 1–14. doi:10.1016/j.cie.2021.107133

Liu, Z., & Li, Z. (2020). A blockchain-based framework of cross-border e-commerce supply chain. *International Journal of Information Management*, *52*(102059), 1–18. doi:10.1016/j.ijinfomgt.2019.102059

Lohmer, J., & Lasch, R. (2020). Blockchain in operations management and manufacturing: Potential and barriers. *Computers & Industrial Engineering*, *149*(106789), 1–15. doi:10.1016/j.cie.2020.106789

Longo, F., Nicoletti, L., Padovano, A., D'Atri, G., & Forte, M. (2019). Blockchain-enabled supply chain: An experimental study. *Computers & Industrial Engineering*, *136*, 57–69. doi:10.1016/j.cie.2019.07.026

Martinus, W., Wahab, M. S., Yudi, & Ham, H. (2021). Data Transmission Using RFID System on Smart Shopping Carts for Checkout Process Efficiency in Supermarket at Indonesia. *Procedia Computer Science*, *179*, 902–912. doi:10.1016/j.procs.2021.01.080

Masuti, P. M., & Dabade, U. A. (2019). Lean manufacturing implementation using value stream mapping at excavator manufacturing company. *Materials Today: Proceedings*, *19*, 606–610. doi:10.1016/j.matpr.2019.07.740

Munim, Z. H., Balasubramaniyan, S., Kouhizadeh, M., & Hossain, N. U. I. (2022). Assessing blockchain technology adoption in the Norwegian oil and gas industry using Bayesian Best Worst Method. *Journal of Industrial Information Integration*, *28*(100346), 1–14. doi:10.1016/j.jii.2022.100346

Occhiuzzi, C., Amendola, S., Nappi, S., D'Uva, N., & Marrocco, G. (2019). RFID Technology for Industry 4.0: Architectures and Challenges. *IEEE International Conference on RFID Technology and Applications (RFID-TA)*, 181 – 186. 10.1109/RFID-TA.2019.8892049

Romero, L. F., & Arce, A. (2017). Applying Value Stream Mapping in Manufacturing: A Systematic Literature Review. *IFAC-PapersOnLine*, *50-1*(1), 1075–1086. doi:10.1016/j.ifacol.2017.08.385

Rožman, N., Diaci, J., & Corn, M. (2021). Scalable framework for blockchain-based shared manufacturing. *Robotics and Computer-integrated Manufacturing*, *71*(102139), 1–14. doi:10.1016/j.rcim.2021.102139

Schmidt, C. G., & Wagner, S. M. (2019). Blockchain and supply chain relations: A transaction cost theory perspective. *Journal of Purchasing and Supply Management*, *25*(100552), 1–13. doi:10.1016/j.pursup.2019.100552

Song, J. M., Sung, J., & Park, T. (2019). Applications of Blockchain to Improve Supply Chain Traceability. *Procedia Computer Science*, *162*, 119–122. doi:10.1016/j.procs.2019.11.266

Stadnicka, D., & Litwin, P. (2019). Value stream mapping and system dynamics integration for manufacturing line modelling and analysis. *International Journal of Production Economics*, *208*, 400–411. doi:10.1016/j.ijpe.2018.12.011

Su, D., Zhang, L., Peng, H., Saeidi, P., & Tirkolaee, E. B. (2023). Technical challenges of blockchain technology for sustainable manufacturing paradigm in Industry 4.0 era using a fuzzy decision support system. *Technological Forecasting and Social Change*, *188*(122275), 1–15. doi:10.1016/j.techfore.2022.122275

Sultan, F. A., Routroy, S., & Thakur, M. (2021). A simulation-based performance investigation of downstream operations in the Indian Surimi Supply Chain using environmental value stream mapping. *Journal of Cleaner Production*, *286*(125389), 1–15. doi:10.1016/j.jclepro.2020.125389

Tao, F., Zhang, Y., Cheng, Y., Ren, J., Wang, D., Qi, Q., & Li, P. (2021). Digital twin and blockchain enhanced smart manufacturing service collaboration and management. *Journal of Manufacturing Systems*, *62*, 903–914. doi:10.1016/j.jmsy.2020.11.008

Teng, Y., Li, L., Song, L., Yu, F. R., & Leung, V. C. M. (2021). Profit Maximizing Smart Manufacturing over AI Enabled Configurable Blockchains. *IEEE Internet of Things Journal*, *9*(1), 346–358. doi:10.1109/JIOT.2021.3098917

Tseng, F. M., Liang, C. W., & Nguyen, N. B. (2023). Blockchain technology adoption and business performance in large enterprises: A comparison of the United States and China. *Technology in Society*, *73*(102230), 1–9. doi:10.1016/j.techsoc.2023.102230

Wang, B., Wang, P., & Tu, Y. (2021). Customer satisfaction service match and service quality-based blockchain cloud manufacturing. *International Journal of Production Economics*, *240*(108220), 1–13. doi:10.1016/j.ijpe.2021.108220

Wang, Z., Wang, T., Hu, H., Gong, J., Ren, X., & Xiao, Q. (2020). Blockchain-based framework for improving supply chain traceability and information sharing in precast construction. *Automation in Construction*, *111*(103063), 1–13. doi:10.1016/j.autcon.2019.103063

Westerkamp, M., Victor, F., & Küpper, A. (2020). Tracing manufacturing processes using blockchain-based token compositions. *Digital Communications and Networks*, *6*(2), 167–176. doi:10.1016/j.dcan.2019.01.007

Yang, A., Li, Y., Liu, C., Li, J., Zhang, Y., & Wang, J. (2019). Research on logistics supply chain of iron and steel enterprises based on block chain technology. *Future Generation Computer Systems*, *101*, 635–645. doi:10.1016/j.future.2019.07.008

Yu, C., Jiang, X., Yu, S., & Yang, C. (2020). Blockchain-based shared manufacturing in support of cyber physical systems: Concept, framework, and operation. *Robotics and Computer-integrated Manufacturing*, *64*(101931), 1–15. doi:10.1016/j.rcim.2019.101931

Zhang, C., Zhou, G., Li, H., & Cao, Y. (2020). Manufacturing Blockchain of Things for the Configuration of a Data- and Knowledge-Driven Digital Twin Manufacturing Cell. *IEEE Internet of Things Journal*, *7*(12), 11884–11894. doi:10.1109/JIOT.2020.3005729

Zhang, L. H., Li, T., & Fan, T. J. (2018). Inventory misplacement and demand forecast error in the supply chain: Profitable RFID strategies under wholesale and buy-back contracts. *International Journal of Production Research*, *56*(15), 5188–5205. doi:10.1080/00207543.2018.1463110

Zhang, Y., & Wang, Z. (2019). Optimal RFID Deployment in a Multiple-Stage Production System Under Inventory Inaccuracy and Robust Control Policy. *IEEE Transactions on Industrial Informatics*, *15*(6), 3230–3242. doi:10.1109/TII.2018.2878638

Zhang, Y., Xu, X., Liu, A., Lu, Q., Xu, L., & Tao, F. (2019). Blockchain-Based Trust Mechanism for IoT-Based Smart Manufacturing System. *IEEE Transactions on Computational Social Systems*, *6*(6), 1386–1394. doi:10.1109/TCSS.2019.2918467

KEY TERMS AND DEFINITIONS

API: Application Programming Interface. It is a set of definitions and protocols for building and integrating application software.

HTTP: HyperText Transfer Protocol. This is standard application-level protocol used for exchanging files on the internet.

IoTs: Internet of Things. This is a system of interrelated computing devices, mechanical and digital machines.

RFID: Radio Frequency Identification. The term would better describe a form of wireless communication that incorporates the use of electromagnetic or electrostatic coupling in the radio frequency portion of the electromagnetic spectrum to uniquely identify an object, animal or person.

Chapter 2
Process-Oriented Model for Managing Software Development Projects Using the PRINCE2 Method

Katja Kous
Faculty of Electrical Engineering and Computer Science, University of Maribor, Slovenia

ABSTRACT

This chapter focuses on the process-oriented model for software development using the PRINCE2 method, and it is divided into two primary parts. The first part offers a theoretical overview of project management, encompassing project definition, the definition and classification of project management, including the characteristics of both traditional and agile project management. Additionally, within this part, the process of software development and the key characteristics of PRINCE2 are presented, including the description of the processes defined by the mentioned method. The second part of the chapter is dedicated to integrating the software development process with the PRINCE2 processes. The constructed process-oriented model includes the nine phases with both the PRINCE2 processes and software development processes intertwined. Based on a critical review of the usefulness of the integration model, the advantages and disadvantages are presented. This well-structured model can significantly contribute to the successful management of software projects.

INTRODUCTION

Project management has been a significant and dynamic field over the past few decades. During this time, many researchers have been investigating different aspects of this complex area of project management, both theoretically and practically. Until today, many project management methods have been developed to address the specific needs and requirements of different projects. These methods serve as indispensable tools in project management, enabling effective progress measurement and task control (Jamali & Oveisi, 2016). Some methods follow traditional management approaches that are not limited

DOI: 10.4018/979-8-3693-0458-7.ch002

to a specific project domain, providing a structured framework for managing projects in a general sense. On the other hand, some approaches are more iterative and incremental, seeking to avoid the standard approaches. They are typically tailored to specific domains, focusing on the unique characteristics and requirements of those industries or project types.

Project management methods can be categorized into two different categories: (I) traditional project management methods and (II) agile methods (Jamali & Oveisi, 2016). Traditional project management methods typically follow a linear process, where all the process phases occur in sequence. This means that one phase should be finished before the next phase starts. Traditional methods highlight the need for comprehensive upfront planning of various project aspects, including crucial factors like cost, scope, and time. Consequently, these methods are frequently labeled as inflexible and less adaptable to change. On the other hand, agile methods present an iterative approach that focuses more on incorporating customer feedback and continuous releases with every iteration of a software development project (Flora & Chande, 2014). Agile methods prioritize individuals and their interactions, teamwork, customer collaboration, and flexibility. They delve into evolving changes and collaborative efforts to bring out results rather than adhering strictly to a predefined process. Adaptive planning is a key characteristic of Agile methods, allowing for flexibility and responsiveness to changing project needs. Although it is believed that agile methods were used only for software development; today, this is no longer the case. Other areas, such as marketing, IT, event planning, and product development, have adapted and modified the agile method to fit their industries (Asana, 2022). In the realm of agile methods in the software development domain, the three most notable representatives of agile methods, which focus on flexibility, iterative development, and continuous improvement, are (I) *Scrum*, (II) *Kanban*, and (III) *Extreme Programming* (XP) (Chaouch, Mejri, & Ghannouchi, 2019), while two prominent representatives of traditional project management methods are (I) *Projects IN Controlled Environments* (PRINCE2) (AXELOS Limited, 2017), and (II) *Project Management Body of Knowledge* (PMBOK) (Project Management Institute, 2017a).

Despite the availability of numerous project management methods also in the Information and Communication Technology (ICT) domain, software development projects often face significant challenges and have a reputation for failure. These projects frequently encounter issues such as exceeding budget constraints, experiencing delays, or failing to meet customer requirements (Cerpa & Verner, 2009; Savolainen, Ahonen, & Richardson, 2015). Moreover, examples from the real world demonstrate that approximately 70% of digital transformations do not achieve their intended objectives (Forth, Reichert, de Laubier, & Saibal, 2020). The 2020 Global Application Modernization Business Barometer Report states that 74% of organizations that initiated a legacy system modernization project failed to complete it, aligning with the 70% failure rate reported by McKinsey & Co. several years ago (Pratt, 2021). These statistics underscore the challenges and complexities involved in managing ICT projects successfully.

Numerous studies have been conducted to investigate and identify factors that can improve the success of IT projects. For example, a study by Iriarte and Bayona (2020) focused on success factors, while Pankratz and Basten (2014) examined success criteria. Bilir and Yafez (2021) and Varajão and Trigo (2016) researched the success achieved in project management and projects. Islam and Evans (2020) explored the key factors of success for software development projects within the PRINCE2 method. Thought the research, 20 factors have been identified as key success factors, such as defined roles and responsibilities, scope management, management by stages, adequate planning, top management support, time management, risk management, monitoring project progress, change management, communication management, quality management, project team competency, managing product delivery, cost management, learn from experience, prioritizing task, assign work to the right person, benefit realization and being agile (Islam & Evans, 2020).

Kruger and Rudman (2013) reported that software projects often fail due to a lack of well-structured project management methods. This indicates that software projects are missing essential steps for effective project management, which are typically well-defined in traditional project management methods. However, project managers have acknowledged that traditional methods can be complex and time-consuming (Kruger & Rudman, 2013). This complexity poses challenges for project managers, particularly in the context of software development projects, making it difficult to apply traditional approaches to project management successfully (Kruger & Rudman, 2013).

In light of this, we suggest to integrate the PRINCE2 method into the software development process. This integration aims to provide a process-oriented model that offers a comprehensive overview of the phases and activities required in a software development project, encompassing both project management and software production perspectives. This model can significantly help all stakeholders, including senior executives, IT project managers, IT team managers, team members, and IT developers. It can bring the procedural process closer to them and enables ease of implementation of project management method in the software development process. Importantly, it also offers a well-structured approach to eliminate unsuccessfully completed projects.

The chapter is organized into seven sections. The next section includes the presentation of the theoretical overview of project management. In the beginning, project definitions and definitions and classifications of project management, including the characteristics of both traditional and agile project management, are presented. The following section is focused on the presentation of the software development processes. The fourth section describes traditional project management methods, called PRINCE2, including a detailed presentation of PRINCE2 processes. The fifth section presents a description of the investigation, including the research objective, methodology, and integration of the Software Development Life Cycle and the PRINCE2 method. Additionally, the section detail the process-oriented approach for the development of software projects with the mentioned method. After that, the advantages and disadvantages of using the model are given, and trends in project management are presented. The chapter is finished with a conclusions section.

WHAT ARE PROJECTS AND PROJECT MANAGEMENT?

The topics of projects and project management have always been relevant and continue to be extensively researched by many authors. The focus of their research is on finding effective ways to ensure projects are successfully completed within the allocated time, budget, resources, and objectives. As a result, numerous definitions of projects and project management have developed over time to capture the evolving understanding of project management practices. Only the most important ones are presented below.

Project Definition

According to the Britannica Dictionary (The Britannica Dictionary, 2023), a project is "a planned piece of work with a specific purpose, such as acquiring information or creating something new, typically requiring a significant amount of time". A more straightforward definition characterizes a project as "a series of tasks that must be completed to achieve a particular outcome" (Kissflow, 2022). PRINCE2 defines a project as "a temporary organization established to deliver one or more business products based on an agreed business case" (AXELOS Limited, 2017). In the 3rd edition of the PMBoK, a project is categorized as a "temporary endeavor with a defined beginning and end, aimed at creating a unique product, service, or result" (Project Management Institute, 2004). However, in the 7th edition, projects are viewed as the primary means through which business value is achieved, enabling the attainment of corporate objectives (Iqbal, 2020).

To summarize, the highlighted definitions of project are mostly similar. Thus, a project represents a temporary process where the project's initiation and conclusion should be clearly defined. This process involves a sequence of activities aimed at achieving a unique purpose and the specific objective of the project within defined constraints, such as time, budget, and resources. Although projects may vary in complexity, size, and intended outcome across diverse industries and sectors, they typically comprise fundamental components such as objectives, scope, constraints, resources, stakeholders, timeline, risk, communication, changes, quality, planning, execution, monitoring and control, and closure. For the integration of all these components into a cohesive entire and the successful execution of a project, a well-structured process is required. This process is referred to as project management, and it is presented in the following subsection.

Project Management Definition

In general, project management can be defined as the process to lead or leading a project performed by a team to achieve certain goals. It involves the use of methods, skills, knowledge, and experience to «coordinate activities to direct and control the accomplishment of agreed objectives» (ISO-International Organization for Standardization, 2021). According to the PRINCE2 method, project management is described as "a temporary organization that is needed to produce a unique and predefined outcome or result at a pre-specified time using predetermined resources" (AXELOS Limited, 2017). PMBoK 3rd edition defines project management as "the application of knowledge, skills, tools, and techniques to a broad range of activities in order to meet the requirements of a particular project" (Project Management Institute, 2004). PMBok 7th edition states that project management involves "the application of processes, methods, skills, knowledge, and experience to achieve specific project objectives according to the project acceptance criteria within agreed parameters. Project management has final deliverables that are constrained to a finite timescale and budget" (Project Management Institute, 2017a). Additionally, ISO 10006, a standard for quality in project management, defines it as a "planning, organizing, monitoring, controlling and reporting of all aspects of a project and the motivation of all those involved in it to achieve the project objectives" (ISO-International Organization for Standardization, 2017).

In summary, project management is the practice of organizing and managing resources to ensure the completion of all the necessary tasks within the predefined scope, timeline, and cost limitations. It involves a sequence of activities such as planning, implementing, and monitoring to meet project objectives. Additionally, it encompasses effectively controlling and balancing the constraints of time, cost, and scope to produce quality deliverables that meet or exceed the expectations of project stakeholders.

Project Management Classification

Project management can be classified into two distinct categories: (I) traditional project management and (II) agile project management (Jamali & Oveisi, 2016). Both categories are presented below.

Traditional Project Management

Traditional project management, also known as Waterfall Methodology, adopts a linear approach where processes unfold in a predictable sequence. This methodology follows a predetermined set of stages, assuming that the project requirements remain unchanged while allowing for adjustments to the budget and project timeline. In this approach, the project lifecycle typically comprises five stages, as presented in Figure 1. Those stages are (Tawfik, 2022):

- Initiation: The requirements, scope, risks, benefits, and feasibility of a project are explored during the pre-planning phase, where the project is assessed.
- Planning: Logical project teams are identified, and the project is divided into smaller work items while creating the project schedule.
- Execute: The project plan is implemented, transforming it into a tangible reality.
- Monitor: The project is continuously monitored to ensure it remains on the right track, and adjustments are made to plans, teams, and activities as necessary.
- Close: The project is concluded, and a comprehensive review is conducted to capture lessons learned. Plans for updates or replacements of outdated products are also established.

Figure 1. A process model of stages in traditional project management

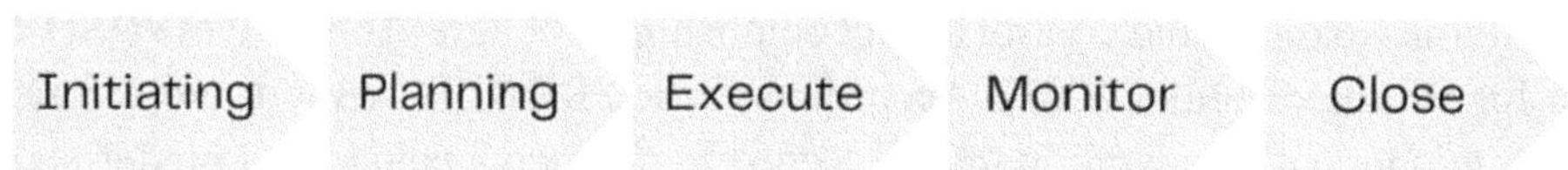

Based on the traditional project approach, two prominent representative methods are (I) *Projects IN Controlled Environments* (PRINCE2) (AXELOS Limited, 2017) and (II) *Project Management Body of Knowledge* (PMBOK) (Project Management Institute, 2017a). Although both approaches are based on their own characteristics, the crucial point is that PMBoK is compatible with PRINCE2 (Williams, 2023). According to Williams (2023), PRINCE2 and PMBoK acknowledge and promote each other's presence in their marketing materials, positioning themselves as complementary approaches that can be utilized together. PRINCE2 is presented as a "method", while PMBoK is positioned as a "standard". However, in practice, organizations choose to adopt either one or both methods based on factors such as the project's nature, location, and associated costs (Williams, 2023). PRINCE2 is widely utilized in the United Kingdom, Australia, and Europe, while PMBoK is more commonly employed in North America (Morjane, Bannari, & Gharib, 2022; Jamali & Oveisi, 2016) and also in Europe Mainland.

Agile Project Management

Agile project management is known as the alternative approach to the traditional software development process (Chaouch et al., 2019). The Association for Project Management defined agile project management as an "iterative approach to delivering a project throughout its life cycle. Iterative or agile life cycles are composed of several iterations or incremental steps towards the completion of a project" (Association for Project Management, 2022). Therefore, agile project management is an iterative and flexible approach to managing software development projects (Association for Project Management, 2022). It prioritizes collaboration, adaptability, and continuous improvement throughout the lifecycle of the software project. It is based on the Agile Manifesto, which outlines a set of values and principles that guide project management practices (Flora & Chande, 2014). Key values defined in the Agile Manifesto are (Kirvan & Pratt, 2023):

- Customer collaboration over contract negotiation: Emphasizing close collaboration with customers or stakeholders to ensure their requirements are understood and addressed throughout the project.
- Responding to change over following a plan: Acknowledging that project requirements and circumstances can change and being able to adapt and respond to those changes effectively.
- Working software over comprehensive documentation: Prioritizing the development of functional software that provides value to users, rather than focusing solely on extensive documentation.
- Individuals and interactions over processes and tools: Recognizing the importance of effective communication, collaboration, and teamwork within the project team.

Agile project management divides projects into several dynamic phases, known as sprints. Those phases are flexible and, as presented in Figure 2, composed by planning, design, development, testing, deployment, and review. Each sprint typically lasts for a few weeks and focuses on delivering a small but functional piece of the overall project. The project requirements and priorities can be re-evaluated and adjusted at the end of each sprint, allowing for flexibility and responsiveness to changes.

Figure 2. Agile development process

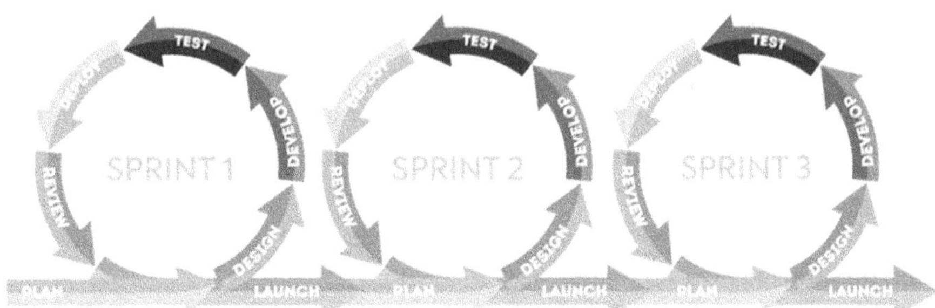

Until today, many agile methods have been developed, such as Kanban, Scrum, Extreme Programming (XP), Adaptive Project Framework (APF), Extreme Project Management (XPM), Adaptive Software Development (ASD), Dynamic Systems Development Method (DSDM), Feature Driven Development (FDD) and each of them has own characteristics and specific. For example, Scrum breaks down extensive projects into smaller tasks that can be completed within short development cycles (Figure 3 (a)). However, it is primarily oriented around products rather than projects. Kanban adopts a visual and incremental approach, representing task statuses on a board as to do, in progress, and done (Figure

3 (b)). Crystal, designed for short-term projects, involves co-located teams. DSDM is a methodology more applicable to large organizations, while FDD is intensely focused on the development team and mandates comprehensive documentation and rigorous organization (Martin & Martin, 2023). From the mentioned crowd of agile methods, the most notable representatives are (I) SCRUM, (II) Kanban, and (III) Extreme Programming (XP) (Chaouch et al., 2019).

Figure 3. (a) Scrum framework; (b) Kanban board example (Martin & Martin, 2023)

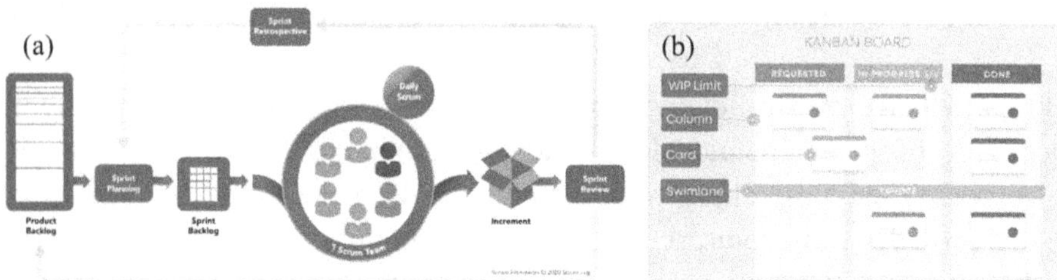

SOFTWARE DEVELOPMENT PROCESS

Overview of the Software Development Process

A software development process refers to a structured and systematic approach used to create software applications. It covers various phases, activities, and methodologies that guide the development team through the entire lifecycle of software creation. The aim of a software development process is to produce high-quality software that meets user requirements while adhering to project constraints such as time, budget, and resources.

Software Development Life Cycle (SDLC) is a specific conceptual framework that outlines the phases and activities involved in developing software, from analysis to maintenance (Rouse, 2011). Therefore, it provides a structured approach employed within the software domain to design, develop, and test high-quality ICT solutions. As presented in Figure 4, SDLC, based on the Waterfall model, comprises six phases and presents the sequential process model where one phase should be concluded before the next phase can commence. It begins with analysis, progresses through design, implementation, testing, and deployment, and finishes with maintenance.

Presentation of SDLC's Phases

The first phase in SDLC is called analysis, where everyone involved gets an answer to the question: What do we need, or what the built software system should provide? Therefore, before the software team can develop the idea into a final software product, it is crucial to gather and analyze the actual requirements of the customer and also business requirements. In this phase, the project manager collaborates with all stakeholders, including customers, users, and business analysts, to collect and understand the requirements of the software. This phase is also focused on identifying the project's needs and objectives, as well as documenting both functional and non-functional requirements and creating a detailed project

Figure 4. The software development life cycle

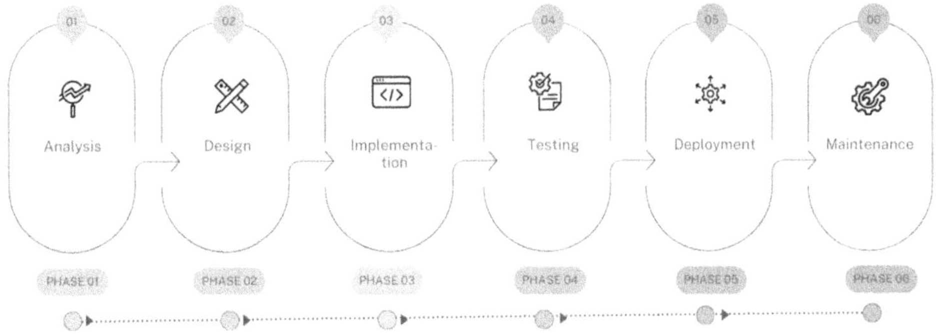

scope. The activities within this phase are not carried out sequentially but simultaneously, and they are divided into two groups:

- Problem analysis – the outcome is a complete understanding of the problem area and
- Product description – the outcome is a consistent and comprehensive document called Software Requirements Specifications (SRS), which outlines the functional requirements, characteristics of the hardware environment, the basic form of user interfaces, and implementation goals or required capabilities.

The next phase in SDLC is called design. This phase can answer the question: How to do it, or how will we satisfy the identified requirements - system behavior? Based on the requirements gathered in Phase 1, the design phase involves creating a design for the software system. This includes defining the architecture, data structures, interfaces, and components. System designers in this phase also consider factors such as scalability, security, and performance. The design process covers the following steps:

- Preliminary planning - this involves breaking down the software system into coherent components and further breaking down these components into smaller sub-components until they are easily understandable. Each module is then documented with descriptions of inputs, outputs, and data transformation functions and
- Detailed planning - in this step, algorithms for each module are defined and documented.

The outcome of this phase is a Software Design Document (SDD) and modular decomposition of the software system, definition of data structures, specification of file formats, and description of the most crucial algorithms.

After the design documents are created, the next phase can begin, known as implementation. In this phase, developers write the actual code based on the design specifications. They use frameworks, programming languages, and tools to build the software application. The primary focus of the phase is the development of perfect codes because the proper coding practices, code documentation, and coding standards are crucial to ensure maintainable and error-free code. This phase is often the longest in the entire process in SDLC.

The fourth phase is very crucial in SDLC and is called testing. In this phase, the software is systematically checked for defects, errors, and inconsistencies. When testing individual modules, the focus is on specific parts of the program to more easily the identification and resolution of errors. At the same time, control of the behavior of the module is also verified against the specified specifications (functional testing). Subsequently, verified modules are integrated or combined into a unified program structure, constituting the whole system. This is followed by system testing, wherein the entire software system is evaluated within a specific hardware environment to ensure its alignment with the given specifications of the software requirements. Therefore, various testing techniques are employed, including unit testing (testing individual components), integration testing (testing interactions between components), system testing (testing the entire system), as well as acceptance testing, and non-functional testing, like performance, security, etc. During this phase, identified bugs and issues are reported and subsequently addressed.

The next phase is deployment, which starts when the software is prepared for release. This means that all the coding errors have been removed during the testing stage, and the software successfully passes testing and quality assurance evaluations. The deployment phase involves releasing the software to the intended environment, which could be a production server, a cloud-based platform, or any other deployment target. During this phase, configuration, setup, and installation are also performed.

Following the deployment phase, the customers start using developed software. During the use of the software, the actual issues may start surfacing with time, and this requires the maintenance of the software. Therefore, after the deployment phase, the software enters the maintenance phase, which is the final phase in the SDLC. In this phase, the software is actively monitored within the live environment. Any arising issues are dealt with, and essential updates and improvements are implemented. Maintenance can include different activities, like bug fixes, performance optimizations, feature enhancements, and updates to accommodate changes in technology or user needs.

PROJECTS IN CONTROLLED ENVIRONMENTS (PRINCE2)

The PRINCE2 method is one of the representatives of a traditional approach to project management. It is a process-oriented method, which is flexible and can be tailored to any project irrespective of scale, complexity, culture, or geography. The current edition from 2017 was developed on the experience of thousands of projects and the contributions of people, academics, project managers, and consultants.

History Background of the PRINCE2 Method

The PRINCE2 method has a long and extensive history starting from 1975. Its initial stage was known as PROMPT II (Project Resource Organization Management Planning Techniques) and was introduced by Simpact Systems Ltd. Subsequently, it received official recognition from the UK Government's Central Computer and Telecommunication Agency (CCTA) (PRINCE2, 2023). In 1989, the CCTA renamed it as PRINCE, retaining the original acronym (PROMPT II IN the CCTA Environment) and utilizing it for IT projects. However, civil servants later changed the name to Projects IN Controlled Environments, which is still used today. The methodology was ripe with problems as it was rigid and lacked the tailorable attributes it possesses today (PRINCE2, 2023). Following consultations with numerous project management experts and approximately 150 organizations, PRINCE2 was formally established in 1996. This version was considered an improved and more adaptable iteration compared to its earlier editions. In 2009, significant revisions were made to the methodology, including the incorporation of seven fundamental principles. Subsequently, in 2013, ownership of PRINCE2 was transferred to AXELOS Ltd (PRINCE2, 2023). AXELOS further updated PRINCE2 with its 2017 edition, where the method was further revised in line with feedback received from world-leading practitioners (PRINCE2, 2023).

Practical Application of the PRINCE2 Method

The PRINCE2 method is useful in various sectors, including Public Sector, Oil and Gas Industry, Construction, IT, Banking, Engineering, Operations Management, and Marketing. In the Public Sector, organizations like the NHS, Home Office, and Metropolitan Police use the PRINCE2 method to manage projects effectively, ensuring optimal resource utilization and justifiable taxpayer expenditure. In Oil and Gas Companies such as Shell, BP, and Transpower New Zealand (Knowledgehut, 2023), PRINCE2-certified project managers enhance project success by maintaining financial viability and resource utilization in complex projects. Similarly, the Construction Industry, like as the UK Highways Agency and IPP Contracting Ltd. (Knowledgehut, 2023), benefits from PRINCE2's adaptable framework, aiding project managers in adhering to budgets, risks, and quality standards. In the Banking Industry, such as Barclays (Knowledgehut, 2023), the PRINCE2 method ensures data protection and financial stability in projects, enhancing employability prospects for Finance Project Managers. For the Engineering sector, the PRINCE2 method offers structured project management, aligning with the key themes of Organization, Quality, Planning, and Risk Management. Operations Management benefits from PRINCE2's process-driven framework, ensuring projects meet quality, time, and budget requirements. In Marketing, the PRINCE2 method helps manage campaigns within predefined budgets and deadlines, providing a flexible method for varying project sizes and complexities. The methodology facilitates clear roles and responsibilities among stakeholders while maintaining a common framework for effective communication (The Knowledge Academy, 2023).

Within the IT sector, the PRINCE2 method enables monitoring and management control processes, regardless of project size, type, or scope. The method's capability to oversee projects and assess progress at every stage empowers IT companies to thoroughly evaluate a project's financial feasibility, aiding decisions on whether to proceed or adapt objectives. The IT industry faces distinct challenges, primarily due to the rapidly evolving nature of technology and customer expectations. The adaptability of the PRINCE2 method suits IT projects for several reasons (The Knowledge Academy, 2023):

- It can be tailored to projects of any scale.
- The PRINCE2 method is responsive to changes in project requirements and goals, regardless of their scope.
- The method enhances the likelihood of projects being completed on time and within budget.
- The PRINCE2 method fosters effective communication among all project stakeholders, regardless of their roles.
- Projects begin with clearly defined outcomes and objectives, ensuring alignment among all contributors.
- The PRINCE2 method promotes the creation of risk contingency plans, minimizing risky practices.
- Its structured approach facilitates project execution to achieve maximum benefits.

IT companies that employ the PRINCE2 method are IBM, HP, Siemens, Philips, Vodafone, and Ericsson Services Ireland, as mentioned in (The Knowledge Academy, 2023).

Components of the PRINCE2 Method

The current edition of the method addresses project management with four integrated elements of principles, themes, processes, and the project environment, as presented in Figure 5. Therefore, PRINCE2 includes (AXELOS Limited, 2017):

- the project environment,
- 7 PRINCE2 principles,
- 7 PRINCE2 thems and
- 7 PRINCE2 processes.

Figure 5. The structure of method PRINCE2
Source: AXELOS Limited (2017)

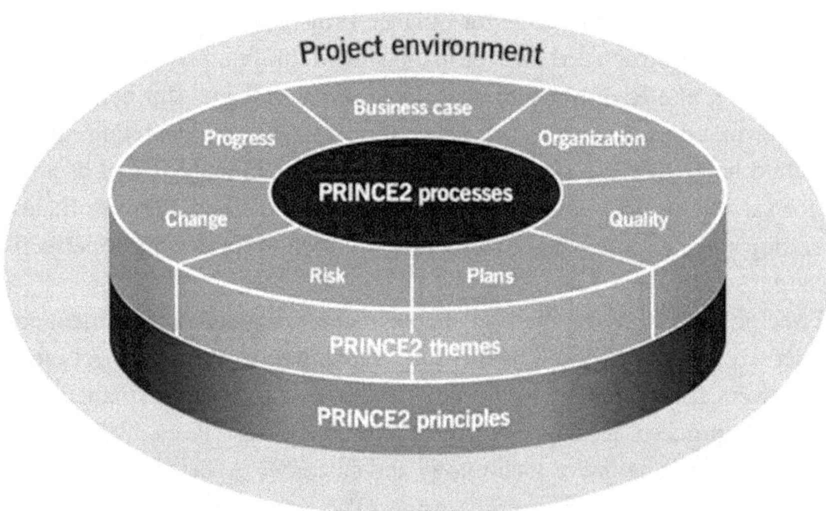

Organizations often want a consistent approach to managing projects. The project environment segment facilitates the organization's customization process of the PRINCE2 method, enabling them to develop their own project management methodology. This tailored method is then integrated into the organization's overall way of working (AXELOS, 2017).

The PRINCE2 principles, derived from lessons learned from past projects, provide the guiding obligations and best practices which determine whether the project is genuinely being managed using PRINCE2. The method encompasses the following seven principles: continuous business justification, learning from experience, defined roles and responsibilities, managing by stages, managing by exception, focusing on products, and tailoring to suit the project (AXELOS Limited, 2017).

PRINCE2 themes describe different areas of project management that should be addressed continually and in parallel throughout the life cycle of the project. They offer insights into how the project should be managed, and they are addressed within the PRINCE2 processes. The following are the themes of PRINCE2 (AXELOS Limited, 2017): business case, organization, quality, plan, risk, change, and progress.

PRINCE2 processes address the chronological flow of the project and describe a progression from the pre-project activity of getting started through the stages of the project lifecycle to the final act of project closure. Each process includes checklists of recommended activities, products, and related responsibilities. PRINCE2 method defines the following processes (AXELOS Limited, 2017):

- starting up a project,
- directing a project,
- initiating a project,
- managing a stage boundary,
- controlling a stage,
- managing product delivery and
- closing a project.

The detail of the processes is presented in the subsection below as they constitute the most crucial component of our integrated process-oriented model.

Process Aspect of the PRINCE2 Method

As we already mentioned, PRINCE2 is a process-based approach to managing the project. It means that it is constructed with a set of activities designed to accomplish a specific objective (AXELOS Limited, 2017). PRINCE2 defines seven processes, which offer the set of activities required to direct, manage and deliver a project successfully (AXELOS Limited, 2017). As presented in Figure 6, the direction of a project is project board oriented and is defined within the process of Directing a Project with some activities within the process of Starting up a Project. The management aspect is project manager oriented and is included in the processes of Initiating a Project, Managing a Stage Boundary, Controlling a Stage, Closing a project, and certain activities within the process of Starting up a Project, while the delivery of the project is responsible for a team manager(s) and is described in the process of Managing Product Delivery.

Starting Up a Project

The Starting up a project process is presented as the first process in PRINCE2. It marks as a pre-project process, designed to ensure that the prerequisites for initiating the project are in place. The information about the project available at the time of start-up is presented in the Project mandate, which is provided by the responsible authority, which could be corporate, program management, or the customer. The project mandate can stem from different sources like a feasibility study or a request for a proposal. The document should include adequate information to identify at least the prospective executive of the project board and establish the project's terms of reference. The Project mandate is further developed into the Project brief to provide the necessary information for the project board to decide on project initiation (AXELOS Limited, 2017).

Figure 6. The PRINCE2 processes (summarized by the figure in AXELOS, 2017)

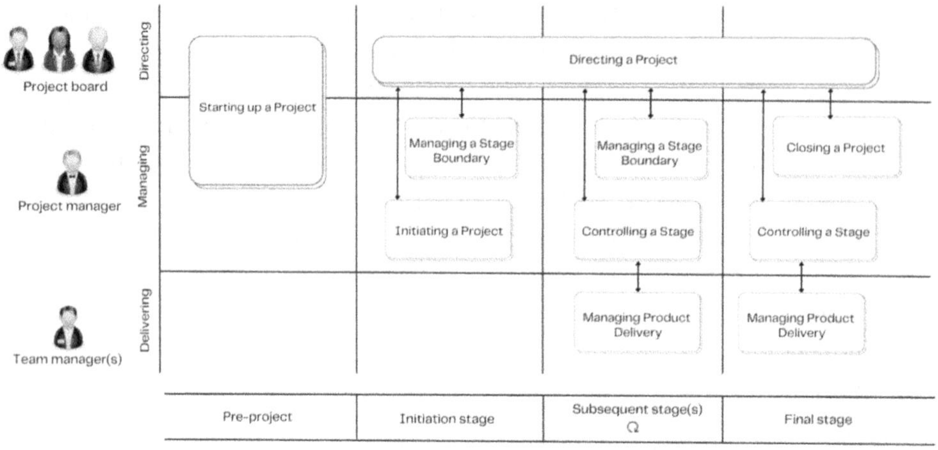

The preparation of the outline business case and the assembly of the project brief involve regular interaction and consultation between the project manager, project board members, and other stakeholders. Investing time in clearly capturing requirements during the project start-up phase leads to time savings during project delivery by preventing issues, exceptions, and the need for extensive replanning. The project brief is subsequently expanded and refined into the Project Initiation Documentation (PID) through the Initiating a Project process (AXELOS Limited, 2017).

The activities within the Starting up a project process are likely to be shared between corporate, programme management or the customer, the executive, and the project manager. The activities are to (AXELOS Limited, 2017):

- appoint the executive and the project manager,
- capture previous lessons,
- design and appoint the project management team,
- prepare the outline business case,
- select the project approach and assemble the project brief and
- plan the initiation stage.

The process of Starting up a project is presented in the following Figure 7.

Directing a Project

The main purpose of the Directing a Project process is to empower the project board with accountability for the project's success (AXELOS Limited, 2017). This is achieved through making critical decisions and exercising overall control by the project board, while the day-to-day management of the project is the obligation of the project manager. Therefore, the project board is responsible for the following (Figure 8) (AXELOS Limited, 2017):

Figure 7. Overview of starting up a project (summarized by the figure in AXELOS, 2017)

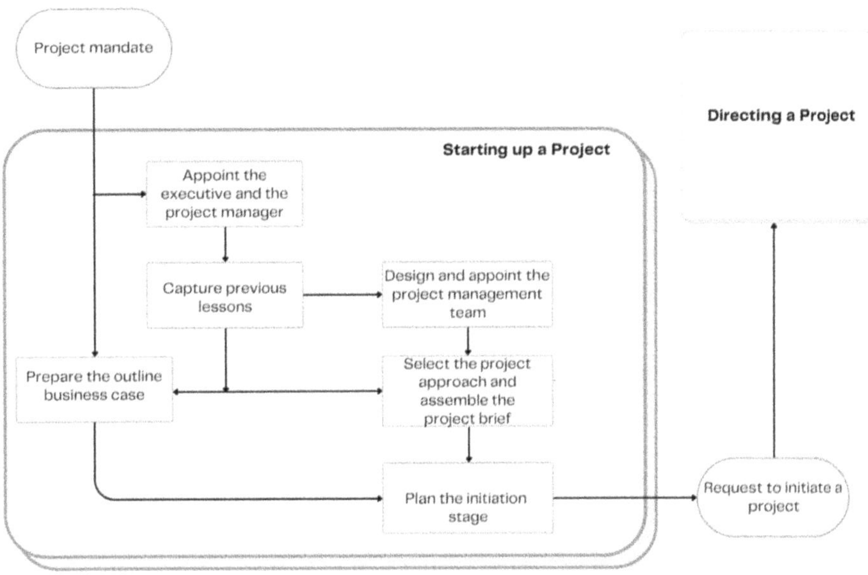

- authorizing the initiation of the project,
- authorizing the project to proceed,
- authorizing a stage plan or exception plan,
- providing ad hoc direction as needed and
- authorizing the closure of the project.

This process is very important and takes place at the end of each phase. Therefore, before the project proceeds to the next phase, the Project board conducts a review of the completed phase and assesses the progress. If the project remains aligned with the scope of the business opportunity, the Project board approves the project to proceed.

Initiating a Project

The purpose of the Initiating a Project process is to establish a strong foundation for the project (AXELOS Limited, 2017). This allows the organization to clearly understand the work required to deliver the project's products before making a significant investment. As a component of the process, approaches for critical project elements, including risk, communication, change management, and quality, must be carefully addressed and formulated. Therefore, within this process, as shown in Figure 9, the project manager is responsible for the following activities (AXELOS Limited, 2017):

- agreeing on tailoring requirements,
- preparing the risk management approach,
- preparing the change control approach,
- preparing the quality management approach,
- preparing the communication management approach,

- setting up project controls,
- creating the project plan,
- refining the business case and
- assembling the project initiation documentation.

Figure 8. Overview of directing a project (summarized by the figure in AXELOS, 2017)

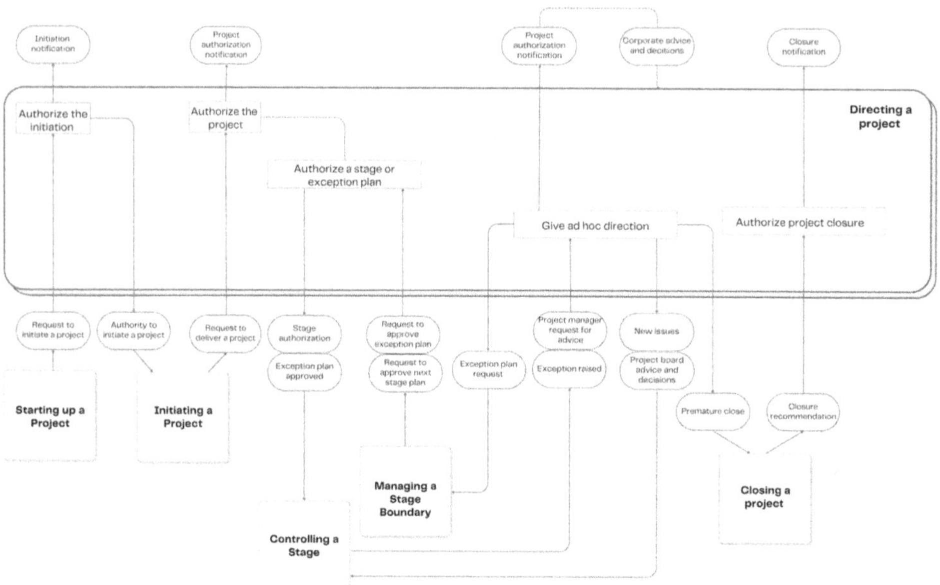

Controlling a Stage

The purpose of the Controlling a Stage process is to allocate tasks, monitor their progress, address any issues that arise, provide progress updates to the project board, and implement corrective actions as necessary. The aim is to ensure that the management stage stays within acceptable tolerance levels. (AXELOS Limited, 2017). This process describes the work of the project manager in handling the day-to-day management of the management stage. This process should be used for each delivery stage of the project, except the final one. Activities within the Controlling a stage process are project manager oriented and comprise (AXELOS Limited, 2017):

- Work packages:
  - authorize a work package,
  - review work package status and
  - receive completed work packages.
- Monitoring and reporting:
  - review the management stage status and
  - report highlights.

Figure 9. Overview of initiating a project (summarized by the figure in AXELOS, 2017)

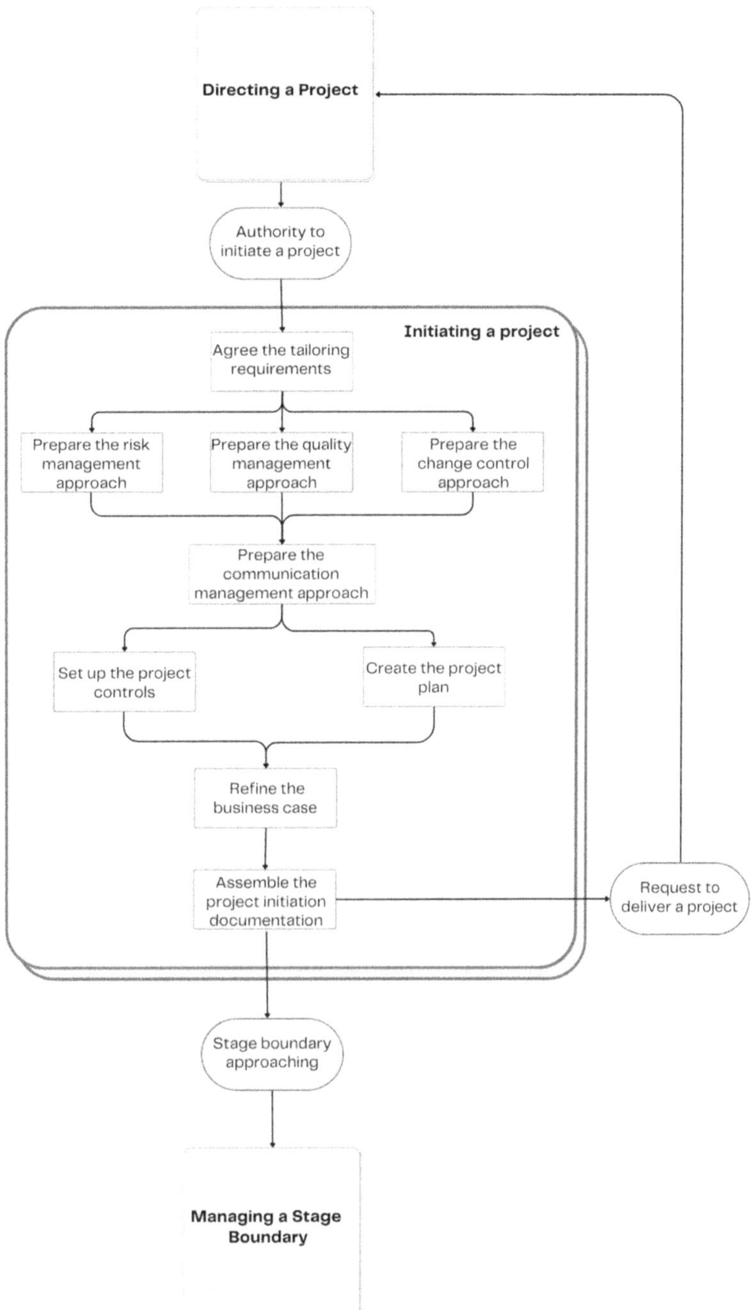

- Issues and risks:
    - capture and examine issues and risks,
    - escalate issues and risks and
    - take corrective action.

Figure 10. Overview of controlling a stage (summarized by the figure in AXELOS, 2017)

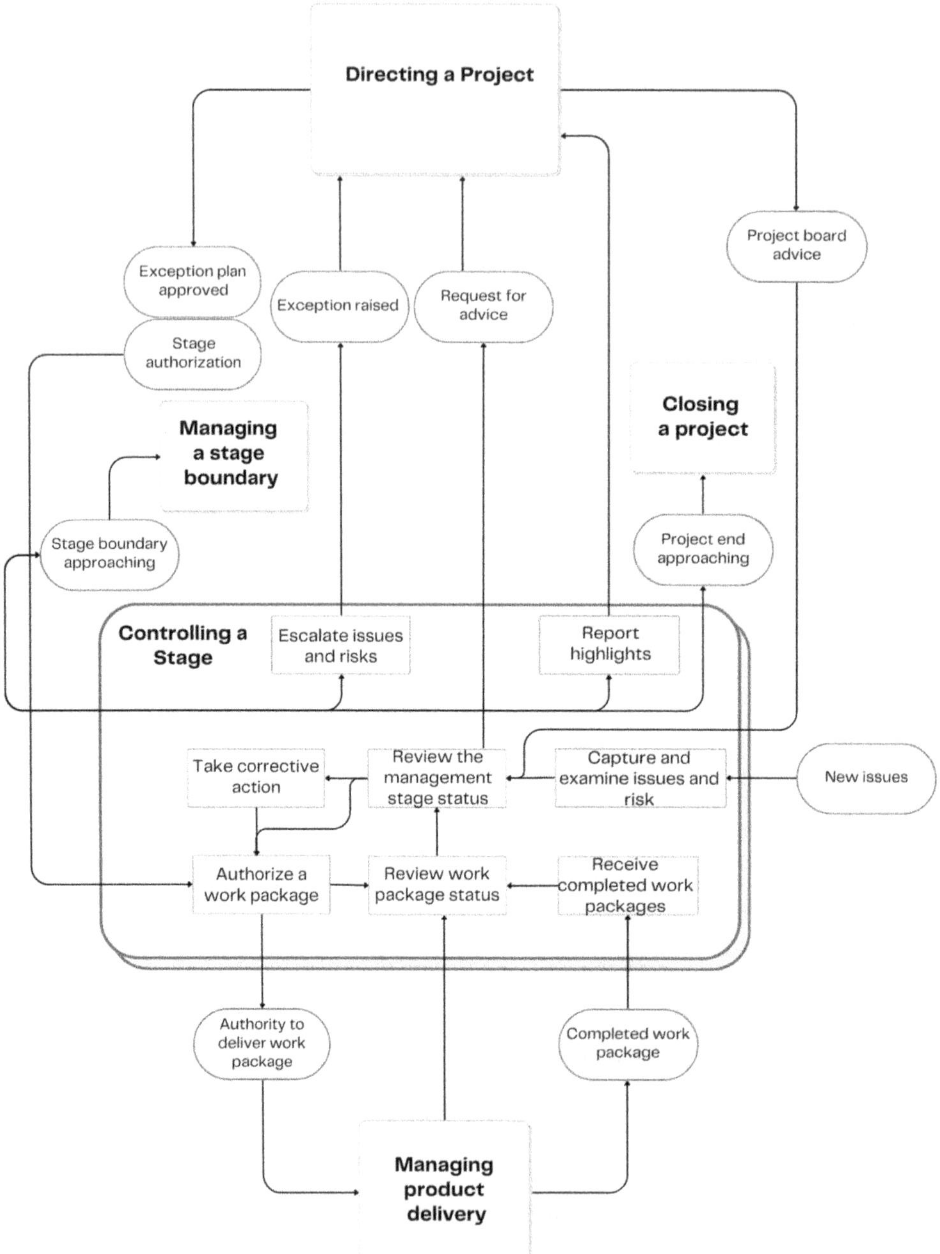

The process is presented in Figure 10.

Managing Product Delivery

The purpose of the Managing Product Delivery process is to establish and maintain effective communication and coordination between the project manager and the team manager(s). This is achieved by agreeing upon the requirements for acceptance, execution, and delivery of the project's products. Managing product delivery focuses on the perspective of the team managers, whose responsibility is to supervise and coordinate a specific area of work that contributes to the delivery of one or more products within the project. Within this process, the team manager(s) should (AXELOS, 2017):

- accept a work package,
- execute a work package, and
- deliver a work package.

The activities within the process are presented in Figure 11.

Figure 11. Overview of managing product delivery (summarized by the figure in AXELOS, 2017)

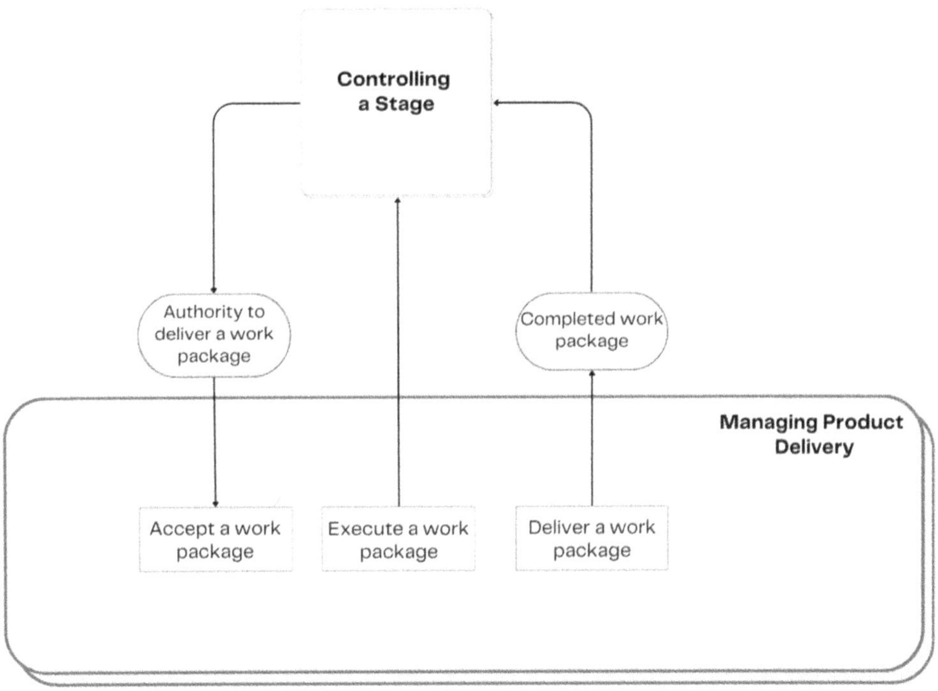

Managing a Stage Boundary

The purpose of Managing a stage boundary process is to enable the project manager to provide the project board with sufficient information to be able to review the success of the current management stage, approve the next stage plan, review the updated project plan, and confirm continued business justification and acceptability of the risks. As presented in Figure 12, The activities within the managing a stage boundary process are project manager oriented and are to (AXELOS Limited, 2017):

- plan the next management stage,
- update the project plan,

- update the business case,
- report management stage end and
- produce an exception plan.

Figure 12. Overview of managing a stage boundary (summarized by the figure in AXELOS, 2017)

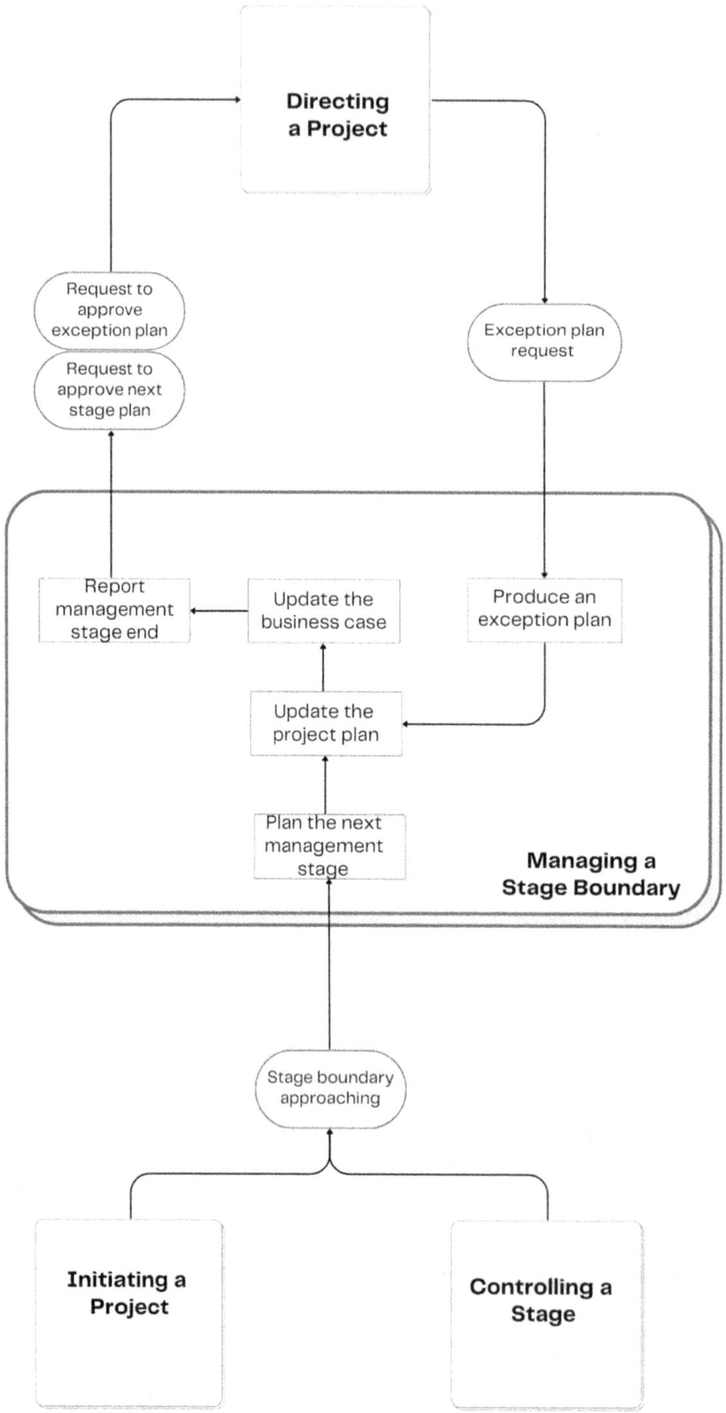

Closing a Project

The purpose of the Closing a Project process is to establish a definitive milestone where the acceptance of the project's deliverables is confirmed. It also serves to acknowledge the achievement of the objectives outlined in the original Project Initiation Documentation (PID) or approved changes to the objectives or recognize when the project has reached its maximum contribution and has no further impact to make.

As presented in Figure 13, the project manager is responsible for the following activities within the mentioned process: preparing for planned closure, preparing for premature closure, handing over the project's deliverables, evaluating the project's performance, and recommending project closure.

Figure 13. Overview of closing a project (summarized by the figure in AXELOS, 2017)

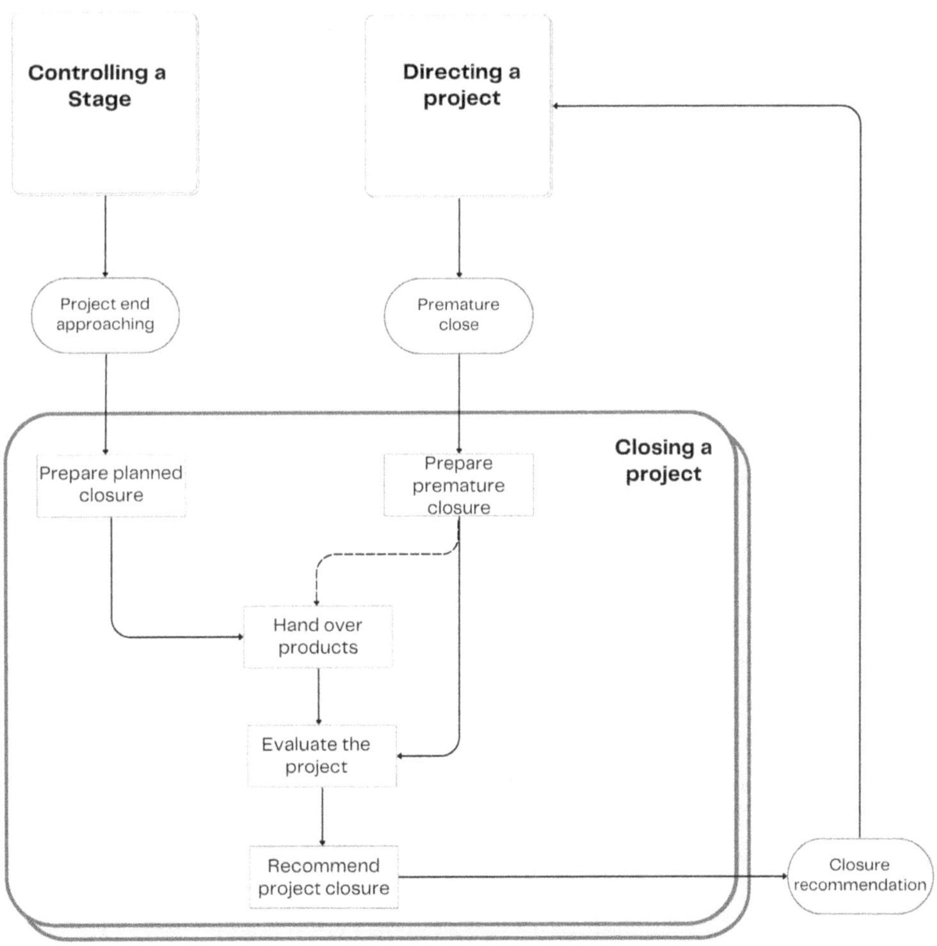

PROCESS-ORIENTED MODEL FOR MANAGING SOFTWARE DEVELOPMENT PROJECTS USING THE PRINCE2 METHOD

The Objective of Model Integration

The main objective is to integrate the PRINCE2 method into the software development process. This integration involves incorporating the project management process following PRINCE2 into the core software development phases. The outcome of this integration is an integration process-oriented model that provides beneficial knowledge of project management to different stakeholders, such as senior executives, IT project managers, IT team managers, team members, and IT developers.

Methodology

The model integration is based on various research methods, including the description method, the analytical method, and the synthesis method. Based on the knowledge obtained from the theoretical background and practical experiences, the integration method was used to create the integration process-oriented model for managing software development projects using PRINCE2 methods.

Figure 14 illustrates the transformed phases model of SDLC. As seen from the mentioned figure, the SDLC phases have been expanded by three additional phases from the project lifecycle: the Pre-project and Pre-analysis phase, the Initiation phase, and the Final phase. As a result, the constructed SDLC model comprises nine phases, where all additional phases are oriented toward project management, except one part of the Pre-project and Pre-analysis phase, where the analysis activities can be related to the content of the software development process.

An Integration Process-Oriented Model of the Software Development Life Cycle and the PRINCE2 Method

This subsection presents the process-oriented model for effectively managing software development projects by integrating SDLC phases and the PRINCE2 method. Before presenting the process-oriented model, the used terminology is described to enhance understanding. For clarity in model presentation, the names of SDLC phases (such as analysis, design, implementation, testing, deployment, and maintenance) and the process names according to the PRINCE2 method (such as Starting up a project, Directing a project, Initiating a project, Managing a stage boundary, Controlling a stage, Managing product delivery, and Closing a project) remain unchanged. As previously mentioned and shown in Figure 14, the SDLC phases are extended by three additional stages from the project lifecycle: the Pre-project and Pre-analysis phase, the Initiation phase, and the Final phase. Consequently, the resulting SDLC model comprises nine phases.

Figure 15 illustrates the integration of SDLC phases and PRINCE2 processes. The PRINCE2 processes are shown over grey color, whereas the SDLC phases are represented over a white background. The activities related to the SDLC have already been presented in the Software development process section. Therefore, this chapter primarily focuses on management activities.

The software development process begins with the Pre-project and Pre-analysis phases. During this period, both the management process known as Starting up a project (defined by the PRINCE2 method) and Pre-analysis (defined by the software development process) are executed. Therefore, during this phase, the executive and project manager are appointed, previous lessons are reviewed and captured, and the project management team is assembled. The project manager also selects the project approach, prepares the outline business case and project brief, and creates a plan for the initiation stage. The input information is provided through the project mandate document, created by the initiator of the project. Supplementary information can also be obtained from activities carried out during the pre-analysis phase. These activities play a crucial role in enabling stakeholders to acquire a comprehensive grasp of the project's goals, scope, and feasibility.

Figure 14. Transformed model of SDLC

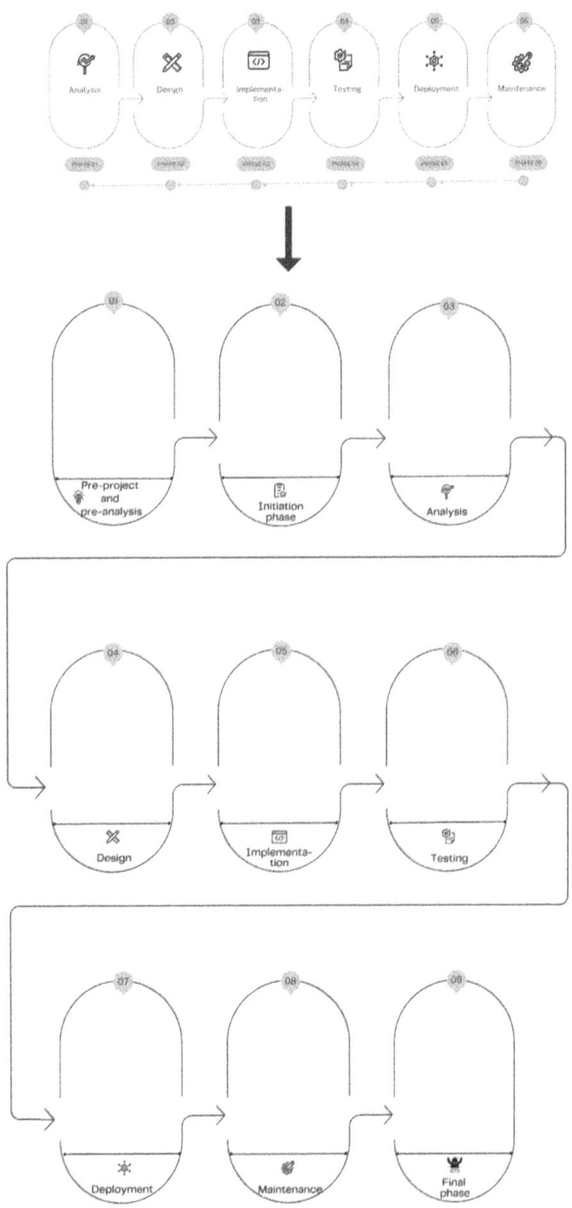

Figure 15. Integration process-oriented model of the software development life cycle and the PRINCE2 method

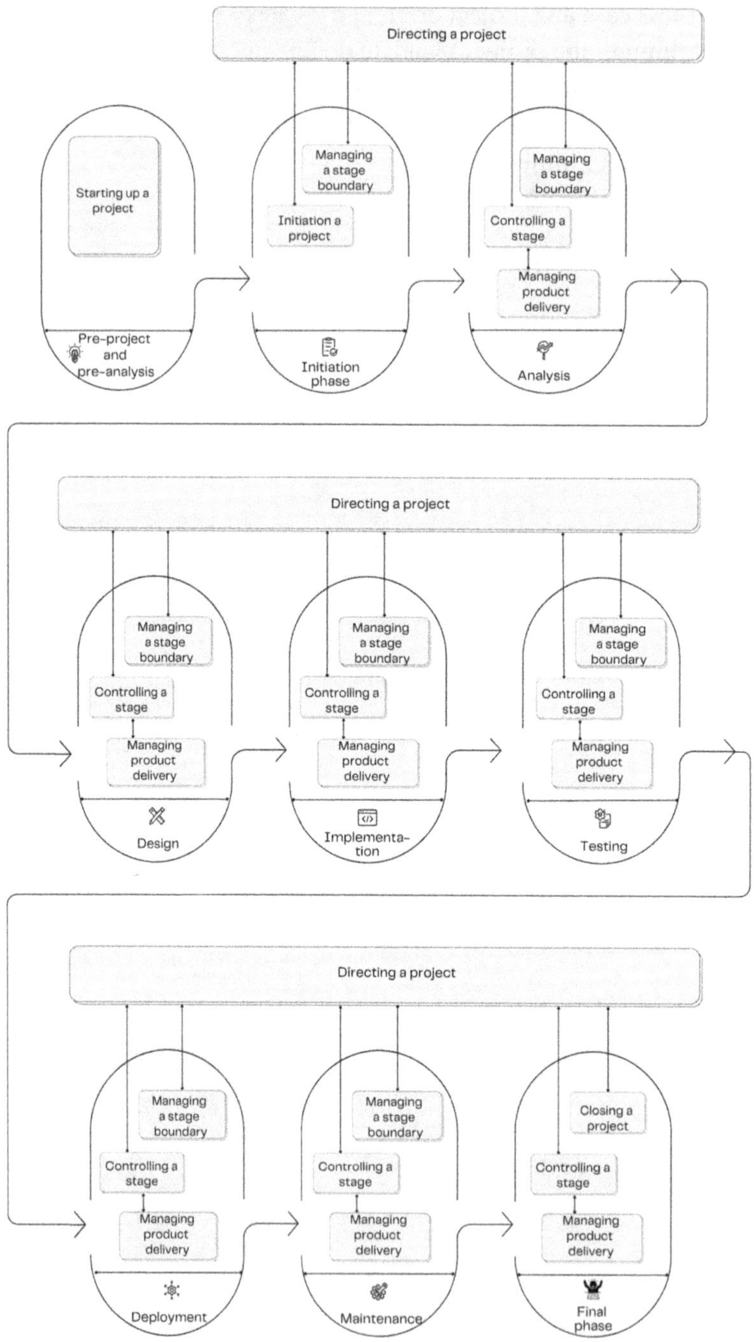

Before the Initiation phase begins, all relevant results are submitted to the project board. If the project holds a substantial business case, the project board approves of project execution, marking the project's initiation. Following the Initiation phase, both the Initiating a project process and the Managing a stage boundary process, as defined by the PRINCE2 method, are undertaken. During the Initiating a project process, the project manager should prepare the approach for key project management components (such as risk management, change control, quality management, and communication management), create a project plan, refine the business case, and assemble the project initiation documentation. Within the Managing a stage boundary process, the project manager is responsible for creating a plan for the upcoming management stage, updating the project plan and the business case, and reporting the end of the management stage. If there are any exceptions to the project, the project manager is also tasked with preparing an exception plan.

Upon completion of the Initiation phase, the outcomes again are committed to the project board through the PRINCE2 Directing a project process. After the project board approves the continuation of the project execution, the phase of analysis, as defined by SDLC, begins. After completion of the analysis phase it follows design, implementation, testing, deployment, and maintenance phases. Throughout all of these mentioned phases, the same processes defined by the PRINCE2 method are carried out. Those processes are: Managing a stage boundary, Controlling a stage, and Managing product delivery.

During the phases of analysis, design, implementation, testing, deployment, and maintenance, the most crucial outcomes related to the final product(s) are developed. In each of those phases, the collaboration between the project manager and team manager(s) is deeply intertwined. The responsibilities of a team manager (s) involve accepting the work package from the project manager, executing it, and delivering the work package according to agreed-upon deadlines. Additionally, the project manager is responsible for authorizing a work package, reviewing the status of the work packages and receiving completed work packages. Additionally, the project manager is tasked with monitoring the management stage status and reporting, which includes reviewing the management stage's status and highlighting key points. When it comes to issues and risks, the project manager's role involves capturing and assessing issues and risks, escalating them when necessary, and taking corrective actions as required. Besides those responsibilities, the project manager also carries out activities within the Managing a stage boundary process (described above).

For the transition from one phase to another, the approval of the project board is required. This ensures a controlled progression through the mentioned phases. Therefore, upon receiving approval from the project board for progressing to the next phase, the transition from the analysis phase to the design phase occurs. This is followed by a progression to the implementation phase, which leads to the deployment phase and then to the maintenance phase.

After the maintenance phase, the final phase involving PRINCE2 processes, such as Managing product delivery, Controlling a stage, and Closing a project, is executed. The project can officially be completed if the project board confirms the project's conclusion (the last activity in the Directing a project). It is important to note that the project completion process can also be carried out at any time during project execution if the project board determines, based on outcomes and reports, that the project is not meeting desired objectives or has deviated from its intended course.

A CRITICAL REVIEW OF THE USEFULNESS OF THE INTEGRATION MODEL FOR MANAGING SOFTWARE DEVELOPMENT PROJECTS USING PRINCE2 METHODS

In this section, the advantages and disadvantages of the usefulness of the integration model for managing software development projects using PRINCE2 methods are presented, which are based on a critical review. The process-oriented model for managing software development projects using the PRINCE2 method offers several followed advantages. First, the model provides a comprehensive approach that combines the structured framework of PRINCE2 with the practical phases of SDLC. This holistic perspective ensures that both management and technical considerations are adequately addressed, contributing to a well-rounded project management strategy. Second, the constructed process-oriented model helps align project objectives with the software development process, restriction the risk of scope expansion and deviations from the intended path. By structuring the project into clear phases and milestones, the model enables detailed progress monitoring, achievement tracking, and identifying potential bottlenecks. This transparency empowers stakeholders to stay informed and make informed decisions. Third, the robust risk management processes inherent in the PRINCE2 method contribute to effective risk mitigation when integrated into software development projects. Early identification and strategic management of risks minimize their impact on project outcomes and foster a proactive approach to addressing potential challenges. A clear definition of responsibilities between project managers and team managers is another significant advantage. This allocation of roles fosters effective collaboration, fosters a sense of ownership, and ensures accountability throughout the project's lifecycle. With defined roles, team members can work cohesively and leverage their expertise to achieve project objectives efficiently. Additionally, effective communication and collaboration are underscored by the model. Through well-defined roles, responsibilities, and communication channels, misunderstandings are minimized, and teamwork is enhanced. This alignment leads to improved project outcomes and stakeholder satisfaction. Controlled progression also presents one of the advantages of using the model. The requirement for project board approval at key transition points introduces a controlled progression mechanism, preventing hasty decisions and promoting thorough evaluation before moving to the next phase. This measured approach contributes to the project's overall success and quality.

During the critical review, the following challenges and disadvantages were also identified. First, integrating SDLC phases and PRINCE2 processes can lead to increased complexity in project management. This added complexity might need more effort to effectively execute and manage the model, possibly requiring extra time and resources for its successful implementation and comprehensive training. The organization might need to allocate additional resources, including conducting training programs for project managers and team members to inform them of both SDLC and PRINCE2 methodologies. This investment in training could impact budgets and timelines. Additionally, the integrated model's emphasis on Resource Intensiveness through detailed processes and comprehensive documentation might require additional time and resources. This complexity of the integrated model could particularly impact smaller projects with limited capacities, where the administrative overhead might overshadow the benefits of the model's implementation. Lastly, the model's structured approach might limit flexibility in handling dynamic changes or rapidly evolving requirements. The predefined processes might struggle to accommodate sudden shifts in scope or emerging priorities, potentially affecting the project's adaptability to changing circumstances.

PROJECT MANAGEMENT TRENDS IN THE FUTURE

Software project management has been transforming significantly due to technological advancements, changing work dynamics, and evolving customer expectations. Several trends have emerged in recent years, shaping how software projects are managed. Here are some significant trends in software project management (Kevin D. Davis, 2023a; Patra, 2023):

Artificial Intelligence (AI): AI and automation impacted the project management process. Businesses are leveraging AI to ensure the successful completion of projects through various strategies. Firstly, AI assists in obtaining performance insights, enabling teams to understand project progress and identify areas for improvement. Secondly, AI aids in estimation and prediction analysis, enhancing the accuracy of project timelines and resource allocation. Moreover, AI-powered tools support decision-making by providing data-driven recommendations for optimal project strategies. Additionally, AI facilitates data visualization, transforming complex project data into understandable visuals that aid in comprehension and decision-making. Another crucial application is AI-driven risk analysis, where algorithms assess potential risks and suggest mitigation strategies. Lastly, AI optimizes resource scheduling by considering factors like team availability and task dependencies, leading to more efficient project planning and execution.

Data Analytics for Data-Driven Project Management: Big Data analytics is a rapidly emerging trend in the field of project management. Organizations, regardless of their size, generate amounts of data on a daily basis. Thus, harnessing this data for decision-making is a smart strategy. Data and its management and analytics are significant in making quick and informed decisions for project managers. It is used in project scheduling, risk estimation, quality management, client, etc.

Hybrid Approaches: Hybrid approaches involve the combination of two or more methods. These approaches often merge elements from Agile and traditional methodologies to address specific project requirements. The Agile approach contributes flexibility, teamwork, and customer collaboration, while the traditional approach offers a linear project management route with a greater emphasis on planning and strategizing to ensure the precise completion of processes.

Remote Working: Remote work was already increasing in popularity, but in recent years, there has been a significant surge in its adoption. The global pandemic compelled organizations to implement remote work for safety reasons, and remote work will probably persist in the coming times. In such situations, cloud-based project management software emerges as a pivotal solution. These tools offer convenient deployment for hybrid or remote teams, facilitating efficient task and project management. Such software effectively gathers essential data that requires monitoring, validation, and utilization by project managers. This empowers them to make well-informed real-time decisions, irrespective of different work shifts and geographical locations.

Demand for Soft Skills - According to a report by PMI, there will be a need for around 88 million project-management-related professionals by 2027 (Project Management Institute, 2017b). The role of a project manager has evolved significantly, moving from simply task completion to strategic leadership that drives organizational change (Kevin D. Davis, 2023b). This is supported by the PMI survey, which highlights the high demand for professionals with a blend of competencies, including technical and leadership skills, as well as strategic and business management abilities (Project Management Institute, 2017b). Additionally, there's a growing shift towards emphasizing soft skills in organizations. This trend in project management is understandable, given the increasing capabilities of AI-powered solutions to handle complex technical aspects. This leaves managers with more capacity to focus on other responsibilities, making soft skills like conflict resolution, stakeholder engagement, negotiation, mentoring and training, decision-making, and team building even more essential.

CONCLUSION

This chapter offers insights into the realm of project management. The evolution of project management over the past decades has driven extensive theoretical and practical exploration. A diverse range of project management methods has arisen to address varying project needs, serving as tools for progress tracking and progress control. Despite the availability of project management methods within the ICT domain, software development projects frequently grapple with challenges contributing to their failure rate. These challenges often originate from the absence of well-structured project management methods. To fill this gap, this chapter introduces a process-oriented model for managing software development projects using the PRINCE2 method. This model provides a comprehensive perspective, encompassing both project management and software development aspects. Although integrating the process-oriented model using the PRINCE2 method offers advantages, organizations must carefully evaluate potential challenges in the context of model usage for their projects. Addressing challenges through effective planning and adaptation will enable organizations to maximize the model's benefits while minimizing its potential weaknesses.

ACKNOWLEDGMENT

The authors acknowledge financial support from the Slovenian Research Agency (research core funding No. P2-0057).

REFERENCES

Asana. (2022). *Waterfall vs. Agile vs. Kanban vs. Scrum: What's the difference?* Retrieved from https://asana.com/resources/waterfall-agile-kanban-scrum

Association for Project Management. (2022). *What is agile project management?* Retrieved from https://www.apm.org.uk/resources/find-a-resource/agile-project-management/

AXELOS Limited. (2017). Managing Successful Projects with PRINCE2 (6th ed.). Norwich: The Stationery Office.

Bilir, C., & Yafez, E. (2021). Project success/failure rates in Turkey. *International Journal of Information Systems and Project Management*, *9*(4), 24–40. doi:10.12821/ijispm090402

Cerpa, N., & Verner, J. (2009). Why Did Your Project Fail? *Communications of the ACM*, *52*(12), 130–134. doi:10.1145/1610252.1610286

Chaouch, S., Mejri, A., & Ghannouchi, S. A. (2019). A framework for risk management in Scrum development process. *Procedia Computer Science*, *164*, 187–192. doi:10.1016/j.procs.2019.12.171

Flora, H. K., & Chande, S. V. (2014). A Systematic Study on Agile Software Development Methodologies and Practices. *International Journal of Computer Science and Information Technologies*, *5*(3), 3626–3637. http://www.ijcsit.com/docs/Volume 5/vol5issue03/ijcsit20140503214.pdf

Forth, P., Reichert, T., de Laubier, R., & Saibal, C. (2020). *Flipping the Odds of Digital Transformation Success.* Retrieved from https://www.bcg.com/publications/2020/increasing-odds-of-success-in-digital-transformation

Iqbal, M. (2020). *The Standard of Project Management and PMBOK 7.* Retrieved from https://mudassiriqbal.net/the-standard-of-project-management-and-pmbok-7/

Iriarte, C., & Bayona, S. (2020). It projects success factors: A literature review. *International Journal of Information Systems and Project Management*, *8*(2), 49–78. doi:10.12821/ijispm080203

Islam, S., & Evans, N. (2020). Key Success Factors of PRINCE2 Project Management Method in Software Development Project. *International Journal of Engineering Materials and Manufacture*, *5*(3), 76–84. doi:10.26776/ijemm.05.03.2020.02

ISO-International Organization for Standardization. (2017). *ISO 10006:2017(en) Quality management — Guidelines for quality management in projects.*

ISO-International Organization for Standardization. (2021). *ISO 21500:2021 Project, programme and portfolio management — Context and concepts.*

Jamali, G., & Oveisi, M. (2016). A Study on Project Management Based on PMBOK and PRINCE2. *Modern Applied Science*, *10*(6), 142. doi:10.5539/mas.v10n6p142

Kevin, D. (2023a). *Future of Project Management: Future Trends and Skills.* Retrieved from https://www.knowledgehut.com/blog/project-management/future-of-project-management

Kevin, D. (2023b). *Project management Demand: Career Opportunities.* Retrieved from https://www.knowledgehut.com/blog/project-management/project-management-demand

Kissflow. (2022). *What is a Project in Project Management?* Retrieved from https://kissflow.com/project/what-is-a-project/

Knowledgehut. (2023). *ITIL Certification vs PRINCE2 – Understanding the Differences.* Retrieved from https://www.knowledgehut.com/blog/it-service-management/itil-vs-prince2

Kruger, W., & Rudman, R. (2013). Strategic Alignment Of Application Software Packages And Business Processes Using PRINCE2. *The International Business & Economics Research Journal*, *12*(10), 1239. doi:10.19030/iber.v12i10.8134

Martin, A., & Martin, A. (2023). Introduction to an agile framework a for the management of technology transfer projects. *Procedia Computer Science, 219*(2022), 1963–1968. doi:10.1016/j.procs.2023.01.496

Morjane, W., Bannari, R., & Gharib, J. (2022). Overview of Project Management Methodologies: Traditional Versus Agile Approach. *European International Conference on Industrial Engineering and Operations Management, 5*, 783–794. 10.46254/EU05.20220157

Pankratz, O., & Basten, D. (2014). Ladder to success – Eliciting project managers' perceptions of IS project success criteria. *International Journal of Information Systems and Project Management*, *2*(2), 5–24. doi:10.12821/ijispm020201

Patra, A. (2023). *12 Project Management Trends Emerging in 2023*. Retrieved from https://www.replicon.com/blog/project-management-trends/

Pratt, M. K. (2021). *Why IT projects still fail*. Retrieved from https://www.cio.com/article/230427/why-it-projects-still-fail.html

PRINCE2. (2023). Retrieved from https://www.prince2.com/eur

Project Management Institute. (2004). A Guide to the Project Management Body of Knowledge (3rd ed.). Project Management Inst).

Project Management Institute. (2017a). *A Guide to the Project Management Body of Knowledge* (7th ed.). Project Management Institute.

Project Management Institute. (2017b). *Job Growth and Talent Gap 2017-2027*. Retrieved from https://www.pmi.org/-/media/pmi/documents/public/pdf/learning/job-growth-report.pdf?sc_lang_temp=en

Rouse, M. (2011). *Software Development Life Cycle Model*. Retrieved from https://www.techopedia.com/definition/25976/software-development-life-cycle-model-sdlc

Savolainen, P., Ahonen, J. J., & Richardson, I. (2015). When did your project start? - The software supplier's perspective. *Journal of Systems and Software*, *104*, 32–40. doi:10.1016/j.jss.2015.02.041

Tawfik, D. (2022). *Traditional project management vs. Agile: How to choose*. Retrieved from https://monday.com/blog/project-management/traditional-project-management/

The Britannica Dictionary. (2023). *Project*. Retrieved from https://www.britannica.com/dictionary/project

The Knowledge Academy. (2023). *What sectors use PRINCE2?* Retrieved from https://www.theknowledgeacademy.com/courses/prince2-training/what-sectors-use-prince2/

Varajão, J., & Trigo, A. (2016). Evaluation of IS project success in InfSysmakers: An exploratory case study. *2016 International Conference on Information Systems, ICIS 2016*, 1–10.

Williams, R. T. (2023). Software project management. Thesis Commons *Vbax2, Center for Open Science*. Retrieved from https://ideas.repec.org/p/osf/thesis/vbax2.html

ADDITIONAL READING

Cerdeiral, C. T., & Santos, G. (2019). Software project management in high maturity: A systematic literature mapping. *Journal of Systems and Software*, *148*, 56–87. doi:10.1016/j.jss.2018.10.002

Islam, S., & Evans, N. (2020). Key Success Factors of PRINCE2 Project Management Method in Software Development Project. *International Journal of Engineering Materials and Manufacture*, *5*(3), 76–84. doi:10.26776/ijemm.05.03.2020.02

Project Management Institute. (2017a). *A Guide to the Project Management Body of Knowledge* (7th ed.). Project Management Institute.

Project Management Institute. (2017b). *Job Growth and Talent Gap 2017-2027*. Retrieved from https://www.pmi.org/-/media/pmi/documents/public/pdf/learning/job-growth-report.pdf?sc_lang_temp=en

Varajão, J., Magalhães, L., Freitas, L., & Rocha, P. (2022). Success Management – From theory to practice. *International Journal of Project Management*, *40*(5), 481–498. doi:10.1016/j.ijproman.2022.04.002

KEY TERMS AND DEFINITIONS

Agile Project Management: An iterative, flexible approach to managing projects focused on collaboration, adaptability, and delivering customer value

Process: A collection of tasks, assignments, or activities carried out in a specific sequence, transforming inputs into outputs.

Project: A temporary endeavor with clearly defined initiation and conclusion.

Project Board: A mandatory entity within PRINCE2's organizational structure consisting of Senior User(s), the Executive, and Senior Supplier(s). It is responsible for performing the process Directing a Project with some activities within the process of Starting up a Project.

Project Management: The practice of organizing and managing resources to ensure task completion within predefined scope, timeline, and cost limits.

Project Manager: A distinct role within PRINCE2's organizational structure, responsible for overseeing the project on a daily basis. He/she is accountable for executing the processes of Initiating a Project, Managing a Stage Boundary, Controlling a Stage, and Closing a Project, as well as certain activities within the process of Starting up a Project.

SDLC: A systematic process used by software developers and organizations to analyze, design, implement, test, deploy, and maintain software solutions.

Software Development Process: A systematic approach to creating software applications.

Team Manager(s): A role within PRINCE2's organization structure that is responsible for the creation of products that have been assigned by the project manager. The team manager receives guidance from and reports to the project manager. This role can be assigned either to the project manager or a distinct individual.

Traditional Project Management: A linear, structured approach to managing projects where phases occur sequentially.

Chapter 3
Towards Achieving a Sustainable Lean Transformation:
Measuring Tangible and Intangible Gains

Azim Azuan Osman
https://orcid.org/0000-0002-9078-3154
Universiti Malaysia Pahang, Malaysia

Ahmad Nazif Noor Kamar
https://orcid.org/0000-0002-1130-1285
Universiti Malaysia Pahang, Malaysia

Syed Radzi Rahamadulla
https://orcid.org/0000-0002-6555-9919
Universiti Malaysia Pahang, Malaysia

ABSTRACT

Toyota Motor's success as a global brand automobile manufacturer has inspired manufacturing organizations worldwide to pursue lean transformation. However, a lack of understanding of lean sustainability hampers their progress towards achieving true lean organization status like Toyota. Without proper measurement, the gains from lean improvements remain unknown, leading to inaccuracies in strategy deployment. This chapter aims to define sustainable lean transformation gains and propose indicators to measure them. Extensive literature review reveals the importance of tangible and intangible indicators. To validate the proposed measurements, a survey involving 7 lean experts and 92 practitioners was conducted. Data analysis utilized content validity index, inter-rater agreement, and measurement model analysis. The chapter concludes by suggesting research opportunities to enhance lean management knowledge.

DOI: 10.4018/979-8-3693-0458-7.ch003

INTRODUCTION

Lean Manufacturing (LM) is an improvement strategy that originated from the Toyota Production System (TPS). Toyota Motor Manufacturing's sustainable success in facing the 1973 global oil crisis inspired manufacturing organizations around the globe to transition from traditional mass and batch production to the LM system. This conversion from traditional methods to the LM system is referred to as "lean transformation" (Grigg et al., 2018; Mann, 2015; Roth, 2011). The term "lean transformation" describes the necessary changes made to achieve desirable gains associated with lean practices. The term transformation implies a significant, holistic, and profound change that organizations need to fully embrace lean thinking as a new operational philosophy, replacing a profit-based mindset (Mann, 2015; Roth, 2011).

However, organizations that have successfully initiated lean transformation may encounter difficulties and challenges in sustaining this initiative in the long run (Costa et al., 2019; Pearce & Pons, 2019). Logically, no organization would embark on a transformation program with the intention to fail. Despite numerous studies demonstrating the significant and positive effects of LM on various performance measures (Hardcopf et al., 2021; Iranmanesh et al., 2019; Susanty et al., 2021), the field has struggled with a lack of clarity on how to consistently achieve such performance from lean transformation and what indicators should be considered to measure it. This gap in knowledge within the LM literature requires urgent attention from lean scholars and practitioners (Jadhav et al., 2014; Mohd Yusof & Aoki, 2016).

Therefore, the objectives of this chapter are as follows: First, the authors attempt to resolve the lexical confusion surrounding "lean sustainability" and explain the different perspectives in defining this term. Second, in their pursuit of a clear and consensus definition of lean sustainability, the authors propose an operational definition that encompasses its underlying multidimensional concept. Finally, based on an extensive literature review, this chapter proposes a set of sustainable lean transformation gains that include both tangible and intangible indicators. Operational performance and business performance indicators represent the tangible indicators, while continuous improvement capability represents the intangible indicators. These indicators were then validated through a survey involving lean experts and practitioners.

LITERATURE REVIEW

This literature review section commences with an examination of short-term and long-term gains and objectives arising from lean transformation results. Subsequently, a spectrum of real-world scenarios across industries is presented, illustrating both the successes and challenges that organizations have encountered on their journeys of lean transformation. These narratives serve as a repository of rich insights, offering valuable lessons for practitioners and scholars alike. This section also engages in a comprehensive exploration of the concept of lean transformation sustainability, rooted in the broader context of sustainable organizational change. Building upon this conceptual foundation, the chapter shifts its focus towards the formulation of measurement indicators designed to evaluate sustainable gains in lean transformation endeavors. The concept of lean transformation sustainability underscores the consistent attainment of performance objectives and the enduring capability to derive benefits and enhancements from lean initiatives. Through an in-depth exploration of the measurement of sustainable gains, this chapter aspires to provide insights into the assessment of the efficacy and enduring impact of lean transformation efforts, encompassing both tangible and intangible outcomes.

Assessing Gains From Lean Transformation

Many manufacturers attempting lean transformation face a recurring issue: securing its sustainability over time (Association for Manufacturing Excellence, 2009). Various sources including failure statistics (Ahmed Soliman, 2013; Costa et al., 2019; Jadhav et al., 2014; Madsen et al., 2019; Pearce & Pons, 2019; Sisson & Elshennawy, 2015; Van Landeghem et al., 2013) and case studies highlighting downturns in lean transformation (Grigg et al., 2018; Murti, 2009; Pentlicki, 2014; Turesky & Connell, 2010) consistently reinforce this challenge. This issue partly stems from inadequate measurement criteria and poor review systems for assessing an organization's progress in lean transformation (Ahmad et al., 2017; Mohd Rose et al., 2013; Sahwan et al., 2012). Despite this recognized challenge, numerous current studies have failed to address a critical aspect: the attainment of long-term success in lean transformation. Consequently, a noticeable gap exists within the Lean Management literature. To bridge this gap, it becomes evident that comprehensive assessment indicators are necessary. These indicators should encompass not only short-term accomplishments but also the crucial factor of long-term sustainability.

While lean transformation should be embraced as a long-term strategy for sustainable purposes, the importance of quick wins or short-term gains cannot be understated. These short-term victories remain indispensable to motivate employees and foster their trust in supporting the lean strategy (Hines et al., 2011; Lucey et al., 2005). The significance of quick wins lies in the message they convey to all employees: that the lean strategy is yielding tangible outcomes for the organization. Consequently, quick wins act as catalysts, spurring greater commitment to persistently pursuing lean transformation for the long term.

Nonetheless, it is essential to note that while lean practitioners should never forsake long-term goals in favor of fleeting short-term gains to sustain lean transformation (Al Najem et al., 2012; Liker, 2004; Mohd Yusof & Aoki, 2016), the pursuit of quick wins holds substantial value. Quick wins play an instrumental role in transformation efforts by building momentum and substantiating the feasibility of the transformation process. While quick wins serve as crucial motivation, they also fit into the broader context of realizing long-term goals (Burnes, 2017; Tracey & Flinchbaugh, 2009). Achieving short-term objectives is pivotal as they constitute integral stepping stones along the transformation journey, thereby complementing the ultimate attainment of long-term goals. This dynamic interaction is not a mere trade-off; it represents a complementary and mutually reinforcing relationship.

To sum up, the literature underscores the nuanced interplay between quick wins, short-term goals, and the fundamental principles of long-term lean transformation. While quick wins offer immediate motivation, validate lean concepts, and build momentum, their pursuit should align harmoniously with the enduring tenets of lean thinking, including fostering a culture of continuous improvement and embracing sustainable, long-term changes. Navigating this balance requires lean practitioners to skillfully integrate short-term gains into a larger framework of transformative, lasting improvement, consistent with the principles of continuous improvement philosophy and the vision of sustainable transformation. This extensive discourse serves to underscore the paramount importance of scrutinizing essential indicators that lean practitioners should consider to measure lean transformation's effectiveness and sustainability. This chapter attempts to effectively bridges the gap between short-term gains and long-term aspirations, forging a path toward sustainable transformation.

Success Stories and Case Studies of Failed Lean Transformations

In the pursuit of competitive advantage, organizations have increasingly embraced lean principles as a strategy to streamline processes, eliminate waste, and enhance overall efficiency. The essence of lean principle lies in its commitment to continuous improvement, where every individual within the organization plays an integral role in identifying and implementing enhancements. Nevertheless, despite the clear benefits of lean transformation, ensuring its long-term sustainability remains a formidable challenge. This section explores the intricacies of sustaining lean transformation by drawing upon a diverse array of both successful and unsuccessful cases.

Popoola (2000) conducted a longitudinal case study to unveil the factors that dictate the sustainability of lean transformation in Kodak Canada Inc. (KCI). These factors encompass tools and technology, employee involvement, learning from previous Lean Projects, the promotion and awarding system, expansion and alignment of lean behaviour, and performance metrics. Among these factors, some have been instrumental in KCI's sustained lean transformation, while others warrant further improvement to ensure the continuous success of KCI's lean journey. Meanwhile, Taylor et al. (2013) scrutinized three factors that contribute to the endurance of the Lean System in a UK assembly plant of a global car manufacturer. These factors encompass leadership from top management, workforce attitude and attributes, and the infrastructure of the corporate system. Notably, the Lean System had been integrated into the case plant for nearly 16 years at the time of the study.

Sisson and Elshennawy (2015) undertook an analysis of four well-established lean organizations that have exhibited sustainable success for over a decade. These organizations, namely Autoliv Inc., Boeing Company, Danaher Corporation, and United Technologies Corporation, provide valuable insights into the enduring factors behind effective lean practices. Across these firms, they identified 17 concrete actions that are deemed pertinent for sustaining lean efforts. These actions encompass a range of strategies, from securing support from top leadership and leveraging outsourcing consultants/sensei, to extending lean principles beyond manufacturing, integrating suppliers, maintaining a dedicated lean improvement team, fostering consistent communication on lean, aligning human resource policies, providing comprehensive training in lean principles, cultivating internal lean champions, utilizing tools like value stream mapping (VSM) and standard work, implementing hoshin kanri (policy deployment) to align strategy, incorporating the Voice of Customer (VOC) to drive process enhancement, conducting regular Kaizen Events to foster a culture of continuous improvement, utilizing visual management for tracking progress, adapting the lean system to the organization's unique context, and recognizing that lean transformation is an ongoing journey rather than a static destination. The findings drawn from these case analyses affirm the applicability of all 17 actions in real-world scenarios. Nevertheless, Sisson and Elshennawy (2015) underscore the utmost importance of accountability and a robust follow-up process, facilitated by standard work practices and effective performance metrics, as underscored by the respondents.

Consistent with the work of Sisson and Elshennawy (2015), Hogan (2009) also conducted an examination of the Autoliv Production System (APS). Hogan's research highlights the achievement of the Autoliv Ogden Airbag (AOA) assembly plant in upholding its Lean Culture through a single case study. The elements contributing to the sustainability of lean success, as identified by Hogan (2009) and Sisson and Elshennawy (2015), largely overlap. Moreover, Rentes et al. (2009) documented success stories from two leading manufacturers of glass products and a major power turbine manufacturer in Brazil. In a similar vein, many of the factors attributed to sustaining success align closely with the findings of Sisson and Elshennawy (2015).

Meanwhile, Marchwinski (2014) presents a case study derived from a medical device manufacturer's five-year experience in pursuing and maintaining lean transformation and culture. The study's outcomes underscore the importance of the 'Golden Triangle'—comprising standardized work, accountability management, and visual control—as the linchpin for sustaining the Lean Operation System and nurturing the Lean Culture. Similarly, Schlichting (2009) underscores the critical role of standardized work and visual management in maintaining a robust lean culture, as exemplified by the MAHLE Inc. engine cylinders manufacturing plant. Additionally, the essentiality of accountability management as a keystone for sustaining lean initiatives finds substantiation in the cases of a pumping components manufacturer (Turesky & Connell, 2010) and a kitchen cabinet manufacturing facility (Mann, 2015).

Overall, common determinants of lean transformation sustainability are found in the literature. For example, leadership and top management commitment, employee engagement and involvement, employee training and development, daily management accountability and standard work practices.

On the contrary, from the perspective of failed transformation, Murti (2009) studied lean transformation among nine manufacturers who were participants in the New Zealand Trade and Enterprise (NZTE) Lean Programs. After two years of deployment, the researcher concluded that NZTE's Lean Programs were successful in promoting lean but proved inadequate in ensuring sustainable improvements. Only one organization seemed likely to sustain improvements due to several common problems experienced by other participants. Even after a follow-up study in 2018, all but one of the firms had failed to successfully implement lean. The successful firm was the one predicted as potentially capable of sustaining lean transformation in 2009 (Grigg et al., 2018). The findings of the follow-up study confirmed the findings of the original study: out of the nine companies, only one was strongly sustaining the lean transformation. Two declined to be interviewed but stated the lean program had been aborted. Two others were willing to be interviewed but had also aborted the lean program. Two were attempting to sustain lean transformation, while two were restarting the transformation.

In contrast to the accounts of successful lean transformations, several instances depict the challenges and obstacles that hinder the sustainability of such initiatives. For example, Murti (2009) delved into lean transformation within nine manufacturers participating in New Zealand Trade and Enterprise (NZTE) Lean Programmes. Despite an initial promotion of lean principles, sustainable improvements proved elusive for most organizations, with only one exhibiting potential for long-term success. This follow-up study in 2018 further confirmed the struggles, as most firms failed to fully implement lean practices. These findings are echoed by Turesky and Connell (2010), whose case study highlighted the two-steps-forward, one-step-back nature of lean transformations. Even though improvements were made, they often eroded over time.

In particular, the study conducted by Turesky and Connell (2010) offers valuable insights into the intricacies of sustaining lean transformation by highlighting the significant challenges encountered by a Northern New England company specializing in pumping components for the automotive and industrial sectors. Within this context, the researchers meticulously identified eight distinct factors that contributed to the reversion, including a lack of top management support and communication, no formal training provision, bias in project selection, unengaged employees, employee resistance to change, and sole reliance on lean project team representatives.

Another example of reported barriers inhibiting manufacturers from sustaining lean transformation is evident in the case of Colorado's SME manufacturing organizations, as studied by Pentlicki (2014). Three organizations with a minimum of two years' experience in implementing lean manufacturing were included in the study. The researcher identified nine common barriers to sustaining lean transformation experienced by all respondent organizations. Some of these barriers were consistent with previous findings from Lucey et al. (2005). In Lucey et al.'s study, three groups of experts, including consultants, academics, and authors with well-versed knowledge and experience in change management, were interviewed to provide a balanced perspective on reasons for lean transformation failure. In total, nine experts (three from each respective group) were interviewed. The summary of these common barriers and problems is presented in Table 1.

Table 1. Barriers and challenges to sustain lean transformation

Barriers/ Challenges	Lucey et al. (2005)	Murti (2009)	Turesky and Connell (2010)	Pentlicki (2014)
Leadership	Lack of executive leadership.	Poor senior management commitment. Lack of leadership skill.	Lack of top management support and communication before, during, and after lean project completion.	Senior leaders unaware of their role in leading lean transformation Senior leaders have low degree of leadership knowledge.
	Failure to fully mobilise change champions. Using an outsider to transact change.	Fail to develop the lean champion's capabilities. Rely too much on external champions (consultants). No entry or exit plan from external consultant. No focus on customer value (Voice of Customer).		Utilising outside trainers that do not really understand the organisation's culture.
Understanding on lean concept and philosophy	Lack of clear executive vision. Absence of dedicated and fully resourced implementation team.	Poor understanding of lean philosophy. For leader, lean is viewed as short-term productivity improvements rather than as a philosophy and long-term strategy. For employees, lean is another management fad which cause them excess workload and excuse to reduce labours.	Large gaps in training caused the understanding of lean and the reasons employees need embrace lean transformation are very different within the organization.	Lean is deployed depends on organisation context. Struggle to expand lean manufacturing implementation into supporting departments Too busy to allocate time and other resources for lean programmes.
Employee Engagement	Failure to engage employees Failure to plan and manage quick wins.	High staff resistance. High staff turnover.	Resistance to change from employees that are not a part of process improvement decision making.	Resistance to change from employees. Front line workers need trainings to apply lean tools and concepts. Front line workers acceptance and ownership.

In summary, the wealth of knowledge gleaned from both successful lean transformation stories and the hard-earned lessons of failed attempts provides invaluable guidance for organizations embarking on their own lean journeys. These narratives offer a roadmap of best practices, emphasizing the crucial role of leadership, employee engagement, standardized work, accountability management, and visual control, among other factors. However, despite this rich tapestry of insights, an evident gap remains in these narratives. None of the studies, whether highlighting successes or failures, explicitly addresses the critical question of how to measure a sustainable lean transformation. The absence of a dedicated focus on this aspect leaves organizations without a clear compass to navigate the uncharted waters of lean sustainability assessment. To bridge this gap effectively, there is an urgent need to develop a robust assessment tool that encompasses the criteria and indicators necessary to gauge lean transformation sustainability comprehensively. Such assessment tool would not only empower organizations to measure the lasting impact of their lean initiatives but also facilitate the refinement and optimization of their lean practices over time. It is through this holistic understanding of lean transformation, encompassing both its enduring spirit and its measurable impact, that organizations can chart a course towards sustained excellence in the dynamic landscape of modern industry.

Lean Transformation Sustainability

In recent years, the application of Lean Production Systems (LPS) has become closely linked to sustainability. Scholars such as Benkarim and Imbeau (2021) and Madsen et al. (2019) have identified two main perspectives in discussing sustainability within LPS research. The first perspective focuses on how LPS adoption can contribute to environmental sustainability by reducing waste and energy consumption, as demonstrated in studies by Habidin et al. (2020). The second perspective revolves around sustaining the momentum of lean transformation beyond initial pilots and blitzes, as discussed by Jørgensen et al. (2007). This chapter primarily addresses the latter perspective.

In previous literature, various terms have been used to describe the concept of Lean Transformation Sustainability (LTS), such as "sustaining lean gains," "sustaining lean transition," and "sustaining lean conversion." However, these terms have been used without clear definitions, leading to confusion and ambiguous interpretations of LTS. To address this issue, the present chapter aims to provide a comprehensive and explicit definition of LTS.

Some studies have linked the origin of LTS to the concept of sustainable organizational change. Buchanan et al. (2005) define sustainable change as the ongoing maintenance of new working methods, achievement of performance goals, and continuous improvement over a suitable timeframe within a given context. Building upon these three facets of sustainable organizational change, the authors formulate an all-inclusive definition of LTS. Additionally, simple definitions of LTS from existing literature were considered during the formulation process (refer to Table 2).

Table 2. Lean transformation sustainability definitions

Authors	Definitions
Alukal (2006)	Obtaining enduring success with lean transformation.
Jørgensen et al. (2007)	Maintaining the momentum of lean transformation once initial pilots and blitzes are completed.
Ruffa (2011)	Achieving the highest level of lean maturity and advancing at a strong but cautious pace.
Grigg et al. (2018)	The final stage of the process improvement, focused on how to maintain the momentum of lean transformation within firms.

Table 2 provides insights into four distinct definitions of Lean Transformation Sustainability (LTS) that shed light on different aspects of the concept. Alukal's definition focuses on sustaining success in lean transformation, which is closely tied to achievement of performance goals throughout the lean journey.

This aligns with Buchanan et al.'s (2005) emphasis on persistent goal achievement and explains why terms like "sustaining lean gains" and "sustaining lean improvements" have been used by previous scholars.

In contrast, Jørgensen's and Grigg's definitions place emphasis on maintaining the momentum of lean transformation over time. This aspect is related to the stability of work methods, specifically the extent to which an organization adopts lean tools and techniques. Ruffa's definition of lean maturity level also aligns with this perspective, reflecting an organization's progression in lean adoption and the duration of implementation. To address work method stability, previous scholars have used terms such as "sustaining lean transition," "sustaining lean conversion," "sustaining lean initiatives," and "sustaining lean ideology" in relation to the LTS concept.

Although there is no specific LTS definition that directly addresses consistent improvement trajectories, studies by Burch (2008), Schlichting (2009), and Grigg et al. (2018) highlight the importance of continuous improvement capability as a measure of LTS gains. However, many studies tend to overlook this criterion and instead focus on operational or financial performance as the primary measures of LTS gains. This neglects the aspect of consistent improvement trajectory highlighted by Buchanan et al. (2005). Burch (2008) emphasizes that while performance goals represent tangible gains from lean transformation, continuous improvement capabilities represent the intangible gains that should not be ignored. The significance of continuous improvement capability is reinforced by seminal works in the field of lean transformation. The Toyota Way pillars, particularly the emphasis on continuous improvement, as popularized by Liker (2004), lay a foundational understanding of the perpetual advancement intrinsic to successful lean practices. Additionally, the pursuit of perfection, which stands as one of the core lean principles, was introduced by Womack and Jones (1996), underlining the unending journey of enhancement inherent to lean thinking.

Another crucial aspect in defining LTS is determining the start and end of the sustaining phase. In the context of Total Quality Management (TQM), the sustaining phase begins after completing the pilot phase, which involves implementing quality management practices and tools. Similarly, in Lean Production Systems (LPS), the sustaining phase can be considered to start after completing the lean pilot project, which involves implementing basic lean elements into the manufacturing system. The duration of the sustaining phase may vary, but visible improvements are typically observed within six months. The ending period of the sustaining phase is indefinite, as long as the organization intends to continue its lean efforts.

Based on these considerations, the authors conceptually define LTS as the maintenance of lean transformation momentum in an organization's production system to achieve persistent performance goals while consistently pursuing continuous improvement. The sustaining phase begins after completing the lean pilot project and continues for a duration appropriate to the specific context. The newly proposed LTS definition draws upon the facets of sustainable organizational change and takes into account lean practices that require less investment and are feasible for implementation, even in small and medium-sized enterprises (SMEs). This definition builds upon the foundation of sustainable organizational change and provides a comprehensive understanding of LTS (refer to Table 3 for a summary).

Table 3 presents the coherence between the concept of sustainable organizational change (Buchanan et al., 2005) and LTS definitions extracted from previous studies (Alukal, 2006; Grigg et al., 2018; Jørgensen et al., 2007; Ruffa, 2011). The newly proposed definition comprehensively covers the entire meaning of the LTS concept by addressing all the characteristics of sustainable organizational change. Additionally, it justifies the use of diverse terms found in previous studies. This detailed definition provides stronger evidence of content validity compared to existing LTS definitions.

Table 3. Coherence between the concept of sustainable organisational change, LTS definitions, and synonym terms used in previous studies

Sustainable Organisational Change	Lean Transformation Sustainability	Synonym Terms
Stability of work methods	Momentum of lean transformation (Grigg et al., 2018; Jørgensen et al., 2007; Ruffa, 2011)	1. Sustaining lean initiatives 2. Sustaining lean transition 3. Sustaining lean conversion
Persistent achievement of performance goals	Enduring success (Alukal, 2006)	1. Sustaining lean improvements 2. Sustaining lean gains
Consistent improvement trajectory	Continuous improvement capabilities (Burch, 2008; Grigg et al., 2018; Schlichting, 2009)	1. Sustaining lean improvements 2. Sustaining lean gains

Sustainable Lean Transformation Gains

The assessment of sustainable gains proposed in this chapter can be attributed to the concept of "holding the gains" introduced by Joseph M. Juran, a renowned Quality Guru (Dale, 1996). It aligns with the notion of "persistent achievement of performance goals" advocated by (Buchanan et al., 2005) in the concept of sustainable organizational change. Sustaining gains refers to the ability to consistently acquire benefits and improvements from lean transformation efforts. Assessing sustainable gains serves as a constant stimulus to validate the effectiveness of improvement efforts and test an organization's commitment to continuous improvement (Dale, 1996; Davies, 1992). It is essential to ensure that the gains achieved through improvement strategies are not short-lived or lost (Burch, 2008; Rentes et al., 2009).

Gains derived from lean transformation primarily manifest as tangible improvements, including operational performance and business performance. Operational performance relates to the internal operations of the organization and focuses on eliminating waste, while business performance encompasses financial and non-financial metrics such as return on assets and the ability to develop a competitive profile (Jayaraman et al., 2012). Indicators of operational performance include cost savings, space optimization, product quality, employee and equipment productivity, product and volume flexibility, and on-time delivery fulfillment (Hernandez-Matias et al., 2020; Jayaraman et al., 2012; Onofrei et al., 2019). Business performance indicators encompass revenue growth, net profits, return on assets, competitive profile, new product development, and market development (Jayaraman et al., 2012; Losonci & Demeter, 2013; Nawanir et al., 2016).

However, it is worth noting that these tangible gains alone do not fully capture the sustainability of lean transformation. Studies have acknowledged the importance of considering intangible gains, particularly the continuous improvement (CI) capability, to assess lean transformation sustainability (Burch, 2008; Grigg et al., 2018; Jørgensen et al., 2007). CI capability refers to a set of competitive abilities that enable organizations to learn, innovate, and renew (Aloini et al., 2011). It is a dynamic concept demonstrated through ongoing activities focused on incremental changes in processes to improve organization-wide performance (Galeazzo et al., 2017).

Scholars such as Jørgensen et al. (2007) argue that a balanced approach, considering both tangible and intangible gains, creates synergy between the two indicators of improvement. Furthermore, a mixed-methods study conducted on 11 manufacturing organizations in Western Massachusetts found that most organizations regarded CI capability as a positive by-product of their lean transformation initiatives

(Burch, 2008). However, none of the organizations in Burch's study actually assessed changes in CI capability improvements. Therefore, Burch (2008) suggests that assessing intangible gains related to CI capability provides a better understanding of the efficacy of lean transformation. Similarly, Grigg et al. (2018) emphasizes the significance of a well-established CI capability as the true measure of lean transformation sustainability. However, the results of Grigg's study on nine manufacturing organizations in New Zealand revealed a lack of CI capability, leading to stagnated lean transformation and hindering the sustainability of the improvement efforts.

Given these considerations, the present study aims to assess sustainable gains in three dimensions: operational performance, business performance, and CI capability. While operational and business performance represent tangible gains, CI capability serves as the intangible gain that reflects the organization's ability to continuously improve and adapt. Table 4 provides a summary of the operational definitions for each dimension of Sustainable Lean Transformation Gains.

Table 4. Operational definitions of sustainable lean transformation gains

Construct / Dimension	Definition
Sustainable Gains	The ability to persistently acquire benefits and improvements from lean transformation efforts that include both tangible and intangible gains.
a. Operational Performance	Gains from internal operation of the company in terms of cost reduction, product quality improvement, flexibility enhancement, delivery performance, and productivity increment (Jayaraman et al., 2012).
b. Business Performance	Gains from financial aspects, such as revenue growth, net profits, return on assets, and non-financial aspects, such as capacity to develop a competitive profile, new products, and market shares (Jayaraman et al., 2012).
c. Continuous Improvement Capability	Competitive abilities that allows organisations to learn, innovate and renew (Aloini et al., 2011).

Furthermore, based on these definitions, the authors assigned a range of six to eight indicators to each dimension. The effectiveness of measurement lies in the successful representation of abstract constructs through a set of meaningful questions or items. It has been suggested that three items per construct or dimension are sufficient to achieve this purpose (Carpenter, 2018; Hair, Black, et al., 2019). However, Boateng et al. (2018) argue that researchers should initially generate at least twice the number of desired final items to allow for the necessary flexibility in selecting the optimal combination of items. Therefore, the authors believed that having six to eight items per dimension, which is twice the minimum requirement for meaningful measurement, is appropriate and relevant. These indicators were derived from a range of previous studies, as documented in Table 5.

VALIDATION PROCEDURES

To ensure the goodness of the proposed measurement indicators, the authors undertook a two-phase validation process. The first phase focused on content validity analysis, which involved seeking input from experts in the field. Through this analysis, the experts provided valuable insights and feedback on the relevance and appropriateness of the indicators. In the second phase, the authors conducted a construct validity analysis using statistical methods. The data for the statistical test was obtained from a survey administered to lean practitioners in the manufacturing industries. This analysis enabled them to evaluate the relationships and consistency between the indicators and the underlying constructs they were intended to measure. By employing both content and construct validity analyses, the authors obtained a comprehensive validation of the measurement indicators.

Table 5. Assessment indicators of sustainable lean transformation gains

Dimensions	Code	Assessment Indicators	Sources
Operational Performance	OP01	Cost saving	Jayaraman et al. (2012)
	OP02	Value-added activities	
	OP03	Product quality	
	OP04	Employee productivity	
	OP05	Machine productivity	
	OP06	Volume flexibility	
	OP07	Product flexibility	
	OP08	Delivery performance	
Business Performance	BP01	Revenue growth	Jayaraman et al. (2012) and Fullerton et al. (2014)
	BP02	Net profits	
	BP03	Return on assets	
	BP04	Competitive profile	
	BP05	New product development	
	BP06	Market development	
Continuous Improvement Capability	CI01	Ability to proactively adapt to changes in the business environment	Gaiardelli et al. (2019) and van Assen (2020)
	CI02	Ability to establish well-defined processes to implement improvements based on lessons learned	
	CI03	Ability to establish mechanisms to capture and share lessons learned from both successful and unsuccessful improvement initiatives	
	CI04	Ability to actively share knowledge and collaborate cross-functionally within the organization	
	CI05	Ability to actively implement feedback from employees at all levels	
	CI06	Ability to integrate continuous improvement efforts into the organization's performance evaluation and recognition systems	
	CI07	Ability to actively utilize recent technologies to enhance continuous improvement efforts	

Expert Validation: Content Validity Index and Inter-Rater Agreement

Evaluations by panel of experts are intended for producing content validity evidences. Content validity refers to the extent to which an instrument logically measures the intended variable (Fraenkel et al., 2012). In line with the literature (Carpenter, 2018; Fisher, 2020; Rubio et al., 2003), this study sought professional opinions from two groups of experts:

i. Topic experts with extensive knowledge and practical experience in the subject matter.
ii. Survey methodologists who could provide credible advice on collecting accurate data for answering research questions.

Experts' evaluations were systematically employed using formalized scaling (Boateng et al., 2018) with clear instructions (Carpenter, 2018) to minimize bias and subjective assessments. The study utilized a content validation rubric that required the panel of experts to review and rate each item's representativeness and clarity on a four-point Likert scale (1 = item is not representative, 2 = item needs major revisions, 3 = item needs minor revisions, and 4 = item is representative). This content validation rubric adheres to the standard format for reporting content-oriented evidence as advocated by The American Educational Research Association, American Psychological Association, and National Council on Measurement in Education (2014). The rubric also provided space for experts to comment on word choices and other content validity aspects such as double-barreled, leading, difficult, redundant, or sensitive questions.

For this study, a panel of 15 experts well-versed in lean manufacturing studies and/or possessing in-depth practical experiences in lean transformation programs was approached. The panel comprised eight academic scholars with doctoral degrees or pursuing doctoral degrees in the field, three lean consultants, and four lean practitioners from industries. Additionally, one of the academic scholars was skilled in scale development and statistical analyses, specifically requested to evaluate the scale appropriateness and statistical potential of the proposed questionnaire set. Initially, the experts were given one week to return the validation rubric, but due to their busy schedules, the authors spent approximately one month gathering feedback. Reminders were sent via WhatsApp messages and phone calls once or twice a week until the rubric was returned.

Ultimately, feedback was obtained from 11 experts. Among them, four did not rate the items but provided general comments on improving the indicators. The four experts who responded but did not rate the items included two lean consultants, one practitioner from the automotive manufacturing industry, and one senior lecturer. Thus, only seven completed validation rubrics from seven experts remained for analysis (see Table 6).

Table 6. Profile of lean experts

Expert Code	Gender	Education	Designation	Relevance
Expert #1	Male	PhD	Senior lecturer	10 years' experience in lean manufacturing research and lean industrial collaboration
Expert #2	Female	PhD	Senior lecturer	8 years' experience in lean manufacturing research and lean industrial collaboration
Expert #3	Male	PhD	Senior lecturer	5 years' experience in lean manufacturing research and the winner of public university's lean project competition
Expert #4	Female	Masters	Senior lecturer	6 years' experience in lean manufacturing research and the winner of public university's lean project competition
Expert #5	Male	Degree	Lean executive	10 years experienced practitioner
Expert #6	Male	Degree	Manufacturing engineer (Electrical & electronics manufacturing)	9 years experienced practitioner
Expert #7	Male	Masters	Deputy Director	5 years' experience as the lead consultant of lean transformation projects

Boateng et al. (2018) suggest that a range of five to seven experts is sufficient for content validation, considering they should come from different backgrounds. As mentioned earlier, the present study gathered seven experts comprising academic lean scholars (subject-matter experts and methodologists), a lean consultant (subject-matter expert), and lean practitioners (experts from the target population), fulfilling the recommended number of experts and background diversity as suggested in the literature.

Most experts rated the questionnaire items with a score of 3 (item needs minor revisions) or 4 (item is representative) to represent the construct. The ratings given by the panel of experts for each questionnaire item are provided in Table 7. Content validity index (CVI) and inter-rater agreement (IRA) were calculated to determine whether to retain, revise, replace, or remove the rated items based on objective measures (Polit & Beck, 2006; Rubio et al., 2003). CVI and IRA were calculated using the following formulas for item-level CVI (I-CVI) and item-level IRA (I-IRA).

Table 7. Content validity ratings by panel of experts

Item Code	Expert #1	Expert #2	Expert #3	Expert #4	Expert #5	Expert #6	Expert #7	n_r	$\sum n_a$
OP01	4	4	4	4	4	4	4	7	7
OP02	4	4	3	2	4	4	4	6	6
OP03	4	4	4	4	4	4	4	7	7
OP04	4	4	4	4	4	4	4	7	7
OP05	4	4	4	4	4	4	4	7	7
OP06	4	4	4	4	4	4	4	7	7
OP07	4	3	4	4	4	4	4	7	6
OP08	4	4	4	4	4	4	4	7	7
BP01	4	4	4	4	4	3	4	7	6
BP02	4	4	4	4	4	3	4	7	6
BP03	4	4	4	4	4	3	4	7	6
BP04	4	4	4	4	4	3	4	7	6
BP05	4	4	4	4	4	3	4	7	6
BP06	4	4	4	4	4	3	4	7	6
CI01	4	4	4	4	4	4	4	7	7
CI02	4	4	4	4	2	4	4	6	6
CI03	4	4	4	4	4	4	4	7	7
CI04	4	4	4	3	2	4	4	6	5
CI05	4	4	4	4	2	4	4	6	6
CI06	4	4	4	3	2	4	4	6	5
CI07	4	4	4	4	4	4	4	7	6

The study also calculated scale-level CVI (S-CVI) and scale-level IRA (S-IRA) by averaging across all items. Averaging for S-CVI and S-IRA is recommended when the number of experts exceeds five (Rubio et al., 2003), which was the case for this study, as evaluations were gathered from seven experts. The results of CVI and IRA calculations for both item-level and scale-level are presented in Table 8.

Table 8. Content validity ratings by panel of experts

Dimensions	Item Code	n_r	I-CVI	S-CVI	$\sum n_a$	I-IRA	S-IRA
Operational Performance	OP01	7	1.000	.982	7	1.000	.964
	OP02	6	.857		6	.85	
	OP03	7	1.000		7	1.000	
	OP04	7	1.000		7	1.000	
	OP05	7	1.000		7	1.00	
	OP06	7	1.000		7	1.000	
	OP07	7	1.000		6	.857	
	OP08	7	1.000		7	1.00	
Business Performance	BP01	7	1.000	1.000	6	.857	.857
	BP02	7	1.000		6	.857	
	BP03	7	1.000		6	.857	
	BP04	7	1.000		6	.857	
	BP05	7	1.000		6	.857	
	BP06	7	1.00		6	.857	
Continuous Improvement Capability	CI01	7	1.000	.918	7	1.000	.857
	CI02	6	.85		6	.85	
	CI03	7	1.00		7	1.00	
	CI04	6	.85		5	.71	
	CI05	6	.85		6	.85	
	CI06	6	.85		5	.71	
	CI07	7	1.00		6	.85	

According to Davis (1992), a content validity index (CVI) of 0.80 is considered adequate to establish content validity for a variable. Similarly, Lynn (1986) suggested that an inter-rater agreement (IRA) of 0.80 indicates acceptable reliability in measuring a variable. Applying these standards, all dimensions in this study demonstrated sufficient evidence of content validity and inter-rater reliability. As a result, no indicators were removed from the list due to lack of representativeness or clarity.

The results obtained from the evaluation process provided further supporting evidence for validating the measurement of sustainable lean transformation gains, which encompasses both tangible and intangible indicators. The inclusion of both types of indicators enhances the comprehensiveness of the measurement approach. Moving forward, the next step in this research is to obtain construct validity evidence, which will allow for a complete claim of validity for the measurement of Sustainable Gains.

Practitioners Survey: Construct Validity

To validate the proposed Sustainable Gains indicators using statistical methods, the authors conducted a cross-sectional survey among lean practitioners in the manufacturing industry in Malaysia. The survey specifically targeted manufacturing organizations in Malaysia that are practicing lean principles. As there was no existing directory available, the authors compiled their own sampling frame using a self-compilation directory provided by the Malaysia Productivity Corporation (MPC). This directory was derived from the list of organizations that participated in MPC's Lean Transformation Program and Assessment between 2015 and 2018, encompassing 213 manufacturing organizations from 11 different industries classified by the Ministry of International Trade and Industry (MITI). The study focused on organizations that had implemented lean transformation for at least two years, based on previous research highlighting the importance of this duration for developing necessary capabilities and sustaining lean practices (Galeazzo, 2019; Madsen et al., 2019; Van Landeghem et al., 2013).

The eligible respondents for the study were managerial-level staff, including top, middle, and first-line managers, who were actively involved in lean transformation initiatives within their respective organizations. Following previous studies (Netland et al., 2020; van der Merwe, 2016), these managerial-level staff were considered qualified individuals to provide insights into lean transformation inquiries. In successful lean organizations, the strategy is deployed from top to bottom, while the execution works from bottom to top (Mann, 2015; Poksinska & Swartling, 2018; Sisson & Elshennawy, 2015). Hence, all managerial staff members were directly involved in the lean transformation program according to their designated roles.

The authors utilized a voluntary sampling technique and distributed the survey questionnaire to all manufacturing organizations listed in the sampling frame. Using the G*Power calculator and following Memon et al.'s (2020) recommendation, the calculated sample size for the study was determined to be 77, which provided sufficient statistical power. The self-completed questionnaires were distributed via email and social media channels such as WhatsApp and Telegram. The questionnaire was prepared in both Microsoft Word format and an online electronic form created with Google Forms. Initial contact with the respondents was made via email to explain the purpose of the study and request their voluntary participation. The email included attachments of both the Word document and a link to access the Google Forms questionnaire. Personal phone numbers listed in the sample frame were not used initially to respect respondents' privacy. Out of the 213 organizations listed in the MPC's lean practitioners' directory, a total of 92 questionnaires were returned from eligible respondents. Thirty organizations indicated that they were no longer practicing lean principles, resulting in a response rate of 50.27%, which exceeded the required sample size.

As a result, the survey successfully captured the diversity of the manufacturing sector in Malaysia by obtaining respondent organizations from 11 different industrial classifications established by MITI. The majority of eligible respondents were involved in the production of food and beverages (F&B) products (20.7%), while aerospace components manufacturers constituted the minority (1.1%). Other major respondent industries included wood-based products (18.5%), electrical and electronics devices (15.2%), and automotive parts (9.8%). Chemical and petrochemical product manufacturers, iron and steel producers, and pharmaceutical manufacturers accounted for 8.7% of the total eligible samples each. The remaining industries in the sampled dataset were machinery and equipment (5.4%), rubber (2.2%), and textile (2.2%) manufacturing. Compared to previous research studies in Malaysia that focused on a single industry such as aerospace components (Puvanasvaran et al., 2008), E&E devices (Wong et al., 2009), automotive parts (Habidin et al., 2020), machinery and equipment (Chong et al., 2020), and food and beverages (Khusaini et al., 2014) this study demonstrated that lean principles were being adopted beyond these specific industrial settings.

Importantly, all 92 organizations included in the study were confirmed to be lean practitioners. The majority of these companies had been implementing lean practices for approximately four to five years (55.4%), and none had less than two years of experience, as targeted during the data collection process.

Furthermore, 40.2% of the respondents' organizations had adopted lean practices for four to five years, while the rest had implemented lean practices for two to four years (4.4%). Therefore, this information confirms the eligibility of all respondents' companies as lean practitioners. To provide further insight into the demographics of the respondents, the study also analyzed the personal information of the individuals who completed the questionnaires on behalf of their organizations. The main respondents consisted of middle managers (68.5%), followed by top managers (29.3%), and a small percentage of first-line managers (2.2%). Middle managers held positions such as general manager, plant manager, head of departments, engineers, and executives. Examples of job titles acquired in the present study included Head of System and Sustainability, Operations Manager, Production Manager, Project Manager, Plant Manager, Factory Manager, Administration Executive, Industrial Engineer, Manufacturing Engineer, Lean Engineer, and Lean Specialist.

Top management positions included directors, presidents, chairmen, senior executives, and senior managers of an organization. Job titles obtained from top management respondents included Managing Director, Executive Director, Director of Manufacturing, Chief Executive Officer, Chief Operating Officer, and Senior Manager (Manufacturing). The minority of first-line managers sampled in this study held the title of Production Supervisor. It is worth noting that, contrary to prior local studies that did not consider administrative personnel such as Human Resource Managers and Administration Executives as eligible respondents (Hasan, 2021; Iteng, 2013; Mohamed Ismail, 2014), this study took a different approach. In line with international lean scholars' viewpoints emphasizing the role of the human resource department in supporting lean transformation sustainability (Hines et al., 2011; Jørgensen et al., 2007; Marshall, 2014; Tracey & Flinchbaugh, 2009), this study considered both Human Resource Managers and Administration Executives as eligible respondents. The involvement of these personnel indicates that the sampled organizations had integrated human resource functions to the extent of assigning human resource managers and administration executives as individuals in charge of the lean transformation program. Furthermore, the present study focused on the strategic perspective of the organization's lean transformation, unlike previous local studies that emphasized the technical perspective. The aim was not to assess the extent of lean tools and techniques application, which was the primary focus of prior studies. Therefore, all acquired respondents were considered eligible based on the defined qualification criteria.

Since Sustainable Gains is a multi-dimensional variable consisting of operational performance, business performance, and continuous improvement capability, a higher-order measurement model assessment was conducted to evaluate construct validity. This assessment was carried out using the SmartPLS 4 software, a statistical analysis tool specializing in partial least squares structural equation modelling (PLS-SEM) (Ringle et al., 2022). PLS-SEM is a variance-based structural equation modeling (SEM) approach commonly used when a small population restricts the sample size or when the research model includes formative constructs (Hair, Risher, et al., 2019). The authors' choice of utilizing SmartPLS 4 aligns well with their objective of validating Sustainable Gains as a reflective-formative higher-order construct. SmartPLS 4 is specifically designed to handle PLS-SEM analysis, making it suitable for their aim. Operational performance, business performance, and continuous improvement capability are considered formative dimensions of Sustainable Gains. This choice is justified as formative measurement is appropriate when the construct represents a broader concept that can be captured by different dimensions or aspects (Xu et al., 2019). By employing SmartPLS 4, the authors can effectively assess the relationships between Sustainable Gains as the latent construct and its reflective indicators and formative dimensions (see Figure 1). The software provides the necessary analysis to evaluate the construct's validity and reliability which enables a comprehensive understanding of Sustainable Gains as a multi-dimensional construct.

Figure 1. Sustainable gains as a reflective-formative higher order construct

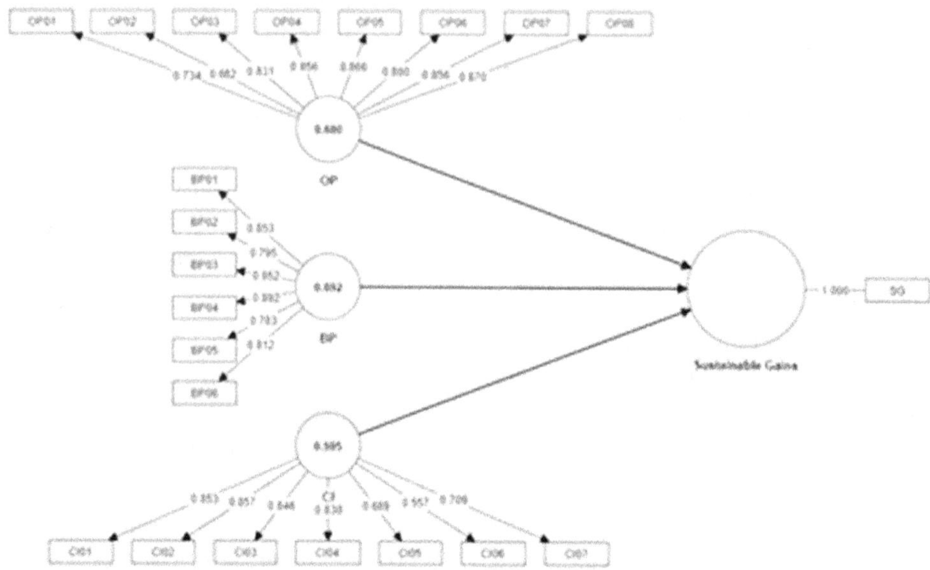

Figure 1 portrays Sustainable Gains as a reflective-formative higher-order construct, with its dimensions operational performance (OP), business performance (BP), and continuous improvement capability (CI) depicted as lower-order constructs. The indicators measuring OP, BP, and CI are connected reflectively to their respective constructs. Conversely, OP, BP, and CI are connected formatively to Sustainable Gains. The values shown on the indicators' arrows represent the outer loadings, while the values inside the construct represent the average variance extracted (AVE) statistics.

The assessment of the measurement model for reflective constructs involves evaluating AVE statistics to indicate convergent validity, the rho c coefficient (composite reliability) to establish internal consistency reliability, and the heterotrait-monotrait (HTMT) ratio to demonstrate discriminant validity (Hair et al., 2022). On the other hand, for the formative measurement model, redundancy analysis is conducted between the formative higher-order Sustainable Gains indicators and its global single-item measure to assess convergent validity (refer to Figure 2). In addition to convergent validity, the assessment of the formative measurement model includes examining collinearity between indicators and the significance of outer weights. The results of these assessments are summarized in Table 9, Table 10 and Table 11.

Figure 2 depicts the path model used for redundancy analysis in SmartPLS 4. It shows that operational performance (OP), business performance (BP), and continuous improvement capability (CI) form the construct named Sustainable Gains, which is depicted as the predictor variable. The global single-item measure of Sustainable Gains is depicted as the criterion variable.

Figure 2. Redundancy analysis

Table 9. Convergent validity and internal consistency reliability assessments

Dimensions	Item Code	Loading	Rho c	AVE
Operational Performance	OP01	.744	.944	.679
	OP02	.692		
	OP03	.838		
	OP04	.855		
	OP05	.865		
	OP06	.868		
	OP07	.847		
	OP08	.865		
Business Performance	BP01	.868	.932	.695
	BP02	.814		
	BP03	.857		
	BP04	.895		
	BP05	.752		
	BP06	.809		
Continuous Improvement Capability	CI01	.859	.910	.595
	CI02	.870		
	CI03	.849		
	CI04	.837		
	CI05	.698		
	CI06	.543		
	CI07	.683		

Table 9 presents the results of internal consistency reliability and convergent validity for all constructs. The minimum requirement for convergent validity of a construct is an average variance extracted (AVE) statistic of 0.5 or higher (Fornell & Larcker, 1981; Hair et al., 2022). Furthermore, a satisfactory level for the rho c coefficient is equal to or greater than 0.7 (Gefen et al., 2000; Hair et al., 2022). As a result, all dimensions of Sustainable Gains have achieved the threshold for convergent validity, with AVE values ranging from 0.595 to 0.695. None of the items in the measurement model need to be removed in order to fulfill the requirement for convergent validity. Although items such as OP2, CI05 and CI06 displayed outer loadings below the standard threshold of r < 0.708, these items were retained based on the opinions of other scholars. Researchers are permitted to retain items with outer loadings as low as 0.50 (Byrne, 2016) as long as the particular construct has achieved its convergent validity requirement (AVE ≥ 0.50).

Table 10. Discriminant validity assessment

Dimensions	1	2	3
1. Operational Performance			
2. Business Performance	.662		
3. Continuous Improvement Capability	.415	.448	

Table 10 presents the results of the HTMT ratio, which is used to assess discriminant validity. A HTMT ratio greater than 0.85 indicates a potential problem with discriminant validity (Kline, 2015). The results in Table 10 demonstrate that all ratios were below 0.85, confirming that there are no issues with discriminant validity among all dimensions of Sustainable Gains.

Table 11. Sustainable gains formative dimensions assessment

Construct	Dimensions	Convergent Validity	Weights	VIF	t-Value Weights	Outer Loadings
Sustainable Gains	Operational Performance	.591	.559	1.716	2.311*	.793
	Business Performance		-.063	1.750	.383	.574
	Continuous Improvement Capability		.677	1.267	3.848**	.876

To validate the formative dimensions of Sustainable Gains, convergent validity is assessed using redundancy analysis as suggested by (Chin, 1998). As shown in Table 11, the formative construct of Sustainable Gains yields a path coefficient of 0.591, which is not significantly different from 0.7 (97.5% percentile confidence interval: [0.434; 0.688]) (Sarstedt et al., 2019). Thus, the formatively measured construct demonstrates sufficient degrees of convergent validity. Furthermore, collinearity between indicators is assessed. Based on the results presented in Table 10, all dimensions of the formative Sustainable Gains construct satisfy the variance inflation factor (VIF) values, consistently remaining below 3.3 (Diamantopoulos & Siguaw, 2006). Therefore, it can be concluded that collinearity does not reach critical levels in any of the formative dimensions, and it is not an issue for the estimation of the PLS-SEM. Lastly, the significance of the outer weights of the formative dimensions is examined. The results indicate that all dimensions are significant except for Business Performance. However, the outer loading for Business Performance is above 0.5. Hence, Business Performance can be retained in the Sustainable Gains construct based on its absolute contribution (Cheah et al., 2018; Hair et al., 2022).

CONCLUSION

The assessment of content validity index (CVI) and inter-rater agreement (IRA) provides a solid foundation for the measurement model. The obtained CVI values demonstrate that the dimensions in the model have achieved adequate content validity, surpassing the minimum threshold of 0.80. This indicates that the indicators included in the measurement model accurately represent the underlying constructs of Sustainable Gains. Additionally, the IRA values indicate a high level of agreement among the raters, ensuring the reliability and consistency of the measurement model across different evaluators.

Moving on to the assessment of convergent validity, the results demonstrate that all dimensions of Sustainable Gains have achieved the threshold for convergent validity. The AVE values above 0.5, provide sufficient evidence of convergent validity. None of the items in the OP, BP or CI needed to be removed, as all indicators contribute to the overall measurement of the construct. Furthermore, the assessment of discriminant validity using the HTMT ratio confirms that there are no issues with discriminant validity among all dimensions of Sustainable Gains. All HTMT ratios were below the threshold of 0.85, indicating a clear distinction between the dimensions in the Sustainble Gains.

In validating the formative dimensions of Sustainable Gains, redundancy analysis was conducted, resulting in a path coefficient of 0.591. This coefficient demonstrates sufficient degrees of convergent validity for the formatively measured construct. Additionally, collinearity between indicators was assessed, and the results indicate that all dimensions of the formative Sustainable Gains construct satisfy VIF values, remaining consistently below 3.3. This confirms that collinearity does not reach critical levels and does not pose an issue for the estimation of the proposed formative dimensions. Finally, the significance of the outer weights of the formative dimensions was examined. Although Business Performance did not reach significance, it can still be retained in the Sustainable Gains construct based on its absolute contribution.

Overall, the comprehensive assessment of the measurement model, including content validity, inter-rater agreement, convergent validity, discriminant validity, and formative construct assessments, supports the robustness and validity of the proposed approach for measuring Sustainable Lean Transformation Gains. These findings provide valuable insights for practitioners and researchers seeking to evaluate and enhance the effectiveness of lean transformation initiatives.

In light of the findings and conclusions of this study, several recommendations for future research can be made. Firstly, replication studies are essential to validate the proposed measurement model and indicators of Sustainable Gains in different contexts. Replicating the study in diverse industries, cultural settings, or geographical regions can provide valuable insights into the generalizability and applicability of the indicators. This will contribute to the robustness and reliability of the measurement model across different organizational and cultural contexts.

Furthermore, exploring the potential to adopt or adapt the Sustainable Gains indicators in different settings is an important avenue for future research. Investigating the transferability of the indicators to other sectors or industries can help identify their effectiveness and relevance beyond the manufacturing sector. This can include service industries, healthcare organizations, or even non-profit sectors where lean principles and practices are increasingly being embraced.

Lastly, longitudinal studies can be conducted to assess the sustainability and long-term impact of lean transformation initiatives. By monitoring the changes in Sustainable Gains over an extended period, researchers can gain insights into the dynamics of lean implementation and its effects on organizational performance and continuous improvement capability. This will provide a deeper understanding of the long-term benefits and challenges associated with sustaining lean practices. Overall, conducting replication studies, exploring different settings, and conducting longitudinal studies will contribute to advancing the field of sustainable lean transformation and refining the measurement and assessment of Sustainable Gains.

REFERENCES

Ahmad, M. F., Toh, L. Y., Chan, S. W., Ahmad, A. N. A., Raja Mohd Rasi, R. Z., Abdul Rahman, N. A., Muhd Nor, N. H., Hassan, M. F., & Hashim, F. A. (2017). Continuous improvement and its barriers in electrical and electronic industry. MATEC Web of Conferences 135, Langkawi, Malaysia. doi:10.1051/matecconf/201713500045

Ahmed Soliman, M. H. (2013). Lean transformation guidance: Why organizations fail to achieve and sustain excellence through lean improvement. *International Journal of Lean Thinking*, *4*(1), 31–40.

Al Najem, M., Dhakal, H., & Bennett, N. (2012). The role of culture and leadership in lean transformation: A review and assessment model. *International Journal of Lean Thinking*, *3*(1), 119–138.

Aloini, D., Martini, A., & Pellegrini, L. (2011). A structural equation model for continuous improvement: A test for capabilities, tools and performance. *Production Planning and Control*, *22*(7), 628–648. doi:10.1080/09537287.2010.508759

Alukal, G. (2006, October). 2006). Keeping lean alive. *Quality Progress*, *39*(10), 67–69. https://asq.org/quality-progress/articles/lean-lessons-keeping-lean-alive?id=b90de437aa374da689bba4c848cb6ef1

American Educational Research Association, American Psychological Association, & National Council on Measurement in Education. (2014). Standards for educational and psychological testing. American Education Research Association.

Association for Manufacturing Excellence. (2009). Sustaining lean: Case studies in transforming culture. CRC Press.

Benkarim, A., & Imbeau, D. (2021). Organizational commitment and lean sustainability: Literature review and directions for future research. *Sustainability (Basel)*, *13*(6), 3357. doi:10.3390u13063357

Boateng, G. O., Neilands, T. B., Frongillo, E. A., Melgar-Quiñonez, H. R., & Young, S. L. (2018). Best practices for developing and validating scales for health, social, and behavioral research: A primer. *Frontiers in Public Health*, *6*(149), 1–18. doi:10.3389/fpubh.2018.00149 PMID:29942800

Buchanan, D., Fitzgerald, L., Ketley, D., Gollop, R., Jones, J. L., Lamont, S. S., & Whitby, E. (2005). No going back: A review of the literature on sustaining organizational change. *International Journal of Management Reviews*, *7*(3), 189–205. doi:10.1111/j.1468-2370.2005.00111.x

Burch, M. K. (2008). *Lean longevity: Kaizen events and determinants of sustainable improvement.* University of Massachusetts Amherst.

Burnes, B. (2017). *Managing change* (7th ed.). Pearson Education Ltd.

Byrne, B. M. (2016). Structural equation modeling with AMOS: Basic concepts, applications, and programming (3rd ed.). Routledge, Taylor & Francis Group.

Carpenter, S. (2018). Ten steps in scale development and reporting: A guide for researchers. *Communication Methods and Measures*, *12*(1), 25–44. doi:10.1080/19312458.2017.1396583

Cheah, J.-H., Sarstedt, M., Ringle, C. M., Ramayah, T., & Ting, H. (2018). Convergent validity assessment of formatively measured constructs in PLS-SEM. *International Journal of Contemporary Hospitality Management*, *30*(11), 3192–3210. doi:10.1108/IJCHM-10-2017-0649

Chin, W. W. (1998). The partial least squares approach for structural equation modeling. In *Modern Methods for Business Research* (pp. 295–336). Lawrence Erlbaum Associates Publishers.

Chong, J. Y., Puvanasvaran, A. P., & Feng, C. J. (2020). Exploring critical success factors for the implementation of lean manufacturing in machinery and equipment SMEs. *Engineering Management in Production and Services, 12*(4).

Costa, F., Lispi, L., Staudacher, A. P., Rossini, M., Kundu, K., & Cifone, F. D. (2019). How to foster sustainable continuous improvement: A cause-effect relations map of lean soft practices. *Operations Research Perspectives*, *6*, 100091. doi:10.1016/j.orp.2018.100091

Dale, B. G. (1996). Sustaining a process of continuous improvement: Definition and key factors. *The TQM Magazine*, *8*(2), 49–51. doi:10.1108/09544789610114867

Davies, P. (1992). Holding the gains. *The TQM Magazine*, *4*(3). Advance online publication. doi:10.1108/09544789210034347

Davis, L. L. (1992). Instrument review: Getting the most from a panel of experts. *Applied Nursing Research*, *5*(4), 194–197. doi:10.1016/S0897-1897(05)80008-4

Diamantopoulos, A., & Siguaw, J. A. (2006). Formative versus reflective indicators in organizational measure development: A comparison and empirical illustration. *British Journal of Management*, *17*(4), 263–282. doi:10.1111/j.1467-8551.2006.00500.x

Fisher, S. (2020). *7 Ways to pretest your survey before you send it.* Qualtrics. Retrieved July 17th from https://www.qualtrics.com/blog/6-ways-to-pretest-your-survey-before-you-send-it/?fbclid=IwAR0BVDBgLceDDBqhRDoHNtDVHxsiUg-IMt416h_TUTLS52gW39Qszbyo8v0

Fornell, C., & Larcker, D. F. (1981). Evaluating Structural Equation Models with unobservable variables and measurement error. *JMR, Journal of Marketing Research*, *18*(1), 39–50. doi:10.1177/002224378101800104

Fraenkel, J. R., Wallen, N. E., & Hyun, H. H. (2012). *How to design and evaluate research in education* (8th ed.). McGraw-Hill Companies, Inc.

Fullerton, R. R., Kennedy, F. A., & Widener, S. K. (2014). Lean manufacturing and firm performance: The incremental contribution of lean management accounting practices. *Journal of Operations Management*, *32*(7), 414–428. doi:10.1016/j.jom.2014.09.002

Gaiardelli, P., Resta, B., & Dotti, S. (2019). Exploring the role of human factors in lean management. *International Journal of Lean Six Sigma*, *10*(1), 339–366. doi:10.1108/IJLSS-08-2017-0094

Galeazzo, A. (2019). Degree of leanness and lean maturity: Exploring the effects on financial performance. *Total Quality Management & Business Excellence*, 1–19. doi:10.1080/14783363.2019.1634469

Galeazzo, A., Furlan, A., & Vinelli, A. (2017). The organizational infrastructure of continuous improvement – an empirical analysis. *Operations Management Research : Advancing Practice Through Research, 10*(1), 33–46. doi:10.100712063-016-0112-1

Gefen, D., Straub, D., & Boudreau, M.-C. (2000). Structural Equation Modeling and Regression: Guidelines for research practice. *Communications of the Association for Information Systems, 4*, 7. doi:10.17705/1CAIS.00407

Grigg, N. P., Goodyer, J. E., & Frater, T. G. (2018). Sustaining lean in SMEs: Key findings from a 10-year study involving New Zealand manufacturers. *Total Quality Management & Business Excellence, 31*(5-6), 609–622. doi:10.1080/14783363.2018.1436964

Habidin, N. F., Mohd Zubir, A. F., Mohd Fuzi, N., & Salleh, M. I. (2020). The relationship between sustainable manufacturing practices, lean improvement and performance. *World Review of Entrepreneurship, Management and Sustainable Development, 16*(1), 92–107. doi:10.1504/WREMSD.2020.105529

Hair, J. F., Black, W. C., Babin, B. J., & Anderson, R. E. (2019). *Multivariate data analysis* (8th ed.). Cengage Learning.

Hair, J. F., Hult, G. T. M., Ringle, C. M., & Sarstedt, M. (2022). *A primer on partial least squares structural equation modeling (PLS-SEM)* (3rd ed.). SAGE Publications Inc.

Hair, J. F., Risher, J. J., Sarstedt, M., & Ringle, C. M. (2019). When to use and how to report the results of PLS-SEM. *European Business Review, 31*(1), 2–24. doi:10.1108/EBR-11-2018-0203

Hardcopf, R., Liu, G., & Shah, R. (2021). Lean production and operational performance: The influence of organizational culture. *International Journal of Production Economics, 108060*. Advance online publication. doi:10.1016/j.ijpe.2021.108060

Hasan, M. Z. (2021). *Relationship between lean manufacturing practices and sustainability in manufacturing organisations: Mediating effect of manufacturing performance and moderating effect of ethical climate*. Universiti Utara Malaysia.

Hernandez-Matias, J. C., Ocampo, J. R., Hidalgo, A., & Vizan, A. (2020). Lean manufacturing and operational performance: Interrelationships between human-related lean practices. *Journal of Manufacturing Technology Management, 31*(2), 217–235. doi:10.1108/JMTM-04-2019-0140

Hines, P., Found, P. A., Griffiths, G., & Harrison, R. (2011). *Staying lean: Thriving, not just surviving* (2nd ed.). Lean Enterprise Research Centre, Cardiff University., https://orca.cf.ac.uk/52764/1/stayinglean.pdf

Hogan, B. J. (2009, December 1). Sustaining a lean culture. *Manufacturing Engineering Magazine, 143*(5), 71-76. http://advancedmanufacturing.org/sustaining-lean-culture/

Iranmanesh, M., Zailani, S., Hyun, S. S., Ali, M. H., & Kim, K. (2019). Impact of lean manufacturing practices on firms' sustainable performance: Lean culture as a moderator. *Sustainability (Basel), 11*(4), 1112. doi:10.3390u11041112

Iteng, R. (2013). *The relationship between lean production, operational performance and business performance in Malaysian manufacturing industry*. Universiti Kebangsaan Malaysia.

Jadhav, J. R., Mantha, S., & Rane, S. B. (2014). Development of framework for sustainable lean implementation: An ISM approach. *Journal of Industrial Engineering International*, *10*(3), 72. doi:10.100740092-014-0072-8

Jayaraman, K., Teo, L. K., & Keng, L. S. (2012). The perceptions and perspectives of Lean Six Sigma (LSS) practitioners: An empirical study in Malaysia. *The TQM Journal*, *24*(5), 433–446. doi:10.1108/17542731211261584

Jørgensen, F., Matthiesen, R., Nielsen, J., & Johansen, J. (2007). Lean maturity, lean sustainability. In J. Olhager & F. Persson (Eds.), *Advances in Production Management Systems* (pp. 371–378). IFIP International Federation for Information Processing. doi:10.1007/978-0-387-74157-4_44

Khusaini, N. S., Jaffar, A., & Yusoff, N. (2014). *A survey on lean manufacturing tools implementation in Malaysian food and beverages industry using rasch model.* Advanced Materials Research, Johor Bahru, MY.

Kline, R. B. (2015). *Principles and practice of structural equation modeling* (4th ed.). The Guilford Press.

Liker, J. K. (2004). *The Toyota way: 14 management principles from the world's greatest manufacturer* (1st ed.). McGraw-Hill Education.

Losonci, D., & Demeter, K. (2013). Lean production and business performance: International empirical results. *Competitiveness Review*, *23*(3), 218–233. doi:10.1108/10595421311319816

Lucey, J., Bateman, N., & Hines, P. (2005). Why major lean transitions have not been sustained. *Management Services*, *49*(2), 9–13.

Lynn, M. R. (1986). Determination and quantification of content validity. *Nursing Research*, *35*(6), 382–385. doi:10.1097/00006199-198611000-00017 PMID:3640358

Madsen, D. Ø., Berg, T., Stenheim, T., Moum, J. V., Bordewich, I. O., & Storsveen, M. (2019). The long-term sustainability of lean as a management practice: Survey evidence on diffusion and use of the concept in Norway in the period 2015–2017. *Sustainability (Basel)*, *11*(11), 3120. doi:10.3390u11113120

Mann, D. W. (2015). *Creating a lean culture: Tools to sustain lean conversions* (3rd ed.). CRC Press.

Marchwinski, C. (2014). *Sustain your lean business system with a "Golden Triangle"*. Lean Enterprise Institute. Retrieved Dec 1st from https://www.lean.org/common/display/?o=2592

Marshall, D. A. (2014). *Lean transformation: Overcoming the challenges, managing performance, and sustaining success*. University of Kentucky.

Memon, M. A., Ting, H., Cheah, J. H., Ramayah, T., Chuah, F., & Cham, T. H. (2020). Sample size for survey research: Review and recommendations. *Journal of Applied Structural Equation Modelling*, *4*(2), 1–20. doi:10.47263/JASEM.4(2)01

Mohamed Ismail, R. (2014). *Mediation impact of manufacturing strategies on external environmental factors and manufacturing performance*. Universiti Utara Malaysia.

Mohd Rose, A. N., Md Deros, B., & Ab Rahman, M. N. (2013). *Lean manufacturing practices implementation in Malaysian's SME automotive component industry*. Applied Mechanics and Materials.

Mohd Yusof, S., & Aoki, K. (2016, March 8-10). *Proposed lean sustained factors*. The 6th International Conference on Industrial Engineering and Operations Management (IEOM 2016), Kuala Lumpur, Malaysia.

Murti, Y. (2009). *Sustaining lean in New Zealand manufacturing organisations*. Massey University.

Nawanir, G., Lim, K. T., & Othman, S. N. (2016). Lean manufacturing practices in Indonesian manufacturing firms. *International Journal of Lean Six Sigma*, *7*(2), 149–170. doi:10.1108/IJLSS-06-2014-0013

Netland, T. H., Powell, D. J., & Hines, P. (2020). Demystifying lean leadership. *International Journal of Lean Six Sigma*, *11*(3), 543–554. doi:10.1108/IJLSS-07-2019-0076

Onofrei, G., Prester, J., Fynes, B., Humphreys, P., & Wiengarten, F. (2019). The relationship between investments in lean practices and operational performance: Exploring the moderating effects of operational intellectual capital. *International Journal of Operations &amp. International Journal of Operations & Production Management*, *39*(3), 406–428. doi:10.1108/IJOPM-04-2018-0201

Pearce, A., & Pons, D. (2019). Advancing lean management: The missing quantitative approach. *Operations Research Perspectives*, *6*, 100114. doi:10.1016/j.orp.2019.100114

Pentlicki, J. H. (2014). *Barriers and success strategies for sustainable lean manufacturing implementation: A qualitative case study*. University of Phoenix.

Poksinska, B., & Swartling, D. (2018). From successful to sustainable lean production: The case of a Lean Prize Award Winner. *Total Quality Management & Business Excellence*, *29*(9-10), 996–1011. do i:10.1080/14783363.2018.1486539

Polit, D. F., & Beck, C. T. (2006). The content validity index: Are you sure you know what's being reported? Critique and recommendations. *Research in Nursing & Health*, *29*(5), 489–497. doi:10.1002/nur.20147 PMID:16977646

Popoola, O. A. (2000). Developmeny of a methodology for the rapid implementation of a sustainable lean manufacturing system. Massachusetts Institute of Technology (MIT).

Puvanasvaran, A. P., Tan, B. H., Megat Ahmad, M. H., Tang, S. H., Muhamad, M. R., & Hamouda, A. M. (2008). Degree of leanness and managerial commitment in an aerospace company. *Journal of Statistics and Management Systems*, *11*(4), 653–673. doi:10.1080/09720510.2008.10701336

Rentes, A. F., Araujo, C. A. C., & Rentes, V. C. (2009). Best practice examples in sustaining improvements from Lean implementation. *Proceedings of the 2009 Industrial Engineering Research Conference*.

Ringle, C. M., Wende, S., & Becker, J.-M. (2022). *SmartPLS 4*. SmartPLS. http://www.smartpls.com

Roth, G. (2011). Sustaining lean transformation through growth and positive organizational change. *Journal of Enterprise Transformation*, *1*(2), 119–146. doi:10.1080/19488289.2011.579228

Rubio, D. M., Berg-Weger, M., Tebb, S. S., Lee, E. S., & Rauch, S. (2003). Objectifying content validity: Conducting a content validity study in social work research. *Social Work Research*, *27*(2), 94–104. doi:10.1093wr/27.2.94

Ruffa, S. A. (2011). Going lean fieldbook - A practical guide to lean transformation and sustainable success. American Management Association (AMACOM).

Sahwan, M. A., Ab Rahman, M. N., & Md Deros, B. (2012). Barriers to implement lean manufacturing in malaysian automotive industry. *Jurnal Teknologi*, *59*(2), 107–110. doi:10.11113/jt.v59.2571

Sarstedt, M., Hair, J. F. Jr, Cheah, J. H., Becker, J.-M., & Ringle, C. M. (2019). How to specify, estimate, and validate higher-order constructs in PLS-SEM. *Australasian Marketing Journal*, *27*(3), 197–211. doi:10.1016/j.ausmj.2019.05.003

Schlichting, C. (2009). *Sustaining lean improvements*. Worcester Polytechnic Institute.

Sisson, J. A., & Elshennawy, A. (2015). Achieving success with lean. *International Journal of Lean Six Sigma*, *6*(3), 263–280. doi:10.1108/IJLSS-07-2014-0024

Susanty, A., Sumiyati, L. S., Syaiful, S., & Nihlah, Z. (2021). The impact of lean manufacturing practices on operational and business performances at SMES in the wooden furniture industry. *International Journal of Lean Six Sigma*. doi:10.1108/IJLSS-08-2020-0124

Taylor, A., Taylor, M., & McSweeney, A. (2013). Towards greater understanding of success and survival of lean systems. *International Journal of Production Research*, *51*(22), 6607–6630. doi:10.1080/00207543.2013.825382

Tracey, M. W., & Flinchbaugh, J. (2009). How human resource department can help lean transformation. In Sustaining lean: Case studies in transforming culture (pp. 119-128). CRC Press.

Turesky, E. F., & Connell, P. (2010). Off the rails: Understanding the derailment of a lean manufacturing initiative. *Organizational Management Journal*, *7*(2), 110–132. doi:10.1057/omj.2010.14

van Assen, M. F. (2020). Training, employee involvement and continuous improvement – the moderating effect of a common improvement method. *Production Planning and Control*, 1–13. doi:10.1080/09537287.2020.1716405

van der Merwe, K. R. (2016). Leadership behaviours and lean culture attainment in automotive component manufacturers. *Journal for New Generation Sciences*, *14*(3), 259–278.

Van Landeghem, H., Bauters, K., & Limère, V. (2013). A management system for sustainable lean implementation. *IIE Annual Conference. Proceedings*, 941-950. http://eserv.uum.edu.my/scholarly-journals/management-system-sustainable-lean-implementation/docview/1471958596/se-2?accountid=42599

Womack, J. P., & Jones, D. T. (1996). *Lean thinking: Banish waste and create wealth in your organisation* (Vol. 397). Simon & Schuster.

Wong, Y. C., Wong, K. Y., & Ali, A. (2009). A study on lean manufacturing implementation in the Malaysian electrical and electronics industry. *European Journal of Scientific Research*, *38*(4), 521–535.

Xu, L., Peng, X., & Prybutok, V. (2019). Formative measurements in operations management research: Using partial least squares. *The Quality Management Journal*, *26*(1), 18–31. doi:10.1080/10686967.2018.1542287

ADDITIONAL READING

Boateng, G. O., Neilands, T. B., Frongillo, E. A., Melgar-Quiñonez, H. R., & Young, S. L. (2018). Best practices for developing and validating scales for health, social, and behavioral research: A primer. *Frontiers in Public Health*, *6*(149), 1–18. doi:10.3389/fpubh.2018.00149 PMID:29942800

Hair, J. F., Hult, G. T. M., Ringle, C. M., & Sarstedt, M. (2022). *A primer on partial least squares structural equation modeling (PLS-SEM)* (3rd ed.). SAGE Publications Inc.

Hines, P., Found, P. A., Griffiths, G., & Harrison, R. (2011). *Staying lean: Thriving, not just surviving* (2nd ed.). Lean Enterprise Research Centre, Cardiff University. https://orca.cf.ac.uk/52764/1/stayinglean.pdf

Mann, D. W. (2015). *Creating a lean culture: Tools to sustain lean conversions* (3rd ed.). CRC Press.

Osman, A. A., Che Mamat, R., & Mat Ali, M. (2020). Lean transformational sustainability models: A critical review. *Advances in Business Research International Journal*, *6*(2), 1–18. doi:10.24191/abrij.v6i2.10581

Rubio, D. M., Berg-Weger, M., Tebb, S. S., Lee, E. S., & Rauch, S. (2003). Objectifying content validity: Conducting a content validity study in social work research. *Social Work Research*, *27*(2), 94–104. doi:10.1093wr/27.2.94

Ruffa, S. A. (2011). *Going lean fieldbook - A practical guide to lean transformation and sustainable success. American Management Association*. AMACOM.

Sarstedt, M., Hair, J. F. Jr, Cheah, J. H., Becker, J.-M., & Ringle, C. M. (2019). How to specify, estimate, and validate higher-order constructs in PLS-SEM. *Australasian Marketing Journal*, *27*(3), 197–211. doi:10.1016/j.ausmj.2019.05.003

KEY TERMS AND DEFINITIONS

Construct Validity: Construct validity is established when a measurement tool consistently and accurately captures a distinct concept. This type of validity encompasses various elements, including content validity, convergent validity, and discriminant validity.

Content Validity: The extent to which an instrument convincingly appears to assess the intended variable in a logical manner.

Convergent Validity: The degree of similarity or correlation among indicators that have been employed to measure the same construct.

Discriminant Validity: The level at which a construct is genuinely different from other constructs, both in terms of its correlation with other constructs and the extent to which its indicators solely represent that specific construct.

Inter-Rater Agreement: The degree of consensus or consistency among two or more raters (experts) in their assessments of a particular measurement instrument. It measures the extent to which multiple raters or judges, who are independently evaluating the same indicators or criteria, provide similar ratings or scores.

Internal Consistency Reliability: The extent to which items within a measurement instrument consistently measure the same construct or attribute. It is commonly assessed using statistical coefficients such as Cronbach's alpha and rho c.

Lean Pilot Project: The process of installing basic lean elements into the organisation's operations system.

Lean Transformation: The conversion from traditional operations system to lean operations system. This conversion reflects necessary changes to achieve the gains associated with lean practices.

Lean Transformation Sustainability: Maintaining the momentum of lean transformation in organisation's operations system to achieve persistent performance goals while having consistent direction towards continuous improvement.

Sustainability: The ability to be maintained at a certain level or standard over time.

Sustainable Gains: The ability to persistently acquire benefits and improvements from lean transformation efforts that include both tangible and intangible gains.

Chapter 4
The Method RAB2/E Matrix:
An Approach for Effective Program and Project Portfolio Prioritization Procedures

Altino José Mentzingen de Moraes
https://orcid.org/0000-0002-0303-9192
Lisbon University, Portugal

ABSTRACT

This chapter presents a method, applicable to the program and project portfolio prioritization procedures, named RAB2/E matrix (rapidity, autonomy and benefit / extended), where the letter "E" means "extended," since this new approach is derived from another original matrix (RADAR DE PROJETOS 2015) with new features. After performing these procedures related to portfolio prioritization, any project management methodology—such as PMBoK©, PRINCE2®, and ZOPP—can be applied to control the tasks which have to be done. The already mentioned new features were implemented in the prior matrix according to the aspects of internal and external influences perceived. In order to get better comprehension of how this new method was planned, and which were its foundations, this chapter also describes some techniques that can be used as tools for program and project portfolio prioritization. A statistic sample about the implementation of this method RAB2/E matrix are in its conclusions.

INTRODUCTION

Nowadays, and never before with the technology growing faster in an incredible rhythm, the Corporations has a so concurrent environment around they which pushes forward innovation and, consequently, Business Processes transformation as well.

The challenger, to keep the development and to maintenance the acquired market position (in order to reach a minimum target), is to balance the resources (Humans, Financials, and Technical) to extract the best possible return of investment to attend the Boad of Directors directives and their shareholders expectations.

DOI: 10.4018/979-8-3693-0458-7.ch004

The modern way to handle this challenger is to manage every action as a task, as part of a main Project included in a major Programme (with the principal target to build a product or to make available a service to be offer to the Corporate's external Clientele), under a holistic view (allocating and deallocating the Resources as necessary or not anymore) aiming to optimize the costs and time schedule.

But, applying this way of handling this challenger by the implementation of a Program and Project Management, arises a new issue what is how to define the Programs and Projects most important (according to some rules and criteria) to be done first than another.

That is when, the technique to manage a Portfolio gets high focus and special attention, promoted with the sponsorship by the Strategic Planning Area/Sector which needs the feedback of this type of management to subsidize its governance.

It is recognized that an effective Program and Project Portfolio Management, inside the Organization, can provide strong support that can collaborate to administrate the constant and growing need of the Corporate World in to be able to meet the demands of their Clientele, as well as, to keep ahead of the competition regarding the functionalities and the quality of the services and products provided.

In the 2000 decade, in its beginning, the subject of Program and Project Portfolio Control became more prominent in the Program and Project Management literature.

Partly due to the growing importance of activities in the Project Area in Corporations and partly due to the problems arising by the coexistence of multiplex Programs and Projects, simultaneous and concurrent, inside the same Organization.

An effective Program and Project Portfolio Management System should provide elements for the Organization's Executives can decide which initiatives best reflect business needs.

That is, "do the right thing," according to Drucker (1963, pp. 50-60), which in its context of Program and Project Portfolio Management, means mapping the most relevant opportunities and selecting the Programs and Projects most aligned with the Organizational Strategy.

The alignment between the Enterprise's Business Strategy and its Program and Project Portfolio – exemplified by PMI (2006), Ghapanchi, Tavana, Khakbaz & Low (2012, pp. 791-803), Costantino, Di Gravio & Nonino (2015, pp. 1744-1754) and Böhle, Heidling & Schoper (2016, pp. 1384-1392) – has been debated with interest by students and by organizations and some models have emerged in both Academic and Corporate scenarios.

This must happen, always when the PMO – Project Management Office is actioned to respond to this scenario, by making available new solutions that correspond to these expectations of the Business Areas.

Other examples of authors that researched this theme are Dye & Pennypacker (1999), Reyck, Grushka-Cockayne, Lockett, Calderini, Moura & Sloper (2005, pp. 524-537) and Carvalho & Rabechini Jr. (2006).

Additionally of to this Chapter Section "Introduction", the exposition of the text of this chapter will follow the below Nomenclature Table as presented in below Table 1.

In the topic "Problem approach" are presented the questions that this chapter intends to propose a way of workaround and solution. In the topic "Author Expertise" it is described the academic and professional conceptualization that the author possesses for subsidizing the formalization of his proposal driven by this chapter. In the topic "Methodology applied" is defined how the proposed solution was constructed.

In the topic "Theory references" a fundamental literature is presented on the techniques of Program and Project Portfolio Prioritization discussed. The topic "RAB^2/E Matrix" address the points those drove up the proposal of extended the original RAB Matrix to this new version. In the topic "Method implementation" it is exposed how RAB^2/E Matrix could be placed in practice, in a real Corporate' world, applying its artefacts. In the topic "Method application" is defined the relationship between the

RAB^2/E Matrix and Project Management Methodologies, such as, PMBoK© (PMI, 2022), PRINCE2© (OGC, 2018), and ZOPP© (GTZ, 2006).

In the topic "Conclusions" are analyzed and highlighted the contributions that this work intends to offer to the field of this research. In the topic "Future works" point out other alternatives that can be aggregated to evolve this study. And finally, at the end of this chapter in the topic "References", are described the textual materials researched to support the assembly of this proposal.

Table 1. Chapter sections nomenclature table

Nomenclature
Problem approach
Author expertise
Methodology applied
Theory references
RAB^2/E Matrix
Method implementation
Method application
Conclusions
Future works
References

PROBLEM APPROACH

An issue that is always under discussion in Organizations is how to decide, with a scientific method, which strategy is the better to follow – what means – where to invest money with fast financial feedback.

As a way to be followed, the PMO – Project Management Office can help with this issue by effectively administrating the Program and Project Portfolio, by applying Prioritization Techniques that consider as important some strategic factors, such as the "fast financial feedback", to organize the development order of these.

The point here is that the most known Prioritization Techniques, including in the group of Multi-Criteria Decision-Making (MCDM), did not consider these "important some strategic factors" (called as "*exogeneous*") which can interfere in a Program and Project Portfolio Prioritization.

This was the target of this Article: to review the Prioritization Techniques, try to find one that can match the goal to aggregate mathematics science (statistics rules) and also social science (*exogenous* criteria), and if it is found, study – whether or not – the criteria were enough to assistant an effective and right decision in Strategic Planning tasks.

Also, after evaluating if the existent *exogenous* criteria found – in the Prioritization Techniques found which aggregates mathematics and also social sciences – were enough or not to assistant an effective and right decision, this chapter will propose to insert some new *exogenous* criteria to enhance the level of possible analysis.

As an academic contribution, the author of this chapter presents some new criteria to be included in one already existent Prioritization Techniques known as *Matriz RAB^2/E* (RAB^2/E Matrix) for Program and Project Portfolio Management, in order to achieve the goal, of better support the Organizations in its decision for investment in the development of one Program or Project instead of another.

These criteria are presented, in the Figure 10, in the form of a Table of Criteria of Prioritization (built in a MS®-Excel© Spreadsheet from Microsoft) and are described in this Chapter and commented in the text body.

AUTHOR EXPERTISE

The perception of the criteria, which were the focus of this chapter, was the result of the accumulation of experiences throughout the professional career of more than forty nine years of the author in software projects of various types, besides additional Technical Certifications in the field of Project Management (PMP© – Project Management Professional/PMI© – Project Management Institute) and Process Management (CBPP® – Certification in Business Process Professional/ABPMP® – Association of Business Process Management Professional).

METHODOLOGY APPLIED

This chapter is the result of several years of work in the area of IT – Information Technology, where in his activities, the author encountered problems existents in this theme related to how to decide which Program or Project will return faster the results for the attending of the expectations and requirements.

Therefore, the author used his procedures/*constructs* designed to solve these issues that were presented in this work, also having been these, validated as effective in several opportunities.

However, to be able to justify which Scientific Methodology was applied to the execution of this Chapter, one can say that these were the Bibliographic Research (to relate the practice to the theory), the Data Survey (to understand the criteria that should be considered for setting up the new proposal for a Program and Project Portfolio Prioritization Technique) and the Laboratory (since the theory studied was applied in practice in the real world on several occasions).

THEORY REFERENCES

As already presented in RADAR DE PROJETOS (2015), besides proposing a new version for the *Matriz RAB – Rapidez, Autonomia e Benefício* (in English, RAB Matrix – Rapidity, Autonomy and Benefit, as a free translation since was not found any publication in English referring this theme), which will be called as "*Matriz RAB^2/E – Rapidez, Autonomia e Benefício / Estendida*" ("RAB^2/E Matrix – Rapidity, Autonomy and Benefit / Extended") throughout this text, this Chapter also intends to introduce some techniques applicable to Program and Project Prioritization defined as Multi-Criteria Decision-Making (MCDM).

Multi-Criteria Decision-Making (MCDM)

According to Taherdoost & Madanchian (2023), the Multi-Criteria Decision-Making (MCDM) is "one of the main decision-making problems which aims to determine the best alternative by considering more than one criterion in the selection process. MCDM has manifold tools and methods that can be applied in different fields from finance to engineering design."

Also, about Decision-Making Process, these same authors define that "there is no decision that can be addressed without referring to the Decision-Making Process. Decision-Making, as a mental complex process, is a problem-solving program that aims to determine a desirable result considering different aspects. This process can be rational or irrational, and on the other hand, it can use implicit or explicit assumptions that are influenced by several factors such as physiological, biological, cultural, social, etc.".

They concluded their exposition with "All these aspects together with authority and risk levels can affect the complexity level of a decision-making process. Nowadays, complex decision-making problems can be solved by utilizing mathematical equations, manifold statistics, mathematics, economic theories, and computer devices that help to calculate and estimate the solutions to decision-making problems automatically".

A survey done by both, and included in their literature, is in the Figure 1 and the Figure 2, which explain: Figure 1= how much the Multi-Criteria Decision-Making (MCDM) has been referenced in the decade from 2012 to 2021; Figure 2= in which Areas of Knowledge the Multi-Criteria Decision-Making (MCDM) can be applied.

Figure 1. Number of articles from 2012 to 2021 (Taherdoost & Madanchian, 2023)

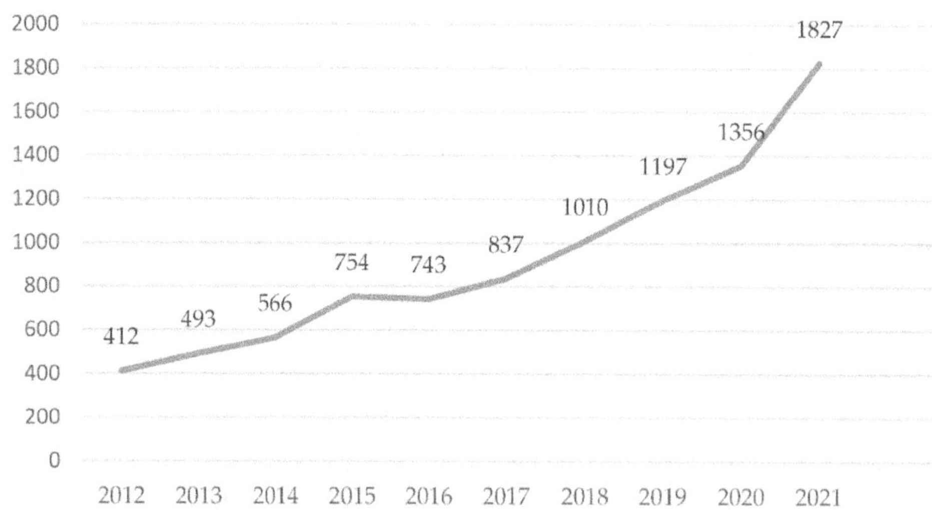

Still interpretating the words of Taherdoost & Madanchian (2023), they say that "There are several types of MCDM methods that are developed or improved by different authors during the last decades. The main differences between these methods are related to the complexity level of algorithms, the weighting methods for criteria, the way of representing preferences evaluation criteria, uncertain data possibility, and finally, data aggregation type".

Figure 2. Number of articles based on the subject area (Taherdoost & Madanchian, 2023)

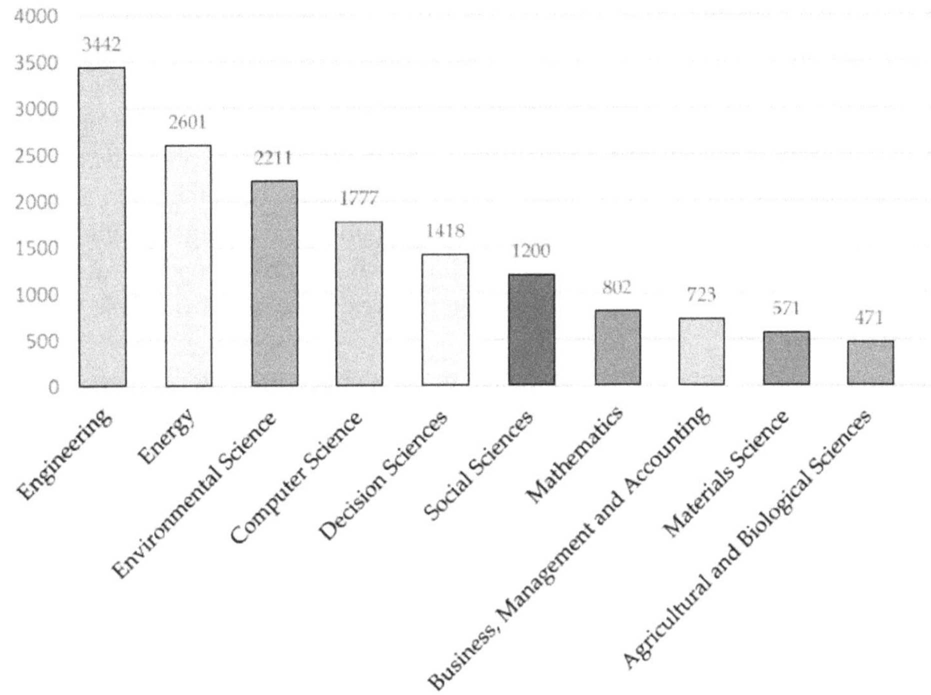

That is the same logic this chapter follows, which means, others existent Techniques are part of a set of tools which can support the Decision-Making Process as well.

Regarding the mentioned existent Techniques related to Multi-Criteria Decision-Making (MCDM), that can be applicable to Program and Project Prioritization and which this Chapter will also present in detail in the following topics, these are listed in alphabetical order for not imply any indication of one be better than another.

Their names are: AHP – Analytic Hierarchy Process by Saaty (1980), BWM – Best-Worst Method by Rezaei (2016, pp. 126-130), Électre by Roy, Bernard (1968), Fuzzy Logic by Martino, Perfilieva & Sessa (2021), MACBETH – Measuring Attractiveness by a Categorical-Based Evaluation Technique by Bana e Costa & Vansnick (1994, pp. 489-500), PROMETHEE – Preference Ranking Organization MeTHod for Enrichment Evaluations by Almeida, Almeida & Costa (2014, pp. 275-299] and TOPSIS – Technique for Order of Preference by Similarity to Ideal Solution by Tan, Shen, Langston & Liu (2010, pp. 302-315).

AHP: Analytic Hierarchy Process

The AHP – Analytic Hierarchy Process, from an American management professor Saaty (1980), is an internationally recognized decision-making technique. It is intended to help people or organizations make the right choice in complex decisions. A concrete choice can be made using a prescribed calculation and based on seemingly abstract Decision-Making criteria.

A comment and short definition from this Author about AHP are that it is possible "…to plan, to set and to prioritize resource allocation using the multicriteria decision making approach of the AHP - Analytic Hierarchy Process".

According also to him, it is possible as well "…to discover how to structure complex multi-person, multi-criteria, multi-time period problems with uncertainty & risk in hierarchic form, set priorities for the elements in each level according to their impact on the criteria or objectives of the next higher level, to articulate your judgments through a series of pairwise comparisons, obtaining a precise numerical measurement of the priority of each element, & synthesize all the judgments within the hierarchy to reach a best decision. The AHP – Analytic Hierarchy Process is a simple, yet powerful decision-making tool for planning, structuring priorities, weighing alternatives, allocating resources, analyzing policy impacts & resolving conflicts".

A value is assigned to the criteria relevant to making the right choice, after which possible solutions are mathematically calculated and determined. The Analytic Hierarchy Process is, therefore, both a psychological and mathematical method.

Figure 3 shows a Diagram about this Technique.

Figure 3. AHP flow (Saaty, 1980)

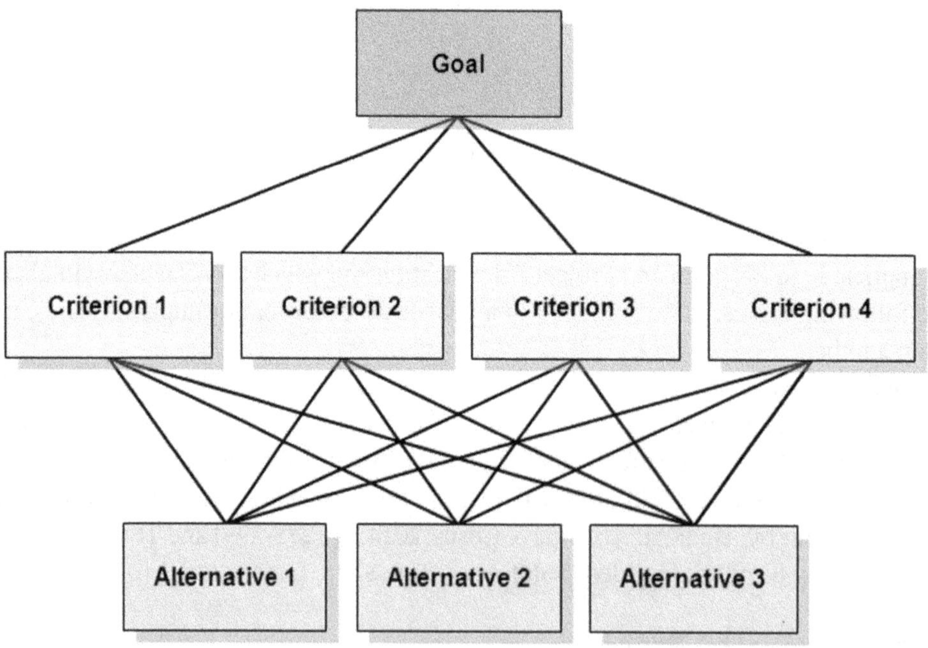

BWM: Best-Worst Method

The BWM – Best-Worst Method, by Rezaei (2016, pp. 126-130), is a Multi-Criteria Decision-Making Method that uses two Comparison Vectors in pairs to determine the Weights of Criteria.

First, the Best (e.g., most desirable, most important) and the Worst (e.g., least desirable, least important) criteria, are identified by the Decision-Maker, and after that, the Best Criteria are compared for choosing the Best Criterion Criteria of all.

This Author defines that "The BWM is an MCDM Method which can be used in several phases of solving an MCDM problem. More specifically it can be used to evaluate the alternatives with respect to the criteria (especially in the cases where objective metrics are not available to evaluate the alternatives). It can also be used to find the importance (weight) of the criteria which are used in finding a solution to satisfy the main goal(s) of the problem".

He concluded his definition with "The BWM has been used to solve many real-world MCDM problems in the areas such as Business and Economics, Health, IT, Engineering, Education and Agriculture. In principle, wherever the aim is to rank and select an alternative from among a set of alternatives, this method can be used. It can be used by one Decision-Maker or a group of Decision-Makers".

Figure 4 shows a Diagram which refers to this Technique.

Figure 4. BWM group decision-making model (adapted from Rezaei, 2016)

ÉLECTRE: ÉLimination Et Choix Traduisant la REalité (Elimination and Choice Translating Reality)

The *ÉLECTRE* Method was formally first proposed by Bernard Roy (1968), widely recognized as the father of the *ÉLECTRE* Method, in Europe in the mid-1960s. This Method also is a part of Multi-Criteria Decision-Making (MCDM) group. The focus of *ÉLECTRE* Method is to balance the alternatives and finds the one which "dominates" the others.

It was first applied in 1965 when Bernard Roy was working in a concrete, multiple criteria, real-world problem, of how firms could decide on new activities and had encountered problems using a weighted sum Technique.

The *ÉLECTRE* Method was to choose the best action(s) from a given set of actions, but it was soon applied to three main problems: choosing, ranking, and sorting.

There are two main parts to an *ÉLECTRE* application:

- 1st. the construction of one or several outranking relations which aims at comparing in a comprehensive way each pair of actions;
- 2nd. an exploitation procedure that elaborates on the recommendations obtained in the first phase.

Rmk.: The nature of the recommendation depends on the problem being addressed under the already mentioned three main problems: choosing, ranking or sorting.

The version of ÉLECTRE started in *ÉLECTRE* I and the evolutions have continued with *ÉLECTRE* II, *ÉLECTRE* III and *ÉLECTRE* IV to mention a few. These are used in the fields of Business, Development, Design, and small hydropower.

The flow of the *ÉLECTRE* Method is presented in Figure 5 and this figure is adapted from Bernard Roy (1968) paper about this theme.

Fuzzy Logic

The Fuzzy Logic is an approach that allows multiple possible values of a variable to be processed through a single variable. This tries to solve issues that have a broad scope and no data precision by applying a Heuristic Analysis that makes it possible to obtain a series of precise and assertive conclusions. The Fuzzy Logic is aimed at solving problems by making the best possible decision given the input and considering all available information.

According to Martino, Perfilieva & Sessa (2021), there is a practical model of Fuzzy Logic implementation name as Fuzzy Transform (F-transform) and the abstract of this work of them describes it as following:

Fuzzy Transform is a Technique applied to approximate a function of one or more variables applied by Researchers in various image and data analysis. In this work we present a summary of a Fuzzy Transform method proposed in recent years in different data mining disciplines, such as the detection of relationships between features and the extraction of association rules, time series analysis, data classification. After having given the definition of the concept of Fuzzy Transform, in one or more dimensions in which the constraint of sufficient data density with respect to, Fuzzy Partition is also explored, the data analysis approaches recently proposed in the literature based on the use of the Fuzzy Transform are analyzed. In particular, the strategies adopted in these approaches for managing the constraint of sufficient data density and the performance results obtained, compared with those measured by adopting other methods in the literature, are explored.

Figure 6 shows the Fuzzy Transform Processing Structure.

Figure 5. ÉLECTRE method flow (Adapted from Roy, 1968)

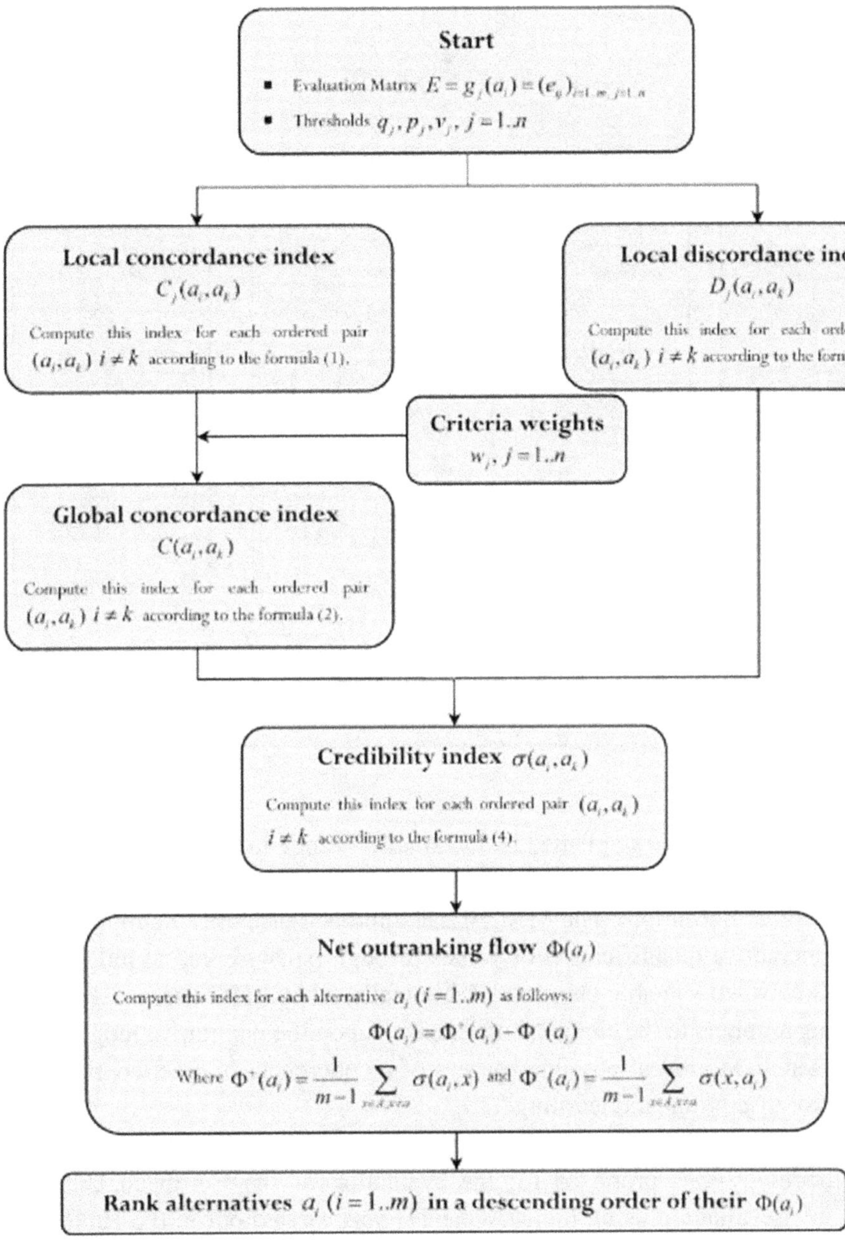

MACBETH: Measuring Attractiveness by a Categorical-Based Evaluation Technique

The MACBETH, by Bana e Costa & Vansnick (1994, pp. 489-500), is an interactive multi-criteria Decision-Support approach used to create a Quantitative Value (numerical, determined by real data) and Qualitative Measure (non-numeric, determined by subjective judgment) model.

Figure 6. Fuzzy f-transform processing structure (Martino, Perfilieva, & Sessa, 2021)

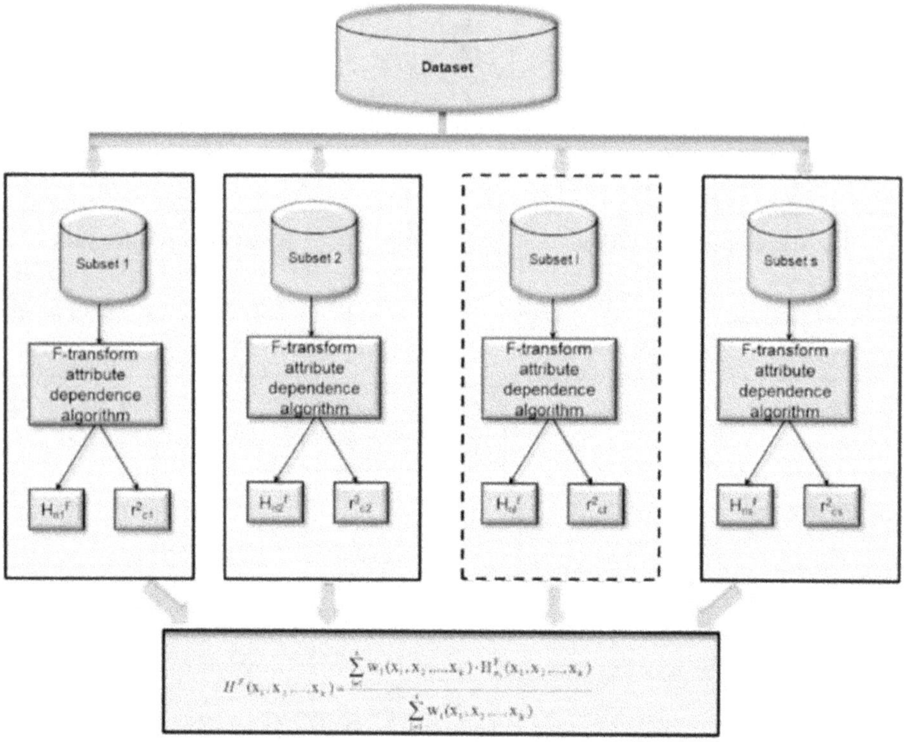

The Degree of Attractiveness is established by the smallest range in the Measure Scale (by Criteria Category) of numerical and non-numerical compilation.

Regarding both Authors definition "The MACBETH approach proposes a simple questioning procedure to drive the interactive quantification of values through pairwise verbal judgements of difference of attractiveness between valuable elements. Technically, MACBETH uses a chain of four linear programs for assigning numbers to the elements of set based upon the qualitative judgements expressed by a interviewed person and to reveal possible sources of incoherence. In practice, this information is to be used as a basis for discussion and learning".

As an example of MACHBETH approach implementation, in 1995 under the framework of MEANS[1] a multicriteria methodology was proposed for the evaluation of the European Union's Structural Programmes and a pilot evaluation using the MACBETH was carried out in the Hainaut province of Belgium. The Hainaut Program was a typical Structural Program that involved 1.5 billion of Euros of public spending over six years. It was made up of forty-five Measures that aimed at relaunching Socio-Economic development.

Figure 7 shows an Application Screen, named as M-MACBETH, which can be search in the link https://m-macbeth.com/.

Figure 7. MACBETH application screen (m-macbeth.com)

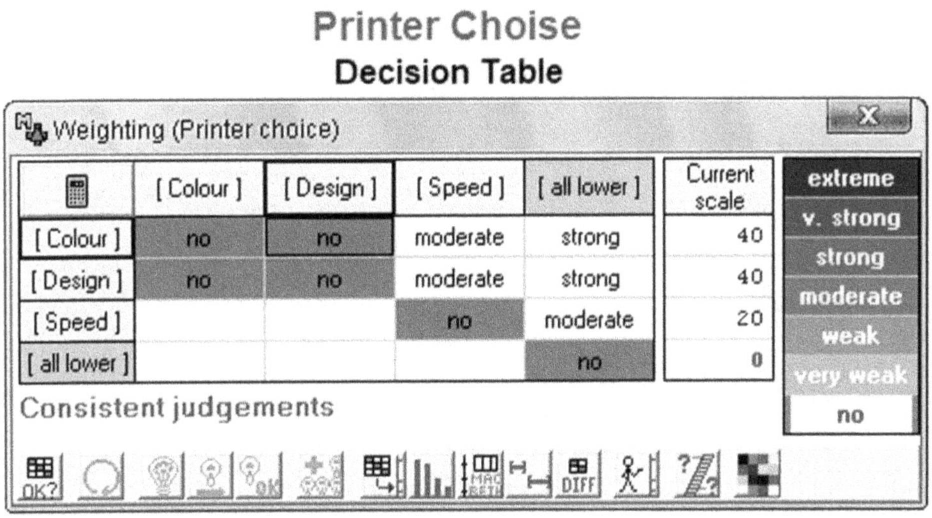

PROMETHEE: Preference Ranking Organization Method for Enrichment Evaluations

The starting point of the PROMETHEE Method, by Almeida, Almeida & Costa (2014, pp. 275-299), is an evaluation matrix of the alternatives with respect to a set of criteria. Then, a Preference Function is assigned to each of the criteria.

In these Authors description of PROMETHEE Method, they define that it starts when "…the Decision-Maker establishes the relative weights for the criteria, and the general criterion to establish his/her intensity of preference between the alternatives for each criterion. The Decision-Maker further establishes the parameters associated with each general criterion: the limit of preference (p) and the limit of indifference (q). The general criteria, the weights of the associated criteria and parameters, are items of information obtained directly from the Decision-Maker. The evaluation of each alternative for each criterion, within the context of the results to be achieve and the methodology used, must be obtained from the evaluation of these points of this structure".

The Preference Function of a criterion describes how the preference of the decision maker changes with the difference between the Performance Levels of the possible alternatives to this criterion.

Figure 8 shows a Software Screen about this Technique.

TOPSIS: Technique for Order of Preference by Similarity to Ideal Solution

This Method, proposed by Tan, Shen, Langston & Liu, Y. (2010, pp. 302-315) which is very similar to BWM – Best-Worst Method, refers to making choice of the best alternative from among a finite set of Decision Alternatives in terms of multiple criteria, usually conflicting. The TOPSIS selects the alternative closest to the ideal solution and the farthest from the negative alternative.

Figure 8. PROMETHEE software screen (visual-promethee.html)

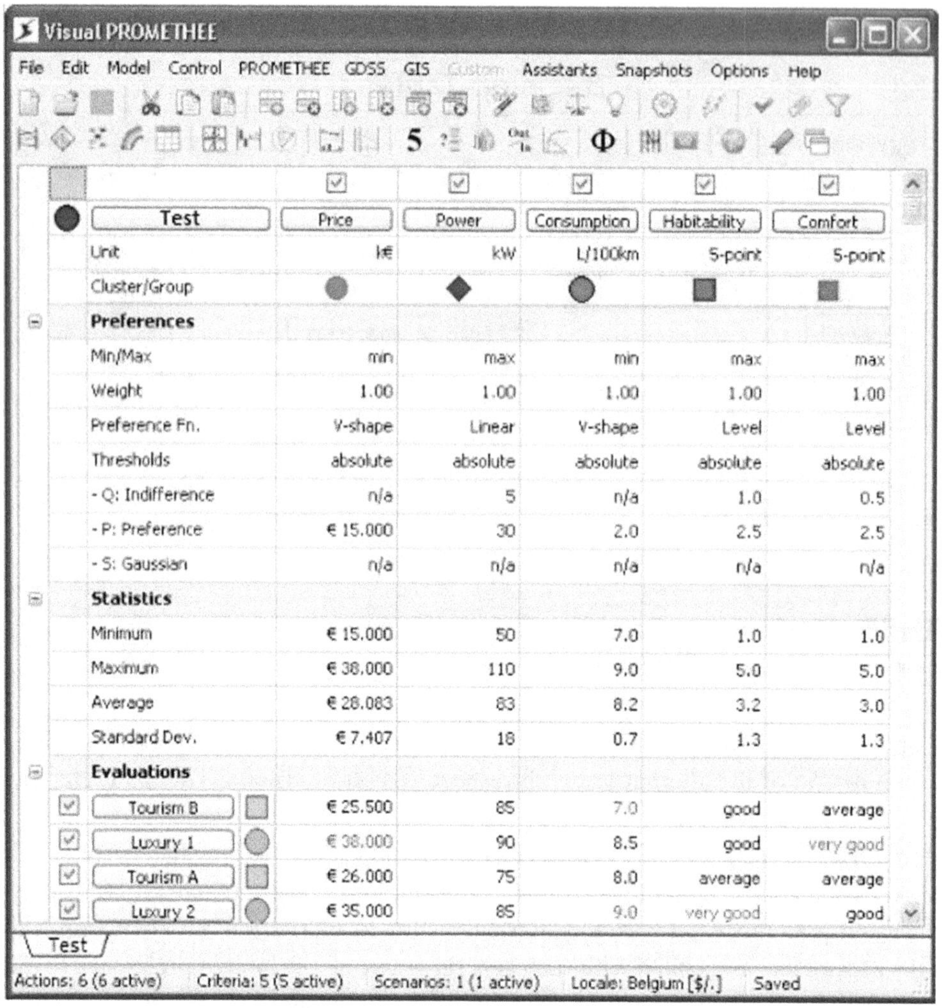

The Method is based on capturing information about attributes provided by the Decision Maker, such as, numeric data. Its purpose is to evaluate, prioritize and select inputs by assigning weights to subjective criteria.

Figure 9 shows a Flow Diagram according to this Technique built by a software named ArcGIS which can assist to handle the TOPSIS data.

The four above Authors explain that "The TOPSIS method is used to help contractors make decision on project selection and the linguistic terms are defined for representing the triangular numbers for ratings of alternatives and weights of criteria. The selection of appropriate projects for bidding is a multiple attribute group decision-making exercise. In a real decision process, there are many uncertainties and ambiguities, and time limitations mean that decision makers cannot always make precise judgments. The TOPSIS approach can be used to simulate the decision process in project selection, and the results provide contractors with valuable insight into the project selection problem".

Figure 9. TOPSIS ArcGIS flow (www.arcgis.com)

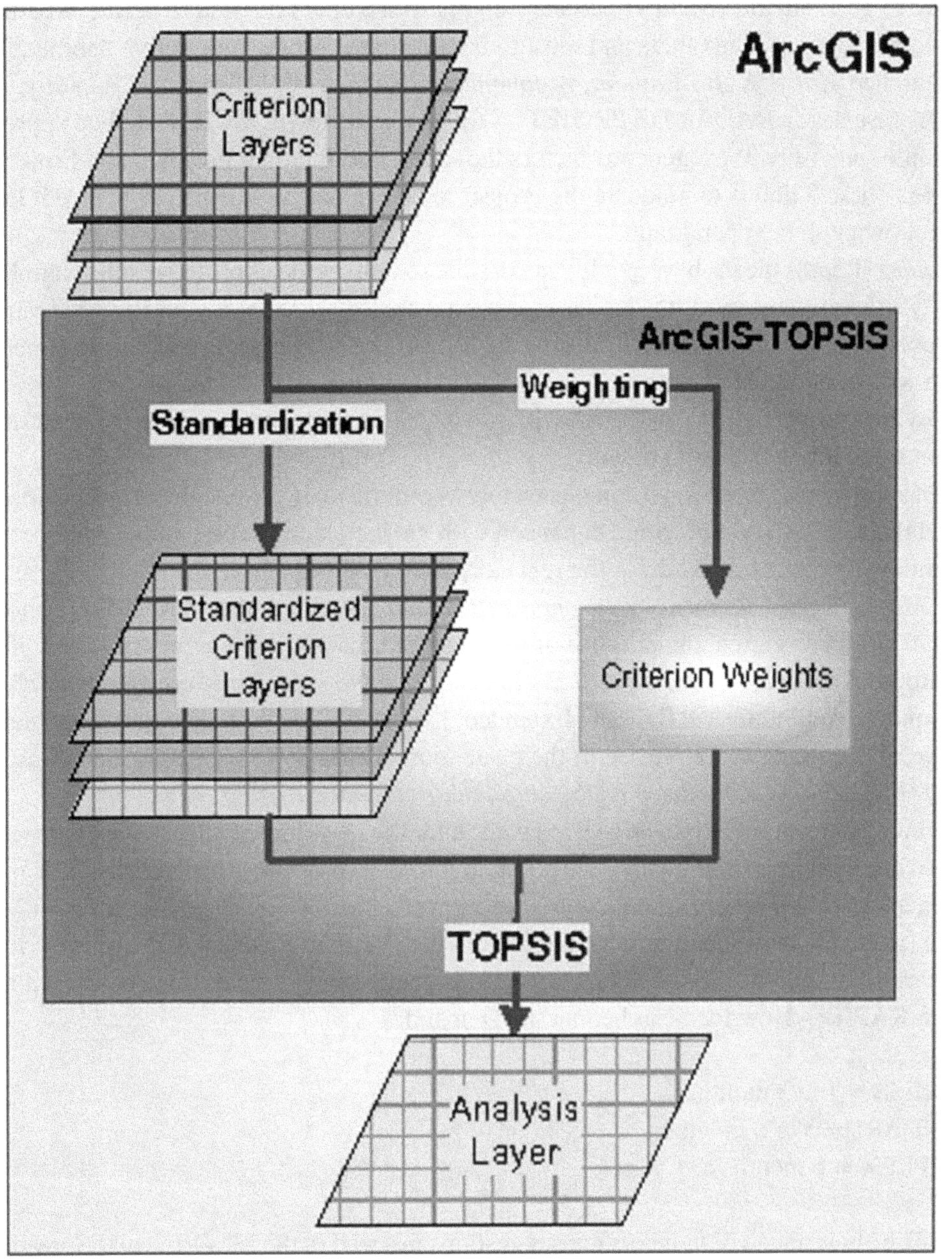

RAB²/E Matrix

As one can see, all those Techniques went very deeply in mathematics and statistics sciences and methods to drive the support to the Decision-Make Process, but they did not approach how have to be the treatment according to values (representing the criteria) which can be considered and balanced when the final decision will be made in order to prioritize a Project.

Thus, this is the crucial point – what means – to define which are the criteria to be applied – in each case – before to go to attribute values to create weights which could be used to define, whether or not a project is more important than others and must to be prioritized for be built before another.

The researched *Matriz RAB - Rapidez, Autonomia e Benefício* (RAB Matrix - Rapidity, Autonomy and Benefit) presented in RADAR DE PROJETOS (2015) is a different MCDM Method approach which considers some (precisely 3) exogeneous factors those can interfere in a Program and Project Portfolio Prioritization. These 3 points to graduate the Project to be evaluate in order to prioritize it later are described as following in next paragraph.

The *Rapidez* (Rapid) means how quickly is possible to deliver the expected results from Project, the *Autonomia* (Autonomy) means if it is necessary external contributions or if your Project Team can solve it themselves and the *Benefício* (Benefit) means the level of positive impacts that will be generated when the solution will be putted in place.

Hence, by measuring these three points with grades, is possible better define the need of prioritize and focus on some Projects than in others.

But, even approaching these 3 exogeneous factors as criteria to determine the Project Prioritization, it was realized that the RAB Matrix could enhanced with the inclusion of some more criteria, to establish a more useful and practical method, for the real Corporate environment.

For the *Matriz RAB – Rapidez, Autonomia e Benefício* (RAB Matrix – Rapidity, Autonomy and Benefit) in its original version, the purpose of this chapter is to propose a new version for it. This new version is proposal named as "*Matriz RAB²/E – Rapidez, Autonomia e Benefício / Estendida*" ("RAB²/E Matrix – Rapidity, Autonomy and Benefit / Extended"), in which, newer three points were included with the objective of becoming more precise in the evaluation. These new three points are: Cost, Risk and Availability (Financial) (*Custo, Risco e Disponibilidade (Financeira)*).

For the three points of the original RAB, as well as for the new three points of the proposed RAB²/E, are presented one direct question – with three possible answers – those have different Significance Values, representing a higher *status*, a medium *status*, and a lower *status*, which also have different Mathematical Weights (to enable their measurement and rank in the Portfolio Program and Project Priority List).

For the three points of the original RAB, the three direct questions, and its three possible answers, are:

Criterion RAPID: - How long can be met the Demand?

1. EXPRESS = 1 to 3 months;
2. STANDARD= 3 to 6 months;
3. COMPLEX = 6 months to 1 year.

Rmk.: - The above range of numbers are suggestions inserted in the MS®-Excel© Spreadsheet from Microsoft presented in Figure 10 (shown forward), which can be changed to fit new realities.

Criterion AUTONOMY: - What is the involvement of the Areas to meet the Demand?

1. MAXIMUM= Your Area can perform alone;
2. AVERAGE = Needs other Areas;
3. MINIMUM = Needs Higher Decision.

Criterion BENEFIT: - How far will the results go by meeting Demand?

1. EMBRACING= For all Organization.
2. RESTRICTED= Only for one Area;
3. PERSONAL = Only for own use.

For the new three points of the proposed RAB^2/E, the three direct questions, and its three possible answers, are:

Criterion COST: - What is the investment to meet the Demand?

1. SMALL = 100,000;
2. NORMAL= 500,000;
3. BIG = 1,000,000.

Rmk.: - The above range of numbers are suggestions inserted in the MS®-Excel© Spreadsheet from Microsoft presented in Figure 10 (shown forward), which can be changed to fit new realities, in the same way that, the Cost Unit must be defined.

- Choose the number closest the value that was informed.

Criterion RISK: - Is there any factor that impacts meeting the Demand?

1. NONE = Unidentified.
2. FORECASTED= During the Project.
3. IMMEDIATE = At the beginning of the Project development.

Criterion AVAILABILITY: - Are resources already available to meet the Demand?

1. ALL = No Exception.
2. MOST = More than 50% of the necessary.
3. MINORITY= Less than 50% of the necessary.

Note: - The "Minimum" and "Maximum" fields in the "Prioritization Level" (in the MS®-Excel© Spreadsheet) table are for establishing the Score Range for High, Medium, and Low prioritization.

- Also, in this same Spreadsheet, the data (graphics) and the procedure actions are shown in its tabs.

Of course, *exogeneous* factors can interfere in the initial grades – for more or less – before achieving the final grades to be considered for sorting the Project Portfolio list in an order that suggests what should be developed first.

For more details about the possible kinds of exogeneous factors those can interfere in a Program and Project Portfolio Prioritization, some articles of the same Author of this chapter can be researched, listed in References as Moraes (1985, 1989, 2011, 2015, 2017).

METHOD IMPLEMENTATION

In Figure 10, Figure 11 and Figure 12 are presented the "RAB^2-E Matrix= Portfolio Prioritization Spreadsheet {V.02h} Scope= .... – Scenario= .... .xlsx" ("Matriz RAB^2-E= Planilha de Priorização de Portfólio {V.02e} Escopo= .... – Cenário= .... .xlsx"), in MS®-Excel, what is a real contribution from the author. The two "...................." fields can be used to better define the context of the Spreadsheet (which can be copied to simulated more than one Scope and Scenario). This information is also included in the spreadsheet header.

The mentioned Spreadsheet (which has in its name the "/" character changed to "-" per Windows restriction) is available for download in the Google Drive link "https://drive.google.com/drive/folders/10XI_q6X7Kh7PZerhwuG4vuo102fPPLEJ?usp=sharing". If any support is needed, a contact can be done directly to the author.

This Spreadsheet has three Tabs – which will be described in the follow of this same Chapter – and has been used in several Organizations with different realities, aiming to collaborate, with the Decision-Making Process based on a strongly structured Priority List and related to the management of a Program and Project Portfolio.

The Spreadsheet is prepared to handle and treat up to 100 Projects. If the Corporation has more Project than this number, the 100 Projects most relevant should be prioritized by this tool and this list can be updated since some Projects are being closed or change its *status* to "no more relevant". The 100 Projects can be inserted in the Project List of the Tab #1 and can be visualized in the columns of the Graphics in the Tab #2 and the Tab#3.

As is explain – inside the Spreadsheet – "1. Best visualization at 60% of Zoom", "2. Only gray background fields can be updated" and "3. The light-yellow background fields can be updated by Administrator". This last point is only applied to Tab #1 since is in this Tab that we have the data insertion and parameters to calculate these data. So, if the Administrator has the Spreadsheet Open/Access Password, it is possible to change the Mathematical Weight (and even its initial and proposed names) and evaluate different situations.

Portfolio Prioritization Spreadsheet Tab #1

The Figure 10 shows the Tab #1, and in this Tab, the columns have comments about the column data to be inserted in these. An orange colour square, with the number 1 inside the square in the column named as "Risk", highlights this information as an example. For seeing these comments, it is only needed to pass the mouse over the column name.

Because of the screen visualization restriction, only the initials Projects lines (from the "Project #001" to the "Project #005"), from the total of 100 Projects (see "TOTAL of PROJECTS" field) listed in this simulation, can be seen in Figure 10.

In the line for each Project, there is a Listbox (in each column) where is possible to find the three Options referred to the Grades 1, 3, and 5 for each one of the six Criteria, which are, Rapidity, Autonomy, Benefit, Cost, Risk and Availability (Financial).

This point, mention in the last paragraph, can be seen in the orange colour oval circle, as an example, in the first line (related to the "Project #001") in the column "Rapid", where the three Options ("EXPRESS= 1 to 3 months", "STANDARD= 3 to 6 months" and "COMPLEX= 6 months to 1 year"), were listed.

It is necessary to fill all these six fields, related to the six Criteria, to get the Final Graduation shown in the column named as "GRADUATION [RAB] [RAB^2-Extended]" and highlighted with an orange colour square with the number 2 inside the square.

About the orange colour square with the number 3 inside – which, in reality, there are three of these ones (noted as "a", "b", and "c" outside the square) – it means the possibility of the User to define what is the acceptable quantity of Total Percentage of High Priority (field with this context and noted as "3c" outside in an orange square with number 3 inside) found according to its capability to manage technically.

The square bordered by a line and with a flag inside, below the field named as "HIGH Acceptable %", is the icon which will show the status found, for the analysis based on the User definition, about the percentage of projects it is possible to be handled by the Project Team. When this field "HIGH Acceptable %" is blank or equal to 0 (zero), the icon flag in the square bordered by a line below this field is in yellow colour.

If the acceptable quantity of Total Percentage of High Priority, inserted in the field with the orange colour square noted as "3a" outside, is greater than the quantity of Total Percentage of High Priority calculated in the column noted as "3b" outside in another square in orange colour (which, as already mentioned, is also presented in the field Total Percentage of High Priority with this context and noted as "3c" outside) the icon flag will turn to green colour.

It means that the acceptable quantity of Total Percentage of High Priority, defined and possible to be handled, is greater than the field Total Percentage of High Priority found. Otherwise, the icon flag will turn to red colour, what means that, the quantity of Total Percentage of High Priority found is not acceptable under its capability to manage.

In this sample, if the acceptable quantity of Total Percentage of High Priority inserted in the field with the orange colour square noted as "3a" outside was 12, the flag will turn to green colour, since 12 is greater than 11 presented in the field Total Percentage of High Priority noted as "3c" outside.

Still analysing this sample, if the acceptable quantity of Total Percentage of High Priority inserted in the field with the orange colour square noted as "3a" outside was 11 or less, the icon flag will turn to red colour, since 11 is minor than 12 inserted in the field noted as "3a" outside.

A way to workaround, when a red flag icon happens for trying to reduce the "HIGH Acceptable %", can be the following below alternatives:

- To Mitigate the Risk Criterion and to perform the revisions, of the others five criteria applied, in order to input low values than the already applied;
- To Increase the resources in the Project Team and in the Executor Area, such as, Human Technicians, Financial Budget, Technological Equipment and others;
- To Eliminate, at this moment, some Projects with no actual condition to begin without extra and additional efforts.

Rmk.: These Alternatives can also be checked in the Tab #1 since there is a comment in "HIGH Acceptable %" field that can be open and visualized (just pass over the field name with the mouse).

Continuing the analyse of the Tab #1, the orange colour square with the number 4 inside the square, highlights the column named as "PRIORITIZATION 1 [RAB^2-Extended]". This is an automatic calculation of the Percentage of Prioritization according to the 3 (three) Options choose by the six Criteria. There is a Percentage Total in a field in the bottom of this Tab #1 (not visualized in the Picture 9) and each percentage, for each line of Projects, is a part of the total of 100%.

In fact, since this sample in this Tab #1 is with its all 100 lines of Projects filled, its normal to have a range of 0%, 1% and 2%, with could be interpreted that all 100 of Projects are equal (in other words, that all have the same Level of Prioritization). It occurs because in this "PRIORITIZATION 1 [RAB^2-Extended]" field is not showing the percentage value with decimal places.

But in the Tab #2, which will be explained in the next Topic with the name of "Portfolio Prioritization Spreadsheet Tab #2" and where is expressed graphically this "PRIORITIZATION 1 [RAB^2-Extended]" field, the decimal places are considered in order to expose the differences among all Projects.

If this criterion was not applied, in this sample case where there are all the 100 Projects filled, all graphic columns of the Tab #2 would be 0%, 1% and 2%, what would be not showing any significant discrepancies. Thus, a precise analysis about the Prioritization Levels, would be impossible to be performed.

As can be seen, in the tab #2, the decimal places interfere in the graphic exposition and insert weights to the values and then, in such way, is possible to distinct real differences among all values and support better the Decision-Making Process.

Concluding the analyse of the Tab #1, the orange colour square with the number 5 inside the square, highlights the column named as "PRIORITIZATION 2 [USER]". This is an option for the User defines and inserts the own vision about the Project Prioritization additional to the automatic definition of the Levels of Prioritization the spreadsheet calculates based in the column named as "PRIORITIZATION 1 [RAB^2-Extended]" already mentioned in prior paragraphs. There is no automatic calculation of the Percentage of Prioritization in these columns.

In this sample, were used a Scale of 10, from 10 to 100, to sort the Levels of Prioritization. Also, it can be seen in this same sample, that some Projects could be without this graduation. It is also a choice for the Users. An example, when it could happen, is when the User prefer not sort Projects those are not in real execution and that are still waiting some decision to be started, such as, missing budget release, people allocation, internal authorization from the BU - Business Unit/Area and another issues.

Another possibility to use this "PRIORITIZATION 2 [USER]" column is just to insert a sequential number, in ascending order, in the List of Projects from 1 (one) to "n" (adding 1 [one] to each one of Projects of the list), in order to define the Levels of Prioritization. In this suggestion, there will be not different Projects with the same number, and so, the Levels of Prioritization would be more precise.

As a point to emphasize, in this another suggestion of how to use this same "PRIORITIZATION 2 [USER]" column, the User could also prefer not to sort all Projects and only will apply the numbers to the Projects those are effectively already driven to enter under real execution and not to those ones that are still in the Planning Phase. That is the reason why was defined "n", as the last number in the last paragraph, since this could be between 1 as the initial and 100 as the final.

In the Tab #3, which will be explained in the next Topic with the name of "Portfolio Prioritization Spreadsheet Tab #3", will be expressed graphically this "PRIORITIZATION 2 [USER]" field.

Portfolio Prioritization Spreadsheet Tab #2

The Figure 11 shows a view of the Tab #2, and this Tab is the statistic result, from the column named as "PRIORITIZATION 1 [RAB^2-Extended]", shown in graphic mode. This column is highlighted with orange colour square with the number 4 inside in the Figure 10.

Because of the screen visualization restriction, it is not shown the last lines (in the bottom of this screen) from all graphic data.

The “Scope” field and the “Scenario” field of the header of this Tab #2 are automatic filled by the same field data inserted in the Tab #1. But the “Rmk” field is not automatic filled by the same field data inserted in the Tab #1, and thus, can be inserted to express some special occurrence in this statistic and graphic tab.

The content of this Tab #2 is better described in prior Topic named as “Portfolio Prioritization Spreadsheet Tab #1”.

Portfolio Prioritization Spreadsheet Tab #3

The Figure 12 shows a view of the Tab #3, and this Tab is the statistic result, from the column named as “PRIORITIZATION 2 [USER]”, shown in graphic mode. This column is highlighted with orange colour square with the number 5 inside in the Figure 10.

Because of the screen visualization restriction, it is not shown the last lines (in the bottom of this screen) from all graphic data.

The “Scope” field and the “Scenario” field of the header of this Tab #2 are automatic filled by the same field data inserted in the Tab #1. But the “Rmk” field is not automatic filled by the same field data inserted in the Tab #1, and thus, can be inserted to express some special occurrence in this statistic and graphic tab.

The content of this Tab #3 is better described in prior Topic named as “Portfolio Prioritization Spreadsheet Tab #1”.

Figure 10. RAB²/E matrix MS®-Excel© spreadsheet (Tab #1)

Figure 11. RAB²/E matrix MS®-Excel© spreadsheet (Tab #2)

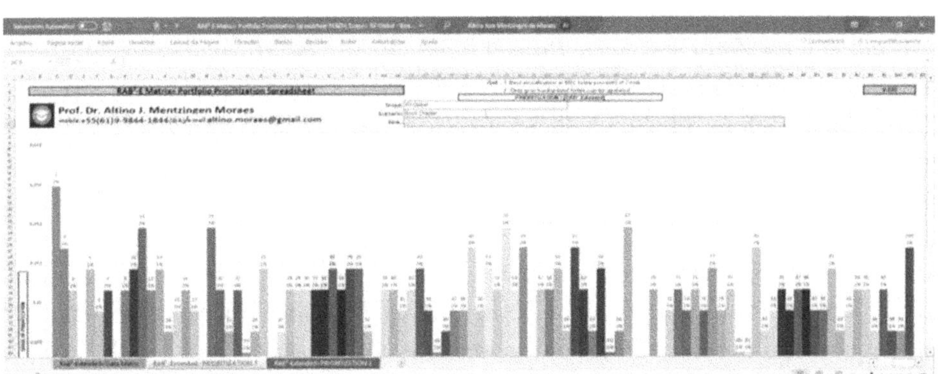

Figure 12. RAB²/E matrix MS®-Excel© spreadsheet (Tab #3)

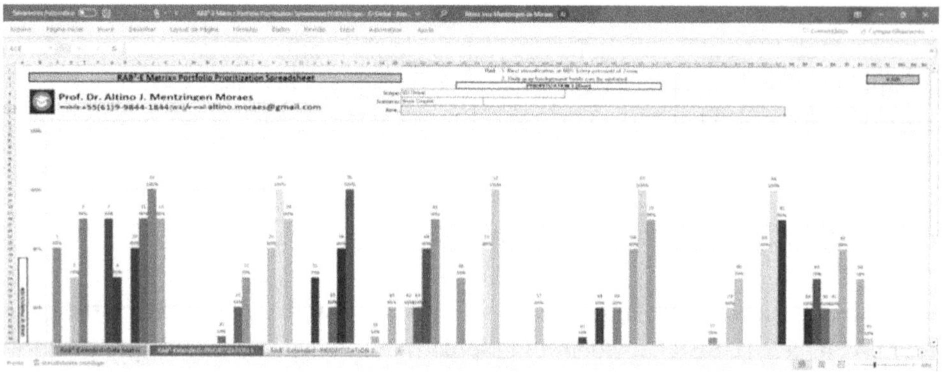

Perhaps, the method that could be consider of little bit similar with the *Matriz* RAB²/E (RAB²/E Matrix), proposed in this Chapter, would be the "Solution Selection Matrix" of Six Sigma (2019) even with the peculiar differences between both and the structured implementation presented in this Chapter for the *Matriz* RAB²/E (RAB²/E Matrix), which defines questions – for each one of six Points – and the respective options of three answers in order to attribute criteria (with Significant Values) and enable to build a Sort List of Programs and Projects development priority.

Indeed, by the supervised manner with that this work was built (long and large research/survey and assembled according to the feedback of the application of its proposition in the field by many year), it is possible to verify the usefulness of the proposal presented.

Also, can be concluded that its results can be considered as effective management and planning tool in corporate real world and, in additional, how practical this proposal is for the reality of Organization in its day-to-day activities.

METHOD APPLICATION

The most recognized Methodologies to manage Programs and Projects are PMBoK© – A Guide to Project Management Body of Knowledge, created by PMI – Project Management Institute (PMI, 2022), PRINCE2® – Project In a Controlled Environment, created by OGC – Office of Government Commerce (OGC, 2018), and ZOPP – *Ziel-Orientierte Projekt Planung* (Target-Oriented Project Planning), created by GTZ – *Gesellschaft für Technische Zusammenarbeit* (Society for Technical Cooperation) (GTZ, 2006).

As per others Methodology structures, these are also made and built by a Work Process Flow using Tools for to be performed. One common Process to all these 3 Methodologies is the Initial Planning Process. There are many Tools, categorized as Multi-Criteria Decision-Making (MCDM), to support this phase tasks.

The RAB²/E Matrix, as other Multi-Criteria Decision-Making (MCDM) Tools, also was created to support the Programs and Projects Methodologies in its Initial Planning Process in the moment of defining the order and sequence of the execution and development of the projects listed in the Project Portfolio.

Its more special characteristic is not to be only a Multi-Criteria Decision-Making (MCDM) Tool which focus only on mathematics science (statistics rules) and not also only on social science (*exogenous* criteria), but in both aspects, which enhance the results and its more precision during the assistance of the Decision-Making Process of how to handle with a Program and Project Portfolio Prioritization questions.

Per has a vision of deal with social science (exogenous criteria) – such as Political Factors, Human Behaviours, External Influences, and etc. – much more than other mathematical sciences – such as Statistics Rules, Mathematics Weight, Graphical Analysis, and etc. – the RAB^2/E Matrix fits better to assist the Corporate Strategic Planning to do its job of organising the budget and the schedules to correspond to the Investor's expectations.

CONCLUSION

With the objective of testing and checking the real usability of this Method, its artefacts (the MS®-Excel© Spreadsheet from Microsoft and the Method RAB^2/E Matrix Manual of Use) were distributed to some interested Users, covering these eight SMEs – Small and Medium Enterprises in Financial Business Area (1), Industrial Business Area (2) and Service Business Area (5).

In this assessment was applied another view of how to rise the evaluation of the acceptation of a new tool, or any new procedures, instead of the common and usual Likert Table created by the sociologist Rensis Likert (Likert, 1932) with five Levels of Grade, what do they mean 1= Lower Value; 2= Lower Intermediate Value; 3= Intermediate Value; 4= Higher Intermediate Value; 5= Higher Value).

This new approach was explained in the Doctorate Thesis of this chapter´s author (Moraes, 2011, p. 180-189) and can be referenced as AJMM Table. It directs the analysis just to three Levels of Grade: 1$^{st.}$= Ok, 2$^{nd.}$= Ok with Restriction or 3$^{rd.}$= Not Ok. For this assessment purposes, these three Levels of Grade were defines as: 1$^{st.}$= Applicable, 2$^{nd.}$= Applicable with Restrictions or 3$^{rd.}$= Not Applicable.

Analysing the evaluations (Figure 13), it was analysed that two evaluations that pointed the Method as classified in the note of "2$^{nd.}$= Applicable with Restrictions" highlighted that these restrictions were in the inability of these own two SMEs to validate the information regarding to the Criterion of AVAILABILITY (one SME of the Industry Business Area), as well as, to the Criterion of AUTONOMY (one SME of the Service Business Area).

In reality, this issue is an internal problem of the Organization that needs to raise the level of political power and hierarchical performance of its PMO – Project Management Office, changing this classification level from Weak Relationship Matrix to Strong/Projectized Relationship Matrix (Figure 14) as recommended by the PMI (2006).

This analysis also demonstrated how much the inclusion of this new Criterion of AVAILABILITY, in the extended version of the previous Matrix which now has the new and current name of RAB^2/E Matrix, helped to present this problem, and direct its solution.

With this evaluation, which covered these three Business Areas, it was possible to confirm that the Method can be actually useful for the purpose it proposes, that is, to prioritize the Projects of a Portfolio in such a way that the initiatives can have more assertiveness and produce more consistent results.

Figure 13. Statistic results

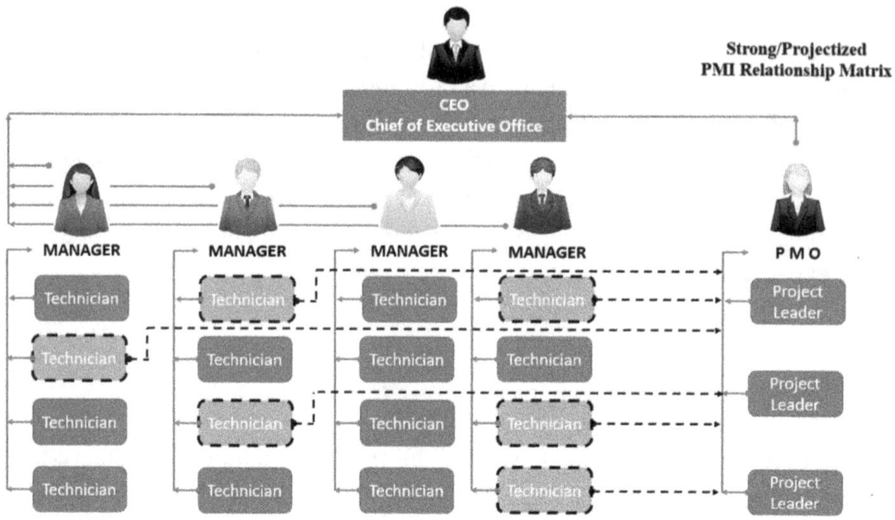

Rmk.: The Technicians, in the Dashed Border Box, are allocated to a Project conducted by PMO.

Figure 14. PMI© model

Method RAB^2/E Matrix Usability Survey

			1st. Applicable	2nd. Applicable with Restrictions	3rd. Not Applicable
Financial Business Area	=	1	1	0	0
Industry Business Area	=	2	1	1	0
Service Business Area	=	5	4	1	0
TOTAL=	=	8	6	2	0

FUTURE WORKS

Among suggestions for future works, one of these could be the study of new criteria to implement more the current sixPoints of "Matriz RAB²/E – *Rapidez, Autonomia e Benefício / Estendida*" ("RAB²/E Matrix – Rapidity, Autonomy and Benefit / Extended"), what means, the previous threePoints: Rapidity, Autonomy and Benefit (*Rapidez, Autonomia e Benefício*) – from the original Matriz RAB (RAB Matrix) – and the new three points: Cost, Risk and Availability (Financial) (*Custo, Risco e Disponibidade [Financeira]*) – from the new proposal of Matriz RAB²/E (RAB²/E Matrix).

These new candidate criteria can be perceived during more utilization of the Matriz RAB²/E (RAB²/E Matrix), in the next PMO – Project Management Office implementations. However, even with the possibility of studying the inclusion of some more criteria to be added to the current proposal of RAB²/E, this should not be too complex in order to maintain the original idea of RAB, which is to be direct and simple, although its original three Points are very subjective, what is resolved, by the inclusion of the new three points proposed by RAB^2/E.

REFERENCES

Almeida, J. A., Almeida, A. T., & Costa, A. P. C. S. (2014). Portfolio selection of information systems projects using PROMETHEE V with c-optimal concept. *Pesquisa Operacional, 34*(02), 275–299. doi:10.1590/0101-7438.2014.034.02.0275

Bana e Costa, C. A., & Vansnick, J. C. (1994). MACBETH - An interactive path towards the construction of cardinal value functions. *International Transactions in Operational Research, 1*(4), 489–500. doi:10.1016/0969-6016(94)90010-8

Böhle, F., Heidling, E., & Schoper, Y. (2016). A new orientation to deal with uncertainty in projects. *International Journal of Project Management, 34*(07), 1384–1392. doi:10.1016/j.ijproman.2015.11.002

Carvalho, M. M., & Rabechini, R. Jr. (2006). *Construindo competências para gerenciar projetos: teoria e casos [Building competeences to manage projects: theory and cases].* Atlas.

Costantino, F., Di Gravio, G., & Nonino, F. (2015). Project selection in project portfolio management: An artificial neural network model based on critical success factors. *International Journal of Project Management, 33*(08), 1744–1754. doi:10.1016/j.ijproman.2015.07.003

Drucker, P. F. (1963). Managing for business effectiveness. *Harvard Business Review, 41*(3).

Dye, L. D., & Pennypacker, J. S. (1999). *Project portfolio management: selecting and prioritizing projects for competitive advantage*. Center for Business Practices.

Ghapanchi, A. H., Tavana, M., Khakbaz, M. H., & Low, G. (2012). A methodology for selecting portfolios of projects with interactions and under uncertainty. *International Journal of Project Management, 30*(07), 791–803. doi:10.1016/j.ijproman.2012.01.012

GTZ – Gesellschaft für Technische Zusammenarbeit. (2006). *ZOPP – Ziel-Orientierte Projekt Planung*. German Government. Available in: https://pmkb.com.br/uploads/2013/08/cartilha-zopp-portugues.pdf

Likert, R. (1932). A Technique for the Measurement of Attitudes. *Archives de Psychologie, 140*, 1–55.

Martino, F., Perfilieva, I., & Sessa, S. (2021). *A Summary of F-Transform Techniques in Data Analysis*. Available in: https://www.researchgate.net/publication/353461547

Moraes, A. J. M. (1985). *Alocação de Recursos em Projetos de Processamento de Dados - Fatores Determinantes* [Resource Allocation in Data Processing Projects - Determinant Factors]. MMFV/1a. Versão. VII Congresso Regional e IV Feira Nacional da SUCESU / BR - Sociedade dos Usuários de Computadores e Equipamentos Subsidiários, Sao Paulo/State of Sao Paulo/Brazil.

Moraes, A. J. M. (1989). *Alocação de Recursos em Projetos de Processamento de Dados - Fatores Determinantes* [Resource Allocation in Data Processing Projects - Determinant Factors]. MMFV/2a. Versão). XXII Congresso Nacional e IX Feira Internacional da SUCESU / BR - Sociedade dos Usuários de Computadores e Equipamentos Subsidiários., Sao Paulo/State of Sao Paulo/Brazil.

Moraes, A. J. M. (2011). *Proposta do M2A3-GovTI – Modelo de Maturidade para Análise do Alinhamento das Atividades relacionadas à Governança da TI em conformidade com as expectativas de resultado planejadas pela Organização* [2M3A-GovIT Proposal – Maturity Model for Analysis of the Alignment of Activities related to IT Governance in accordance with the expectations of results planned by the Organization]. Production Engineering Doctorate Thesis. PPGEP - Programa de Pós-Graduação *Stricto-Sensu* em Engenharia de Produção. Universidade Paulista (UNIP). 406 p. São Paulo; Brazil.

Moraes, A. J. M. (2015). *Worksheet of Exogenous Variables that Impact the Success of Validation Stage of Product Delivery of a Project.* 6th International Multi-Conference on Complexity, Informatics and Cybernetics: IMCIC 2015. Available in https://www.iiisci.org/Journal/SCI/Abstract.asp?var=&id=ZA646OI15

Moraes, A. J. M. (2017). *Interpretation of the results of a Case Study about Impacts and Influences of Exogenous Variables in the planning of Chronogram and Budget in Software Projects.* 21st World Multi-Conference on Systemics, Cybernetics and Informatics: WMSCI 2017. Available in https://www.iiisci.org/Journal/SCI/Abstract.asp?var=&id=SA820QW17

OGC – Office of Government Commerce. (2018). *PRINCE2® – Project In a Controlled Environment.* Available in: https://www.leansixsigma.com.br/acervo/26181926.pdf

PMI. (2006). *The Standard for Portfolio Management.* Project Management Institute.

PMI. (2022). *PMBoK© – A Guide to Project Management Body of Knowledge* (7th ed.). PMI – Project Management Institute.

RADAR DE PROJETOS. (2015). *Matriz RAB - Rapidez, Autonomia e Benefício* [RAB Matrix - Rapidity, Autonomy and Benefit]. Available in: http://www.radardeprojetos.com.br/2015/04/matriz-de-priorizacao-rab-rapidez.html

Reyck, B., Grushka-Cockayne, Y., Lockett, M., Calderini, S. R., Moura, M., & Sloper, A. (2005). The impact of project portfolio management on information technology projects. *International Journal of Project Management, 23*(7), 524–537. doi:10.1016/j.ijproman.2005.02.003

Rezaei, J. (2016). Best-worst multi-criteria decision-making method: Some properties and a linear model. *Omega, 64*, 126–130. doi:10.1016/j.omega.2015.12.001

Roy, B. (1968). Classement et choix en présence de points de vue multiples (la méthode ÉLECTRE). *La Revue d'Informatique et de Recherche Opérationelle*, (8), 57–75.

Saaty, T. L. (1980). *The Analytic Hierarchy Process: Planning, Priority Setting, Resource Allocation.* McGraw-Hill.

Sigma, S. (2019). *Solution Selection Matrix.* Available in: https://goleansixsigma.com/solution-selection-matrix/

Taherdoost, H., & Madanchian, M. (2023). *Multi-Criteria Decision Making (MCDM) Methods and Concepts*. Available in: https://www.mdpi.com/2673-8392/3/1/6#

Tan, Y. T., Shen, L. Y., Langston, C., & Liu, Y. (2010). Construction project selection using fuzzy TOPSIS approach. *Journal of Modelling in Management*, *5*(3), 302–315. doi:10.1108/17465661011092669

ADDITIONAL READING

Hasan, G., Ashraf, Z., & Khan, M. F. (2021). *Multi-choice best-worst multi-criteria decision-making method and its applications*. Available in: https://onlinelibrary.wiley.com/doi/10.1002/int.22663

Novák, V., Perfilieva, I., & Močkoř, J. (1999). *Mathematical principles of fuzzy logic*. Kluwer Academic. doi:10.1007/978-1-4615-5217-8

PROMETHEE & GAIA. (2023). *Multicriteria decision aid methods*. available in: http://en.promethee-gaia.net/promethee.html

Saracoglu, B. O. (2015). An Experimental Research Study on the Solution of a Private Small Hydropower Plant Investments Selection Problem by ELECTRE III/IV, Shannon's Entropy, and Saaty's Subjective Criteria Weighting. *Advances in Decision Sciences*, *2015*, 1–20. doi:10.1155/2015/548460

Sulaimon, A., Kupolati, E. O., & Oyenuga, O. G. (2023). *Measuring attractiveness by a categorical based evaluation technique (Macbeth) for churn and retention of decision of subscribers in the Nigeria Telecommunication Industry*. Available in: https://www.researchgate.net/publication/373238665_Measuring_attractiveness_by_a_categorical_based_evaluation_technique_macbeth_for_churn_and_retention_of_decision_of_subscribers_in_the_Nigeria_telecommunication_industry

Vincke, P. (1992). *Multicriteria Decision-Aid*. Wiley.

Yadav, V., Karmakar, S., Kalbar, P., & Dikshit, A. K. (2021). *PyTOPS: A Python based tool for TOPSIS*. Available in: https://ui.adsabs.harvard.edu/abs/2019SoftX...9.217Y/abstract

KEY TERMS AND DEFINITIONS

Case: A way to validate an Idea or Project testing its effectiveness, in a real world Organizational environment implementation, according to the obtaining results found.

Exogeneous: External factors, from outside limits of a System or of a Process, which can interfere in its expected results.

Management: Holistic view of all the work to be carried out, considering positive and negative impact factors on whether or not it is carried out, aiming to make the allocated Return on Investment more productive and profitable.

Methodology: Set of rules organized, sequentially by Processes, for building a Product or obtaining a Result.

Planning: Sequential organization of Work Stages, with the prediction of allocation of Human and Financial Resources, in order to achieve a Goal.

Portfolio: CATALOG of Services or Products, offered by the Organization or Area, which can meet the demands of Clients or Users.

Prioritization: Organization of actions in descending order, based on the calculated Importance of Delivery index within established criteria, to guide the focus of initiatives.

Programme: GROUP of Projects which has the same target and those will be development together to achieve the same objective.

Project: Sequencing of Activities and Tasks in the form of a Schedule, with the definition of Technicians and the Costs involved, with the aim of achieving a goal.

Risk: Evaluation of the possibilities of occurrence of Situations or Facts, which generate impact in the execution of a planning, with the definition of applicable Workaround Solutions.

Strategy: Coordinated actions for execution in the Medium Term, which aim to achieve the result targets planned by the organization.

ENDNOTE

1 MEANS is a programme of the European Commission. It aims at improving Methods for Evaluating Actions of Structural Nature.

Chapter 5
Attaining CMMI Level 3 With Agile Development in Small-Medium Firms

Pitiphat Joembunthanaphong
https://orcid.org/0009-0001-6992-5971
Faculty of Information Technology and Digital Innovation, North Bangkok University, Thailand

ABSTRACT

This research chapter outlines an improvement process for software development and requirements management in small to medium-sized software companies with teams up to 25 members. It integrates elements from the Waterfall Model and Agile to address challenges in developing software for home loan services in Thai commercial banks. The study aims to achieve Capability Level 3 in the CMMI model, analyzing projects in the Thai software industry. Specific practices SP1.1 – SP1.5 and generic goals GP1.1 – GP3.2 of the requirements management process group are considered, referencing IEEE 12207-2008 and IEEE 1074-2006 standards. The outcomes include developed processes, guidelines, and tested tools. SCAMPI assessment by three experts shows improved benefits realization (avg. score: 4.373), work performance (avg. improvement: 34.34%), and process capability (avg. score: 88.22%), affirming Capability Level 3.

INTRODUCTION

This research is an extension of the work originally presented at the 2022 26th International Computer Science and Engineering Conference (Joembunthanaphong & Sriharee, 2022). The focus is on the challenges encountered by small and medium-sized software development companies with teams of up to 25 members in effectively managing software requirements (Ardana & Suharjito, 2017). Specifically, it addresses the complexities encountered in developing software, such as home loan services for commercial banks in Thailand. The primary drivers for requirements changes are legal regulations and policy adjustments regarding the criteria for approving bank home loans, which can arise before and during the software development process (Chuphet et al., 2020). These changes pose various impacts and risks,

DOI: 10.4018/979-8-3693-0458-7.ch005

including the possibility of low-quality software products, delayed deliveries, and potential project failure (Dennis et al., 2009). To overcome these challenges and enhance customer confidence in the software product's quality, small and medium-sized software companies must establish standardized requirements management processes to systematically control requirements changes. The paper also discusses findings from the Software Industry Benchmark Study (2019), revealing that approximately 50% of companies face significant issues and obstacles related to requirements management.

In Thailand, the current standard related to requirements management processes for small and medium-sized organizations is ISO/IEC 29110. This standard focuses on designing the work process based on the software development lifecycle (International Organization for Standardization, 2011) with an emphasis on addressing overall project management issues. However, it may not fully cover specific challenges related to requirements changes (Chaiyan et al., 2017). Although the CMMI 2.0 model, which follows the SEMAT (Software Engineering Method and Theory) model, offers a more flexible approach to accommodate requirements changes, it is more suitable for larger software companies, particularly at Capability Level 3, which requires teams of 30 or more members (SEI, 2018). Therefore, small-sized software companies may find it challenging to reach CL3 with this requirements. Nevertheless, planning for the assessment and process improvement should be done in advance to prepare for such a transition in the future when the company expands and meets the criteria, making it easier to achieve CL3. As a result, the author proposed improvements to the software development and requirements management processes by analyzing and developing from the ISO/IEC 29110, IEEE 1074, and IEEE 12207 standards. The study focused on the challenges of requirements changes in home loan services software for commercial banks. The author presented:

1. A method for defining the software development and requirements management processes.
2. A blended approach to the work process, incorporating elements of the Waterfall model and Agile (Scrum) to accommodate requirements changes.
3. Development of generic and specific best practice tools for the process group to achieve Capability Level 3 in the CMMI 2.0 model.

Section 2 provides essential context, beginning with the study's motivation and an exploration of challenges faced by Small-Medium companies in software development. It offers a concise literature review and introduces the CMMI model and SCAMPI method. Section 3 outlines the research methodology, including sample group definition, participant outreach, company selection, and the description of the Improvement Process. It also highlights the development of a supportive requirements management tool and the evaluation process using SCAMPI. Section 4 presents research results, incorporating empirical data from sample companies and expert assessments using SCAMPI. Finally, Section 5 summarizes key findings, discusses their implications, suggests future research directions, and underscores contributions to the field.

FRAMEWORK AND BACKGROUND

Motivation

This research was driven by the pressing challenges encountered by small and medium-sized software development teams in Thailand as they undertook the development of home loan services software for commercial banks. The central focus of this study was to enhance the management of software requirements, particularly in the context of evolving and dynamic requirements. The primary motivation behind this research was to offer comprehensive guidelines to these teams, enabling them to establish a standardized and internationally endorsed approach to requirements management.

The study placed a significant emphasis on the critical need for flexibility when handling the fluid landscape of software requirements, a necessity arising from the ever-changing regulatory framework governing bank home loans. By implementing a standardized approach to requirements management, the research sought to drive improvements in both efficiency and software quality.

In essence, this research was motivated by a profound desire to empower Thai software development teams in effectively navigating the intricacies of managing requirements for home loan services software. Its ultimate objective was to equip these teams with the tools and knowledge needed to adopt a standardized and globally recognized approach to requirements management.

Background

This research commenced with interviews of project managers within the Thai software industry, focusing on small to medium-sized software development firms with teams of up to 25 members. These interviews revealed notable challenges in the realm of software requirements management, corroborating findings from the 2019 Software Industry Benchmark Study shown in Figure 1.

Figure 1. Software problems arise from requirements management issues

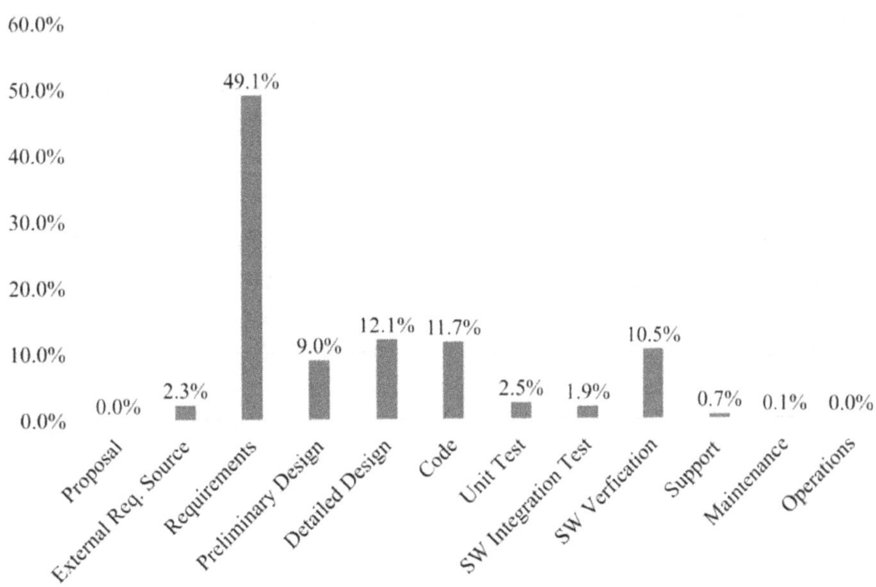

The investigation delved into two completed projects concerning home loan services software for commercial banks spanning from 2017 to 2022. Both projects encountered delays attributable to complexities in handling evolving requirements. To gauge the current state of requirements management, the author meticulously compared project plans, work procedures, and the tangible outcomes of the requirements management process across both projects. The objective was to assess the process's existing capabilities and pinpoint areas necessitating enhancement.

Initially, consideration was given to ISO/IEC TR 29110-1:2016, a standard tailored for small and medium-sized software development teams. However, it became evident that this standard predominantly centered on project management and software implementation, with requirements development and management constituting only a fraction of the overarching process. Compounding the challenge, certification bodies in Thailand exclusively conferred certifications at the highest capability level prescribed by ISO/IEC TR 29110-1:2016, rendering it unsuitable for addressing the research problem at hand. Consequently, the decision was made to revamp the process framework by drawing upon the CMMI standard with the objective of achieving Capability Level 3. CMMI was deemed apt for systematizing and overseeing the requirements management process at an organizational level (Lina & Dan, 2012). Nevertheless, realizing Capability Level 3 within the CMMI framework, commencing from Level 2, posed a formidable challenge for small and medium-sized teams grappling with finite resources. Consequently, the author undertook the task of adapting and enhancing the process in accordance with the CMMI V1.3 standard to ultimately attain Capability Level 3

Literature Review

Software Process Improvement (SPI) is a critical component of software development, contributing to enhanced product and service quality while aligning organizations with their strategic objectives (Pressman, 2010). While SPI is commonly associated with larger organizations, its relevance extends to small and Small-Medium companies as well. This literature review explores the importance of SPI in Small-Medium companies, emphasizing the shared goals of achieving excellence in software project execution, improving product quality, satisfying customers, and avoiding project overruns and failures.

SPI is equally vital for Small-Medium companies, which strive for excellence in software project execution, product quality, and customer satisfaction. However, Small-Medium companies face distinct challenges due to limited resources, necessitating external support to implement effective improvement strategies. The study conducted by Saastamoinen and Tukiainen (2004) provides empirical evidence of SPI's positive impact on product and service quality, demonstrating its effectiveness in collaboration with small and Small-Medium companies.

This literature review draws inspiration from prior research efforts that have aimed to define processes for enhancing organizational capability within the context of the Capability Maturity Model Integration (CMMI). These studies encompass various domains and have yielded valuable insights into improving software development processes. Notable contributions include studies such as Scrum-Based Practices (Lina and Dan, 2012), which focused on practices tailored for a Scrum-based software development model and their alignment with the CMMI Model. Similarly, the work of Tariq and Iftikhar (2014) proposed process definitions for Software as a Service (SaaS) and highlighted general practices for Requirements Management (REQM), emphasizing the importance of mapping often-overlooked activities in requirements management. Another study by Kamal Najjar and Al-Sarayreh (2015) proposed goals, practices, and activity descriptions to enhance requirements management, introducing a flow-based activity for the generic practice of REQM. Furthermore, Ardana and Suharjito (2017) proposed the evaluation of software development processes using CMMI-Dev, targeting limited-resource companies to achieve capability level 2 of CMMI 1.3. Their work emphasized the enhancement of requirements management and employed the SCAMPI method for class C assessments.

The present research work integrates principles from prior contributions, particularly those by Ardana and Suharjito (2017), to define processes in alignment with CMMI and the SCAMPI assessment method (SEI, 2011). This research extends the principles established by Tariq and Iftikhar (2014) and defines both generic and specific practices for process improvement. Moreover, it addresses the specific domain of software development for home-loan services within the banking sector. While the initial software development process adhered to a Waterfall approach, this research introduces Scrum-based activities to enhance the flexibility of requirements management.

In conclusion, this literature review underscores the significance of SPI in Small-Medium companies, emphasizing the importance of external support and the adaptation of best practices from prior research to enhance organizational capability in achieving software development objectives. It provides the foundation for understanding the context of SPI in Small-Medium companies and highlights the integration of prior work into the current research's framework.

CMMI Model Structure

The CMMI (Capability Maturity Model Integration) comprises five levels, each marking a distinct stage of process maturity (SEI, 2018). Level 1 - Initial is characterized by unpredictable, reactive processes. At Level 2-Managed, processes become stable with basic project management practices. Level 3-Defined denotes well-documented, standardized processes. Level 4-Quantitatively Managed involves processes measured and controlled with quantitative data. Level 5-Optimizing focuses on continuous improvement based on performance data. Organizations progress through these levels by demonstrating process maturity, aiming for higher performance.

The progress of process improvement is measured by the capability level (CL) achieved, and each CL for the selected process group must result from successful completion of the defined generic practices (GPs) at that level, as shown in Figure 2. Each process group comprises two main components: Goals and Practices.

Goals are categorized as Generic Goals (GGs) and Specific Goals (SGs). Practices are grouped as Generic Practices (GPs) and Specific Practices (SPs) (SEI, 2011). Generic Goals, as shown in Table 1, emphasize clear, integrated processes, with numeric sequences indicating increasing capability levels. Specific practices and goals are labeled as SP x.y, where x matches the SG number, and y represents the practice's sequence. For instance, achieving CL3 for requirements development and management (RDM) requires implementing specific practices SP1.1-SP1.5, as shown in Table 2. Generic Practices (GPs), like GP3.1, "Establish a Defined Process," ensure process effectiveness.

Figure 2. CMMI continuous structure (SEI, 2018)

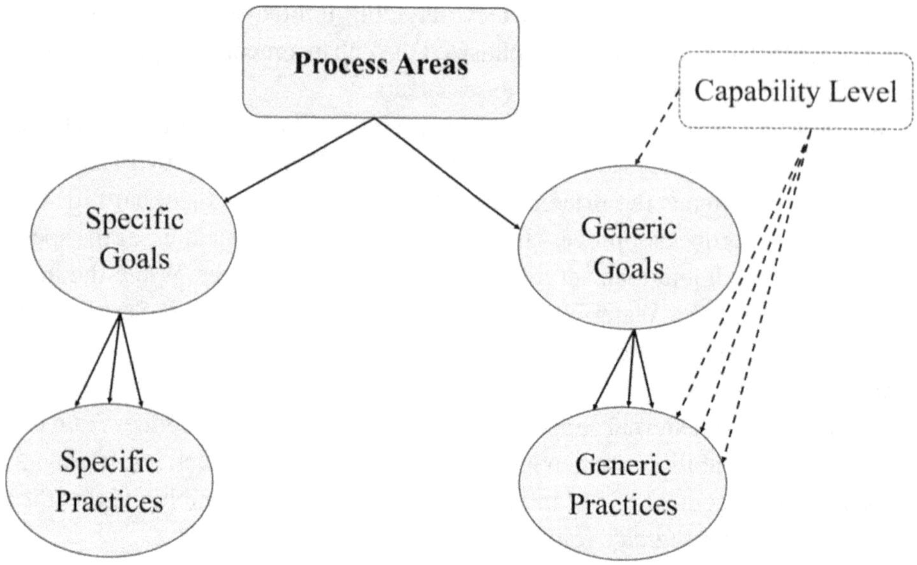

Table 1. Generic goal and progression of processes (SEI, 2011)

Generic Goal & Title	Progression of Processes
GG1: Achieve Specific Goals	Performed process
GG2: Institutionalize a Managed Process	Managed process
GG3. Institutionalize a Defined Process	Defined process
GG4: Institutionalize a Quantitatively Managed Process	Quantitatively Managed process
GG5: Institutionalize an Optimizing Process	Optimizing process

Standard CMMI Appraisal Method

SCAMPI (SEI, 2011), the CMMI evaluation method, tracks the outcomes of model practices. These outcomes act as indicators of practice implementation, like footprints in the sand. Practice Implementation Indicators (PII) take three forms:

1. Direct Artifacts: Tangible results directly produced by practice implementation, such as work products.
2. Indirect Artifacts: Evidence or indicators of actions taken, like meeting minutes or reports.
3. Affirmation: Verbal or written confirmation of practice implementation through interviews or questionnaires.

Table 2. Practices to achieve CL3 of the RDM process area (SEI, 2011)

Specific Practices	Generic Practices (CL1)
SP1.1: Obtain and Understanding of Requirements	GP1.1: Perform Specific Practices
SP1.2: Obtain Commitment to Requirements	
SP1.3: Manage Requirements Changes	
SP1.4: Maintain Bidirectional Traceability of Requirements	
SP1.5: Identify Inconsistencies Between Project Work and Requirements	
Specific Practices	Generic Practices (CL2)
All the SPs	All CL1 GPs Plus
	GP2.1: Establish an Organizational Policy
	GP2.2: Plan the Process
	GP2.3: Provide Resources
	GP2.4: Assign Responsibility
	GP2.5: Train People
	GP2.6: Manage Configurations
	GP2.7: Identify and Involve Relevant Stakeholders
	GP2.8: Monitor and Control the Process
	GP2.9: Objectively Evaluate Adherence
	GP2.10: Review Status with Higher Level Management
Specific Practices	Generic Practices (CL3)
All the SPs	All CL1 & CL2 GPs Plus
	GP3.1: Establish a Defined Process
	GP3.2: Collect Improvement Information

The evaluation process (Figure 3) involves analyzing requirements, comparing project outcomes to the defined process, identifying gaps, and recommending improvements. SCAMPI assesses effective practice implementation by examining direct and indirect evidence and affirmations related to those practices.

RESEARCH METHODOLOGY AND PROCESS

The research methodology (Figure 4) started with defining characteristics for a random sample of small to medium-sized software development teams experienced in home mortgage service software (1). Questionnaires were sent to select companies, their responses analyzed (2), and qualifying companies were chosen (3). Relevant software development integration standards, such as IEEE/EIA 12207-2008 and IEEE 1074-2006, were reviewed, and processes defined (4). Tools were developed and applied to two sample projects (5), with data collected for comparative analysis (6). Finally, satisfaction and process capability were assessed using the SCAMPI method by expert assessors (7).

Figure 3. CMMI appraisal method for process improvement (Tachanunachanun et al., 2012)

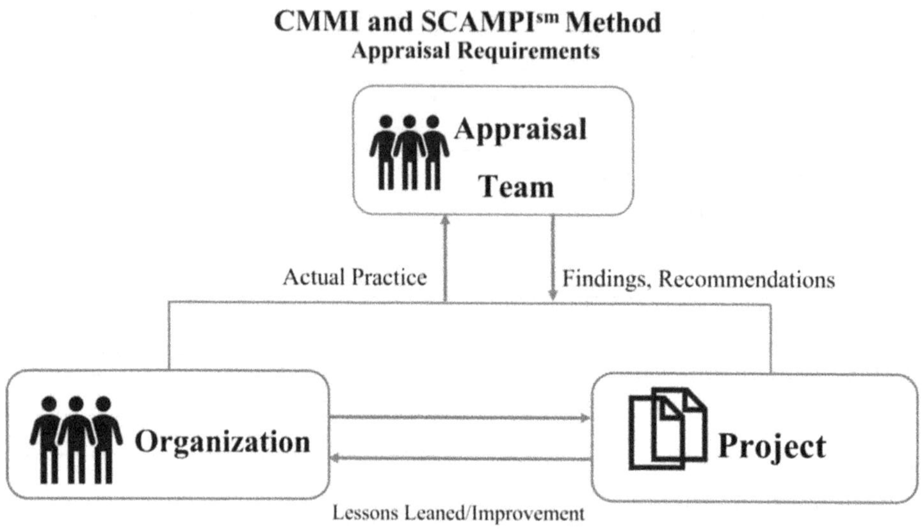

1. Establish the Criteria for the Random Sample Selection and Create the Questionnaire

This research addresses software demand management challenges in 8 small to medium-sized software companies with fewer than 25 members. These firms were randomly selected from 37 registered software developers in the Pak Kret District's industrial zone, operating from 2017 to 2021. Data was gathered through surveys of 30 individuals, including project managers and team members, with 5 of them representing companies struggling with recent project demands. After analyzing the questionnaires, 15 individuals were purposively chosen for interviews to explore project characteristics and issues. All interviewees had 3-5 years of software project management experience and managed over 4 projects. The questionnaire covered various aspects, including software development processes, project management practices, compliance with industry standards, challenges, and improvement initiatives. Its aim was to comprehensively assess current practices and identify areas for enhancement, informing the design of an effective improvement process for better project outcomes.

2. Send a Letter to the Random Sample Group

Data was collected over a three-month period, from May 15, 2021, to July 15, 2021. In this study, the researcher utilized randomly distributed questionnaires to collect data from project managers, software development team members, and 30 experts across all eight companies. All 30 questionnaires were returned, resulting in a 100 percent response rate.

Figure 4. Research methodology

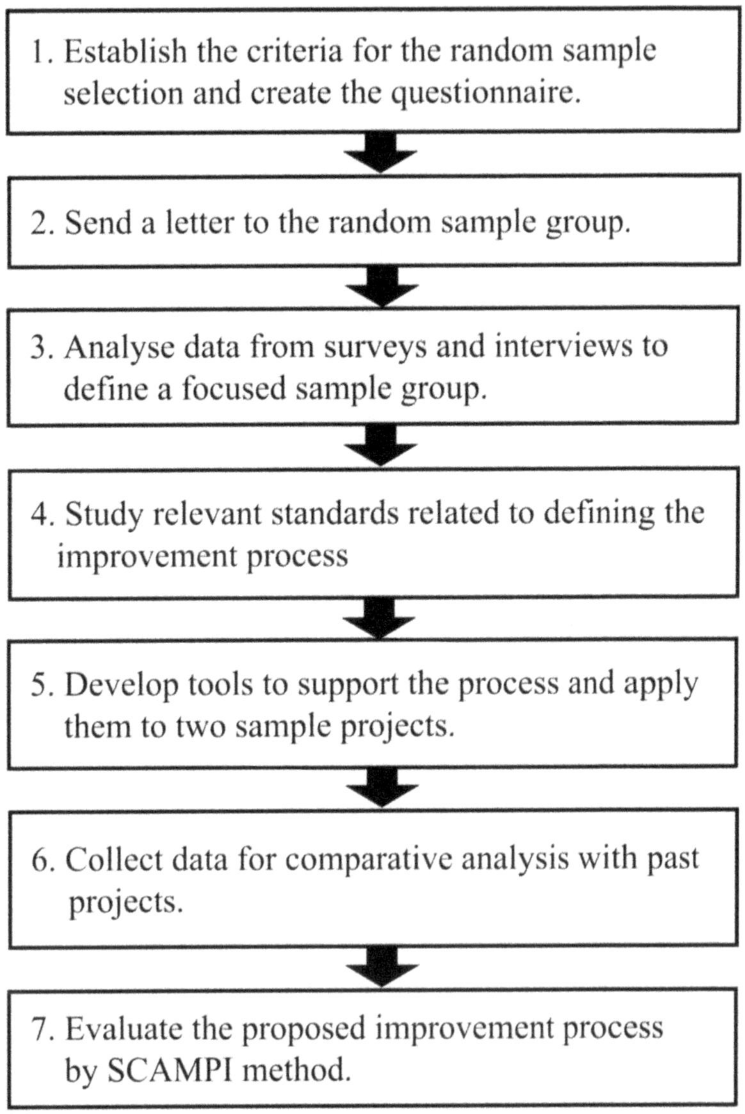

3. Selection of Companies That Meet the Specified Criteria

The questionnaire data, collected from 30 respondents, was analyzed to determine the study samples. The results were presented, highlighting specific questions and their top-three responses, as shown in Figure 5. For example, when asked about the total number of team members involved in their projects, the majority (86.66%) had 20 to less than 25 team members, while 6.67% mentioned 15 to less than 20 members, and another 6.67% had 20 to less than 30 team members.

Figure 6 shows the impact of changes on different phases. The requirements analysis phase was the most affected, mentioned by 53.33% of respondents. The system design phase followed with 20%, and the implementation phase had a 13.33% impact.

Figure 5. Results for the total number of team members involved in the project

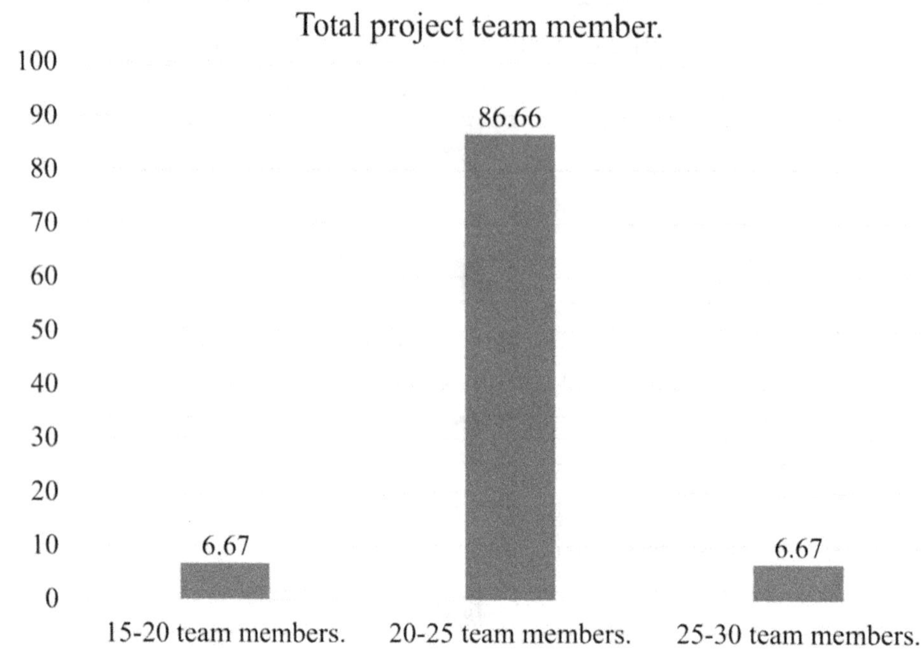

Figure 6. Results specifying which phase in the SDLC was affected by changes

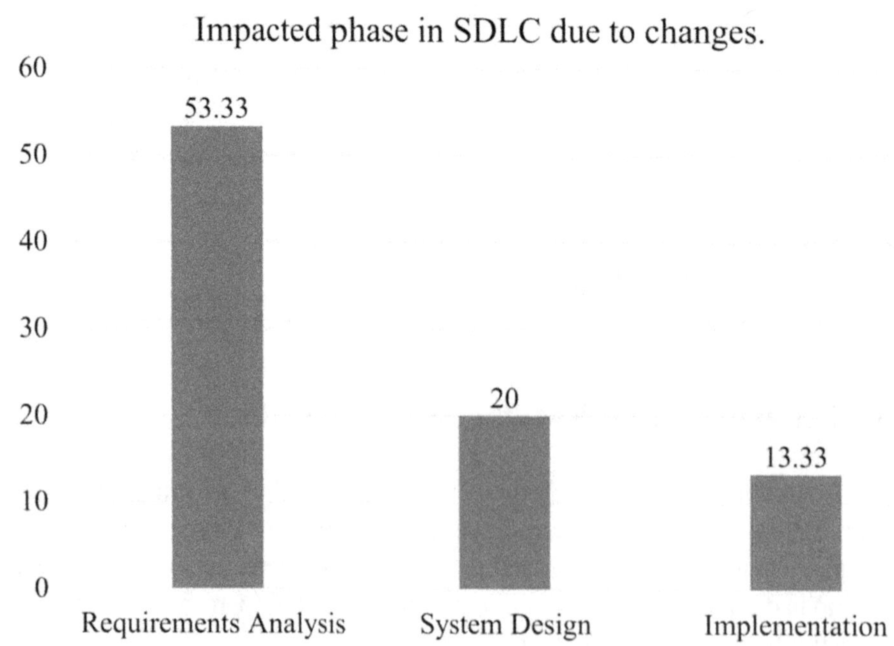

Figure 7 highlights that requirements management issues were widespread. Respondents faced challenges during different phases, with 53.33% encountering problems in the management phase, 26.67% during the change phase, and 20% during the traceability phase. These insights pinpoint areas requiring improvements in requirements management.

Figure 7. Results of requirements analysis phase challenges

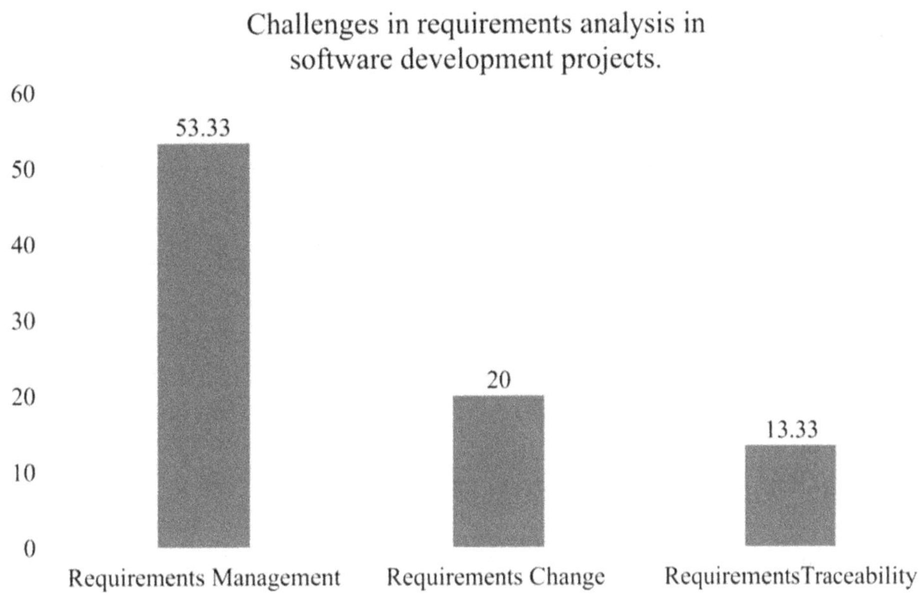

Interviews with team members unveiled key factors contributing to project delays:

1. Economic Changes: Frequent shifts in financial policies, laws, and regulations from 2017 to 2021, possibly exacerbated by the Covid-19 situation, had a substantial impact on both past projects.
2. Lack of Standardization: Inconsistent approaches to change management across projects due to the absence of standardized procedures led to inefficiencies.
3. Compliance with Customer Requirements: Strict adherence to customer banks' formal processes and policies was essential, requiring alignment with specific banking procedures.
4. Balancing Flexibility and Documentation: Striking a balance between flexibility and robust documentation was crucial, especially in handling requirements change documents according to banking document requirements.

These insights emphasize the need to address these challenges for enhanced development processes and project success.

4. Define the Improvement Process

In section 4., the author focused on studying two crucial standards in software engineering: IEEE 12207 (IEEE, 2008) and IEEE 1074 (IEEE, 2006). IEEE 12207 outlines software development life cycle processes and established industry practices, serving as a foundation for defining an improvement process aligned with industry best practices. IEEE 1074 emphasizes verification and validation activities throughout the software development life cycle, providing insights to integrate robust verification and validation practices into the proposed improvement process. By studying these standards, the author aimed to enhance the Hybrid Software Development Methodology (HSDM) with Scrum-based Agile practices (4.1) and tailor the improvement process (4.2) to the specific needs of participating organizations, ultimately improving performance, efficiency, and quality in future projects.

4.1 Improving Waterfall Model by Scrum-Based Agile

The section enhances the traditional waterfall model with Scrum-based Agile practices, improving software development flexibility. The steps include defining the process, selecting the project life cycle model, creating the software project life cycle, aligning activities, prioritizing them, and conducting reviews for effectiveness. This hybrid approach combines traditional and Agile methods for better project outcomes. The improvement process is structured in six steps, as shown in Figure 8.

Step 1: Define the definition of the improvement process

Table 3 presents data on customizing the software development process to meet specific company requirements. For instance, requirement SIES01 mandates alignment with home loan service software development.

Table 3. Requirements for the software development life cycle of the project

ID	Definition
SIES01	This is in line with the development of software for home loan services.
SIES02	Corresponds to a team of small to medium software developers.
SIES03	Compliant with Hybrid Software Development Methodology.
SIES04	Change requirements, and uncertainly.

Step 2: Select the life cycle of the software project (SPLCM)

The author selected a compatible software project life cycle model (SPLCM) that matched the improvement process's objectives and requirements, serving as the foundation for integrating Scrum-based Agile practices.

Figure 8. Improving software and project life cycle step

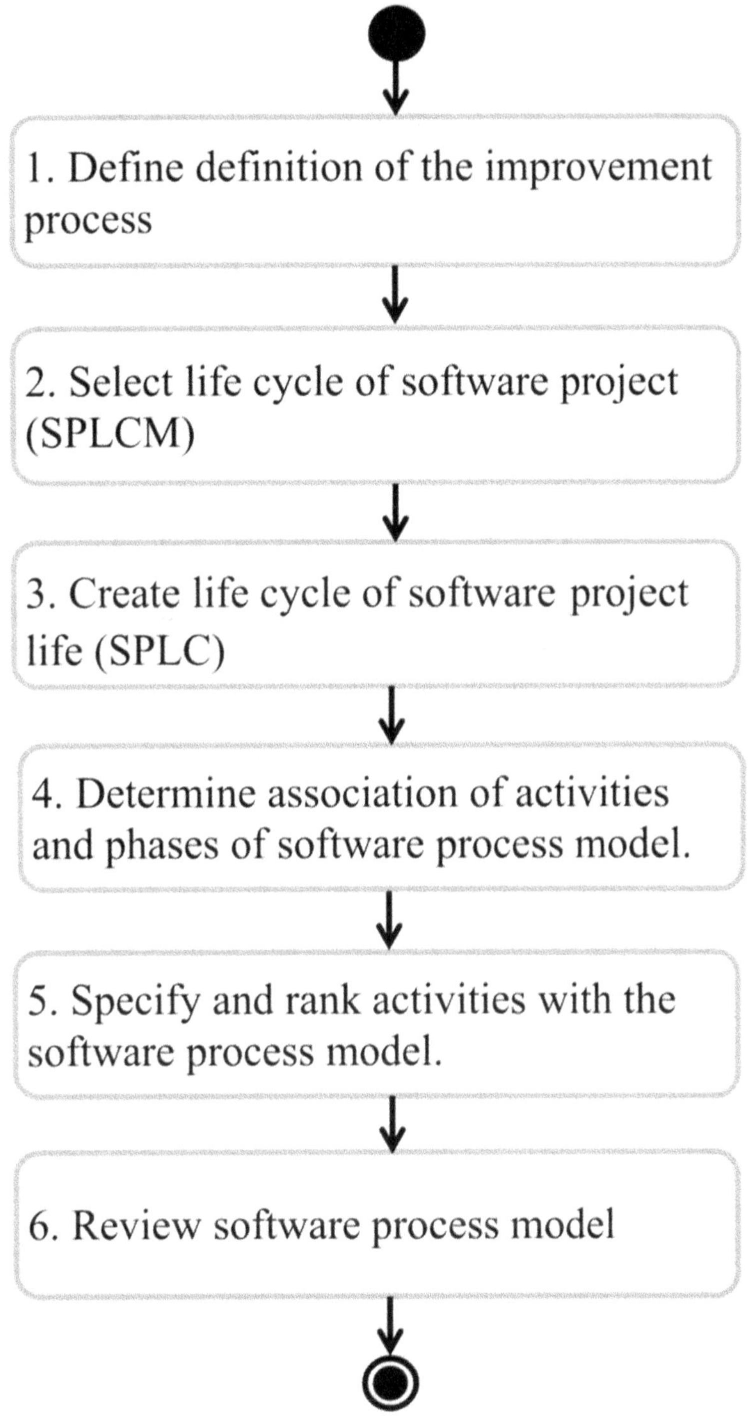

Step 3: Create the life cycle of the software project life (SPLC)

In this phase, the author developed a customized Software Project Life Cycle (SPLC) by integrating Scrum-based Agile methodology. This hybrid approach aimed to leverage the strengths of both the traditional waterfall model and Agile practices (Sommerville & Sawyer, 1997). The resulting Hybrid Software Development Methodology (HSDM), shown in Figure 9, included planning, requirements gathering, requirements analysis, system design, and implementation phases. These phases were enriched with Scrum-based Agile activities. Team members engaged in daily brief meetings, lasting fifteen to thirty minutes, to discuss progress and address task-related issues. Additionally, the product was delivered to customers weekly, emphasizing iterative development and timely delivery. The HSDM aimed to enhance efficiency and responsiveness in the software development process.

Combining the Waterfall model with Scrum-based Agile involves incorporating Agile practices and principles into each phase of the Waterfall model. Here's how each phase can be adapted:

- **Planning:** Utilize Agile techniques like Sprint Planning to break down the project into smaller iterations. Develop a backlog of tasks and prioritize them based on customer requirements and feedback.
- **Requirements Gathering:** Involve stakeholders, including customers and end-users, throughout the process to gather and refine requirements collaboratively. Use user stories and personas to capture and document requirements in a more Agile manner.
- **Requirements Analysis:** Analyze and prioritize requirements based on customer value and feedback. Use Agile techniques like MoSCoW (Must have, Should have, Could have, Won't have) to categorize and prioritize requirements.
- **System Design:** Utilize Agile principles of continuous integration and continuous delivery to iteratively design and develop the system. Conduct frequent design reviews and encourage open communication among team members.
- **Implementation:** Break the implementation phase into smaller increments (Sprints) and focus on delivering a working product in each iteration. Use daily Scrum meetings to monitor progress, identify roadblocks, and plan for the day's tasks.

Throughout the process:

- Emphasize collaboration, open communication, and flexibility in responding to changing requirements and customer feedback.
- Regularly conduct Sprint Reviews to showcase the developed features to stakeholders and gather feedback for future iterations.
- Encourage self-organizing and cross-functional teams that work together to achieve project goals

By integrating Agile practices into the Waterfall model, the development team can benefit from increased adaptability, shorter feedback loops, and improved customer satisfaction. The result is a more efficient and customer-centric software development process.

Figure 9. Hybrid software development methodology

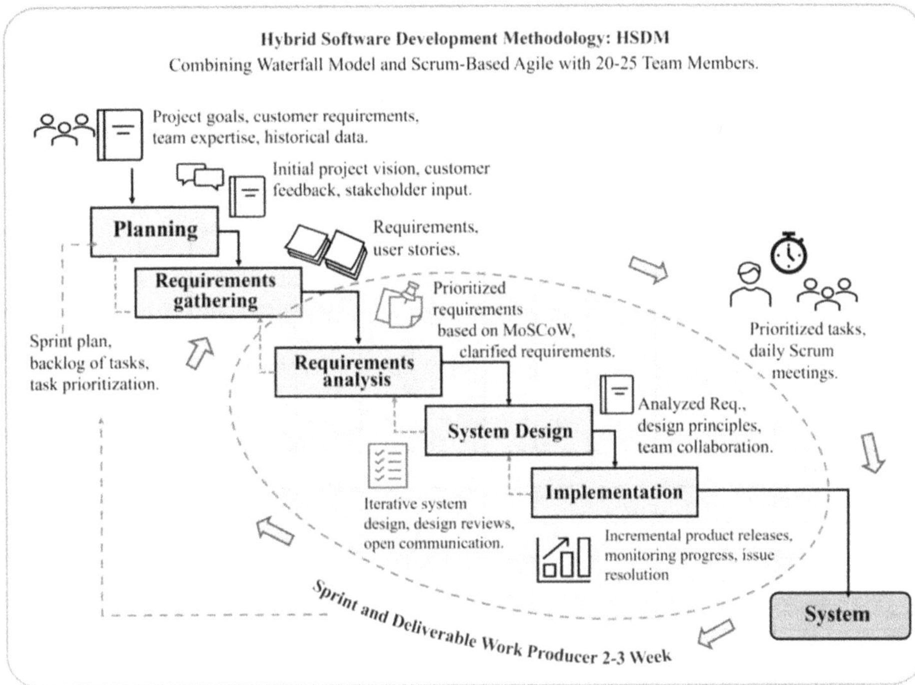

Step 4: Determine association of activities of software process model

The author performed the following steps to seamlessly integrate Agile practices into the existing software development process (As shown in Table 4): Identified key activities and phases in the software process model (Step: 1) Established interconnections and relationships within the Software Project Life Cycle (SPLC) (Step: 2). Associated selected models with activities specified in IEEE 1074 with managers and software development team members (Step: 3). Prioritized and merged the selected activities according to four levels of importance: NU (Not Used), H (High Importance), M (Medium Importance), and L (Low Importance) (Step: 4). Mapped project operations to established and refined processes (Step: 5). Analyzed the importance of these activities in various phases of the Integrated Software Development Process Model (SPLCM Version1), such as demand collection phase 1 and Requirements Analysis phase (Step: 6).

Table 4 presents identified activities and their importance levels in each software development phase. "High Importance" activities take precedence in the integration process, ensuring effective incorporation of Agile practices into the existing framework. This enhances flexibility and adaptability, improving productivity and customer satisfaction in future development cycles. Mapping project operations to established processes, such as "Prioritize and Integrate Software Requirements" (A.3.1.3) from IEEE 1074, highlights their high importance in the Integrated Software Development Process Model during Demand Collection phase 1 (SPLCM Version1) and the Requirements Analysis phase, emphasizing their significance in the improvement process.

Table 4. Activities of IEEE Std. 1074 and SPLC

Activities of IEEE Std 1074 (Preceded by Corresponding Subclause number)	SPLCM Version 1					SPLCM Version N					SPLCM Version End				
	1. Planning	2. Requirements Gathering	3. Requirements analysis	4. system design	5. Implementation	1. Planning	2. Requirements Gathering	3. Requirements analysis	4. system design	5. Implementation	1. Planning	2. Requirements Gathering	3. Requirements analysis	4. system design	5. Implementation
A.2.1 Concept Exploration Activity Group															
A.2.1.1 Identify Ideas or Needs (Required)		H	M	L	L		H	M	L	L		H	M	L	L
A.2.1.2 Formulate Potential Approaches (Required)			M	H	M			M	H	M			M	H	M
A.2.1.3 Conduct Feasibility Studies (Required)	H	L	L			M	L				L	L			
A.2.1.4 Refine and Finalize the Idea or Need (Required)			H	M				H	M				H	M	
A.2.2 System Allocation Activity Group															
A.2.2.1 Analyze System Functions		M	H	L			M	H	L			M	H	L	
A.2.2.2 Develop System Architecture				H					M					M	
A.2.2.3 Allocate System Requirements		H	M				M	M				M	M		
A.2.3 Software Importation Activity Group															
A.2.3.1 Identify Imported Software Requirements		H	M				H	M				H	M		
A.2.3.2 Evaluate Software Import Sources	NU	NU	NU	NU	NU	NU	NU	NU	NU	NU	NU	NU	NU	NU	NU
A.2.3.3 Define Software Import Method	NU	NU	NU	NU	NU	NU	NU	NU	NU	NU	NU	NU	NU	NU	NU
A.2.3.4 Import Software				M	M				M	M				M	M
A.3.1 Software Requirements Activity Group															
A.3.1.1 Define and Develop Software Requirements		H	H				H	H				H	H		
A.3.1.2 Define Interface Requirements		H	H	H			H	M	M			H	M	M	
A.3.1.3 Prioritize and Integrate Software Requirements		H	H				H	H				H	H		
A.3.2 Design Activity Group															
A.3.2.1 Perform Architectural Design				H					H					M	
A.3.2.2 Design Database				H					M					M	
A.3.2.3 Design Interfaces				H					M					L	
A.3.2.4 Perform Detailed Design				H					M					M	
A.3.3 Implementation Activity Group															
A.3.3.1 Create Executable Code					H					H				H	
A.3.3.2 Create Operating Documentation					M					L				M	
A.3.3.3 Perform Integration					H					H				H	
A.3.3.4 Manage Software Releases					M					L				M	

Legend: NU = not used; H = Mapped Activity (High importance); M = mapped activity (Medium importance); L = Mapped Activity (Low Importance)

Step 5: Specify and rank activities with the software process model

Figure 5 summarizes the selected activities for each development phase, identified and prioritized collaboratively by project managers and development team representatives. An example is Model Phase SPLC 2.7: Requirements management, linked to IEEE 1074 activity A.3.1.1: Define and Develop Software Requirements. This linkage follows an iterative and invocative mapping, marked with "H" for High Importance in all iterations of the software development phases within the Hybrid Software Development Methodology. This information was instrumental in defining the development and requirements management process, aligning it with the Generic Practices of CMMI and the resulting work products.

Table 5. Life cycle segment or phase and IEEE Std. 1074 activities mapping

ID	HSDM Life Cycle Phase	IEEE 1074 Activities	Mapping Type	Importance		
				First	N	End
2.0	Requirements gathering					
2.1	Plan to gather requirements	A.2.1.1 Identify Ideas or Needs (Required)	Iteration	H	H	H
2.2	Specify how to collect requirements	A.2.1.1 Identify Ideas or Needs (Required)	Iteration	H	H	H
2.3	collection of requirements	A.1.3.4 Retain Records (Required)	Iteration	M	M	M
2.4	Requirements analysis and negotiation	A.2.1.1 Identify Ideas or Needs (Required)	Iteration	H	H	H
2.5	Requirement documentation	A.3.1.1 Define and Develop Software Requirements	Iteration	H	H	H
2.6	Requirements validation	A.5.1.1 Conduct Reviews (Required)	Iteration	H	M	M
2.7	Requirements management	A.3.1.1 Define and Develop Software Requirements	Iteration	H	H	H
2.8	Deliver software requirements specification documents to stakeholder	A.5.3.2 Produce and Distribute Documentation (Required)	Invocation	M	M	M

Step 6: Review the software process model

This is a validation process to verify the alignment of the customized software development process with the company's requirements. It includes confirming whether selected activities match the model as specified. For example, requirements ID SIES04, "Change requirements and uncertainty" (Table 3), must correspond with activities in the HSDM Life Cycle Phase (Table 5). Validated results are then effectively utilized.

4.2 Improving Waterfall Model by Scrum-Based Agile

The process of defining work products and practices for software development and requirements management involves five key activities, as shown in Figure 10:

Figure 10. Process definition step

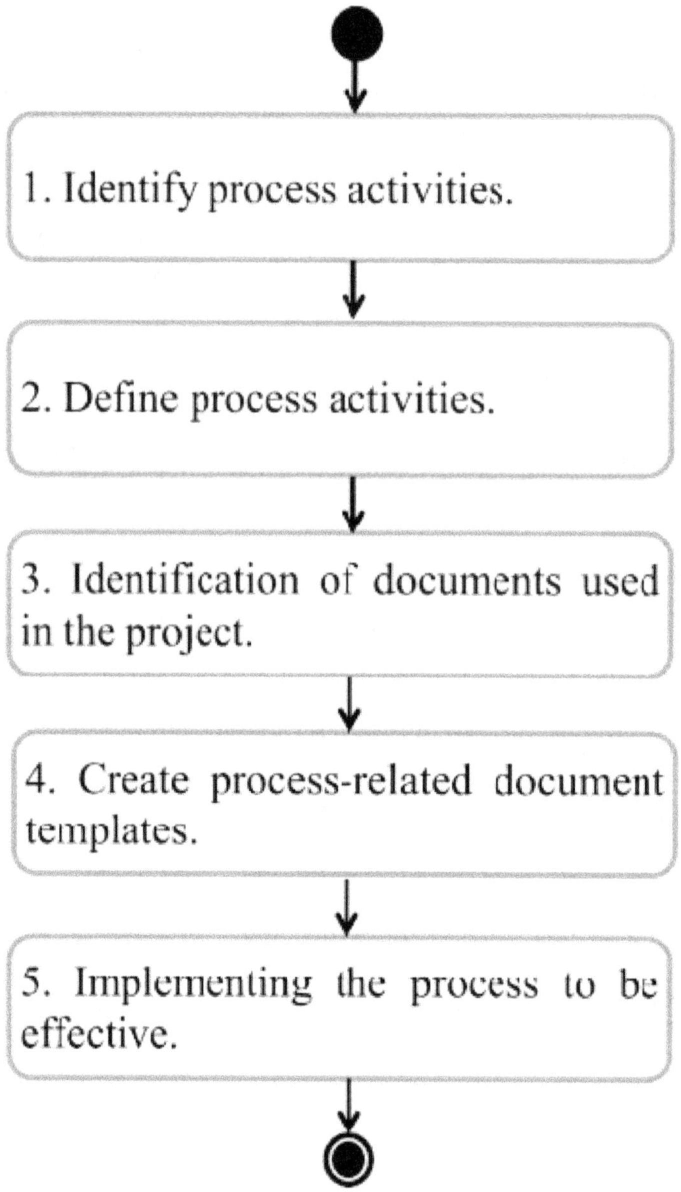

Step 1: Identify process activities

In this initial phase, essential activities for improving the software development process are identified. The selection is based on a thorough study of standards like IEEE 12207-2008 and IEEE 1074-2006, specifically focusing on requirements management in HSDM and IEEE 1074's A.3.1.1 Define and Develop Software Requirements. These activities serve as a foundation for subsequent process enhancements.

- The process entails specifying activities, input work products, and output work products in software development and requirements management, as detailed in Table 6. For instance, Activity SP1.1: Establish organization-wide requirements management policies and procedures serves as an Expected output in a specific CMMI process. It involves input work products like Project plan and Requirements management policy, and output work products such as Requirements management policy and Requirements management procedure.
- In total, there are 24 activities for software development and requirements management, including 14 input and 14 output work products. Four activities have both input and output work products. This comprehensive list is essential for establishing a well-defined and efficient improvement process, enhancing the organization's software development and requirements management practices to attain CMMI level 3 capability.

Step 2: Define process activities

The study identified weaknesses in software development and requirements management processes in Thai commercial banks during home loan software projects. To address these, the author defined activities aligning with IEEE 1074, CMMI practices, and specific process outputs, as seen in Figure 6. For example, O2: Requirements management procedure aligns with GP1.1 and SP1.1, while I12: Change Request Forms align with GP2.6 and SP1.4. These correlations indicate successful CMMI model practice implementation and desired outcomes.

Step 3: Identification of documents used in the process

Generic Practices ensure process repeatability and effectiveness. They are crucial for achieving improvement goals and follow a continuous usage model. To assess capability level 3, organizations must adhere to 13 generic practices, such as GP2.6: Develop plans, track, and control requirements changes, explained in Figure 7 based on IEEE 12207.

Clear process definition aligns with generic goals, particularly at capability level 3, where processes are well-defined. This includes Input I12: Change Request form specified in GP2.6, as shown in Figure 11. These aspects foster mutual understanding and continuous learning for improvement.

Step 4: Create process-related document templates

Document templates maintain consistency and standardization in documentation by providing guidelines for capturing project information. They ensure standardized practices for software development teams and facilitate quality assessment based on CMMI practices. Figure 8 provides an example, showing the Change Request Form (I12) aligned with a process activity for requesting a system change, as shown in Figure 11.

Table 6a. Process definition for improvement

Process Area	Requirements Development and Management: RDM	Capability Level	The Things That Need to Be Done
Generic goal Type: Required	GG1: Define the process for managing requirements and controlling changes to the requirements of organizational operations to efficiently and effectively meet the agreed-upon customer requirements.	CL1	all SPs or implement GP1.1
	GG2: Evaluate whether the implementation conforms to the process description specified in GG1 and adapt it to align with organizational policies. This entails planning, controlling work, conducting inspections, and communicating with relevant stakeholders to ensure alignment with mutual benefits.	CL2	GP1.1 to GP2.10
	GG3: Develop standardized tools to support the processes outlined in GG2, which will be consistent across the entire organization. Each distinct project will then be assigned the organization's standardized processes tailored for its use.	CL3	GP1.1 to GP3.2
Practice for generic process Type: Expected	GP1.1: Develop policies and procedures for requirements management. GP2.1, GP2.2: Establish objectives and goals for requirements management. GP2.3, GP2.4, GP2.5: Define roles and responsibilities for requirements management. GP2.6: Develop plans, track, and control requirement changes. GP2.7: Assess and report customer satisfaction. GP2.8: Review the status of product and service quality related to requirements management. GP2.9: Review the project's requirements management plan. GP2.10: Plan corrective actions for unmet requirements management control objectives and record corrections within a defined cycle. GP3.1: Establish process and requirements management standards as defined. GP3.2: Acquire tools to support the activities, products, and data needed for continuous process improvement.		
Expected output for specific process Type: Expected	SP1.1: Establish organization-wide requirements management policies and procedures. SP1.2: Define objectives and achieve agreements related to requirements management. SP1.3: Manage requirement changes, assign responsibilities, and define positions for requirements management. SP1.4: Trace the sources of requirements and monitor customer satisfaction status. SP1.5: Take action to identify and address inconsistencies between project outcomes and requirements to enhance quality and meet established goals.		

Table 6b.

Inputs Work Product	Outputs Work Product
I1: Project Plan (GP1.1, GP2.6, GP2.8-GP2.9, SP1.1-SP1.3, SP1.5) I2: Contract (GP1.1, GP2.6, GP2.8-GP2.9, SP1.1-SP1.3, SP1.5) I3: Requirements Specification Document (GP1.1, GP2.1-GP2.6, GP2.8-GP2.9, SP1.1-SP1.3) I4: Software Testing and Quality Assurance Plan Document (GP1.1, GP2.6-GP2.8, SP1.1-SP1.2, SP1.5) I5: Requirements Management Policy (GP1.1, GP2.1-GP2.2, GP2.8-GP2.9, GP3.1-GP3.2, SP1.1) I6: Requirements Management Procedure (GP1.1, GP2.1-GP2.2, GP2.8-GP2.9, GP3.1-GP3.2, SP1.3) I7: Requirements Management Objectives and Goals (GP1.1, GP2.1-GP2.2, GP2.8-GP2.9, GP3.1-GP3.2, SP1.2) I8: Company Structure (GP1.1, GP2.1-GP2.2, SP1.3) I9: Customer Satisfaction Data (GP2.7, GP2.10, SP1.4) I10: Project Progress Reports (GP2.8, SP1.4) I11: Meeting Reports (GP2.10, GP3.1-GP3.2, SP1.1-SP1.5) I12: Change Request Forms (GP2.6, SP1.4) I13: Customer Satisfaction Reports (GP2.6, GP2.8-GP2.9, SP1.4) I14: Problem Records (GP2.8-GP2.10, GP3.1-GP3.2, SP1.5) I15: Review Records (GP2.8-GP2.10, GP3.1-GP3.2, SP1.5)	O1: Requirements Management Policy (GP1.1, SP1.1) O2: Requirements Management Procedure (GP1.1, SP1.1) O3: Requirements Management Objectives and Goals (GP2.1-GP2.2, SP1.2) O4: Requirements Management Team Structure (GP2.3-GP2.5, SP1.3) O5: Customer Satisfaction Reports (GP2.6-GP2.7, SP1.4) O6: Requirements Management Plan Review Reports (GP2.8-GP2.10, GP3.1, SP1.5) O7: Quality Improvement Plan for Requirements (GP2.6, GP2.8-GP2.10, GP3.1, SP1.5) O8: Change Request Records (GP2.6, SP1.5) O9: Analysis of Requirement Modification Reports (GP2.9-GP2.10, SP1.5) O10: Version Control Reports (GP2.9, SP1.5) O11: Requirements Backtracking Reports (GP2.6, SP1.4, SP1.5) O12: Statement of Work and Process Description (GP3.1, SP1.1-SP1.5) O13: Project Repository for Requirements (GP3.2, SP1.1-SP1.5)

Table 7. Process example, GP2.6: Develop plans, track, and control requirements changes

Purpose	To create a requirements management plan in line with the requirements management policy, follow these key practices: 1. Traceability: Maintain consistent requirements with backward tracing. 2. Requirement Elicitation: Define stakeholder input procedures. 3. Change Control: Establish change management procedures. 4. Change Reporting: Develop a system for documenting and communicating changes. 5. Customer Satisfaction Analysis: Implement methods to assess customer satisfaction.
Entry criteria	The requirements document agreement, defined in the contract involving the customer, procurement, development, and support teams, serves as a baseline for referencing activities in software development, requirements management, testing, quality assurance, and project plan progress analysis.
Input work products	I1: Project Plan Project Plan I3: Requirements Specification Document I4: Software Testing and Quality Assurance Plan Document I12: Change Request Forms I13: Customer Satisfaction Reports
Process	1. Stakeholders, including software engineers, project managers, customers, and support teams, establish baseline requirements together. 2. Ensure unique identification of each requirement to prevent duplication and enable cross-referencing. 3. Define criteria for assessing requirement changes, considering factors like scope, cost, and schedule, ensuring they pass a cost-benefit analysis. 4. Trace requirement change origins to inform change management planning and assess design areas affected. 5. Regularly review and update the requirement management plan based on customer feedback. 6. Implement changes based on customer input and ensure their effectiveness.
Output work products	O7: Quality Improvement Plan for Requirements O8: Change Request Records O11: Requirements Backtracking Reports
Exit criteria	1. Requirements plan, tracking, tracing, and change control satisfy customers and align with mutual agreement. 2. Change control committee approves or rejects all requirement changes. 3. Each requirement undergoes full design, development, testing, and quality assurance in line with baseline project requirements.
Responsible	1. Requirements Engineers 2. Customers and Relevant Stakeholders
Supervisor	1. Head of System Development and Software Department 2. Software Project Manager 3. Change Control Committee Member

Step 5: Implementing the process to be effective

The final step involves the practical implementation of the defined improvement process, aligning with IEEE 830 guidelines for effectiveness. These steps result in a well-crafted process tailored to the organization's needs, fostering structured, efficient, and adaptive software development and requirements management practices, ultimately achieving CMMI level 3 capability.

Figure 11. Example of a process activity for requesting a system change (I12)

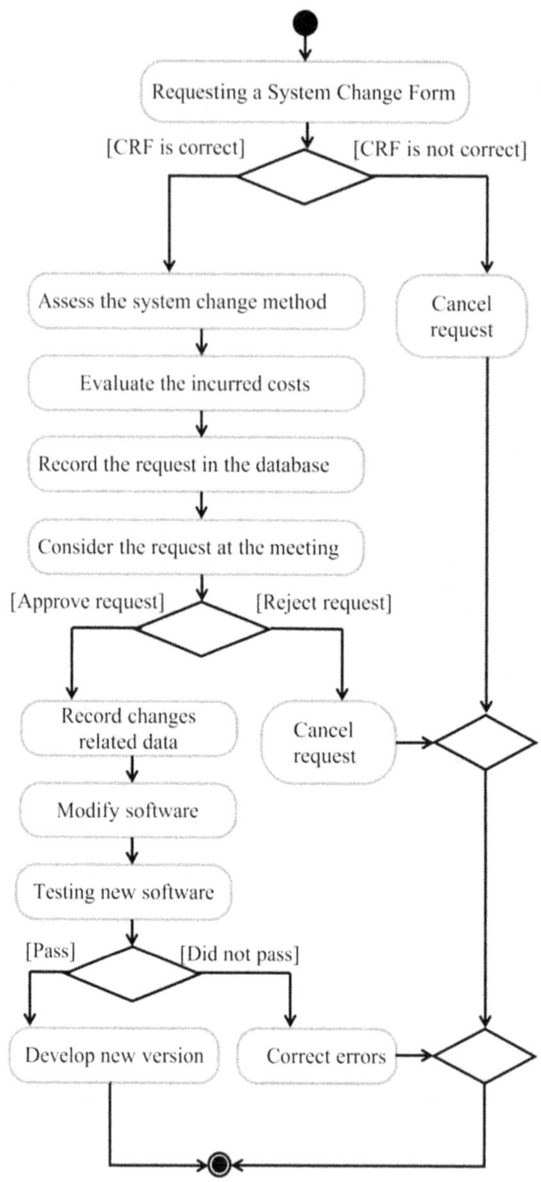

5. Develop the Support Tool for Requirements Management

Supporting tools play a crucial role in CMMI level 3 practices, particularly in GP3.2, which requires at least two projects in the company to use defined processes. For example, O13 involves a project repository for requirements, storing artifacts. Figure 12 illustrates the six steps in designing and developing these tools: studying workflow problems (Step 1), gathering requirements (Step 2), designing the tool's workflow (Step 3), creating detailed interactions (Step 4), and testing and adapting with a sample group (Step 5).

Table 8. Example change request form document template (I12)

Change Request Form (CRF)				
CRF#	*[CR-XXX]*			
Type of CRF	☐ Feature Addition CRF ☐ Bug Fix CRF ☐ Performance Improvement CRF ☐ Simplification CRF ☐ Requirement Change CRF ☐ Security Enhancement CRF ☐ Deprecation CRF ☐ Feature Removal CRF ☐ Other................................			
Project/System Name	*[Full/Official Name per the attached contract]*			
Requester's Name	*[First Name, Last Name]*			
Recipient's Name	*[First Name, Last Name]*			
Brief Description of Request	*[Enter a detailed description of the requested changes]*			
Request Date	*[Date (dd/mm/yyyy)]*			
Desired Date	*[Date (dd/mm/yyyy)]*			
Priority	☐ Low	☐ Moderate	☐ High	☐ Mandatory
Reason for Change	*[Description of the details of the reason for requesting the change]*			
Other Impacts	*[List any other items affected by this change]*			
Assumptions and Notes	*[Hypotheses or comments regarding the requested change]*			
Comments	*[Add additional comments]*			
Attachments or References	☐ Have	☐ Don't have		
	Link:			
Approval Signature	*[Approver's Signature]*		Date	*[MM/DD/YYYY]*

Table 9. Functions, user role, and practices CMMI

Functions	User Roles	Practices CMMI
Manage Software Project Data	Project manager	SP1.1, SP1.2, SP1.5, GP2.3, GP2.6, GP3.2
Manage Requirements Data	Project manager	SP1.1, SP1.2, SP1.4, SP1.5, GP2.6, GP3.2
Manage Test Case Data	Project manager	SP1.1, SP1.4, GP2.6, GP2.8, GP3.2
Manage Requirements Change Data	Project manager	SP1.3, GP2.6, GP2.8, GP3.2
Define Project Status	Project manager	SP1.1, SP1.2
Define Requirements Change Status	Project manager	SP1.3
Create Requirements Traceability Matrix	Project manager	SP1.1, SP1.3, SP1.4, SP1.5, GP2.6, GP3.2
Print System Version Change Reports	Project manager	SP1.1, SP1.3, SP1.5, GP2.6, GP3.2
Check Project Progress Status	Customer	SP1.1, SP1.2, SP1.5, GP2.3, GP2.6, GP3.2
Request Requirements Change	Customer, Project manager	SP1.3, GP2.6, GP2.8, GP3.2
Check Requirements Change Status	Customer	SP1.3, GP2.6, GP2.8, GP3.2
Approve Requirements Change Requests	Committees (CCB)	SP1.3, GP2.6, GP2.8, GP3.2

Table 9 summarizes functions, user privileges, and their alignment with CMMI practices based on input from 30 individuals in a focused sample group across two projects.

Figure 13 shows the functional use case model of the tool, designed using UML(Dennis et al., 2009)., to ensure its alignment with CMMI level 3 practices and enhance efficiency and customer satisfaction.

Figure 12. Design and develop support tool step

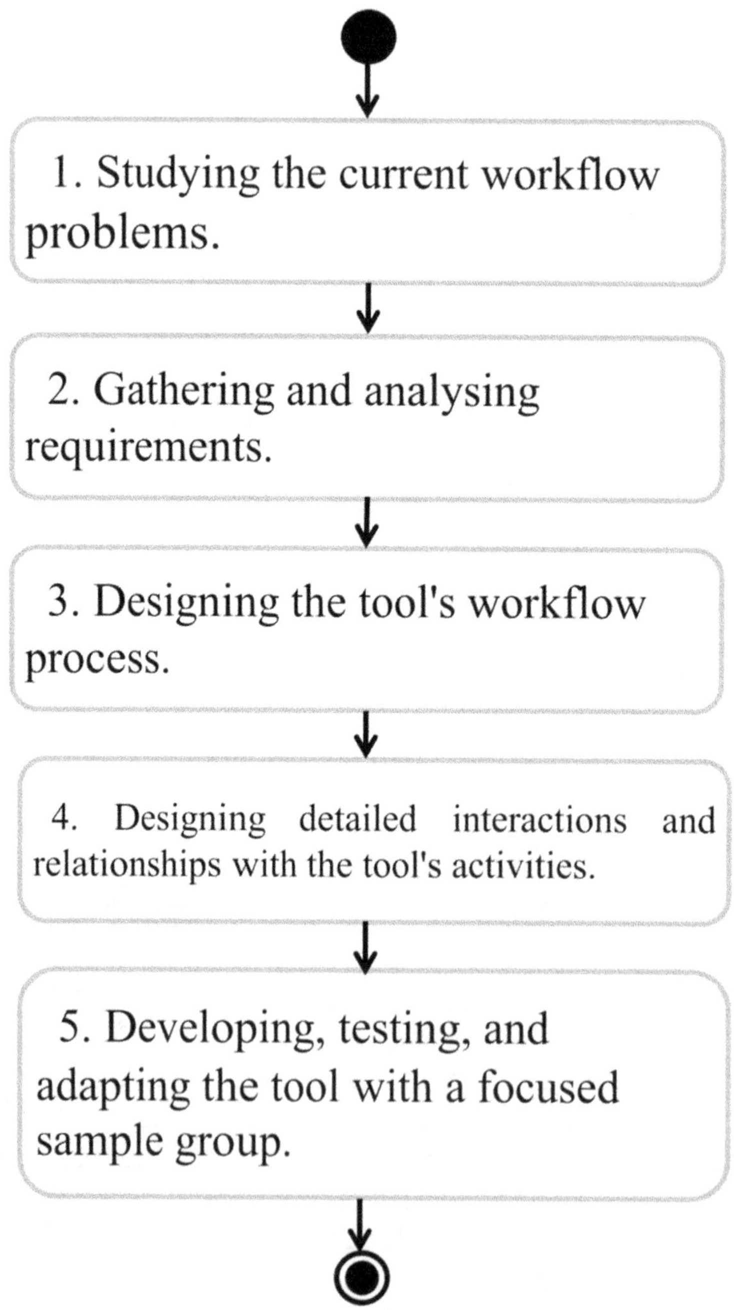

Figure 13. Design and develop support tool step

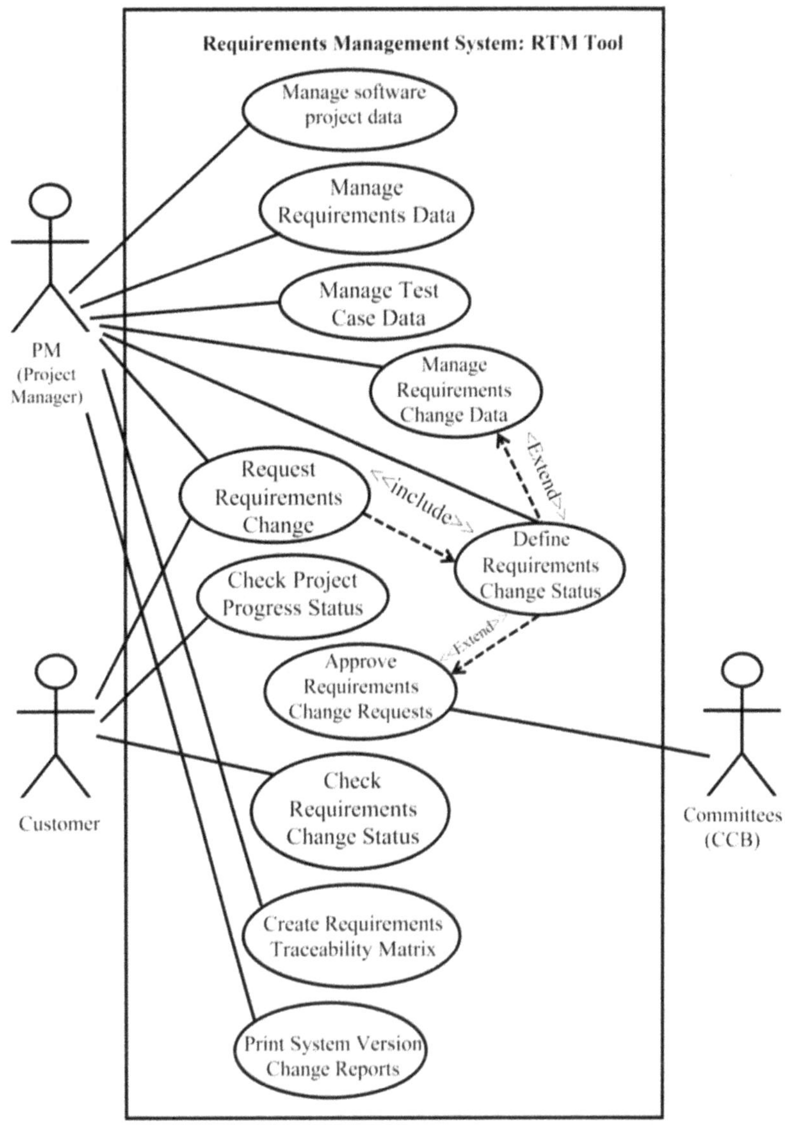

6. Evaluate the Proposed Improvement Process

To evaluate the proposed improvement process, it is essential to involve stakeholders who are directly or indirectly impacted by the process changes. Here is a step-by-step method to evaluate the proposed improvement process by stakeholders:

6.1 Analyze and Compare Results

The evaluation of the proposed improvement process involves analyzing and comparing the outcomes before and after implementing the process in different projects.

- Define process capability (1): Define process capability characteristics, metrics, evaluation methods, and responsible parties.
- Plan analysis and evaluation (2): Plan to analyze process capability by comparing pre- and post-implementation results in four similar home loan service software development projects conducted between 2017-2022. These projects share characteristics such as function, development time, and budget.
- Analyze variance (3): Analyze project performance variance from the estimation plan, encompassing cost, time, scope, and effort. This data complements process capability evaluation using calculation formula 1.

$$v = \frac{x-\mu}{\sigma} \tag{1}$$

6.2 Assessment of Satisfaction From the Implementation of the Improved Process

- Develop data collection Tool (1): Create a tool for collecting feedback on the improved process implementation. Gather input from project managers, developer team members, customers, and demand oversight directors through surveys or interviews.
- Calculate satisfaction percentage (2): Use formula 2 to quantify satisfaction levels with the improved process implementation.

$$= \frac{F \times 100}{n} \tag{2}$$

- Calculate average satisfaction (3) (Likert, 1961): Compute the average satisfaction level using formula 3 to gauge stakeholders' overall satisfaction with the implemented process.

$$\bar{X} = \frac{\sum x}{n} \tag{3}$$

7. Evaluate the Proposed Improvement Process by SCAMPI Method

The evaluation of achieving Capability Level 3 (SEI, 2011; Tachanunachanun et al., 2012) requires passing the assessments and achieving Capability Level 2 first, following the sequence of Level 1 and Level 2. At each level, the evaluation report must receive specific rankings, namely: For Capability Level 1 (CL1): The report must receive a majority or full score (Largely or Fully). For Capability Level 2 (CL2): The report must receive a full score (Fully). For Capability Level 3 (CL3): The report must receive a full score (Fully). Table 10 illustrates the scoring ranges and their corresponding symbols and meanings. There are four ranges, each denoting different levels of achievement: Score percentage 0-15: Symbol N, meaning Not Achieved. Score 16-50%: Symbol P, meaning Partially Achieved. Score 51-85%: Symbol L, meaning Largely Achieved. Score 86-100%: Symbol F, meaning Fully Achieved.

Table 10. Score range, symbol and description

Score Range (%)	Symbol	Description
0–15	N	Not achieved
16–50	P	Partially achieved
51–85	L	Largely achieved
86–100	F	Fully achieved

The report must receive a The evaluation of process capability is reported based on the results of the assessment of CMMI process practice outcomes (Ehsan et al., 2010), to achieve Capability Level 3, the organization must undergo assessments and meet the specified ranking criteria for each level (CL1, CL2, and CL3) based on the percentage scores, as outlined in Table 10. The evaluation process is crucial to determine the maturity and effectiveness of the implemented process and its alignment with CMMI standards.

MEASUREMENT OF PROCESS IMPROVEMENT

Small and medium-sized software companies have implemented the improved process in two home loan service software development projects. The duration of these projects was six months, during which data was collected, analyzed, and evaluated to assess the process improvement objectives. The comprehensive assessment covered four aspects: (1) Evaluation of Supporting Tools and Specific Practices. (2) Evaluation of satisfaction of using the improvement process. (3) Measurements of the process capability before and after applying the proposed improvement process. (4) Assessment of the proposed process of improvement using SCAMPI method.

1. Evaluation of Supporting Tools and Specific Practices

The assessment of tools and practices aligned with the defined requirements management process aimed to ensure their effective utilization in the projects. Expert assessors from external organizations, project managers, and development team representatives evaluated these tools based on CMMI practices, leading to the following findings:

1. Seamless User Interaction: The tools effectively supported all five specific practices (SP1.1-SP1.5) of the requirements management process and four generic practices (GP2.3, GP2.6, GP2.8, and GP3.2), resulting in the creation of 12 essential work products. These tools facilitated the storage and management of data, inputs, and outputs required for process evaluation.
2. Suitable for Small and Medium-sized Organizations: The assessed tools were deemed suitable for small and medium-sized software companies. They provided flexibility in tailoring to project-specific characteristics, promoting standardized software development and requirements management aligned with CMMI Level 3 capabilities.

Table 11. User satisfaction with project tools' capabilities

Evaluation Topics	Mean	S.D.
1. Project management data handling tools.	4.00	0.53
2. Requirements management data handling tools.	4.31	0.54
3. Test case management data handling tools.	4.37	0.66
4. Change request management data handling tools.	4.52	0.51
5. Project progress status tracking tools.	4.28	0.59
6. Change request status tracking tools.	4.55	0.51
7. Tools to create requirement traceability matrices.	4.37	0.60
8. Tools for generating various reports related to requirement management.	4.48	0.56
9. Tools for checking the status of requirement change requests.	4.59	0.57
10. Tools for approving requirement change requests.	4.44	0.58
Average	**4.391**	**0.565**

In Table 11, the evaluation demonstrates the efficiency of these tools in supporting requirements management, enhancing collaboration among project stakeholders, and ensuring compliance with CMMI standards. The results consistently show high user satisfaction ratings for project tools' capabilities, further affirming their effectiveness in improving the software development process.

2. Evaluation of Satisfaction of Using the Improvement Process

The satisfaction of project teams and stakeholders, which includes project managers, developers, customers, and demand controllers, was measured to assess the benefits resulting from the process implementation, for both the projects and the organization as a whole. Table 12 displays the user satisfaction results for the improvement process and requirements management, with an average score of 4.306 and a standard deviation of 0.580. Furthermore, Table 13 outlines the findings of a survey conducted to evaluate the adoption of the hybrid model in the software development process, with an average rating of 4.423 and a standard deviation of 0.599.

Table 12. User satisfaction of process and requirements management

Evaluation Topics	Mean	S.D.
1. Software project management.	4.00	0.53
2. Software requirements documentation	4.31	0.54
3. Software requirements change control	4.52	0.57
4. Software test case management	4.17	0.66
5. Software requirements traceability.	4.31	0.66
6. Software project progress tracking.	4.28	0.59
7. Preparing evidence for process capability assessment	4.55	0.51
Average	**4.306**	**0.580**

Table 13. User satisfaction of improved process model (HSDM)

Evaluation Topics	Mean	S.D.
1. Suitable for the home loan software service project of the bank.	4.38	0.62
2. Appropriate for small to medium-sized software development teams.	4.55	0.51
3. Flexibility in adapting work practices to fit the requirements of the bank's home loan software service.	4.52	0.57
4. Prioritizing process execution and deliverable generation equally.	4.28	0.65
5. Having activity steps that align with the RTM Tool for process improvement in CMMI.	4.41	0.63
6. Capable of accessing and understanding the real work practices of the software development team.	4.45	0.63
7. Suitable for iterative work and project software evolution.	4.17	0.58
Average	**4.423**	**0.599**

Overall, user satisfaction, as shown in Table 11, 12, and 13, was found to be at a good level, with an average score of 4.373 and a standard deviation of 0.581. This indicates that the implemented changes and the adoption of the hybrid model were well-received by the users and met their expectations. The positive feedback from users demonstrates the effectiveness of the improvement process and its impact on requirements management in software development projects. The average score reflects the overall contentment and approval of the users with the enhanced process and the hybrid model, validating their successful integration into the organization's practices.

3. Process Capability Measurements: Before and After Improvement

The author conducted an experiment on two software projects, the Mortgage Loan System and Home Loan Tracing, as shown in Table 14. The author analyzed the measurements of the improved software development process in comparison with two previous projects. All four projects offered similar functionality for home loan services but were developed for different customers, namely banks. The duration of these software projects ranged from 6 to 8 months, and the budget for each project did not exceed 18,000 USD.

Table 14. Measurements of the process before and after improvement

Evaluation Topics	Difference of Capability				Average
	1: Mortgage Loan System		2: Home Loan Tracing		
	Before	After	Before	After	
1. Flexibility of small teams to align with CMMI standards.	47.98	85.89	48.11	85.54	37.67
2. Capability to assess process capabilities.	47.58	86.00	48.28	85.20	37.67
3. Ability to measure process efficiency.	47.25	83.53	45.51	83.23	37.00
4. Capability to continuously improve team workflows.	63.16	88.16	63.00	88.00	25.00
Average					**34.34**

Table 14 illustrates the evaluation results for each project. Figure 14 showcases an example of the outcomes, comparing the projects before and after implementing the proposed improvement process.

Figure 14. Difference of capability

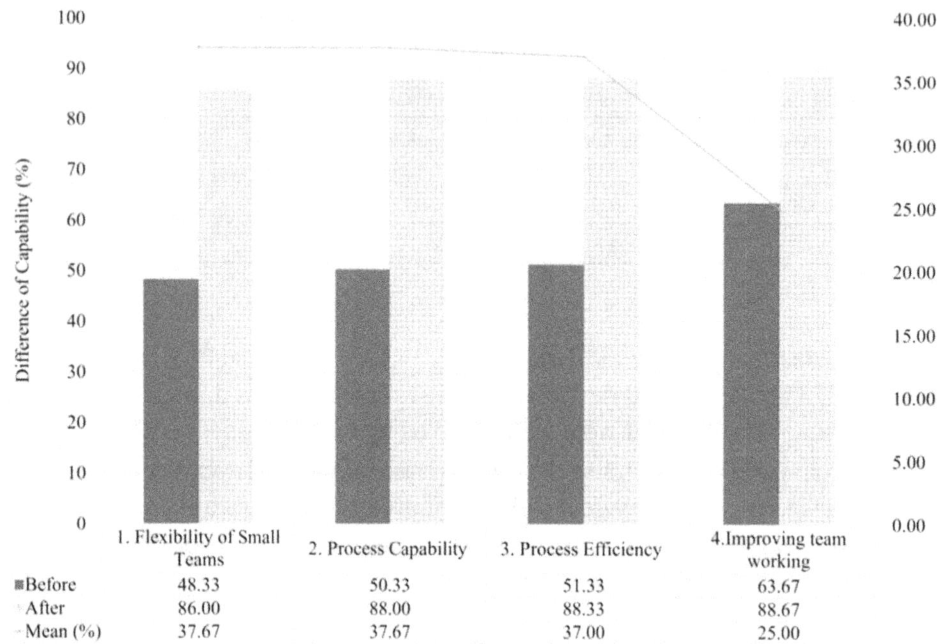

In summary, the evaluation of the software projects after implementing the proposed improvement process showed significant positive results. The comparison between projects before and after the improvement process demonstrated an overall difference of 34.34%, indicating a substantial improvement in the software development process. The improvement process led to remarkable advancements in various aspects:

- Flexibility: The projects exhibited a notable increase of 37.67% in their flexibility, allowing for better adaptation to changing requirements and business needs.
- Process Capability: The process capability saw a significant improvement of 37.67%, indicating better control and predictability in project execution.
- Efficiency: The projects became 37.00% more efficient, leading to faster development cycles and improved resource utilization.
- Team Working: The improvement process resulted in a 25.00% enhancement in team collaboration and coordination, promoting a more cohesive and productive working environment.

Overall, the results demonstrated that the adoption of the proposed improvement process positively impacted the software projects' performance and contributed to achieving the organization's objectives more effectively and efficiently.

4. Assessment of the Proposed Process of Improvement Using SCAMPI Method

The author evaluated the capability of the improved process using SCAMPI. This evaluation involved checking the results obtained from following the defined process and activities in the HSDM, including examining the work products from the tool's responsory evaluation. The purpose of the assessment was to ensure that the project implemented the recommended practices in the CMMI component structure Class C. The evaluation team consisted of three skilled and experienced assessors, including the lead appraiser, who person trained, and experienced. It is important to note that this assessment was solely intended to report the achievement of the research work's objectives and not to seek certification from the SEI institute. Table 15 presents the results of the process capability assessment, indicating that the improvement process has successfully achieved Capability Level 3 according to the CMMI standards.

Table 15. Results of process capability assessment

Capability Level (CL)	Generic Goals	Assessment Score (%)	Rating
CL1	GG1: Achieve Specific Goals	100.00	Fully
CL2	GG2: Institutionalize a Managed Process	86.67	Fully
CL3	GG3. Institutionalize a Defined Process	88.22	Fully

- The generic goal GG1, which involves defining the requirements management process and controlling changes to improve efficiency and meet customer needs, scored 100% (Fully), demonstrating the process's capability at Level 1.
- Goal GG2 focused on evaluating whether development aligns with the defined process in GG1 and complies with organizational policies through planning, monitoring, and stakeholder cooperation, scoring 86.67% (Fully), indicating the process capability at Level 2.
- Additionally, GG3, centered around developing tools to support GG2 and enforcing the practice throughout the organization, with projects aligning their processes and procedures to the organization's standard, scored 88.22% (Fully), showcasing the process capability at Level 3.

In conclusion, the assessment reveals that the software development and requirements management process has achieved Capability Level 3, in line with the research objectives. More detailed assessment results for different capability levels are available in Table 16.

Based on the evaluation results in Table 16, 15 out of 17 CMMI indicators were successfully implemented, resulting in an 88.22% score, contributing to achieving Level 3 process capability. However, some issues were identified, particularly in the team's requirements management practices, where the team's structure lacked clarity. The assessor suggested addressing Generic Practice GP2.3 and GP2.5 to establish clear positions and responsibilities at the organizational level to improve requirements management across projects.

Table 16. Capability levels assessment results

<table>
<tr><th colspan="3">Process Area Components</th><th rowspan="2">Indicator</th><th rowspan="2">Score</th><th rowspan="2">CL</th></tr>
<tr><th>Type: Required</th><th>Type: Expected</th><th>Type: Expected</th></tr>
<tr><td>GG1</td><td>GP1.1</td><td>SP1.1-SP1.5</td><td>5</td><td>5</td><td>1</td></tr>
<tr><td colspan="6">Summary Rating value: (5/5) x 100 = 100%
Process Rating: ☐ N ☐ P ☐ L ☑ F
Summary Capability Level 1 ☑ Pass ☐ Not pass</td></tr>
<tr><td>GG2</td><td>GP1.1, GP2.1-GP2.10</td><td>All SP</td><td>15</td><td>13</td><td>2</td></tr>
<tr><td colspan="6">Summary Rating value: (13/15) x 100 = 86.67%
Process Rating: ☐ N ☐ P ☐ L ☑ F
Summary Capability Level 2 ☑ Pass ☐ Not pass</td></tr>
<tr><td>GG3</td><td>GP1.1, GP2.1-GP2.10, GP3.1-GP3.2</td><td>All SP</td><td>17</td><td>15</td><td>3</td></tr>
<tr><td colspan="6">Summary Rating value: (15/17) x 100 = 88.22%
Process Rating: ☐ N ☐ P ☐ L ☑ F
Summary Capability Level 3 ☑ Pass ☐ Not pass</td></tr>
</table>

Additionally, Generic Practice GP2.8, involving direct confirmation of software product quality from monitoring and requirements management activities, was not fully met. The assessor recommended improving the relationship between requirements management and software product quality assurance in future improvement cycles.

Despite these observations, the process achieved 86.67% in Level 2 and 88.22% in Level 3, demonstrating that the improvement process aligns with CMMI objectives for both levels.

CONCLUSION

The evaluation of the proposed improvement process aimed at achieving CMMI Level 3 in requirements development and management has yielded positive results. The tools and practices demonstrated effective alignment with CMMI standards, rendering them suitable for small and medium-sized companies. User satisfaction with the process and HSDM model was notably high, averaging a score of 4.373, with requirements management receiving the highest satisfaction rating at 4.550, particularly among small and medium-sized teams. The implemented improvements have notably enhanced flexibility (37.67%), process capability (37.67%), efficiency (37.00%), and team collaboration (25.00%). The SCAMPI assessment has successfully confirmed the process's attainment of Capability Level 3, with generic goals GG1, GG2, and GG3 scoring 100%, 86.67%, and 88.22%, respectively, representing levels 1, 2, and 3. However, it's worth noting that while most CMMI indicators were met (88.22%), certain areas, such as team structure within requirements management (GP2.3, GP2.5) and product quality assurance (GP2.8), require further attention.

In summary, the evaluation and assessment unequivocally endorse the effectiveness of the proposed improvement process in software development and requirements management. Future research should encompass benchmarking studies and comparative analyses with other organizations to identify best practices. Drawing insights from successful implementations in similar industries can inform effective strategies. Furthermore, evaluating the long-term impact of the improvement process on software projects and organizational performance is of paramount importance. Continuous monitoring and measuring outcomes over time can validate the sustained benefits, ensuring its enduring success.

Additionally, exploring the integration of agile methodologies and DevOps practices into the improvement process holds the potential to enhance adaptability, collaboration, and continuous delivery. This optimization of the entire software development lifecycle can lead to higher-quality products, improved project outcomes, and greater organizational success. Nonetheless, it's essential to acknowledge that this research, despite its adaptability and industry specificity, may have limitations in terms of generalizability due to its narrow focus and limited sample size. Moreover, the absence of a comparative analysis and potential subjectivity in expert evaluations pose certain constraints. Nonetheless, this research represents a commendable effort in addressing challenges in a specific industry and providing insights into hybrid process improvement methodologies.

REFERENCES

Ardana, I. M. S., & Suharjito. (2017). Software development evaluation process using CMMI-Dev on limited resources company. In *2017 3rd International Conference on Science in Information Technology (ICSITech)* (pp. 319-324). . doi:10.1109/ICSITech.2017.8257132

Chaiyan, P., AnuKul, T., & Ployravee, K. (2017). Standard interpret: ISO/IEC TR 29110 management and engineering guide: basic profile (1st ed.). Ministry of Information and Communication Technology, Bangkok, Thailand.

Dennis, A., Wixom, B. H., & Tegarden, D. (2009). *System Analysis Design UML Version 2.0: An Object-Oriented Approach*. John Wiley & Sons.

Ehsan, N., Perwaiz, A., Arif, J., Mirza, E., & Ishaque, A. (2010). CMMI / SPICE based process improvement. In *2010 IEEE International Conference on Management of Innovation & Technology* (pp. 859-862). IEEE. 10.1109/ICMIT.2010.5492803

IEEE. (1998). *IEEE Guide for Software Requirements Specification (ANSI/IEEE Std. 830-1998)*. Institute of Electrical and Electronics Engineers, Inc.

IEEE. (2006). *ANSI/IEEE Standard for Developing a Software Project Life Cycle Process (IEEE Std. 1074-2006)*. Institute of Electrical and Electronics Engineers, Inc.

IEEE. (2008). *ANSI/IEEE Standard Information Technology-Software Life Cycle Process, IEEE/EIA Std*. Institute of Electrical and Electronics Engineers, Inc.

International Organization for Standardization. (2011). ISO Technical report for Systems and software engineering — Lifecycle profiles for Very Small Entities (VSEs) — Part 4-1: Profile specifications: Generic profile group (ISO/IEC 29110-4-1) (1st ed.).

International Organization for Standardization. (2016). *ISO/IEC TR 29110-1*. Systems and Software Engineering - Lifecycle profiles for Very Small Entities (VSEs) - Part 1: Overview.

Joembunthanaphong, P., & Sriharee, G. (2022). The Improvement Process for The Software Development and Requirements Management to Achieve Capability Level 3 of CMMI. In *2022 26th International Computer Science and Engineering Conference (ICSEC)* (pp. 296-301). 10.1109/ICSEC56337.2022.10049356

Kamal Najjar, S., & Al-Sarayreh, K. T. (2015). Capability Maturity Model of Software Requirements Process and Integration (SRPCMMI). ACM.

Likert, R. A. (1961). *New Patterns of Management*. McGraw-Hill Book Company, Inc.

Lina, Z., & Dan, S. (2012). Research on Combining Scrum with CMMI in Small and Medium Organizations. In *2012 International Conference on Computer Science and Electronics Engineering* (pp. 554-557). 10.1109/ICCSEE.2012.477

Pressman, R. S. (2010). *Software Engineering: A Practitioner's Approach* (7th ed.). McGraw-Hill, Inc.

Saastamoinen, I., & Tukiainen, M. (2004). Software Process Improvement in Small and Medium Sized Software Enterprises in Eastern Finland: A State-of-the-Practice Study. In T. Dingsøyr (Ed.), *EuroSPI 2004* (pp. 69–78). Springer-Verlag Berlin Heidelberg. doi:10.1007/978-3-540-30181-3_7

SEI. (2011). Method Definition Document of Standard CMMI Appraisal Method for Process Improvement. SCAMPIsm. Software Engineering Institute, Carnegie Mellon University.

SEI. (2018). *Capability Maturity Model Integration. CMMI® V2.0 for Development, Version 2.3*. Software Engineering Institute.

Sommerville, I., & Sawyer, P. (1997). *Requirements Engineering: A Good Practice Guide* (1st ed.). John Wiley & Sons Ltd.

Tachanunachanun, K., Apinporn, M., & Chayakorn, P. (2012). Technical Challenges of CMMI-based Assessment Team. *International Journal of Digital Content Technology and its Applications, 6*(21), 101-110. doi:10.4156/jdcta.vol6.issue21.10

Tariq, A., Khan, S. A., & Iftikhar, S. (2014). Remapping of CMMI level-2 KPA's for development process improvement of Software-as-a-Service (SaaS) cloud environment. In *2014 International Conference on Open Source Systems & Technologies* (pp. 43-51). 10.1109/ICOSST.2014.7029318

ADDITIONAL READING

Hunter, R. B., Thayer, R. H., & Paulk, M. C. (2001). *Software Process Improvement*. Wiley-IEEE Computer Society Press.

Kotonya, G., & Sommerville, I. (1998). *Requirements Engineering: Processes and Techniques*. Wiley.

KEY TERMS AND DEFINITIONS

Agile (Scrum): An iterative and flexible software development approach that emphasizes collaboration, adaptability, and customer feedback.

CL3 (Capability Level 3): A maturity level within CMMI that indicates a high level of process maturity and capability in an organization, often requiring specific criteria and practices.

CMMI (Capability Maturity Model Integration): CMMI is a framework that helps organizations improve their processes and systems. It provides a set of best practices and guidelines for achieving higher levels of maturity and capability in various domains, including software development.

Home-Loan Services Software: Streamlines and manages home loan processes for banks. It includes credit assessment, interest rate calculations, document management, and customer communication to improve efficiency.

HSDM (Hybrid Software Development Methodology): Is a customized approach for small to medium-sized software companies with 25-30 team members, ideal for projects with frequent changes and unclear requirements, like banking software development. It blends Waterfall Model and Agile (Scrum) elements to create a flexible and efficient development process.

Process Improvement: Refers to the enhancement and refinement of software development and requirements management processes.

Requirements Management: The systematic process of documenting, analyzing, and controlling software requirements throughout the development lifecycle to ensure they are well-defined and meet stakeholder needs.

SCAMPI (Standard CMMI Appraisal Method for Process Improvement): Uses the CMMI model to assess an organization's process maturity and capability. In research, it's the method used to evaluate process improvement effectiveness.

Waterfall Model: A traditional linear software development approach where each phase must be completed before the next one begins, typically used for projects with well-defined requirements.

Chapter 6
Digital Transformation Risks and Uncertainties in European Union and Indian Industry

Anitha Kumari
https://orcid.org/0000-0002-8343-8926
GITAM University (Deemed), India

ABSTRACT

The speed of digital transformation and disruptive technologies influence a company's competitive edge. The fourth industrial revolution and digitalization have the potential to touch all areas of an organisation at the same time. This creates a conflict between digitalizing an existing, successful business and creating new, fully digitalized enterprises. The aim of the study is to determine the risks and uncertainties of digital transformation in the European Union and the Indian industry. The literature review provides insight into the concept of digital transformation in businesses. This study developed a digital strategy model and a digital transformation risks and uncertainties framework. Secondary data and statistics on business digitization in the European Union and Indian industries are presented. This chapter focuses on mitigating risks and uncertainties associated with the digital transformation of the European Union and Indian industry as a whole, including research that provides the direction for digitalization in all businesses.

1. INTRODUCTION

Technological innovation is rapidly changing the world. The industrial revolution paved the way for globalisation, connection, and the foundations of modern society and wealth. Digital transformation is the process of integrating new digital technologies into all business sectors, resulting in a dramatic shift in how the firm functions. Digital disruption raises the emergence of new competitors or new entrants who have mastered digital business skillsets and have developed solutions, business models, and approaches that have a significant impact on customer behaviour and market context, forcing existing players to change their strategies as a result. The solution had the biggest market share based on a component,

DOI: 10.4018/979-8-3693-0458-7.ch006

while the services had the fastest growth rate. Digital technologies and approaches are penetrating every aspect of business. The internet of things, ubiquitous connectivity, big data and analytic capabilities, cloud computing, blockchain, artificial intelligence, and robotics are significantly changing nearly all industries. Corporate governance and business models have all been affected as a result of digitization. Improvements in infrastructure and analytical skills in information technologies (IT) during the last decade have spurred new business model innovations at all levels. This has given corporations an advantage in nearly every economic sector (Grover and Kohli, 2013; Bleicher and Stanley, 2016).

Digital transformation is accelerating on a large scale that has never been seen before, introducing new risks and uncertainties. People, businesses, and governments planning for the future can no longer rely on the idea that the future will be much like the present. Instead, they must plan for a wide range of possible futures as well as the new possibilities and challenges that may arise. A strategy and policy framework formed today can withstand and adapt to the changes brought about by digital transformation and the direction, pace, and extent of those changes if they are developed using this approach. This way, they can be resilient and adaptable (OECD, 2020). Transformational changes within a company are in high demand in order to expand the business and compete in today's changing business environment. Enhancing the customer experience, operational agility, and the integration of digital technologies are all part of the transformative process as a whole. In countries like Europe and India, cloud computing and big data analytics are two digital transformation solutions that have contributed significantly to the rapid growth of the digital transformation market.

The European Union's institutions, as well as its capacity for cross-border collaboration, are crucial for both supporting and implementing the digital economy. To ensure that this collaboration is operative and produces the desired outcomes, it must be customised to the characteristics and diversity of particular European Union member states. Indian institutions have made real progress in integrating new technology into numerous sectors, and a number of industries are undergoing digital transformation. Alternatively, the level of penetration varies according to the requirements of different industries. The Indian business environment is being reshaped by megatrends such as technology, globalisation, exponential technology usage, and demographic changes, among other things. The concept of Industry 4.0 and digitalization processes are receiving more attention in academic research (Osterrieder, 2020; Nick G, 2020; Castro HF, 2020; Basl, 2017; Castelo-Branco, 2019; Moeuf et al., 2017; Hofmann, 2017; Santos et al., 2017; Smit, 2016). Only the most relevant articles on the subject were included in this study. The purpose of this review was to familiarise authors with studies that examined the digitalization, robotics, and automation processes of businesses, sectors, and countries, as well as the evaluation methods applied so far to assess these developments.

The objective of the research is to determine the risks and uncertainties of digital transformation in the European Union and Indian industry. This study focuses on organisational performance management, such as technical, economic, socio-cultural, political, and environmental perspectives. Existing organisations in various industries have the possibility to become more digital with new technologies. Changes to essential company activities, organisational structures, goods, and services are required to manage these complex shifts. Society as a whole is undergoing immense change as a result of the growth of digital technologies and their widespread use across all industries. This study identifies the key perspectives for action that emerge from the scenario analysis of digital transformation. Furthermore, the digitalization of business has become a growing focus in the European Union and Indian industry. This paper focuses on mitigating risks and uncertainties associated with the digital transformation of the European Union and Indian industry as a whole, including research that provides the direction for digitalization in all businesses. The paper is structured into five parts. The introduction to the study is presented in the first section. The second part presents the literature review with emphasis on the proposed business strategy model and digital risk evaluation framework. The third part presents the methodology. The fourth part is dedicated to the discussions on the perspectives and viewpoints on mitigating risks and uncertainties associated with digital transformation in businesses in the EU and India. The fifth part is dedicated to the conclusions based on the perceptions.

2. REVIEW OF LITERATURE

2.1 Digital Transformation

The term "digital transformation" refers to the process of changing business and organisational processes, competencies, and models. These transformations take advantage of the changes and possibilities inherent in the digital technology mix, accelerating their effect in a strategic manner that takes current and future shifts into account. Digital transformation is crucial for most firms, large and small. Businesses must evolve to stay competitive and relevant in an increasingly digital world. Digital transformation presents a challenge for management since the ramifications extend beyond industry structures and strategic positioning to the entire value chain. Digital transformation has resulted in a rapidly changing corporate environment that offers exponentially expanding potential for new capabilities and initiatives. It is very important for businesses today to be able to adapt quickly to changes in the digital world. It's possible for businesses to plan a long-term digital journey that can be scaled and changed. This includes a well-defined digital strategy, a good business case, and a personal and flexible method. With digital transformation, companies must also keep an eye on the risks that come into the environment and how they might change the ecosystem. This way, they can get the most out of their digital activities. Businesses can't ignore the opportunities and threats that the changing environment presents, but they also can't ignore how important going digital will be to them and how important it will be for them (Deloitte, 2018).

Global economic growth and citizen well-being can both benefit greatly from the digital transformation that has already begun in many countries and areas. Although its consequences will be seen in practically all aspects of technical, economic, social, cultural, political, and environment. It is expected to have an impact in both positive and negative ways (El Massah, 2020; Jafari, 2021; Kraus, 2021). The most important digital transformation technologies, which have found widespread useful application, are primarily communication technologies, data collection technologies, as well as technologies for processing and analysing data (Javaid et al., 2020; Szabo et al., 2020; Yuksel, 2020). The process of digital transformation has emerged as a critical instrument for increasing the productivity and competitiveness of businesses, which are continuously on the lookout for new and inventive ways to improve the efficiency and competitiveness of their operations. New business structures, product definitions, and consumer interaction styles are required to attain this goal (Dery, 2017). The digital transformation of businesses and complete economies that is related to the concept of Industry 4.0 affects a wide range of their activities and all of their resource allocation decisions (Ashrafi, 2015; Mithas, 2013).

2.2 Industry 4.0 and Business Digitalization in European Union

Industry 4.0 innovation has facilitated the development of new technologies such as collaborative robots, single-axis robots, SCARA robots, and AI-powered robots. They have enabled the robotics sector to streamline processes, increase efficiency, and reduce mistake rates. Businesses are investing heavily in robotic systems in order to increase workplace safety and manufacturing capability. As a result, industrial robotics will become a new trend in the market for digital transformation. The growing demand for industrial automation is one of the factors driving the digital transformation market's rise. The growing adoption of wireless communication and other advanced technologies across a variety of industries and verticals is likely to drive demand for and growth in the digital transformation market. Numerous sectors, including banking, healthcare, energy, power, education, and manufacturing, are investing heavily in automation services in order to see immediate and positive results in terms of process improvement. These sectors have begun the journey to total digitalization by integrating smart systems and Internet of Things sensors into their processes.

Europe's digital transformation industry is expected to have strong growth in upcoming years as a result of factors such as increased adoption of digital services across multiple sectors. However, the increased frequency of security breaches, cyber-attacks, and growing privacy concerns may limit the regional market's growth. The regional digital transformation market is categorised due to the region's diverse industries and competitive environment. Additionally, various government-led projects are underway to accelerate the digital transformation industry in the European region. The goal of digital transformation is to use smart technology to build new business models, processes, and software that are more profitable, competitively advantageous, and successful than the ones that currently exist.

2.3 Industry 4.0 and Business Digitalization in India

For Industry 4.0 as the technological revolution, it may be beneficial to take a systemic approach and analyse three key components of each revolution: technological advancements, economic scenarios, and demographic situations. In recent years, a new collection of technologies has arisen. This is the fourth industrial revolution's starting point. Cyber Physical Systems (CPS) are Industry 4.0's primary technology. It is a synthesis of cybernetic and physical systems (Lee et al., 2015), in which the two systems operate as a single unit. It is applicable to a wide variety of industries. The CPS was developed in response to significant technological advancements in the domains of the internet, computer science, embedded systems, and artificial intelligence (AI). The convergence of these technologies has the potential to create havoc. Industry 4.0 adoption requires both private and public sector investment. Despite advancements in information technology and electronics, expenditures on infrastructure, equipment, education, and training are important (Kagermann et al., 2013). The trade-off between investments and gains is context-dependent. The rivalry to innovate has created an active market, which has eroded competitive advantages. It puts pressure on businesses to continuously adopt. Simultaneously, teamwork is becoming increasingly vital in order to innovate (Chesbrough, 2006).

There are a number of benefits. For example, it boosts productivity growth in a variety of industries while also improving worldwide competitiveness. Aside from these two benefits, enhanced analytics would also aid in increasing manufacturing capability and improving product quality. This manufacturing strategy would shift toward failure prevention and prediction via data analytics. Automation and robotics would shorten the manufacturing cycle, reduce time to market, and remove unnecessary resource usage.

This digitization of numerous company operations will result in cost savings as well as a better customer and staff experience. The Internet of Things, along with machine-to-machine and machine-to-machine connections, would tighten the supply chain and minimise wait times. According to McKinsey, implementing Industry 4.0 across functions like manufacturing, supply chain, logistics, and procurement may enhance operational profits by 40% while spending only 10% of the capital budget. However, India's adoption of Industry 4.0 is still in its early stages (Engineer Souls, 2019). Widespread deployment seems to be years away because it needs a big initial investment, there are not enough experts, the infrastructure is not good enough, and there are no rules about cyber security.

2.4 Digital Strategy

The object of digital strategy is to harness technology to improve corporate performance, whether through new product development or product redesign. It defines an organization's plan for generating new competitive advantages through technology, as well as the tactics it will use to accomplish this goal. Changes in business models are prevalent when new technology enables innovative firms to supply previously inaccessible services. Today, technology is so integrated into business that it transcends hardware and software. In the next few years, as digital technology becomes more prominent and firms embark on a journey of digital transformation, the terms "digital strategy" and "business strategy" will become interchangeable. For the time being, it is still appropriate to refer to digital strategy as such, since it is used to direct attention to digital activity. Always remember that digital strategy is both a concept and a physical object; that is, it should ultimately result in the construction of a precise plan or roadmap. Digital strategy must become the foundation of company strategy. There is a tendency to use the terms "digital transformation" and "digital strategy" interchangeably. The two names are related but have different meanings. Change is driven by digital transformation in three areas: customer experience, operational procedures, and business models. A collaborative approach throughout the whole organisation is required, as is a shift in corporate culture as part of the digital transformation process.

However, digital strategy is concerned with technology rather than culture. When it comes to shifting business models, digital strategy is particularly essential since it makes use of technology to build digital business capabilities. Setting a plan ensures that technology is applied in a way that supports business objectives. While digital strategy seeks to use technology to transform activities and thus the company, IT strategy seeks to transform technology in isolation. Traditionally, IT strategy has determined which technologies to invest in based on the current business orientation. Instead, digital strategy focuses on transforming activities and processes to better serve customers. Then it searches for the ideal mix of technologies and techniques to produce these experiences. This shift in strategy has given digital leaders new competitive advantages and growth prospects (Christine Reyes, 2021). Instead, digital strategy focuses on transforming activities and processes to better serve customers. It's common for digital strategy to examine whether new technology will truly complement or grow the existing business. Digital transformation aims to establish a solid basis for digital business. This means building a company that can constantly reinvent itself to meet changing customer needs and expectations. A company's digital strategy should have enough foresight to keep up with the rapid developments in the digital market.

Figure 1. Digital strategy model
Source: Christine Reyes (2021)

2.6 Digital Transformation Risks and Uncertainties Framework

A framework based on digital transformation to analyse digital risks and uncertainties in business strategies is presented in this section and illustrated in Figure 2. The approach uses the digital transformation of the EU and India to determine the benefits and risks associated with the development of industries. The impact of new constraints on the digital disruption of industries. This knowledge is used to determine the risks and uncertainties of digital transformations in the European Union and Indian industries, which include overall benefits and variances. This framework effectively captures the difficulties associated with determining risks and uncertainties, guided by a proven scenario method (Yadong Luo, 2021).

Digital risk refers to the likelihood of a bad event occurring as a result of external or internal vulnerabilities that endanger the operation of a company's operations. When it comes to international business, we describe "digital risk" as uncertainty or disruption induced by digitalization pressures in nations where the multinational enterprise (MNE) operates or competes and which has a negative influence on the company's operations. Globalization is entering a new era of disruptions and adversities that are increasing both new and old business risks. Digital connectivity, on the other hand, is a double-edged sword that may both allow and impede cross-border operations. Digitized connectedness is made possible by digital platforms, information and communication technologies (ICT), internet and intranet access, and other digital technology enablers such as cloud services, big data, as well as data analytics and artificial intelligence. Cross-border transactions are strengthened as a result of digitalization, which also transmits a rich stream of innovation and ideas around the world (Banalieva & Dhanaraj, 2019;

Hennart, 2019; Kano, 2018; Tallman, Luo, & Buckley, 2018). However, in addition to the benefits, there are inherent hazards associated with digital technology, with the following three types of digital risks deserving of further discussion:

Figure 2. Digital risk evaluation framework
Source: Yadong Luo (2021)

2.6.1 Digital Interdependence

Digital interdependence risks manifest themselves as unexpected contagions, interruptions, and breakdowns caused by digital interconnectivity between a focal MNE and its worldwide business partners, corporate members, vendors, distributors, suppliers, and customers in a variety of locations across the globe. International companies are becoming increasingly reliant on one another as a result of digital globalisation, and as a result, they are becoming more vulnerable to the consequences of all threats facing them and their partnering units (McKinsey, 2020). The consequences of external shocks are expanded in a more interconnected, digital world, and current effects spread more quickly as a result. The global financial crisis of 2008 showed how quickly contagion may spread when there are connections between the world's major markets. Digital connectivity speeds up and spreads the bad effects of a global platform's failure, whether it affects the whole platform or just a part of it. This shows the digital fragility caused by interdependence and interconnection.

2.6.2 Global Cybersecurity

Global cybersecurity risk refers to the possibility of loss or injury as a result of an MNE's information and communication systems being vulnerable to cyberattacks or data breaches. Digitization opens up worldwide markets and makes MNEs increasingly reliant on data, information, and ICT infrastructure. Global clients are wary of using a digital outlet that does not protect their privacy and gives the best performance, security, availability, and dependability (UNCTAD, 2015; Nambisan et al., 2017). With new technology comes new risks, including security breaches, fraud, service disruptions, and service level failures. Many MNEs have already experienced internal and external security breaches, a new type of IB risk with economic and social repercussions (World Bank, 2016). Indirect harm from such breaches can be huge and difficult to repair, including loss of important data, business reputation, and consumer trust. For these reasons, businesses must address hazards beyond physical security.

Cybercrime, cyberterrorism, and cyberespionage are well-known threats to national security. However, information security cyber-attacks are a new IB risk for nearly all MNEs. As worldwide transactions and procedures grow more digital, so do global organisations' vulnerabilities to cyber-attacks (Kshetri, 2005). Many of the world's major firms have previously been hacked. It is estimated that cybercrime damages the world economy by around US$400 billion every year. Cyber-attacks will almost certainly increase in number and impact more firms in the future, especially those lacking in technology and security skills. While tools like firewalls have become commonplace for safeguarding devices and zones, modern risk management demands a managed-service strategy to cover entire IT ecosystems. Development and operations (DevOps) have become a service in cyber security.

2.6.3 Regulatory Complexity

Digital regulatory complexity risk is caused by the many different regulations, rules, and standards that are in place in the countries where an MNE does business. This creates a lot of regulatory multiplicity, variance, and incompatibility, which makes cross-border activities more difficult (Oxley & Yeung, 2001). However, many governments, both in developed and developing countries, are getting stricter about how they protect people's data. This includes a wide range of things. The scope of regulations is getting bigger, with more attention being paid to things like digital taxes, customer protection, national security, and information security. It is because of these regulations that people need to be ready for digital risks. For example, to get ready for the General Data Protection Regulation (GDPR) in Europe, banks and other financial organisations must take the necessary steps to improve their digital capabilities, such as putting in place advanced systems for managing client master data. Govindarajan et al. (2019) state that data generated by Indian citizens would be treated as a national asset. It would be kept safe inside India's borders and used to protect India's strategic and defence interests.

3. METHODOLOGY

The study's goal is to identify the risks and uncertainties associated with digital transformation in European Union and Indian industries. This study uses a descriptive approach to understand the effects of the risks and uncertainties brought on by the digital transformation on the economies of the European Union and India. The risks and uncertainties associated with the European and Indian industries were analysed through a thorough literature review and unobtrusive research methods. By reviewing secondary data and statistics on business digitalization in the European Union and Indian provinces across time and across economic sectors, we may draw conclusions (Saldana, Johnny, 2003). This study includes a review of the literature, which provides insight into the concept of digital transformation in businesses. The purpose of this study is to highlight the risks and uncertainties associated with the digital transformation of the European Union industry as a result of the changes brought about by the use of smart technology in all business sectors. This analysis is important because it highlights new potential for businesses in terms of observation in society and technology that will set the outline for efficiency in the new digital age and in the future. The research is structured to take into account the secondary data that has been chosen, thereby incorporating all of the conditions that make up the European Union's and India's technological, economic, socio-cultural, political, and environmental perspectives. This paper discusses mitigating risks and uncertainties associated with the digital transformation of the European Union and Indian industry as a whole, including research that provides the direction for digitalization in all businesses. The study identifies the developing industries in terms of digitalization for businesses as well as the most actual ways in which digitalization delivers enhanced value for organisations.

4. RESULTS AND DISCUSSION

Implementing disruptive technology to boost value creation, efficiency, and social welfare is at the heart of digital transformation. Corporate strategy studies have been conducted by several national governments, multilateral institutions, and industry associations to help guide their long-term strategies (Christof and Carlos, 2018). Digital transformation is accelerating change on a global scale never seen before, posing new risks and uncertainties. An interdisciplinary task force on the risks and uncertainties of integrated digital systems could look into a wide range of current and possible future risks related to building a stronger and more integrated digital information system. However, the economy's digital sector will expand. New technology, applications, and services are inevitable, but no one can foresee how and where these developments will manifest. Much depends on a company's adaptability in order to profit from this continuous array of risks and uncertainties. Today, it is essential to identify and coordinate all business components. For digital to become a reality and be maintained, corporate executives must adopt an enterprise-wide perspective. Companies must realise that digitization is not an IT issue, but rather an organisational revolution that affects every aspect of the organisation and must be controlled by the entire workforce.

4.1 Perspectives

Technological solutions could integrate mechanisms to separate data and store them in multiple locations, mechanisms to control and track access to information, mechanisms to extract only the minimum data required for a given need, and others. This includes situations related to both cybersecurity and the potential abuse of the system by users who gain access both illegally and legally. It is developing mitigation solutions in collaboration with key stakeholders that would feed into integrated data safeguarding solutions (OECD, 2021). Global competitiveness is explicitly emphasised in the European Commission's communication on industrial digitalisation. Europe must develop legislative measures that bolster its industrial leadership and capture the opportunities inherent in the platform economy. There is the potential to increase cognitive diversity and collective intelligence, allowing human workers to do a broader range of tasks, increase their efficiency, and engage in more creative, meaningful employment. The digitization of the economy and society has also had a dramatic effect on the functioning of their free market liberal democracies. It is important to change the way people learn in order to give them new skills and a focus on the future that will help them do well in digital work and society.

The European Commission is aware that administrative and legal uncertainties are a main inhibitor for industry concerning the use of big data in digitalisation. This group will work on a standardisation plan to identify and specify important standardisation priorities, with a focus on new technologies and domains critical to the digital economy. Political solutions could include partnerships with other governments to mutually audit each other's national safeguards. Cultural solutions could involve a high degree of awareness among citizens of the risks and signs of abuse, such that the population will not tolerate moves to weaken or remove safeguards (Fabian, 2021). The European Commission focuses on getting things done because it knows that there is no clear line between digitalizing industry and digitalizing other areas.

Table 1. Perspectives of risks and uncertainties of digital transformation

Perspective	Objective	Risks and Uncertainties
Technological	Improve the technical standards and regulatory framework. Maximize digital data security, transparency, autonomy, and trust.	Cybersecurity Potential abuse of the system Using new technologies
Economical	Develop and implement cutting-edge business models. Boost economic income, productivity, and value addition.	Cost or complexity of meeting regulations Lack of financial resources
Socio-cultural	Encourage a more innovative and collaborative culture in business and in the world at large.	Distribution channels Low demand for the innovative goods and services Lack of marketing expertise
Political	Improve the accessibility and quality of digital services that the public can use.	Administrative issues Legal issues
Environmental	Make and keep up digital communication infrastructures that are cheap, accessible, and reliable.	Market dominated by established competitors

4.2 Mitigating Risks and Uncertainties in European Union

New technologies are being used to establish or improve industrial practices, culture, and customer understandings in order to satisfy ever-changing market and corporate needs. As a result, businesses will operate and provide value to customers in fundamentally different ways going forward. A lot of new technologies are helping businesses transform, like blockchain technology and the internet of things (IoT), as well as cloud computing, big data, and artificial intelligence (AI). The digital transformation market may be segmented into artificial intelligence, IoT, cloud-based, and others based on type. Cloud computing is expected to account for 49.38 percent of the market. From 2021 to 2026, the global digital transformation market is expected to grow at a rate of 13%. In 2019, the market was worth US $330.6 million. By the end of 2026, the market is expected to be worth $784.96 million. Organizations can use digital transformation to mitigate risks and deal with shocks, including market fluctuations, company reorganisation, and the geopolitical climate. The transition from traditional to new digitised business models encourages the development of increasingly technologically inventive products and services. This research examines the current state of the worldwide digital transformation, as well as future projections, growth possibilities, important markets, and key actors. An overview of the digital transformation in North America, Europe, China, Japan, South Korea, and Central and South America is included in the report.

According to the Strategic Policy Forum on Digital Entrepreneurship, 81% of executives believe that platform-based business models are critical to their company's long-term success. 91% of chief executives in the automotive and healthcare industries acknowledge that data analytics has a strong potential for generating significant revenue. According to the report, digital platforms are on the verge of reaching a total market value of 4 trillion euros, and 1.3 million people work directly for these platforms. The application of Industrial Internet of Things (IIoT) technologies shows enormous potential, but companies still hesitate to use these platforms and their possibilities, even if they are aware of them (Fabian, 2021). According to an article published by Eurostat, the Europe 2020 strategy sets an ambitious goal of strengthening the circumstances for innovation, research, and development. By 2020, the target is to boost combined public and private investment in research and development to 3% of GDP, from the current level of 2%. This gives competitors around the world a chance to catch up quickly, even in areas where European companies have been strong in the past.

With a compound annual growth rate (CAGR) of 26% from the years 2018 to 2025, the digital transformation industry in Europe is expected to increase from $92.7 billion in 2017 to $520.4 billion by the year 2025 (ReportLinker, 2019). The European digital transformation business is being driven by a variety of factors, including the increasing acceptance of digital solutions across a diverse range of industries. In the future, cyber-attacks and security breaches could get worse, as well as privacy concerns. This could slow the growth of the European digital transformation market in the future. Digital solutions are rapidly gaining traction in a variety of industries, including manufacturing, automotive, healthcare, banking and financial services, retail, media, and entertainment. These industries continue to reap the benefits of digital transformation. Analytics enables them to comprehend and service clients more effectively. The digital transformation market in Europe is split up because there are so many different industries. The competitive dynamics of the industry are expected to change in the next few years. The government is also working on a number of projects to help the digital transformation market in Europe grow even faster.

4.3 Mitigating Risks and Uncertainties in India

There are several risks involved with the implementation of fourth industrial revolution. India continues to be underdeveloped in terms of physical and digital infrastructure. Despite continued attempts by the government, the country continues to lack critical infrastructure such as roads and electricity. Additionally, India's telecommunications network continues to suffer from slow data speeds and unreliable connections. According to the KPMG India Cybercrime Survey Report 2017, cyber security is one of the top five corporate threats in India. The regulatory environment controlling data privacy would also need to be tightened. Digital technology is also expensive. Building the linked factories of the future may require a huge investment. Bajpai and Biberman (2019) stated that access to digital technology for MSME's, the backbone of India's manufacturing economy, remains a challenge due to high costs. There is still a leadership change. India's aim at widespread adoption will be impeded by a lack of prepared corporate executives for the Industry 4.0 era. Despite strong conventional leadership in Indian organisations, there is a scarcity of digital specialists with a clear vision for Industry 4.0 adoption. India's existing workforce is technologically deficient in skills in additive manufacturing, data analytics, and the Internet of Things. An industry-ready workforce requires collaboration between industry, government, and academia. They need the necessary abilities for success. People, particularly at the strategic leadership and production levels, can be a big issue for Indian businesses as they move towards Industry 4.0 maturity. All stakeholders must plan, invest, and collaborate to produce leaders who can manage their organisations in the digital age (PWC and FICCI, 2019).

The traditional organisational structure based on human-to-human hierarchy is anticipated to be gradually phased out in favour of functions involving strategic and operational interaction between humans and robots. To prepare for the fourth industrial revolution, Indian businesses must reinvent leadership and produce new leaders capable of interacting with a network of teams in a fast-paced technology environment. Most importantly, the company must transform entrenched mindsets and manage change efficiently. As Industry 4.0 automates most technical tasks, the focus may move to soft skills. This reengineering at the executive level is critical. The global Industry 4.0 market is estimated to reach $214 billion in value by 2023. The industrial revolution has been implemented by the United States, China, Japan, the United Kingdom, and a number of European Union member states. Germany chose Industry 4.0 as a strategic goal in 2010 in order to position itself as a leader in modern manufacturing technologies. Additionally, it identified a three-dimensional technique for progressing in an orderly fashion. The government has done this by giving small and medium-sized businesses information and resources and by making deals with countries like China and Japan to work together (Bajpai and Biberman, 2019).

According to India's "Make in India" development plan, it is the world's sixth biggest manufacturer. The government plans to raise manufacturing's proportion of GDP from 16–17 percent to 25 percent by 2022. The administration has enacted a number of policy reforms, including the introduction of the GST and the liberalisation of FDI rules. Industry 4.0, in general, provides an opportunity for India's manufacturing industry. India is presently lagging behind its global rivals in terms of Industry 4.0 implementation. A significant sector of the industrial industry remains post-electrified, with technology restricted to stand-alone systems. Industry 4.0's underlying assumption of integrating physical systems with cyber platforms is still developing (Aulbur and Singh, 2014). Due to high costs, the MSME group has limited access to modern technologies. India's success in two important Industry 4.0 enabler technologies, IoT and Big Data, appears to be establishing the ideal framework for its "tiny factories." By 2020, India will own 20% of the worldwide IoT market, worth $3 billion (GOI, 2018). The industrial segment of the Indian LoT market currently accounts for 60% of the market. The Indian big data analysis industry is anticipated to reach $1.6 billion by 2025, with a CAGR of 26%. "Made in India" commands 32% of the worldwide market (Nishimura, T, 2018).

India is digitalising several industries. However, penetration varies per sector. Some industries are experimenting with networked manufacturing floors and assembly lines. Some of these businesses are testing or developing small-scale Industry 4.0 solutions. Many countries in Europe and Asia are also exhibiting a strong commitment to Industry 4.0 research and application. Industry 4.0 is only getting started. Despite the adoption of some technology, there are still major advancements to be made. The institutional setting presents its own set of issues. It could take two or three decades to reap the full benefits, and there could be side effects as well. India benefited from advances in information technology, the internet, renewable energy, mobile phones, and connected gadgets during the Third Industrial Revolution. During this time, India's way of life was transformed by astounding advancements. This leads to the question: what exactly is Industry 4.0? Across the company's value chain, it combines sophisticated analytics, AI, big data, the internet of things (IoT), robots and automation, and process digitization.

4.4 Contribution

Many top executives are seeking to understand how digitalisation affects their organisation in an increasingly digital environment (Bjorkdahl, 2020), and they are focusing on building new practises, competencies, and strategies to create and capture value. However, many firms are still unaware of the impact of digitalisation on performance, and as a result, they invest in information technology without a well-thought-out strategy. Companies that invest in digitisation may beat their competitors in terms of sales growth and company efficiency. Many organisations are motivated to develop new business models based on digital technology in order to expand their opportunities and benefits (Bresciani et al., 2018). Several businesses recognise the advantages and favourable performance consequences. These insights can help managers and practitioners understand how the level, benefits, impacts, and potential future directions of digitization affect organisational performance. This study adds to the literature on digitalization in organisations and its implications on performance by bridging the gap and recommending future research areas, as well as providing many stimulants for researchers (Ricci et al. 2020). The findings indicate a growing interest in digital transformation, which can assist organisations in achieving improved performance, primarily at the organisational level; they also provide a global overview of potential connected risks and uncertainties. The benefits and costs of digital transformation are examined, along with the management skills and advanced technology needed to achieve the desired results (Chouaibi et al., 2022).

5. CONCLUSION AND RECOMMENDATIONS

Digital technologies and the transformation of all economic sectors will revolutionise market structure and governance, resulting in a dramatic reconfiguration of labour and employment. The digital transformation allows for the deep integration of systems, resulting in seamless digitalised value chains that are more efficient overall. The European Commission is aware that digital technologies and systems need to work together seamlessly. But to achieve this, they have to bring together the industry and the standardisation communities on a global level. Investments from the public and private sector will be key enablers, especially for new technologies, reskilling the workforce, and innovative business models. The same applies to European Union-wide standards for digital technologies and systems. New technologies and standards have to be implemented that allow data to flow seamlessly, which could help overcome existing problems and accelerate the modernization process in industries. The successful application of industrial IoT will help improve the competitiveness of European industry. The study is crucial in showing the importance of digitization in new worker skill sets and business process re-engineering. On the other hand, there are European and national initiatives to both privately and publicly invest in the deployment of new digital technologies. It provides considerable potential for industries to access new benchmarks and establish new standards.

A digitised India will become a global industrial powerhouse. Digital technologies like IoT and robotics are changing the global industry. Cost reduction, quality improvement, customisation, and performance improvements are all driving productivity increases. However, digital technology penetration in the Indian industry is relatively young. India gains a lot from this. Numerous advantages exist, including a vast and developing domestic market, a wide pool of workers with varied talents, and a large start-up technology base. While digital technologies can stimulate progress, they can also be disruptive, affecting productivity and employment. A new policy is required to encourage digital adoption, build a digital ecosystem, boost competitiveness, and leapfrog into the digital twenty-first century while filling skill gaps and providing jobs for millions of unemployed Indians. With the help of Make in India and the Industrial Revolution 4.0, the government aims to increase manufacturing's proportion of the GDP to 25%. Advancing technologies such as 5G cellular networks and wireless sensor networks, as well as industrial e-commerce, will influence industrial competitiveness. Global industries are on the cusp of a new era. Intelligent machines, modern connectivity, big data, and cloud computing are transforming industrial production. It's all about Industry 4.0 and the Industrial Internet. It will rewrite global competitive dynamics and laws. The drive for better industrial output could affect the future of big businesses and the economy as a whole.

REFERENCES

Ashrafi, R., & Mueller, J. (2015). Delineating IT resources and capabilities to obtain competitive advantage and improve firm performance. *Information Systems Management*, *32*(1), 15–38. doi:10.1080/10580530.2015.983016

Aulbur, W., & Singh, H.V. (2014). *Next Generation Manufacturing: Industry 4.0: A Look at the Changing Landscapes in Manufacturing.* CII and Roland Berger.

Bajpai, N., & Biberman, J. (2019). *The Future Work in India: Adopting to the Fourth Industrial Revolution.* ICT Working Paper No. 11.

Banalieva, E., & Dhanaraj, C. (2019). Internalization theory for the digital economy. *Journal of International Business Studies*, *50*(8), 1372–1387. doi:10.105741267-019-00243-7

Basl, J., & Kopp, J. (2017). Study of the Readiness of Czech Companies to the Industry 4.0. *Journal of Systems Integration*, *8*, 40–45.

Bjorkdahl, J. (2020). Strategies for digitalisation in manufacturing firms. *California Management Review*, *62*(4), 17–36. doi:10.1177/0008125620920349

Bleicher, J., & Stanley, H. (2016). Digitization as a catalyst for business model innovation a three-step approach to facilitating economic success. *Journal of Business and Management*, *8*, 62–71.

Bresciani, S., Ferraris, A., & Del Giudice, M. (2018). The management of organisational ambidexterity through alliances in a new context of analysis: Internet of Things (IoT) smart city projects. *Technological Forecasting and Social Change*, *136*, 331–338. doi:10.1016/j.techfore.2017.03.002

Castelo-Branco, I., Cruz-Jesus, F., & Oliveira, T. (2019). Assessing Industry 4.0 readiness in manufacturing: Evidence for the European Union. *Computers in Industry*, *107*, 22–32. doi:10.1016/j.compind.2019.01.007

Castro, H. F., Carvalho, A. R. F., Leal, F., & Gouveia, H. (2019). Assessing Industry 4.0 Readiness of Portuguese Companies. In H. Almeida & J. Vasco (Eds.), Progress in Digital and Physical Manufacturing, ProDPM 2019. Academic Press.

Chesbrough, H. W. (2006). *Open Innovation: The New Imperative for Creating and Profiting from Technology*. Harvard Business Press.

Chouaibi, S., Festa, G., Quaglia, R., & Rossi, M. (2022). The risky impact of digital transformation on organizational performance – evidence from Tunisia. *Technological Forecasting and Social Change*, *178*, 121571. doi:10.1016/j.techfore.2022.121571

Deloitte. (2018). *Managing risk in digital transformation*. Deloitte.

Dery, K., Sebastian, I. M., & van der Meulen, N. (2017). The digital workplace is key to digital innovation. *MIS Quarterly Executive*, *16*, 135–152.

EIU. (2014). *Networked manufacturing: The digital future*. Economist Intelligence Unit.

El Massah, S., & Mohieldin, M. (2020). Digital transformation and localizing the sustainable development goals (SDGs). *Ecological Economics*, *169*, 106490. doi:10.1016/j.ecolecon.2019.106490

GOI. (2018). *Internet of Things (IoT)*. IoT India Magazine.

Govindarajan, V., Srivastava, A., & Enache, L. (2019). How India Plans to Protect Consumer Data. *Harvard Business Review*.

Grover, V., & Kohli, R. (2013). Revealing your hand: Caveats in implementing digital business strategy. *Management Information Systems Quarterly*, *37*, 655–663.

Hennart, J. F. (2019). Digitalized service multinationals and international business theory. *Journal of International Business Studies*, *50*(8), 1388–1400. doi:10.105741267-019-00256-2

Hofmann, E., & Ru¨sch, M. (2017). Industry 4.0 and the current status as well as future prospects on logistics. *Computers in Industry*, *89*, 23–34. doi:10.1016/j.compind.2017.04.002

Jafari-Sadeghi, V., Garcia-Perez, A., Candelo, A., & Couturier, J. (2021). Exploring the impact of digital transformation on technology entrepreneurship and technological market expansion: The role of technology readiness, exploration and exploitation. *Journal of Business Research*, *124*, 100–111. doi:10.1016/j.jbusres.2020.11.020

Javaid, M., Haleem, A., Vaishya, R., Bahl, S., Suman, R., & Vaish, A. (2020). Industry 4.0 technologies and their applications in fighting COVID-19 pandemic. *Diabetes & Metabolic Syndrome*, *14*(4), 419–422. doi:10.1016/j.dsx.2020.04.032 PMID:32344370

Johnny. (2003). *Longitudinal Qualitative Research: Analyzing Change through time*. Altamira Press a Division of Rowman & Littlefield Publishers Inc.

Kagermann, H., Wahlster, W., & Helbig, J. (2013). *Recommendations for Implementing the Strategic Initiative Industrie 4.0, Final Report of the Industrie 4.0 Working Group*. Forschungs Union and Acatech.

Kano, L. (2018). Global value chain governance: A relational perspective. *Journal of International Business Studies*, *49*(6), 684–705. doi:10.105741267-017-0086-8

Kraus, S., Schiavone, F., Pluzhnikova, A., & Invernizzi, A. (2021). Digital transformation in health care: Analyzing the current state-of-research. *Journal of Business Research*, *123*, 557–567. doi:10.1016/j.jbusres.2020.10.030

Kshetri, N. (2005). Pattern of global cyber war and crime: A conceptual framework. *Journal of International Management*, *11*(4), 541–562. doi:10.1016/j.intman.2005.09.009

Lee, J., Bagheri, B., & Kao, H. (2015). A Cyber-Physical Systems Architecture for Industry 4.0.-based on manufacturing systems. *Manufacturing Letters*, *3*, 18–23. doi:10.1016/j.mfglet.2014.12.001

Luo, Y. (2021). A general framework of digitalization risks in international business. *Journal of International Business Studies*.

Manyika, J., Lund, S., Bughin, J., Woetzel, J., Stamenov, K., & Dhringra, D. (2016). *Digital globalization: The new era of global flows*. McKinsey Global Institute.

McKinsey. (2020). *Risk, resilience, and rebalancing in global value chains*. McKinsey Global Institute.

Mithas, S., Tafti, A., & Mitchell, W. (2013). How a firm's competitive environment and digital strategy posture influence digital business strategy. *Management Information Systems Quarterly*, *37*(2), 511–536. doi:10.25300/MISQ/2013/37.2.09

Moeuf, A., Pellerin, R., Lamouri, S., Tamayo-Giraldo, S., & Barbaray, R. (2017). The industrial management of SMEs in the era of Industry 4.0. *International Journal of Production Research*, *7543*, 1–19.

Nambisan, S., Lyytinen, K. J., Majchrzak, A., & Song, M. (2017). Digital innovation management: Reinventing innovation management research in a digital world. *Management Information Systems Quarterly*, *4*(1), 223–238. doi:10.25300/MISQ/2017/41:1.03

Nick, G., Szaller, A., Bergmann, J., & Va'rgedő, T. (2019). Industry 4.0 readiness in Hungary: Model, and the first results in connection to data application. *IFAC-PapersOnLine*, *52*(13), 289–294. doi:10.1016/j.ifacol.2019.11.185

Nishimura, T. (2018). *Big Data Analytics Market – Future Scope in India*. Silicon India.

OECD. (2021). Key future uncertainties in digital transformation and potential implications for Latvia. In *Going Digital in Latvia*. OECD Publishing.

Osterrieder, P., Budde, L., & Friedli, T. (2020). The smart factory as a key construct of industry 4.0: A systematic literature review. *International Journal of Production Economics*, *2020*(221), 107476. doi:10.1016/j.ijpe.2019.08.011

Oxley, J., & Yeung, B. (2001). E-commerce readiness: Institutional environment and international competitiveness. *Journal of International Business Studies*, *32*(4), 705–723. doi:10.1057/palgrave.jibs.8490991

PWC & FICCI. (2019). *Fast Forward: Relevant Skill for a Buoyant Indian Economy*. Author.

ReportLinker. (2019). *Europe Digital Transformation Market to 2025 - Regional Analysis and Forecasts by Components; Deployment Type; and End-User*. The Insight Partners.

Reyes, C. (2021). *What is Digital Strategy?* Liferay.

Ricci, F., Scafarto, V., Ferri, S., & Tron, A.,(2020). Value relevance of digitalisation: the moderating role of corporate sustainability. An empirical study of Italian listed companies. *Journal of Cleaner Production*, *276*, 123–282. https://doi.org/.jclepro.2020.123282 doi:10.1016/j

Santos, M. Y., Oliveira, J., Andrade, C., Lima, F. V., Costa, E., & Costa, C. (2017). A big data system supporting Bosch Braga industry 4.0 strategy. *International Journal of Information Management*, *37*(6), 750–760. doi:10.1016/j.ijinfomgt.2017.07.012

Schiopu, R. (2020). *Business Digitalization in the European Union*. Sciendo.

Souls, E. (2019). *Industry 4.0: Importance and Necessity in India Fabian Wanke (2021). EU Digital Transformation Challenges*. ARC Advisory Group.

Strategic Policy Forum on Digital Entrepreneurship. (2016). Accelerating the digital transformation of European industry and enterprises. *European Union*.

Szabo, R., Vuksanović, I., Herceg Hana'k, R., Hortovanyi, L., Romanova´, A., Mocan, M., & … . (2020). Industry 4.0 Implementation in B2B Companies: Cross-Country Empirical Evidence on Digital Transformation in the CEE Region. *Sustainability (Basel)*, *19*(22), 9538. doi:10.3390u12229538

Tallman, S., Luo, Y., & Buckley, P. (2018). Business models in global competition. *Global Strategy Journal*, *8*(4), 517–535. doi:10.1002/gsj.1165

UNCTAD. (2015). Information economy report: Unlocking the potential of E-commerce for developing countries. UNCTAD.

Wang, S., Wan, J., Zhang, D., Li, D., & Zhang, C. (2016). Towards smart factory for industry 4.0: A self-organized multiagent system with big data based feedback and coordination. *Computer Networks*, *101*, 158–168. doi:10.1016/j.comnet.2015.12.017

World Bank. (2016). World Development Report 2016: Digital dividends. Author.

Yu¨ksel, H. (2021). An empirical evaluation of industry 4.0 applications of companies in Turkey: The case of a developing country. *Technology in Society*, *63*, 101364. doi:10.1016/j.techsoc.2020.101364

Chapter 7
Optimizing Patient Flow in Emergency Care Units and Lean Healthcare

Andrei Bonamigo
https://orcid.org/0000-0002-6670-9755
Fluminense Federal University, Brazil

Patricia Mendonça Maia Bernardes
Fluminense Federal University, Brazil

Luiz Felipe Conrado
https://orcid.org/0000-0001-7537-3336
Fluminense Federal University, Brazil

Robisom Damasceno Calado
https://orcid.org/0000-0003-3349-0344
Fluminense Federal University, Brazil

ABSTRACT

The healthcare industry faces challenges in delivering high-quality care with limited resources. Inefficiencies like long waiting times and excessive staff workload contribute to patient dissatisfaction. Lean methodology, specifically Lean Healthcare, offers improvement opportunities. However, barriers to implementation exist, including resistance from healthcare practitioners. This chapter proposes solutions for implementing Lean principles in healthcare. It suggests adapting vocabulary and symbols for a patient-centered approach, grouping patients into "patient pathways" for process efficiency, addressing employee feedback, collecting process data for evidence-based decision-making, and maximizing human resources. Clear communication, employee motivation, and ongoing improvement efforts are crucial. Implementing Lean effectively improves efficiency, patient satisfaction, and healthcare quality.

DOI: 10.4018/979-8-3693-0458-7.ch007

INTRODUCTION

The goal of the healthcare field is, for all intents and purposes, to maximize the value of services provided to clients and patients (Singh et al., 2022; Costa et al., 2022). When thinking about hospitals, clinics, and other healthcare facilities, it's important to remember that the outcomes and items given are health and treatments for patients, who are the focus of the healthcare industry (Maione et al., 2020).

One of the ways to achieve this while meeting organizational goals is through the Lean methodology adoption (Davis, 2010; Bonamigo et al., 2022), which can be applied in healthcare facilities through the Lean Healthcare use. Providing reliable, safe, and quality care while constantly seeking efficiencies is one of the challenges in healthcare that require careful consideration of Lean Healthcare principles (Hallam & Contreras, 2018). Combined with the Lean approach to cost and waste reduction, Lean Healthcare offers great opportunities to become a significant area of research for healthcare organizations and researchers alike.

In healthcare, there are many inefficient systems that cause more harm than good for patients (Singh et al., 2022). These inefficiencies are often deeply ingrained in the daily operations of healthcare businesses and are the main source of patient dissatisfaction (Leite et al., 2020). One of the key factors that reduces the value of service for patients is long waiting times, which are associated with negative experiences (Barlow, 2002; Bielen & Demoulin, 2007). The Single-Minute Exchange of Die (SMED) technique is a Lean tool that focuses on optimizing setup activities and reducing idle time. While SMED is widely used in manufacturing, there are few studies on its implementation in healthcare. Some criticize its origins in manufacturing and caution against the cultural differences between manufacturing and healthcare operations (Chiarini & Baccarani, 2016).

Most hospitals use conventional management thinking, which prioritizes local improvement of individual healthcare activities rather than process improvement. In contrast, Lean Thinking focuses on improving the entire process of care, from determining the need for a service to delivering that service without interruption. The focus must be shifted from individual tasks to the patient pathway, defined as a set of activities that must be performed in the appropriate sequence and at the appropriate time to meet the patient's needs (de Souza & Pidd, 2011).

The healthcare industry faces numerous challenges, including limited resources, increased demand due to population growth and unhealthy lifestyles, and economic crisis (Maione et al., 2020). Due to the indeterministic nature of healthcare systems, which makes it difficult to anticipate future states and configurations, it is crucial to find new ways to provide care effectively while also meeting customer expectations (Crema & Verbano, 2021).

Delivering and financing high-quality healthcare services has been a major global goal recently, mainly because healthcare quality reflects citizens' perceptions of their quality of life. However, according to Maione et al. (2020), this ecosystem faces important challenges such as:

- **Rising Costs:** this might be due to a variety of circumstances, such as an unanticipated increase in demand due to an aging population or lifestyle-related disorders (mainly alcohol, smoke, drugs, and obesity). The advent of new technologies and medicines, which may increase demand — but also expenses — associated with their implementation, is another factor driving up demand (Hurst, 2000).
- **Shift from Supply-Driven to Demand-Driven:** patients frequently demand the finest possible service quality at the lowest possible cost and with the fastest possible processing times. Customers

have easier access to the medical information on the internet, which raises their awareness of their medical needs and desires and reduces information asymmetry. As a result, healthcare firms should place a greater emphasis on what customers desire.

- **Cybersecurity:** the health department has become an easy target for cybercrime, given the amount of sensitive information about patients collected by information systems. Not only to guarantee the confidentiality of medical records, but also to avoid injunctions for violations of security standards, healthcare organizations should strengthen their reaction to cybercriminals.

Inefficiencies in healthcare systems often result in more harm than good for patients. One major contributing factor is the issue of long wait times, which has negative impacts on patient satisfaction and overall healthcare quality. To address this problem, Lean philosophy provides various strategies for optimizing management. Among these strategies, Single-Minute Exchange of Die (SMED) is a promising tool for reducing set-up and changeover times (Bin Che Ani & Bin Shafei, 2013).

Based on the Toyota Kata, this study presents a guide to evaluating and managing SMED in the health context. Through a literature review and content analysis, Bardin (2011) developed a base method for the implementation of the aforementioned tools. As a consequence of this study, waste found in the ECUs will be evaluated and mitigated.

The analysis focused on identifying the major challenges in Lean implementation in both manufacturing and healthcare sectors, as well as the specific differences between the two sectors. Based on the results, the authors developed guidelines that consider the unique characteristics of each healthcare facility and the diverse needs of individual patients (Peimbert-García et al., 2021).

The organization of this chapter is as follows: First, a comprehensive review of Lean Management, Lean Healthcare, SMED, and Kata is presented. Next, the focus shifts to examining the primary challenges, controversies, and dilemmas linked to the healthcare industry's integration of Lean and other manufacturing techniques. Lastly, potential solutions to the aforementioned issues are proposed, alongside suggestions for future research directions, conclusions, and additional reading recommendations.

BACKGROUND

Lean Management (LM)

The term originated in the Toyota Production System, introduced by Japanese engineers Taiichi Ohno and Shigeo Shingo (Arnheiter & Maleyeff, 2005). Traditional production focused on high volumes, large batches, and long waiting times, leading to quality issues discovered late in the process. In contrast, Lean production emphasizes small batch sizes and a make-to-order approach (Arnheiter & Maleyeff, 2005).

The LM philosophy aims to "eliminate waste and reduce variability across suppliers, customers, and the company" (Rotter et al., 2019, p. 368). However, due to an ongoing debate in operations management (OM), there is no single definition of LM (Pettersen, 2009).

LM can be seen as a systematic and focused approach to teach employees Lean principles, promoting their application within the organization. It involves a comprehensive plan for Lean change management, encompassing both individual and collective organizational transformation (Charron et al., 2014).

In addition to small batch sizes and reducing inventory, the main pillars of Lean are defined as the following:

- **Waste Elimination:** Lean prioritizes customer value over performance optimization. Customers only value activities that directly contribute to the end product (Hallam & Contreras, 2018). Therefore, non-value-adding activities should be identified and promptly eliminated (Tlapa et al., 2020).
- **Reduction of Variability:** This encompasses variations in product quality characteristics (e.g., length, width, thickness), delivery times, and working hours (specifically downtime, absenteeism, and lack of employee qualifications). Standardized work processes and collaborations between suppliers and producers can enhance improvement in these areas (Arnheiter & Maleyeff, 2005).
- **Zero Quality Control (ZQC):** Quality requirements are crucial in Lean's pursuit of perfection. Yet, traditional quality control can be inefficient and burdensome, offering limited value to the process. Crosby (1989) defines quality as "conformance to requirements." In a Lean enterprise, the goal is for every part to meet quality requirements without relying on extensive quality control. This can be achieved by employing defect assurance systems (Poka-Yoke), automated inspections, audits, statistical process control, and halting production when defects occur.
- **Perfection:** Represents the core of LM, and is achieved through continuous improvement (kaizen). For this to be possible, processes must be standardized, stable, and transparent (Bauer et al., 2018).

Lean Healthcare (LH)

LH is a philosophy centered around optimizing hospital organization and management using principles, techniques, and tools (Graban & Toussaint, 2018). It emerged as a service strategy to eliminate waste and non-value-adding activities in healthcare processes. Implementing LH can enhance clinical care efficiency, lower costs, and enhance patient outcomes (Tlapa et al., 2020).

LH has seen successful implementation in various settings, such as intensive care units (ICUs), cardiology, surgery, gynecologic oncology, colonoscopy, pathology, radiology, psychiatric units, ophthalmology, otolaryngology, ultrasound otolaryngology, organ transplant centers, and clinical laboratories (Tlapa et al., 2020). In the United States, around 70% of hospitals have integrated LH into their care plans or related strategies, as shown in a national study (Shortell et al., 2018).

The tactics of LH begin with examining a healthcare process and determining what is of value to the patient (Tlapa et al., 2020), which in itself is commonly interpreted as quality divided by cost (Ken Lee et al., 2016). In addition, value in health care is "activities that enhance the quality of healthcare and promote patient well-being so as to achieve better outcome" (Tlapa et al., 2020, p. 261).

The LH approach and its tools have demonstrated the ability to expedite patient recovery in healthcare settings, leading to improved quality of life and cost reduction (de Amaral et al., 2021). Lean, when effectively applied, facilitates the measurement of activity value and identifies variations, leading to positive and consistent outcomes (Vats et al., 2011).

Bolton Hospitals in the United Kingdom implemented Lean principles and tools like *kaizen*, value stream mapping, standardized work, pulled systems, and continuous flows in their operations. As a result, they achieved significant improvements, including a 38% reduction in hospital length of stay for hip fractures, a 33% decrease in patient turnaround time, and a 36% reduction in mortality rate (Fillingham, 2007).

A Thai hospital (Trakulsunti, 2022) implemented multiple Lean Six Sigma tools, including cause-and-effect diagrams, spaghetti diagrams, five-why analysis, project charters, brainstorming, control charts, and hypothesis testing. These tools were used to identify the root causes of medication errors and develop solutions to prevent them. The implementation of Lean Six Sigma resulted in a reduction of monthly dispensing errors from 29 incidents to 6 incidents over 14,000 total inpatient days between March 2018 and November 2019, and improved patient safety.

Based on their work at Flinders Medical Center (Australia), McGrath et al. (2008) presented a set of principles to increase the success rate of Lean Healthcare projects, which are as follows:

- **Customer Specification:** In contrast to other sectors, the healthcare industry faces challenges in identifying its primary customer due to its complex system. Processes often prioritize internal customers like physicians, hospitals, healthcare facilities, and the government. However, the authors argue that the value stream should be centered around the ultimate customer: the patient.
- **Leadership Efforts Made by Directors:** Employees need to perceive the commitment of managers at the upper levels of the hierarchy. The Lean program should be considered a priority.
- **Multidisciplinary Teams:** Problem-solving should be carried out in teams comprising members who are directly involved in the analyzed work. These teams should be supervised by process optimization specialists.
- **Implementation:** According to the authors, this is the most difficult part of the process, and the managers entrusted with this task should have change management skills.
- **Focus on Patient Flow:** Patients should be sorted by similar service delivery needs to facilitate the redesign process, e.g., elderly patients with comorbidities, patients requiring emergency care, and patients who can be sent home immediately after evaluation. The value stream must be designed to meet the needs of patients and their operators.
- **Data:** Solutions should be evidence-based. The redesign process involves gathering diverse perspectives from involved parties regarding the problem and its causes, and then aligning them with available data. This data should be easily accessible, presented in a straightforward and visible manner, and provided in real-time to facilitate the analysis and correction of errors.
- **Goals and Deadlines:** The desired results should be ambitious, but at the same time realistic. Achieving goals can motivate employees and inspire innovation, which together can lead to amazing results.
- **Process Management:** Training and external support should be considered. The use of external consultants can be an effective tool to overcome obstacles in an employee's mindset and facilitate the team's work.
- **Project Selection:** Initially, the deliberate selection of simple, quick-win projects can encourage employee engagement. High-volume patient family improvements are also a good starting point.
- **Flexibility and Persistence:** The PDSA (plan-do-study-act) method is ideal for making the implementation of improvement projects more flexible and creating space for continuous learning.
- **Sustainability:** A process of continuous review and improvement of health services is essential to meet the clients' needs. This ongoing improvement process should be integrated into the overall change process to ensure sustainability and achieve higher levels of quality and efficiency.

Finally, the authors suggest a sustainability cycle — as described below:

1. **Standardization:** New processes should be thoroughly documented, clearly outlining responsibilities, particularly for new or temporary personnel. Eliminating variance from the process is a critical

aspect of standardized work, and regular performance checks should be conducted to ensure that procedures are being followed as intended.

2. **Maintenance:** Each value stream should have a designated process leader responsible for consistently monitoring, measuring, and revising the work using performance indicators. Spending time at the location where work is executed effectively allows the process leader to observe task completion and identify areas for potential improvement.
3. **Continuous Improvement:** Needed to meet demand growth, technological innovation, and quality standards.

Single-Minute Exchange of Die (SMED)

Shigeo Shingo introduced the SMED technique in his book "Revolution in Manufacturing: The SMED System" in 1985. Its aim is to enable quick and efficient transitions between products by reducing set-up times, with the "running product" in the healthcare context being the sick or injured patient (Bin Che Ani & Bin Shafei, 2013; Karam et al., 2018). This method suggests a maximum set-up time of 10 minutes, achievable through work rationalization by the machine operator (Rosa et al., 2017).

According to Shingo (2019), a process is defined as "a continuous flow through which raw materials are transformed into finished items," while an operation (or activity) is "any action performed on raw materials, intermediate, or finished products by man, machine, or equipment."

Shingo's pioneering technique provides a comprehensive approach to achieving small-batch, flexible production systems. It encompasses both the theoretical background of the methodology and practical applications required to reduce set-up time to under 10 minutes (Tekin et al., 2019).

SMED comprises four stages to minimize set-up time: preliminary stages, separation of internal and external set-up, conversion of internal to external set-up, and streamlining every aspect of set-up (Bin Che Ani & Bin Shafei, 2013). External set-up refers to activities that can be performed while the equipment is not in operation, typically before or after the production process. Internal set-up, on the other hand, includes activities that can only be carried out when the equipment is stopped and not running, leading to downtime during the setup process (Bonamigo et al., 2022).

The aforementioned steps are outlined as follows:

1. **Preliminary Stages:** In traditional processes, internal and external set-up procedures are often combined, leading to unnecessary idle time for machines. To address this issue, the responsible person must thoroughly investigate the actual workplace conditions. Conducting a detailed analysis involves continuous production observations using a stopwatch, work sampling research (especially in repetitive processes), worker interviews, and recording the complete set-up operation. These alternatives provide valuable insights for the study and help identify opportunities for improvement.
2. **Separation of Internal and External Set-Up:** The implementation of SMED reaches its most critical stage here because even though most people acknowledge that stopping a process for specific activities is inefficient, they often fail to recognize their own behavior when executing such tasks. Transforming as much of the set-up operation into external activities can help reduce the time required by 30 to 50%. Shingo emphasizes that understanding the distinction between internal and external set-up is vital to achieving successful SMED implementation. Separation can be achieved by employing a checklist or check-table for all tasks involved in an activity, avoiding generic lists for the entire process. Instead, detailed checklists should be utilized to ensure effectiveness.

3. **Conversion of Internal to External Set-Up:** Even though the decrease indicated above is excellent for process optimization, it is insufficient to meet the SMED target. This step entails two key concepts: examining activities to see whether any tasks are incorrectly considered to be internal and figuring out how to change such chores to external. Internal set-up operations can frequently be transformed into external set-up by re-evaluating their genuine purpose. Following the analysis, trial shots should be taken, and the activity should then be transitioned to the external.
4. **Streamlining Every Aspect of Set-Up:** To ensure that the obtained set-up is already at its bare minimum, a thorough examination of each part is essential. Although steps 3 and 4 are separate, they do not need to be executed in a specific order; they can be carried out almost simultaneously. While improving the storage and transportation of components and tools can enhance external activities, it is not sufficient on its own. Internal operations can benefit from various methods, such as simultaneous operations, using functional clamps for easy positioning, eliminating adjustment requirements, and implementing recommended combinations of tasks (indicated relations).

Although the SMED approach is renowned for optimizing manufacturing processes, it's essential to acknowledge that it was not originally designed for the healthcare industry. As a result, it may not be entirely compatible with healthcare operations. While there has been extensive research on SMED implementation, it's crucial to customize the approach to suit the specific environment and infrastructure of the healthcare processes in which it will be applied.

For example, the "unfinished product" in this case is the patient who has not yet received adequate treatment; while the "final product" is that same patient after release, healthy, after being treated. Set-up processes can be traditional machine adjustments (such as setting up an X-ray machine and sterilizing rooms for surgical procedures), or they can be directly related to the patient, such as the triage process.

Toyota Kata

The concept of Toyota Kata was first introduced by Rother (2009) based on his research into the continuous improvement practices of Toyota (de Souza et al., 2020; Ferenhof et al., 2018). Rother (2009) defines Kata as a means of aligning or synchronizing two elements with a third. The term originates from Japanese martial arts, where it refers to fundamental movement patterns passed down from master to student across generations.

The core idea behind the Toyota Kata approach is that organizations can create a method, or kata, to adapt to unpredictable internal and external conditions (Rother, 2009). Essentially, Kata can be viewed as a repetitive pattern of improvement, empowering individuals to adjust their thoughts and actions in response to dynamic circumstances (W. de Souza et al., 2020; Rother, 2009).

There are two main types of Kata utilized to achieve optimal conditions within Toyota: Improvement Kata and Coaching Kata (de Souza et al., 2020; Rother, 2009), as exemplified by Figure 1.

The Improvement Kata is a recurring routine employed by Toyota to continuously enhance, adapt, and evolve their processes. Conversely, the Coaching Kata is a repeated routine where Toyota leaders teach the Improvement Kata to all members of the organization.

The Improvement Kata, which can be implemented at all levels of the organization, consists of four distinct steps (de Souza et al., 2020):

Figure 1. Improvement kata and coaching kata
Adapted from Rother (2009).

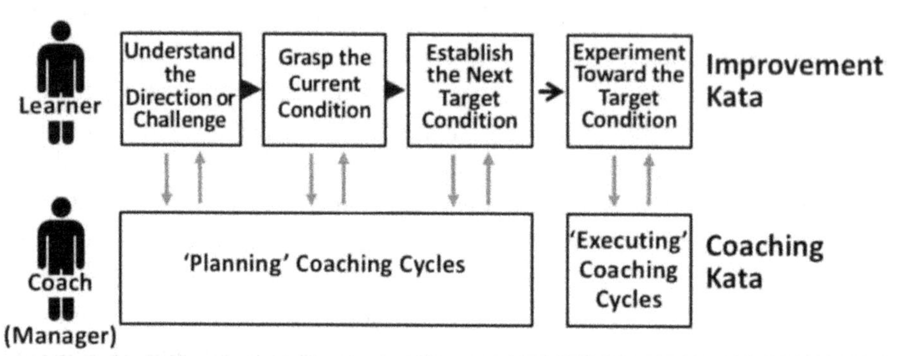

1. **Understand Direction:** In this step, the organization's long-term objective, known as the direction, must be clearly defined. It should align with the company's Vision and be selected by leadership. A specific challenge, along with its attainability, needs to be identified and communicated clearly during this process.
2. **Understand the Current Condition:** Here, the focus is on comprehending the current state by gathering data to establish a desirable future condition. Rather than conducting an extensive and detailed analysis, emphasis is placed on utilizing existing knowledge through observations and measurements within the system.
3. **Establish the Desired Future Condition:** Based on the understanding of the current situation, an achievable future state is defined within a short timeframe, starting from a point that can be immediately approached. This future state is known as the Target Condition, and it should be more detailed and quicker to achieve than the original Challenge. Once the Target Condition is reached, it becomes the new current condition, prompting the establishment of a new Target Condition for the next proposed Challenge.
4. **Iteration Towards the Target Condition:** The Apprentice and their team conduct small experiments using the scientific method and the PDCA (Plan, Do, Check, Act) cycle to progress towards the Target Condition. They identify and address obstacles one by one. At the end of each stage, they reflect on the outcomes, which forms the basis for planning subsequent stages.

Both the Improvement Kata and Coaching Kata are documented on a board called the Storyboard, which serves as a living document placed near the process and visible to all involved. This board helps visualize the four steps of the Improvement Kata and the cycles of the Coaching Kata. In organizations, the concept of knowledge waste refers to the neglect of relevant knowledge during the knowledge conversion process (Ferenhof et al., 2018).

The Coaching Kata routine is applicable across all organizational levels. It involves assigning a more experienced mentor or coach to guide employees, including the coach themselves, through real improvement efforts or work-related situations (de Souza et al., 2020; Rother, 2009).

In summary, the Improvement Kata and the Coaching Kata work together in a coordinated manner. The initial focus is on developing individuals' problem-solving abilities, and then the emphasis shifts towards establishing a strong connection between the learner and the system to enhance work processes (de Souza et al., 2020).

ISSUES, CONTROVERSIES, AND PROBLEMS

The healthcare industry faces a crucial challenge of managing the growing demand while maintaining service quality (Cerdeira, 2020). As a result, many organizations experience overcrowding and prolonged waiting periods, leading to increased patient mortality rates. These delays also lead to inefficient resource utilization, negatively impacting patient and staff satisfaction (Improta et al., 2018).

These challenges manifest in problems such as excessive staff workload, extended user wait times, breakdowns in communication between patients and healthcare professionals, and compromised care for urgent cases. Additionally, conflicts arise due to a lack of comprehension in risk assessment and extended waiting periods for medical care or procedures, as everyone seeks prompt attention regardless of the severity of their conditions (Riquetta, 2018).

Many healthcare practitioners are not familiar with the Lean mindset, and when they learn that it originated in the manufacturing industry, they often dismiss it as inappropriate for a field as varied as healthcare (Chiarini & Baccarani, 2016). Additionally, they worry about relinquishing their autonomy and flexibility in patient treatment, as they hold the belief that adopting a method with standardized work, such as SMED, would restrict their ability to propose nonstandard treatments. They fear that this approach may lead to treating patients, who are human beings, as mere "pieces of metal," compromising the essential human touch required in healthcare provision (de Souza & Pidd, 2011; Erthal et al., 2021).

The management area presents obstacles to the adoption of Lean and SMED, primarily due to managers' preference for a "fire-fighting" approach to problem-solving. Instead of proactively preventing issues from occurring, they tend to address them as they arise (de Souza & Pidd, 2011). Furthermore, physicians and nurses can perceive the project to be something forced on them if they were not involved in some way (Chiarini & Baccarani, 2016).

While the primary objective for healthcare professionals and managers is patient recovery and delivering the best possible treatment conditions, it is crucial to acknowledge the financial situation of healthcare facilities as an influential factor (Erthal et al., 2021). Private hospitals have a responsibility to generate profits for their shareholders, which can make them cautious about investing in costly strategies without a clear understanding of the potential returns. On the other hand, public health services may not be universally accessible and rely entirely on government budget allocations. The availability of funding determines their sustainability and ability to continue operating effectively.

Furthermore, it is important to consider that numerous public hospitals lack the essential infrastructure required to operate their procedures with optimal efficiency. This factor should be taken into account before proposing enhancements that may be incompatible with the financial realities of such hospitals (Levinson & Shojania, 2011).

In this regard, the primary challenges lie in finding appropriate terminology that aligns closely with the healthcare domain. Additionally, there is a need to facilitate the transition for doctors and nurses between different models, as they may perceive the change as a potential loss of service autonomy and resource allocation.

SOLUTIONS AND RECOMMENDATIONS

Drawing from the findings of the literature review, specific guiding principles have emerged to facilitate the implementation of SMED and Kata in a healthcare context. These principles will now be presented in the form of guidelines that should be adhered to when transitioning from the initial state to an optimized state.

Adapting Vocabulary and Symbols

In the initial stages, it is important to prevent alienation and foster acceptance among team members when introducing the new strategy. To achieve this, the language and symbols used should be tailored and adapted to the new environment (Erthal et al., 2021; Ferenhof et al., 2018).

It is recommended to avoid using terminologies such as "defect" and "completed product" and instead opt for concepts like "error" and "recovered patient." This shift in language helps create a more patient-centered and process-improvement-oriented approach (Chiarini & Baccarani, 2016). Furthermore, it is advisable to refrain from referencing the Toyota Production System and utilizing technical jargon associated with Lean strategies. Instead of explicitly mentioning terms like "Toyota Kata," it is more effective to communicate the concept as a "cyclical learning and improvement method". This helps to ensure clearer understanding and engagement among the staff (de Souza & Pidd, 2011).

Nonetheless, it is crucial to establish a standardized vocabulary to be universally applied throughout the organization for SMED and Kata implementation. Terminological inconsistencies across departments can result in significant misunderstandings. While the focus should be on conveying the idea rather than fixating on specific labels, certain terms may need to be modified to ensure clarity and alignment (de Souza & Pidd, 2011).

Grouping Patients in "Patient Pathways"

The notion that a Lean-based healthcare model treats patients as mere "pieces of metal" is a misconception. In reality, patients are not treated as identical entities, but rather receive similar treatments when they fall into similar categories. This approach allows for efficient and effective care delivery while still recognizing the unique needs and characteristics of each individual patient (de Souza & Pidd, 2011).

This type of model is projected to work along with the idea of patient pathways, which can be defined as a sequence of care operations (procedures) shared by a group of patients (cluster or 'patient-care family' that are sufficiently similar to one another (Ben-Tovim et al., 2007). This indicates that patients are still treated on an individual basis by physicians and are not compelled to fit into predefined clusters. However, it is common for patients to naturally fall into similar groups based on their conditions or circumstances.

Put simply, while patients are not viewed as completely identical, there are often similarities in the tasks they need to undertake to receive treatment based on their specific needs. As these tasks are frequently repeated for multiple patients, implementing standardized work and SMED techniques can decrease their set-up time, leading to a substantial reduction in overall process set-up time due to the repetitive nature of these activities.

It's also important to remember that enhancing a particular patient pathway may not be sufficient. In geriatric care, for example, a decrease in bed occupancy (from 100% to roughly 80%) paradoxically created a problem by retaining unoccupied beds. Empty beds were occupied by non-elderly patients who couldn't find a bed anywhere else in the hospital after they were available on the bed management system. It's critical to optimize parallel patient paths by carefully evaluating how they interact (de Souza & Pidd, 2011; Graban & Toussaint, 2018).

Implementing Cultural Enhancement and Addressing Employee Feedback

To ensure the success of the new system, it is crucial for all staff members, regardless of their level, to undergo thorough training and fully understand the advantages it brings. Striking a balanced approach to training, avoiding both rushing through it and causing unnecessary delays, is vital to achieve optimal outcomes (de Souza & Pidd, 2011).

When implementing LH, it is crucial to actively listen to the concerns and complaints of the staff and consider their suggestions. Even if their input cannot be immediately applied in the current context, it may hold value for other departments. Adopting a gradual approach to implementation can result in substantial benefits, as Lean does not necessarily require a sudden and all-encompassing effort. By involving all stakeholders in the process improvement effort, Lean Healthcare can help increase staff engagement and motivation, leading to a more positive work environment and better patient care (Kam, 2021).

During the implementation of LH practices, it is crucial to take into account the hospital's existing infrastructure and funding (Peimbert-García et al., 2021). The provided instructions should be regarded as guidance for shaping the action plan while considering the available resources and constraints, rather than rigid rules that must be strictly adhered to. By adopting a more flexible and adaptable approach, the desired outcomes can be achieved effectively. In order to sustain the gains made and identify potential opportunities following the implementation of the LSS approach, healthcare managers need to be motivated to develop a continuous improvement philosophy (Rathi, 2022).

Collecting Process Data and Acquiring Technical Expertise

Shifting the attention of healthcare managers from problem-solving and firefighting to in-depth analysis, as well as transforming their decision-making approach from experience-based to evidence-based, continues to be a challenge. Implementing SMED in healthcare requires a combination of quantitative and qualitative abilities, implying that healthcare providers may need to acquire quantitative skills. These skills may be necessary to enhance healthcare productivity as part of a broader performance measurement initiative (de Souza & Pidd, 2011).

To successfully implement SMED and Kata in healthcare, it is crucial to have adequate knowledge of technical aspects, equipment, work organization, and a thorough understanding of the method itself (Rosa et al., 2017). Following Shingo's original concept, the initial crucial step in applying SMED in healthcare involves defining the complete process that requires improvement and streamlining.

To effectively improve a process, it is necessary to identify all its activities and known bottlenecks, utilizing Key Performance Indicators (KPIs) to determine which parts require immediate attention, improvement, and goal setting. This process should encompass a comprehensive list of activities to leverage KPIs for process improvement (Erthal et al., 2021; Régis et al., 2019).

Maximizing the Utilization of Human Resources

The healthcare industry heavily relies on the specialized skills of doctors and nurses, who possess valuable but limited labor time (Peimbert-García et al., 2021). To optimize their time, it is crucial to delegate tasks that can be handled by other departments, reducing unnecessary burden and freeing up doctors and nurses to focus on specialized work. Furthermore, other departments can support the emergency department by assisting in patient setup and preparation, ensuring readiness for the next patient, minimizing waiting time, and avoiding idle time for healthcare professionals (Hallam & Contreras, 2018; Rosa et al., 2017).

It is important to avoid idle time for all employees, particularly physicians who require regular intervals to rest between demanding treatment sessions. Incorporating active breaks into the work schedule has shown to improve productivity, well-being, and health, as long as they are well-controlled and integrated with the tasks at hand (Gallis, 2013). By recognizing the value of labor time, delegating tasks, and managing fatigue, healthcare organizations can optimize resources, improve employee well-being, and enhance the quality of patient care.

Promoting Clarity, Motivation, and Engagement in Achieving Expectations

To ensure a successful implementation, it is crucial for all individuals involved to have a clear understanding of the expectations placed upon them. Motivation and engagement should be nurtured among the team members, encouraging their genuine commitment to meeting these expectations. This approach emphasizes the collective benefit of the system rather than relying solely on managerial directives (Davis, 2010).

Before initiating practical work, forthcoming changes should be effectively communicated to all employees, including physicians, nurses, and staff from other departments. They should also be informed about the expected behaviors that will contribute to the successful implementation of these changes (Chiarini & Baccarani, 2016; Davis, 2010). However, this communication should not be overly authoritative. Instead, participants should be incentivized to actively contribute to process improvement through mechanisms like monetary bonuses or other benefits tied to ranking systems (Chiarini & Baccarani, 2016).

By fostering clarity, motivation, and engagement, organizations can enhance the effectiveness of their processes while creating an environment that encourages active participation and continuous improvement.

Creating an Integrated Lean System

Individual methods have the capacity to enhance processes in diverse ways. Nevertheless, each method comes with its own set of pros and cons. Therefore, implementing a strategy that integrates multiple methodologies and tools is usually the most appropriate approach to tackle optimization problems effectively (Priori & Saurin, 2020).

While SMED proves to be a valuable approach in reducing waste within healthcare processes, it may not encompass all the necessary solutions to address every issue comprehensively (Rosa et al., 2017). Based on the exposed, the authors suggest combining the implementation of SMED with a Kata approach to achieve better results. Depending on the context of the healthcare facilities, other Lean techniques such as poka-yoke, kanban, and value stream mapping can be employed in conjunction with SMED and Kata (Ferenhof et al., 2018; Peimbert-García et al., 2021; Régis et al., 2019).

In this context, Kata serves as a means to integrate SMED standards into the daily routine and offer continuous training to uphold the implementation of these strategies. It also ensures regular audits are conducted to verify adherence to the processes. Any deficiencies should be addressed through further education rather than disciplinary measures (Hallam & Contreras, 2018).

FUTURE RESEARCH DIRECTIONS

The implementation of LM in healthcare has the potential to reduce patients' journey time, decrease costs, and enhance user satisfaction. However, it is crucial to recognize that LM alone is insufficient and requires a combination of mindset transformation and organizational cultural changes to foster continual improvement. Unlike static tools, SMED and Kata are dynamic instruments that should be adaptable to the evolving processes and operations.

To ensure the sustainability and longevity of SMED in healthcare organizations, future research should focus on cultivating a Lean organizational culture. This research should explore the effective use of terminology and symbols, which significantly contribute to the ease of adoption for healthcare professionals.

Despite the potential benefits of SMED, there is a lack of detailed studies on its implementation in healthcare facilities, including information about the installation process, complementary tools utilized, the pre-intervention infrastructure situation, encountered challenges, specific achieved results, and statistical evidence. Therefore, case study research can contribute to expanding the knowledge base in this area.

CONCLUSION

In conclusion, the healthcare industry is grappling with the complex task of managing increased demand while maintaining service quality. The resulting overcrowding and prolonged waiting periods not only lead to higher patient mortality rates but also contribute to resource inefficiency and diminished patient and staff satisfaction. Challenges such as excessive staff workload, communication breakdowns, and compromised care for urgent cases further exacerbate the situation.

The adoption of Lean, Kata and SMED methodologies faces resistance from healthcare practitioners who may view them as incompatible or restrictive, raising concerns about standardized treatments and the human touch in healthcare. Management's preference for a reactive problem-solving approach and the need for financial considerations further impede the adoption of these strategies.

Additionally, public hospitals may face infrastructure limitations and financial constraints, while private hospitals balance profitability and investment decisions. Overcoming these challenges necessitates, an appropriate terminology, cultural change promoting motivation and engagement, facilitating the transition for healthcare professionals, ensuring they perceive the changes as improvements rather than losses.

ACKNOWLEDGMENT

The authors would like to thank the Brazilian Ministry of Health, UFF - Universidade Federal Fluminense, and Euclides da Cunha Foundation. This Research is part of the" Lean Project in UPA 24h" that has been funded by the Brazilian Ministry of Health (TED 15/2021, number: 25000.103452/2021-14).

REFERENCES

Arnheiter, E. D., & Maleyeff, J. (2005). The integration of lean management and Six Sigma. *The TQM Magazine*, *17*(1), 5–18. doi:10.1108/09544780510573020

Bardin, L. (2011). Análise de Conteúdo (1° ed, Vol. 1). Edições 70.

Barlow, G. L. (2002). Auditing hospital queuing. *Managerial Auditing Journal*, *17*(7), 397–403. doi:10.1108/02686900210437507

Bauer, H., Brandl, F., Lock, C., & Reinhart, G. (2018). Integration of Industrie 4.0 in Lean Manufacturing Learning Factories. *Procedia Manufacturing*, *23*, 147–152. doi:10.1016/j.promfg.2018.04.008

Ben-Tovim, D. I., Bassham, J. E., Bolch, D., Martin, M. A., Dougherty, M., & Szwarcbord, M. (2007). Lean thinking across a hospital: Redesigning care at the Flinders Medical Centre. *Australian Health Review*, *31*(1), 10. doi:10.1071/AH070010 PMID:17266483

Bielen, F., & Demoulin, N. (2007). Waiting time influence on the satisfaction-loyalty relationship in services. *Managing Service Quality*, *17*(2), 174–193. doi:10.1108/09604520710735182

Bin Che Ani, M. N., & Bin Shafei, M. S. S. (2013). The Effectiveness of the Single Minute Exchange of Die (SMED) Technique for the Productivity Improvement. *Applied Mechanics and Materials*, *465–466*, 1144–1148. . doi:10.4028/www.scientific.net/AMM.465-466.1144

Bonamigo, A., Bernardes, P. M. M., Conrado, L. F., Torres, L. F., & Calado, R. D. (2022). Patient Flow Optimization: SMED adoption in Emergency Care Units. *IFAC-PapersOnLine*, *55*(10), 204–209. doi:10.1016/j.ifacol.2022.09.391

Cerdeira, A. K. (2020). *SisperaH: Sistema Inteligente de Gestão de Lista de Espera Hospitalar: regulação de leitos, lista de espera, gestão e inovação em saúde*. Universidade Federal do Rio Grande do Norte. https://repositorio.ufrn.br/handle/123456789/31857

Charron, R., Harrington, H. J., Voehl, F., & Wiggin, H. (2014). *The Lean Management Systems Handbook*. Productivity Press., doi:10.1201/b17201

Chiarini, A., & Baccarani, C. (2016). TQM and lean strategy deployment in Italian hospitals. *Leadership in Health Services*, *29*(4), 377–391. doi:10.1108/LHS-07-2015-0019 PMID:27707152

Costa, H. G., da Silva, M. H. T., Santos, G. N., Bonamigo, A., & Callado, R. D. (2022). Clustering Brazilian Public Emergency Healthcare Units. *IFAC-PapersOnLine*, *55*(10), 566–571. doi:10.1016/j.ifacol.2022.09.454

Crema, M., & Verbano, C. (2021). Simulation modelling and lean management in healthcare: First evidences and research agenda. *Total Quality Management & Business Excellence*, *32*(3–4), 448–466. doi:10.1080/14783363.2019.1572504

Crosby, P. (1989). Let's Talk Quality: 96 Questions You Always Wanted to Ask (1° ed, Vol. 1). McGraw-Hill.

Davis, B. M. (2010). Applying Lean to the Perioperative Environment. *AORN Journal*, *92*(S6). Advance online publication. doi:10.1016/j.aorn.2010.09.012

de Amaral, L., Calado, R., Teixeira, A., da Silva, M. H., Bourguignon, S., & Costa, H. (2021). *Systematic review and meta-analysis of the use of lean methods and tools in healthcare services: an alternative to improve care during the pandemic*. Research Square.

de Souza, L. B., & Pidd, M. (2011). Exploring the barriers to lean health care implementation. *Public Money & Management*, *31*(1), 59–66. doi:10.1080/09540962.2011.545548

de Souza, W., Buss, L., Candido, D., Carrera, J.-P., Li, S., Zarebski, A., Pereira, R. H., Prete, C., Santos, A., Parag, K., Belotti, M. C., Vincenti-Gonzalez, M., Messina, J., da Silva Sales, F. C., Andrade, P., Nascimento, V., Ghilardi, F., Abade, L., Gutierrez, B., ... Faria, N. (2020). Epidemiological and clinical characteristics of the COVID-19 epidemic in Brazil. *Nature Human Behaviour*, *4*(8), 856–865. doi:10.103841562-020-0928-4 PMID:32737472

Erthal, A., Frangeskou, M., & Marques, L. (2021). Cultural tensions in lean healthcare implementation: A paradox theory lens. *International Journal of Production Economics*, *233*, 107968. doi:10.1016/j.ijpe.2020.107968

Ferenhof, H. A., Da Cunha, A. H., Bonamigo, A., & Forcellini, F. A. (2018). Toyota Kata as a KM solution to the inhibitors of implementing lean service in service companies. *VINE Journal of Information and Knowledge Management Systems*, *48*(3), 404–426. doi:10.1108/VJIKMS-11-2017-0083

Fillingham, D. (2007). Can lean save lives? *Leadership in Health Services*, *20*(4), 231–241. doi:10.1108/17511870710829346 PMID:20698096

Gallis, C. (2013). ncreasing productivity and controlling of work fatigue in forest operations by using prescribed active pauses: A selective review. *Croatian Journal of Forest Engineering: Journal for Theory and Application of Forestry Engineering*, *34*(1), 103–112.

Graban, M., & Toussaint, J. (2018). *Lean Hospitals*. Productivity Press. doi:10.4324/9781315380827

Hallam, C. R. A., & Contreras, C. (2018). Lean healthcare: Scale, scope and sustainability. *International Journal of Health Care Quality Assurance*, *31*(7), 684–696. doi:10.1108/IJHCQA-02-2017-0023 PMID:30354875

Hurst, J. (2000). Challenges for health systems in member countries of the Organisation for Economic Co-operation and Development. *Bulletin of the World Health Organization*, *78*(6), 751–760. PMID:10916912

Improta, G., Romano, M., Di Cicco, M. V., Ferraro, A., Borrelli, A., Verdoliva, C., Triassi, M., & Cesarelli, M. (2018). Lean thinking to improve emergency department throughput at AORN Cardarelli hospital. *BMC Health Services Research*, *18*(1), 914. doi:10.118612913-018-3654-0 PMID:30509286

Kam, A. W., Collins, S., Park, T., Mihail, M., Stanaway, F. F., Lewis, N. L., Polya, D., Fraser-Bell, S., Roberts, T. V., & Smith, J. E. (2021). Using Lean Six Sigma techniques to improve efficiency in outpatient ophthalmology clinics. *BMC Health Services Research*, *21*(1), 1–9. doi:10.118612913-020-06034-3 PMID:33413381

Karam, A.-A., Liviu, M., Cristina, V., & Radu, H. (2018). The contribution of lean manufacturing tools to changeover time decrease in the pharmaceutical industry. A SMED project. *Procedia Manufacturing*, *22*, 886–892. doi:10.1016/j.promfg.2018.03.125

Ken Lee, K. H., Matthew Austin, J., & Pronovost, P. J. (2016). Developing a Measure of Value in Health Care. *Value in Health*, *19*(4), 323–325. doi:10.1016/j.jval.2014.12.009 PMID:27325323

Lawal, A. K., Rotter, T., Kinsman, L., Sari, N., Harrison, L., Jeffery, C., Kutz, M., Khan, M. F., & Flynn, R. (2014). Lean management in health care: Definition, concepts, methodology and effects reported (systematic review protocol). *Systematic Reviews*, *3*(1), 103. doi:10.1186/2046-4053-3-103 PMID:25238974

Leite, H., Bateman, N., & Radnor, Z. (2020). Beyond the ostensible: An exploration of barriers to lean implementation and sustainability in healthcare. *Production Planning and Control*, *31*(1), 1–18. doi:10.1080/09537287.2019.1623426

Levinson, W., & Shojania, K. G. (2011). Bad experiences in the hospital: The stories keep coming. *BMJ Quality & Safety*, *20*(11), 911–913. doi:10.1136/bmjqs-2011-000474 PMID:21964611

Liker, J. (2004). The Toyota Way: 14 Management Principles from the World's Greatest Manufacturer (1° ed). McGraw Hill.

Maione, E., Bruno, G., & Lombardi, F. (2020). *Lean healthcare application for patient flow analysis in Cardiology department*. Politecnico di Torino, Corso di Laurea Magistrale in Ingegneria Gestionale. https://webthesis.biblio.polito.it/id/eprint/14000

McGrath, K. M., Bennett, D. M., Ben-Tovim, D. I., Boyages, S. C., Lyons, N. J., & O'Connell, T. J. (2008). Implementing and sustaining transformational change in health care: Lessons learnt about clinical process redesign. *The Medical Journal of Australia*, *188*(7, S6), 422. Advance online publication. doi:10.5694/j.1326-5377.2008.tb01692.x PMID:18341474

Peimbert-García, R. E., Gutiérrez-Mendoza, L. M., & García-Reyes, H. (2021). Applying Lean Healthcare to Improve the Discharge Process in a Mexican Academic Medical Center. *Sustainability (Basel)*, *13*(19), 10911. doi:10.3390u131910911

Pettersen, J. (2009). Defining lean production: Some conceptual and practical issues. *The TQM Journal*, *21*(2), 127–142. doi:10.1108/17542730910938137

Plenert, G. J. (2011). *Lean Management Principles for Information Technology*. CRC Press. doi:10.1201/b11549

Priori, F. R., & Saurin, T. A. (2020). Solução de problemas em uma emergência hospitalar: Avaliação dos métodos A3 e análise de causa raiz. *Revista Produção Online*, *20*(1), 63–94. doi:10.14488/1676-1901.v20i1.3258

Rathi, R., Vakharia, A., & Shadab, M. (2022). Lean six sigma in the healthcare sector: A systematic literature review. *Materials Today: Proceedings*, *50*, 773–781. doi:10.1016/j.matpr.2021.05.534 PMID:35155129

Régis, T. K. O., Santos, L. C., & Gohr, C. F. (2019). A case-based methodology for lean implementation in hospital operations. *Journal of Health Organization and Management*, *33*(6), 656–676. doi:10.1108/JHOM-09-2018-0267 PMID:31625821

Riquetta, A. C. B. (2018). *Aplicativo para dispositivo móvel direcionado aos usuários das Unidades de Pronto Atendimento (UPA) 24 horas de Curitiba*. Universidade Tecnológica Federal do Paraná. http://repositorio.utfpr.edu.br/jspui/handle/1/3932

Rosa, C., Silva, F. J. G., Ferreira, L. P., & Campilho, R. (2017). SMED methodology: The reduction of setup times for Steel Wire-Rope assembly lines in the automotive industry. *Procedia Manufacturing*, *13*, 1034–1042. doi:10.1016/j.promfg.2017.09.110

Rother, M. (2009). The Toyota Kata: Managing People for Improvement. Adaptiveness and Superior Results (1° ed, Vol. 1). McGraw Hill.

Rotter, T., Plishka, C., Lawal, A., Harrison, L., Sari, N., Goodridge, D., Flynn, R., Chan, J., Fiander, M., Poksinska, B., Willoughby, K., & Kinsman, L. (2019). What Is Lean Management in Health Care? Development of an Operational Definition for a Cochrane Systematic Review. *Evaluation & the Health Professions*, *42*(3), 366–390. doi:10.1177/0163278718756992 PMID:29635950

Shingo, S. (2019). *A Revolution in Manufacturing: The SMED System*. Routledge. doi:10.4324/9781315136479

Shortell, S. M., Blodgett, J. C., Rundall, T. G., & Kralovec, P. (2018). Use of Lean and Related Transformational Performance Improvement Systems in Hospitals in the United States: Results From a National Survey. *Joint Commission Journal on Quality and Patient Safety*, *44*(10), 574–582. doi:10.1016/j.jcjq.2018.03.002 PMID:30243359

Singh, S., Verma, R., & Koul, S. (2022). A collaborative method for simultaneous operations: Case of an eye clinic. *OPSEARCH*, *59*(2), 711–731. doi:10.100712597-021-00513-9

Tekin, M., Arslandere, M., Etlioğlu, M., Koyuncuoğlu, Ö., & Tekin, E. (2019). An Application of SMED and Jidoka in Lean Production. In *Proceedings of the International Symposium for Production Research 2018* (p. 530–545). Springer International Publishing. 10.1007/978-3-319-92267-6_45

Tlapa, D., Zepeda-Lugo, C. A., Tortorella, G. L., Baez-Lopez, Y. A., Limon-Romero, J., Alvarado-Iniesta, A., & Rodriguez-Borbon, M. I. (2020). Effects of Lean Healthcare on Patient Flow: A Systematic Review. *Value in Health*, *23*(2), 260–273. doi:10.1016/j.jval.2019.11.002 PMID:32113632

Trakulsunti, Y., Antony, J., Edgeman, R., Cudney, B., Dempsey, M., & Brennan, A. (2022). Reducing pharmacy medication errors using Lean Six Sigma: A Thai hospital case study. *Total Quality Management & Business Excellence*, *33*(5-6), 664–682. doi:10.1080/14783363.2021.1885292

Vats, A., Goin, K. H., & Fortenberry, J. D. (2011). Lean analysis of a pediatric intensive care unit physician group rounding process to identify inefficiencies and opportunities for improvement. *Pediatric Critical Care Medicine*, *12*(4), 415–421. doi:10.1097/PCC.0b013e3181fe2e3c PMID:20975612

Womack, J. P., & Jones, D. T. (1997). Lean Thinking: Banish Waste and Create Wealth in your Corporation. *The Journal of the Operational Research Society*, *48*(11), 1148–1148. doi:10.1057/palgrave.jors.2600967

ADDITIONAL READING

Ahmed, S. (2019). Integrating DMAIC approach of Lean Six Sigma and theory of constraints toward quality improvement in healthcare. *Reviews on Environmental Health*, *34*(4), 427–434. doi:10.1515/reveh-2019-0003 PMID:31314742

Leite, H., Bateman, N., & Radnor, Z. (2020). Beyond the ostensible: An exploration of barriers to lean implementation and sustainability in healthcare. *Production Planning and Control*, *31*(1), 1–18. doi:10.1080/09537287.2019.1623426

Parkhi, S. S. (2019). Lean management practices in healthcare sector: A literature review. *Benchmarking*, *26*(4), 1275–1289. doi:10.1108/BIJ-06-2018-0166

Polancich, S., & Pilon, B. (2019). The application of the Toyota Production System LEAN 5S methodology in the operating room setting. *Nursing Clinics*, *54*(1), 53–79. PMID:30712545

Prado-Prado, J. C., García-Arca, J., Fernández-González, A. J., & Mosteiro-Añón, M. (2020). Increasing competitiveness through the implementation of lean management in healthcare. *International Journal of Environmental Research and Public Health*, *17*(14), 4981. doi:10.3390/ijerph17144981 PMID:32664355

Rodgers, B., & Antony, J. (2019). Lean and Six Sigma practices in the public sector: A review. *International Journal of Quality & Reliability Management*, *36*(3), 437–455. doi:10.1108/IJQRM-02-2018-0057

Rotter, T., Plishka, C., Lawal, A., Harrison, L., Sari, N., Goodridge, D., Flynn, R., Chan, J., Fiander, M., Poksinska, B., Willoughby, K., & Kinsman, L. (2019). What is lean management in health care? Development of an operational definition for a Cochrane systematic review. *Evaluation & the Health Professions*, *42*(3), 366–390. doi:10.1177/0163278718756992 PMID:29635950

Sunder, M. V., Mahalingam, S., & Krishna, M. S. N. (2020). Improving patients' satisfaction in a mobile hospital using Lean Six Sigma–a design-thinking intervention. *Production Planning and Control*, *31*(6), 512–526. doi:10.1080/09537287.2019.1654628

KEY TERMS AND DEFINITIONS

Continual Improvement Process: A systematic and ongoing approach used by organizations to enhance their products, services, processes, and overall performance over time. It involves identifying areas for improvement, setting objectives, implementing changes, and evaluating the results in a continuous cycle.

Flow: Refers to the progressive achievement of tasks along a value stream so that a product proceeds from design to launch, order to delivery, and raw materials into the hands of the customer with no stoppages, scrap, or backflows (Womack & Jones, 1997).

Lead Time: Total time from the moment the customer places an order to the moment that customer receives the order (Womack & Jones, 1997).

Lean Healthcare: A methodology that focuses on improving healthcare delivery through the adoption of lean principles, which include eliminating waste, enhancing value for patients, improving patient flow, reducing waiting time, increasing efficiency, enhancing quality and safety, empowering employees, and promoting continuous improvement (Lawal et al., 2014).

Lean Management: A systematic approach to identify and eliminate waste through continuous improvement by flowing the product at the pull of the customer in pursuit of perfection (Plenert, 2011).

Set-Up Time: The time required to change a process or machine from the last part of a production lot to the first good part of the next lot (Shingo, 2019).

SMED: A system for dramatically reducing the time it takes to complete equipment changeovers. The essence of the SMED system is to convert as many changeover steps as possible to "external" (performed while the equipment is running), and to simplify and streamline the remaining steps (Shingo, 2019).

Toyota Production System: A philosophy of manufacturing that emphasizes the elimination of waste in all forms and respects the fact that constantly improving this system is a never-ending process. It is a set of principles and practices that focus on designing out overburden and inconsistency so that work is performed smoothly, and the result is that workers develop a deep commitment to the goals of the organization (Liker, 2004).

Value: Any action or process that a customer would be willing to pay for (Womack & Jones, 1997).

Waiting Time: Idle or non-productive time during which a product, service, or information is delayed or held up in a process, often due to inefficiencies, bottlenecks, or interruptions. It is a form of waste that does not add value to the customer and is targeted for elimination or reduction in lean thinking.

Chapter 8
A Review of Governance Frameworks for National Spatial Data Infrastructure

Munir Ahmad
https://orcid.org/0000-0003-4836-6151
Survey of Pakistan, Pakistan

Asmat Ali
https://orcid.org/0000-0002-8804-2285
Survey of Pakistan, Pakistan

ABSTRACT

This chapter examined the governance framework of National Spatial Data Infrastructures in five South Asian countries: Bangladesh, India, Nepal, Pakistan, and Sri Lanka. It analyzed six key components—participation and consensus orientation, responsiveness and transparency, equity and accountability, effectiveness and efficiency, rule of law, and strategic vision—underpinning NSDI programs. The diverse strategies and structures employed by these countries are explored. Bangladesh's collaborative NSDI Steering and Technical Committees promote geospatial data sharing. India's two-tier structure involves the National Spatial Data Committee and the NSDI Executive Committee for policy setting and implementation. Nepal's lack of a designated NSDI agency hampers coordination. Pakistan's NSDI is in the feasibility study phase, while Sri Lanka emphasizes its NSDI within its Digital Policy. Overall, it was observed that some characteristics of good governance are evident across the majority of the countries examined in this chapter; however, the level of maturity remains relatively weak.

INTRODUCTION

Geospatial information pertains to data concerning entities, occurrences, or phenomena situated on the Earth's expanse. This encompasses geographic coordinates, descriptive attributes, and frequently, temporal particulars (Stock & Guesgen, 2016). Spatial data offers diverse utility across multiple sectors,

DOI: 10.4018/979-8-3693-0458-7.ch008

encompassing realms like disaster response, agriculture risk assessment, environmental strategizing, and safeguarding water resources (Zhang et al., 2021). Skillful handling of spatial data stands as a pivotal factor in enhancing the efficiency of urban planning endeavors, yielding benefits in terms of both cost-effectiveness and time conservation (Ostadabbas et al., 2021). In recent times, we have witnessed a swift expansion in the multitude of sources and accessibility of geospatial data and information. This surge presents fresh new prospects and challenges the boundaries of scientific understanding and timely technological resolutions (Filchev et al., 2020).

Embracing geospatial data and leveraging advanced tools such as satellite imagery, GIS, and GNSS, geospatial technology emerges as a pivotal player in propelling the journey toward sustainable development. It empowers informed decision-making regarding land management, resource management, and infrastructure growth, all the while amplifying efficiency and precision in the allocation of resources (Joshi, 2023; Kyle, 2022). The true value of geospatial information emerges when it becomes easily accessible, shared, and put into practical application (Simmons, 2018). Thus, to fully realize the promise of geospatial data in promoting sustainable development, informed decision-making, and effective resource allocation, a Spatial Data Infrastructure needs to be established.

The concept of the Spatial Data Infrastructure encompasses the essential technology, policies, standards, and skilled personnel needed to acquire, process, retain, distribute, and enhance the effective application of geospatial information. Functioning as a structured framework, it streamlines the administration and collaborative dissemination of geographical data (Binder Maitra, 2015). Spatial Data Infrastructures frequently amalgamate information from diverse origins, either physically housed in a central repository or virtually linked via a central catalog that connects to the source data overseen and provided by its proprietors. SDIs can be established across a spectrum of magnitudes and intricacies. Individual entities can oversee Enterprise SDIs; governing bodies can administer regional, state, or sectoral SDIs; or entire countries can steward National SDIs (NSDI) (Simmons, 2018).

Ensuring the triumph of an NSDI and fostering active engagement from stakeholders demands the establishment of an effective governance framework. A governance framework is "an organized structure established as authoritative within the institution, comprising processes and rules established to ensure projects meet their purpose" (Ole et al., 2009). The megaprojects' governance framework strives to harmonize governmental effectiveness, credibility, and accountability. Finding a balance between these goals is a complex task that involves managing conflicts within and among various tiers of the framework (Brunet, 2021; Brunet & Aubry, 2016).

According to Crompvoets et al., (2018), governance of SDI encompasses the "structures, policies, actors and institutions by which the infrastructure is managed pertaining to decisions made for accessing, sharing, exchanging and using the relevant available spatial information". This endeavor seeks to mitigate disparities, redundancies, inconsistencies, and unutilized prospects that often arise within a multi-stakeholder setting, impacting the creation, administration, dissemination, and utilization of spatial data.

Across the globe, nations are actively developing their own NSDIs, each potentially shaped by unique governance structures. Hence, the primary objective of this study is to examine the governance systems of national SDIs within different countries. To achieve this objective, the chapter is structured as follows: Section 2 provides the theoretical background on NSDI and governance framework, succeeded by the importance of governance framework in SDI outlined in Section 3. Section 4 describes the methodology adopted in this chapter. The subsequent Section 5 presents the results of the review of governance framework in the South Asian countries. Ultimately, the chapter concludes by summarizing key findings and proposing recommendations for further research.

THEORETICAL BACKGROUND

This section presented a detailed description of two fundamental concepts: governance framework and spatial data infrastructure to provide a comprehensive comprehension of the research topic.

Spatial Data Infrastructure

The concept of "Spatial Data Infrastructure" has gained significant recognition within the domains of geographic information systems and spatial data management. It traces its roots back to the inception of the National Spatial Data Infrastructure, first introduced at the Canadian Conference on Geographic Information Systems in 1991 (J. D. McLaughlin, 1991). This notion was further elaborated upon through Executive Order 12906, signed by President Clinton the subsequent year, titled 'Coordinating Geographic Data Acquisition and Access: The National Spatial Data Infrastructure.' This directive notably heightened the awareness regarding the imperative for governmental initiatives to advance the collection, management, and utilization of geospatial data. Its influence extended beyond just the United States federal agencies, resonating at both national and global echelons (Masser, 2005).

Spatial data infrastructure embodies the foundational physical and organizational framework necessary to facilitate the efficient and effective utilization of spatial data (Rajabifard et al., 2006). To harness spatial data from diverse sources and fully unlock its potential, an SDI must encompass a holistic understanding of its applications, transcending the technical elements and data models (Ahmad et al., 2022; Ali et al., 2021). Governments at various tiers—local, national, and international—have embarked on SDI initiatives to facilitate the amalgamation and dissemination of spatial data for multifarious objectives (Crompvoets et al., 2004; Masser, 2005; Rajabifard et al., 2006). The initial focal point of national and regional spatial data infrastructures was to centralize databases with geospatial data primarily sourced from authoritative origins (Groot & McLaughlin, 2000; Jacoby et al., 2002; Masser, 1999).

A fundamental element within SDI is its interoperability, enabling the seamless exchange and application of spatial data across diverse platforms, applications, and entities, regardless of their origin, structure, or format. This seamless interaction is accomplished through the adoption of standardized protocols and specifications, exemplified by the directives established by entities such as the Open Geospatial Consortium (OGC) and the International Organization for Standardization (ISO). These universally accepted standards streamline the fusion of disparate datasets and promote effortless data sharing and cooperative efforts among SDI stakeholders (Chaturvedi et al., 2019; Corti et al., 2019).

An additional notable aspect of SDI is its inclusiveness, which concerns the ease with which users can reach, uncover, and fetch spatial data. To fulfill this objective, web-driven gateways, repositories, and utilities have been established, endowing users with a diverse array of resources and features to explore, interrogate, and procure spatial data. These online interfaces streamline the process of users finding and attaining the specific spatial data they need, thereby contributing to a wide array of applications and scenarios (Giuliani et al., 2017; Vancauwenberghe & van Loenen, 2018).

SDI Architecture

The structure of SDI encompasses multiple constituent parts that collaborate harmoniously to facilitate the exchange and administration of spatial data. These distinct SDI elements share several fundamental attributes. In line with their unique intentions, ideologies, and priorities, various scholars and institutions have formulated their own distinct components for NSDI. Illustrated in Figure 1, (Rajabifard et al., 2002) introduced five pivotal SDI components: policy, access network, standards, personnel, and data.

Within Figure 1, the dynamic technological facets of SDI—such as access networks, regulations, and standards—impact the fundamental interplay between the two other segments, namely geographical data, and individuals. The model's dynamic nature signifies that a comprehensive SDI encompasses crucial considerations of interoperability, regulations, and networks, extending beyond the mere presence of spatial data and individuals (Rajabifard et al., 2002). A more intricate exploration of SDI components was provided by the GSDI Cookbook (GSDI, 2004). delving into elements like metadata, catalogs, and web applications. This nuanced perspective presents a more holistic understanding of the constituents of an SDI, as depicted in Figure 2.

Figure 1. Components of SDI
Source: Rajabifard et al. (2002)

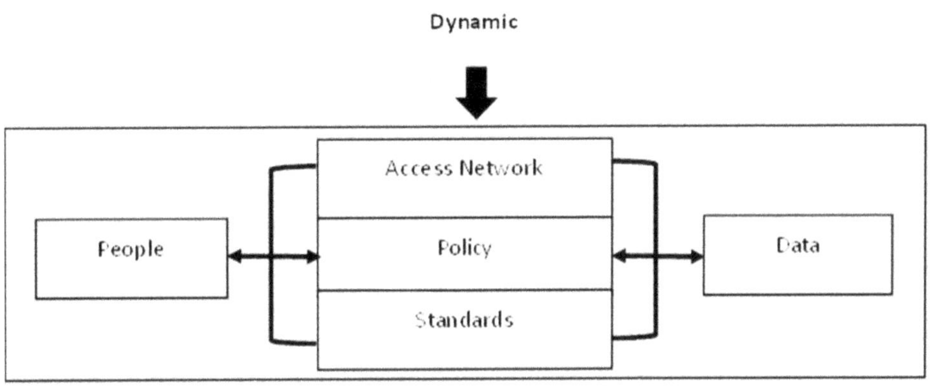

Figure 2. Elements of SDI
Source: GSDI (2004)

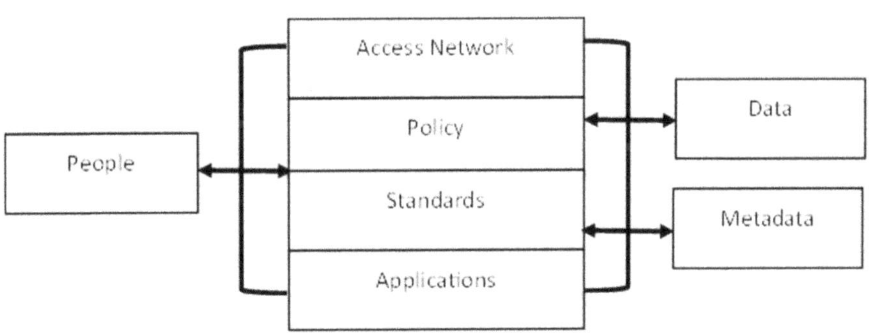

As the concept and progression of the SDI framework have evolved, the significance of several additional elements has surfaced. Capacity building, spatial data sharing, partnerships, and governance have been acknowledged as influential contributors to the efficacy and triumph of SDIs (Mohammadi, 2008).

Governance Framework

A governance framework denotes a structured methodology or system that steers the decision-making and managerial processes within an organization or project. This framework offers a set of principles, policies, and protocols that delineate the approach to decision formulation, delegation of duties, and establishment of accountability. Its purpose is to establish clear objectives, define roles and obligations, oversee performance, and evaluate outcomes. In addition, it encompasses mechanisms for harmonization, adjustment, and preservation of interactions in networks spanning multiple organizations. This governance framework is versatile and can be adapted to diverse domains, including brain data acquisition and processing, project networks, antimicrobial resistance, decentralized exchange, and information systems. Its primary objective is to optimize advantages, mitigate risks, and ensure conscientious advancement and safeguarding of human rights (Anderson et al., 2019; Ienca et al., 2022; Kujala et al., 2021). A governance framework for major public projects is a tool to enhance performance by improving government efficiency, legitimacy, and accountability (Brunet & Aubry, 2016). Governance frameworks can face a challenge in designing a suitable user interface for network infrastructures (Galani et al., 2013).

A governance framework encompasses four key domains of regulatory involvement: obligatory regulations, ethical considerations and informal norms, responsible innovation, and upholding human rights (Ienca et al., 2022). Moreover, establishing an effective risk governance structure for nanomaterials necessitates advanced methodologies for making decisions based on risk assessment, a comprehensive model predicting human behavior and choices, and adherence to legal and regulatory mandates (Stone et al., 2018). When addressing the issue of antimicrobial resistance, a governance framework for national action plans encompasses three focal points: devising policies, deploying tools for execution, and overseeing progress through monitoring and evaluation (Anderson et al., 2019). For an examination of governance within public spaces, a framework should encompass the identification of actors and stakeholders, delineation of governance structure, utilization of governance tools, and execution of governing tasks (Zamanifard et al., 2018). In the realm of project networks, governance can be classified into dimensions such as defining objectives, establishing incentives, overseeing progress, assigning roles and making decisions, synchronizing efforts, and enhancing capabilities (Kujala et al., 2021).

Mao et al., (2022) introduced an innovative framework for governing government data, which revolves around a central data intermediary platform. This framework caters to the requirements of modern digital governance, unlocking the potential value of data assets, enhancing auditing and supervision processes, and facilitating improved communication channels.

Deploying Big Data analytics within information services necessitates a distinct data governance framework, one that diverges from conventional data governance practices. This specialized framework places emphasis on qualities such as timeliness, dependability, significance, adequacy, and safeguarding of personal information (Kim & Cho, 2018).

IMPORTANCE OF GOVERNANCE FRAMEWORK IN SDI

Spatial Data Infrastructures have emerged as transformative tools that hold the promise of enhancing governance structures and bolstering their effectiveness. SDIs have gained recognition for their potential to revolutionize decision-making processes, streamline public service delivery, and foster sustainable development (Ayanlade et al., 2008a; GSDI, 2004). While SDIs are perceived as endeavors that contribute to improved governance or the efficacy of governance, a significant hurdle in the creation of SDIs lies in managing the governance of the infrastructure itself (Crompvoets et al., 2018).

SDIs encompass an intricate amalgamation of technological, policy, and organizational facets that collectively contribute to the efficient collection, management, sharing, and utilization of spatial data (Rajabifard et al., 2002). However, without effective governance, these individual components may operate in isolation, leading to fragmentation, inefficiencies, and the inability to fully harness the potential of spatial data. Thus, efficient and well-orchestrated governance of Spatial Data Infrastructures stands as a pivotal determinant in ensuring the seamless integration and consistent operation of its diverse components (Craglia & Johnston, 2004).

By implementing effective governance practices, SDIs can bridge the gaps between various stakeholders, including government bodies, private enterprises, research institutions, and citizen contributors. (Kleijn et al., 2014). A well-structured governance framework ensures that objectives, roles, responsibilities, and decision-making processes are clearly defined and aligned. This, in turn, enables a harmonious coordination of efforts, facilitates data interoperability, minimizes redundancy, and promotes the equitable distribution of benefits among stakeholders. According to (Castelein et al., 2013) effective cooperation plays a pivotal role in the evolution of spatial data infrastructures, encompassing the concerted efforts of stakeholders to pool resources, exchange insights, and leverage their expertise. The triumph of SDIs hinges upon the artful fusion of structured collaborative frameworks and the organic spontaneity inherent in informal cooperative methods.

Effective governance enhances transparency, accountability, and credibility, which are fundamental aspects in garnering trust and collaboration among diverse participants (Bertelli, 2008; Johnston, 2006). As SDIs often involve complex interactions and interdependencies among technological, institutional, and social factors, a well-governed system helps to navigate challenges, resolve conflicts, and adapt to evolving needs and opportunities.

The efficacy of spatial data infrastructures in addressing the complexities brought about by emerging technologies and evolving user requirements is intricately tied to the establishment of robust governance mechanisms (J. Sjoukema et al., 2020). To illustrate, the utilization of agent-based modeling emerges as a potent tool for delving into the multifaceted realm of SDI governance. Through simulations, it becomes conspicuously clear that a network-oriented governance strategy outperforms conventional hierarchical or laissez-faire approaches (J. W. Sjoukema et al., 2021). This underscores the pivotal role of governance paradigms in ensuring the adaptability, responsiveness, and efficiency of SDIs in an ever-changing landscape.

METHODOLOGY

The scope of governance extends beyond political boundaries, permeating into the realms of social and economic spheres. It encompasses not just governmental entities, but also encompasses a wider spectrum of participants, including civil society organizations and private sector entities (UNDP, 1997). Within the NSDI framework, governance transcends the realm of government bodies, weaving a tapestry that involves dynamic interactions with civil society organizations and private sector stakeholders. This multifaceted approach to governance ensures that the NSDI thrives as a collaborative ecosystem, fostering effective data sharing, interoperability, and sustainable development for the betterment of society at large (Ayanlade et al., 2008b; Feeney et al., 2001; J. McLaughlin & Nichols, 1994).

Spatial data infrastructure serves as a pivotal enabler for enhancing good governance, as emphasized by studies conducted by Ali & Ahmad, (2012); Ali & Imran, (2021); Singh & Pandey, (2018). In line with this, the United Nations Development Programme (UNDP, 1997) has meticulously outlined essential attributes encapsulating the essence of good governance such as participation, rule of law, transparency, responsiveness, consensus orientation, equity, effectiveness and efficiency, accountability, strategic vision. The assessment of the governance framework of the National Spatial Data Infrastructure within this chapter intricately integrates these delineated characteristics as a guiding lens. A comprehensive exploration of the definition and comprehension of these specific attributes in relation to the NSDI is unfolded below, thereby illuminating the profound interconnection between the principles of good governance and the NSDI's structure. Nine characteristics of good governance, as endorsed by the UNDP in 1997, have been consolidated for the purpose of this chapter's analysis. The examination is focused on a subset of these traits, resulting in a refined set of six components that are used to assess the governance framework of NSDI.

This chapter aims to evaluate the governance structures of NSDI in various nations, focusing on South Asian countries such as India, Bangladesh, Sri Lanka, Nepal, and Pakistan. Countries like Bhutan and Maldives are not considered in this analysis, as despite the passage of over twenty-five years, Bhutan has encountered challenges in making substantial strides in NSDI development. This predicament can be attributed to a dearth of dedicated resources, limited capacity, and the absence of a universally embraced national policy, as highlighted in the India Geospatial Forum of 2015. The assessment of various components as defined above is executed through the literature review method.

REVIEW OF GOVERNANCE FRAMEWORK

In this section, the status of the 06 components chosen as a methodology in the 05 countries namely Bangladesh, India, Nepal, Pakistan, and Srilanka is briefed in Table 1 and elaborated as below:

Participation and Consensus Orientation

Within the NSDI framework, participation holds a crucial role, denoting the engaged participation of all stakeholders in the process of decision-making. This takes place within an inclusive environment where every participant is afforded the opportunity to influence outcomes and gain insights into the underlying processes. To facilitate effective decision-making, the NSDI employs consensus-building mechanisms that prioritize alignment with the broader community's perspectives. This approach ensures that decisions are collaborative, inclusive, and well-informed. An apex body, vested with authority, often oversees these consensus-building efforts, while continuous monitoring ensures that the established decisions and processes remain in line with the evolving needs and expectations of stakeholders. The situation of participation and consensus orientation in five countries is described below.

Regarding Bangladesh, Rahman & Szabó, (2023) argued that the Survey of Bangladesh (SoB) has been energetically engaged in fortifying the foundational structure essential for the seamless execution of NSDI. This encompasses the inception of both the NSDI Steering Committee and the Technical Committee. These dedicated panels bear the responsibility of shaping policies, delineating guidelines, and setting benchmarks for the meticulous management of geospatial data, all while fostering a climate of effective collaboration among pertinent stakeholders.

Similarly, as far as India is concerned, Acharya & Pandey, (2018) endorsed that at the national level, NSDI operates under a two-tier coordination structure in India. The apex body, known as the National Spatial Data Committee (NSDC), is chaired by the Minister of Science and Technology, with relevant government secretaries as members. NSDC sets policy direction, offers guidance, and oversees the NSDI's overall implementation, including necessary adjustments. The Surveyor General of India and the Director of the National Remote Sensing Centre serve as member secretaries, along with domain experts in geospatial technologies. On a lower tier, the NSDI Executive Committee (EC), co-chaired by the Surveyor General of India and the Director of the National Remote Sensing Centre, includes heads of central government data-providing agencies as members. The EC is responsible for implementing NSDI policies and decisions established by NSDC, managing day-to-day operations, and supervising Working Groups/Technical Committees focused on thematic domains such as geospatial metadata, data content standards, interoperability, national data registry, geospatial cloud, and administrative boundary harmonization.

In Nepal, the situation regarding the participation and consensus orientation component is not encouraging. No agency is designated to oversee the matters pertaining to NSDI. The absence of significant backing for harmonized efforts across governmental bodies and the absence of a formally appointed agency to oversee NSDI pose substantial threats to Nepal's resilience. Furthermore, this situation presents a significant barrier to Nepal's journey toward sustainable development. A Council for NSDI coordination at the Ministerial or Secretary level should be expeditiously established under an officially endorsed mandate. This Council should receive guidance from a technical committee, consisting of senior officials from all government ministries. It is paramount that the agency responsible for spearheading NSDI endeavors is formally designated and acknowledged (Bell et al., 2020).

Regarding Pakistan, the NSDI is currently in the feasibility study stage (Ahmad & Khiyal, 2023), which implies the absence of an apex body to foster consensus development.

The governing framework of the Sri Lanka National Spatial Data Infrastructure comprises two pivotal committees: the Executive Committee and the Executive Steering Committee (ESC). These committees hold indispensable significance in providing guidance and oversight over the NSDI program's policies, activities, and standards (nsdi.gov.lk, 2023a). Under the leadership of the Prime Minister of Sri Lanka, the Executive Committee assumes a central role. This committee, inclusive of pertinent cabinet members, bears the responsibility of offering guidance, direction, and authoritative decision-making power concerning the program's policies and activities (nsdi.gov.lk, 2023a). The Executive Steering Committee assumes a prominent role in championing the NSDI program, orchestrating guidance and support. This committee operates within the purview of the Department of National Planning (NPD) and is co-chaired by two esteemed figures: the Secretary of the Ministry of National Policies & Economic Affairs and the Surveyor General (nsdi.gov.lk, 2023a; UNGGIM, 2019).

Responsiveness and Transparency

The NSDI operates with a keen awareness of evolving demands, swiftly adapting its mechanisms to cater to the dynamic needs of stakeholders. This agility is particularly vital in meeting the evolving demands of users, ensuring that the NSDI remains a robust platform for the provision of spatial data. As new data emerges and user requirements shift, the NSDI stands committed to facilitating a seamless flow of information, actively contributing to well-informed decision-making processes. This commitment to staying responsive and accommodating is pivotal in not only fulfilling user demands but also fostering a comprehensive and effective spatial data-sharing ecosystem. Below is a description of the state of the Responsiveness and Transparency components in five different countries.

In the context of Bangladesh, according to Rahman & Szabó, (2023), the Survey of Bangladesh has been instrumental in the creation of a dedicated national geospatial data hub that can be accessed via https://nsdi.gov.bd/. This platform has been strategically designed to facilitate the seamless dissemination of geospatial data to a diverse spectrum of government bodies, as well as external organizations and individuals. By centralizing the sharing and interchange of geospatial information, this innovative initiative serves as a pivotal conduit for decision-makers and various stakeholders to effortlessly obtain and apply this valuable data. The dynamic accessibility offered by this platform is poised to streamline decision-making processes and foster greater collaboration across multifaceted sectors. According to Rahman & Szabó, (2023), ensuring the precision and excellence of geospatial data encounters complexities within the context of Bangladesh. This is attributed to resource constraints, a scarcity of comprehensive technical assistance, constraints on data sharing, and the lack of a well-defined metadata framework.

P. K. Singh, (2009) endorsed that in 2008, a significant milestone was achieved as the India Geoportal (https://www.nsdi.gov.in) made its debut under the NSDI's auspices. However, a notable observation emerged: the scope of available spatial metadata for the country remained confined. A crucial revelation highlighted the scenario wherein numerous government and private entities were actively engaged in generating spatial data. Curiously, by March of the subsequent year, only a mere 17 government entities aligned themselves with the NSDI, with only a handful contributing their metadata to the NSDI servers.

Regarding Nepal, the National Geoportal (https://nationalgeoportal.gov.np) serves as the central hub for Nepal's comprehensive NSDI Clearinghouse delivering seamless accessibility to verified geospatial datasets, maps, and tools curated by the Survey Department. It stands as a unified online platform, streamlining the exploration and application of diverse geospatial information and services. Prominently, the National Geoportal showcases a repertoire of user-intuitive data search mechanisms, data retrieval capabilities, and dynamic data depiction on interactive maps. The Geoportal extends its reach across multiple domains, encompassing Geographic Information Infrastructure, Topographic Survey, Geodetic Survey, and Cadastral Survey, all the while furnishing indispensable datasets and services. Impressively, the interface presents a wealth of 54 datasets, captures a substantial count of 10,045 data views, and logs an impressive 12,126 downloads (nationalgeoportal.gov.np, 2023).

Although, a website regarding NSDI exists for Pakistan (www.nsdi.gov.pk). However, there is no data-sharing activity or mechanism available on this website.

According to (UNGGIM, 2019) since the year 2001, the Survey Department of Sri Lanka has embarked on a proactive endeavor aimed at instituting a comprehensive national spatial data infrastructure within the nation's borders. Remarkably, the NSDI has garnered recognition as a pivotal endeavor within the broader framework of the Government of Sri Lanka's National Digital Policy, specifically falling under the strategic banner of "Digitalization of the Economy. The inauguration of the NSDI platform (https://

www.nsdi.gov.lk/) has effectively paved the way for public access to geospatial data. Through this platform, individuals can conveniently retrieve geographical information pertaining to specific locations. The platform encompasses a website, an associated metadata catalogue, and a user-friendly geo-portal, collectively streamlining the process of data retrieval.

Equity and Accountability

The NSDI harmonizes the principles of equity and accountability to ensure that all stakeholders enjoy equal access to spatial data resources. Concurrently, the NSDI upholds a rigorous commitment to responsibility and transparency in its functions. Accountability extends throughout decision-making processes across diverse entities, assuring that actions are fair and in harmony with the NSDI's foundational principles. Below, you will find a description of the status of the equity and accountability component in five distinct countries.

According to Rahman & Szabó, (2023) imposing a comprehensive mandate, the SoB orchestrates harmonious NSDI development endeavors spanning governmental bodies, private enterprises, educational institutions, and civil society entities. Furthermore, the SoB has proactively instituted a National Geospatial Data Sharing Policy, strategically charting the course for data interchange amongst the multifaceted array of stakeholders.

According to Acharya & Pandey, (2018) in Indian NSDI, there exists a Steering Committee and multiple Technical Committees. These committees comprise members selected from prominent research and development institutions, including IITs, universities, and laboratories.

Serving as the secretariat, the Survey Department of Nepal plays a pivotal role within the National Mapping Committee, which has been established to oversee and regulate all surveying and mapping endeavors within the nation. A significant mandate bestowed upon this committee involves the endorsement of all geospatial products created within the country, irrespective of their origins in governmental or private sectors. The Director General of the Department assumes the crucial dual role of being the Member Secretary of the committee and the Coordinator of the Technical Sub-committee (UNGGIM, 2012).

In 2021, the Survey of Pakistan took a significant stride by establishing a coordination committee. This initiative was launched during a gathering held at the headquarters of SoP, signifying the initial phase of orchestrating collaborative NSDI implementation. The committee consists of a panel of 16 representatives encompassing a diverse range of federal ministries, governmental bodies, and private enterprises, including the Survey of Pakistan itself (Ali & Imran, 2021).

Within the framework of the Sri Lanka NSDI, the Technical Committee consists of representatives drawn from various participating organizations, spanning both governmental and non-governmental entities. This committee serves a pivotal role by offering input, counsel, and recommendations to the GeoCentre. Its primary focus encompasses technical policy considerations, fostering inter-agency collaboration, and the formulation of shared standards and quality assurance tools. Technical Committee undertakes the crucial task of harmonizing technical concerns across the wider NSDI community. It champions the cause of standards and interoperability, fostering a cohesive landscape for data exchange. The committee also assumes a role in evaluating business processes, ensuring their efficiency and relevance (nsdi.gov.lk, 2023a).

Effectiveness and Efficiency

This embodies the optimization of resources and efforts to achieve impactful outcomes. By harnessing data and spatial insights, the NSDI aims to meet diverse needs while utilizing resources judiciously. This synthesis of effectiveness and efficiency underscores the NSDI's commitment to delivering tangible results while maximizing its operational efficiency through capacity building and awareness campaigns. The evaluation of the effectiveness and efficiency component in five countries is outlined as follows:

According to Hussain, (2016) within the context of Bangladesh, ongoing endeavors are directed towards fortifying the capacity-building initiatives associated with NSDI advancement. However, there exists a scope for further augmentation, particularly concerning the enrichment of expertise and insights among the cadre of professionals deeply engaged in the progression of NSDI. Rahman & Szabó, (2023) argued that a prominent hurdle intertwined with the endeavor of enhancing capacity for NSDI development in Bangladesh lies in the constrained pool of adept professionals obtainable for this purpose. Rahman & Szabó, (2023) explored that the prevailing situation concerning NSDI awareness within Bangladesh exhibits a dual narrative of progress and identifiable areas necessitating heightened attention. Over time, the Survey of Bangladesh (SoB) has dedicated substantial endeavors towards cultivating a deeper understanding of NSDI and its advantages among the diverse stakeholders within the country. Workshops, instructional sessions, and proactive engagement initiatives have been orchestrated by the SoB to enlighten government entities, non-governmental bodies, academic institutions, and private organizations about the pivotal role of geospatial data and its applications in steering decisions and orchestrating effective planning endeavors. However, Hussain, (2016) noted that notwithstanding these concerted efforts, there persists a challenge in establishing comprehensive and widespread cognizance and comprehension of NSDI among the pivotal stakeholders of Bangladesh.

In 2003, a comprehensive assortment of materials concerning Indian NSDI was in place. These encompassed directives on NSDI metadata standards, NSDI exchange standards, NSDI application protocols, and the foundational NSDI network framework (Rao, 2007; P. K. Singh, 2009). UNGGIM, (2022) highlighted that, over the past decade, the Department of Science and Technology's National Geospatial Program (NGP) has been diligently organizing a series of educational initiatives. These endeavors encompass both 3-day orientation programs and comprehensive 21-day capacity-building programs. These programs are thoughtfully designed to cater to decision-makers, encompassing a range of topics. This includes providing a foundational understanding of geospatial technologies as well as delivering specialized training tailored to specific themes.

The "International FIG Workshop on The Role of Land Professionals and SDI in Disaster Risk Reduction" occurred in Kathmandu, Nepal, through a collaborative endeavor involving FIG Commission 2, Commission 7, ISPRS Working Group IV/4, Nepal Institution of Chartered Surveyors (NICS), and Nepal Remote Sensing and Photogrammetric Society (NRSPS). This event, which took place from November 25-27, 2015, had the objective of leveraging worldwide expertise in disaster risk reduction and its post-impact application following the 2015 Nepal earthquake. Its primary aim was to enhance the capacity of professionals to contribute to disaster risk reduction initiatives in Nepal and to explore advancements in geospatial education and SDI concepts. The workshop facilitated meaningful exchanges centered around image-based emergency management, challenges tied to land, and the cultivation of spatially empowered societies. The orchestrating of this event was significantly driven by the International Federation of Surveyors (FIG), a notable non-governmental organization, contributing to the progression of professional practices and global standards within the surveying community (Bhatta et al., 2016).

In March of 2023, the 2nd Conference on Exploring the Feasibility of Establishing a National Spatial Data Infrastructure for Pakistan was convened. This gathering was strategically orchestrated to cultivate synergies among the realms of academia, industry, and seasoned professionals, all with the overarching goal of unveiling the latent potential that NSDI holds for Pakistan. Spanning across a span of two days, the conference encompassed an array of focal points. These encompassed delving into the nexus between Science, Technology, and Innovation (STI) and the development of NSDI, gauging success benchmarks, identifying risk variables, discerning emergent trajectories, canvassing avenues for financial support, and mapping out the trajectory of advancement (Munir et al., 2023).

The objective of the Outreach Strategy for Sri Lanka's NSDI is to elevate consciousness, encourage cooperative efforts, and amplify involvement in the NSDI initiative. This comprehensive strategy entails forging alliances, crafting informative content, harnessing the power of social media, delivering informative talks, and actively participating in conferences. The spectrum of endeavors spans from evaluating outreach resources to orchestrating cross-departmental functions and establishing affiliations to procure data. The ultimate aspiration revolves around enriching public consciousness, facilitating harmonious stakeholder collaboration, and accentuating the potential influence of the initiative (nsdi.gov.lk, 2023c).

Rule of Law

This entails that the NSDI functions within a fair and equitable system, adhering to laws that govern spatial data management, sharing, and utilization. The rule of law underscores the NSDI's commitment to operating within ethical boundaries and upholding the rights of all stakeholders. The assessment of the rule of law component in five countries is detailed as follows:

Rahman & Szabó, (2023) underscored that the Geospatial Data and Services Act serves as a cornerstone, endowing a lawful scaffold governing the compilation, application, exchange, and circulation of geospatial data in Bangladesh in the context of NSDI. This legislation simultaneously introduces a Geospatial Data Committee, entrusted with the responsibility of supervising the unfolding NSDI journey across the nation. Nonetheless, the practical enactment of this legal provision has encountered its share of obstacles. A substantial hurdle can be attributed to a deficiency in widespread awareness and comprehension among the pertinent stakeholders, thus impeding the broader execution of the Geospatial Data and Services Act.

In India, the NSDI initiative was officially inaugurated via a cabinet resolution in June 2006. Its primary aims were to enhance accessibility to systematically gathered geospatial data, render these resources searchable and discoverable through accompanying metadata, and raise awareness among end-users about the advantages of NSDI (GOI, 2006).

In Nepal, no law exists regarding NSDI as far as the available literature is concerned. An absence of an endorsed all-encompassing government strategy for NSDI is noticeable within Nepal. To achieve this, the formulation of an NSDI policy is essential, encompassing facets such as comprehensive governmental synchronization, establishment of a lead agency, identification of data custodian agencies, establishment of fundamental datasets, allocation of resources, establishment of data standards, and formulation of protocols for accessibility and data sharing (Bell et al., 2020).

In 2014, the Government of Pakistan entrusted the Survey of Pakistan (SoP) with the task of formulating NSDI and fostering collaboration with pertinent entities within the nation (Surveying and Mapping Act, 2014). Regrettably, the SoP's commencement of implementation remains contingent on the awaited allocation of funds by the government. Moreover, a comprehensive law related to NSDI Pakistan that encompasses different facets of the NSDI is missing.

The Government of Sri Lanka has successfully instituted a National Spatial Data Infrastructure (NSDI) program. This endeavor has been designated as a pivotal undertaking within the National Digital Policy framework, specifically under the banner of "Digitalization of the Economy." This recognition underscores the strategic importance that the Government of Sri Lanka places on the NSDI as a fundamental initiative to drive digital transformation within the country's economic landscape (nsdi.gov.lk, 2023b). However, after the exploration of available literature, relevant law or act related to Sri Lankan NSDI has not been found.

Strategic Vision

This entails a comprehensive and forward-looking perspective on spatial data governance and its role in societal development. This perspective is grounded in an understanding of historical, cultural, and social complexities. It ensures that the NSDI operates with a holistic, long-term perspective, considering the evolving needs and aspirations of the community it serves. The evaluation of the strategic vision component in five countries is elaborated upon below:

The inception of Bangladesh's NSDI commenced in 2016 when a dedicated task force was established by the government. This task force was entrusted with the responsibility of crafting a comprehensive roadmap for the successful implementation of the NSDI. Within this roadmap, pivotal elements crucial to the NSDI's effectiveness were outlined by the task force. These elements encompassed data-sharing policies, precise technical standards, and the establishment of suitable institutional frameworks. Subsequently, the government has steadily progressed in the execution of the NSDI, reflecting its dedication to enhancing data integration and accessibility (Rahman & Szabó, 2023).

In 2001, the Indian National Spatial Data Infrastructure emerged, championed by the collaborative efforts of the Department of Science and Technology (DST) and the Department of Space within the Government of India (P. K. Singh, 2009). The overarching aspiration behind NSDI's inception revolved around crafting a comprehensive nationwide framework. Its primary goal encompassed the provision of structured spatial data, fostering its accessibility, and encouraging the utilization of this geospatial information as a cornerstone for effective planning (GOI, 2011) cited in Praharaj & Bandyopadhyay, (2019). According to (Praharaj & Bandyopadhyay, 2019) India introduced the National Data Sharing and Accessibility Policy (NDSAP) in 2012 (GOI, 2012). This strategic move was aimed at facilitating the availability of such data for valid and officially registered purposes. The core objective of this policy centers around enhancing the accessibility and dissemination of non-sensitive data among authorized users, fostering its application for scientific advancement, economic progress, and social development endeavors.

UNGGIM, (2012) highlighted that since 2001, the Survey Department of Nepal has been at the forefront of a pioneering endeavor to establish a comprehensive national spatial data infrastructure within the country. Orchestrated under the umbrella of the National Geographic Information Infrastructure Project (NGIIP), this initiative is entrusted with a pivotal responsibility. The NGIIP diligently strives to foster collaboration, inclusively engaging a diverse spectrum of stakeholders. This encompasses governmental, non-governmental, and private sector entities actively involved in the realm of geospatial information. While commendable progress has been achieved, the Department remains committed to exerting persistent efforts in order to realize the full potential of this sector.

Table 1. Status of governance of NSDI in five countries

Components	Bangladesh	India	Nepal	Pakistan	Sri Lanka
Participation and Consensus Orientation	In Bangladesh, the NSDI Steering Committee and the Technical Committee shape policies and guidelines while fostering collaboration (Rahman & Szabó, 2023).	India operates under a two-tier structure, with the National Spatial Data Committee (NSDC) setting policy direction and the NSDI Executive Committee (EC) managing implementation (Acharya & Pandey, 2018).	Nepal lacks a designated agency for NSDI oversight, hindering coordinated efforts. The establishment of a coordinating Council and technical committee is crucial (Bell et al., 2020).	The NSDI in Pakistan is at the feasibility study stage, without a formal apex body for consensus development (Ahmad & Khiyal, 2023).	Sri Lanka's NSDI governance involves the Executive Committee and Executive Steering Committee, guiding policies and activities (nsdi.gov.lk, 2023a).
Responsiveness and Transparency	Bangladesh's NSDI offers a geospatial data hub nsdi.gov.bd/ for stakeholders.	India's NSDI Geoportal www.nsdi.gov.in showcases data.	Nepal's National Geoportal nationalgeoportal.gov.np streamlines access to datasets.	Pakistan's NSDI website www.nsdi.gov.pk lacks data-sharing mechanisms.	Sri Lanka's NSDI platform www.nsdi.gov.lk offers public access to geospatial data.
Equity and Accountability	The Survey of Bangladesh coordinates NSDI development (Rahman & Szabó, 2023).	India's NSDI involves committees for policy and oversight (Acharya & Pandey, 2018).	Nepal's National Mapping Committee and Survey Department oversee NSDI (UNGGIM, 2012).	Survey of Pakistan formed a coordination committee for NSDI (Ali & Imran, 2021).	Sri Lanka's Technical Committee represents participating entities (nsdi.gov.lk, 2023a).
Effectiveness and Efficiency	Capacity-building for NSDI in Bangladesh is progressing. (Hussain, 2016)	India's National Geospatial Program offers education initiatives. (UNGGIM, 2022)	Nepal's capacity-building efforts include workshops and conferences. (Bhatta et al., 2016)	Pakistan's NSDI feasibility study is ongoing. (Ahmad & Khiyal, 2023)	Sri Lanka's Outreach Strategy aims to enhance awareness and collaboration (nsdi.gov.lk, 2023c).
Rule of Law	Bangladesh's Geospatial Data and Services Act governs NSDI operations (Rahman & Szabó, 2023).	India's NSDI was established through a cabinet resolution (GOI, 2006).	Nepal lacks comprehensive NSDI laws (Bell et al., 2020).	Pakistan's NSDI implementation awaits government funding (Surveying and Mapping Act, 2014). No comprehensive law exists.	Sri Lanka's NSDI is aligned with the National Digital Policy (nsdi.gov.lk, 2023b). But no formal law exists.
Strategic Vision	Bangladesh's NSDI development began in 2016 with a task force (Rahman & Szabó, 2023).	India's NSDI aims for structured spatial data and accessibility (P. K. Singh, 2009).	Nepal's NGIIP fosters collaboration among diverse stakeholders (UNGGIM, 2012).	Pakistan's NSDI is in the feasibility evaluation stage (Ahmad & Khiyal, 2023).	Sri Lanka's NSDI has a strategic roadmap within the Digital Policy (nsdi.gov.lk, 2023b).

Concerning Pakistan, the NSDI is presently in the phase of evaluating its feasibility (Ahmad & Khiyal, 2023). This suggests that a concrete strategic vision has not been established at this point in time.

Udagepola, (2016) endorsed that the draft report for the Sri Lanka Infrastructure Framework was unveiled in June 2014, followed by the issuance of the Sri Lanka Spatial Data Infrastructure Road Map on the 26th of November 2014. Yet, the landscape in Sri Lanka remains relatively unchanged, mirroring the situation prior to 2014. In a proactive role, the Department of Survey (SoD) is spearheading efforts towards the establishment of the National Spatial Data Infrastructure. The Sri Lanka Spatial Data Infrastructure Road Map outlines a range of themes, each meticulously crafted to cater to the pragmatic necessities of government, industry, and the wider community.

CONCLUSION

The establishment and effective operation of a National Spatial Data Infrastructure play a vital role in harnessing the potential of geospatial data for informed decision-making and sustainable development. The chapters presented a comprehensive analysis of the governance framework within the NSDI context, examining the principles of good governance and their interplay with the NSDI's structure. This investigation sheds light on the intricate connections between governance, data sharing, accountability, and efficiency, all of which are essential for the success of an NSDI.

The methodology employed in this study explored the multifaceted dimensions of governance, extending beyond political boundaries to encompass a diverse array of stakeholders, including governmental bodies, civil society organizations, and private sector entities. This comprehensive approach underscores the collaborative nature of the NSDI, where active engagement and transparent processes are crucial for effective data sharing and interoperability. The review of governance frameworks within South Asian countries highlighted the diverse strategies employed by each nation to foster consensus, ensure transparency, and promote equitable access to geospatial resources.

Participation and consensus orientation emerged as key principles that drive the NSDI's governance structure. The active involvement of stakeholders in decision-making processes facilitated through consensus-building mechanisms ensures that decisions resonate with the broader community and contribute to collaborative outcomes. The existence of apex bodies, such as the NSDI Steering Committee and Technical Committees, further strengthens the governance framework, enabling effective policy development and coordination.

The responsiveness and transparency of the NSDI are pivotal in addressing evolving user demands and facilitating the seamless flow of spatial data. By promptly adapting its mechanisms to accommodate changing requirements, the NSDI ensures that stakeholders have access to up-to-date and relevant information for informed decision-making. Initiatives like the NSDI platforms in various countries, such as Bangladesh and Sri Lanka, exemplify the commitment to data sharing and accessibility while acknowledging the challenges in achieving comprehensive awareness and utilization.

Equity and accountability are cornerstones of the NSDI's governance framework, ensuring that all stakeholders have equal opportunities to benefit from spatial data resources. By upholding principles of responsibility and transparency, the NSDI enhances its credibility and effectiveness in supporting decision-making processes. The establishment of National Mapping Committees and endorsement procedures for geospatial products further reinforce accountability and harmonization.

The emphasis on effectiveness and efficiency underscores the NSDI's commitment to optimizing resources and efforts to achieve impactful outcomes. Through capacity-building initiatives and awareness campaigns, the NSDI empowers stakeholders to harness the full potential of geospatial data. Future work in this area could focus on strengthening capacity-building programs, fostering greater collaboration among stakeholders, and refining the governance framework to adapt to evolving technological advancements and user requirements.

Thus, the governance framework is a critical component of the NSDI, ensuring the effective coordination, data sharing, and accessibility necessary for informed decision-making and sustainable development. The principles of good governance, coupled with responsive data-sharing mechanisms, set the stage for a successful NSDI that caters to the diverse needs of stakeholders and contributes to the advancement of society at large. As countries continue to develop and refine their NSDIs, the lessons learned from this study can provide valuable insights for shaping effective governance structures and realizing the full potential of geospatial data.

REFERENCES

Acharya, P. S., & Pandey, S. (2018). National spatial data infrastructure India (NSDI-India)-present status and the future strategies. Geospatial Infrastructure, Applications and Technologies: India Case Studies. doi:10.1007/978-981-13-2330-0_2

Ahmad, M., Khayal, M. S. H., & Tahir, A. (2022). Analysis of Factors Affecting Adoption of Volunteered Geographic Information in the Context of National Spatial Data Infrastructure. *ISPRS International Journal of Geo-Information*, *11*(2), 120. Advance online publication. doi:10.3390/ijgi11020120

Ahmad, M., & Khiyal, M. S. H. (2023). Assessment of land administration in Pakistan and the potential role of volunteered geographic information. In Handbook of Research on Driving Socioeconomic Development With Big Data. doi:10.4018/978-1-6684-5959-1.ch014

Ali, A., & Ahmad, M. (2012). Is SDI Development, Waste of Time and Money for Pakistan? In *Global geospatial conference 2012 - Spatially enabling government, industry and citizens* (p. 13). Academic Press.

Ali, A., & Imran, M. (2021). National Spatial Data Infrastructure vs. Cadastre System for Economic Development: Evidence from Pakistan. *Land (Basel)*, *10*(2), 188. doi:10.3390/land10020188

Ali, A., Imran, M., Jabeen, M., Ali, Z., & Mahmood, S. A. (2021). Factors influencing integrated information management: Spatial data infrastructure in Pakistan. *Information Development*. Advance online publication. doi:10.1177/02666669211048483

Anderson, M., Schulze, K., Cassini, A., Plachouras, D., & Mossialos, E. (2019). A governance framework for development and assessment of national action plans on antimicrobial resistance. In The Lancet Infectious Diseases (Vol. 19, Issue 11). doi:10.1016/S1473-3099(19)30415-3

Ayanlade, A., Orimoogunje, I. O. O., & Borisade, P. B. (2008). Geospatial data infrastructure for sustainable development in sub-Saharan countries. *International Journal of Digital Earth*, *1*(3), 247–258. doi:10.1080/17538940802149940

Bell, K., Lamb, A., Lipej, B., Evtimov, V., Hilton, A., Galic, Z., Hunter, G., Shreesh, R., Dhakal, S., & Rawal, N. (2020). *Technical Assistance to Develop the Land Administration and Geospatial Information Systems of Nepal*. doi:10.13140/RG.2.2.13525.78564

Bertelli, A. M. (2008). Credible governance? Transparency, political control, the personal vote and British quangos. *Political Studies, 56*(4), 807–829. doi:10.1111/j.1467-9248.2007.00713.x

Bhatta, G. P., Dangol, S., & Sapkota, R. K. (2016). Role of Land Professionals and Spatial Data Infrastructure in Disaster Risk Reduction: In the Context of Post 2015 Nepal Earthquake: General Review. *Nepalese Journal on Geoinformatics, 15*, 59–65. doi:10.3126/njg.v15i1.51187

Binder Maitra, J. (2015). National Spatial Data Infrastructure (NSDI). In S. Shekhar, H. Xiong, & X. Zhou (Eds.), *Encyclopedia of GIS* (pp. 1–7). Springer International Publishing. doi:10.1007/978-3-319-23519-6_860-2

Brunet, M. (2021). Making sense of a governance framework for megaprojects: The challenge of finding equilibrium. *International Journal of Project Management, 39*(4), 406–416. Advance online publication. doi:10.1016/j.ijproman.2020.09.001

Brunet, M., & Aubry, M. (2016). The three dimensions of a governance framework for major public projects. *International Journal of Project Management, 34*(8), 1596–1607. Advance online publication. doi:10.1016/j.ijproman.2016.09.004

Castelein, W. T., Bregt, A. K., & Grus, L. (2013). The role of collaboration in spatial data infrastructures. *URISA Journal, 25*(2).

Chaturvedi, K., Matheus, A., Nguyen, S. H., & Kolbe, T. H. (2019). Securing Spatial Data Infrastructures for Distributed Smart City applications and services. *Future Generation Computer Systems, 101*, 723–736. Advance online publication. doi:10.1016/j.future.2019.07.002

Corti, P., Bartoli, F., Fabiani, A., Giovando, C., Kralidis, A. T., & Tzotsos, A. (2019). GeoNode: An open source framework to build spatial data infrastructures. *PeerJ*, 7.

Craglia, M., & Johnston, A. (2004). Assessing the impacts of spatial data infrastructures: methods and gaps. *7th AGILE Conference on Geographic Information Science*.

Crompvoets, J., Bregt, A., Rajabifard, A., & Williamson, I. (2004). Assessing the worldwide developments of national spatial data clearinghouses. *International Journal of Geographical Information Science, 18*(7), 665–689. doi:10.1080/13658810410001702030

Crompvoets, J., Vancauwenberghe, G., Ho, S., Masser, I., & Vries, W. T. (2018). Governance of national spatial data infrastructures in Europe. *International Journal of Spatial Data Infrastructures Research Citation, 13*.

De Kleijn, M., van Manen, N., Kolen, J., & Scholten, H. (2014). Towards a User-centric SDI Framework for Historical and Heritage European Landscape Research. *International Journal of Spatial Data Infrastructures Research*, 9.

Feeney, M., Rajabifard, A., & Williamson, I. P. (2001). Spatial data infrastructure frameworks to support decision-making for sustainable development. *5th Global Spatial Data Infrastructure Conference.*

Filchev, L., Pashova, L., Kolev, V., & Frye, S. (2020). Surveys, Catalogues, Databases/Archives, and State-of-the-Art Methods for Geoscience Data Processing. In P. Škoda & F. Adam (Eds.), *Knowledge Discovery in Big Data from Astronomy and Earth Observation* (pp. 103–136). Elsevier. doi:10.1016/B978-0-12-819154-5.00016-3

Galani, A., Koutsouris, N., Poulios, G., Tsagkaris, K., & Demestichas, P. (2013). Designing the governance framework for network and service management in Future Networks. *2013 Future Network & Mobile Summit*, 1–8.

Giuliani, G., Lacroix, P., Guigoz, Y., Roncella, R., Bigagli, L., Santoro, M., Mazzetti, P., Nativi, S., Ray, N., & Lehmann, A. (2017). Bringing GEOSS Services into Practice: A Capacity Building Resource on Spatial Data Infrastructures (SDI). *Transactions in GIS*, *21*(4), 811–824. Advance online publication. doi:10.1111/tgis.12209

GOI. (2006). *Resolution on "Constitution of National Spatial Data Infrastructure (NSDI).* GOI.

GOI. (2011). *NSDI working Groups Report*. GOI.

GOI. (2012). *National Data Sharing and Accessibility Policy*. Ministry of Science and Technology, Government of India.

Groot, R., & McLaughlin, J. (2000). Geospatial data infrastructure : concepts, cases and good practice. In R. Groot & J. McLaughlin (Eds.), *GeoSpatial Data Infrastructure: Concepts, Cases and Good Practice*. Oxford University Press. https://research.utwente.nl/en/publications/geospatial-data-infrastructure-concepts-cases-and-good-practice

GSDI. (2004). Developing Spatial Data Infrastructures: The SDI Cookbook. GSDI/Nebert.

Hussain, F. (2016). Digital contradictions in Bangladesh: Encouragement and deterrence of citizen engagement via ICTs. *Information Technologies and International Development*, *12*(2).

Ienca, M., Fins, J. J., Jox, R. J., Jotterand, F., Voeneky, S., Andorno, R., Ball, T., Castelluccia, C., Chavarriaga, R., Chneiweiss, H., Ferretti, A., Friedrich, O., Hurst, S., Merkel, G., Molnár-Gábor, F., Rickli, J. M., Scheibner, J., Vayena, E., Yuste, R., & Kellmeyer, P. (2022). Towards a Governance Framework for Brain Data. *Neuroethics*, *15*(2), 20. Advance online publication. doi:10.100712152-022-09498-8

Jacoby, S., Smith, J., Ting, L., & Williamson, I. (2002). Developing a common spatial data infrastructure between state and local government - An Australian case study. *International Journal of Geographical Information Science*, *16*(4), 305–322. Advance online publication. doi:10.1080/13658810110096001

Johnston, M. (2006). *Good governance: Rule of law, transparency, and accountability*. United Nations Public Administration Network.

Joshi, P. P. K. (2023, April). *Geospatial Technology for Sustainable Development*. Geospatial World. https://www.geospatialworld.net/prime/prime-opinion/geospatial-technology-for-sustainable-development/

Kim, H. Y., & Cho, J. S. (2018). Data governance framework for big data implementation with NPS Case Analysis in Korea. *The Journal of Business and Retail Management Research, 12*(3), 36–46. doi:10.24052/JBRMR/V12IS03/ART-04

Kujala, J., Aaltonen, K., Gotcheva, N., & Lahdenperä, P. (2021). Dimensions of governance in interorganizational project networks. *International Journal of Managing Projects in Business, 14*(3), 625–651. Advance online publication. doi:10.1108/IJMPB-12-2019-0312

Kyle, W. (2022, May). *Not Just Who, But Where: The need for geospatial data to achieve the Sustainable Development Goals*. International Institute for Sustainable Development. https://www.iisd.org/articles/insight/not-just-who-where-need-geospatial-data-achieve-sustainable-development-goals

Mao, Z., Wu, J., Qiao, Y., & Yao, H. (2022). Government data governance framework based on a data middle platform. *Aslib Journal of Information Management, 74*(2), 289–310. Advance online publication. doi:10.1108/AJIM-03-2021-0068

Masser, I. (1999). All shapes and sizes: The first generation of national spatial data infrastructures. *International Journal of Geographical Information Science, 13*(1), 67–84. doi:10.1080/136588199241463

Masser, I. (2005). GIS worlds: creating spatial data infrastructures (Vol. 338). ESRI Press.

McLaughlin, J., & Nichols, S. (1994). Developing a national spatial data infrastructure. *Journal of Surveying Engineering, 120*(2), 62–76. doi:10.1061/(ASCE)0733-9453(1994)120:2(62)

McLaughlin, J. D. (1991). Towards national spatial data infrastructure. *Proceedings of the Canadian Conference on GIS*, 1–5.

Mohammadi, H. (2008). *The Integration of multi-source spatial datasets in the context of SDI initiatives* [PhD thesis]. Department of Geomatics, The University of Melbourne.

Munir, A., Asmat, A., Donald, G., Walter, T. D. V., Giles, F. D., & Muhammad, I. (2023). *2nd Workshop on Feasibility Study for Establishment of National Spatial Data Infrastructure (NSDI) for Pakistan*. Researchgate. https://www.researchgate.net/publication/369021769_2nd_WORKSHOP_ON_FEASIBILITY_STUDY_FOR_ESTABLISHMENT_OF_NATIONAL_SPATIAL_DATA_INFRASTRUCTURE_NSDI_FOR_PAKISTAN

nationalgeoportal.gov.np. (2023). *National Spatial Data Center*. https://nationalgeoportal.gov.np/

nsdi.gov.lk. (2023a). *Governance Structure*. https://nsdi.gov.lk/governance-structure

nsdi.gov.lk. (2023b). *NSDI*. https://nsdi.gov.lk/nsdi

nsdi.gov.lk. (2023c). *Outreach Plan*. https://www.nsdi.gov.lk/outreach-plan

Ole, J. K., Terry, M. W., Terry, W., & Ole, M. M. (2009). *Governance Frameworks for Public Project Development and Estimation*. Project Management Institute.

OstadabbasH.MerzH.WeippertH. (2021). Integration of urban spatial data management and visualization with enterprise applications using open-source software. *International Archives of the Photogrammetry, Remote Sensing and Spatial Information Sciences - ISPRS Archives, 43*(B4-2021). doi:10.5194/isprs-archives-XLIII-B4-2021-307-2021

Praharaj, S., & Bandyopadhyay, S. (2019). Understanding the open data challenge for building smart cities in India. In *Open Cities | Open Data*. Collaborative Cities in the Information Era. doi:10.1007/978-981-13-6605-5_16

Rahman, M., & Szabó, G. (2023). Assessing the Status of National Spatial Data Infrastructure (NSDI) of Bangladesh. *ISPRS International Journal of Geo-Information, 12*(6), 236. Advance online publication. doi:10.3390/ijgi12060236

Rajabifard, A., Binns, A., Masser, I., & Williamson, I. (2006). The role of sub-national government and the private sector in future spatial data infrastructures. *International Journal of Geographical Information Science, 20*(7), 727–741. Advance online publication. doi:10.1080/13658810500432224

Rajabifard, A., Feeney, M. E. F., & Williamson, I. P. (2002). Future directions for SDI development. *International Journal of Applied Earth Observation and Geoinformation, 4*(1), 11–22. doi:10.1016/S0303-2434(02)00002-8

Rao, M. (2007). NSDI – then, now and whenever. *Coordinates: A Resource on Positioning, Navigation and Beyond*. https://mycoordinates.org/nsdi-%E2%80%93-then-now-and-whenever/all/1/

Simmons, S. (2018). Metadata and Spatial Data Infrastructure. In B. Huang (Ed.), *Comprehensive Geographic Information Systems* (pp. 110–124). Elsevier. doi:10.1016/B978-0-12-409548-9.09611-1

Singh, B., & Pandey, S. (2018). Geospatial policies in India and their implementation in good governance. In Geospatial Infrastructure, Applications and Technologies: India Case Studies. doi:10.1007/978-981-13-2330-0_1

Singh, P. K. (2009). Spatial Data Infrastructure in India : Status, Governance Challenges, and Strategies for Effective Functioning. *International Journal of Spatial Data Infrastructures Research*, 4.

Sjoukema, J., Bregt, A. K., & Crompvoets, J. (2020). Understanding governance dynamics: The governing system of spatial data infrastructures. *International Journal of Spatial Data Infrastructures Research*, 15.

Sjoukema, J. W., Samia, J., Bregt, A. K., & Crompvoets, J. (2021). Governance interactions of spatial data infrastructures: An agent-based modelling approach. *International Journal of Digital Earth, 14*(6), 696–713. Advance online publication. doi:10.1080/17538947.2020.1868585

Stock, K., & Guesgen, H. (2016). Geospatial Reasoning With Open Data. In R. Layton & P. A. Watters (Eds.), *Automating Open Source Intelligence* (pp. 171–204). Syngress. doi:10.1016/B978-0-12-802916-9.00010-5

Stone, V., Führ, M., Feindt, P. H., Bouwmeester, H., Linkov, I., Sabella, S., Murphy, F., Bizer, K., Tran, L., Ågerstrand, M., Fito, C., Andersen, T., Anderson, D., Bergamaschi, E., Cherrie, J. W., Cowan, S., Dalemcourt, J. F., Faure, M., Gabbert, S., ... Poortvliet, P. M. (2018). The Essential Elements of a Risk Governance Framework for Current and Future Nanotechnologies. *Risk Analysis*, *38*(7), 1321–1331. Advance online publication. doi:10.1111/risa.12954 PMID:29240986

Surveying and Mapping Act (2014).

Udagepola, K. P. (2016). A Framework for Spatial Data Visualization: Sri Lanka Globe (S-Globe). *37th Asian Conference on Remote Sensing,* 17–21.

UNDP. (1997). *Governance for sustainable human development - A UNDP policy document*. United Nations Development Programme.

UNGGIM. (2012). *Country Report - Nepal*. https://ggim.un.org/country-reports/documents/Nepal-2012-country-report.pdf

UNGGIM. (2019). *Country Report - Sri Lanka*. http://ggim.un.org/docs/meetings/GGIM5/GGIM5 Report Draft 14Aug.pdf

UNGGIM. (2022). *Country Report - India*. https://ggim.un.org/country-reports/documents/India_Country_Report-2022.pdf

Vancauwenberghe, G., & van Loenen, B. (2018). *Exploring the Emergence of Open Spatial Data Infrastructures: Analysis of Recent Developments and Trends in Europe*. doi:10.1007/978-3-319-59442-2_2

Zamanifard, H., Alizadeh, T., & Bosman, C. (2018). Towards a framework of public space governance. *Cities (London, England)*, *78*, 155–165. Advance online publication. doi:10.1016/j.cities.2018.02.010

Zhang, Z., Wang, Z., Li, A., Ye, X., Usery, E. L., & Li, D. (2021). An al-based spatial knowledge graph for enhancing spatial data and knowledge search and discovery. *Proceedings of the 1st ACM SIGSPATIAL International Workshop on Searching and Mining Large Collections of Geospatial Data, GeoSearch 2021*. 10.1145/3486640.3491393

ADDITIONAL READING

Ahmad, M., Ali, A., & Khiyal, M. S. H. (2023). Fog Computing for Spatial Data Infrastructure: Challenges and Opportunities. In Multi-Disciplinary Applications of Fog Computing: Responsiveness in Real-Time (pp. 152–178). doi:10.4018/978-1-6684-4466-5.ch008

Masser, I. (2011). Emerging frameworks in the information age: The spatial data infrastructure (SDI) phenomenon. In The SAGE Handbook of GIS and Society. doi:10.4135/9781446201046.n14

Masser, I. (2019). The future of spatial data infrastructures. In *Geographic Information Systems to Spatial Data Infrastructure* (pp. 227–252). CRC Press. doi:10.1201/9780429505904-12

KEY TERMS AND DEFINITIONS

Equity: It embodies the principle of fairness, impartiality, and justice in the equitable allocation of resources, opportunities, and advantages to both individuals and groups.

Geoportal: It is a specialized web-oriented platform, that acts as a central nexus for the exploration, revelation, and administration of geospatial knowledge and data.

Governance Framework: It denotes a structured methodology or system that steers the decision-making and managerial processes within an organization or project.

Spatial Data Infrastructure: Spatial data infrastructure plays a vital role by providing the fundamental physical and organizational framework needed to enhance the efficient and ideal utilization of spatial data.

Strategic Vision: It represents the all-encompassing, future-oriented outlook and course of action established by an entity, whether it be an organization or an individual, to attain its desired goals and objectives.

Chapter 9
Promoting Strategic Management Systems for Sustainable Business Models:
Ideas and Guidance

Chukwuemeka Ugboma Azinge
https://orcid.org/0009-0007-6280-8194
Lagos Business School, Pan-Atlantic University, Nigeria

ABSTRACT

This chapter explores how strategic management systems drive sustainable business models. It discusses the link between sustainability and financial success, leveraging frameworks like RBV and Triple Bottom Line. Practical insights from cases like Unilever and Patagonia are examined, emphasizing stakeholder engagement and performance metrics. The role of emerging trends like circular economy and digitalization is highlighted. The chapter underscores the need for integrating sustainability systematically and offers a roadmap for organizations to achieve lasting impact.

INTRODUCTION

In the past couple of years, organisations have been faced with growing calls to focus, not only on financial returns but also on environmental, social, and governance issues within the sphere of the organisation's influence, which implies integrating the notion of sustainability into the organisational framework and operating model. With these renewed calls for sustainability practices and principles in the organisational context, paradigms have shifted, and organisations are beginning to appreciate why financial performance is now inextricably linked to a robust sustainability strategy. A recent report by Mckinsey emphasised the idea that a robust synergy between sustainable business models and strategic management systems creates increased competitive advantage for the organisation. In addition, the

DOI: 10.4018/979-8-3693-0458-7.ch009

Global Reporting Initiative (GRI) found that long-term shareholder value is created when sustainability is integrated into the organisation's overall strategic framework. Tesla, Patagonia, and Unilever are all examples of organisations that have built sustainable business models via strategic management systems.

Structure

This chapter has been structured into roughly 5 major segments: We will consider (1.) **Evolution of Strategic Management Systems and Sustainable Business Models**, looking into how sustainability in business has evolved since the industrial revolution till today. (2.) **Sustainable Business Transformation: Culture, Performance and Concepts**, delving into performance management, the triple bottom line performance measure, sustainability reporting, materiality assessment and multi-stakeholder collaboration. (3.) **Trade-offs and Risks Between Short-term Financial Goals and Long-term Sustainability Objectives**, regulatory fears and critical reputational dangers will be considered as well as guidelines to evade such dangers (4.) We will consider **Case Studies** of Interface Inc., Unilever and Patagonia. In the last major segment, (5.) **Sustainability Models and Innovations in Strategic Management** with a focus on importance of circular economy, digitalization and technology, then also discussing the role of organisational leadership in driving the needed change.

Overall, this chapter covers various topics around Strategic Management Systems for Sustainable Business Models, from historical perspectives to contemporary challenges and innovative solutions. It provides a well-rounded view of the topic and incorporates case studies for practical illustration.

EVOLUTION OF STRATEGIC MANAGEMENT SYSTEMS AND SUSTAINABLE BUSINESS MODELS

The Industrial Revolution, which began in the mid-18th century, necessitated the emergence of the concept of Sustainability in business operations. Though sustainability in business has taken on different names and evolved in forms over several decades. Sustainability and the industrial revolution are interdependent upon each other as sustainable goals induce industrial revolution and industrial revolution facilitates sustainability (Vivek et al., 2022).

In the 19th and early 20th century, some early environmentalists, such as John Muir and Henry David Thoreau, raised concerns about the impact of industrialization on the natural environment, leading to environmental awareness.

The mid-20th century ushered in more hope for sustainability as governments began to introduce environmental regulations in response to growing pollution and environmental degradation. The environmental movement in the United States, which is broad in scope, responded to growing industrialization, population, and pollution, as well as to resource exploitation (Lazarus, 2004), resulting in the establishment of agencies like the U.S. Environmental Protection Agency (EPA) in 1970 and landmark environmental laws like the Clean Air Act (1970) and Clean Water Act (1972) in the United States.

In the 1970s and 1980s, some corporations started to pay attention to environmental issues due to regulatory pressures and public awareness. Businesses began to adopt environmental management systems and practices, often driven by cost-saving opportunities, risk management, and corporate reputation concerns. The publication of the Brundtland Report, also known as "Our Common Future" in 1987 by the

World Commission on Environment and Development, introduced the concept of sustainable development. It emphasized the need to balance economic growth, social equity, and environmental protection.

In the late 20th century and early 21st century, Corporate Social Responsibility (CSR) gained prominence as companies recognized the importance of not only environmental sustainability but also social responsibility. CSR encompassed initiatives related to philanthropy, ethical business practices, and community engagement. Haidar (2021) believes that the historical origin of sustainability however can be traced to environmental accounting, as premised on the ideals of corporate social responsibility (CSR) and corporate management practices, in tandem with the demands of external stakeholders on the environmental, economic, and social dynamics of businesses.

The 21st century saw a significant increase in corporate sustainability efforts, with more companies integrating sustainability into their core business strategies. Sustainability became more mainstream in the business world during the 2010s. Factors like climate change, resource scarcity, and changing consumer preferences pushed sustainability to the forefront of corporate agendas. Many companies began integrating sustainability into their core business strategies, products, and supply chains.

The Paris Agreement and the Sustainable Development Goals adopted in 2015, reflected a new social contract in which corporations are expected to play a relevant role in the global efforts to achieve the SDGs (Latapí Agudelo et al., 2019) which are gaining importance in all the industrial sectors and the attainment of SDGs will lead to simultaneous betterment of human lives, environment and economic prosperity (Agrawal et al., 2022). Businesses' contribution to the Goals will be key to their achievement. Each government will have its own set of priorities which will drive the action it needs to take. A PwC (n.d.) article suggests that businesses would want to align with the SDGs so as to make an impact that helps, not hinders, a country to achieve its goals. With 193 governments agreeing to deliver 17 goals tackling major world issues by 2030, change lies ahead for business, not only to rethink strategy and business behaviour to align with the goals, but also to assess and evidence their impact.

In recent years, companies have been under increasing pressure from consumers, grassroots and community organizations, governments, and shareholders to develop and practise sustainable business practices (Hou et al., 2023). This has necessitated the concepts and practise of Sustainability Reporting and the adoption of international standards, such as the Global Reporting Initiative (GRI), the United Nations Global Compact, green bonds, sustainable investment funds, and environmental, social, and governance (ESG) metrics for evaluating companies.

Today, advances in technology, such as renewable energy, clean transportation, data analytics, artificial intelligence (AI), blockchain and the internet of things (IoT) amongst other innovations continues to provide businesses with tools to reduce their environmental footprint and operate more sustainably. The fourth industrial revolution (4IR) is here. Previous industrial revolutions have radically improved the standards of living for human beings, but not only are these gains unevenly distributed across geographies and demographics, they have come with the degradation of our planet's health (Steffen et al., 2015; World Economic Forum, 2020). Today's technological revolution must break this pattern and, for the first time, deliver sustainable, inclusive economic growth (World Economic Forum, 2020, p. 5)

The evolution of sustainability in business continues, driven by a combination of regulatory requirements, consumer demand, investor pressure, advancement in technology and a growing recognition of the long-term business benefits of sustainable practices. It has evolved from a peripheral concern to a strategic imperative for many organizations, influencing how they operate, innovate, and interact with the world around them.

Strategic Management Systems

Strategic management is the planned use of a company's resources to reach its goals and objectives (Indeed Editorial Team, 2023). Koteen (1989) defines strategic management as a broad concept that "embraces the entire set of managerial decisions and actions that determine the long-run performance of an organisation" (p. 18).

Strategic management is a multidimensional discipline that strengthens organisations by integrating various management processes. It fosters alignment, coordination, and synergy across functional divisions and organisational levels. By connecting internal processes to external outcomes and linking operational decisions to strategic objectives, strategic management enables organisations to navigate complexity, drive growth, and achieve sustainable success. Strategic management is crucial in enhancing organisations' long-term sustainability and effectiveness by addressing substantive policies and management capabilities. It is a comprehensive framework that integrates various management processes, offering a systematic, coherent, and practical approach to establishing, achieving, monitoring, and updating an agency's strategic objectives. At its core, strategic management embraces an integrative nature that extends beyond individual functions and organisational levels (Poister & Streib, 1999). Firstly, it fosters a unified focus across functional divisions and different levels of an organisation, aligning efforts towards common goals, themes, and issues. By promoting a shared vision and purpose, strategic management ensures that all stakeholders work harmoniously towards achieving long-term objectives.

Secondly, strategic management establishes a vital link between internal management processes, program initiatives, and desired outcomes in the external environment. It recognises the interconnectedness between an organisation's internal operations and the dynamic external landscape in which it operates. By understanding and responding effectively to external factors such as market trends, customer needs, and competitive forces, strategic management enables organisations to adapt, innovate, and remain competitive in the ever-changing business environment. Finally, strategic management bridges the gap between day-to-day operational decisions and the broader strategic objectives of an organisation. It emphasises the need to align tactical actions with the long-term vision, ensuring daily decisions contribute to the overall strategic direction. This integration ensures that short-term efforts are not made at the expense of long-term goals and that all decisions and actions are driven by a clear understanding of the organisation's strategic intent.

A strategic management system is a tool used to manage the direction and operations of a business. This system is beneficial to any business because it allows the organization to create and implement strategies that will ensure the success of the business (Wozniak, n.d.). Implementing such a system offers numerous advantages to the organisation's overall success. Here are the benefits of integrating a strategic management system:

Establishing Clear Direction: A strategic management system provides a clear roadmap by defining long-term objectives and strategies that align with the company's mission and vision. This ensures everyone works towards the same goals, enhancing cohesion and focus.

Cultivating Accountability: The system fosters a culture of accountability by enabling management to measure and track performance against previously established objectives. This allows for regular progress assessment and identifying areas that require improvement, ultimately promoting a sense of responsibility among employees.

Adapting to Changing Markets: A strategic management system equips the organisation to anticipate and respond to future competition and evolving market dynamics. By analysing opportunities and threats, the system helps the organisation to proactively plan and adjust strategies to stay ahead of the curve.

Encouraging Collaboration: The strategic management system encourages collaboration and cooperation among departments and staff members through its comprehensive approach. Aligning efforts towards shared goals facilitates effective communication, knowledge sharing, and teamwork, enhancing efficiency and outcomes.

Fostering Innovation and Creativity: The system creates an environment conducive to innovation and creativity by promoting, developing and implementing new ideas and strategies. Encouraging exploration and experimentation stimulates fresh thinking and allows the organisation to adapt to changing circumstances with innovative solutions.

Identifying Areas for Improvement: A strategic management system offers transparency by providing a comprehensive view of the organisation and its performance. This enables the identification of areas that need improvement, whether in processes, resource allocation, or performance metrics. By highlighting weaknesses, the system supports informed decision-making and facilitates continuous improvement efforts.

The strategic management system works in close conjunction with various other management subsystems. It can be enhanced by incorporating additional approaches like the balanced scorecard, SWOT analysis, Porter's five forces model, corporate social responsibility, and strategic marketing planning. These complementary approaches assist organisations in identifying their strengths and weaknesses, evaluating the competitive landscape, and formulating effective strategies. By integrating these approaches, organisations gain valuable insights and tools to strategically navigate their internal and external environments (Dess et al., 2010).

In recent times, strategic management can be defined through three significant concepts: resilience, agility, and sustainability. One of the mandatory elements to be considered in strategic management is sustainability as defined through environmental, social, and governance (ESG) criteria, which is already making its mark in many business mindsets (Păun & Pinzaru, 2021). Sustainable strategic management is often described as "a veritable tool for improving the competitiveness, performance levels and structural development of organisations" (Momanyi, 2020). According to Chladek (2019), sustainable strategic management entails a structured future vision that integrates sustainability into business strategies. While it may appear altruistic or idealistic, it goes beyond that, as it offers tangible benefits that enhance organisational performance. Beyond the well-known "three Ps" - people, planet, and profit - adopting sustainability in business strategies provides several significant advantages. Incorporating sustainability practices safeguards the corporate brand and mitigates risks. By proactively addressing environmental and social concerns, organisations can protect their reputation and avoid potential backlash from stakeholders. This approach minimises negative impacts and positions the organisation as a responsible and ethical entity in the eyes of customers, investors, and the public.

Embracing sustainability in strategic management as a core principle can yield a new competitive advantage. Organisations can differentiate themselves from competitors by aligning business goals with a larger purpose. Consumers increasingly favour companies that demonstrate a commitment to sustainability, leading to improved brand loyalty, customer satisfaction, and increased market share. A purpose-driven approach attracts like-minded employees and fosters a positive work culture, further contributing to organisational success. Additionally, sustainable strategic management opens up opportunities in emerging markets for sustainable goods. As global awareness and demand for environmentally friendly products and services grow, organisations prioritising sustainability can tap into these markets and gain a competitive edge. By offering innovative and sustainable solutions, organisations can capture new customer segments and expand their revenue streams. Sustainable strategic management encourages collaboration and cooperation. Addressing sustainability challenges often requires partnerships with suppliers, government bodies, NGOs, and local communities. By working together, organisations can share knowledge, resources, and expertise to drive positive changes at a larger scale. This collaborative approach fosters innovation, enables shared learning, and creates a more sustainable ecosystem for all parties involved.

Sustainable Business Models

"A business model that prioritises sustainability is one that, at a minimum, considers all stakeholders, assesses and addresses environmental impacts, and is transparent and thorough in its reporting." Colabello

The term "model" refers to an abstract depiction of how a company's business operations operate and the term "business" refers to the structured conversion of input components into goods and services (Gomes et al., 2019). By using a thorough aggregated picture of reality that can integrate political, legal, economic, sociocultural, technological, and ecological aspects into the transparent architecture to manage complexity, a business model offers a simplified representation of value-creation processes, roles, and interactions to create customer value by ensuring competitive advantage and generating revenue (Doleski, 2015).

The concept of a business model revolves around three fundamental components: value proposition, value creation and delivery, and value capture (Okano et al., 2019) and value creation is the heartbeat of a business model (Beltramello et al., 2013). The value proposition is the unique offering or benefit that a business provides to its customers. It answers the question of why customers should choose a particular product or service over competitors. The value proposition highlights the offering's value, relevance, and differentiation in meeting customer needs or solving their problems. Value creation and delivery refer to the processes and activities undertaken by a business to create and deliver the promised value to customers. It involves designing and producing products or delivering services that align with the value proposition. This element encompasses various aspects, including production, operations, distribution, customer service, and any other activities that contribute to delivering the desired value to customers. Value capture entails the strategies and mechanisms a business employs to capture and monetise the value created. It encompasses revenue generation models, pricing strategies, cost structures, and profit mechanisms. Value capture ensures that the business can sustainably generate revenues that exceed the costs incurred in creating and delivering the value proposition.

Together, these three business model elements form a cohesive framework that outlines how a company creates, delivers, and captures value in its operations. Businesses can optimise their overall performance and achieve long-term success by focusing on developing a compelling value proposition, establishing efficient value creation and delivery processes, and implementing effective value capture strategies. Sustainable business models allow for a holistic view of how business is conducted, considering the interests of shareholders and environmental and social sustainability metrics.

SUSTAINABLE BUSINESS TRANSFORMATION: CULTURE, PERFORMANCE AND CONCEPTS

The study by Linnenluecke and Griffiths (2010) emphasises the significance of the formulation and execution of Sustainable Management Systems (SMS) in the context of sustainable business models. Establishing and carrying out an SMS is deeply intertwined with the overall culture of an organisation. To effectively achieve corporate sustainability, embracing changes in business management practices and corporate behaviours is imperative.

In sustainable business practices, more than merely implementing tools, techniques, and change strategies are needed to guarantee the success of corporate environmental management endeavours. Vodonik (2018) highlights that a major obstacle to achieving organizational change programs is the existing organisational culture. Even the most well-structured approaches can only succeed if an organisation's culture resists change. Organisational culture plays a pivotal role in shaping a company's attitudes, behaviours, and norms. If the prevailing culture is not receptive to sustainability practices or is inherently resistant to change, the adoption of SMS can encounter significant challenges. Vodonik's insights underline that the inherent resistance of organisational culture can act as a formidable barrier to the effective implementation of initiatives focused on corporate environmental management.

To successfully transition towards sustainable business models and ensure the viability of SMS, it is imperative to address not only the technical and strategic aspects but also the cultural dimensions within an organisation. This requires a comprehensive approach that involves altering the processes and tools and influencing employees' and stakeholders' attitudes, values, and norms. In essence, embracing sustainability necessitates a holistic transformation encompassing changes in organisational culture, management practices, and corporate paradigms.

Performance Management

Organisational Performance Management Systems and their metrics have been enhanced to enhance business performance and competitiveness. Outstanding examples are the Performance Prism of Neely et al. (2002) and the Balanced Scorecard (BSC) of Kaplan and Norton (1992). Organisations seek to improve their performance indicators internally. They must also evaluate their performance in relation to each indicator to determine whether what is being measured is also being applied by the market and whether the outcomes are what are influencing the choices of customers. Both Kaplan and Norton (1998) and Neely (2002) emphasise the need to examine the key performance indicators and, if necessary, stop using them or develop new ones.

The balanced scorecard measures four strategic dimensions of the business in integrating performances into the organisation's goals and objectives. It includes the financial dimension - this is explained by Kaplan and Norton (1992) as metrics for this revenue, profitability, return on investment, and cost management (finances), the customer aspect, which evaluates the consumer's needs and satisfaction (customer base), the organisation's internal process - which examines the efficiency and effectiveness of business operations and processes (improvement in operations and innovation) and finally the people dimension - this implies employees learning and growth (employees satisfaction and well-being). The balanced scorecard measures emphasises the need for financial and non-financial measures for business information and performance indicators. Still, it was limited and criticised for its traditional economic value performance reporting, lacking focus and importance on sustainability and corporate social responsibility (CSR).

The Performance Prism of Neely, on the other hand, seeks to explain the performance of an organisation from five facets; its focus was on stakeholders' satisfaction, contributions, organisation strategies, organisation process and capabilities (Neely et al., 2002). Its emphasis on stakeholder satisfaction, including the satisfaction of investors, suppliers, employees, customers and regulators, would have a great import on the financial performance of the organisation (Neely et al., 2002). This prism also demands what is wanted from the stakeholders, how profitable a customer is to the organisation (Neely et al., 2001). So more broadly, the prism seeks the needs of stakeholders and the organisation's needs from them to enhance and measure performance. It also aids organisations to manage their performance and meet the needs of all stakeholders.

Figure 1. Performance Prism, Neely (2002)

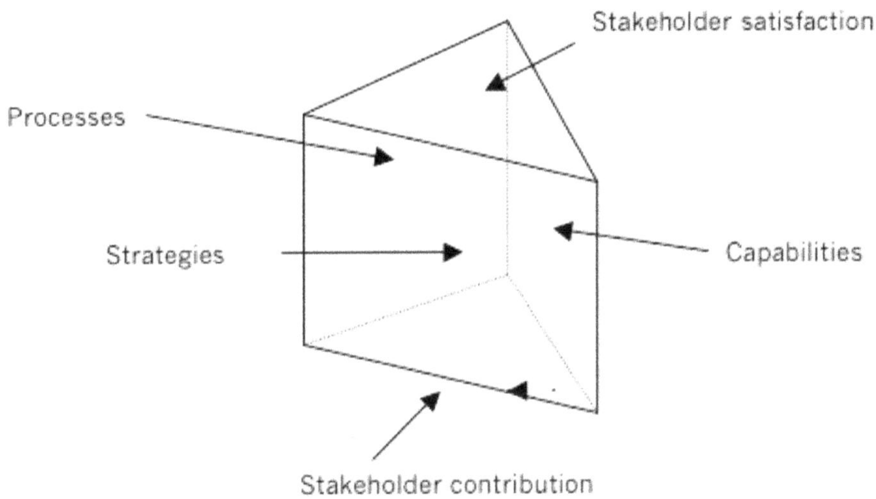

The Triple-bottom-line Performance Measure and Sustainability

More suitable in the measure of performance in relation to business sustainability, the triple-bottom-line approach by Elkington (1998), emerged as a potential measure for business sustainability. It has been widely accepted by scholars, organisations and the society (Lacy et al., 2010). This is because there is an increased focus on sustainability and its implication for performance management. In traditional performance measurements, financial information is considered, but the social and environmental aspects of business performance are now very essential. Therefore, the triple bottom line approach measures the economic value-added and the value addition or destruction businesses or organisations have made socially and environmentally (Neri et al., 2021). The phrase "people, planet and profit" describes the goal of the triple bottom line and sustainability goals (Elkington, 1994).

Figure 2. Illustration of the triple bottom line (Elkington, 1994)

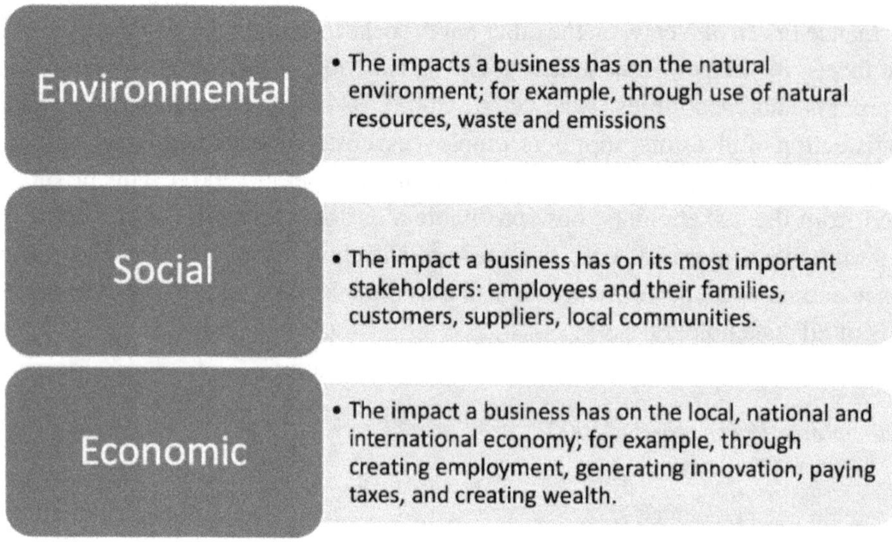

To Elkington (1998), the triple bottom line approach could lead to organisational performance in economic prosperity, quality of the environment and social justice, it creates value addition in their products and services to cater for the three concepts (McDonough & Braungart, 2002). For more viability of the triple bottom line approach, the economic indicators could be measured with the balanced scorecard to integrate actions on financial and non-financial performance (Hourneaux Jr. et al., 2018). To achieve sustainability, the practices of green purchasing and green capabilities must influence the triple-bottom-line performance of organizations (Khan et al., 2022).

Sustainability reporting

Strategic Management Systems must include sustainability reporting. The emergence of sustainability reporting across time, from its early beginnings to its current importance, has taken a good shape. Sustainability reporting has transformed from a novel idea to a crucial pillar of corporate transparency and accountability as societies and business organisations increasingly recognise the necessity of ethical behaviour. This trip charts the transition from conventional/traditional financial reporting to a multifaceted model that includes aspects of government, social interaction, and the environment, illuminating the shared commitment to a more just and sustainable future. The primary objective of sustainability performance management is to establish a strong linkage between the management of environmental and social aspects and the strategic direction of the business. This involves seamlessly integrating environmental and social considerations into the broader business strategy and competitiveness framework. Additionally, it entails the seamless fusion of environmental and social data with conventional economic business information. This integration of diverse information sources then serves as the foundation for comprehensive sustainability reporting, as highlighted by Dienes et al. (2016).

Figure 3. Elkington's Triple Bottom Line Model

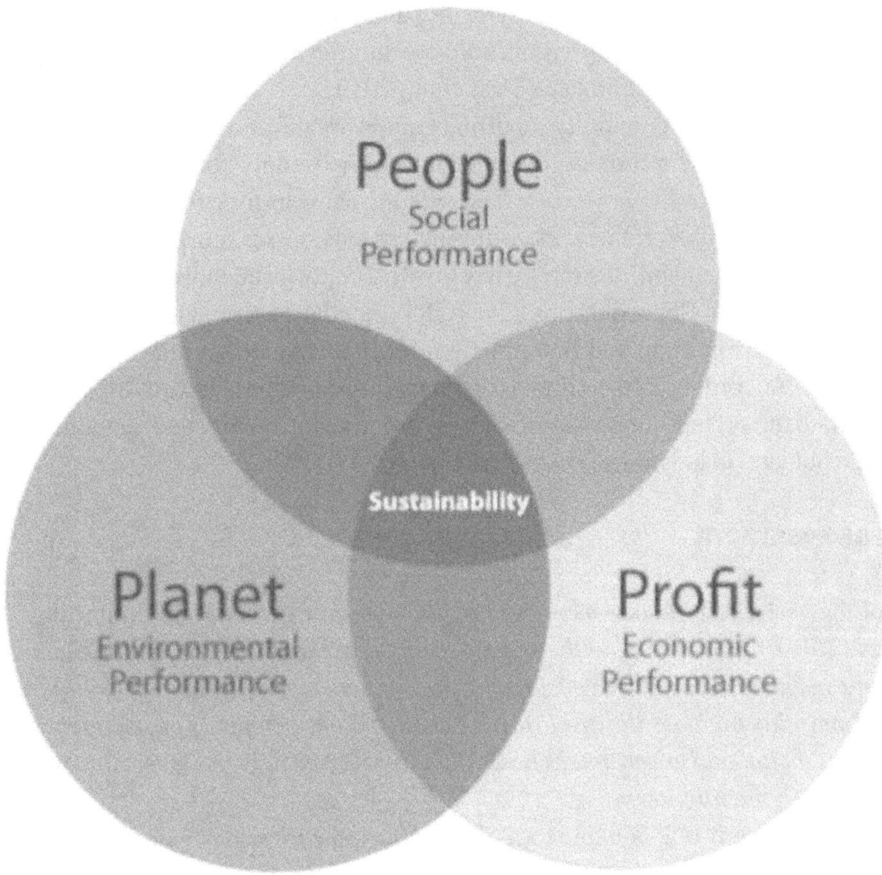

Sustainability reporting offers organisations, an increased capacity to monitor accomplishments towards specific goals; facilitate environmental strategy implementation; increase awareness of general environmental issues within the organisation; capability of clearly communicate corporate messages both internally and externally; increase reliability in general due to greater accountability; capability of communicating endeavours and norms; and standards; goodwill, reputation and business development (Kolk, 2004). In its early realise of sustainability reporting, some organisations gave some reasons for not reporting sustainability, and this includes; that competing organisations are not reporting, do not influence sales since their consumers do not take interest in it, the organisation already has a reputation for its environmental performance, it is prohibitively costly, the difficulty of data gathering based on organisation operations, it could also cause legal repercussions and harm the organisation's reputation (Sustainability/UNEP, 1998).

Sustainability reporting is a sort of non-financial disclosure that enables organisations to describe their progress in various sustainability-related areas. These include measurements related to the environment, society, and governance, as well as potential hazards and future effects. The main objective of sustainability reporting is to inspire concrete actions supporting these initiatives. It provides a platform for businesses to communicate the complex effects of their actions, whether they have positive or bad effects on the environment, society, and economy. This, in turn, helps to define priorities clearly. The reporting structure might include various features, such as pictures, data, graphs, and infographics, to ensure transparency in expressing sustainability strides and initiatives. Sustainability reporting is useful because it allows a company to identify risks and opportunities that may affect its long-term viability and increase transparency and brand image (Shad et al., 2019)

In general, the practice of sustainability reporting equips organisations to evaluate both risks and opportunities. It acts as a channel for promoting environmentally friendly company practices, coordinating with corporate social responsibility objectives, and creating chances for cost-saving measures. The need for an internationally recognised framework within which businesses, corporations, and organisations may communicate their sustainability strategy has grown due to sustainability's importance as a major worldwide issue. The Global Reporting Initiative (GRI) Standards give organisations a clear direction on what data they should report on and best practices for reporting on various economic, environmental, and social facets. According to the Global Sustainability Standards Board, the report must include themes that illustrate the organisation's significant environmental, social, and economic impacts or the influence of stakeholders' evaluations (GRI, 2016).

Materiality assessment

The concept of the Materiality Assessment is in alignment with sustainability reporting. According to AccountAbility (2018), "*Materiality, in the sustainability context, relates to identifying and prioritising the most relevant sustainability topics, considering the impact each topic has on the organisation and its stakeholders. Materiality includes the disclosure of risks and opportunities posed by these issues affecting environmental, social, and governance (ESG) domains that have impacts on corporate performance and on stakeholders in the long-term.*"

A materiality assessment is a valuable tool offering insights to enhance understanding and ranking of diverse sustainability considerations. This includes integrating stakeholder viewpoints regarding the organisation's offerings. Nevertheless, the core objective of such an evaluation is to pinpoint the pivotal social and environmental matters that hold the utmost significance for your company, investors, and stakeholders. The prominence of materiality assessments is rising, aligning with the global movement towards heightened transparency and a more substantial commitment to sustainability. The concept of materiality helps you identify the social and environmental issues that are most important to the organisation and its stakeholders. Of notable importance, especially for companies aiming to communicate their Corporate Social Responsibility (CSR), is the principle of materiality.

Stakeholder engagement as part of an inclusive materiality process can result in numerous beneficial outcomes, including:

Ensure that important environmental and social concerns are considered in corporate strategy and that sustainability management is integrated into larger business and organisation processes and operations.

Discerning trends that could have a big influence on the ability of the organisation to generate wealth in the long run.

Enable different business units to be prepared to seize opportunities to create new products or services and beat off competition.

Organising the organisation's resources such that they are prioritised for the sustainability concerns that are most essential to the organisation and its stakeholders will allow the organisation to spend time and resources on the areas that are most crucial.
Identifying the areas the organisation needs to handle and keep an eye on crucial yet unaddressed concerns
Determining the topics that interest those who are significant stakeholders, allows you to deliver succinct information that gives those who require it a relevant picture of progress.
Assisting in determining the areas where the organisation is increasing or decreasing its importance to society.

KPMG (2014, p. 6) provides a seven-step approach to conducting a materiality assessment and it is presented in the table below.

Table 1. Approach to Materiality Assessment

Phase 1:	Defining the purpose and scope of materiality
Phase 2:	Identifying the potential material topics
Phase 3:	Categorizing potential material topics
Phase 4:	Gathering information about the impact and importance of topics
Phase 5:	Prioritizing material topics based on the strategic importance to the business and the stakeholders
Phase 6:	Testing the materiality result with key internal audience
Phase 7:	Seeking stakeholder's feedback on the reported material topics

Source: KPMG (2014 p. 6). Sustainable Insight: the essentials of materiality assessment

The procedure for defining the material aspects and boundaries of an organisation's activities summarized in figure 4 below. According to GRI (2013), It is divided into four steps, they are;

Identification of the Aspects and any other relevant topics, and their Boundaries; Prioritization of the Aspects and any other relevant topics from Step 1, to identify those that are material and therefore to be reported; Validation where the Principles of Completeness and Stakeholder Inclusiveness are applied to finalize the identification of the report contenton; Finally, after the report has been published, it is important that the organization undertakes a review of its report. (pp. 32-33)

Multi-stakeholder collaboration

In the new systems of sustainability models and governance, multi-stakeholder collaboration and partnership are exalted as sustainable development. The role and relevance of multi-stakeholder collaboration have very high expectations. The collaboration is expected to address the issues of regulatory deficit, implementation deficit, and participation deficit in sustainability governance. All stakeholders, including governments, intergovernmental organisations, and non-state actors in all spheres of society, are urged to get involved and work collaboratively to create value for sustainability for the benefit of society due to the scope, intricacy, and mutual dependence of the sustainable development goals included in the 2030 Agenda (Grainger-Brown & Malekpour, 2019; Melo, 2018). To effectively address the complex issues of sustainable development that are beyond the capability of organisations required or the ability to address them on their own, collaborative obligations to sustainable development are acknowledged as being essential at all levels (Ayala-Orozco et al., 2018; Fobbe, 2020; Lozano et al., 2021).

Figure 4. Process for Defining Material Aspects and Boundaries
(Source: GRI, 2013, p. 32)

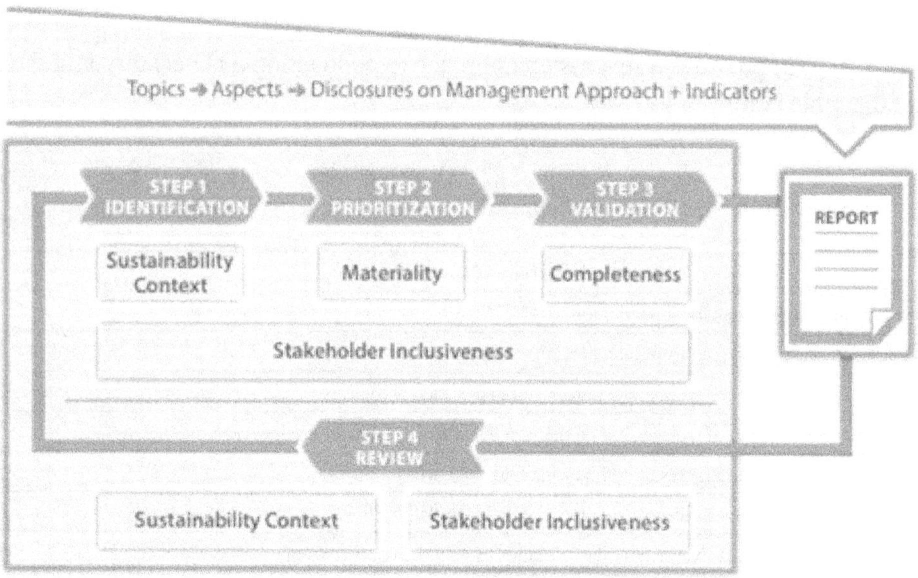

Multi-stakeholder partnerships are seen as an effective way to address current challenges in sustainable development because they bring together actors from various societal sectors (non-profit, public, and private), incorporating resources and collaborating on risk-sharing. A large coalition of international and national actors from the public and private sectors, non-governmental organisations, and academia that support the achievement of the Sustainable Development Goals (SDGs) are behind these partnerships, which can act locally, nationally, regionally, and globally. Researchers emphasised the significant added value of collaborative actions to support the SDGs, while providing benefits for everyone involved, related to the simpler access to information, materials, connections, prospects, and an improved understanding of the various aspects of sustainability affecting the society (Fruedenrich et al., 2020; Kuenke & Aitken, 2015).

TRADE-OFFS AND RISKS BETWEEN SHORT-TERM FINANCIAL GOALS AND LONG-TERM SUSTAINABILITY OBJECTIVES

To meet changing societal demands, organisations must adapt their long-term strategies and incorporate environmental and social aspects into their product offerings and decision-making. However, at the same time, companies must satisfy short-term profitability interests and demands from shareholders. The adoption of corporate sustainability addresses integrating sustainability into organisational processes and operations from a profit perspective (Haessler, 2020). While profitability is viewed as businesses' primary concern and output, business managers sometimes face a trade-off between sustainability, especially in value creation and profits (Epstein, 2015). Most managers, if in conflict, will choose profitability over sustainability. A study by Graham et al. (2005), investigating 400 organisations, indicated that managers will prefer to forgo long-term value creation to meet short-term profit targets.

RISKS INTRINSIC TO INTEGRATING SUSTAINABILITY INTO BUSINESS MODELS

Integrating sustainability into business models can bring numerous benefits, both for the environment and the business's long-term success. However, this process also comes with several inherent risks and challenges. Two key risks are explained below:

Regulatory Fears

Sustainability practices are often subject to evolving regulations and standards. Failing to comply with these regulations could lead to fines, legal action, or reputational damage. Keeping up with changing requirements across various regions can be complex. Regulatory fear" refers to the concern and uncertainty that businesses may have about the potential regulatory changes and requirements related to sustainability as they integrate these practices into their business models.

The following suggests how regulatory fear can be an intrinsic risk to integrating sustainability:

Changes in Regulations. Environmental protection, social responsibility, and sustainability regulations can change quickly. Organisations that have made investments in specific procedures or technologies can find themselves unexpectedly subject to new regulatory requirements that call for more adjustments or expenditures.

Costs of Compliance. Adopting new regulations frequently entails expenses. To achieve compliance, businesses may need to set aside resources for process adjustments, technological upgrades, or additional staff training. Budgets may be strained, and profitability may suffer, especially for smaller businesses.

Planning Under Uncertainty. It might be difficult to anticipate regulatory changes, which makes long-term planning difficult. Businesses may be hesitant to make sizable expenditures in sustainability if they worry that future legislation may deem those efforts outmoded or insufficient.

Competitive Disadvantage. Businesses that adopt sustainable practices proactively before legislative requirements may have an advantage. In contrast, organisations that put off taking action because of regulatory uncertainty may later find themselves at a disadvantage and unable to catch up to more prepared rivals.

Lack of Alignment. Aligning with existing and prospective future legislation is necessary to integrate sustainability business models. If legislative changes are not anticipated, strategies and investments may be made that are not in line with the changing legal environment.

Reputation Risk. Failure to comply with regulations can lead to bad press, harming a company's reputation. This could erode investor and customer confidence, which would be detrimental to the company's long-term viability.

Multijurisdictional Operations Complexities. Managing compliance with various regulatory frameworks can be challenging for organisations operating across different regions and nations. As businesses must operate in various legal frameworks, the potential of regulatory dread rises.

Conflict Between Short-Term and Long-Term Objectives. Businesses may be forced to choose between short-term financial objectives and long-term sustainability objectives that are required by regulatory changes. Making immediate financial advantages more important than sustainability enhancements could result in missed opportunities and difficulties in the future.

Resource Allocation and Adaptation. Organisations may need to allocate resources more quickly to fulfil fresh compliance standards if regulations change quickly. This could disrupt existing workflows and take resources away from other critical operations.

By taking the following steps, businesses can navigate the uncertainty of regulations and enhance their sustainable business models:

The organisation must stay up-to-date with regulatory changes related to sustainability.

The organisation must incorporate scenario development that anticipates potential regulatory changes and their implications for their business.

Sustainability strategies must be flexible to allow for response adjustments to regulation changes.

Early actions to align with regulatory expectations whenever possible.

Engagement with the regulatory authorities to provide input on potential regulations and their practical implications.

Collaboration with all stakeholders to collectively address regulatory challenges and influence positive changes.

Reputational Dangers

If sustainability initiatives are perceived as "greenwashing" or insincere attempts to appear environmentally friendly without substantial changes, it can lead to reputational damage and loss of trust among customers, investors, and other stakeholders. These forms of how these can manifest and have an impact on the organisation include;

Perception of "Greenwashing". Greenwashing is the practice of a firm overstating or misrepresenting its environmental initiatives to appear more sustainable than it actually is. A firm may lose credibility and confidence if stakeholders believe it dishonestly markets its environmental activities. This could harm the company's reputation, particularly in light of the growing concern investors and consumers have for social and environmental issues.

Negative Effects on Brand Value. Consistent messaging and great experiences help brands grow over time. The brand's perceived value may be diminished if sustainability efforts are thought to be false. Customers' loyalty and revenues may decline due to consumers associating the company with hypocrisy.

Lack of Transparency. For sustainability efforts to succeed, transparency is essential. When an organisation is secretive about its successes, difficulties, and failures, stakeholders may assume the worst and think the company is unreliable. For credibility to remain intact, both accomplishments and mistakes must be discussed openly.

Investor Confidence. Nowadays, many investors consider a firm's sustainability performance when making investment decisions. Investor trust may erode if a business's sustainability promises are refuted or if its activities fall short of expectations, which could have an adverse financial impact.

Long-term Repercussions. Damage to one's reputation extends beyond just immediate consequences. It may impact investor relations, corporate relationships, employee morale, and customer loyalty. It might take time and money to restore a reputation that has been tarnished.

Loss of Competitive Advantage. Organisations prioritising sustainability can gain a competitive edge by courting customers who care about the environment and the community. If an organisation's image suffers due to accusations of greenwashing, it may lose this advantage and find it difficult to set itself apart from rivals.

By taking the following steps, businesses can mitigate the risk of reputational damage and enhance their credibility in the eyes of stakeholders;

Genuinity and authenticity in sustainability claims that can be substantiated with organisation actions and data to back them.

Setting clear and realistic goals for the organisation to avoid under-delivery and over-promising. Therefore, organisations must set sustainable goals that are achievable and must be transparent in reporting their progress.

Sustainability efforts must be addressed and communicated properly by stating progress, achievements and various obstacles and uphills in its attainment to all stakeholders.

Active stakeholder involvement to ensure that sustainability initiatives align with their expectations of the organisation.

Continuous show and demonstration of Improvement in sustainability practices and the organisation's adaptation to sustainability challenges.

External Validation of sustainability efforts by third-party organisations with reputable sustainability practices.

Develop a crisis management plan that will address reputational issues and help resolve and respond to false publicity of the organisation.

CASE STUDIES: BUFFERING CORPORATE PROCESSES BY INTEGRATING SUSTAINABILITY

Few case studies highlight the challenges organisations face that have successfully advanced SMS for sustainability integration into their existing corporate models, as well as methods and strategies employed to overcome such challenges and resulting consequences (Lozano et al., 2020). There would be discussions around three firms that have advanced their sustainability models into their corporate processes' operations.

Interface Inc.

In the design and manufacture of sustainable modular flooring, suitable for any education environment, A global carpet manufacturer has portrayed real-time strategic management systems that empower incorporating sustainability theories and values into its business model, resulting in increased competitiveness. Interface Inc. is recognised as a global leader in sustainability. In 1994 we were one of the first companies to commit to sustainability, known as Mission Zero publicly, to eliminate any negative environmental impact by 2020.

For 21 years, Interface relied significantly on fossil fuels for its manufacturing, transportation, and product production, operating instinctively on the old industrial paradigm of "take-make-waste". The pivotal moment occurred in 1994 when Ray C. Anderson realised how little thought was being given to the future and the pioneering role the company could play in forging a new course that would try to create an industrial model and society that was more sustainable. Interface aimed to demonstrate that any corporation can reinvent itself and that there is no longer any justification for anyone not to do so if even a heavily dependent on oil company can do it. The idea that emphasising sustainability has a detrimental impact on the bottom line has been debunked by Interface. Interface cut the amount of industrial waste the company sends to landfill by 84% between 1996 and 2013. Currently, 36% of yarn and 51% of carpet backing are made from recycled or biodegradable materials, making up around 49% of all raw resources. $450 million in waste expenditures may have been saved. The total energy used at the factories worldwide has decreased by 39% per unit. Additionally, 100% renewable energy accounts for 36% of the energy used worldwide (7 out of 9 facilities use 100% renewable energy). The amount of greenhouse gas emissions has decreased by 41%. The first US company to use The Natural Step's Framework was Interface. The new Interface vision was developed under the direction of The Natural Step and other sustainability visionaries, using the metaphor of Mount Sustainability as outlined by The Natural Step's four principles. The illustration below demonstrates their sustainability initiatives.

Figure 5. The natural step: Interface Case Study

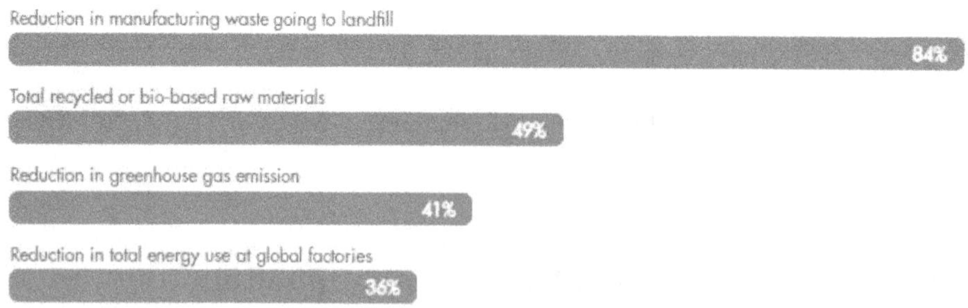

The Net-Works programme of Interface Inc. collaborates with local communities in poor nations to recover abandoned fishing nets from the sea and other bodies of water. The recycled yarn made from these nets is subsequently utilised to make carpet tiles. The programme offers local populations employment opportunities in addition to aiding in the cleanup of maritime habitats. Interface's product design and manufacturing procedures are influenced by nature. The business incorporates biomimicry principles, which model tactics from nature, into its innovation process. The development of Interface's products places a strong emphasis on biophilic design, which aims to reconnect people with nature. The sustainability initiatives of Interface Inc. often show a thorough commitment to social and environmental responsibility, taking into account many aspects of the company's operations, product development, and community engagement. The company exemplifies how businesses may successfully incorporate sustainability into their core operating models and positively impact society and the environment.

Climbing the 7 fronts of Mount Sustainability to reach Mission Zero

Eliminate Waste. Restoring natural habitats by reclaiming and recycling old fish nets and turning them into carpet tiles

Benign Emissions. Introducing new systems such as the revolutionary TacTiles™ stickers, which allow for the installation of carpets without glue.

Renewable Energy. Collaborating to build a biogas plant to convert methane from landfills into energy

Close the Loop. ReEntry 2.0™, which separates the fibres and backings of old carpet tiles. The fibre is then recycled into new threads, which are combined with recycled yarn from discarded fishnets, to produce Biosfera™, a carpet with 100% recycled yarn

Efficient Transport. Interface applies carbon offset programs for both product shipping and employee commuting

Sensitising Stakeholders. Equipping everyone within Interface's network with knowledge about sustainability and the 7 Fronts, offering tools and opportunities to promote that agenda

Redesign commerce. Tile exchange and Tile care programs aim to extend the life of a carpet through maintenance, reducing both costs for clients and environmental impact, as well as creating new jobs and markets

Unilever

As part of its business strategy, Unilever incorporated sustainability into its model via a Sustainable Living Plan that aimed to improve its social and environmental impact. Furthermore, Unilever has employed a multi-stakeholder engagement approach that has heightened understanding of stakeholders' expectations and apprehensions to fuse these into the organisation's strategy. The Sustainable Living Plan by Unilever is a good illustration of how a business may include sustainability in its main business plan. The strategy is integrated into the company's business model, decision-making procedures, and performance measures for assessing staff performance. With this strategy, Unilever can ensure that sustainability is an integral element of its business strategy rather than an afterthought.

Unilever's Sustainable Living Plan offers a comprehensive framework outlining the company's commitment to sustainable development. Since its inception in 2010, it has significantly influenced Unilever's corporate strategy in favour of more responsible and long-lasting practices. The three central tenets of this plan are improving livelihood prospects, reducing environmental impact, and enhancing health and well-being. Unilever's Sustainable Living Plan is an excellent example of how a company may use corporate social innovation to balance its financial performance with its societal goals. Unilever has completely embraced this attitude as an essential component of its business model because it recognises the relationship between its profitability and the welfare of both the Earth and humanity. Unilever strives to achieve a harmonious blend of profitability and societal impact by innovating advanced products and services designed to address sustainability challenges. For instance, within its lineup, the laundry brand OMO has launched the product OMO EcoActive, an example. This innovation delivers effective cleaning and reduces water and energy consumption. Unilever's creation, The Vegetarian Butcher, presents another illustration of this approach, offering consumers a conscientious and ecologically sound alternative for meals through its plant-based meat substitute.

Unilever is utilising its size and impact to foster favourable transformations throughout its value network. The company maintains close collaboration with its suppliers, guaranteeing their alignment with its sustainability criteria. Additionally, Unilever has introduced endeavours like the Unilever Sustainable Living Young Entrepreneurs Awards, an initiative designed to endorse and nurture young entrepreneurs creating inventive resolutions to address sustainability issues.

Patagonia

Patagonia, on the other hand, equally merged sustainability with its business model. Outdoor and adventure clothing manufacturer Patagonia is well known for setting the bar for environmental responsibility. With a mission statement to *"build the best product, cause no unnecessary harm, use business to inspire and implement solutions to the environmental crisis"*.

Patagonia shows how profit-making does not have to cost the Earth, the use of ecologically friendly products, ethical production methods, and support for environmental concerns all reflect the company's commitment to sustainability. Patagonia has demonstrated a strong commitment to environmental preservation and conservation through their active engagement. Their activism encompasses endeavours to safeguard public lands, address the challenges of climate change, and promote sustainable agricultural practices. An integral part of Patagonia's sustainability strategy is the implementation of the 1% for the Planet initiative, wherein the company allocates 1% of their sales towards supporting environmental organisations (Patagonia, 2022).

The Common Threads Initiative includes reducing by not purchasing unnecessary items, Repair, which involves assisting consumers in fixing malfunctioning equipment, Reuse the item by giving it to someone who might need it. Recycle the useless items and create a connection with eBay so that people may purchase pre-owned Patagonia goods rather than brand-new ones. Customers can trade in wearable used items for shop credit, allowing them to replace old products in a sustainable way.

Patagonia has established a comprehensive strategy based on the five iterative steps Nimudolu (2009) articulated for the transition to sustainability. According to this philosophy, compliance is a prerequisite and an entry point into sustainable technology. The journey of Patagonia includes changing its value chains to ensure sustainability at every stage. To lessen the influence on the environment, the corporation is also strongly committed to redesigning the way its products are made.

Patagonia is also actively involved in the development of innovative business models that place a significant emphasis on sustainability. By challenging traditional norms and practises, they raise the bar for innovative approaches to balancing business with social and environmental responsibility. This commitment also includes the creation of ground-breaking next-practice platforms that serve as templates for organisations to emulate, raising the standard for sustainability both inside and outside the sector.

Figure 6. Patagonia sustainability model (medium.com, 2021)

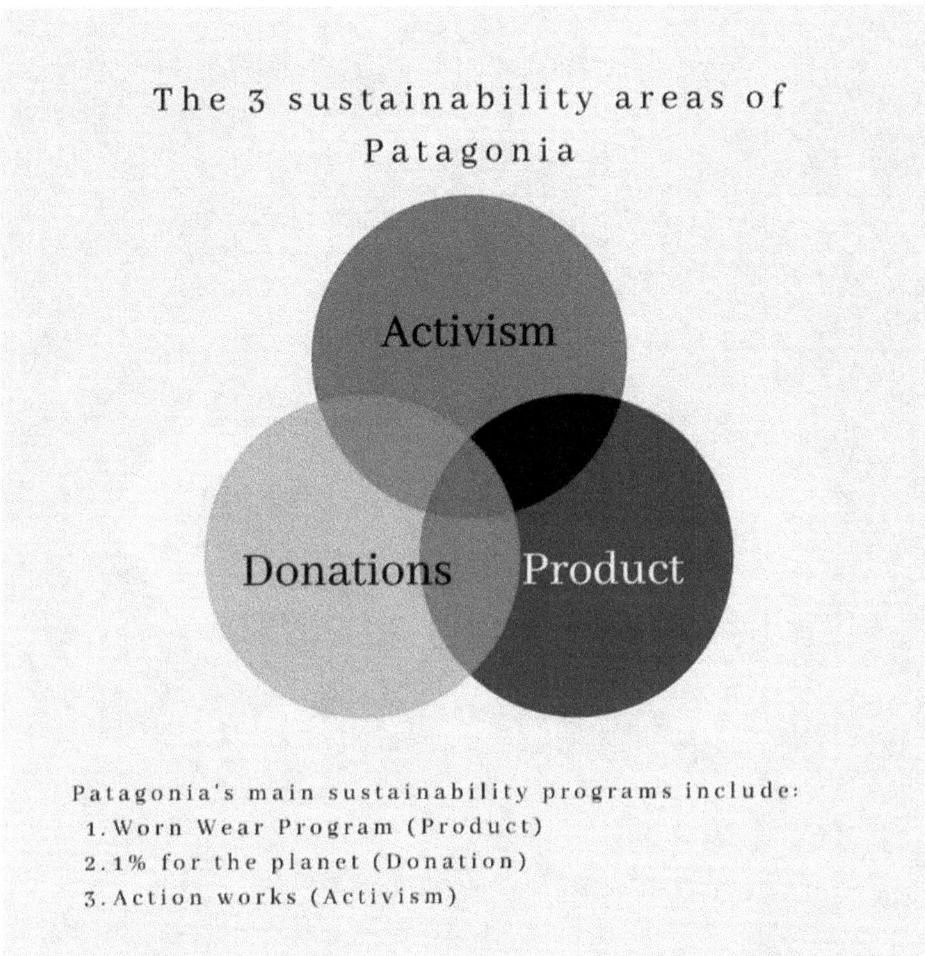

Sustainability Models and Innovations in Strategic Management

Organisations can use certain methods to overcome obstacles when leveraging strategic management systems to build sustainable business models. These include sustainability models like;

The Circular Economy

The goal of the Circular Economy is to reduce the amount of waste generated and promote a more sustainable approach to resource use. In comparison with the linear economy which drives an increment in the use of natural resources by trapping them as waste, the circular economy helps eliminate waste and regenerate natural resources. The rationale behind how a company produces, delivers, and collects value for a wider range of stakeholders while minimising environmental and social costs is expressed in a circular business model.

Figure 7. Linear Economy (Boxall, 2023)

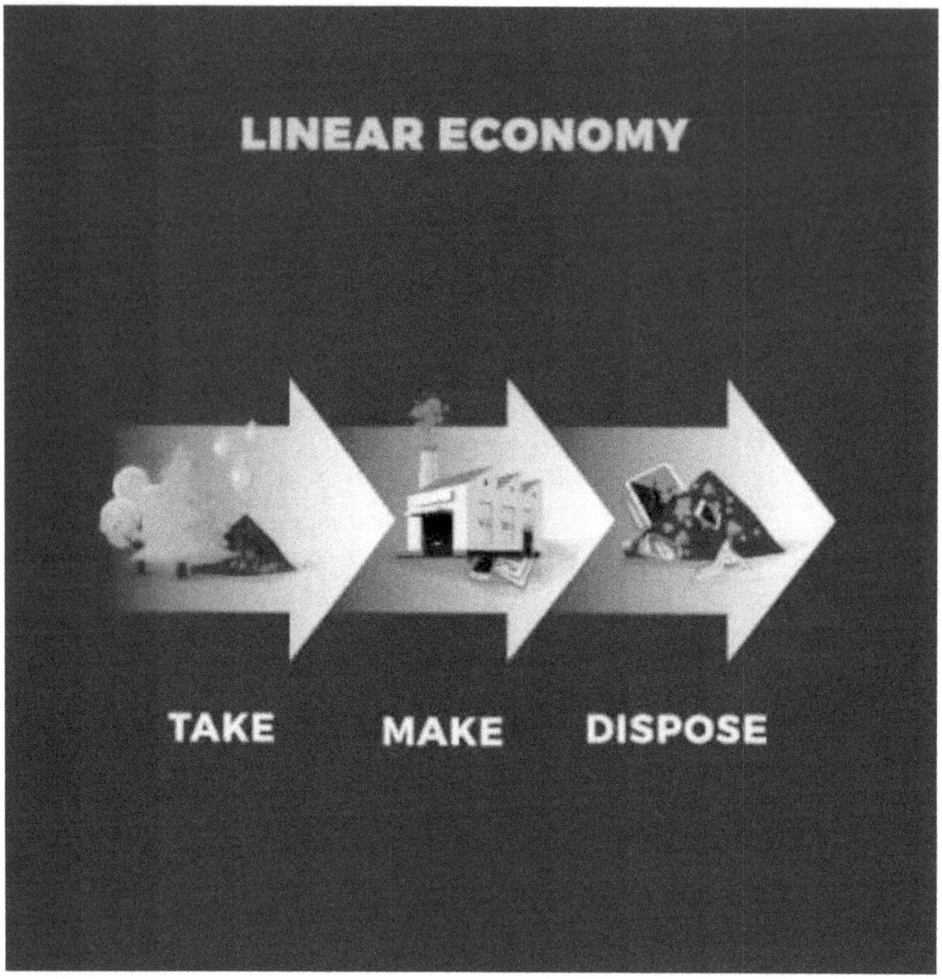

A paradigm shift of applying circular economy to achieve sustainable manufacturing is progressively accepted by different manufacturing industries (Geissdoerfer et al., 2017; Gusmerotti et al., 2019; Jia et al., 2020; Korhonen, 2004; Kun et al., 2021; Lieder & Rashid, 2016). Central to this shift is the recognition of the imperative to embed sustainability principles within the fabric of circular economy business models, as underscored by the insights of Alhawari et al. (2021). However, successfully establishing a circular economy necessitates a comprehensive grasp of the intricate infrastructure that underpins recycling and remanufacturing processes. Geissdoerfer et al. (2017) have meticulously illuminated the multifaceted interplay between sustainability and the circular economy, elucidating a spectrum that ranges from synergistic interdependence to instances of delicate trade-offs.

In essence, the converging goals of sustainable development and circular economy practices are to forge a symbiotic relationship with potential mutual benefits. The realisation of these benefits hinges upon a strategic amalgamation of sustainability principles within circular business frameworks bolstered by a nuanced comprehension of the intricate mechanisms supporting recycling and remanufacturing, as expounded by pertinent scholarly research.

Figure 8. Circular Economy (Boxall, 2023)

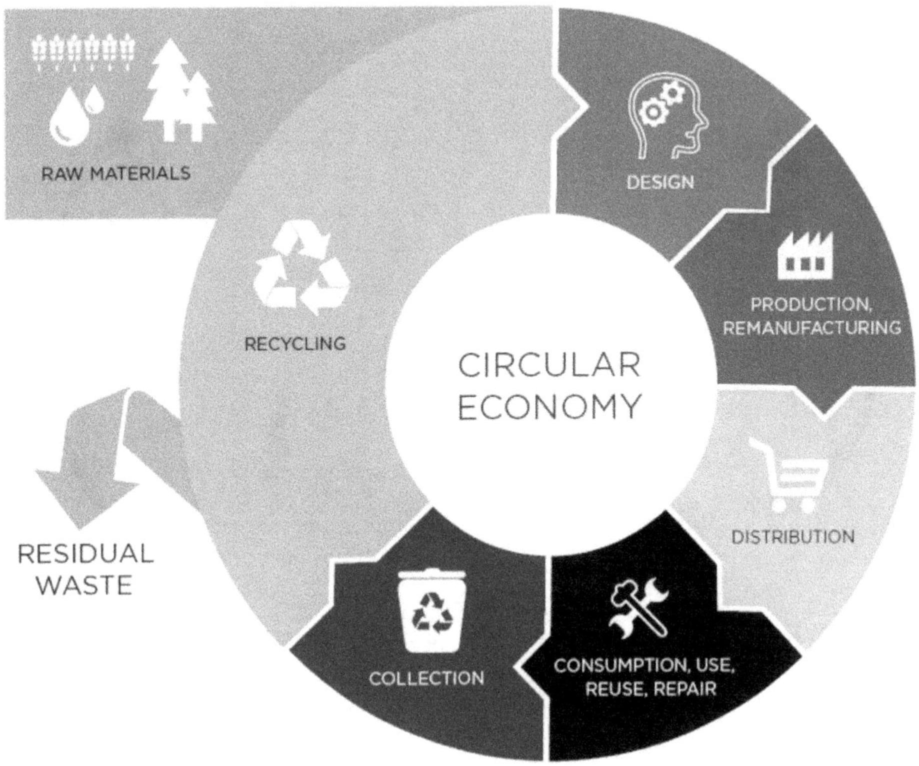

Digitalisation and Technology

This enables a merger between sustainability and organisational structures. Technology and digitalisation have had a tremendous impact on how firms run and have created new prospects for creating sustainable business models. When a firm seeks to increase its value while simultaneously taking into account its effects on the economy, society, and the environment, it is said to be using a sustainable business model. This shift towards sustainable business models involves new digital technologies like the Internet of Things, big data and related analytics, and virtual and augmented reality. These technologies do form the foundation of what is known as the fourth industrial age. Additionally, they fundamentally alter how businesses produce goods or provide services, easing the transition to sustainability (Bressanelli et al., 2018).

According to Ross et al. (2017), the systematic application of these technologies causes businesses to undergo a digital transformation or to redefine their business procedures and methods. As stated by Watanabe et al. (2018), the process of digitalization has the potential to enhance production procedures, making way for cost reductions. This can be achieved through benefits such as comprehensive visibility across the supply chain, enhanced precision in deliveries, optimization of stock levels, and synchronization with demand planning efforts. "Blockchain, integrated with AI and data shared across cellular networks via Internet of Things (IoT) devices, can help companies monitor and expedite the identification of bottlenecks in the supply chain, thereby mitigating transport risks. This, in turn, can allow businesses to better anticipate the possibility and extent of delays" (Deloitte, 2023, p. 4)

Figure 9. Representation of digitalisation and transformation to sustainable business models, Adapted from Broccardo et al., (2023)

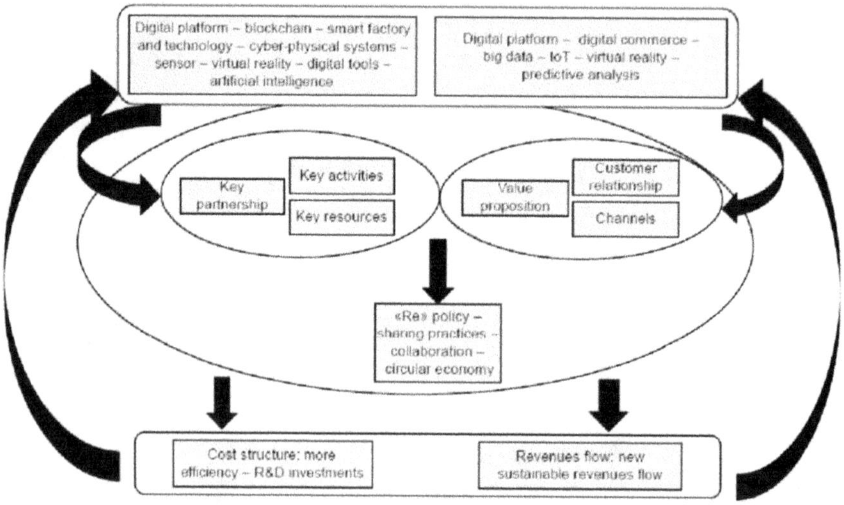

Data-driven analysis of water consumption, energy usage and waste generation with digital technology can help with resource usage optimisation, it also facilitates the reduction and reliance on fossil fuels and minimises the carbon footprint of the organisation. Businesses can build, test, and refine goods in virtual environments using digital tools like simulations and computer-aided design (CAD) software. This iterative process can result in the development of more sustainable, durable, recyclable, and resource-efficient goods. Thanks to blockchain technology and other digital platforms, the ability to track goods and resources in real time improves supply chain transparency. This transparency promotes ethical sourcing, lowers the possibility of social and environmental abuses, and increases consumer confidence. Large datasets can be analysed, and firms can extract insights using data analytics and artificial intelligence. This entails seeing trends, comprehending consumer behaviour, and foreseeing market demands—all of which can help business strategists create sustainable business plans. The integration of digitalization and technology into sustainable business models necessitates a comprehensive strategy that takes into account how environmental, social, and economic concerns are interconnected. Businesses that effectively use these technologies can boost stakeholder participation, reduce environmental impact, increase operational efficiency, and improve the planet's and its people's well-being.

Some of the applications of these cutting-edge technologies are further presented moving forward.

Big Data Analytics (BDA) in Business Sustainability

Big data is a collection of massive and complex data sets and data volumes that include huge quantities of data, data management capabilities, social media analytics and real-time data. Big data analytics (BDA) is the process of examining large amounts of data (Ishwarappa & Anuradha, 2015)

By tapping into extensive datasets, companies can enhance decision-making, pinpoint resource efficiency prospects, minimize waste, and tackle environmental and societal issues more effectively. BDA enables businesses to make decisions based on facts and evidence rather than intuition or guesswork. Almost 60% of healthcare organizations already use big data and nearly all the remaining ones are open to adopting big data initiatives in the future (Baturina, 2019). By analyzing large volumes of data, patterns and trends that may not be apparent at a smaller scale can be identified. This leads to more accurate forecasts, precise predictions, and a deeper understanding of customer behavior, market dynamics, and operational efficiencies (Afreen, 2023).

A case study analysis by Ciccullo et al. (2022) based on secondary sources, shows that some startup business models leverage Big Data Analytics (BDA) to avoid food waste by optimizing an existing linear supply chain, while other business models create value out of food waste by leveraging a circular food supply chain. We found that the latter business models are not fully exploiting the potential of BDA. Hence BDA can be used for efficient resource utilization and reduce waste. Big Data Analytics assumes a pivotal role in propelling sustainability in the corporate world.

Blockchain in Supply Chain Transparency

Blockchain technology allows the integration of all supply chain members into a single secure network while sharing data and information (Difrancesco et al., 2023; Dutta et al., 2020). Due to this, businesses can now track and verify the sustainability and origin of products in their supply chains. This enhances transparency and traceability. For companies looking to cement their place in tomorrow's economy, there is a pressing need to seek out innovative technological tools like blockchain that can deliver the foundational supply chain transformations necessary to ensure competitiveness (Back, 2017). A more recent report by World Economic Forum (2023, p. 9) pointed out that blockchain can enable the transparent tracking of products and materials in supply chains. Blockchain can help reduce the environmental damage caused by illegal or unsustainable practices, such as deforestation, overfishing or hazardous waste disposal.

In practical terms blockchain technology has been used by De Beers, one of the largest diamond producers in the world. De Beers implemented a blockchain-based tracking system called Tracr. Tracr allows De Beers to track diamonds from the point where they are mined, through the cutting and polishing process, and ultimately to the end consumer. This technology provides tamper-proof source assurance at scale, encourages consumers' confidence in the ethical sourcing of their diamonds, and helps to combat the trade in conflict diamonds (Bulbulia, 2022; Deloitte, 2023, p. 5).

With supply chain transparency and traceability being addressed by blockchain technology, businesses can surmount the issues of greenwashing and other related hurdles which can cause reputational damage, thus increasing their competitiveness and overall profitability in a sustainable way.

Internet of Things (IoT) and Artificial Intelligence (AI) in Product Sustainability

A straightforward way to view the combination of AI and IoT treats the IoT system as a means of channeling data into intelligent monitoring or decision-making application (Figueredo, 2021). Products equipped with IoT-enabled sensors continuously gather data on their usage and performance throughout their lifespan. This data informs product improvements and reduces environmental impact. Additionally, AI-driven product design optimizes sustainability by considering factors such as materials, energy efficiency, and recyclability. These technologies enhance the overall environmental and economic sustainability of products.

Nest Labs' smart thermostats can adapt the system operations to the users' routines. In this way, an optimal balance between comfort and energy savings can be found. Another organization, AGCO Agcommand monitors the use, condition of farm equipment, as well as environmental parameters, to optimize overall farm performance (Ingemarsdotter et al., 2019, p. 16).

In these and other ways, businesses can harness IoT and AI to enhance product sustainability. There are still a lot of possibilities yet to be discovered with these technologies.

THE ROLE OF ORGANISATIONAL LEADERSHIP IN DRIVING SUSTAINABILITY

This is crucial and needs to be considered. Employee engagement is another crucial component of properly integrating sustainable principles into a firm. Sustainability is a complex problem that necessitates considerable organisational adjustments. As sustainability demands, corporate business strategies and thinking must change to incorporate long-term goals. Successful implementation of this will significantly affect company missions, value chains, cultures, operations and strategies (Millar et al., 2012). According to Gomez-Trujillo and Gonzalez-Perez (2021), creating an organisational culture that is focused on sustainability may be a way to address the organisational change that sustainability demands of businesses. In the writings of Baumgartner (2009), *"if aspects of sustainable development are not part of the mindset of leaders and members of the organisation, corporate sustainability activities will not affect the core business efficiently and are more likely to fail."* (p. 102)

Therefore, employees must be engaged with adequate and proper leadership. In order to successfully incorporate sustainability into organisations, there must be both top-down and bottom-up strategies, as well as manager-employee relationships, that support this process. Organizations must ensure that employees have the necessary resources to engage with sustainability change. This includes time, information, moral support, and technical and financial resources (Markos & Sridevi, 2010). After encouraging employees to take responsibility and personally commit to the company's sustainability goal, giving them the tools they need to get involved with sustainability is crucial. Organisations must ensure that their staff members have a solid understanding of sustainability and how the company's sustainability vision and plan will affect their everyday tasks and work. Employee engagement is pivotal in sustainability, and leadership is the torchbearer. Leaders should cultivate a culture of sustainability among employees through education, training, and recognition of their contributions to sustainability efforts. Leadership necessitates a steadfast commitment to the long-term perspective of sustainability (Hargreaves & Flink, 2012). Employees can better connect their workplace behaviours and values with the change by being informed about its reasons. This increases the likelihood that they will embrace a more sustainable business approach. By creating an environment that supports and rewards sustainable practices, leaders encourage employees to embrace sustainability as a core aspect of their work.

Establishing the organisation's vision and fundamental principles is mostly the responsibility of the leadership. Sustainability becomes integral to organisational culture when enshrined in these guiding principles (Benn et al., 2014). In order to ensure alignment with the organisation's broader purpose, leaders must passionately express their commitment to sustainability. Another essential component of leadership's function in sustainability is strategic planning. Executives are responsible for defining and expressing sustainability objectives, integrating them smoothly into the organisation's overall business plan (Arjaliès & Mundy, 2013). Stakeholder engagement is a crucial aspect of leadership. Building support for sustainability initiatives requires active participation from internal and external stakeholders, which effective leaders do (Dobele et al., 2014). Stakeholder participation in decision-making processes and open communication about the organisation's sustainability efforts are essential elements in this attempt. The management of sustainability performance monitoring and reporting is also committed to leaders. They are entrusted with creating key performance indicators (KPIs) and regularly assessing how well sustainability goals are progressing.

By incorporating sustainability into the organization's culture, strategy, and everyday operations, organizational leadership plays a crucial role in improving sustainability. Effective leaders understand that in the modern corporate climate, where environmental and societal issues hold increasing influence over consumers, investors, and regulatory authorities alike, sustainability is not only a moral necessity but also a competitive advantage.

CONCLUSION

In summary, this chapter buttressed how sustainable business models develop and are implemented in the business world and how new components make appropriate changes to the theoretical business model representation that could serve as a foundation for business models that satisfy all economic, social, and environmental goals of organisations. Businesses and organisations focus on business profit, they need to start gradually replacing their business goals with sustainable business models, focusing on the triple bottom line simultaneously, the companies have to redesign processes, production, activities and several structures to align with the sustainability principles even with profit-making. As a result, successful long-term business operations and socially and environmentally responsible business models are essential. Businesses are essential in bringing about change as the globe struggles with urgent issues including climate change, resource depletion, social injustice, and ethical questions. Sustainability integration is more than just a fad; it is a strategic requirement that considers economic, environmental, and social factors.

Sustainable business models are based on the virtues of accountability, openness, and moral conduct. They seek to strike a balance between corporate profitability and global and human well-being. These models place a strong emphasis on innovation, technology, efficiency and teamwork to generate wealth for all parties involved, not just shareholders. Businesses may help create a more just and sustainable society by implementing socially conscious initiatives, ethical sourcing, and circular economy practices. Furthermore, incorporating sustainability into business operations calls for a comprehensive strategy. It includes lowering environmental consequences through waste reduction, energy efficiency, and ethical supply chain management. Prioritizing employee wellbeing, diversity, and inclusion are additional requirements. Businesses can gain the trust of their customers, investors, and the community by being truthful in their communications. Even if there are obstacles like limited resources, opposition to change, and potential trade-offs, they can be overcome with visionary leadership, strategic planning, and a dedication to ongoing progress. Sustainable business practices can raise a company's profile, boost client retention, open doors to new markets, and strengthen resilience in the face of adversity. In the end, adopting sustainable business models and practises is not just an option; it is necessary for companies to prosper in a world that is changing quickly. Businesses may help create a better future for everyone by balancing financial success with social responsibility, environmental stewardship, and ethical behaviour. Collaboration, innovation, and creativity may lead the path for a more inclusive, equitable, and sustainable global economy.

Although the models of sustainability are efficient for business growth, the challenges, limitations, and criticisms of the integration of strategic management systems and sustainable business models are still imminent in their applications in business operations today. The need for organisations to remain deliberate about overcoming challenges and staying sustainable in the long term will improve the efforts towards sustainability. The challenges, limitations and critics of applying sustainable business models are explained below.

Challenges

Due to the diverse nature of sustainability issues, integrating strategic management systems with sustainable business models can be challenging. Planning and coordination must be done carefully to balance economic, environmental, and social goals.

If implementing sustainable practices upsets established routines, procedures, or conventional business models, there may be resistance from staff, stakeholders, and even management.

Sustainable business models frequently emphasise long-term advantages, which might conflict with the short-term financial objectives that some organisations emphasise on.

It can be difficult to measure and report sustainability performance accurately. Compared to traditional financial measures, indicators for social and environmental impacts may be less standardised and more difficult to define.

Making the switch to sustainable practises may necessitate initial investments in infrastructure, training, and technology, which can be a deterrent to expenditures of the organisation, but it will save costs in the long term.

If there is insufficient market demand or if customers are hesitant to pay more for sustainable solutions, the adoption of sustainable products and services may be slowed.

Limitations

There may be conflicts between social, environmental, and economic objectives. One facet of sustainability may be incompatible with another, for instance.

Sustainability must consider global variables like the complexity of the supply chain, varying regulatory requirements, and cultural differences.

It is difficult to evaluate performance across industries and businesses since globally recognised standards for sustainable business models have yet to be reached.

Compared to larger corporations, SMEs may experience more resource limitations when striving to implement sustainable practices.

The performance of sustainable business models can be impacted by factors beyond the control of a business, such as alterations to legislation, fluctuations in the market, or catastrophes caused by nature.

Criticisms

Some businesses may need to change their method to exploit sustainability as a marketing gimmick. "Greenwashing" is referred to as this, and it can damage the reputation of sustainable business methods.

According to critics, businesses may downplay or remove negative consequences from their reporting while highlighting favourable sustainability factors.

Some businesses may embrace token sustainable practices rather than making significant adjustments to their fundamental business practices, which will lessen the impact of sustainability initiatives (tokenism)

According to detractors, organisations' main goal is to maximise profits, therefore, pursuing sustainability goals could be regarded as taking resources away from this objective.

Some argue that incorporating sustainability may complicate decisions too much and remove focus from essential business operations.

Potential Areas for Future Research

The potential areas of research are to know how recent methods and technology can be applied strategically to improve sustainability business models and aid organisations towards achieving sustainability. Some studies need to be industry-specific to help organisations in that industry measure, evaluate and refine their processes to become more sustainable. The technological tools to aid sustainable businesses must also be studied individually to explore more ways they can be incorporated.

REFERENCES

AccountAbility. (2018). *AA1000 Accountability Principles 2018.* AccountAbility. https://www.accountability.org/static/6b3863943105f2a5c4d5fc96affb750d/aa1000_accountability_principles_2018.pdf

Afreen, S. (2023). *The Role of Big Data Analytics in Business Decision Making.* The Times of India. May 26, 2023. https://timesofindia.indiatimes.com/blogs/voices/the-role-of-big-data-analytics-in-business-decision-making/

Agrawal, R., Majumdar, A., Majumdar, K., Raut, R. D., & Narkhede, B. E. (2022). Attaining sustainable development goals (SDGs) through supply chain practices and business strategies: A systematic review with bibliometric and network analyses [November.]. *Business Strategy and the Environment, Wiley Blackwell, 31*(7), 3669–3687.

Alhawari, O., Awan, U., Bhutta, M. K. S., & Ülkü, M. A. (2021). Insights from circular economy literature: A review of extant definitions and unravelling paths to future research. *Sustainability, 13*(2), 859.

Arjaliès. Diane-Laure & Mundy, Julia. (2013). The Use of Management Control Systems to Manage CSR Strategy: A Levers of Control Perspective. *Management Accounting Research.* 24. http://dx.doi.org/10.1016/j.mar.2013.06.003

Awan, U., Sroufe, R., & Shahbaz, M. (2021). Industry 4.0 and the circular economy: A literature review and recommendations for future research. *Business Strategy and the Environment, 30*(4), 2038–2060.

Ayala-Orozco, B., Rosell, J. A., Merçon, J., Bueno, I., Alatorre-Frenk, G., Langle-Flores, A., & Lobato, A. (2018). Challenges and strategies in place-based multi-stakeholder collaboration for sustainability: Learning from experiences in the Global South. *Sustainability, 10*(9), 3217.

Back, A. (2017, Nov 6). Using Blockchain for Supply Chain Transparency and Traceability. Medium. https://medium.com/blockchain-review/the-visible-supply-chain-ab73a80863fd

Baturina, O. (2019, May 2). *40 Stats and Real-Life Examples of How Companies Use Big Data.* ScienceSoft. https://www.scnsoft.com/blog/big-data-use-cases-stats-and-examples#1

Baumgartner, R. J. (2009). Organizational Culture and Leadership: Preconditions for the Development of a Sustainable Corporation. *Sustainable Development, 17*, 102–113.

Beltramello, A., Haie-Fayle, L., & Pilat, D. (2013). Why New Business Models Matter for Green Growth (No. 2013/1). OECD Publishing.

Benn, S., Edwards, M., & Williams, T. (2014). *Organizational Change for Corporate Sustainability* (4th ed.). Routledge.

Boxall, N. (2023, April 20). Circular economy roadmap for plastics, glass, paper and tyres - Circular Economy. Circular Economy. https://research.csiro.au/circulareconomy/circular-economy-roadmap-for-plastics-glass-paper-and-tyres/

Bressanelli, G., Adrodegari, F., Perona, M., & Saccani, N. (2018). Exploring how usage-focused business models enable circular economy through digital technologies. *Sustainability, 10*(3), 639.

Broccardo, L., Zicari, A., Jabeen, F., & Bhatti, Z. A. (2023). How digitalization supports a sustainable business model: A literature review. *Technological Forecasting and Social Change, 187*, 122146.

Bulbulia, T. (2022, May 5). *De Beers Introduces Pioneer Blockchain-backed Diamond Source Platform at Scale.* Mining Weekly. https://www.miningweekly.com/article/de-beers-introduces-pioneer-blockchain-backed-diamond-source-platform-at-scale-2022-05-05

Ceulemans, K., Scarff Seatter, C., Molderez, I., Van Liedekerke, L., & Lozano, R. (2020). Unfolding the complexities of the sustainability reporting process in higher education: a case study in the university of British Columbia. *International business, trade and institutional sustainability*, 1043-1070.

Chladek, N. 2019. Why you Need Sustainability in your Business Strategy. [online] Harvard Business School. *Business Insights.* https://online.hbs.edu/blog/post/business-sustainability-strategies

Cicculo, F., Fabbri, M., Abdelkafi, N., & Pero, M. (2022). Exploring the potential of business models for sustainability and big data for food waste reduction. *Journal of Cleaner Production.* Vol. 340, 130673, ISSN 0959-6526. https://doi.org/10.1016/j.jclepro.2022.130673

Deloitte. (2023). *Using blockchain to drive supply chain transparency.* Deloitte. Pp. 4-5. https://www2.deloitte.com/content/dam/Deloitte/us/Documents/us-ent-supply-chain-pov.pdf

Dess, G. G., Lumpkin, G. T., & Eisner, A. B. (2010). Strategic management: Creating competitive advantages. 5 Hill Irwin.

Dienes, D., Sassen, R., & Fischer, J. (2016). What are the drivers of sustainability reporting? A systematic review. *Sustainability Accounting. Management and Policy Journal*, 7(2), 154–189.

Difrancesco, R. M., Meena, P., & Kumar, G. (2023). How blockchain technology improves sustainable supply chain processes: a practical guide. Oper Manag Res 16, 620–641 https://doi.org/10.1007/s12063-022-00343-y

Dobele, A. R., Westberg, K., Steel, M., & Flowers, K. (2014). An examination of corporate social responsibility implementation and stakeholder engagement: A case study in the Australian mining industry. [Crossref.]. *Business Strategy and the Environment*, *23*(3), 145–159.

Doleski, O. D. (2015). *Integrated Business Model: applying the St. Gallen Management concept to business models*. Springer.

Dutta, P., Choi, T., Somani, S., & Butala, R. (2020) Blockchain technology in supply chain operations : Applications, challenges and research opportunities. Transp Res Part E 142:102067. https://doi.org/10.1016/j.tre.2020.102067

Elkington, J. (1994). Towards the sustainable corporation: Win-win-win business strategies for sustainable development. *California Management Review*, *36*(2), 90–100.

Elkington, J. (1998). Partnerships from cannibals with forks: The triple bottom line of 21st-century business. *Environmental Quality Management*, *8*(1), 37–51.

Epstein, M. J., Buhovac, A. R., & Yuthas, K. (2015). Managing social, environmental and financial performance simultaneously. *Long Range Planning*, *48*(1), 35–45.

Figueredo, K. (2021, March 10). *Product Management Implications of AI for IoT.* IoT For All. https://www.iotforall.com/product-management-implications-of-ai-for-iot

Fobbe, L. (2020). Analysing organisational collaboration practices for sustainability. *Sustainability*, *12*(6), 2466.

Freudenreich, B., Lüdeke-Freund, F., & Schaltegger, S. (2020). A stakeholder theory perspective on business models: Value creation for sustainability. *Journal of Business Ethics*, *166*, 3–18.

Geissdoerfer, M., Savaget, P., Bocken, N. M., & Hultink, E. J. (2017). The Circular Economy–A new sustainability paradigm? *Journal of Cleaner Production*, *143*, 757–768.

Gomes, J. G. C., Okano, M. T., Guerra, R. S., Cordeiro, D. D. S., Santos, H. C. L. D., & Fernandes, M. E. (2022). Analysis of Sustainable Business Models: Exploratory Study in Two Brazilian Logistics Companies. *Sustainability*, *14*(2), 694.

Gomes, S. B., Santoro, F. M., Da Silva, M. M., & Iacob, M. E. (2019, October). A reference model for digital transformation and innovation. In *2019 IEEE 23rd International Enterprise Distributed Object Computing Conference (EDOC)* (pp. 21-30). IEEE.

Gomez-Trujillo, A. M., & Gonzalez-Perez, M. A. (2021). Digital transformation as a strategy to reach sustainability. Smart Sustain. Built Environ. (2021). https://doi.org/10.1108/sasbe-01-2021-0011

Graham, J. R., Harvey, C. R., & Rajgopal, S. (2005). The economic implications of corporate financial reporting. *Journal of Accounting and Economics*, *40*(1-3), 3–73.

Grainger-Brown, J., & Malekpour, S. (2019). Implementing the sustainable development goals: A review of strategic tools and frameworks available to organisations. *Sustainability*, *11*(5), 1381.

GRI. (2016). *Global Sustainability Standards Board.* Global Reporting Initiative. https://www.globalreporting.org/standards/global-sustainability-standards-board/

GRI. (2013). *G4 Sustainability Reporting Guidelines.* Global Reporting Initiative. https://respect.international/wp-content/uploads/2017/10/G4-Sustainability-Reporting-Guidelines-Implementation-Manual-GRI-2013.pdf

Gusmerotti, N. M., Testa, F., Corsini, F., Pretner, G., & Iraldo, F. (2019). Drivers and approaches to the circular economy in manufacturing firms. Journal of Cleaner Production, Volume 230, Pages 314-327, ISSN 0959-6526. https://doi.org/10.1016/j.jclepro.2019.05.044

Haessler, P. (2020). Strategic decisions between short-term profit and sustainability. *Administrative Sciences*, *10*(3), 63.

Haidar, H. (2021). Historical Perspectives and the Emergence of the Sustainability Concept in Organizations. *Open Journal of Business and Management*, *9*, 2277–2298. doi:10.4236/ojbm.2021.95123

Hou, Y., Khokhar, M., Sharma, A., Sarkar, J. B., & Hossain, M. A. (2023). Converging concepts of sustainability and supply chain networks: a systematic literature review approach. Environ Sci Pollut Res 30, 46120–46130 https://doi.org/10.1007/s11356-023-25412-y

Hourneaux, F. Jr, Gabriel, M. L. D. S., & Gallardo-Vázquez, D. A. (2018). Triple bottom line and sustainable performance measurement in industrial companies. *Revista de Gestão*, *25*(4), 413–429.

Indeed Editorial Team. (2023, March 11). Strategic Management: Definition, Purpose and Example. Indeed. https://www.indeed.com/career-advice/career-development/what-is-strategic-management

Ingemarsdotter, E., Jamsin, E., Kortuem, G., & Balkenende, R. (2019). Circular strategies enabled by the Internet of Things—A framework and analysis of current practice. *Sustainability (Switzerland)*, 11(20), 5689. https://doi.org/10.3390/su11205689

Ishwarappa, K., & Anuradha, J. (2015). A Brief Introduction on Big Data 5Vs Characteristics and Hadoop Technology. Procedia Computer Science 48 (2015) 319 – 324. https://doi.org/10.1016/j.procs.2015.04.188

Jerry, T. (2021, December 27). What Makes Patagonia A World Leader In Sustainability. *Medium*. https://medium.com/climate-conscious/what-makes-patagonia-a-world-leader-in-sustainability-486073f0daa

Jia, F., Yin, S., Chen, L., & Chen, X. (2020). The circular economy in the textile and apparel industry: A systematic literature review. Journal of Cleaner Production, Volume 259, 120728,ISSN 0959-6526. https://doi.org/10.1016/j.jclepro.2020.120728

Kaplan, R., & Norton, D. (1992). The Balanced Scorecard—Measures That Drive Performance. *Harvard Business Review*, •••, 79. PMID:10119714

Kaplan, R. S., & Norton, D. P. (1998). Putting the Balanced Scorecard to Work. In T. Siesfeld, J. Cefola, & D. Neef (Eds.), *The Economic Impact of Knowledge*. Butterworth Heinemann.

Kennerley, M., & Neely, A. (2002). Performance measurement frameworks: A review. *Business performance measurement. Theory into Practice*, *2*(3), 145–155.

Khan, S., Yu, Z., & Farooq, K. (2022). Green capabilities, green purchasing, and triple bottom line performance: Leading toward environmental sustainability. *Business Strategy and the Environment*. Advance online publication. doi:10.1002/bse.3234

Kolk, A. (2003). Trends in sustainability reporting by the Fortune Global 250¢. *Business Strategy and the Environment*, *12*(5), 279–291.

Kolk, A. (2004). A decade of sustainability reporting: Developments and significance. *International Journal of Environment and Sustainable Development*, *3*(1), 51–64.

Korhonen, J. (2004). Industrial ecology in the strategic sustainable development model: strategic applications of industrial ecology. Journal of Cleaner Production, Volume 12, Issues 8–10, Pages 809-823. ISSN 0959-6526. https://doi.org/10.1016/j.jclepro.2004.02.026

Koteen, J. (1989). *Strategic Management in Public and Nonprofit Organizations: Thinking and Acting Strategically on Public Concerns*. Praeger.

KPMG. (2014). *The essentials of materiality assessment*. KPMG Sustainable Insight. p. 32-33. https://assets.kpmg.com/content/dam/kpmg/pdf/2014/10/materiality-assessment.pdf

Kun, L. A., Eng, T. S., Wei, H., Xuecheng, D., & Seeram, R. (2021). Sustainability framework for pharmaceutical manufacturing (PM): A review of research landscape and implementation barriers for circular economy transition, Journal of Cleaner Production, Volume 280, Part 2, 124264, ISSN 0959-6526. https://doi.org/10.1016/j.jclepro.2020.124264

Lacy, P., Cooper, T., Hayward, R., & Neuberger, L. (2010). *A new era of sustainability. UN Global Compact*. Accenture.

Latapí Agudelo, M. A., Jóhannsdóttir, L., & Davídsdóttir, B. A literature review of the history and evolution of corporate social responsibility. Int J Corporate Soc Responsibility 4, 1 (2019). https://doi.org/10.1186/s40991-018-0039-y

Lazarus, R. J. (2004). *The Making of Environmental Law*. University of Chicago Press.

Lieder, M., & Rashid, A. (2016). Towards circular economy implementation: a comprehensive review in context of manufacturing industry. Journal of Cleaner Production, Volume 115, Pages 36-51. ISSN 0959-6526. https://doi.org/10.1016/j.jclepro.2015.12.042

Linnenluecke, M. K., & Griffiths, A. (2010). Corporate Sustainability and Organizational Culture. *Journal of World Business, 45,* pp. 357-366. https://doi.org/10.1016/j.jwb.2009.08.006

Lozano, R., & Carpenter, A., & Sammalisto, K. (2020). Analysing Organisational Change Management in Seaports: Stakeholder Perception, Communication, Drivers for, and Barriers to Sustainability at the Port of Gävle. (In book: European Port Cities in Transition) DOI: . doi:10.1007/978-3-030-36464-9_12

Lozano, R., Barreiro-Gen, M., & Zafar, A. (2021). Collaboration for organizational sustainability limits to growth: Developing a factors, benefits, and challenges framework. *Sustainable Development*, *29*(4), 728–737.

Markos, S., & Sridevi, M. S. (2010). Employee Engagement: The Key to Improving Performance. *International Journal of Business and Management*, *2*(12), 89–96.

McDonough, W., & Braungart, M. (2002). Design for the triple top line: New tools for sustainable commerce. *Corporate Environmental Strategy*, *9*(3), 251–258.

Melo, V. (2018). Collaborative Efforts for Sustainable Development: Surveying the Literature on Multi-Stakeholder Initiatives to Realize the Sustainable Development Goals. *Task Team on CSO Development Effectiveness and Enabling Environment, 10.*

Millar, C., Hind, P., & Magala, S. (2012). Sustainability and the need for change: Organizational change and transformational vision. *Journal of Organizational Change Management*, *25*(4), 489–500.

Momanyi, C. (2020). Influence of Sustainable Strategic Management Practices on the Performance of Technical and Vocational Education and Training: A Literature Based Review. *Journal of Strategic Management*, *4*(3), 10–29.

Neely, A. D., Adams, C., & Kennerley, M. (2002). *The performance prism: The scorecard for measuring and managing business success* (pp. 159-160). London: Prentice Hall Financial Times.

Neely, A., Adams, C., & Crowe, P. (2001). The performance prism in practice. *Measuring Business Excellence*, *5*(2), 6–13.

Neri, A., Cagno, E., Lepri, M., & Trianni, A. (2021). A triple bottom line balanced set of key performance indicators to measure the sustainability performance of industrial supply chains. *Sustainable Production and Consumption.* Vol 26. pp. 648-691,ISSN 2352-5509. https://doi.org/10.1016/j.spc.2020.12.018

Nidumolu, R., Prahalad, C. K., & Rangaswami, M. R. (2009). Why sustainability is now the key driverof innovation? *Harvard Business Review*, (September), 56–64.

Okano, M. T., Antunes, S., Langhi, C., & Simões, E. (2019). Digital Transformation: News Technologies and Business Model. *Ijsrm.Human,* 2019; Vol. 13 (3): 81-100. https://ijsrm.humanjournals.com/wp-content/uploads/2019/10/6.Marcelo-T-Okano-Samira-Antunes-Celi-Langhi-Eliane-Sim%C3%B5es.pdf

Patagonia. (2022). The Activist Company. Retrieved from https://www.patagonia.com/the-activist-company.html

Păun, T., & Pinzaru, F. (2021). Advancing strategic management through sustainable finance. *Management Dynamics in the Knowledge Economy*, *9*(2), 279–291.

Poister, T. H., & Streib, G. D. (1999). Strategic management in the public sector: Concepts, models, and processes. *Public Productivity & Management Review*, •••, 308–325.

PwC. (n.d.). Sustainable Development Goals (SDG) - Impact on business. https://pwc.to/3as3Vid

Ross, J. W., Beath, C. M., & Sebastian, I. M. (2017). How to develop a great digital strategy. *MIT Sloan Management Review*, *58*(2), 7.

Shad, M. K., Lai, F. W., Fatt, C. L., Klemeš, J. J., & Bokhari, A. (2019). Integrating sustainability reporting into enterprise risk management and its relationship with business performance: A conceptual framework. *Journal of Cleaner Production*, *208*, 415–425.

Steffen, W., Richardson, K., Rockström, J., Cornell, S. E., Fetzer, I., Bennett, E. M., Biggs, R., Carpenter, S. R., De Vries, W., De Wit, C. A., Folke, C., Gerten, D., Heinke, J., Mace, G. M., Persson, L. M., Ramanathan, V., Reyers, B., & Sörlin, S. (2015). Planetary Boundaries: Guiding Human Development on a Changing Planet: https://science.sciencemag.org/content/347/6223/1259855

Sustainability/UNEP. (1998). *The non-reporting report.*

Vivek, C. M., Ramkumar, P., & Srividhya, P. K. (2022). Sustainability and the Industrial Revolution. In *The Palgrave Handbook of Global Sustainability*. Palgrave Macmillan., .https://doi.org/10.1007/978-3-030-38948-2_147-1

Vodonick, J. (2018). The key to Organizational Sustainability. Nurturing a Culture of Change. *Systems Research and Behavioral Science*, *35*(4), 458–468.

Watanabe, C., Naveed, N., & Neittaanmäki, P. (2018). Digital solutions transform the forest-based bioeconomy into a digital platform industry-A suggestion for a disruptive business model in the digital economy. *Technology in Society*, *54*, 168–188.

World Economic Forum. (2020). Unlocking Technology for the Global Goals. https://www3.weforum.org/docs/Unlocking_Technology_for_the_Global_Goals.pdf

World Economic Forum. (2023). Guidelines for Improving Blockchain's Environmental, Social and Economic Impact. p. 9. https://www3.weforum.org/docs/WEF_Guidelines_for_Improving_Blockchain%E2%80%99s_Environmental_Social_and_Economic_Impact_2023.pdf

Wozniak, K. (n.d.). Strategic management system. CEOpedia. https://ceopedia.org/index.php/Strategic_management_system#:~:text=A%20strategic%20management%20system%20is,the%20success%20of%20the%20business

DEFINITIONS OF KEY TERMS

Sustainable business model: A business strategy that puts long-term economic, social, and environmental sustainability first is a sustainable business model.

Sustainability: The ability to preserve or endure a system or process, through time without significantly harming the environment, society, or future generations is called sustainability.

Strategic Management Systems: Organisations utilise structured procedures, structures, and tools known as strategic management systems to create, carry out, and evaluate their strategic plans and activities in a way consistent with their goal.

Circular Economy: A circular economy is a type of economy that seeks to reduce waste and maximise the use of resources.

Corporate Social Responsibility (CSR): Corporate Social Responsibility (CSR) is the term used to describe the ethical and socially conscious practises and acts that organisations and corporations voluntarily engage in to benefit society and the environment.

Corporate Sustainability: Corporate sustainability refers to a business strategy that incorporates environmental, social, and governance (ESG) issues into the operations of an organisation and business strategy.

Greenwashing: When a firm or organisation makes overstated or fraudulent claims about the environmental friendliness or sustainability of its products, services, or general business practices, it engages in greenwashing, a dishonest marketing technique.

Sustainability reporting: Sustainability reporting is a means organisations communicate their environmental, social, and governance performance and impact to diverse stakeholders.

Stakeholder collaboration: This is the process an organisation uses to communicate, exchange knowledge, and work as a collective to accomplish shared goals, frequently connected to social, environmental, or corporate objectives.

Chapter 10
Consumer Perception of Robotic Mobile Fulfillment Systems:
A Netnographic Case Study of Amazon

Badr Bentalha
https://orcid.org/0000-0003-1339-542X
National School of Business and Management, Sidi Mohammed Ben Abdellah University, Morocco

ABSTRACT

The chapter aims to understand customer perception after the introduction of robots in the robotic mobile fulfillment system (RMFS) storage areas for Amazon. Based on a netnographic analysis focused on the use of RMFS by the American company Amazon, the work is mainly aimed at improving our understanding of the performance of RMFS and the perception of this technology by customers of service companies in general and retail companies in particular. Improved productivity, reduced operation time, agility and flexibility, improved picking accuracy, optimal space utilization, cost of capital, and work ergonomics are the main motivations perceived and discussed by the virtual community behind the introduction of RMFS in Amazon's storage areas. Several risks of RMFS robotization are discussed based on the qualitative study conducted. Finally, a classification of the customers' perception of this new technology is made by distinguishing the variables of perceived usefulness and ease of use.

INTRODUCTION

In the current era, robotics offers several technical and business opportunities. Some companies have chosen robotization to increase the cost-effectiveness of their products and services. Several industries are adopting robotics to perform various tasks. Service companies in general and retail companies, in particular, have followed these technological advancements to evolve their business and logistics systems (Mende et al., 2019). To gain a competitive edge and trigger innovation processes in retail, they have chosen to opt for the technological advances offered by robotization and the integration of these technologies in several phases of the value chains.

DOI: 10.4018/979-8-3693-0458-7.ch010

Warehouse order picking is a set of operations that requires a large amount of manual work. These are several related tasks that aim to prepare customer orders in warehouses. Its role is becoming more and more important, especially in the distribution and e-commerce logistic chains. Automation of these chains is possible. Indeed, several companies have already implemented automated or robotized systems to facilitate the preparation of customer orders. Changing lifestyles, exponential advances in technology, and innovation in retail are encouraging service companies to adopt robots to perform their daily operations.

The acceleration of global demand for online commerce and ongoing changes in transportation and telecommunication mechanisms have increased the number of transactions conducted and created new requirements, particularly for warehousing and storage systems (Bentalha et al., 2023). Manual order-picking systems were relatively operational and reliable with large and predictable orders. However, e-commerce orders are generally small and unpredictable. In addition, warehouse sizes are often large with huge variations that tire operators and require them to travel repetitive distances every day. Automated order-picking systems aim to reduce delivery times and ensure certain ergonomics for the order pickers.

The Robotic Mobile Filling System (RMFS) is an automated order-picking system. It is based on robotic technology and seems to be very suitable for online retail companies especially given their large warehouse sizes (Merschformann et al., 2019). In this system, robots, not operators, pick orders using mobile shelves of different sizes and dimensions, called pods, and bring the requested goods to the workstations. The goal is to minimize time loss, reduce picker distances, and consequently increase productivity rates.

Amazon is a global online shopping giant. It offers remote sales of several products on an international scale. It is also an innovative company given the introduction of several technological or organizational innovations (Amazon go, Amazon Key, etc.). In this sense, it is a very advanced company in terms of the use of robots in different parts of the value chain. The use of these robots comes in response to several issues concerning product delivery, labor shortages, and situational breaks between supply and demand. There are approximately 100,000 in its warehouses (Wingfield, 2017).

Thus, the analysis of the introduction of robotization in supply chains seems to be a highly topical theoretical theme. Indeed, there are currently several gaps in the understanding of the motives and effects of robotization in supply chains. Also, from a more practical point of view, we have identified an empirical gap concerning the perception of customers on the introduction of robotization that could serve as a question to the identified research problem. Robotic Fulfillment Systems for Smart Service Supply Chains represent a phenomenon that deserves the attention of service scholars and practitioners.

Therefore, how do customers perceive the introduction of robots in Amazon's corporate storage areas? To what extent does digital feedback vary in content and discourse in terms of opportunities and threats of using Robotic Mobile Fulfillment Systems for Amazon?

To deepen our reflection, we will first analyze the process and possible interrelationships between the Smart Service Supply chain, IoT, and IoRT. Then, we will talk about our netnographic methodological approach and the possibilities offered by this method to discuss the issues of interference of the optimization logic and customer perception. Finally, we will support our reflection on the results obtained by our qualitative netnographic study to show the different relationships and possibilities.

THEORETICAL FRAMEWORK

Smart Service Supply Chain, Internet of Things, and Internet of Robotic Things

A supply chain is a group of companies that transmit materials to each other (La Londe & Masters, 1994). These are several independent actors who contribute to the manufacture of a product and its delivery to the end user. The service supply chain is a rapidly expanding scientific field (Bentalha, 2020). The structural singularity of these chains lies in their specific characteristics. Thus, several authors (Choudhury et al., 2020; Rasolofo-Distler & Distler, 2018) have distinguished service logistics chains by calling them Services Supply Chains (SSC). Iakovaki et al. (2009) define SSC as, "A network of interconnected organizations that use resources and transform their inputs (skills and knowledge) into a service offering, to augment the delivery of a flexible customized solution."

In services, the activity is usually initiated by customers. Therefore, SSCs involve these customers as active participants (Hmioui & Bentalha, 2021). Hence, he or she acts as a provider for the service supplier. This dual function of the customer is called customer-supplier duality or bidirectional relationships (Sampson & Spring, 2012).

One of the characteristics of service supply chains is the presence of customers and the strong interaction between the customer and the supply chain components. This is because the customer can offer certain components of the service and therefore evaluate the outcome and the service process (Sharma et al., 2014). A second characteristic of these chains is the high fragmentation of operations and processes related to service delivery. SSC partners are involved in the operations of the service process, including handling customer inputs and interacting directly with them (Wynstra et al., 2015). Also, the number of references to be managed in SSCs is frequently higher, estimated to be ten to one hundred times higher, given the diversity of equipment. A third characteristic of SSCMs is the strong presence of staff. Indeed, services tend to be much more labor-intensive than manufacturing (Hmioui & Bentalha, 2021). The particular management of SSCs creates coordination, collaboration, and integration mechanisms adapted to these chains.

Today's service supply chains must be flexible, efficient, and intelligent. Intelligent logistics involves the comprehensive application of integrated intelligent technology to achieve logistics and warehousing automation, visualization, control, intelligence, and network management. The purpose is to raise the rate of exploitation of the assets, and the level of productivity and to diminish the expenses of the logistics (Dou Xin-Xin, 2016). Smart logistics is mainly aimed at "the realization of a logistics distribution system with high efficiency and low smart operating cost" (Tong, 2015). Smart logistics aims at several improvements in enterprises (Dou Xin-Xin, 2016). First, reducing the cost of logistics by lowering the bottleneck, enhancing communication, diminishing the use of labor, material, and resources, and improving coordination mechanisms. Secondly, it improves companies' competitiveness by accelerating information transmission, modifying and adapting management tools permanently, and strengthening coordination throughout the value chain. Finally, it promotes the development of smart territories. Indeed, intelligent logistics seems to be favorable for the development of informational exchanges for the benefit of cities and territories. Smart logistics is linked to using the Internet of Things (IoT). This technology offers a great advantage in terms of instant communication between the different components of the value chain. To this end, managers, workers, machines, and products are linked by a coherent logistical and informational process. The optimization of these processes depends on the combination of several technological applications to link the purchasing, storage, warehousing, and delivery components (Bentalha et al., 2020). Therefore, IoT connects people, processes, and technology tools and aims to create complex and seamless systems. This comprehensive integration of IoT with humans in communication, collaboration, and technical analysis enables real-time decision-making. This explains the current craze for this technology. In fact, according to IDC (International Data Corporation, 2022), the total number of linked IoT products will grow to 55.9 billion in 2025.

IoT is a core component of smart logistics. Indeed, the various IoT applications enable instant and remote monitoring of the connected parts of the supply chain and data (Kim et al., 2017; Liu et al., 2020). Accordingly, this allows for quick decision-making and tailored solutions through the various connected sensors and devices.

Currently, the use of digital technologies in supply chains is usually associated with the progressive integration of different technologies (Bentalha et al., 2019). It's about having systems that combine IoT, AI, automatic application, and deep learning. The integration of these technologies with robots creates a new technological system called Internet the the of Robotic Things (IoRT). Thus, different robots can work in the logistics area for loading/unloading, production operations, and quality control (Ray, 2016; Afanasyev et al., 2019). According to Stratistics MRC (Strategy Market Research Consulting, 2017), the IoRT marketplace represented approximately \$4.37 billion as of 2016 and is expected to grow to \$28.03 billion by 2023. Several factors can explain this upward trend. These include the emphasis on online business operations, Industry 4.0, and the sustained connectivity of people and territories (Batth et al., 2018; Sharma et al., 2020; Bentalha, 2022). Therefore, we can say that robotics and the digital age will change the managerial mechanisms and strategic orientations of value chains.

ROBOTIC MOBILE FULFILLMENT SYSTEMS FOR SMART LOGISTIC

Over the past few decades, logistics has undergone a threefold leap from manual operation to mechanization to automation. In this sense, the integration of robotization was primarily aimed at achieving productivity gains over manual labor (Fu et al., 2021). The initial idea is that the integration of robots will produce more speed and less cost (Edward et al., 2017) while providing greater autonomy and versatility (Sousa & Rocha, 2019). With artificial intelligence, this idea will be expanded and will be oriented to the fact that even cognitive or non-programmed activities will be performed efficiently by these robots. The speed of growth of e-commerce brings new challenges to warehouse operations, among which order picking plays a crucial role and directly affects the overall efficiency of order fulfillment (Lamballais et al., 2017; Shen et al., 2020).

The Mobile Robotic Fulfillment System (RMFS) is an integrated model for automated and robotic order picking. The goal is to reduce the manual part of the work in warehouses and improve productivity. These systems also aim to support large volumes of demand and seasonal increases in business.

The principle is to reduce picker trips and travel by using automatic vehicles and support equipment (Merschformanna et al., 2019). These digital and interconnected tools pick mobile shelves containing the desired storage and transport them to manual picking stations (Yudiansyah et al., 2020). This is one of the fundamental trends in the future development of smart logistics (Wu & Gu, 2019). The robots pick the following shelves from stock-keeping units (SKUs). This is a barcode on labels in the stores (Lamballais et al., 2017).

RMFS was invented to improve picking efficiency and reduce labor costs by leveraging mobile robots moving in shelving (Boysen et al., 2017). The cooperation between robots and mobile shelving eliminates unproductive picker movements in pick-to-room systems (Battini et al., 2017). In addition, an RMFS aims at reducing the execution time in the warehouses, which will have an impact on the delivery time of the orders (Yuan & Gong 2017). Thus, one of the best examples of this new form of store management is made by Amazon with a remarkable robotization of the different logistic functions.

In the context of the IT and robotics, the logistics and warehousing industry have produced a smart warehouse bot, that has been extensively applied in several logistics platforms. Amazon's sites now have more than 350,000 robots of all kinds deployed around the world. Amazon has purchased and developed several models and technical devices. These include Kiva, Hercules, Pegasus, Xanthus, Bert, Ernie, Scooter, Kermit, and Scout. The KIVA system consists of four basic components to enable the picking function, namely mobile storage racks, picking workstations, multiple pickers, and mobile robots (Nussbaum, 2015; Boysen et al., 2017; Weidinger et al., 2018; Yang et al., 2021). An integrated camera system is used to continuously read barcodes and robot positions. The rotation is easily provided by a mechanism that allows the robot to move linearly on all sides. (D'Andrea et al., 2008; Enright & Wurman, 2011). In addition, Kiva can track orders in real time with its Wi-Fi connectivity (Jun-tao Li, 2016; Hanson et al., 2018). The introduction of this robot to Amazon's warehouses has resulted in significant gains. Order fulfillment quality has been estimated at 99% (Li & Liu, 2016); productivity increase at 20% (Bogue, 2016), and storage space management improvement at 50% (Lee, 2019).

Apart from these considerable gains, the analysis of customer and consumer perception of this technology is rarely discussed either theoretically or empirically.

CUSTOMER PERCEPTIONS OF ROBOTIC MOBILE FULFILLMENT SYSTEMS

Robots have been gradually introduced into customer service. This has resulted in the presence of discussions about the causes of robotization adoption and the strategic and operating consequences sought. These discussions point to a profound change in certain activities for customers (Claro & & Ramos, 2018). The areas of robotic extension are many. These include robotic applications in hotels and homes (Huang & Rust, 2021), vital e-commerce extensions and book service (Choudhury, 2016; Adhikari, 2017; Adhikari, 2017; Fluss, 2017; Prakash, 2017), robots in stocking areas (Ackerman, 2016; Calfas, 2019) and financial supports for asset managers (Javelosa, 2017).

This rapid and continuous introduction of robotization is primarily aimed at the stability of delivery to ensure a fixed customer experience and relatively standardized service (Aron et al. 2011). The presence of robots in the delivery locations impact the customer who seems to feel more speed of delivery (He et al., 2018), improved quality of delivery (Doorn et al., 2017; Hoffman & Novak, 2018), and more interaction in the retail spaces (Mende et al., 2019). Nevertheless, the bulk of studies dealing with customer perception of new robotic technology remain elementary and fragmented. In addition, empirical studies dealing with robots in real-world contexts are rarer (Herrmann et al., 2015).

Customer approval and perception of robots depend on perceived usefulness and ease of use (Xiao & Kumar, 2021). The first reflects the utility released by the application of the novel and emerging technology, while the second relates to the ease of using the new technology (Davis et al., 1989). The initial scale consists of 7 items while additional scales have more items (Venkatesh & Bala, 2008) (Table 1).

Table 1. Factors influencing perceived usefulness and perceived ease of use

Determinants of Perceived Usefulness		Determinants of Perceived Ease of Use	
Determinants	**Definitions**	**Determinants**	**Definitions**
Perceived Ease of Use	The level perceived by a user that will not require any effort.	Computer Self-Efficacy	The level of achievement of a specific task using innovation.
Subjective Norm	The perceived level of influence of other users	Perception of External Control	The level at which resources are thought to be sufficient.
Image	The perceived level of technology use and its ability to improve social status.	Computer Anxiety	The level of fear associated with the utilization of technology.
Job Relevance	The perceived level of applicability of the technology system to the job	Computer Playfulness	The level of cognitive spontaneity with the new technology
Output Quality	Perceived level of accurate application of job tasks	Perceived Enjoyment	The perceived level of appreciation in itself in using the new technology.
Result Demonstrability	The level of outcome measurement (tangibles, observables, and communicables).	Objective Usability	A comparison of systems according to the real effort needed to complete jobs

Source: adapted from Venkatesh & Bala (2008) p. 277 & p. 279

SURVEY DESIGN: OBJECTIVES, FIELDS, AND METHODOLOGY

The main question of the work is related to the introduction of robots in the storage areas and the perception of this technological novelty by the customers. The question we want to clarify in this work using netnography is the customers' perception of the introduction of robots in RMFS. Indeed, the use of robots has shown its advantages on time, cost, and flexibility. Nevertheless, we have noticed a weakness in the work that has dealt with the effects of these technological advances on consumer perception. For example, how do Amazon customers perceive the introduction of various intelligent robots in the Robotic Mobile Fulfillment System? Does the introduction of these robots have a favorable effect on the smart service supply chain in terms of positive impacts on customers and favorable perceptions of external actors?

To understand customer perception, we opted for a netnographic approach. This method of data collection allows us to understand representative online communities. The Internet has turned into a significant spot for research, with individuals partaking in gatherings, digital broadcasts, long-range interpersonal communication locales, recordings, sites, newsgroups, photograph-sharing networks, and virtual universes.

Kozinets (2015) stated that 'netnography was a name given to a specific set of related data collection, analysis, ethical and representational research practices, where a significant amount of data collected and participant observational research conducted originates in and manifested through that data shared freely on the Internet, including mobile applications'. Netnography dissects the open demonstrations of the clients who are individuals from virtual networks by attempting to give them importance. It is an "ethnography applied to the Internet" (Alla et al., 2020). A netnography approach principally centers around the point that concerns the members, the gathering, and the informal organization site by using the exploration theory.

Netnography is a qualitative method of tracking digital communities. It is therefore an ethnographic conducted online. Its main focus is the study and analysis of consumer activities via online behaviors, comments, and reviews (Bartl et al., 2016). It is based on leveraging Internet information sources as a vehicle for qualitative data collection (Lamsiah et al., 2021). It uses researcher involvement by integrating a virtual community and learning the attitudes or behaviors shared. Nowadays, most operators are very connected, especially with customers. They share opinions, discuss issues, and analyze buying experiences (Heinonen & Medberg, 2018).

Each new online immersion thus requires a rethinking of its tools to adapt to the particularities of the collectives under study. Netnography thus presents itself more as a flexible methodological framework in that it "cannot extract itself from the consideration of the device under study" (Jouët & Le Caroff, 2016). It is thus marked from the outset by the relative freedom it offers the researcher. Netnography is therefore an empirically driven method of immersing into the customer's domain and gaining a deep understanding of human behavior (Piller et al., 2011). While listening to the natural dialogue of consumers in online communities, netnography provides unbiased information about consumers.

The advantage of this strategy is that the specialist is in the position of a spectator who does not influence the observed. One of the primary benefits of netnography is the capacity to grow the geographic extent of the pursuit, associate internationally scattered organizations, and increment the scientist's availability to the populace under study (Chan & Li, 2010; Addeo et al., 2019; Bentalha & Hmioui, 2021). Nevertheless, netnography has some limitations related to the lack of control or choice over the target population, as well as the inability to pre-create a survey, interview plan, or any other exploration plan or procedure for collecting information (AlDajani, 2020). One more basic part of netnography depends on the powerlessness to catch the scope of disconnected collaborations between local area individuals, taking into consideration disharmony among on the web and disconnected portrayals of respondents (Morais et al., 2020).

In the context of Amazon's use of robots for fulfillment, the consumer cannot perceive the robots, as they are behind the line of sight. To detect the customers' perception of the robotization of the storage area we chose to see the reactions of Amazon customers after viewing videos about the RMFS technology. For our study, we chose to focus on Internet users using YouTube channels. Thus, several online discussions are related to the topic under study. Each online community contains a multitude of comments and allows the analysis of different opinions.

The research refers to a netnographic approach, with a choice to focus on the data of Internet users using YouTube channels. This choice is justified by the number of comments present on the videos of this channel. The chosen approach is justified by the central question of our theme. Indeed, the introduction of customers in storage areas is not possible and the reading of online videos by customers seems to allow the creation of an online community capable of producing relevant and valid comments. The decision to focus on data from Internet users of YouTube channels is also justified by the impossibility of obtaining qualitative information through direct contact between the customer and the robots since the latter operate on the storage site. Certainly, the random filtering of comments requires a large size of comments to limit the selected and analyzed opinions by respecting the criteria of relevance, relation with the subject, and random choice. Also, the videos posted on the YouTube channel have a relatively long duration and therefore allow to give more details and sources of information to the Internet users. Also, the employee working in these premises is involved in the man-machine relationship and the qualitative data that can be derived from the discussion is biased by his involvement in the work. Finally, the analysis of the customer comments is carried out on relatively long videos, offer several points of view on the theme treated and adop,t a relatively neutral approach. In the same vein, the methods of random sampling conducted of comments within each virtual community were carried out by operating on criteria of content, topic, relevance,e, and comprehensiveness of approach. The objective is to achieve by a random and stratified sampling a segmentation of the studied population to have the different profits of the customers.

The connections and judgments that occur online, such as comments, opinions, or responses to messages, and expression of views and dislikes on content produce important useful information about the topic under study. The use of recurrence, verb, tense, word, and judgment analysis in the conducted netnographic study will help us to better understand how customers perceive the robotic technology introduced in Amazon's RMFS stores, the possible hindrances, and the possible extensions.

The first step is to aggregate all comments from several topics related to the research. In the second step, a double coding of the corpus was performed to group the messages by theme. The objective is to perform a contextualized analysis of the different exchanges between the members of the virtual community. In order to avoid bias, comments were not selected based on their content, but rather by random sampling within each virtual community. Once key phrases expressing experiences and opinions were extracted from the comments for qualitative analysis, the meanings of each phrase were summarized into meaningful words, which would then be used as variables for future numerical analyses and discussions.

The analysis of the 612 opinions allowed us to deduce the important opinions and comments related to our study topic. The criterion used to determine the number of samples was theoretical saturation, which was obtained by analyzing the retained number of comments. Theoretical saturation is reached when further analysis of the comments and opinions no longer generates new data so that the researcher decides to stop the process. The research was stopped once the results showed very high similarities in the profiles requested. The opinions were statistically processed using the IRAMUTEQ software.

The netnographic approach should be organized (Figure 1). The main aim of the netnographic approach is to set up an in-depth examination by organizing the practical aspect of the work (Kozinets, 2010), where the scientist should characterize an unmistakable and exact risky to work with the recognizable proof of the virtual local area relating to the object of study, by organizing and contextualizing the peculiarity being contemplated (Rabahi, 2020).

Figure 1. The method followed for our netnographic study
Source: Kozinets (2010)

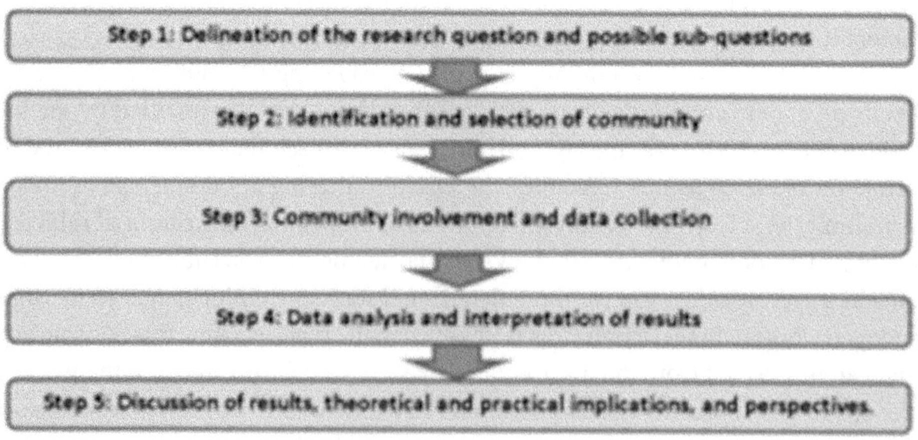

RESULTS

The first step of our empirical study consisted of delimiting the field of the desired analysis by outlining the central research question. In our case, it is to understand the current perceptions of customers regarding the robotization of Amazon's storage areas. Indeed, this technology has shown several advantages in terms of costs, space management, and speed. Nevertheless, few studies have focused on the customers' perception of this technology. Indeed, the customer cannot see the internal part of the storage operation, contrary to studies dedicated to the robotization of sales areas, delivery spaces, or after-sales services.

In addition to the main research question mentioned above, we have identified several subsidiary questions. These are to understand the factors of perceived effectiveness for the customer of the effectiveness of RMFS, barriers, concerns or fears regarding this new technology and finally, the level of perceived usefulness and perceived ease of use of the technology of RMFS robotization.

The second step concerns the selection of the netnographic study community. The choice is made to limit the analysis to Internet users using YouTube channels. This digital community seems relevant insofar as the interaction observed is rich in terms of debates, arguments, and analyses. Indeed, the length and precision of the videos allowed for the presence of a virtual study ground of the phenomenon. The random filtering of comments requires a large number of responses and opinions in order to limit the opinions selected and analyzed by respecting the criteria of relevance, relationship with the subject, and random choice. The objective is therefore to carry out a random and stratified sampling of the population studied to have the different categories of customers. The study involved 6 videos with the collection of 612 opinions. The criterion used to determine the number of samples was the theoretical saturation.

The third step was to group all the selected comments into a single "text corpus" file. A double coding of the corpus was done to group the messages by theme. To avoid bias, comments were not selected based on their content, but rather by random sampling within each virtual community. Data were collected after several interactions between the community under study. Indeed, we tried to guide the discussions via the desired themes without forcing the discussions or influencing the perception of the Internet users. At the end of this process, we were able to obtain the basic text file that will be used for the qualitative research conducted.

For the analysis and interpretation of the results, we have chosen to use the IRAMUTEQ software to extract the expected automatic treatments in terms of redundancy of occurrences, presence of keywords, or distribution of the present themes.

Our empirical analysis through IRAMUTEQ aims first at identifying the main factors of appreciation and perception of the introduction of robots and the process of creating experiences (Figure 2).

The discussions analyzed highlighted several performance areas related to robotization and RMFS performance (Table 2).

The reading of the different comments and the analysis of the words and occurrences allowed us to make several observations about the choice of robotization in service supply chains. Firstly, it is a positioning about commercial rivals. Currently, reducing time and improving efficiency seem to be two major themes shared by businesses and consumers. This result is confirmed by the presence of several temporal concepts in the different opinions of the virtual community. The occurrence of the words time, hour, day and week is visible among the most repeated and discussed expressions by Internet users. Second, robotization allows for better inventory management. The size of inventories and the delivery of a high number of models and variants have also become unmanageable. Most of the time, employees spend their time on customer orders and preparing shipments. Third, the distribution network and shipping service are improved. Previously, e-commerce employees working in stores had to travel miles each day to deliver clients' orders. This situation has always posed serious problems whether for the employee, the e-commerce company, or the customer. Indeed, we can count the non-respect of deadlines, the decrease of profitability indicators, and also the fatigue and stress of the operators (Robin, 2016; Jain & Sharma, 2017). Fourth, robotization helps in improving customer experience and order delivery. The discussions of the Internet users were focused in several directions regarding possible improvements after robotization. These main improvements deal with the aspects of productivity and efficiency, uptime, flexibility, picking precision, space utilization, investment cost and ergonomics.

The manual grouping of the above items allowed us to assess and extract the main dimensions of measuring the degree of perceived effectiveness and their perceptions of the robotization of RMFS (Table 3).

Figure 2. Cloud of appreciation items from the virtual community regarding the introduction of robots in RMFS (Source: Results of the statistical study)

Table 2. Main topics discussed by the virtual community around the introduction of robots in Amazon's RMFS

Items	Occurrence
work	119
amazon	108
item	52
warehouse	50
robot	45
time	42
hour	36
person	35
day	34
job	33
box	33
employee	27
order	26
need	24
week	22
pay	22
lot	22

Source: Results of the statistical study

Table 3. Virtual community's perceived effectiveness in introducing robots into RMFS

Category	Items	Score	Global Frequency (%)	Frequency (%)
Productivity	Automate - energy Gain - Quikly	39	1,13%	4,86%
Uptime	Time – Hour - day Week - minute	382	11,07%	47,63%
Flexibility	Fast – change move	86	2,49%	10,72%
Picking accuracy	Deliver - box	71	2,06%	8,85%
Space utilization	place environment floor	142	4,11%	17,71%
Investment cost	Cost	64	1,85%	7,98%
Ergonomics	Easy	18	0,52%	2,24%
		3452	-	100%

Source: Results of the statistical study

The results of the qualitative analysis show 7 main motivations for robot use discussed by the online community. First, some of the analysis focuses on productivity. Indeed, the main feature mentioned for RMFS is their high capacity in automatic picking, which significantly reduces manual tasks. Secondly, the management of the unavailability or the failure of the robots is noticed instantaneously. Indeed, if a robot seems to have any problem, the system quickly removes it and replaces it without altering the dynamics of the whole. For the optimal use of space, the RMFS allows high flexibility because the integrated automatic system allows to calculation the best combinations according to the dimensions and the storage space. On another level of analysis, RMFS allows for greater accuracy in order picking. The error rate seems to be reduced and a faster use of resources is observed. This results in greater flexibility because the storage areas are adapted to the size of the orders. In addition, RMFS can adjust orders according to availability and order types. Ergonomics is also discussed because the working conditions of the operators are a very recent subject. Indeed, the reduction of travel and picking at fixed stations can improve working conditions.

To elucidate the attitudes of each of these motivations of customers and Internet users, we present in the following table extracts of the verbatim taken from the opinions and comments of the online community (Table 4).

Table 4. Excerpt from customer and web user verbatim to illustrate motivations for Amazon's RMFS robotization

Category	Illustrative Verbatim
Productivity	✓ *'Increasing the burden of maintaining production for the people who can't afford to go home'* ✓ *'Of course they will schedule you at the most automated facility'.* ✓ *'Floating fulfillment will be the future We need to focus on energy improvement to power drones'* ✓ *'these tasks were repetitive anyway humans can now turn their attention towards bigger tasks'*
Uptime	✓ *'and extremely difficult to like a job they tell you all the time that you need to perform faster all they care about is numbers and they track your time off task which is the time you are not scanning'* ✓ *'From 4 days' time to deliver past year to within 18 hour of orderinginsane without even paying any delivery charge just wow'* ✓ *'If you were picking as a employee of amazon can you pick 400 products in a hour is that fast or slow'* ✓ *'Amazon is such an online platform where all the needs of the people are met very quickly'*
Flexibility	✓ *'So any complaining about can't move fast enough should be out the door keep up or move on'* ✓ *'Once they get the technology for that I guarantee their human to robot ratio will change drastically'*
Picking accuracy	✓ *'I could better understand why it took so long Thank you to all the Amazon & Delivery workers for continuing to work and deliver for us during these times'* ✓ *'Amazon's boxes need recalibration because they are way too big for the merchandise that they carry'*
Space utilization	✓ *'every item is placed by a picker on the shelves no it's not they are placed by Stowers pickers take the items off the shelves'* ✓ *'To all the negative comments the work at Amazon is easier than at other warehouse jobs from experience place is clean'*
Investment cost	✓ *'for the inconvenience of going an extra day or week without shaving cream Less boxes less delivery madness less package pilfering less costly claims etc'* ✓ *'When a small product sells it cost Amazon money to ship it out'*
Ergonomics	✓ *'i've worked at amazon LCY2 in tilbury let me explain for whoever applies at amazon this is not a full list cheap wages but big expectations working like a robot to reach their targets which with long periods of time causes health issues'*

Source: Results of the statistical study

Discussions also focused on the doubts, fears, and drawbacks present around the robotization of Amazon's warehouses. Indeed, many members of the virtual community presented doubts and fears about multiple aspects of the robotization of RMFS. Thus, we were in a position to pinpoint a set of challenges and obstacles to the use of robots in Amazon's service chains (Table 5).

Table 5. Barriers to using robots in Amazon's RFMS according to the online community

Category	Items	Verbatims	Occurence
Salary and social	Employees – Union – unemployment – jobs – hurt - depressing warehouses – injured - hurt our back - pressure - depressed	✓ *'Amazon Employees Need To Unionize'* ✓ *'Impressive bad for humans jobs'* ✓ *'Can we appreciate the fact that some Amazon workers get hurt from making sure we get the products we want/need'* ✓ *'Just imagine the pressure i would get depressed by working there'*	226
Pollution	co2 emissions – pollution - environment	✓ *'All the extra energy / co2 emissions required to build and run those robots when workers would have used zero extra net co2'* ✓ *'Amazon does way to much pollution They don't care about the environment at all'*	14
Reluctance to use smart technology	robots Rise -	✓ *'These robots were made by bigger robots Rise of the machines is eminent'*	9
Problem of coordination and collaboration	scanned simultaneously	✓ *'The worst is getting 2 unidentifiable items scanned simultaneously by accident and you don't know which one got the correct beep Anyone know how to know'*	12
Lack of understanding of the implications of smart technology	technical name Lack of digital literacy - complicated - difficult	✓ *'someone knows the technical name of the white elastic bands'* ✓ *'The key thing missing with current robots is hands and accurate vision placement'* ✓ *why i left them Instead of making it easier for their employees they make it so complicated and extremely difficult'*	25

Source: Results of the statistical study

Social barriers are widely discussed in the various comments. Indeed, several discussions focused on social risks such as the dismissal of employees or the risk of injuries. The introduction of robots has pushed several Internet users to show doubts and fears in terms of loss of jobs, risks of accidents and the possibility of weakening humans because of this technology. These doubts are widely present in several comments and take up most of the observed risks of using robots in Amazon's RMFS.

Also, the negative externalities of robots are analyzed especially in terms of their impact on the environment. Indeed, several discussions pointed to robotization as a source of pollution and loss of natural resources. For other Internet users, there is a certain reticence towards the new digital technology. For them, it is likely that this new technology is taking the place of Man and that he will no longer be able to control it in the future. In addition, the problems of coordination and collaboration generated by this technology are present. For some members of the online communities, the problem is the management of the Man-machine relationship and the possible conflicts in terms of coordination, liaison and collaboration. This is complemented by the possibility of having a poor understanding of the implications of smart technology. Finally, the fears about this technology are amplified by the reluctance of some Internet users to have the capacity to understand how this technology works and to have the necessary skills to interact with this new robotic, digital, and connected world.

The approval and perception of robots by customers were also analyzed based on perceived usefulness and ease of use (Xiao & Kumar, 2021). We used the scale developed by Venkatesh & Bala (2008) to derive an assessment of the perception of robotization by Internet users. At the level of perceived usefulness, we noted the predominance of certain aspects of usefulness, especially at the level of Job Relevance and Output Quality (Table 6).

From the analysis of the perceived usefulness of the RMFS by the members of the virtual community, we noted several observations. First, there is some agreement on the ease of use of the RMFS system and its advantages in terms of speed, cost and modernization. Also, robotization positions Amazon as a leader in terms of innovation strategy as several opinions discussed the positive image offered by robotization and also found current examples of this technology in the market except for the case of Tesla. Finally, the logistical and technical improvement offered by the presence of robots in the storage areas is appreciated especially in two criteria, namely the speed and accuracy of deliveries.

Thus, to complete the study of the client's perception, we conducted a parallel analysis of the ease of use of the technology in the virtual community studied (Table 7).

In terms of ease of use of the technology, we found a weakness in the analyses of this variable. Indeed, the customers do not have direct contact with the robots and believe that the greatest benefits will be in terms of speed and precision. Nevertheless, the ease of operation with these robots is evoked and also the importance of mastering the technological aspect to work with these robots now and to interact with this technology in the future. Discussions also focused on the ergonomic aspect and the advantages for employees of reducing the distance traveled.

Table 6. Excerpt from customer verbatim to illustrate perceived usefulness for Amazon's RMFS robotization

Determinants of Perceived Usefulness	
Determinants	**Verbatims**
Perceived Ease of Use	✓ *'a Prime membership Tough job Mad respect for anyone Amazonian who works at a fulfillment center It is far from easy if you are a picker like me* ✓ *'You had to have a package stowed in at least 8 seconds and have a package scanned in less than 2 seconds'*
Subjective Norm	✓ *'Tesla's factories have the same issue'*
Image	✓ *'I can't wait for the future That's amazing these tasks were repetitive anyway humans can now turn their attention towards bigger tasks'*
Job Relevance	✓ *'I don't like the poor ergonomic design that these amazon robots force the person to stoop bending down to fetch items off the lower shelves'*
Output Quality	✓ *'This is insane say what you want about how they treat their workers but the logistical and technological genius here is mind blowing'*
Result Demonstrability	✓ *'This is insane How well a warehouse is configured will have a bearing on how successful a business will be in the speed and accuracy with which it can achieve order fulfilment for its customers'*

Source: Results of the statistical study

Table 7. Excerpt from customer verbatim to illustrate ease of use for Amazon's RMFS robotization

Determinants of Perceived Ease of Use	
Determinants	**Definitions**
Computer Self-Efficacy	✓ *'It's wild to think that almost anyone in the US could order an item and within hours get it at their doorstep hand delivered'*
Perception of External Control	✓ *'This is an amazing opportunity for those who seek to work with robots at this great company'*
Computer Anxiety	✓ *'they are literally turning humans into robots'*
Computer Playfulness	✓ *'If a person has an associate degree in robotics How does one go about getting a job in a fulfillment center'*
Perceived Enjoyment	✓ *'We won't have to do anything the planet would become a safer place We can then enjoy life'*
Objective Usability	✓ *'That certainly helps I walk over 12 miles per day at work Shit sucks That's not including bending lifting twisting standing squatting jumping reaching'* ✓ *'Amazon should hire a professional people who knows about computer'*

Source: Results of the statistical study

CONCLUSION

In today's era, robotics offers many technical and business opportunities. Warehouse picking appears to be a critical activity, especially for service supply chains. Theoretical and empirical discussions around this topic are largely amplified due to the remarkable development of online commerce. This activity has been for several years' manual. The introduction of robots has changed the functioning of service companies by bringing new methodological and managerial discussions. Intelligent logistics aims to integrate new digital and robotic technologies to improve logistics performance (Bentalha, 2023). The Robotic Mobile Fulfillment System (RMFS) is a set of automatic, digital, and robotic picking activities in the warehouse areas.

The article sought to understand the perception of customers and consumers of the introduction of robots in the storage areas of the company Amazon. We highlighted through a netnographic study the possible opportunities and evidentiary threats related to the use of digital and connected robots in Amazon's RMFS. An online netnographic survey was conducted to identify Internet users' perceptions of the use of robots in RMFS. The analysis of the 612 opinions allowed us to deduce the important opinions and comments related to our study topic. Based on a netnographic analysis of Amazon's application of an RMFS, our work gives insight into the performance of RMFS and how customers and consumers perceive this technology in service companies in general and retail companies in particular.

The results of the study showed that robotization offers many opportunities. This study guides managers on how to develop performance relationships in the smart and connected supply chain of the service business. The different aspects of digital technologies are linked and discussed simultaneously to get an overview of the robotization of service companies' warehouses to design a framework that is stable and coherent. We have tried to fill a research gap in the field of robotization of service supply chains, particularly from a client's perspective. Most of the previous works are relatively partial.

This study provides insight and understanding into the limited previous work on the relationship between the digital transformation of service firms and storage areas and warehouses. It provides a new perspective on the growing literature on the uses of bots and social networks in the marketing and media literature at the intersection with robotization, revealing opportunities and additional avenues for future research. Collecting data through a netnographic study and analyzing it based on perceptions could introduce bias and lack of generalizability in the results. Future empirical work is desirable to complete this work.

Our article proposes an original approach in terms of netnograpgy methodology. The different aspects of digital technologies are linked and discussed simultaneously to have a global vision of the robotization of service companies' warehouses.

This study has some limitations and perspectives. Indeed, collecting data through a netnographic study and analyzing them based on perceptions could introduce a bias and a lack of generalization in the results. Indeed, the sampling method chosen and the size of the sample seem to limit the generalizability of the work. Also, the relatively short period of the study seems to limit the opinions collected and may bias the information gathered. We may suggest in future studies to conduct research in different countries and to complement our qualitative study with a confirmatory quantitative study. Finally, additional studies can be conducted in different contexts to compare Amazon's robotic technology with that of its competitors or other service companies to identify the specifics of different contingent contexts.

REFERENCES

Ackerman, E. (2016). *Walmart and Five Elements Robotics Working on Robotic Shopping Cart*. IEEE. https://spectrum.ieee.org/automaton/robotics/industrial-robots/walmart-and-five-elementsrobotics-working-on-robotic-shopping-cart

Addeo, F., Delli Paoli, A., Esposito, M., & Ylenia Bolcato, M. (2019). Doing social research on online communities: The benefits of netnography. *Athens Journal of Social Sciences*, *7*(1), 9–38. doi:10.30958/ajss.7-1-1

Adhikari, R. (2017). *Robots May Become Go-To Customer Service Reps*. CRM Buyer. https://www.crmbuyer.com/story/84765.html

Afanasyev, I., Mazzara, M., Chakraborty, S., Zhuchkov, N., Maksatbek, A., Yesildirek, A., Kassab, M., & Distefano, S. (2019). Towards the Internet of robotic things: Analysis, architecture, components, and challenges. In *2019 12th International Conference on Developments in eSystems Engineering (DeSE)* (pp. 3-8). IEEE. 10.1109/DeSE.2019.00011

AlDajani, I. M. (2020). Phronetic Netnography Research Design. In *Internet Communication Technology (ICT) for Reconciliation* (pp. 155–201). Springer. doi:10.1007/978-3-030-41203-6_7

Alla, L., Hmioui, A., & Bentalha, B. (2020). La netnographie dans les recherches marketing: La communauté virtuelle comme consom'acteur vecteur d'efficacité marketing. *Alternatives Managériales Economiques*, *2*(4), 631–652. doi:10.48374/IMIST.PRSM/ame-v2i4.23559

Aron, R., Shantanu, D., Ramkumar, J., & Praveen, A. P. (2011). The Impact of Automation of Systems on Medical Errors: Evidence from Field Research. *Information Systems Research*, *22*(3), 429–446. doi:10.1287/isre.1110.0350

Bartl, M., Kannan, V. K., & Stockinger, H. (2016). A review and analysis of literature on netnographie research. *International Journal of Technology Marketing*, *11*(2), 165–196. doi:10.1504/IJTMKT.2016.075687

Batth, R. S., Nayyar, A., & Nagpal, A. (2018). Internet of robotic things: driving intelligent robotics of future-concept, architecture, applications and technologies. In *2018 4th International Conference on Computing Sciences (ICCS)* (pp. 151-160). IEEE. 10.1109/ICCS.2018.00033

Battini, D., Calzavara, M., Persona, A., & Sgarbossa, F. (2017). Additional effort estimation due to ergonomic conditions in order picking systems. *International Journal of Production Research, 55*(10), 2764–2774. doi:10.1080/00207543.2016.1190879

Bentalha, B. (2020). Big-Data et Service Supply Chain Management: Challenges et Opportunités. *IJBTSR International Journal of Business And Technology Studies and Research, 1*(3). Advance online publication. doi:10.5281/zenodo.3607357

Bentalha, B. (2022). Green transportation Balanced scorecard model: a fuzzy-delphi approach during COVID-19. In *Computational Intelligence Techniques for Green Smart Cities* (pp. 107–127). Springer International Publishing. doi:10.1007/978-3-030-96429-0_5

Bentalha, B. (2023). A Framework for Exploring the Global Performance of Service Supply Chain Management: A Qualitative Study. *Government Impact on Sustainable and Responsible Supply Chain Management*, 106-129.

Bentalha, B., & Hmioui, A. (2021). Smart Service Supply Chain and Just Walk Out Technology: A Netnographic Approach. In *The Proceedings of the International Conference on Smart City Applications* (223-236). Springer.

Bentalha, B., Hmioui, A., & Alla, L. (2019). The digitalization of the supply chain management of service companies: a prospective approach. In *Proceedings of the 4th International Conference on Smart City Applications* (pp. 1-8). 10.1145/3368756.3369005

Bentalha, B., Hmioui, A., & Alla, L. (2020). The global performance of a service supply chain: a simulation-optimization under arena. In *The Proceedings of the Third International Conference on Smart City Applications* (pp. 489-502). Cham: Springer International Publishing.

Bentalha, B., Hmioui, A., & Alla, L. (2023). Green Transportation Balanced Scorecard: A VIKOR Fuzzy Method for Evaluating Green Logistics Initiatives. In *International Conference on Digital Technologies and Applications* (pp. 916-925). Cham: Springer Nature Switzerland. 10.1007/978-3-031-29857-8_91

Bogue, R. (2016). Growth in e-commerce boosts innovation in the warehouse robot market. *The Industrial Robot, 43*(6), 583–587. doi:10.1108/IR-07-2016-0194

Boysen, N., Briskorn, D., & Emde, S. (2017). Parts-to-picker based order processing in a rack-moving mobile robots environment. *European Journal of Operational Research, 262*(2), 550–562. doi:10.1016/j.ejor.2017.03.053

Calfas, J. (2019). *Robots Are Coming to Walmart and Making Employees Scared for Their Jobs' Money.* https://money.com/money/5641542/walmart-jobs-robot-union

Chan, K. W., & Li, S. Y. (2010). Understanding consumer-to-consumer interactions in virtual communities: The salience of reciprocity. *Journal of Business Research, 63*(9-10), 1033–1040. doi:10.1016/j.jbusres.2008.08.009

Choudhury, S. R. (2016). *SoftBank's Pepper Robot Gets a Job Waiting Tables at Pizza Hut.* CNBC. https://www.cnbc.com/2016/05/24/mastercardteamedupwithpizzahutrestaurantsasiatobringrobotsint

Choudhury, T. T., Paul, S. K., Rahman, H. F., Jia, Z., & Shukla, N. (2020). A systematic literature review on the service supply chain: Research agenda and future research directions. *Production Planning and Control, 31*(16), 1363–1384. doi:10.1080/09537287.2019.1709132

Claro, D. P., & Ramos, C. (2018). Sales intrafirm networks and the performance impact of sales cross-functional collaboration with marketing and customer service. *Journal of Personal Selling & Sales Management, 38*(2), 172–190. doi:10.1080/08853134.2018.1437353

D'Andrea, R., & Wurman, P. (2008). Future challenges of coordinating hundreds of autonomous vehicles in distribution facilities. In *Proceedings of 2008 IEEE International Conference on Technologies for Practical Robot Applications* (pp. 80-83). IEEE. 10.1109/TEPRA.2008.4686677

Davis, F. D. (1989). Perceived Usefulness, Perceived Ease of Use, and User Acceptance of Information Technology. *Management Information Systems Quarterly, 13*(3), 319–340. doi:10.2307/249008

Dong-yuan, Ga-oan, & Zhong-shun (2018). Exploration of Key Technologies of Smart Logistics Based on Big Data. *Proceedings of 2nd International Conference on Education Science and Economic Management (ICESEM 2018)*, 1256-1259.

Doorn, J. V., Mende, M., Noble, S. M., Hulland, J., Ostrom, A. L., Grewal, D., & Petersen, J. A. (2017). Domo Arigato Mr. Roboto: Emergence of Automated Social Presence in Organizational Frontlines and Customers' Service Experiences. *Journal of Service Research, 20*(1), 43–58. doi:10.1177/1094670516679272

Dou. (2016). Based on the background of smart logistics Kiva warehouse robot Application analysis and prospect. *Global Journal of Engineering, Design, and Technology, 5*(3), 1-4.

Enright, J. J., & Wurman, P. R. (2011). Optimization and coordinated autonomy in mobile fulfillment systems. *Proceedings of the 25th AAAI Conference on Artificial Intelligence.*

Fluss, D. (2017). The AI Revolution in Customer Service, Customer Relationship Management. *January, 38.* https://www.destinationcrm.com/Articles/Columns-Departments/Scouting-Report/The-AI-Revolution-in-Customer-Service-115528.aspx

Fu, X. M., Bao, Q., Xie, H., & Fu, X. (2021). Diffusion of industrial robotics and inclusive growth: Labour market evidence from cross country data. *Journal of Business Research, 122*(1), 670–684. doi:10.1016/j.jbusres.2020.05.051

Hanson, R., Medbo, L., & Johansson, M. I. (2018). Performance characteristics of robotic mobile fulfilment systems in order picking applications. *IFAC-PapersOnLine, 51*(11), 1493–1498. doi:10.1016/j.ifacol.2018.08.290

He, Z., Aggarwal, V., & Nof, S. Y. (2018). Differentiated service policy in smart warehouse automation. *International Journal of Production Research, 56*(22), 6956–6970. doi:10.1080/00207543.2017.1421789

Heinonen, K., & Medberg, G. (2018). Netnography as a tool for understanding customers: Implications for service research and practice. *Journal of Services Marketing, 32*(1), 657–679. doi:10.1108/JSM-08-2017-0294

Herrmann, P. N., & Dennis, O. (2015). Beating Irrationality: Does Delegating to IT Alleviate the Sunk Cost Effect? *Management Science*, *61*(4), 831–850. doi:10.1287/mnsc.2014.1955

Hmioui, A., & Bentalha, B. (2021). Service supply chain management: A literature review. *International Journal of Logistics Systems and Management*, *40*(3), 332–353. doi:10.1504/IJLSM.2021.120253

Hoffman, D. L., & Novak, T. P. (2018). Consumer and Object Experience in the Internet of Things: An Assemblage Theory Approach. *The Journal of Consumer Research*, *44*(6), 1178–1204. doi:10.1093/jcr/ucx105

Huang, M. H., & Rust, R. T. (2021). A strategic framework for artificial intelligence in marketing. *Journal of the Academy of Marketing Science*, *49*(1), 30–50. doi:10.100711747-020-00749-9

Iakovaki, A., Srai, J. S., & Harrington, T. (2009), *Service supply chain integration in multiorganisation networks. Applying integration enablers and aligning process capabilities*. 14th Cambridge International Manufacturing Symposium. Configuring manufacturing value chains. Responding to an uncertain world, The Moller Center, Cambridge.

Jain, D., & Sharma, Y. (2017). Adoption of next generation robotics: A case study on Amazon. *PERSPECTIVA A Case Research Journal*, *3*(1), 9–23.

Javelosa, J. (2017). *Major Firm Announces It's Replacing Its Employees with A.I.* Futurism. http://advice.careerbuilder.com/posts/6softskillseveryprofessionalneeds

Jouët, J., & Le Caroff, C. (2016). L'observation ethographique en ligne. *Future Generation Computer Systems*, *76*(1), 159–162.

Kozinets, R. V. (2010). *Netnography. Doing Ethnographic Research Online*. Sage Publications.

Kozinets, R. V. (2015). Netnography: Redefined. *Sage (Atlanta, Ga.)*.

La Londe, B. J., & Masters, J. M. (1994). Emerging Logistics Strategies. *International Journal of Physical Distribution & Logistics Management*, *24*(7), 35–47. doi:10.1108/09600039410070975

Lamballais, T., Roy, D., & De Koster, M. B. M. (2017). Estimating performance in a robotic mobile fulfillment system. *European Journal of Operational Research*, *256*(3), 976–990. doi:10.1016/j.ejor.2016.06.063

Lamsiah, A., Benabderrazik, Y., & Bentalha, B. (2021). The Economic and political components of diplomatic discourse: State actors in Morocco-UK Free Trade Agreement as a case study. *Alternatives Managériales Economiques*, *3*(4), 496–517.

Lee, S. H. (2019). An analysis on the changes of logistics industry using internet of things. *Journal of Advanced Information Technology and Convergence*, *9*(1), 57–66. doi:10.14801/JAITC.2019.9.1.57

Li, J. T., & Liu, H. J. (2016). Design optimization of amazon robotics. *Automation, Control and Intelligent Systems*, *4*(2), 48–52. doi:10.11648/j.acis.20160402.17

Liu, Y., Zhang, W., Pan, S., Li, Y., & Chen, Y. (2020). Analyzing the robotic behavior in a smart city with deep enforcement and imitation learning using IoRT. *Computer Communications*, *150*(1), 346–356. doi:10.1016/j.comcom.2019.11.031

Mende, M., Maura, L. S., Van Doorn, J., Grewal, D., & Shanks, I. (2019). Service Robots Rising: How Humanoid Robots Influence Service Experiences and Elicit Compensatory Consumer Responses. *JMR, Journal of Marketing Research, 56*(4), 535–556. doi:10.1177/0022243718822827

Merschformann, M., Lamballais, T., De Koster, M. B. M., & Suhl, L. (2019). Decision rules for robotic mobile fulfillment systems. *Operations Research Perspectives, 6*(1), 100128. Advance online publication. doi:10.1016/j.orp.2019.100128

Morais, G. M., Santos, V. F., & Gonçalves, C. A. (2020). Netnography: Origins, Foundations, Evolution and Axiological and Methodological Developments and Trends. *Qualitative Report, 25*(1), 441–455. doi:10.46743/2160-3715/2020.4227

Nussbaum, R. (2015). *Changing the tooth-to-tail ratio using robotics and automation to beat sequestration. Air And Space Power,* Journal Maxwell Afb Al. Technical Report.

Piller, F., Ihl, C., & Vossen, A. (2011). Customer co-creation: Open innovation with customers. New forms of collaboration and Innovation in Internet, 31-63.

Prakash, A. (2017). Robots in Retail: Amazon Go Heralds New Customer Service Era. *Robotics Business Review.* https://www.roboticsbusinessreview.com/retail-hospitality/robots-retail-amazon-go-heralds-new-customer-service-era

Rabahi, N. (2020). De l'éthnographie à la netnographie: «Les communautés virtuelles» un nouveau terrain de recherche. *Journal of Social and Human Science Studies, 9*(2).

Rasolofo-Distler, F., & Distler, F. (2018). Using the balanced scorecard to manage service supply chain uncertainty: Case studies in French real estate services. *Knowledge and Process Management, 25*(3), 129–142. doi:10.1002/kpm.1572

Ray, P. P. (2016). Internet of robotic things: Concept, technologies, and challenges. *IEEE Access : Practical Innovations, Open Solutions, 4*(1), 9489–9500. doi:10.1109/ACCESS.2017.2647747

Robin, K., (2016). Robotics in the Real World. *Juvenile Nonfiction*, 48-56.

Sampson, S. E., & Spring, M. (2012). Customer roles in service supply chains and opportunities for innovation. *The Journal of Supply Chain Management, 48*(4), 30–50. doi:10.1111/j.1745-493X.2012.03282.x

Sharma, P., Jain, K., Kingshott, R. P., & Ueno, A. (2020). Customer engagement and relationships in multi-actor service ecosystems. *Journal of Business Research, 121*(1), 487–494. doi:10.1016/j.jbusres.2020.07.031

Sharma, P., Sivakumaran, B., & Marshall, R. (2014). Exploring impulse buying in services: Toward an integrative framework. *Journal of the Academy of Marketing Science, 42*(2), 154–170. doi:10.100711747-013-0346-5

Shen, M., Tang, C. S., Wu, D., Yuan, R., & Zhou, W. (2020). Jd. com: Transaction-level data for the 2020 msom data driven research challenge. *Manufacturing & Service Operations Management*, msom.2020.0900. doi:10.1287/msom.2020.0900

Sousa, M. J., & Rocha, A. (2019). Skills for disruptive digital business. *Journal of Business Research, 94*(1), 257–263. doi:10.1016/j.jbusres.2017.12.051

Strategy Market Research Consulting. (2020). *Internet of Robotic Things- Global Market Outlook 2017-2023*. https://www.strategymrc.com/report/internet-of-robotic-thingsmarket-2017

Tong J. (2015). Wisdom logistics development present situation and countermeasure research in China. *Journal of Lanzhou Institute of Education, 31*(9), 50-51.

Venkatesh, V., & Bala, H. (2008). Technology Acceptance Model 3 and a Research Agenda on Interventions. *Decision Sciences, 39*(2), 273–315. doi:10.1111/j.1540-5915.2008.00192.x

Wang, Y., & Zhang, W. (2018). Development Strategy of Intelligent Thinking System Based on Big Data. *Logistic Engineering and Management, 40*(12), 14–16.

Weidinger, F., Boysen, N., & Briskorn, D. (2018). Storage assignment with rack-moving mobile robots in KIVA warehouses. *Transportation Science, 52*(6), 1479–1495. doi:10.1287/trsc.2018.0826

Wingfield, N. (2017). As amazon pushes forward with robots, workers find new roles. *The New York Times*. https://nyti.ms/2xUhVgM

Wu, Y., & Ge, D. (2019). Key technologies of warehousing robot for intelligent logistics. *1st Int. Symp. Manage. Social Sci. (ISMSS),* 13-14. 10.2991/ismss-19.2019.16

Wynstra, F., Spring, M., & Schoenherr, T. (2015). Service triads: A research agenda for buyer–supplier–customer triads in business services. *Journal of Operations Management, 35*(1), 1–20. doi:10.1016/j.jom.2014.10.002

Xiao, L., & Kumar, V. (2021). Robotics for customer service: A useful complement or an ultimate substitute? *Journal of Service Research, 24*(1), 9–29. doi:10.1177/1094670519878881

Yang, X., Hua, G., Hu, L., Cheng, T. C. E., & Huang, A. (2021). Joint optimization of order sequencing and rack scheduling in the robotic mobile fulfilment system. *Computers & Operations Research, 135*(1).

Yuan, Z., & Gong, Y. (2017). Bot-In-Time Delivery for Robotic Mobile Fulfillment Systems. *IEEE Transactions on Engineering Management, 64*(1), 83–93. doi:10.1109/TEM.2016.2634540

Yudiansyah, A., Keke, Y., & Veronica, V. (2020). Can the mobile robot be a future order-picking solution?: A case study at Amazon fulfillment center. *Advances in Transportation and Logistics Research, 3*(1), 800–806.

ADDITIONAL READING

Dang, V. T., Nguyen, N., & Wang, J. (2021). The impact of retailers' indoor environmental quality on consumer purchase decision. *International Journal of Retail & Distribution Management, 49*(6), 772–794. doi:10.1108/IJRDM-04-2020-0130

Frank, D. A., & Otterbring, T. (2023). Being seen… by human or machine? Acknowledgment effects on customer responses differ between human and robotic service workers. *Technological Forecasting and Social Change*, *189*, 122345. doi:10.1016/j.techfore.2023.122345

Li, Y., & Wang, C. (2022). Effect of customer's perception on service robot acceptance. *International Journal of Consumer Studies*, *46*(4), 1241–1261. doi:10.1111/ijcs.12755

Liu, Y., Wang, X., & Wang, S. (2022). Research on service robot adoption under different service scenarios. *Technology in Society*, *68*, 101810. doi:10.1016/j.techsoc.2021.101810

Wang, C., Liu, Y., & Zhou, H. (2023). Consumer Consumption Behavioral Model for Business Intelligence Using Artificial Intelligence. *Journal of the Knowledge Economy*, 1–27. doi:10.100713132-023-01391-w

KEY TERMS AND DEFINITIONS

Attitudes: Relatively enduring positive or negative evaluations, feelings, and tendencies towards a product, brand, or retailer held by consumers.

Consumer Perception: The way that consumers view, understand, interpret, and organize information about products, brands, companies, or marketing messages to form impressions. Influences purchase behavior.

Expectation: Pre-trial beliefs consumers form about a product or brand that influence satisfaction with actual experiences. Need to be managed.

Fleet Management: Coordinating and optimizing the tasks and paths for a group of robots to avoid congestion and maximize throughput.

Navigation: The ability of RMFS robots to move and steer within facilities using sensors, maps, markers. Enables automation.

Perceived value: Consumer assessment of what is received (benefits, quality, worth) compared to what is given up (price, time, effort).

Picking: The process of selecting and removing items from inventory to fulfill orders or replenish workstations. RMFS automates picking.

Replenishment: Refilling picking stations and transfer points with more inventory when levels run low. Robots deliver additional pods.

Robotic Mobile Fulfillment System (RMFS): Automated robots and associated software that perform warehouse tasks like picking, transporting, and sorting inventory. Increase efficiency.

Warehouse Management System (WMS): Software that handles inventory tracking, order processing, logistics coordination. Provides instructions to RMFS systems.

Chapter 11
ChangeOps:
Strategically Harnessing All Types of Change to Create Increased Effectiveness and Operational Flow

Isolde Genevieve Kanikani
https://orcid.org/0000-0002-8713-8314
Plat4mation, UK

ABSTRACT

There is an overreliance on initiating change in the form of projects. This denies potential strategy, increases risk, and generally disrupts operational flow. With the introduction and recognition of more types of change comes the possibility to strategically harness the right type of change that is fit for purpose, and this is just a start to the potential cost saving that organisations can realise. Operational flow is the life blood of an organisation and the way it delivers value to customers. Too many interruptions will not only slow down flow but can stop it all together. This is not a sustainable possibility for an organisation or the smaller units that form it. Strategically using different types of change to increase flow brings a return on investment at the project level and a cumulative ROI overall as flow brought by ChangeOps increases across the organisation in an interlinked system of influence and output.

INTRODUCTION

The concept of change as something to be managed is so abundant due to the relatively recent recognition of its existence (last 15 years) in the business context and the basic need for management if we are to effectively innovate in our organisations. This means the concept is young in terms of its understanding of how to manage change, particularly when it comes to mass global events like pandemics, economic crises and others that unpredictably show up and ask a lot of organisations who intend to survive the high levels of change that are implied. This stacks up on top of current external and internal changes that need to occur if an organisation is to thrive. Putting the need of speedy decision making together with

DOI: 10.4018/979-8-3693-0458-7.ch011

the adolescence of change management, we end up with a more reactionary, short term and sometimes vague approach to managing change. Operating models and governance soon get out of date in the best of times, and with the speeding up and amount of change needing to be implemented, it's quickly redundant to the point of becoming organisation debt that holds the organisation back from achieving its purpose. This chapter is looking at how change can be broken into clear components that one can operationalise into an effective system. Where flows of change in the form of communication, knowledge sharing, processes and value chains can be first established and second improved.

To understand a particular topic like change we tend to break it down into manageable chunks, giving the opportunity to look closer and get to the heart of any questions, issues or complexities we wish to understand. At times we can stay too high in our view of the things we are working to clarify, and risk creating conclusions based on not much at all that's truly relevant for creating profound comprehension. On the other hand, getting too detailed means we can miss the influencing factors that form part of the system our diminished view is part of. Forgetting the identity and interconnection of the underlying system is to forget that what we are looking at is intrinsically connected and influenced. An example of this is the way we look at change, if we only see change in a project situation, we lose sight of all the other areas where change is formally and informally taking place within the organisation. If we can see that change is inevitable and everywhere, why not train our staff to embrace change as a way of life while connecting changes in a bedrock of an agile governance allowing us to evolve one organism rather than parts that inevitably stop fitting and in some cases start competing.

We need to holistically see the whole, diving in and out of different focuses to really understand what is in front of us, and how this can build strategic advantage and value for the business. Giving attention to the components that make the whole, and a particular focus on the interconnections between these parts while always making sure we don't get lost in activities but keep an eye on outcomes, overall purpose of the organisation and value creation for customers. This is the approach taken within this study, first analysing the different types of change and then combining them into a cohesive picture of interconnections with value orientated best practices and methods.

Governance is pretty much out of date the moment it is finalised unless mechanisms are in place to maintain and update it. Creating a lean governance framework will help lessen the burden of updating while enabling agility to change which is so necessary in these times. The agility amongst other traits of governance maintain a more updated status when it comes to governance. This is a large topic in its own right, but for the purposes of this chapter it will be kept to a brief conceptual outline and related to Objectives and Key Results (OKRs) which is a goal framework that is a great example of what lean governance could look like. The end result of Lean governance would always be determined by the organisation, the purpose and needs to realise this. The concept of lean governance is highly tailored to decrease the wastes involved and at the same time promoting a living breathing structure that enables rather than bogs the organisation down with organisational debt.

BACKGROUND

The Types of Change

Change can occur in many different circumstances, be it as a project, as continuous improvement using *kaizen* principles or methods guided by other Agile frameworks. It can be radical which is harder to monitor and there is often more risk involved because outcomes are harder to predict. Usually more investment is needed to ensure that we win the fight against inertia. It can be iterative, where the goals are easier to define, but significantly less change is realised in a short amount of time but more often a minimum viable product is available sooner than larger more drawn out projects.

Change can be a problem to deal with in Prince 2 and other project methods, or something that's inevitable according to most change managers out there (*Managing Successful Projects With PRINCE2*, 2017). It will be used the following definition of change as a basis for discussion, 'We develop the solution for the organisation, we develop the people in the organisation for the solution (Prosci, n.d.). The case of developing solutions for the organisation directly relates to improving the culture and governance structure. Keeping in mind that improving the organisations ability for value creation is the primary goal here. This is not normally achievable without looking at the flow of day to day operations and the way value or work in progress (WIP) moves through the organisation (Johnson, 2020).

Change takes many forms, and we tend to rely on only a few of the possible forms, theories and best practices available. There is also a tendency to rely on radical change in the form of projects to change rather than more incremental approaches. Due to limits on time and a lack of resources, it's easier to stay with and perpetuate the known change pathways. Change as a project is probably one of the most established, yet we still rush the planning and don't leave enough time to properly integrate the outcomes of the change into business as usual (BAU) when we are done.

Figure 1. The different types of change

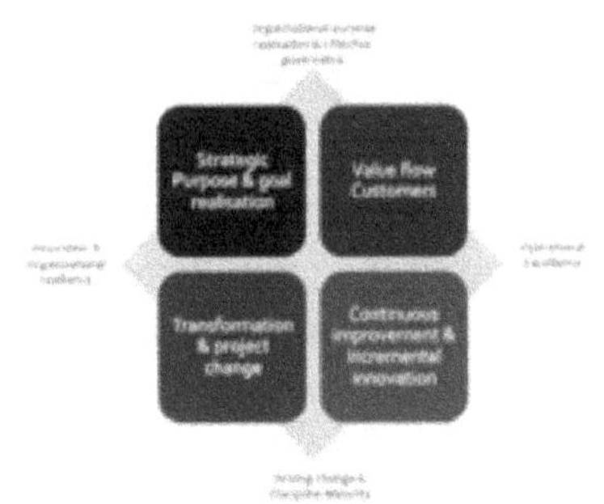

Continuous improvement is another form of change that occurs more in the day to day running of an organisation and as a way to increase quality while reducing waste. Helping keep the standard way of working as up to date as possible, rather than relying on periodic radical change for this. The Toyota company has made many industry significant innovations within this field (Liker, 2004). Together in the coming pages, we will explore how change can take many forms, and how we can strategically make the most of the investments involved in getting people to intrinsically start the process of adapting behaviour to new situations. 'If a company has a strategic advantage, it has a particular characteristic or way of doing things that makes it more successful than others (Cambridge dictionary, 2021).

By combining different types of change while continually updating governance holistically, it is proposed that one can realise greater success, through this create both competitive advantage and real value for our stakeholders. ChangeOps is looking not only at the embedding of project change and continuous improvement into the governance bedrock, but also focusing on the connections that could be further developed to support a holistic adaptive network of integrated change that fundamentally has the opportunity to grow beyond its parts. Besides this, automating and optimising core governance structures and repeatable processes to allow an organisation's people to focus on the intrinsic value they are able to bring, not simply being a machine or static resource. Last but not least, by thinking holistically about change and governance, there are new strategies and advantages to be realised, not to mention greater efficiency. All of which will be discussed in this chapter.

Change Management as a Project: Getting Up to Date and Innovating

There is also some confusion at present around roles and what change management actually is. Put simply, a project is created to make or deliver a particular outcome or deliverable. They aren't busy with the impact this project might have on people or Business as Usual (BAU). The start of a project means getting things done, and the finish is when the new deliverable is ready for some kind of go-live moment usually with some other outcomes. The project manager only needs to tie up a few loose ends and then their task is essentially over. Change management is looking at the project or program of projects,analysing the current situation, the impact the proposed projects might have on the organisation, the people and each other. After the initial executive decision has taken place to initiate the project, the change manager begins their work. Continuing until after go-live and reinforcing the new behaviours established in previous parts of the project. This is a moment when outcomes can be embedded into governance but are often forgotten or not completely integrated. Think on updates to human resources onboarding procedures and contents, checks for how new processes integrate with others still in use. Are there new job descriptions needed, or small additions or details taken away? Can a management role be stopped due to redundancy or does a new one need to be created due to hiring new people for new roles?

The managed part of a change project is traditionally too short to allow for a good transition from Project to BAU. Certainly, a consideration that's interesting when we look at ChangeOps in more detail, mainly because we can make the most of the initial investment to get the project started. In many IT projects, there is also a new role that is commonly put in place, the role of the Adoption specialist. Started in the IT world but has wider possible uses as many industries are finding out. An adoption role is primarily busy with the structuring of an individual project, creating the communication and training needed to support users during an IT implementation or similar. Change management is concerned with the bigger strategic picture as well as how people adopt new tools and project deliverables. Sometimes adoption is simply included in change management and sometimes it's set apart. This depends greatly on the industry and the maturity of the organisation. Change management, particularly when busy with organisation level change, can incorporate whole programs of projects than the typical Project change level its most often associated with. This is where Sponsor coaching, strategy and proper planning are key to success.

Change initiated in the form of projects is as old as time. When organisations want to make something new, or drastically improve something they start a project. Even outside of the context of the organisation. Projects creating new deliverables and that ask for transition in behaviour are essentially changed. Like making a model aeroplane or tidying up the house. As we want to do more with fewer resources within organisations, there is a growing need for this change to be managed by those with specialised knowledge and experience helping to realise the full project benefit. For this reason, the change management profession is becoming more defined and change managers are being brought into projects to

Figure 2. Change in the form of projects

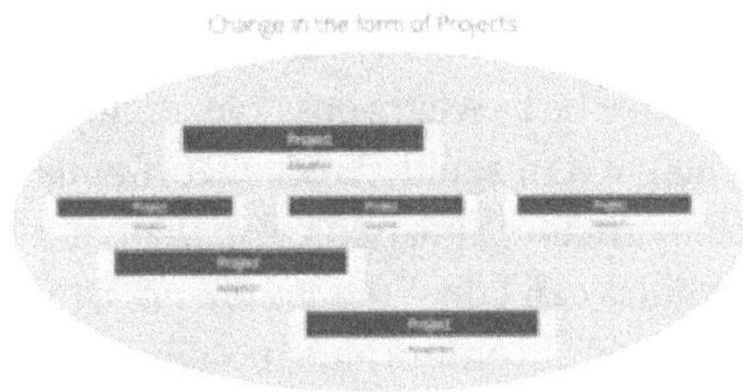

support the people in their process towards realising the new desired future state. The way these projects are initiated, carried out in relation to others within the organisation and how they are re-integrated can mean the difference between success and failure.

When initiating a change project, there are still some challenges that are regularly faced. Like being brought in as a firefighter halfway through a project when there is obvious discontent from impacted stakeholders, rather than at the start when planning and setting up the project for success is truly possible. Due to the fact that change management is relatively new in its modern professional representation, there are all sorts of situations arising around the budget. In some projects, there is the atmosphere that change needs to prove its worth before it gets properly funded, yet it can't do that without the funding. This can go further still with other colleagues not taking change management seriously, either because they consider that they have already been doing change management for years or are simply not quite sure what managing the people's side of change is really about. The way change management and project management are integrated is another area where development could be made. If change is an integrated part of a project team the communication lines are less but change activities can also get easily lost in the project management needs. The better the management of change is the better the success of a project (Creasey). There are more collaboration forms out there, mostly these rely on a recognition of the value of a dedicated change manager and proper funding for this if they are going to be successful.

A lot of resources are used up to fight the inertia of changing something in order to create movement in a situation that is inherently standing still. Not to mention the natural resistance we creatures of habit can have when faced with something new. If we could keep this newly established movement going, directing it towards continuous improvement or the next project, we could gain a lot more from the initial investment. All the stopping and starting uses up a lot of resources and also creates a culture that change is useful sometimes, it's something that happens when necessary and usually last minute. Forcing participants into situations where they are not ready for change, they don't understand what it's trying to achieve and there is generally a lot being asked of them in a short amount of time. Done for survival purposes instead of a natural part of thriving, an infinitely more positive value proposition. (Kotter et al., 2021).

Shifting the focus of change away from the project set-up where possible, could actually allow an organisation's people to see change as a regular part of life, something they can enjoy being part of both in terms of culture, but also the continuous improvement jobs that would become available if the organisation would utilise more types of change within their corporate strategy. Think of situations where people are being employed to create reports from data and the same processes and report content is used every single time. For some this might be a dream job, but for many they would quickly get bored needing more challenge in order to feel achievement and then new motivation (Johnson) (*If Repetitive Work Is Killing Your Creativity, Use These Strategies To Stay Motivated*, 2021)(Friedman, 2015).

Optimising and automating repetitive tasks where possible might seem counterintuitive to motivating people, because this is often attached to a misguided idea that if a machine can do the job for a person no longer exists. It might be true in particular situations. But there is a shift in the areas where we need people in jobs doing work that machines can't do. So if we are open to learning and stop what was probably a depressing job, there is an exciting world of new possibilities out there. If companies can take this a step further and deliberately open up and design new jobs where people can flourish, this would certainly give a competitive edge in this time of great attrition (Cook, 2021).

Prosci's research has shown that Executive sponsorship or lack thereof, is the primary reason why projects fail (Prosci). If we can start to see change in a project as one form of change, bring this together in a holistic picture of the organisation and combine it with a good governance structure. We would see less reliance on change projects, Sponsors can see where the change initiative is coming from and the need is more clear to see. Teaching a leader to be a good sponsor is also vital, no matter the form of change. We often take for granted that a leader will know how to effectively sponsor, but this is a skill to learn. Only through guidance and support can a leader truly become a great sponsor with the exception of a rare few who were born for it.

No clearly defined core processes or an ambiguous governance charter? Then we are not only battling with the trials that come with change as a project, but also with the fact that more needs to be done to show the reason for the project and to get sponsors on board. The need isn't always apparent because the indicators can't be seen in the same way as when the governance structure is visible. One has to dig into situations that can be extremely complex and sometimes we can only guess at possible causes and through this the needs we would like to alleviate. When there is clear governance, the stable structure alone will help to see why some things are not working. Like in a situation when two departments serving the same customers don't have the individual processes aligned. If the two processes are written down and closely followed by each department, it's usually pretty clear why their collaboration is not 100%. If there is no formal form of the process and it's not tangible what the two departments are actually doing in real life. Then the first step is often to create the formal structure and help to identify the possible needs of the present situation.

Most change projects are radical in nature, they create a new road to walk on and require major behaviour shifts in those who will be part of it. The larger the project, the more unpredictable the outcome. Radical change is harder to monitor and generally, the risks involved are considerably more than if change is carried out incrementally. The extended duration of radical change projects means that it takes more to define the goals and vision to work with. They tend also to be more complex, requiring a good amount of time and investment for testing. Some change projects are needed for situations where only a project form of change is appropriate, or where we need to put things in place for then working incrementally. On-premise migration to the 100% cloud project is a good example, once in the cloud, there is a natural movement away from big application updates by software companies which mean that change can then be managed incrementally. There are many more of these situations where a change project can be used to support the new setup needed for good governance and the continuous improvement needed to maintain this.

Figure 3. Continuous improvement and other types of change that occur in organisations

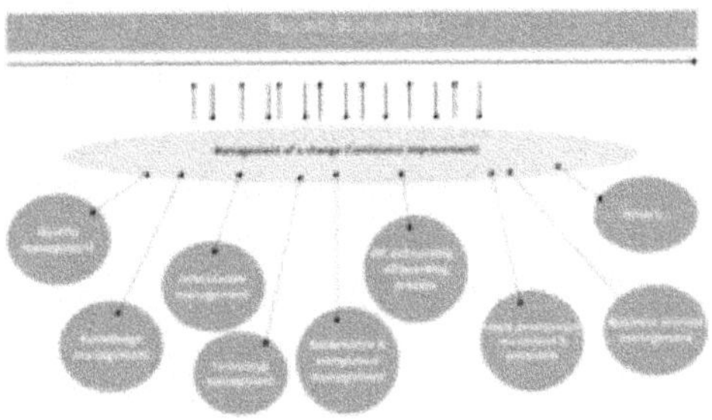

Continuous Improvement: Keeping Up to Date and Driving Quality Improvement

Coming from lean and the Japanese tradition of *Kaizen*, continuous improvement seeks to improve every process in your company by focusing on enhancing the activities that generate the most value for your customer while removing as many waste activities as possible (Kanbanize) (Cane, 1996). Aiming to increase value brought to the customer by first structuring processes and secondly initiating a continuous strategy of improvement. Without the starting point of structured processes that form part of an organisations governance, it's very hard to make real improvements. For example, an organisation wanting to get the ISO 9001 standard within the organisation needs to first show that all-important processes have been structured in a tangible way. Furthermore, these processes have been improved a number of times before an organisation can be audited. Sometimes we fight structure because we seem to lose freedom. Well designed structures that work around the needs of people, facilitated by the right technology, can create greater freedom by giving purpose to our activities and clarity to move in directions that are interesting and healthy for organisational growth.

All in all continuous improvement is the tool we can use to keep governance relevant. Moving away from a stale charter that almost no one reads until there is a need. Governance needs to be a living breathing entity in the organisation, one that is continually updated, improved and refined. Overuse of change projects for this purpose can lead to mass change fatigue and the feeling that change is happening to us, not that we are part of it. With the possibility to automate more of the repeatable tasks in the organisation comes an opportunity to take people away from these mundane roles and get their part of the change by actively making it. People get motivated by feeling that their work is valuable to the company, to the others in their team and that it speaks to their own value systems (Cal & Galindo, 2021). Giving them ownership of structure that is vital to the healthy running of the organisation will often speak to this idea of value. Giving people tasks where they are essentially creating or working on waste areas, things that won't actually be used or could be better done by a computer, won't create the daily satisfaction we search for when going to work. Take the 'Waiting' waste from Lean, and imagine the situation where a manager delegates or assigns more work than they are able to monitor. If assigned work is delivered and waiting for the manager's feedback or sign off, there is a substantial amount of work in progress (WIP) waiting for the manager's response. Assigned employees can't do much more than wait or proactively pick up other work while they wait for the possibility to move with said tasks. In this example, good delegation techniques is not just something good managers do, it's what all managers should be doing in order to cut down WIP and keep value flowing to the customers creating ROI.

There are many models and thoughts out there on continuous improvement that also take on different names. The uniting ideals are greater value creation for customers and other stakeholders by continually improving quality (Garvey, 2019). Some of the better-known ones are ISO 9001, Lean, Six Sigma, and benchmarking to name a few. Due to sharing this ideal, they work incredibly well together as a hybrid quality management structure. One that can be built to meet the organisation's needs. ISO 9001 is a standard framework for managing quality that asks an organisation to formalise many of the basic governance structures needed for the effective running of the organisation. Once this is in place we can begin with continuous improvement measures which are where many of the other models come in. Lean is a method that can be used to improve quality by focusing on the elimination of eight waste areas. "Waste" is commonly defined as any action that does not add value to the customer. Essentially, waste is any unnecessary step in a manufacturing process that does not benefit the customer, therefore, the customer does not want to pay for it (8 Wastes of Lean Manufacturing, 2020) (Streamline, 2019). Six Sigma offers tools and techniques that reduce variance, eliminate defects and help identify the root causes of errors, allowing organisations to create better products and services for consumers (von Rosing et al., 2020). And last but not least, Benchmarking is the practice of comparing business processes and performance metrics to industry bests and best practices from other companies. Dimensions typically measured are quality, time and cost (Benchmarking Definition). All these quality management frameworks and methods can be used to continually update an organisations governance while diminishing the risk of large change projects used for this purpose. Making sure that project change is properly integrated into the governance structure so these new deliverables can also be subjected to continuous improvement.

Governance: Uniting People and Structure

In this study a look at Governance will be taken and the way change is formally and informally occurring in organisations. Taking a high view of governance which will help keep the subject of this chapter within a certain scope. Using the definition ''Governance encompasses the system by which an organisation is controlled and operates, and the mechanisms by which it, and its people, are held to account' (Governance institute Australia). Corporate governance ensures that businesses have appropriate decision-making processes and controls in place so that the interests of all stakeholders (shareholders, employees, suppliers, customers and the community) are balanced. No matter what we name it, identifying the system (the what), engaging employees in how things need to be done (How, Why) and monitoring this means we can create some new value that was not possible when all parts moved in all directions.

Strategic goal defining tools like Objectives and key results (OKRs) are a great way to enforce vision and control at different organisational levels (Akhpah) while getting individuals to become an active part of goal creation within the company. Business as usual (BAU) profit-making activities are often where you can see outward signs that governance is in place, both formal and informal. Governance principles help business outcomes, get us aligned to purpose and are the tools we use to guide us in fulfilling them. How can we implement effective change of any sort, if we don't fundamentally know what we are changing from? A formal governance structure also provides a modus for assessing and then monitoring the organisational system health in relation to percentage likeliness of achieving its purpose. No system or model is perfect and an organisations governance will be no different. So why then do we need governance? Besides the reasons stated above, this imperfect system creates the basic building block we can add to, improve and develop. Without it, these actions aren't possible, something that's important to understand later when we relate to change, Business as usual and various other theories to governance.

The alternative is to keep investing in new imperfect structures that inevitably need to be improved. So why not take up the challenge straight away and build a lean governance that will stay relevant with the fast pace of technological evolution, with the governance framed in such a way as to be reinforced by it. These above definitions can be adapted to work with governance at group, organisation, information, project, team, data and application use levels. For the purpose of this chapter, governance can be seen as an evolving platform, the source of all change and where it is reintegrated. Creating a living breathing heart of the organisation.

Living in VUCA (Volatility, Uncertainty, Complexity & Ambiguity) times, the need for change is more than ever (VUCA World) (Kraaijenbrink, 2018). We can't simply keep adding new projects as and when they are needed. Situations of change fatigue, loss of quality and efficiency of the BAU activities and loss of clarity in situations that are becoming more complex as change after the new change is rolled out over others that haven't been finished yet. Some projects are implemented in a rush, without real clarity of what business goal or need it seeks to relieve. Coming back to the holistic view of the organisation, the interrelatedness of all the parts and definition of a clear stable yet relevant remaining core can give us hope here. For stability bring governance in the form of a charter, a clear set of roles & responsibilities, a clear vision and mission, a way to monitor in order to maintain the organisation rather than let the edges get frayed by the ravages of time and too extended scope.

Governance is often seen as something that is boring, associated with law and finance and not really relevant unless one works with it directly. Then there is an understanding of how having any structure, even an imperfect one, allows the company to function. It allows us to improve core processes because we know what these core processes are. We can train our staff to follow them, we can look to IT to optimise and automate them. If we consider for a moment that there are many jobs out there that rely on people repeating tasks over and over again, some might find this to be heaven but for many who want to know they bring value, this doesn't motivate. In fact, leaving the company looks like a very good option if another role isn't possible. In the time of great attrition, companies are facing difficulties recruiting new quality employees. What if those same companies could automate many of the dull repeating processes, remove some administration and human error to boot, freeing up people for meaningful jobs that make them want to stay. Automatisation and the use of machines don't need to be negative, instead, it gives companies the chance to turn this great attraction into a great attraction if done right (De Smet & Schaninger, 2021). This is one example where sound governance can help company's improve quality and the working lives of many, just by having a clear structure in place.

While considering how best to implement a new learner form of governance, it can be interesting to look at how we can incorporate sustainability measures of people, planet and profit. With many organisations and nations outwardly expressing dedication to lowering CO2 outputs by 2050, and the vast wealth disparities seen globally, there comes a real need to not only address value creation, but value creation done ethically and environmentally friendly to boot. (*Net Zero Targets*) (*Reimagining Capitalism to Better Serve Society*, 2017) (Looney, 2020). Obama's 'The American Jobs act of 2011, was in part designed to spread the wealth amongst the american people and not following the older principle that Shareholders should be king (*Fact Sheet: The American Jobs Act | Whitehouse.gov*, 2011)

Figure 4. Business as usual, operations, governance, and change flow

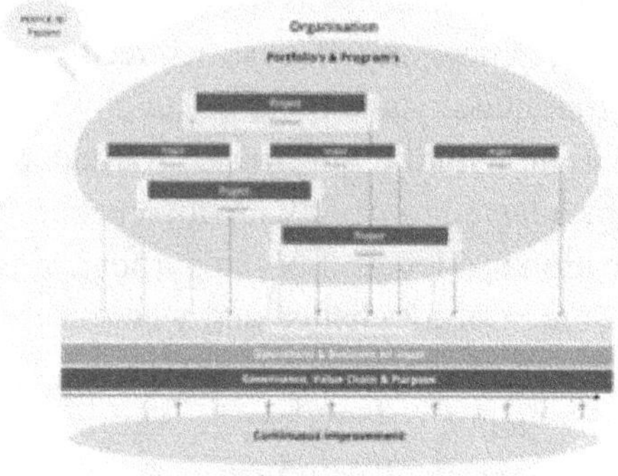

Business as Usual: Opportunity for IT Optimisation, Automation, and Growth of People-Centric Roles

Business as usual (BAU) are the profit activities of the organisation and in many ways the current state of the organisation. BAU activities are also the outcomes of the Governance structure that has been put in place. If there is good governance, then operations will be healthy. Bad governance, like a manager not taking responsibility for their teams or processes not being clearly defined and related across different departments, means the organisation is not running optimally. Sometimes a lack of good governance is due to growing pains, if an organisation grows so quickly that resources are stretched to limits, there is very little attention and time to formalise processes. Another scenario where strong silos exist in the organisation can mean that departmental processes don't relate where they should. An example of this is two departments who share clients and therefore a need to communicate in parts of their process. But each department is improving and changing their own process without checking this against the other. There is a risk of poor design, bad communication between departments, a focus on activities rather than outcomes and bottlenecks within operations. Many of the problems one department might feel, can often be pinpointed by how both departments will be related.

Change carried out as a project often has a big impact on the ability of BAU activities to remain constant and effective. Think of the situation where employees need to start using a new central ERP system that is replacing multiple other programs and places to store information. This change will allow many things to be automated, cut down running costs and enable each employee to gain access to more knowledge in one place. Change in the form of a project has a current, transition and future state phases. During the transition phase, employees are often asked to maintain some of the current state while also learning and using the new future state. Reasons could be that the future state of the ERP system is not yet 100% able to serve all employee needs, maybe employees need to maintain the old system so clients get a smooth transition and don't feel the effects of the change. This could look like maintaining 60% of the old system, 70% of the new system and 5% of the time needed to learn new behaviours and tools. This simply doesn't add up to a stress-free situation for employees and is not manageable long term. Whatever the motivations, employees are often asked to work more than their allotted hours, while learning a new system and keeping clients happy. If the number of mass change projects could be cut down by implementing lean governance and continuous improvement, we can improve the quality of BAU for all our stakeholders.

With the industry 4.0 revolution steadily developing, allied with remote working needs created by the COVID pandemic, there is a growing possibility to optimise and automate many of the repeatable tasks within BAU. Over the last years, many jobs have sprung up that ask employees to do things like data entry or administration that can now be done by connecting formalised processes. On one hand, this leads to a loss of jobs, but on the other hand whole new areas of job roles are opening up. Due to the speed with which industry 4.0 has grown, means there are huge knowledge and experience gaps on the job market. Making employee retention, knowledge management and talent development important topics of these times.

Figure 5. Decrease the need for change as projects with the strategic use of continuous improvement

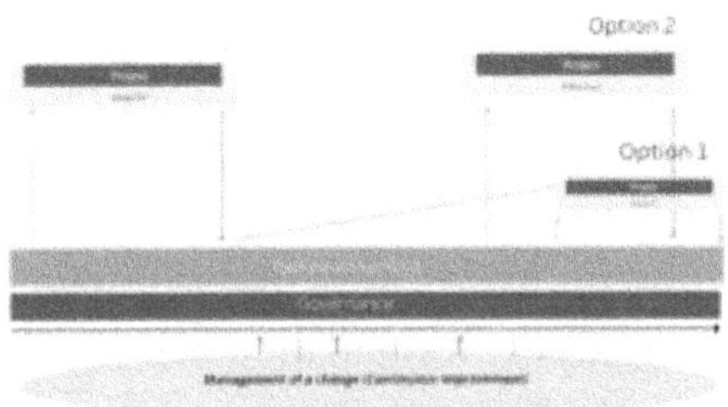

DISCUSSION ON DIFFERENT APPROACHES TO MANAGING AND IMPROVING CHANGE

Operationalizing Change

We canform lean governance and a culture of change in every corner of the organisation by operationalizing change and through this building maturity on the organisational and operational levels. Creating flow for our employees at all levels (Csikszentmihalyi, 2008; Covey, 2004; Pink, 2009; Mausner et al., 1966; Stickdorn et al., 2018), so they can go forward creating flow for our customers. Within an organisation there are a number of types of change that occur at different levels, from organisation wide transformations in the form of programs and projects to operational change created in the process of generating value for customers. When there is talk about Operationalizing Change it means addressing change at all levels and with all types of change. At the organisational level there are two key aspects: the sought after outcomes of transformation, programs and other internal functions, and the second being the change that the delivery of these outcomes creates.

There appears to be less research available on the higher levels of change and outcome creation but there is an abundance on the operational level which focus on improving flow of value that can be adopted for the organisation's wide scope and approach to Change operations. These are mostly originating from the context of manufacturing at the operational level of the organisation and it's good to keep in mind that at this level an organisations operations landscape includes two key aspects: the creation of value in relation to the organisation's primary purpose and the inherent change that is created in this process. This is one type of change occurring in organisations. Some of these approaches will be explored below.

Theory of Constraints

Theory of Constraints (TOC) is a management philosophy that aims to improve the flow of operations by identifying and effectively managing bottlenecks or constraints in processes (Cox & Goldratt, 1986; Goldratt, 2004). It supposes that there is always a constraint (bottleneck) in any given time that will actually deliver business value if solved. A bottleneck refers to any point in the system that limits the overall throughput or slows down the flow. It could be a machine, a department, a specific task, or any other factor that hinders the smooth progression of work. The key benefit of applying TOC is that it helps organisations prevent delays and optimise the utilisation of resources, ultimately improving the overall flow of operations. By identifying and addressing the constraints, organisations can increase throughput, reduce lead times, and enhance overall productivity (Schragenheim, 2000). Moreover, TOC enables organisations to allocate resources strategically to ensure that the bottleneck is given the necessary attention, while also synchronising other parts of the system to support the flow.

In practice, organisations can utilise TOC by following a systematic approach (Theory of Constraints: A Literature Review, 2014). First, they need to identify the critical bottleneck in their operations, which may require careful observation, data analysis, or simulations. Once the bottleneck is identified, strategies such as buffer management can be applied to ensure that work flows smoothly through the constraint. Buffer management involves strategically placing buffers, such as time or inventory buffers, before and after the bottleneck to maintain a continuous flow and absorb any variability or disruptions.

By implementing TOC and effectively managing constraints, organisations can optimise the flow of operations, reduce waste, and enhance overall productivity and customer satisfaction. With a lean and optimised governance in place, this is sustained by structures and monitoring that both maintain and inform about the state of flow (Mabin & Balderstone, 2000;Techt, 2015). Helping us to continuously improve and continuously remain in the optimal state of change. Furthermore, the Theory of Constraints can be applied to organisational change operations by identifying and addressing the constraints or bottlenecks that hinder the change process. By focusing on removing these constraints, organisations can optimise the flow of change initiatives, improve efficiency, and accelerate the pace of organisational transformation. All of this is supported by choosing the right type of change for the job in the first place that could be a potential solution to a bottleneck. An example of this is if we always rely on projects to initiate change which are expensive and have to be prioritised, we create a backlog of projects waiting to be processed, signed off and initiated if successful. If continuous improvement had been used in the lead up to the project, in many cases the level of investment would be greatly decreased and a project might not even be needed getting rid of our 'constraint altogether.

Total quality Management (TQM)

Total Quality Management (TQM) is a management approach that places a strong emphasis on continuous improvement and customer focus. TQM aims to enhance flow in operations by reducing errors, improving customer satisfaction, and optimising processes. It involves the active involvement of all employees in quality improvement efforts to drive overall organisational excellence. Practically, organisations can foster a culture of quality by promoting a shared vision of quality and establishing clear quality objectives. This includes setting quality standards, defining customer expectations, and aligning organisational processes and activities to meet those expectations.

It incorporates Deming's 14 Points, emphasising continuous improvement and customer focus. TQM utilises Statistical Process Control (SPC) techniques to monitor and control processes. It also embraces the philosophy of continuous improvement, borrowing from Kaizen principles. Lean manufacturing principles are incorporated, such as waste reduction and just-in-time production. Customer Relationship Management (CRM) principles are utilised to understand and meet customer needs. TQM emphasises employee empowerment and participation, drawing on theories of motivation and teamwork. It recognizes the importance of Total Employee Involvement (TEI) and the contributions of all employees. Last but not least, it adopts a systems thinking approach to understand and optimise organisational interactions. These theories and approaches collectively form the foundation of TQM, enabling organisations to drive continuous improvement and achieve operational excellence and some of which will be explored in more detail in the next sections.

By creating a culture that values quality, organisations can ensure that every employee understands the importance of their role in delivering high-quality products or services. Furthermore if this employee activity working with customer satisfaction could be extended to include growth mindset and change capability building, it would make everyone an owner of change, flow and customer satisfaction which is a powerful mix if achieved.

Implementing Lean Principles

Lean principles are a set of management principles that focus on eliminating waste and improving efficiency in operations. Waste refers to any activity or process that does not add value to the final product or service. By identifying and eliminating waste, organisations can optimise their processes, improve flow, and enhance overall responsiveness to customer needs.

To practically implement lean principles, organisations can utilise various tools and techniques. Value stream mapping (VSM) is one such tool that helps visualise and analyse the flow of materials and information through a process or value stream. By mapping the current state and identifying areas of waste and inefficiency, organisations can make targeted improvements to streamline processes and enhance flow. VSM enables organisations to optimise value-added activities, reduce non-value-added activities, and eliminate bottlenecks or delays.

Another practical method within lean principles is just-in-time (JIT) production. JIT aims to minimise inventory by producing and delivering products or services just in time when they are needed. This approach reduces carrying costs, avoids overproduction, and enables organisations to respond quickly to changing customer demands. By synchronising production with customer demand, organisations can achieve a smooth and continuous flow, minimising waiting times and reducing lead times.

What does this mean for change? By identifying and addressing areas of waste and inefficiency in the change process, organisations can enhance flow, reduce delays, and improve the overall effectiveness of the change initiatives. Additionally, by embracing a culture of continuous improvement and empowering employees to participate in the change process, organisations can drive sustainable change and create a foundation for ongoing improvement and adaptability. Good value flow means that change flow goes unstopped, but more importantly value doesn't get stuck in some kind of work in progress status. So in many cases good change flow equals value reaching customers more efficiently while making way for still more change. This in turn asks every employee to not only engage with constant flux but get practised in it leading to resilience and improvement to an organisations change maturity. Go one step further and say that this increased maturity cuts costs and increases the % change a company can handle means that there is a double win from the business perspective and a triple one if attrition rates are dropped because people and organisation become changeable.

Figure 6. The 8 wastes of Lean, own depiction

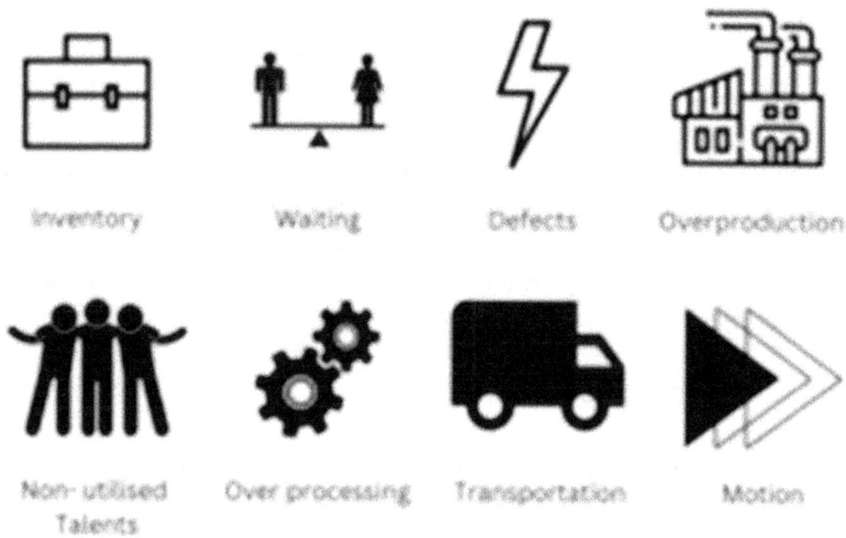

Kaizen

Kaizen, derived from the Japanese term meaning "continuous improvement," is a method that focuses on making small, incremental changes over time to enhance flow in operations. It emphasises the importance of fostering a culture of ongoing improvement within an organisation. By implementing Kaizen, organisations can effectively eliminate waste, optimise processes, and empower employees to contribute to the improvement efforts.

Practically, organisations can utilise Kaizen events, also known as improvement workshops or blitzes, to address specific areas of improvement. These events bring together cross-functional teams to analyse current processes, identify bottlenecks or inefficiencies, and develop solutions. By engaging employees at all levels in these events, organisations can tap into their expertise and encourage collaboration, leading to innovative ideas and process enhancements that improve flow.

Furthermore, organisations can actively encourage employee suggestions for improvement. By providing a platform for employees to share their ideas, organisations can unlock valuable insights and potential improvements from those who are closest to the processes. Employee suggestions can be gathered through suggestion boxes, dedicated improvement platforms, or regular team meetings. This empowers employees, fosters a sense of ownership, and cultivates a culture of continuous improvement.

To support the practical application of Kaizen, organisations can provide training on problem-solving tools and techniques. This equips employees with the necessary skills to analyse processes, identify areas for improvement, and implement solutions effectively. Tools such as root cause analysis, process mapping, and fishbone diagrams can assist in systematically identifying the underlying causes of issues and generating improvement ideas. By equipping employees with problem-solving capabilities, organisations enable them to actively contribute to the flow-enhancement efforts.

Kaizen and Lean are closely related concepts but are not the same. Kaizen represents a philosophy of making small, incremental improvements over time. It focuses on empowering employees to identify and eliminate waste, improve processes, and drive continuous improvement at all levels of the organisation. On the other hand, Lean is a systematic approach to process management that aims to eliminate waste, optimise value-added activities, and improve overall efficiency. Lean incorporates various tools, principles, and techniques to achieve these objectives, such as value stream mapping, just-in-time production, and pull systems. Lean also emphasises the importance of continuous improvement, but it provides a more structured framework and specific methodologies for achieving process optimization.

Some confuse Kaizen with lean methodologies. Kaizen is a mindset or philosophy of continuous improvement, while Lean is a methodology that encompasses a broader set of principles and techniques for waste reduction and process optimization. Kaizen can be seen as an essential component of Lean, as it aligns with the Lean approach of continuous improvement. Both philosophy and framework bring operational improvements that are people-centric, and when applied to change operations we can apply the same concept of wastes when looking to either establish or improve the status quo.

Six Sigma

Six Sigma is a methodology aimed at improving process quality and efficiency initially created by Bill Smith and Mikal Harry (Harry & Schroeder, 2000) . By reducing defects and minimising variations, organisations can enhance flow in operations, leading to improved customer satisfaction and productivity. The DMAIC framework guides the implementation of Six Sigma, involving defining project goals, measuring current performance, analysing data to identify root causes, implementing improvement solutions, and establishing controls to sustain the improvements (Ries, 2023). By using statistical tools and involving cross-functional teams, organisations can proactively identify issues, optimise processes, and achieve operational excellence. Additionally, by aligning the level of Six Sigma quality with strategic goals, organisations can enhance change flow by investing resources where they count the most while still meeting customer needs effectively.

By using Six Sigma, organisations can proactively identify and resolve issues that hinder flow and reduce efficiency. The use of statistical tools and data-driven decision-making enables organisations to make informed choices, eliminate waste, and optimise processes (Juran & Defeo, 2016). Ultimately, Six Sigma promotes a culture of continuous improvement and empowers organisations to achieve and sustain high levels of quality and operational excellence (Zinkgraf, 2006). But the big add from the perspective of change and flow is that we can choose the level of quality that matches the strategic goals of whatever is being developed and delivered. Sometimes it's easy to stuck in the idea of creating the perfect solution, investing hours of time looking for that one elegant way to solve and execute a particular situation or problem case. But does the customer even want this, is their need for a perfect solution more like a six sigma level 3 or 4 with a much higher tolerance for defects? We can increase change flow by gaging the right level of six sigma which supports healthy flow and the remaining effort can either be invested where it counts or be returned a profit.

Theory of Knowledge (TOK)

Theory of Knowledge (TOK) is a management approach that recognizes the significance of knowledge transfer, problem-solving, and innovation within an organisation (Nonaka & Takeuchi, 1995). TOK emphasises the creation of a learning organisation, where individuals and teams continuously improve their skills, share knowledge, and drive innovation (Polanyi, 1966). By implementing TOK, organisations can enhance flow in operations by fostering a culture of continuous learning and improvement. Organisations can establish knowledge-sharing platforms to facilitate the exchange of information and expertise (Wenger, 1998). This can include intranet portals, online forums, or regular team meetings dedicated to sharing best practices and lessons learned. By providing a platform for employees to share their knowledge and experiences, organisations can tap into a wealth of collective wisdom, enabling faster problem-solving, reducing duplication of effort, and promoting continuous improvement.

To support the implementation of TOK, organisations should provide training and development opportunities for their employees. This can involve workshops, seminars, or online courses that enhance skills and knowledge in areas relevant to the organisation's goals and operations. By investing in employee development, organisations equip their workforce with the tools and expertise needed to tackle challenges and contribute to the flow-enhancement efforts (Grant, 1996;Nonaka & Von Krogh, 2009).

Theory of Knowledge (TOK) provides valuable support for organisational change operations by emphasising the importance of knowledge transfer, critical thinking, and continuous learning. Firstly, TOK recognizes that successful change requires a deep understanding of the existing knowledge within an organisation. It encourages stakeholders to question assumptions, challenge prevailing beliefs, and critically evaluate the knowledge that underpins the need for change. By engaging in a comprehensive examination of knowledge, organisations can identify potential gaps or biases that may hinder the change process (Tsoukas, 2003). This awareness enables them to make informed decisions, develop effective change strategies, and mitigate risks associated with incomplete or flawed knowledge.

Community Genogram Mapping

Community genogram mapping is a method that extends the concept of genogram mapping to analyse and understand the relationships and dynamics within a broader community or organisation (Rigazio-DiGilio, 2005). It provides a visual representation of the connections and interactions among individuals, groups, and stakeholders within the community (McGoldrick et al., 1999). By creating community genograms, organisations can enhance flow across people relationships and foster a sense of belonging, collaboration, and shared goals.

Practically, organisations can start by identifying the various individuals and groups that form the community or organisation (Boszormenyi-Nagy & Spark, 1973). This includes employees, leaders, departments, external partners, and other relevant stakeholders. By mapping out these relationships, organisations gain a comprehensive view of the interconnectedness and dependencies within the community, which is essential for fostering effective relationship flow.

Creating a community genogram allows organisations to identify the flow of information, decision-making, and collaboration among different groups or individuals. It helps identify potential bottlenecks, gaps, or areas of limited communication. By analysing the genogram, organisations can gain insights into how information flows through the community, how decisions are made, and how collaboration takes place (Procter & Dalgety, 2004). This understanding enables organisations to implement strategies that enhance communication, streamline processes, and optimise relationship flow.

Furthermore, community genogram mapping provides an opportunity to identify shared goals, common interests, and areas of collaboration within the organisation. By visually representing the connections and relationships, organisations can identify individuals or groups that play crucial roles in facilitating flow and promoting positive relationships. This knowledge allows organisations to leverage these relationships, foster cross-departmental collaboration, and create a sense of community and shared purpose. This may involve creating forums for interdepartmental communication, establishing cross-functional teams, or organising community-building activities to strengthen relationships and promote a sense of belonging.

In summary, community genogram mapping is a powerful tool for understanding and enhancing flow across people relationships within organisations. By visually representing the relationships, analysing information flow, and identifying opportunities for collaboration, organisations can foster effective communication, collaboration, and a sense of community within the organisation. By addressing communication gaps, leveraging shared goals, and fostering relationships, organisations can enhance relationship flow and create a more cohesive and productive working environment. Community genogram mapping in the context of organisations could be a first vital step of any type of change initiation and closely ties in with stakeholder mapping and analysis techniques.

Figure 7. The Lean flow system in organisations, own depiction

Lean Governance

The concept of change operations works together with a modernised lean Governance structure. Why lean and why modernise? Lean governance combines the principles of lean thinking with effective governance practices to drive operational excellence and organisational performance. It emphasises the importance of efficient processes, waste reduction, and continuous improvement, while also ensuring compliance, risk management, and strategic alignment. Lean principles such as value stream mapping, standardised work, and visual management are integrated into governance frameworks to streamline decision-making, enhance transparency, and foster a culture of accountability. The integration of lean and governance enables organisations to achieve a balance between agility and control, optimising resource allocation, and driving sustainable growth. How can we find a balance between formalised governance and culture, making use of the strengths of each while bypassing some of the drawbacks which are natural for any one type of solution?

Imagine a comprehensive governance charter that has taken every measure to document the rules that define a company's approach to people, processes, performance and purpose. Or going to the other extreme of a Latin set-up of governance that's very informal and advocates against written procedures, replacing this with the trust in leadership and the 'family' culture. In the first, you have a continuing need to further document new procedures as new situations arise, and the upside is that there is clear accountability and transparency. Second, not having formalised governance makes it very hard to improve, it's in the heads of a few, and reliance on the 'family' culture and leadership could be both a plus or a potential blindspot in terms of fairness and accountability. So the question that arises is, how to design a governance structure that meets the accountability and transparency needs that enforce responsibility, while not becoming bureaucratically heavy? The more structure you have, whether formal or informal, the more you need to get rid of or update it when changes are being implemented. The idea of a Lean Governance is one that is waste-free and works with managed change to keep the organisation relevant and innovating for greater ROI (Burke et al., 2020;(Lai; Molesky et al., 2020).

In today's rapidly changing business landscape, the concept of modernised governance is gaining recognition as a crucial factor for organisational success. Traditional divisions such as IT and Human Resources are now seen as integral parts of the organisation's ability to stay relevant and effective. IT is no longer limited to a back-office role but is acknowledged as a superhero that streamlines processes and supports centralising information. The roles of the CIO and CTO have become more important than ever in driving IT improvement and innovation. Similarly, Human Resources has evolved from an industrialised efficiency approach to one focused on positive culture and people-centric structuring. Companies like Google have invested in creating a culture that brings out the best in employees, while new governance structures like Holacracy have emerged. By combining theories and methods, organisations can foster cross-functional teams, embrace change as an organisation-wide occurrence, and create self-steering teams that work closely with customers to deliver real value.

The COVID-19 pandemic has further highlighted the need for motivating employees and establishing IT infrastructure that supports remote and hybrid working. The traditional office setup is being replaced by more flexible arrangements, such as Charles Handy's corporate doughnut model, where physical presence is not a constant requirement. However, despite these advancements, organisational approaches, structures, and cultures have been slow to adapt. By starting with a clean slate and incorporating current knowledge, organisations can operate in a way that unleashes human potential and aligns with how people naturally learn and embrace change. This entails shifting the focus from climbing the corporate ladder to creating work environments centred around motivation. Additionally, building a system that embraces lean governance, intelligent structures, thoughtful culture building, and people-centric operations can ensure adaptability and innovation as new knowledge and possibilities emerge.

Overall, the convergence of modernised governance, IT optimization, and people-centric approaches is essential for organisations to thrive in today's dynamic business environment. By reimagining traditional divisions and embracing innovative practices, organisations can create a foundation that fosters progress, adapts to change, and unlocks human potential for greater success.

Objectives and Key Results

OKRs (Objectives and Key Results) provide a framework for setting and aligning organisational goals across all parts of the organisation. OKRs are a shared, lightweight, and dynamic goal-setting approach that helps connect different departments and teams, ensuring that everyone is working towards a common vision (Meehan, 2020). By implementing OKRs, organisations can enhance flow by fostering alignment, transparency, and accountability.

Practically, organisations can start by defining high-level Objectives that represent the overarching goals of the organisation. These Objectives should be aspirational and inspire all employees to work towards a common purpose (Murphy, 2019). Next, Key Results are established for each Objective, which are measurable outcomes that indicate progress and success (Lencioni, 2012). Key Results should be specific, measurable, achievable, relevant, and time-bound (SMART) to ensure clarity and focus.

Connecting all parts of the organisation through OKRs involves cascading the objectives and key results throughout different levels and teams. This ensures alignment between the organisational objectives and the goals of individual departments and teams. By linking each team's objectives to the broader organisational objectives, organisations create a sense of unity and shared purpose, enabling smoother flow across the organisation (Graham & Dennis, 2019).

Furthermore, the dynamic nature of OKRs allows organisations to respond and adjust to shifting priorities or emerging opportunities. OKRs can be revised or updated periodically to reflect new insights, changes in market conditions, or shifts in organisational strategies. This flexibility ensures that the organisational goal framework remains relevant and agile, promoting change flow across the organisation by enabling timely adjustments and alignment. Besides this, OKRs can form part of lean governance offering an agile goal and monitoring approach that can shift easily with change needs and creates flow in the cascade of linked objectives from organisation purpose all the way down to each individual if appropriate strategically.

By defining clear objectives and measurable key results, cascading goals throughout the organisation, implementing regular check-ins and progress tracking, and adapting as needed, organisations can enhance flow by fostering alignment, transparency, and accountability. The use of OKRs enables organisations to connect individual efforts with the broader organisational vision, driving cohesive and focused work towards shared goals. Approaches to goal realisation like KPIs and OKRs as a way of making governance lived rather than hidden somewhere where no one looks. Service design, value propositions through to frameworks that support this at every organisational level (Bernarda et al., 2014).

Strategic Change: One Solution Doesn't Fit All, but the Process of How People Deal With Change Is the Same

When we seek to understand the present, looking at the high holistic level and the detailed specific levels, we can start to organise the possible choices into strategies that will bring us closer to our desired outcomes and benefits realisation. Sometimes these choices are narrowed down too much by tradition, what has been instead what can be healthy and good for the organisation. Many of the present organisational structures can be related back to the industrial revolution of the 1800s and a good ounce of Taylorism can be found too (Taylor, 1998). Governance by power and control rather than empowering employees to be the best they can be through personal leadership development; or Management of people for efficiency rather than putting motivation forefront. Building structures and then pushing people into them, which often doesn't work very well unless the structure has been built around how people work. We have a habit of simply building on old foundations, but with all the change in the world at the moment, these old constructs are becoming less and less relevant. Taking a look at the people-centric structure and how to build this into our governance would not only be a giant leap for the way we see ourselves and our work. So what are some of these strategies and choices we can begin to incorporate?

Combining all change activities throughout the organisation and strongly embedding this into a living breathing governance structure. That is both lean and created for people to excel in, luckily this goes hand in hand with optimising and automating many of the processes people simply just don't need to do anymore. This type of set-up will maintain a formalised form of governance and create a true beating heart of the organisation. A reference for new change projects and continuous improvement initiatives, helping the organisation fulfil its vision and value propositions.

Limiting the number of change projects at any given time, and actively cutting down the reliance we have on these to implement change. Instead where possible, growing the continuous improvement activities that keep our governance relevant and allow a talented workforce to thrive and be part of the change by creating it. Less reliance on projects also help ensure good BAU operations, keep change fatigue to a minimum and grow change maturity in other parts of the organisation.

Radical change is always riskier, uses up more resources to fight inertia and create the necessary movement in people's behaviours needed for success. There are often long time frames involved and due to the size of the projects that can be implemented, the goals and scope can be hard to fathom in the beginning. By making the most of continuous improvements of iterative nature, we can be more sure of what will change and therefore create more effective ways to monitor impact and benefits realisation. Incremental changes done as sprints for example can often deliver working deliverables where larger projects tend to still rely on more waterfall type strategies for delivery of outcomes. Lastly, iterative change gives the organisations people time to grow with the structure that brings them together doing what they do. We can test if solutions really work and often have more possibility for feedback and communication about what's going to happen.

Combining many of the major reasons for the great attrition and the ideals of Future of work, we can see that there is a growing need to put people at the top of the priority list and give places at the heart of the organisation where they can create value. We are moving into a time where repetitive jobs will become a thing of the past, due to the possibilities of today's technology. Many people are working remotely due to the pandemic and many talks of returning back to normal, but maybe this is it. Thinking up a new approach to governance that builds around values like healthy culture, connection and motivation is an exciting prospect and not so out of reach as one might think. We need to shed old ways of working that don't give value anymore and focus on creating new governance structures and change the approach that sets us up for today and a more profound tomorrow. Only in this way can we turn the great attrition into the great attraction for those companies who dare to leave old waste behind.

Traditional Change Management Models and Approaches

We have covered many management models and methods for creating change flow across the different types of change in organisations. While this is the focus of this chapter, it is important to also mention some of the known, tried and tested Change Management methodology. It has already been mentioned that Change Management as a profession is maturing but not as mature as some of the other disciplines existing in organisations. There are many dated models still being used like Elizabeth Kubler-Ross's Change curve based on the grieving cycle (Kübler-Ross, 2014) and Lewin's three stages of change and a number of similar variations on the theme (Burnes, 2019).

Figure 8. ChangeOps, harnessing the power of all types of change to strategically create flow of change and value to customers

The ones that have really inspired movements in the way we work with and think about change have been the 8 Steps of John Kotter (*The 8-Step Process for Leading Change | Dr. John Kotter*), The Association of Change Management Professionals (ACMP) standard, The AIM method (*AIM Change Management Methodology*), McKinsey's 7s (*Enduring Ideas: The 7-S Framework*, 2008) and Prosci's standard method (*Prosci Methodology Overview*) of practice. Much of this change best practice has greatly informed the current approach to project change, helping us to realise more with less impact on people. Furthermore increase speed of adoption, ultimate utilisation and proficiency which in turn increases ROI by saving costs and improving the ability of people to successfully move to the new way of working.

There is also a growing body of Change management knowledge that brings a much more diverse way of thinking about the management of change both on the people, project and organisational levels. An example would include the 6 Batteries of change advocating on the level of organisational transformation and include Leadership, Vision and Strategy, Mobilization, Engagement and Enablement, Governance and Performance Management, and Culture and Mindset (De Prins et al., 2017). John Kotter in his book Accelerate has moved on from the idea of step 1 and a 'burning platform' to talking about Survive and Thrive. Introducing the idea that for people to change they need to be introduced to change in an environment that doesn't put them into survival modus (Kotter, 2014). As the sheer amount of change in organisations is increasing, so too is the need for improved and streamlined change management. Many are incorporating lean principles into the way they manage change, moving away from bulky plans and activity based work toward value focused approach and what is starting to be known as Change Management 2.0 (*Our Philosophy to Modern Change Management*).

CONCLUSION

Harnessing the power of operationalised organisational change relies on this systemic view. If we silo the types of change we only achieve a very small amount of the ROI available from change management activities. In this case change management is taken in the broadest context of the words and meaning of any activity that manages change including all the types of change happening in organisations. Properly managing change at the type of change level is still not something we have mastered with the possible exception of continuous improvement. Giving attention to first understand the types of change within the organisation and then investigate improvement of change management approach would be a great first step.

Seeing that flow between change types equals transfer of value and making the most of any initial investment in getting change started is optimised and thereby creating a cumulative ROI that is not otherwise possible if we keep change siloed. Think Lean manufacturing and the way work in progress (WIP) aims to create an effective flow of change and within this value towards its desired outcome. If there is a stop to flow, then there is a build up of value and other less desirable outcomes like extra costs for storage or a communication and training campaign to re-invigorate the people to start the process when ready to start again. When looking at people dependent aspects like communication and Knowledge sharing that are relied upon for an effective system, the community genogram mapping can be a great way to understand flows between people. If we grow awareness here we can start to develop our approach which will inevitably involve technology and data aspects of transformation going forward in these times. By systemising change we enable a cumulative impact to start to occur where change is not restricted to a particular type, but flows into other types. Why do we want this flow?

Keeping optimising grows change maturity in the people and organisation because people get used to change as a constant rather than the start, manage and stop approach that the overreliance on projects inherent embeds into organisational culture. This stopping and starting is where change resistance can build up. Connecting in a good feedback system where legitimate concerns can be incorporated into outcomes will further enhance this process and diminish the amount of resistance that will be seen.

Viewing change at the organisational and system level, we can start to design flows of change and value whether in the form of processes or value chains. We can also make strategic decisions about the type of change to embrace in particular situations, the balance of change as projects or continuous improvement and the way these can be used to decrease project costs. For example, if we build a continuous improvement process that directly brings project outcomes into the operational level, we maintain a good level of up to date and therefore the need for a new project will be delayed and potentially diminished.

All of these approaches should be properly embedded and agilely interfacing with the organisations governance and operating model in order to maintain structural relevance instead of redundancy that ends up as organisational debt. The next step of this research will be to explore how an agile governance and operationalised change can both interface and reinforce each other for the ultimate elegant realisation of value for customers and fulfilment of organisational purpose.

Put pragmatically, a lot can be achieved with a 'think big, start small' approach. The 'Think big' part is to seek to create change and value flow through the organisation, secondly increasing effectiveness of this. The 'start small' can take a number of forms listed below:

- Map out the different value chains your organisation has and assess where the most value is currently lost and apply what we have learned around constraints.
- When planning new projects, plan the follow-up activities where continuous improvement best practices can be applied and project outcomes can be embedded into business as usual operations.
- Assess the different types of project that typically take place in the organisation, sort them into projects that need to be carried out as projects and those that could be decreased in size by putting continuous improvement measures in place.
- Assess the level of organisational debt present in the operating design, model and governance of the organisation. Clearly identifying debt areas that with different degrees of investment could be updated freeing up budget for new improvements.
- Short term thinking is often the culprit that builds organisational debt and slows down flow of change and value. Identify situations that often bring short term focused decision making and establish best practices that bring the thinking to the longer term or mitigate outcomes of short term thinking.
- Look into inter department relationships where there are vital collaborations that result in value for the customer. Are there clear roles and responsibilities, purpose and alignment with strategic business goals? Overtime even the most elegant processes become dated due to new employees, products and services being added which calls for streamlining in order to get the job done more effectively.

By getting started we smaller initiatives and focus of unlocking value, we create positive impact for the company short term while growing change and value flow for the longer term. Each improvement initiative carried out can be strategically connected to further increase flow. Playbooks can be used to build standard practice that can be reproduced all over the organisation by more individuals. Better yet train people in the ChangeOp's thinking and approach will speed up to process to achieving the 'big picture' result.

We have established the high level different types of change along with their respective challenges, pros and cons. The over reliance on projects as a mechanism for change means that we lose out on utilising other forms of change that might be better suited to the need, or if we had previously started with continuous improvement we might have gotten rid of the need completely positively impacting our investment bottom line. Making use of known methods of creating flow and adding the distinct lens of change to this picture, we can interconnect the different types of change into sub-systems of specific value creation. Whether this is the value delivered to customers or the value of people collaborating and sharing knowledge. Stepping out of the detailed picture that looks only at the short term development, individual change and flow managing approaches is advised here. In conclusion, if we can start working with a think big, act small mentality, we will be able to start embracing some of the concepts in this chapter that come together into a strategic and systemic approach.

REFERENCES

A Brief History of Lean. (n.d.). Lean Enterprise Institute. Retrieved December 29, 2021, from https://www.lean.org/explore-lean/a-brief-history-of-lean/

AIM Change Management Methodology. (n.d.). IMA | Change Management. Retrieved September 3, 2023, from https://www.imaworldwide.com/aim-change-management-methodology

Albert, M. (1993). *Capitalism Against Capitalism*. Wiley.

Benchmarking Definition. (n.d.). iSixSigma. Retrieved December 29, 2021, from https://www.isixsigma.com/dictionary/benchmarking/

Bernarda, G., Pigneur, Y., Osterwalder, A., & Smith, A. (2014). *Value Proposition Design: How to Create Products and Services Customers Want*. Wiley.

Boszormenyi-Nagy, I., & Spark, G. (1973). *Invisible loyalties: Reciprocity in intergenerational family therapy*. Harper & Row.

Burke, C., Fraser, J., & Handler, J. (2020, October 16). *Lean Governance: Just Enough Structure to Secure Great Outcomes from Multiple Agile Teams*. VMware Tanzu. Retrieved December 30, 2021, from https://tanzu.vmware.com/content/blog/lean-governance-just-enough-structure-great-outcomes-multiple-agile-teams

Burnes, B. (2019). The Origins of Lewin's Three-Step Model of Change. *The Journal of Applied Behavioral Science*. https://journals.sagepub.com/doi/full/10.1177/0021886319892685

Cal, P., & Galindo, M. (2021, January 26). *Work motivation: the value behind the task*. BetterUp. Retrieved December 29, 2021, from https://www.betterup.com/blog/work-motivation-the-value-behind-the-task

Cambridge dictionary. (2021, December 22). *Strategic Advantage | Meaning in the Cambridge English Dictionary*. Cambridge Dictionary. Retrieved December 28, 2021, from https://dictionary.cambridge.org/dictionary/english/strategic-advantage

Cane, S. (1996). *Kaizen Strategies for Winning Through People: How to Create a Human Resources Program for Competitiveness & Profitability*. Pitman Pub.

CIO vs CTO: What's the Difference? – BMC Software | Blogs. (2021, November 5). BMC Software. Retrieved December 30, 2021, from https://www.bmc.com/blogs/cio-vs-cto-whats-the-difference/

Covey, S. R. (2004). *The Seven Habits of Highly Effective People*. Audio-Tech Business Book Summaries.

Cox, J., & Goldratt, E. M. (1986). *The goal: a process of ongoing improvement*. North River Press.

Csikszentmihalyi, M. (2008). *Flow: The Psychology of Optimal Experience*. HarperCollins.

Culture Investments. (2019, March 28). Grant Thornton. Retrieved December 30, 2021, from https://www.grantthornton.com/library/articles/advisory/2019/return-on-culture/looking-ROI-in-all-right-places.aspx

De Prins, P., Letens, G., & Verweire, K. (2017). *Six batteries of change: laad je bedrijf op voor verandering*. LannooCampus.

De Smet, A., & Schaninger, B. (2021). *From the great attrition to the great adaptation*. McKinsey & Company. https://www.mckinsey.com/business-functions/people-and-organizational-performance/our-insights/from-the-great-attrition-to-the-great-adaptation?cid=app

Enduring Ideas: The 7-S Framework. (2008, March 1). McKinsey. Retrieved September 3, 2023, from https://www.mckinsey.com/capabilities/strategy-and-corporate-finance/our-insights/enduring-ideas-the-7-s-framework

Forbes. (2018, February 8). *13 Reasons Google Deserves Its 'Best Company Culture' Award*. Forbes. https://www.forbes.com/sites/forbestechcouncil/2018/02/08/13-reasons-google-deserves-its-best-company-culture-award/?sh=72a26b534828

Garvey, J. (2019, May 16). *Total quality management methods to drive team performance*. PeopleGoal. Retrieved December 29, 2021, from https://www.peoplegoal.com/blog/quality-management-techniques-to-drive-team-performance

Goldratt, E. M. (2004). *The Goal: A Process of Ongoing Improvement*. Academic Press.

Governance institute Australia. (n.d.). *What is governance?* Governance Institute of Australia. Retrieved December 28, 2021, from https://www.governanceinstitute.com.au/resources/what-is-governance/

Graham, J., & Dennis, C. (2019). Digital transformation: OKRs as a governance mechanism. *The Journal of Business Strategy*, *40*(1), 36–42.

Grant, R. M. (1996). Toward a knowledge-based theory of the firm. *Strategic Management Journal*, *17*(S2), 109–122. doi:10.1002mj.4250171110

Groth, A., Bognar, S., & Reichert, J. (2018, October 9). *What is holacracy? The management approach tested by Google and Zappos. — Quartz at Work*. Quartz. Retrieved December 30, 2021, from https://qz.com/work/1397516/is-holacracy-the-future-of-work-or-a-management-cult/

Handy, C. B. (1995). *The Empty Raincoat: Making Sense of the Future*. Arrow Business Books.

Harry, M. J., & Schroeder, R. R. (2000). *Six sigma: the breakthrough management strategy revolutionising the world's top corporations*. Currency.

Industrial Revolution: Definitions, Causes & Inventions - History. (n.d.). History.com. Retrieved December 29, 2021, from https://www.history.com/topics/industrial-revolution/industrial-revolution

Johnson, T. (2020). *Lean Methodology Mastery Collection: 8 Books in 1: Lean Six Sigma, Startup, Enterprise, Analytics, Agile Project Management, Kanban, Scrum and Kaizen*. Amazon Digital Services LLC - KDP Print US.

Juran, J. M., & Defeo, J. A. (2016). *Juran's Quality Handbook: The Complete Guide to Performance Excellence* (J. A. Defeo, Ed.; 7th ed.). McGraw-Hill Education.

Kanbanize. (n.d.). *What Is Continuous Improvement? Definition and Tools*. Kanbanize. Retrieved December 29, 2021, from https://kanbanize.com/lean-management/improvement/what-is-continuous-improvement

Kotter, J. P. (2012). *Leading Change*. Harvard Business Review Press.

Kotter, J. P. (2014). *Accelerate: Building Strategic Agility for a Faster-moving World.* Harvard Business Review Press.

Kraaijenbrink, J. (2018, December 19). *What Does VUCA Really Mean?* Forbes. https://www.forbes.com/sites/jeroenkraaijenbrink/2018/12/19/what-does-vuca-really-mean/?sh=6cfcaab17d62

Kübler-Ross, E. (2014). *On Death and Dying: What the Dying Have to Teach Doctors, Nurses, Clergy and Their Own Families*. Scribner.

Lai, E. (n.d.). *Lean Governance - Oxymoron or Essential Strategy?* Cprime. Retrieved December 30, 2021, from https://www.cprime.com/resources/blog/lean-governance-an-oxymoron-or-essential-strategy/

Leibowitz, G. (2017, March 28). *How to Build a Great Company Culture Like Google, According to an Ex-Googler*. Inc. Magazine. Retrieved December 30, 2021, from https://www.inc.com/glenn-leibowitz/how-one-startup-founder-borrowed-the-best-bits-of-googles-culture-for-his-own-co.html

Lencioni, P. M. (2012). *The advantage: Why organisational health trumps everything else in business.* Jossey-Bass.

Liker, J. K. (2004). *The Toyota way*. McGraw-Hill Education.

Managing Successful Projects with PRINCE2. (2017). TSO.

Mausner, B., Herzberg, F., & Snyderman, B. B. (1966). *The motivation to work*. Transaction Publishers.

McGoldrick, M., Gerson, R., & Shellenberger, S. (1999). *Genograms: Assessment and Intervention.* W.W. Norton & Company.

Meehan, P. (2020). Objectives and key results (OKRs): Driving focus, alignment, and engagement in governance. *Corporate Governance Review*, *28*(2), 16–21.

Molesky, J., O'Reilly, B., & Humble, J. (2020). *Lean Enterprise: How High Performance Organizations Innovate at Scale*. O'Reilly Media, Incorporated.

Murphy, S. A. (2019). The power of objectives and key results (OKRs) in corporate governance. *International Journal of Business, Humanities, and Technology*, *9*(5), 63–68.

Nonaka, I., & Takeuchi, H. (1995). The knowledge-creating company. *Harvard Business Review*, *73*(4), 96–104.

Nonaka, I., & von Krogh, G. (2009). Tacit knowledge and knowledge conversion: Controversy and advancement in organisational knowledge creation theory. *Organization Science*, *20*(3), 635–652. doi:10.1287/orsc.1080.0412

Origin of holacracy. (n.d.). Holacracy | Reflect. Retrieved December 30, 2021, from https://www.reflect-beratung.de/en/holacracy/

Our Philosophy to Modern Change Management. (n.d.). Lean Change Management. Retrieved September 3, 2023, from https://leanchange.org/philosophy

Pink, D. H. (2009). *Drive: The Surprising Truth About What Motivates Us*. Penguin Publishing Group.

Polanyi, M. (1966). *The Tacit Dimension*. Routledge & Kegan Paul.

Procter, H. G., & Dalgety, R. (2004). Professional development for culturally competent practice. *Journal of Family Social Work*, *8*(3), 13–27.

Prosci Methodology Overview. (n.d.-a). Prosci. Retrieved September 3, 2023, from https://www.prosci.com/methodology-overview

Prosci. (n.d.-b). *Primary Sponsor's Role and Importance*. Prosci. Retrieved December 28, 2021, from https://www.prosci.com/resources/articles/primary-sponsors-role-and-importance

Prosci. (n.d.-c). *Prosci Methodology*. Prosci. https://www.prosci.com/resources/articles/prosci-methodology

Schragenheim, E., & H. (2000). *Simplified Drum-Buffer-Rope: A Whole System Approach to High Velocity Manufacturing*. William Dettmer.

Schroedel, J. (2019, December 10). *Radical vs incremental change: what is the difference?* CitizenLab. Retrieved December 28, 2021, from https://www.citizenlab.co/blog/e-government/whats-the-difference-radical-vs-incremental-change/

Spindler, R. A. (2019). *Evolution of German corporate governance*. https://eprints.whiterose.ac.uk/141762/1/Evolution%20of%20German%20corporate%20governance.pdf

Stickdorn, M., Hormess, M., Schneider, J., & Lawrence, A. (2018). *This is Service Design Doing: Applying Service Design Thinking in the Real World: a Practitioner's Handbook*. Academic Press.

Streamline. (2019, May 21). *Which should you use – ISO 9001, Six Sigma or Lean?* Streamline. https://streamline.business/which-should-you-use-iso-9001-six-sigma-or-lean

Taylor, F. W. (1998). *The Principles of Scientific Management*. Dover Publications.

The 8-Step Process for Leading Change | Dr. John Kotter. (n.d.). Kotter International. Retrieved September 3, 2023, from https://www.kotterinc.com/methodology/8-steps/

Tricker, B. (2021). *The Evolution of Corporate Governance*. Cambridge University Press.

Tsoukas, H. (2003). Do we really understand tacit knowledge? In E. Chelladurai & R. A. Berger (Eds.), *Strategy and Organization: Realising Strategic Management* (pp. 197–218). Palgrave Macmillan.

von Rosing, M., Scheer, A., & von Scheel, H. (2020, January 9). *What is Six Sigma? Definition, Methodology and Tools*. Six Sigma Daily. Retrieved December 29, 2021, from https://www.sixsigmadaily.com/what-is-six-sigma/

Wastes of Lean Manufacturing. (2020, September 4). TechSolve. Retrieved December 29, 2021, from https://www.techsolve.org/8-wastes-of-lean-manufacturing/

Wenger, E. (1998). *Communities of Practice: Learning, Meaning, and Identity*. Cambridge University Press. doi:10.1017/CBO9780511803932

World, V. U. C. A. (n.d.). *Best practice was yesterday. Best thinking is in demand today and tomorrow*. VUCA.

World - Leadership Skills & Strategies. (n.d.). Retrieved December 28, 2021, from https://www.vuca-world.org/

KEY TERMS AND DEFINITIONS

Business as Usual: Business as usual refers to the normal, ongoing operations and practices of a business or organisation, typically characterised by routine activities, established processes, and the maintenance of existing systems, without significant disruptions or major changes to the standard operating procedures.

Change Flow: Change flow refers to the systematic and coordinated movement of changes within an organisation, encompassing the planning, implementation, and management of multiple change initiatives in a synchronised manner, ensuring smooth transitions, minimising disruptions, and optimising the overall impact and success of change efforts throughout the organisation.

Change Maturity: Organisational change maturity refers to the level of readiness, capability, and effectiveness an organisation possesses in successfully navigating and implementing changes, as well as continuously improving its change management practices and adapting to evolving business environments.

Change Operations: The same as ChangeOps.

ChangeOps: The strategic advance created by connecting different types of change into value-creating flow refers to the synergistic integration of various change initiatives across an organisation, enabling the seamless and efficient generation of value by leveraging the collective impact of these interconnected changes.

Community Genograms: Community genograms are visual representations or diagrams that depict the interconnected relationships, patterns, and dynamics within a community or social system, typically illustrating family relationships, social networks, and other relevant factors to provide a comprehensive understanding of the community's structure, strengths, challenges, and resources.

Continuous Improvement: Continuous improvement is a systematic approach and mindset that focuses on ongoing, incremental enhancements in processes, products, and services, aiming to optimise efficiency, quality, and customer satisfaction by actively seeking and implementing positive changes, fostering a culture of innovation and learning, and embracing feedback and reflection as catalysts for ongoing progress.

Goal Frameworks: Goal frameworks are structured systems or models used to define, organise, and prioritise goals within an organisation or individual context, providing a framework for setting objectives, aligning actions, measuring progress, and ultimately achieving desired outcomes by providing a clear and systematic approach to goal setting and management.

Kaizen: Kaizen is a continuous improvement philosophy and methodology that emphasises small, incremental changes and the involvement of all employees in identifying and implementing improvements in processes, systems, and products, aiming to achieve higher efficiency, quality, and overall organisational performance over time.

Lean: Lean, originally derived from the Toyota Production System, is a management philosophy and methodology that aims to eliminate waste, optimise efficiency, and create value by continuously improving processes, reducing non-value-added activities, empowering employees, and focusing on delivering customer value while maintaining high quality standards and reducing costs.

Operations: Operations, in the context of business, refers to the activities and processes involved in the production, delivery, and management of goods, services, or organisational functions, including aspects such as resource allocation, workflow design, quality control, logistics, and performance optimization, aimed at efficiently and effectively achieving desired outcomes and meeting customer needs.

Systems Theory: Systems theory is an interdisciplinary framework that examines the interrelationships and dynamics of complex systems, considering elements, processes, and interactions as interconnected components within a larger whole, with an emphasis on understanding the systemic behaviour, patterns, and emergent properties that arise from these interactions.

Theory of Constraints: The Theory of Constraints (TOC) is an approach that focuses on identifying and resolving the most critical limiting factors or bottlenecks within a system or process, in order to maximise overall productivity, efficiency, and throughput.

Theory of Knowledge: The Theory of Knowledge, also known as epistemology, is a philosophical discipline that examines the nature, sources, and limits of knowledge, exploring questions such as how knowledge is acquired, justified, and justified beliefs are formed, and what distinguishes knowledge from mere opinion or belief.

Total Quality Management: Total Quality Management (TQM) is a comprehensive management approach that emphasises continuous improvement, customer satisfaction, and employee involvement in all aspects of an organisation's operations, aiming to achieve the highest level of quality in products, services, and processes.

Chapter 12
An Institutional Perspective of CGICTPF Implementation and in the Public Sector

Mampilo Phahlane
University of South Africa, South Africa

ABSTRACT

Much like other governments in the world, the South African government through the Department of Public Service and Administration (DPSA) in collaboration with Government Information Technology Officer Council (GITOC) and the Auditor General (AG) has developed Corporate Governance of Information and Communication Technology Policy Framework (CGICTPF). CGICTPF is based on King III Code of Good Governance, ISO 38500 Standard for the Corporate Governance of ICT, and COBIT as a comprehensive Governance ICT Process Framework and is applicable to all spheres of government. The department of transport was also mandated to implement and use this framework as a government entity to improve the status of ICT government. The chapter is about how CGICTPF was implemented in the public sector using the Department of Transport as a case. Semi-structured open ended interviews data were collected with institutional theory as a lens. It is concluded that management support and proper organizational structures create positive outcomes in environments with high regulatory requirements.

INTRODUCTION

IT governance is a framework which provides direction on how an organization controls and manages its IT assets. IT governance ensures that IT supports and enables an organization to meet its strategic goals and objectives. IT today has risen to prominence as a critical determinant of the growth and survival for companies and governments. Much like other governments in the world, the South African government through the department of public service and administration (DPSA) in collaboration with government information technology officer council (GITOC) and the auditor general (AG) have developed corporate governance of information and communication technology policy framework (CGICTPF). CGICTPF is

DOI: 10.4018/979-8-3693-0458-7.ch012

based on King III Code of Good Governance, ISO 38500 Standard for the Corporate Governance of ICT and COBIT as a comprehensive Governance ICT Process Framework and is applicable to all spheres of government, organs of state and public enterprises (DPSA, 2012).

As part of change management in institutions that implement this mandated framework, they are often implemented to enable an organisation's strategic ability and are developed to influence organisational strategic goals and enhance operational performance (Ako-Nai and Singh, 2019). This has also prompted government institutions to implement these frameworks a way to increase efficiency and better manage IT resources.

According to De Haes and Van Grembergen (2008) the pervasive use of technology has created a serious reliance on IT that demands attention on IT governance, especially so in government where the environment has political, technical, and cultural concerns which in turn influence how things unfold. The success of many organisations is determined by how effectively they manage and control their IT function to realise the expected returns (Bowen et al., 2007). Public sector organisations have also realised the effective governance of IT as important to their performance (Vinten, 2002). The public sector has made considerable IT investments to increase efficiencies and improve service delivery (Devadoss et al., 2002). The ability for government departments to serve citizens better lies in government officials to support the development and implementation of their department specific strategies. Therefore, it is crucial for corporate governance to be well understood and supported as one of the key objectives in government.

The South African government has also made such investments in the development of the CGICTPF for implementation and use by government entities. The premise of this chapter is that CGICTPF was implemented in the department of transport, which is a national department responsible for the regulation and coordination of public, rail transportation, civil aviation, maritime and road transport in South Africa. However, not much is known about the implementation of the CGICTPF in this department when the policy framework was declared as the one to use by government entities for IT governance. The rest of the chapter is structured as follows; change management as a facilitator for CGICTPF is discussed next, followed by studies related to CGICTPF, then the research problem, the underpinning theory, the research methodology, followed by the discussion and findings and the conclusion is discussed last.

CHANGE MANAGEMENT AS A FACILITATOR FOR CGICTPF ADOPTION

Teczke et al (2017) assert that change management cannot be an improvised task that needs thorough planning and should be a structured process of managing people, processes and technology in response to the changing environment, so as to align business strategies with external changes for competitive advantage and viability. The implementation of CGICTPF was also a process that impacted departments, employees and processes, those who were in change of this task had to ensure that all this is taken into consideration during the process.

Anyieni et al. (2013) further discusses that change management means to plan, initiate, realize, control, and stabilize change processes on both corporate and personal levels. This means managers and those involved in the process must be aware of changes in organizational strategy, structure, technology, attitudes, and behaviours. Nickolas (2006) argues that the task of managing change includes its biggest impact on people, and many managers find this difficult. The first step of building change is coalitions of stakeholders, including employees and sponsors or anyone affected by the change at any level or whose support is essential Kanter et al. (1992). A leader must be able to influence others, create a vision and then communicate, empower people, and build teams to make the vision happen so that the planned change could have the necessary buy in from stakeholders and the planned change happens.

Change Management Approaches

Graetz and Smith (2010) discuss ten organizational change philosophies, challenging the notion that change is a finite and discard assumptions about opposing values, instead replacing them with an appreciation of complementary concepts and interactive mix of continuity and change. The change philosophies discussed include the biological, rational, institutional, resource, contingency, the psychological, political, cultural, systems, and postmodern philosophy. The authors further assert that change is neither simple nor straightforward, and unlikely to conform to a formula or a step process, an approach is needed that captures the complexities and dynamics of organizations and actively seeks out the accumulated knowledge, skills, experience and learning of the different communities interacting in them.

Alwadani (2001) suggested phases for change management strategies for ERP implementation, the phases include the knowledge formulation phase, this is where you identify and evaluate the attitudes of individual users and influential groups. Followed by the strategy implementation phase this is where management can use the knowledge regarding potential users from the previous stage to set up strategies that can best overcome users' resistance to the ERP system, and to convince as many users as possible to adopt it. Then the last phase is the status evaluation phase which is the process of monitoring and evaluating change management strategies. Although this strategy for change management is for an ERP implementation, it could be adapted to manage change for any project tat could alter how organizations do things.

Wetzel and Van Gorp (2013) categorised research according to three organizational distinctions which have developed and emerged over time to understand organization change. These distinctions are categorised related closely to theories that focus on the emergence of social order. The distinctions are action or agency vs structure (Reed, 2003). Action or agency is perceiving the organization as individual key actors (agency) and tend to describe organizations as aggregated individualistic action maps or interrelated action, be it on an interactive, an organizational, or even a societal level (structure). Micro vs macro focus is about aspects such as motivation (action-driven) or power games (structure-driven) between individuals and groups within the organization (McKinley and Mone, 2003). Volition vs evolution (voluntarism vs determination) a voluntarist view sees that change occurring through individuals interpreting their experiences in ways that conflict with the dominant establishment perspective whereas a determinist view contrasts this and asserts that individuals are usually seen as determined by the structure of their social relations.

Blackman et al. (2022) discuss managing different forms of conversations can help enact successful organizational change through actively shaping the amendment of new mental models. Meaning that employees in organizations shape their reality through conversations.

Another distinction that decision makes in organizations needs to be aware of is the different between planned and emergent change (Phillips, 2021). Planned change takes a social engineering approach, using a predetermined plan to create the desired change (Marshak and Bushe, 2018). This differs from emergent change, in which an organization experiments with new ideas to see what works. Planned and emergent changes also engage in opposite forms of reasoning. Planned change focuses on the collection and analysis of data, while emergent change looks beyond the data to influence creativity and innovation. Planned change converges on the parts of the change, while emergent change may expand outside the current data to find unconsidered possibilities. As much as CGICTPF implementation was a planned change, management had to accommodate some of the emergent, unplanned, and unforeseen changes that happened around the implementation process.

LITERATURE REVIEW

Most government departments have not been successful in achieving some of their mandates due to poor performance, the world bank (2018) emphasise that poor governance and resistance to structural improvement have eroded pockets of economic returns leaving most of them in a loss-making position. Government departments could be described as ambidextrous (Matheus and Jansen, 2016; Magnusson et al., 2020). Ambidexterity suggests that successful organisations or governments need to exploit existing opportunities to achieve efficiency, while simultaneously exploring new opportunities to achieve innovation (Benner and Tushman, 2003; Magnusson et al., 2020). Ambidexterity thus involves two types of activities: exploitation and exploration (March 1991). So, government department while exploring new opportunities must be efficient by working with what they have, this is what happened during the implementation phase of CGICTPF.

The management of IT resources will improve the quality of operations within government departments. Wilkin et al, (2016) asserted that ICT governance aims to maximise the achievement of the objectives and business value of information technology investments. Some of the challenges faced government departments include weak control environments with lack of internal processes to safeguard assets, promote accountability, stop, or mitigate fraudulent behaviour has been one of the major challenges facing management within government departments (OECD, 2004). Failure to produce credible financial statements, lack of proper accounting standards and inadequate auditing practices (OECD, 2004) have led to low levels of financial disclosure. There is no transparency and accountability to both accounting officers and the public on the performance of most public entities and government departments.

The standard for IT governance for public and private institutions is designed to support any type of institution regardless of size, purpose, design and ownership, there is limited research that investigates its application in the public sector context (Wilkin and Campbell, 2010). It is known that IT investment in a public sector context is deemed to have high rates of failure relate to big projects, often directly impacts the public or business, scrutiny through a public audit body, parliamentary attention, and media coverage (Gershon, 2008). Studies on large-scale investments have shown that IT-enabled change is wasted, challenged, or fails to bring a return to the organization and big projects have a success rate of 2% (Standish Group, 2004), investigation of how IT should be effectively governed, structured and managed in this context is pertinent.

Furthermore, as organizations progress and look to certification to the standard knowledge regarding practice becomes crucial. As study conducted by Wilkin and Campbell (2010) regarding Australian Federal governments investment and management analysis of ICT showed a need for improvement in six areas: ICT governance, efficiencies of ICT operations, skills base management, data centre planning, interaction with industry and sustainability of ICT operations (Gershon, 2008). These confirm the importance of knowledge that is practice-oriented and to prioritise ICT governance especially in government. The challenges for ICT governance in government include complexity of the environment, project initiatives that overlap with other projects, a culture that prioritises correctness over doing the right thing and a focus on managing political risk instead of operational risk (Gershon, 2009). In such environments, ICT governance investments do not always yield the desired results because of the regulatory, political, and cultural nature of government environments (Cloete, 2012).

Definition of Key Terms

IT governance is a framework that provides direction, structure, processes, and standards which would ensure that IT supports and enables the organization to meet its strategic objectives and goals (Campbell et al., 2010). IT governance aims to align business and information technology strategies effectively and efficiently (Wessels and Loggerenberg, 2006). Management within organizations adopt IT governance to ensure efficiency, decreased costs and increased control of IT infrastructures (Van Grembergen, 2003). Further, IT governance is aimed at improving organizational accountability, resulting in increased return on investments. IT governance frameworks such as ITIL (IT Infrastructure Library), CMM (Capability Maturity Model), and COBIT (Control Objectives for Information and Related Technology) are internationally implemented and promote these benefits in organizations. Many organizations also choose to develop their own IT governance models, or choose to employ a combination of models, and develop a customized solution specific to their needs. In the public sector, the focus on IT governance has intensified as governments become large consumers of IT (Tonelli et al., 2017) and have moved toward the modernization of public administration, where questions related to performance, transparency, quality of service, and efficiency have become central concerns (Campbell et al. 2010; Tonelli et al., 2017). However, the implementation and use of these IT governance frameworks have always been a challenge. Letsoalo et al (2006) studied the inhibitors and enablers of IT governance implementation in a South African organization, their study concluded that top management and external support and a project champion are key enablers whereas lack of clear IT processes, inadequate project personnel and stakeholder involvement as inhibitors of IT governance implementation. IT governance framework provides guidance on how governments and organizations can implement, manage, and monitor IT within an organization. It provides means to measures the efficiencies and effectiveness of IT resources and processes. IT governance helps enterprises to create value from IT by maintaining a balance between IT benefits realization and minimizing risk levels and resources (Omari et al., 2012). It enables information and related technology to be controlled and monitored and to be aligned to the organization's strategic objectives and goals.

Corporate Governance of IT (CGIT)

Corporate governance, which has been driven by the imperative to manage organizations' operations more effectively to meet shareholder expectations for financial investment, reputation, competitive edge, and risk management, is the system which directs and controls organizations (OECD, 1999). Corporate governance could also facilitate with data quality and integrity of business transactions, business processes and decisions. Derived from corporate governance, CGIT is defined in the standard as the system by which the current and future use of IT is directed and measured (ISO/IEC 38500, 2008). This involves "evaluating and directing the use of IT to support the organization and monitoring this use to achieve desired outcomes. It includes the strategy and policies for using IT within an organization (ISO/IEC 38500, 2008) Thus, corporate governance lays the foundation for many standards, tools and frameworks that underpin the CGIT.

Standards, Tools, and Frameworks

Several tools, frameworks and standards have been developed and defined to assist organizations maximize potential from their IT investments. These frameworks tool and standards include Val IT, COBIT, Risk IT, ITIL, ISO/IEC 27001 and others. IT provides organizations with the structure they require to measure, monitor and optimise the realization of business value from investment in IT (Val IT 2008). Some of these tools include COBIT2 which is described as a tool that provides a comprehensive framework for the delivery of high-quality information technology-based services" (Val IT 2008). Risk IT is a framework for enterprises to identify, govern and manage IT risk (ITGI, 2009). ITIL is designed to assist organizations in developing a framework for IT service management by providing them with consistent and comprehensive documentation of best practice for IT service management (ITIL, 2009). ISO/IEC 27001(2005) is an information security management system standard that brings information security under the explicit control of management. Other frameworks/tools are organization specific and consultant-defined ones and include CMMI, Prince 2, COSO and ISO17799. The South African government have developed an IT governance framework called CGICTPF and is defined in detail below.

Presidential Review Commission (PRC) Findings

In 1998, Presidential Review Commission (PRC) issued a report which outlined the shortcomings of ICT service delivery in government. Its recommendation was "that all-important ICT-decisions should come from the senior political and managerial leadership of the state and not be delegated to the technology specialists, and further that the management of ICT should be on the same level as the management of other resources. It furthermore advocated a common enabling framework of governance.

To address the recommendations made by the 1998 Presidential Review Commission (PRC) report, parliament approved the creation of a new job role called Government Information Technology Officer (GITO) in the government structures. The role of the GITO was to ensure alignment of the business strategy and the business plan and strategic objectives with IT. However, this role did not achieve its purpose because it was not at a decision-making level. GITO had little to no influence in the management of the IT in government. Because of this, the role of GITO did not improve the status of the management of IT in government. This was further confirmed by the Auditor General's (AG) through the ICT Audits conducted in 2008/09 and again in 2009/10.

The Auditor General of South Africa (AGSA) is the supreme audit institution (SAI) of South Africa. It is the only organisation that has the mandate to audit and report on how the government is using South African taxpayers' money. The mandate of the AGSA is outlined in the Constitution of the Republic of South Africa Chapter 9 (sections 181 & 188).

Auditor General Recommendations

In 2008/09 and again in 2009/10 AGSA reported on the state of IT in government. The AGSA recommendations included the following: "Government should implement a government-wide ICT Governance Framework which will govern ICT. Furthermore, there should be a national ICT strategy to address ICT risks based on defined processes and standards; and The ICT roles and responsibilities should be defined and implemented to ensure adequate ICT enablement" (Department of Public Service and Administration, DPSA 2012:13). In his 2010/11 general report, the AG reported that little to no progress had been made as only 21% of government departments had adequately implemented ICT governance controls and in some instances the suggested controls were not formally documented and adopted. The recommendations by the AG were also supported by internationally accepted good practice, and aligned with King 4, ISO 38500 Standard and COBIT 5. The PSA responded by introducing the CGICTPF.

Corporate Governance of ICT Policy Framework (CGICTPF)

In response to the AGSA's findings and recommendations, the DPSA developed the CGICTPF. According to the DPSA, "The purpose of the CGICTPF project is to institutionalize ICT governance as an importance integral part of corporate governance within departments. This CGICTPF provides set of principles and practices that must be complied with, together with an implementation approach to be utilized for ICT governance within departments. The CGICTPF is applicable all government departments, organs of state and public enterprises (DPSA, 2012). The implementation of CGICTPF was supported by a three-phased implementation guideline which was released in February 2014.

Studies Related to CGICTPF Implementation

Sibanda and Von Solms (2019) addresses the poor performance of IT in municipalities with a phased in approach to include CGICTPF as a guide and suggest a strategy that can be used to implement effective and sustainable IT governance practices in municipalities. De Lange et al., (2015) discussed municipalities and information security management by analysing the CGICTPF and SALGA (South African local government association) documents in relation to what the municipalities are doing and concluded that information security management is a crucial concern for municipalities, as they are not meeting the mandatory requirements set by government leadership. Adeyelure et al (2019) studied the adoption of business intelligence (BI) in a social sector department and CGICTPF was considered during the adoption phase, the study concluded by suggesting a model for BI adoption which included government policies and practices as important during the adoption phase. Mxozi and Flowerday (2021) explored the adoption and use of CGICTPF as a mandatory guide during the adoption phase in a public sector department, the study concluded by proposing a framework for IT adoption and use for the public sector in SA with the aim of improving corporate governance, public administration, and IT compliance.

Improvements in Service Delivery Enabled by CGICTPF

There are issues noted as important and motivated the government to adopt CGICTPF, these include issues related to lack of clear IT roles and responsibilities in the public sector, lack of coordination, incompatibility of systems, inability to retain and attract scarce IT skills, and duplication of systems amongst others. For example, e-governance is implemented through CGICPF, this framework guides information systems behaviour (storage and retrieval) of information from government information systems. Government departments (national and provincial) are heavily reliant on electronic information systems to perform their duties as per their respective mandates and their reporting and administrative functions. These information systems enable the automation of business processes and transaction processing, which contributes significantly to efficient service delivery of the departments. Therefore, the information processed and stored on these systems are regarded as a strategic asset crucial to the achievement of service delivery planning, monitoring, and reporting.

The departments who adopted the framework saw a reduction in overall IT costs, less duplication of tasks, increased IT security, better IT projects and investments monitoring, increased risk management. Before the framework was implemented, government departments were struggling with poor financial management, inaccurate financial and performance information, fruitless and wasteful expenditure, fraud, overall poor performance of IT and non-compliance with applicable IT laws and regulations. Post implementation of CGICTPF, AGSA (2019) reports an increase in the status of IT control from 5% in 2012 to 29% in 2017 and auditees that require intervention down from 49% to 16% over the same period. Although progress is slow, there are other areas of improvement that include streamlined IT processes, head of departments taking responsibility and ownership of ICT delivery, Improved ICT ability and agility to adapt to changing circumstances, and ICT executed in line with legislative and regulatory requirements.

However, the implementation of the framework is not without challenges, there's lack of framework customization for specific departments, overall resistance within departments, and lack of management compliance with controls to regulate the ICT environment due to lack consequence management (EC spending reviews, 2021).

THE RESEARCH PROBLEM

Based on the above studies, there seems to be a lack of literature related to the adoption, implementation of CGICTPF in government departments despite the framework being mandatory in all spheres of government, national government level, provincial and local government (municipalities). Further, the Auditor General report (2019) that discusses security management, user access management and IT continuity discloses that IT controls increased significantly over the past four years from 5% in 2013-14 to 17% in 2016-17(AGSA, 2019). These are relatively low numbers considering the policies and guidelines that government have implemented such as the CGICTPF. So, this study is about the implementation and use of CGICTPF in the department of transport and the study will add to the much-needed literature in understanding how this framework is implemented and used within one of the governments departments.

UNDERPINNING THEORY

The new institutional theory, proposed by Scott (2005), was found to be an appropriate theory for this study. The new institutional theory is regarded as a fit for explaining how established social structures, which include regulations, norms, and cognitive processes, affect social actions and interactions. This theory was adopted because it is deemed suitable for studying the environment of organizations adopting technology and the issues and challenges arising from the use of information technology (Agyei-Ababio, 2023). In this study it meant the adoption of an IT governance framework instead of a technology adoption.

The concept of institutionalization is structured around the maintenance and diffusion of elements such as regulative, normative, and cultural-cognitive processes, referring to an organization as a socio-cultural system that is characterized by either single or multiple. Institutional theory acknowledges three key aspects that variations in institutional contexts arise due to interactions with the environment over time; organizations in different environments develop distinct institutional structures; and these institutional structures tend to endure as they not only provide meaning but also facilitate access to resources from the environment (DiMaggio and Powell, 1983).

RESEARCH METHODOLOGY

The aim of this research was to explore how CGICTPF was implemented in a typical government department in its natural setting. The Department of Transport is responsible for regulation and coordination of Transportation in South Africa that is Public Transport, Rail Transportation, Civil Aviation, Maritime Transport and Road Transport. The department oversees other government entities including Airports company (South Africa), air traffic and navigation services, cross border roads agency, ports regulator of south Africa, passenger rail agency, road accident fund etc. The department has over 3000 employees and more than the IT department where the framework was implemented has over 200 employees. A decentralised IT support structure is followed in the department with each division having its own IT support staff who should be carrying the IT objectives and implementing them in their daily tasks. Using semi structured open ended interview questions, data was collected from employees at the department of transport's headquarters in Pretoria, these included management from the IT department and some of the IT support staff. A purposive sample of employees involved in the implementation of CGICTPF were chosen. Due to ethical considerations, the participants are called participant 1, participant 2, participant 3 and participant 4. The profile of the participants are as follows, participant 1 is a deputy director in the department also called the CIO and has been in this position for five years. Participants 2 and 3 are deputy director general and they are senior managers in the IT department. Participant 4 is a specialist IT personnel and has been with the department for eight years. Interviews took 15-30 minutes in the participants office. The interviewed data was analysed using thematic analysis, the data was transcribed, coded, searched, reviewed, and define themes, The participants were asked questions related to the adoption decisions that influenced the department, the implementation of the framework and how that influenced the way they complete their daily tasks. Most of the participants were not at the department when the framework was implemented but provided recollections about what their colleagues would say about the implementation process. The collected data was analysed using content analysis after it was transcribed. The department of transport

DISCUSSION AND FINDINGS

The study's findings are guided by institutional theory as a lens to understand the institutional environment where CGICTPF was implemented. Using regulative, normative, and cognitive elements to understand the implementation of the framework in a government department, these will be explained and explored in detail below.

Motivation Adoption

Participant 1 *"To put in place system of ICT governance that has functional committees and encompassing top management."* Participant 2 *"They saw it fit to set up ICT governance"*

Motivational factors such as economic benefits, regulation requirements, stakeholder obligations and ethical reasons were considered as influences on adoption of IT governance in the department. The findings are consistent with those of Janahi et al (2015) who studied IT governance in public sector that relational elements are the one's guiding the adoption decisions in organizations. The adoption influences the structure of the IT function and the position of the decision-making authority in the department and to a large part determines the efficacy of IT governance framework, the levels of approvals that were needed for some of the decisions to be approved took longer than expected and this caused low morale and less enthusiasm from those involved in the project

Regulatory adoption influence

Participant 3*"Motivation came from external sources in the form of The DPSA and The Office of the Auditor General (AG)."* Respondent 1*"When organization comply, it will realize benefits for implementing IC governance framework." "We had an Exco that supported the adoption of the IT Governance framework from the department of public services (DPSA)".*

The participants expressed that the adoption decision was to comply to the regulatory requirements of DPSA who are responsible for the development of the framework and ensuring government entities implement it. The findings share similar sentiments too those of Masilela and Nel (2021) whose study investigates how the strategic combination of data governance (DG) and information security governance (ISG) practices and principles could be implemented and incorporated as one of the various approaches in public sector institutions to improve the DISG management functions of an organisation's overall data and information systems and processes and their findings reveal the regulatory nature of the environment makes this process more complex as the implementation process unfolds.

Culture Cognitive Influence

Participant 4*"Culture-cognitive influences have been instrumental in bringing knowledge creation in this organization."* Participant 2 *"Change management process; business process awareness; and risk management committee – were some mechanisms implemented as a result of culture –cognitive influences."*

Culture cognitive influence in the department of transport played an important role during the implementation phase, these include structures, processes and other relational mechanisms influenced this rolling out phase. These structures and processes created an environment in which conflicting priorities could be rationalized and appropriate strategies put in place to achieve positive outcomes for the organization. Similar with the work of Wilkin and Campbell (2010) who looked at variables such as responsibility, strategy influence on a government framework adoption.

How the Framework Was Implemented

Participant 3*"The phase approach proposed by the DPSA helped in ensuring that a project plan is developed for the implementation of the IT governance framework, positive factors came from Involvement by IT and Finance Senior management". "The implementation process Lacked Leadership commitment; poor organizational structures; inadequate role and responsibilities; no clear business processes; and a general lack of segregation of duties. These are the coalition factors that contributed negatively during project implementation".*

The framework was implemented is a phased in approach, the top management and a majority of the team were dedicated and offered support and help when needed. However, there was challenges related to organizational structure and job roles and responsibilities, lack of clear business processes and these made collaborative efforts between team members strained.

Impact of CGICTPF in the Department of Transport

Participant 4 *"Some of the processes which were manually executed have been now automated." "Having defined processes and placing structures in place, the alignment of IT with Business strategy has been achieved."*

The implementation of the framework brought some automation within the department and brought with it overall tracking and accountability of IT assets where there's reports and other formal documentation associated with the process. Overall, there was improved decision making within the department post implementation of the CGICTPF.

CONCLUSION

In this chapter, through the filter of institutional theory, we have looked at the implementation of CGIT in a South African government department and how the implementation has affected the department. The study alludes to the importance of management support and appropriate structures contribute to overall positive outcomes. Moreover, using institutional theory as a it made identifying areas of weakness in the project easier and exposes some of the unique problems faced in government departments, further work is required to evolve practice and to improve outcomes for subsequent projects. The implementation challenges include lack of framework customization as the framework is generic and certain government departments are highly specialised. An emergent risk is adopting new technologies and that means that the framework must be adapted and expanded to accommodate these new developments, further ethical considerations, and alignment with organizational values must be taken into consideration. Much like Graetz and Smith (2010) a multi-philosophy approach reinforces the need to discard assumptions about opposing values, instead replacing them with an appreciation of complementary concepts as one of the ways to approach change management in organizations.

Structural capabilities, process capabilities and relational capabilities are the three key capability structures required for the effective implementation of IT governance (Peterson 2003). Structural capabilities are established at various levels within the organisation as formal structures (such as a committee and advisory board). Process capabilities include formal processes and procedures that enable the development and selection of IT strategies and monitoring them. Relational capabilities are established communication and collaboration mechanisms that enable the active participation of stakeholders in making joint decisions (Ako-nai and Singh, 2019). These structures are highlighted as important as most IT governance frameworks are mostly focused on top management structures and decision making.

According to Padayachee (2013) there is little substantive evidence that corporate governance in South Africa has moved beyond some level of nominal and technical compliance to embrace some of the people-oriented principles that the government is striving for. ICT governance in South Africa is characterised by 'box-ticking', referring to the practice of ticking off certain areas/boxes to indicate that there was compliance with specific aspects, this is one of the challenges that both the private and public sector is struggling with and future research could address this problem.

REFERENCES

Adeyelure, H. M. D. S., & Jokonya, O. (2019). Adoption of Business Intelligence in the South African public social sector Department. In *Proceedings of 4th International Conference on the* (*Vol. 12*, pp. 157-168). Academic Press.

Agyei-Ababio, N., Ansong, E., & Assa-Agyei, K. (2023). Digitalization of revenue mobilization in an emerging economy: The new Institutional Theory perspective. *International Journal of Information Systems and Project Management, 11*(2), 5–22. doi:10.12821/ijispm110201

Ako-Nai, A., & Singh, A. M. (2019). Information technology governance framework for improving organisational performance. *South African Journal of Information Management, 21*(1), 1–11. doi:10.4102ajim.v21i1.1010

Al Omari, L., Barnes, P., & Pitman, G. (2012). Optimising COBIT 5 for IT governance: examples from the public sector. In *Proceedings of the ATISR 2012: 2nd International Conference on Applied and Theoretical Information Systems Research* (pp. 1-13). Academy of Taiwan Information Systems Research (ATISR).

Aladwani, A. M. (2001). Change management strategies for successful ERP implementation. *Business Process Management Journal, 7*(3), 266–275. doi:10.1108/14637150110392764

Anyieni, A. G., Bcom, M., & Campus, N. (2013). Effect of strategic planning on the performance of small and medium enterprises in Kenya: A summary review of the literature. *The International Journal of Professional Management, 8*(6), 1–10.

Auditor-General of South Africa (AGSA). (2019). *Consolidated General Report on the audit outcomes of local government 2017-2018*. Government Printer.

Auditor General South Africa (AGSA). (2019). *12 information technology controls*. Available online at https://www.agsa.co.za/Portals/0/Reports/PFMA/201617/GR/12%20information%20technology%20controls.pdf

Benner, M. J., & Tushman, M. L. (2003). Exploitation, exploration, and process management: The productivity dilemma revisited. *Academy of Management Review, 28*(2), 238–256. doi:10.2307/30040711

Blackman, D. A., Buick, F., O'Donnell, M. E., & Ilahee, N. (2022). Changing the conversation to create organizational change. *Journal of Change Management, 22*(3), 252–272. doi:10.1080/14697017.2022.2040570

Bowen, P. L., Cheung, M. Y. D., & Rohde, F. H. (2007). Enhancing IT governance practices: A model and case study of an organization's efforts. *International Journal of Accounting Information Systems, 8*(3), 191-221.

Campbell, J., McDonald, C., & Sethibe, T. (2010). Public and private sector IT governance: Identifying contextual differences. *AJIS. Australasian Journal of Information Systems, 16*(2). Advance online publication. doi:10.3127/ajis.v16i2.538

Cloete, F. (2012). E-government lessons from South Africa 2001-2011: institutions, state of progress and measurement: Section II: Country perspectives on e-government emergence. *The African Journal of Information and Communication, 2012*(12), 128-142.

De Haes, S., & Van Grembergen, W. (2008). Practices in IT governance and business/IT alignment. *Information Systems Control Journal, 2*, 1–5.

De Lange, J., Von Solms, R., & Gerber, M. (2015, May). *Better information security management in municipalities. In 2015 IST-Africa Conference*. IEEE.

Devadoss, P. R., Pan, S. L., & Huang, J. C. (2002). Structurational Analysis of eGovernment Initiatives: A Case Study of SCO. *Decision Support Systems, 34*(3), 253–269. doi:10.1016/S0167-9236(02)00120-3

DiMaggio, P., & Powell, W. (1983). The Iron Cage Revisited: Institutional Isomorphism and Collective Rationality in Organizational Fields. *American Sociological Review, 48*(2), 147–160. doi:10.2307/2095101

DPSA. (2012). e-Government policy. Department of Public Administration (DPSA).

Eastern Cape Spending Reviews. (2021). *Presented by D Makoni. EC SPENDING REVIEWS 2021 Improving the efficiency and effectiveness of spending on ICT in the Eastern Cape*. Available online at https://www.gtac.gov.za/wp-content/uploads/2022/05/EC_ICT_WebinarSeries.pdf

Gershon, P. (2009). *Review of the Australian Government's Use of Information and Communication Technology*. Department of Finance and Deregulation, The Australian Government Information Management Office.

Graetz, F., & Smith, A. C. (2010). Managing organizational change: A philosophies of change approach. *Journal of Change Management, 10*(2), 135–154. doi:10.1080/14697011003795602

ISO38500. (2008). *Corporate governance of information technology*. International Standards Organization.

ITGI. (2009). *IT Governance Institute*. www.itgi.org

ITIL. (2009). *What is ITIL?* Available at: http://www.itilofficalsite.com/AboutITIL/WhatisITL.asp

Janahi, L., Griffiths, M., & Al-Ammal, H. (2015, July). A conceptual model for IT governance in public sectors. In *2015 Fourth International Conference on Future Generation Communication Technology (FGCT)* (pp. 1-9). IEEE. 10.1109/FGCT.2015.7300242

Kanter, R. M., Stein, B. A., & Jick, T. D. (1992). *The Challenge of Organisational Change*. The Free Press.

Letsoalo, K., Brown, I., & Njenga, K. N. (2006). An investigation of enablers and inhibitors of IT governance implementation: A case study of a South African enterprise. In *Proceedings of the ITG International Conference* (pp. 27-35). Academic Press.

Magnusson, J., Koutsikouri, D., & Päivärinta, T. (2020). Efficiency creep and shadow innovation: Enacting ambidextrous IT Governance in the public sector. *European Journal of Information Systems, 29*(4), 329–349. doi:10.1080/0960085X.2020.1740617

March, J. G. (1991). Exploration and exploitation in organizational learning. *Organization Science, 2*(1), 71–87. doi:10.1287/orsc.2.1.71

Marshak, R. J., & Bushe, G. R. (2018). Planned and generative change in organization development. *OD Practitioner, 50*(4), 9–15.

Masilela, L., & Nel, D. (2021). The role of data and information security governance in protecting public sector data and information assets in national government in South Africa. *Africa's Public Service Delivery and Performance Review, 9*(1), 385. doi:10.4102/apsdpr.v9i1.385

Matheus, R., & Janssen, M. (2016, June). Towards an ambidextrous government: Strategies for balancing exploration and exploitation in open government. In *Proceedings of the 17th International Digital Government Research Conference on Digital Government Research* (pp. 334-341). 10.1145/2912160.2912192

McKinley, W., & Mone, M. A. (2003). Micro and macro perspectives in organization theory: a tale of incommensurability. In W. McKinley, M. Mone, H. Tsoukas, & C. Knudsen (Eds.), *The Oxford Handbook of Organization Theory* (pp. 345–372). Sage.

Nickolas, B. (2006). *Essentials of Change*. Thousands Oak.

Nxozi, M., & Flowerday, S. (2021). IT Governance Adoption and Use by State-owned Entities in South Africa: A Public Administration Perspective. In Interdisciplinary Research in Technology and Management (pp. 181-187). CRC Press. doi:10.1201/9781003202240-29

OECD. (1999). *OECD Principles of Corporate Governance*. OECD.

OECD. (2004). The OECD principles of corporate governance. *Contaduría y Administración*, 216.

Padayachee, V. (2013). Corporate governance in South Africa: from 'Old Boys Club' to 'Ubuntu'? *Transformation: Critical Perspectives on Southern Africa, 81*(1), 260–290.

Peterson, R. R. (2003). Information strategies and tactics for information technology governance. In Strategies for information technology governance. Idea Group Publishing.

Phillips, J. B. (2021). *Change happens: Practitioner use of change management strategies*. The Florida State University.

Reed, M. (2003). Open doors and brick walls: the agency/structure dilemma in organization theory. In H. Tsoukas & C. Knudsen (Eds.), *The Oxford Handbook of Organization Theory* (pp. 289–309). Sage.

Scott, W. R. (2005). Institutional theory: Contributing to a theoretical research program. *Great minds in management: The process of theory development, 37*(2), 460-484.

Sibanda, M., & von Solms, R. (2019). Devising a strategy for IT governance implementation in municipalities. A case study of South Africa. *The Electronic Journal on Information Systems in Developing Countries, 85*(2), e12067. doi:10.1002/isd2.12067

Teczke, M., Sansyzbayevna Bespayeva, R., & Olzhabayevna Bugubayeva, R. (2017). Approaches and models for change management. *Jagiellonian Journal of Management, 3*(3).

(The) Standish Group. (2004). *Third quarter research report: Chaos demographics*. Author.

Tonelli, A. O., de Souza Bermejo, P. H., Aparecida dos Santos, P., Zuppo, L., & Zambalde, A. L. (2017). IT governance in the public sector: A conceptual model. *Information Systems Frontiers*, *19*(3), 593–610. doi:10.100710796-015-9614-x

Val, I. T. (2008). *Enterprise Value: Governance of IT Investments – The Val IT Framework 2.0.* IT Governance Institute.

Val IT. (2009). *Val IT Overview*. Author.

Van Grembergen, W. (2003). Introduction to the minitrack "IT governance and its mechanisms." HICSS 2003. System Sciences, 242.

Vinten, G. (2002). The corporate governance lessons of Enron. *Corporate Governance (Bradford)*, *2*(4), 4–9. doi:10.1108/14720700210447632

Wessels, E., & Loggerenberg, J. V. (2006, September). *IT governance: theory and practice*. In *Conference on Information Technology in Tertiary Education*, Pretoria, South Africa.

Wetzel, R., & Van Gorp, L. (2014). Eighteen shades of grey? An explorative literature review into the theoretical flavours of organizational change research. *Journal of Organizational Change Management*, *27*(1), 115–146. doi:10.1108/JOCM-01-2013-0007

Wilkin, C. L., & Campbell, J. (2010). *Corporate governance of IT: A case study in an Australian government department*. Academic Press.

Wilkin, C. L., Couchman, P. K., Sohal, A., & Zutshi, A. (2016). Exploring differences between smaller and large organizations' corporate governance of information technology. *International Journal of Accounting Information Systems*, *22*, 6–25. doi:10.1016/j.accinf.2016.07.002

World Bank. (2018). *Poverty and shared prosperity 2018: Piecing together the poverty puzzle*. Author.

Wu, S. P. J., Straub, D. W., & Liang, T. P. (2015). How information technology governance mechanisms and strategic alignment influence organizational performance. *Management Information Systems Quarterly*, *39*(2), 497–518. doi:10.25300/MISQ/2015/39.2.10

KEY TERMS AND DEFINITIONS

Corporate Governance of ICT: The system by which the current and future use of ICT is directed and controlled. Corporate governance of ICT involves evaluating and directing the use of ICT to support the organisation, and monitoring this use to achieve plans. It includes the strategy and policies for using ICT within an organisation (ISO/IEC 38500: 2008: 3).

Department: A national department, a national government component, the Office of a Premier, a provincial department or a provincial government component (Public Service Act 103 of 1994, as amended) (PSA) For the purpose of the CGICTPF reference to department includes public administration in all spheres of government, organs of state ix and public enterprises as per Section 195 of the Constitution, Act No 108 of 1996, as amended.

DPSA: Department of Public Service and Administration.

Electronic Government: The use of information and communication technologies in the Public Service to improve its internal functioning and to render services to the public.

Executive Authority: In relation to – (a) the Presidency or a national government component within the President's portfolio, means the President; (b) a national department or national government component within a Cabinet portfolio, means the Minister responsible for such portfolio; (c) the Office of the Commission, means the Chairperson of the Commission; (d) the Office of a Premier or a provincial government component within a Premier's portfolio, means the Premier of that province; and (e) a provincial department or a provincial government component within an Executive Council portfolio, means the member of the Executive Council responsible for such portfolio; (PSA 103 of 1994, as amended) For the purpose of the CGICTPF the Executive Authority as defined in (a) above will refers to the Ministers in the Presidency.

Executive Management: The Executive Management of the Department and could include the Head of Department, Deputy Directors-General (DDGs) /Executive Management of the Department. This normally constitutes the Executive Committee of the Department and should include the GITO.

GITOC: Government Information Technology Officer's Council (Cabinet Memorandum 38(a) of 2000).

Governance of ICT: The effective and efficient management of IT resources to facilitate the achievement of company strategic objectives. (King III Code: 2009: 52) Is the responsibility of executives and the board of directors, and consists of the leadership, organisational structures and processes that ensure that the enterprise's IT sustains and extends the x organisation's strategy and objectives (ITGI 2005) The system by which the current and future use of IT is directed and controlled.

Chapter 13
Role of Customer Experience-Driven Business Innovation Framework for the Modern Enterprises

Vinod Kumar
https://orcid.org/0000-0002-3578-8155
Maharishi Markandeshwar (Deemed), Ambala, India

Deepa Sharma
https://orcid.org/0000-0003-4374-917X
Maharishi Markandeshwar (Deemed), Ambala, India

Sadhna Chauhan
Maharishi Markandeshwar (Deemed), Ambala, India

ABSTRACT

Every day, the business environment is changing rapidly and becoming complex, so organizations must develop new and out of the box strategies and implement such frameworks that can transform the business to another level in this competitive market. In this era, customer preference is the main differentiator, so organizations need to shift their focus to customer experience. Customer experience has become an emerging way of creating a competitive advantage. A customer experience boosts the business growth and drives the revenue for organization by making happy and loyal customers.

INTRODUCTION

Innovation is the process of creating and implementing novel ideas, products, functions, or methods that lead to advancements or improvements. It entails integrating creativity, critical analysis, and problem-solving abilities to create original solutions that solve problems or meet unmet requirements. A variety

DOI: 10.4018/979-8-3693-0458-7.ch013

of industries, including technology, research, business, medicine, education, and more, are all capable of innovation. It might involve small tweaks to current goods or services as well as ground-breaking discoveries that transform entire markets. Innovation is essential to advance and reshape the organization, society, and global future. It stimulates economic expansion, encourages competition, and results in improvements across several industries. Individuals, organizations, and societies may continue to be at the forefront of innovation and adapt to a fast-changing environment by actively searching out new ideas and welcoming change. The innovation focuses on coming up with fresh concepts, assists in spotting openings or gaps, and aids in coming up with workable solutions. It is the readiness to try new things, learn from mistakes, and modify tactics. Innovation involves flexibility and the capacity to adopt new technology, market dynamics, and customer expectations in a world that is changing quickly. The innovative strategies can focus on product innovation; process innovation, business framework innovation, service innovation, and social innovation. Successful innovative strategies make a significant difference through enhancing efficiency, addressing societal issues, providing economic value, or bettering people's lives.

The business environment is constantly evolving and becoming more complex, thus organizations must create innovative strategies and put into practice frameworks that may take their operations to the next level in this cutthroat industry (Peter Drucker, 2001). The primary differentiation in this period is consumer preference, so businesses must turn their attention to the customer experience. Business and customer experience are interwoven and essential to any company's success. Customer experience is the perception and level of happiness a customer has with a company as a result of their interactions, both before and after making a purchase. According to their contacts and experiences throughout the journey, customers form an overall opinion and perspective of a business. Every point of contact and engagement a customer has with a business is covered, including marketing, sales, customer service, and assistance following the sale. Providing exceptional service, creating value, and meeting or exceeding client expectations all contribute to a positive customer experience. It focuses on forming deep connections and enduring relationships with clients. Increased customer happiness, loyalty, good word-of-mouth, and eventually business growth can result from providing an excellent customer experience. Businesses can gain a competitive advantage, enhance customer loyalty, boost customer retention, and boost long-term profitability by prioritizing and delivering excellent client experiences (Horng et al., 2018; Sood and Kumar, 2017). The following important elements must be considered when thinking about your company's operations and clientele that lead to positive customer experience.

a) Personalization: It refers to customers tailored interactions. Businesses may deliver relevant and targeted information, recommendations, and offers by using data and customer insights. Personalization makes a closer connection with clients and improves their experience overall for businesses.
b) Recognizing customer needs: Successful companies put time and effort into recognizing the wants, preferences, and problems of their clients. Businesses can find areas for improvement and modify their goods and services by doing market research, consumer surveys, and feedback analysis.
c) Seamless cross-channel interaction: In the current digital era, customers need a seamless interaction across many touch points and channels, including as websites, mobile apps, social media, and physical stores. To provide a seamless and satisfying experience, businesses should work to deliver consistent messaging, branding, and customer service across all platforms.

d) Increasing client loyalty: Return customers are a company's most valuable resource. Customer loyalty can be increased through loyalty programs, personalized rewards, and proactive involvement. Businesses may create enduring connections with their customers by constantly providing excellent experiences.
e) User-friendly interfaces: Companies should concentrate on designing user-friendly interfaces for all digital products, including e-commerce websites, mobile apps, and customer portals. A positive consumer experience is facilitated by intuitive navigation, concise product descriptions, simple checkout procedures, and responsive design.
f) Outstanding customer service: A positive client experience depends on prompt and efficient customer service. Customers' questions, problems, and complaints should be handled by customer service employees who are well-trained, confident, and empathetic.
g) Constant improvement: Organizations must continually evaluate and enhance their client experiences. It is essential to solicit feedback from customers and actively use it to improve products, services, and processes. Regularly analyzing customer data and implementing changes based on customer insights helps refine the experience.
h) User-Friendliness: It means that organizations must provide simple and seamless interactions across a range of platforms, including websites, mobile apps, and physical storefronts. Process streamlining and reducing consumer effort can significantly improve the experience.
i) Effective communication: It is characterized by timely and accurate communication throughout the client journey. This involves giving access to up-to-date product information, order progress updates, and helpful customer service. Delivering a consistent experience across various touch points and channels is need of the hour. Every time a buyer interacts with an organization, they expect a similar level of experience and quality because consistency fosters reliability and confidence.
j) Empathy and Support: It states that organization must show a sincere interest in comprehending demands and worries of the consumer. Problem-solving skills, proactive support, and compassionate customer service can have a big impact on the overall experience.
k) Employee Engagement: Customers' experiences can be greatly impacted by engaged, empowered staffs that are passionate about providing superior service. Better customer encounters can result from spending money on employee development, rewards, and fostering a happy work atmosphere.

Companies that place a high priority on the customer experience frequently create customer-centric strategies, make investments in technology and tools to improve customer interactions, and set up metrics to gauge and track client loyalty and satisfaction. The customer experience is about more than simply ensuring customer satisfaction—it's also about cultivating brand ambassadors who will help spread the word about and recommend your company to others. Increased customer happiness, brand loyalty, and eventually business success may all be attributed to good customer experiences. The importance of customer experience-driven business innovation in contemporary organizations is highlighted in this chapter. The chapter examines how, in the modern business environment, customer experience has become a key factor in influencing consumer thoughts, satisfaction, loyalty, and advocacy leading to competitive advantage. The background section explores the idea of a business innovation framework that is built around the customer experience. It describes the main elements and principles of the innovation framework, explaining the necessity of customer-centricity throughout the entire innovation process. The chapter also looks at the technological developments that have made it possible for contemporary businesses to efficiently gather, analyze, and use client data. It delves into the use of artificial intelligence, machine learning, and big data analytics to gain deeper customer insights and create personalized experiences. The next section emphasizes the various challenges faced by businesses in incorporating a customer-centric innovation framework along with possible solutions. Real-world case studies are used to further debate regarding customer experience-driven approaches to innovation. These examples show how companies have used data, customer feedback, and insights to pinpoint problems and new trends, and then transformed those findings into creative solutions, or business models. The last section emphasizes that successful modern businesses use customer experience as a strategic differentiator. With the adoption of a customer experience framework businesses will experience long-term growth and sustained success in a highly competitive business environment. The organization can focus on emerging technologies like augmented reality, virtual reality, and the Internet of Things (IOT) that will influence customer experience frameworks in the future. These study fields can offer insightful information about enhancing and developing customer experience frameworks. Organizations can continue to improve consumer experiences and create competitive advantage by filling in these research gaps.

BACKGROUND

The rise of commerce and the evolution of business practices are both entwined with the history of customer experience (CX). Although the idea of putting the needs of consumers first has been around for centuries, the formalization and acknowledgment of customer experience as a separate field is a relatively recent development. Figure 1 represents a synopsis of customer experience history.

Figure 1. History of customer experience

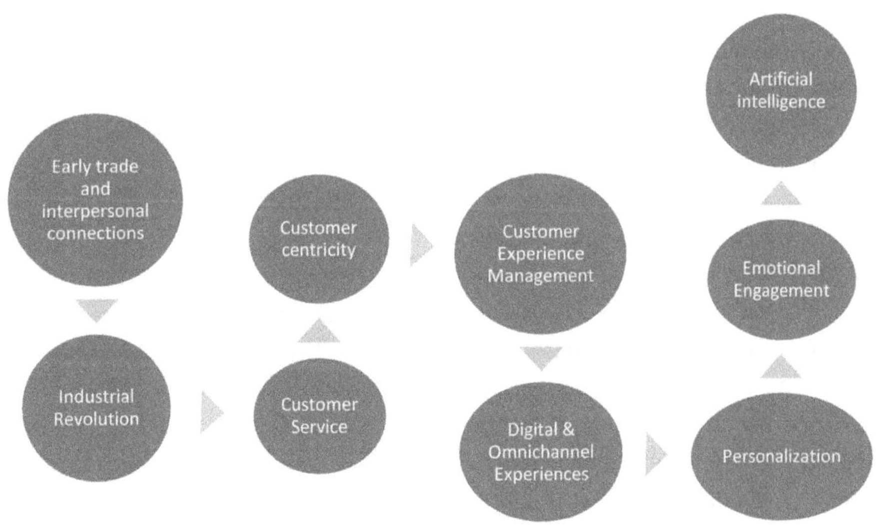

Stage 1 - Early Trade and Interpersonal Connections: Personal connections were very important in ancient times when trade and commerce were done through bartering and small-scale transactions. Direct interaction between buyers and sellers occurred, and word-of-mouth marketing, reputation, and trust were frequently crucial to a company's success.

Stage 2 - Industrial Revolution and Mass Production: The Industrial Revolution brought tremendous changes in trade and manufacturing during the 18th and 19th centuries. The progress of department stores and early retail chains was facilitated by the ability for corporations to produce things on a massive scale through mass production. Customer encounters, however, grew less personal and less frequently personalized.

Stage 3 - Development of Customer Service: At the beginning of the 20th century, companies realized the value of attending to the requirements and concerns of their clients. The idea of assisting, settling grievances, and assuring customer pleasure became popular. During this period, call centers and customer service divisions were established.

Stage 4 - Customer-Centricity: As rivalry grew in the late 20th century, firms began to recognize the need to place customers at the center of their operations. They started to realize that happy customers may be loyal, do business again, and spread good word of mouth. The emergence of customer-centric strategies and practices was a result of this transformation.

Stage 5 - Customer Experience Management's Development: Customer Experience Management (CEM) emerged as a strategic strategy in the late 1990s and early 2000s. CEM placed a strong emphasis on the comprehensive management of all customer touchpoints and interactions with a business for generating dependable and memorable experiences. To collect consumer input, analyze data, and improve customer experience efforts, businesses began investing in technologies.

Stage 6 - Digital Revolution and Omni-Channel Experiences: The internet and mobile devices, in particular, have revolutionized how customers interact with brands. Businesses are now able to communicate with customers through a variety of digital channels thanks to e-commerce and internet platforms. The idea of Omni-channel customer experiences emerged when the emphasis switched to delivering seamless and integrated experiences across many touch points.

Stage 7 - Personalization and Customization: Companies started using customer insights to personalize and customize their offers as a result of the abundance of data and advanced analytics. By adjusting experiences depending on customers' interests, behavior, and demographics, businesses were able to increase customer happiness and loyalty.

Stage 8 - Experience Economy and Emotional Engagement: Creating emotionally compelling experiences has become increasingly important in recent years. Businesses have realized that customers want unique and meaningful interactions and that those that can arouse good feelings and create emotional bonds will stand out in the market.

Stage 9 - Future Trends: Augmented Reality (AR), Virtual Reality (VR), Chatbots, and Artificial Intelligence (AI) are likely to play a larger role in customer experience in the future. Key factors are anticipated to include hyper-personalization, real-time responsiveness, and the ethical use of client data.

In general, the history of customer experience illustrates how businesses and customers' relationships have changed through time, with a rising understanding of the significance of providing outstanding experiences at every stage of the customer journey. Businesses may stand out from rivals, cultivate client loyalty, and ultimately promote corporate success by putting a strong emphasis on delivering a great customer experience.

Literature Review

The paradigm that drives value in marketing has seen a substantial transformation over the previous few decades. It is shifting from creating brands to delivering excellent marketing to currently creating compelling customer experiences. In order to increase the intrinsic utility of the products and services, Payne & Frow (2005) advocated a change in organizational strategies that would focus the customer service component. The authors believed that while product marketing alone was not sufficient for competitive advantage organizations should focus primarily on customer relationship management as a way to create value. Shortly after this significant transition, the expansion of the Internet prompted a second one. Relationship marketing became a common component of goods and services thanks to the Internet's lower entry barrier for relationship-centric strategy implementation (Ngai, 2005). The advent of the internet made it possible for users to communicate and share their experiences on online forums frequently without the company's involvement, which made it more difficult to create a successful customer relationship strategy (Vermeulen et al., 2009; Duan et al., 2008).

Although researchers agree that customer experience should be of utmost importance for organizations, there were fewer consensuses among them on both its exact definition and its measurement. Customer experience refers to the learning that occurs as a result of participating in or observing an event (Collins, 2007); others have defined experience as how a customer feels about the company at each point of contact (Swinyard, 1993). Gentile et al., (2007) described customers' experiences as "strictly personal and imply the customer's involvement at different levels (rational, emotional, sensorial, physical, and spiritual)". Verhoef et al. (2009) acknowledged that customers may perceive value through any part of this journey, including those elements that are not directly under the company's control, such as other consumers, culture, and the overall state of the economy. Customer experience (CX) is defined as the psychological, physiological, bodily, sensory, and social reactions elicited by one or more market actors (De Keyser et al., 2015). The fundamental experience concept is based on consumer engagement with employees and technology and a certain degree of individuality for better-personalized experiences.

The framework for optimizing the customer experience through enhanced business processes was introduced by Botha, Kruger, and De Vries in 2010. By combining numerous well-known strategies into a single complete framework, they created the Enhanced Customer Experience Framework (ECEF) based on simulation, business process re-engineering (BPR), and quality function deployment (QFD). QFD, prioritized business processes from the viewpoint of the customer and to ascertain the association between consumer requirements and business processes. The simulation model was used to assess the effects of process improvements on the experience of customers and BPR along with the benchmarking steps to meet customer needs. A Customer Experience Framework (CEF) that explains the customer's journey has been proposed by Nasution et al. (2014). In their framework, there were five interconnected layers: (1) Accumulated Customer Experience: (2) Customer Values, Needs, and Wants; (3) Experiential Marketing Strategy; (4) Customer Experience Stages; (5) A shift in consumer behavior.

To identify parallels and contrasts across various techniques of customer experience analysis, (Havir, 2017) examined their outcomes. In the first phase, the dimensions and components of the customer experience were taken from the seven models to analyze the customer experience and were compared. A collection of dimensions and factors were produced as a result. The last phase involved extracting customer experience elements and dimensions from 17 applicable customer experience research articles. To create a new universal set of dimensions and address the fragmentation problem, the dimensions and factors were finally grouped based on their descriptions and discovered similarities. Keiningham et al.

(2020) conceptualization of the connection between business framework and customer experience made a positive contribution to the literature on CX. They highlighted the potential for research to further innovate and gave managers a practical framework to model customer framework that supports customer experience-driven new offerings.

Customer experience is a key factor in ensuring customer happiness, establishing benchmarks for expectations, winning over loyal customers, and generating bonds with customers (Singh et al., 2021). Mihardjo, et al. (2019) proposed an Online Customer Experience-Attitude Behaviour Context model for online grocery retailing. The outcomes showed that the convenience, recuperation, and delivery experiences had a substantial influence on the attitude. To improve online consumers' attitudes and repurchase intentions, it may be a good approach for online grocery retailers to periodically include customers in co-creating a delightful online customer experience. Nuseir, M., & Elrefae, G. (2022) found that customer experience also influences social media marketing and consumer-based brand equity in the hospitality industry. Trivedi, J. (2019) & Barbu, et al. (2021) found that fintech companies can provide enhanced technological options (chatbots) on their websites for enhancing customer experience. Customers who are comfortable with technological advancements can drastically cut down on customer support expenses for banks, thereby improving profitability.

Customer Experience and Business Innovation

A key factor in determining a company's success and expansion is the interaction between customer experience and business innovation. When a customer interacts with a business, their impression and pleasure as a whole are referred to as their customer experience. This includes how they feel about the company's products, services, support, and overall brand interactions. Business innovation, on the other hand, refers to the development and use of novel concepts, procedures, goods, or services that enhance an organization's performance, give it a competitive edge, or provide value. The relationship between customer experience and business innovation is explained based on parameters like Customer-driven innovation that assesses the needs of the customer which serves as a rich source of knowledge and ideas for innovation. Businesses can find possibilities for innovation that directly address the wants, problems, and preferences of their customers by knowing those needs, issues, and preferences. Survey results, data analytics, and customer feedback are all excellent sources of inspiration for creative solutions. It provides differentiation and competitive advantage to the organization. A modern enterprise can stand out from its rivals by providing great customer service. Businesses may boost customer retention, foster customer loyalty, and draw in new clients by continually providing excellent experiences. Innovation is essential for developing distinctive, memorable experiences that distinguish a business and provide it with a competitive advantage.

Today's consumers need experiences that are customized to their specific demands and tastes. Businesses can innovate by creating cutting-edge technology, data analytics tools, and customer relationship management platforms that enable mass personalization. Companies can provide tailored experiences that resonate with their customers by utilizing cutting-edge solutions. Business innovation aids organizations in keeping up with rapidly evolving consumer preferences and industry trends. Businesses can respond to changing market dynamics by proactively innovating and launching new products, services, or processes to satisfy rising client needs. Companies may remain competitive and relevant by adopting this forward-thinking strategy. New strategies like gamification, social media platforms, and interactive technologies can greatly increase customer engagement. Businesses may boost customer involvement, build brand support, and produce favorable word-of-mouth recommendations by developing distinctive and interactive experiences. Innovation is fueled by a customer-centric mindset, and innovation improves the customer experience. Businesses may create extraordinary experiences, set themselves apart in the market, and enjoy long-term success by utilizing new tactics, technology, and procedures.

Customer Experience-Driven Business Innovation Framework

It is a tactical strategy that centers the innovation process on the customer experience. It places a strong emphasis on identifying and satisfying customer requirements, problems, and desires as the main engine of corporate innovation.

Figure 2 represents the main steps of the Customer experience-driven business innovation framework strategy.

1. Customer Insight: It refers to knowing your customers well before hand. Organizations must conduct market research, gather customer feedback, and analyze customer data for determining customers' requirements, preferences, and issues. Business can use tools like customer journey mapping for visualizing the customer experience and pinpoint opportunities for improvement.
2. Brainstorming: Business must promote cross-functional cooperation and ideation sessions to provide creative solutions that specifically address the uncovered customer insights. This can be achieved by establishing a culture that values and promotes feedback from all organizational levels.
3. Prioritization: The Company must assess and rank the developed ideas and analyze how well they might affect your company's objectives and the client experience. The account elements like market trends, competitive advantage, market viability, and customer value can be considered.
4. Prototyping: Create minimum viable products (MVPs) or prototypes to test and validate your concepts. Physical items, digital user interfaces, and even process changes can all be included in these prototypes. To guarantee that the prototypes meet the needs and expectations of the customers, involve them in the testing and feedback process.
5. Iterative Development: Business must continuously refine and iterate on the prototypes based on customer feedback and insights. They should use an agile development approach to quickly adapt and make improvements. This iterative process helps ensure that the final product or service aligns with customer expectations.
6. Implementation: It means to put the prototype into practice on a larger scale after it has been approved. Create a thorough execution plan, taking into account variables like available resources, the time frame, and any potential effects on current systems and procedures. All necessary departments and stakeholders should be included to guarantee a smooth transfer.
7. Measurement and Feedback: Create key performance indicators (KPIs) to gauge how the innovation has affected customer satisfaction. Gather consumer feedback regularly to gauge happiness and spot any areas that could have improvement. Utilize this criticism to improve and streamline the innovation. Keep up a culture of continuous improvement by analyzing and revising your innovation plan frequently in light of industry changes and customer input. Leverage new technologies, industry best practices, and customer feedback to stay ahead of the competition and consistently deliver an exceptional customer experience.

Figure 2. Customer experience-driven business innovation framework strategy

Keep in mind that the framework for customer experience-driven business innovation is a continuous activity. It calls for a dedication to comprehend client wants and preferences, as well as openness to innovation and a readiness to change. Businesses may stand out, encourage customer loyalty, and achieve sustainable growth by utilizing the customer experience as a driver for innovation.

Models of Customer Experience-Driven Business Innovation Framework

The multiple models have been defined by various researchers and organizations for enhancing the customer experience.

Customer Experience Business Innovation Model - To match customer values and business strategic needs, Keiningham *et al.*, (2020) suggested a framework for customer experience-driven business model innovation. This model consists of two parts: Component 1 is a Customer Experience Profile based on the cognitive, sensory, physical, emotional, and social dimensions of the customer experience. Component 2 is based on the Strategic Orientation Profile, which focuses on cost leadership, differentiation, and focus strategies. Both components are brought into alignment to improve the consumer experience.

Deloitte: Customer Experience Model – This framework has identified four components: a) Structure and functions b) People & talent c) Governance & power d) Data & Systems. The model states that the organization's customer experience initiatives and cross-functional collaboration are required to change as per the need of the hour. Businesses may develop internal competencies, and agile teams, and sustain a high retention rate through continuous development programs for employees. A transparent measuring and reporting culture, along with clear incentives and enablement supported by resources and budgets, are necessary for an effective governance style. Clear processes for value creation and ownership of data management are required in digital organizations. The firm must make sure that the initiatives support the broad business objectives and are unmistakably related to the brand strategy. The objective is to produce quantifiable value for the business and its clients. Businesses must make sure that their strategy translates their brand strategy into the ideal brand experience across all touch points.

McKinsey: Customer Experience Framework - The formula for implementing customer experience transformations was provided by McKinsey also. It consists of three fundamental building blocks: understanding customer aspiration; transforming the business based on aspirations of customers and implementing the business. The company's purpose and brand promise are delivered when the vision for the customer experience is well understood. For instance, BMW aims to provide the pinnacle of driving experiences, Starbucks aims to deliver nurturing experiences, and Nike aims to create inspirational experiences. In the new normal, customer experience is a competitive advantage. Companies can hope to come out of the crisis with a sustainable edge over their rivals only by committing to the three CX transformation building blocks.

Customer Experience (CX) Metrics

CX metrics are key performance indicators (KPIs) that companies use to monitor and evaluate the caliber of client interactions and experiences with their brands, goods, and services. Depending on their objectives and sector, many organizations may concentrate on various CX indicators; however some of the more typical ones are as follows: a) Customer Satisfaction Score (CSAT): The CSAT asks consumers to rate their satisfaction on a scale, such as 1 to 5 or 1 to 10, to determine how satisfied they are with a particular contact or experience. b) Net Promoter Score (NPS): The NPS asks customers a single question: "On a scale of 0 to 10, how likely are you to recommend our product/service to a friend or colleague?" NPS gauges customer loyalty and satisfaction. Customers are divided into Promoters (9–10), Passives (7-8), and Detractors (0–6) based on their responses. By deducting the percentage of Detractors from the percentage of Promoters, NPS is derived. c) Customer Lifetime Value (CLV): It is a measure of the overall value that a customer is projected to contribute to a business throughout their relationship. It aids companies in prioritizing their efforts to keep valuable clients. d) Customer engagement: It is a metric that assesses how actively customers engage with a business, whether through website visits, social media interactions or app usage. Higher engagement frequently denotes a happier experience. e) Customer Retention & Churn Rate: Customer retention metric counts the proportion of customers a business has kept over a given period. It illustrates the business's capacity to keep a devoted clientele whereas churn rate measures the rate at which clients leave a business over a given time frame. High turnover rates may be a sign of unhappiness or a lack of effort to keep customers. f) Customer Feedback - Monitoring and analyzing client complaints and feedback provide insightful information about areas that want improvement and aid in comprehending customer pain spots. g) Customer Referral Rate: This statistic measures the volume of new customers brought in by way of customer recommendations, revealing the degree of happiness and loyalty among current clients.

To make informed decisions and continuously enhance the customer experience, organizations must constantly measure and analyze key CX KPIs. These indicators assist businesses in determining customer satisfaction levels, pinpointing areas for development, and assessing the success of their customer service and support initiatives. To select the most applicable CX metrics for their organization, firms should also take into account their unique aims, sectors, and clientele.

CHALLENGES

A customer experience framework's implementation can be a difficult task that comes with several difficulties. There are some typical issues that organizations could experience while implementing the framework such as a) Organization alignment: One of the major problems is making sure that all departments and stakeholders are committed to providing a uniform customer experience. To do this, silos must be dismantled, cross-functional communication must be established, and a common understanding of the customer experience must be developed. b) Data Integration & Analysis: Customer experience frameworks rely on data integration and analysis to get insights and make defensible decisions. However, organizations frequently experience difficulties integrating data from many systems and sources. It can sometimes be difficult to analyze and get useful insights from the data, particularly when working with massive amounts of data. c) Understanding customer expectations: Organizations may also struggle with effectively capturing and utilizing customer feedback to drive improvements. Customers' preferences and needs are constantly evolving, and organizations must continually gather feedback, conduct research, and monitor trends to stay ahead. d) Employee engagement and training: Employees plays an essential role in providing a pleasant client experience. However, organizations frequently struggle to motivate and develop their workforce so that they can regularly exceed client expectations. It calls for effective communication, continual training, and fostering a customer-centric culture throughout the entire organization. e) Technology implementation and integration: Implementing a customer experience framework frequently entails the use of a variety of technologies, including customer relationship management (CRM) systems, tools for gathering customer feedback, analytics platforms, and more. It can be difficult to integrate these technologies and make sure they perform well together; this requires technical know-how and careful planning. f) Measurement issues: Determining opportunities for improvement in a customer experience framework requires measuring the framework's efficacy. Organizations may find it difficult to define and apply the right metrics and key performance indicators (KPIs) for evaluating the effectiveness of their activities. It might be difficult to match these indicators with organizational objectives and make sure they truly reflect customer experience. g) Change management: Putting in place a customer experience framework frequently necessitates adjustments to organizational culture, systems, and processes. It might be difficult to properly manage change and win over staff members of all ranks. Organizations must communicate, involve workers, and resolve their worries and opposition for successful implementation. A comprehensive and strategic strategy, leadership commitment, continual monitoring, and adjustments based on consumer feedback and data analyses are necessary for overcoming these problems. Iterative processes call for constant adjustment and improvement to meet changing client expectations.

SOLUTIONS

Several variables can affect implementation of customer experience framework. The adoption of a customer experience framework can be substantially impacted by the current culture inside an organization. The framework is more likely to be accepted and successfully applied if the business has a customer-centric culture that values and prioritizes customer pleasure. The successful deployment of a customer experience framework depends on strong leadership support. It helps to create a feeling of urgency and motivates staff to adopt the framework when executives show their dedication and actively promote a customer-centric mindset throughout the organization. Implementing a customer experience framework depends critically on employee involvement and engagement. Employees must be aware of the significance of providing excellent client experiences and have access to the resources. Employees are more likely to adopt the framework and provide superior client experiences when they are motivated and engaged. Employee understanding of the customer experience framework's goals, objectives, and expectations depends on effective communication. Employees and stakeholders can be brought together via clear and consistent communication to ensure that everyone is working towards the same goals. Accurate and timely customer insights and data should serve as the foundation of any customer experience strategy. The framework's design and implementation can benefit from the market research, data analytics, and customer feedback that are gathered and analyzed. Across numerous teams and departments within an organization, cooperation and coordination are frequently necessary for the successful implementation of a customer experience framework. The seamless delivery of consistent and great client experiences can be hampered by siloed approaches. A customer experience framework should be adaptable and flexible because customer expectations and preferences are always changing. It needs to permit ongoing development based on comments and altering consumer requirements. Organizations that prioritize continual framework review, measurement, and optimization are more likely to be successful in doing so. The capacity to deploy a customer experience framework depends on the infrastructure's readiness and efficiency. Business must facilitate effective communication, and support the delivery of seamless and personalized experiences for gathering and analyzing consumer data. Organizations must have the required tools and processes in place. The customer experience framework must be implemented with sufficient financial, human, and time resources. The proper implementation and durability of the framework may be hampered by insufficient resources. The competitive environment and industry dynamics may also have an impact on how a customer experience framework is implemented. Organizations can set realistic goals and stand out in terms of customer experience by being aware of rivals' strategies and industry benchmarks. Organizations can improve their chances of a successful implementation and reap the rewards of a customer experience framework by taking these elements into account and effectively addressing them.

Applications of Customer Experience-Driven Business Innovation Framework

Computer programs are some cutting-edge marketing tools that assist marketers in enhancing the customer experience through the use of artificial intelligence (AI) techniques. These tools can aid with task automation, campaign optimization, data analysis, and improved decision-making. AI-powered chatbots, such as ChatGpt may assist businesses for interacting with clients, responding to questions, giving individualized advice, and even complete transactions. The AI-based content generation technologies makes blog posts, social media captions, and product descriptions content writing easy. They can provide subject recommendations, grammar checks, and even writing style impersonation. AI-powered social media management platforms provide tools including content scheduling, sentiment analysis, social listening, and automated answers for increasing engagement and performance. AI-powered voice assistants, like Amazon's Alexa or Google Assistant, can do this. AI is used by modern CRM systems to collect and analyze customer data, forecast consumer behavior, and give sales and marketing teams actionable insights. It's crucial to remember that new tools are being created on continuous basis due to changing AI marketing tools and their environment.

Amazon Go Stores

One of the best examples of customer experience innovation is found in Amazon Go stores. Customers benefit from a smooth and seamless buying experience at these convenience stores without cashiers. Tillman (2020) refers to it as "a new kind of store with no checkout required". There are no store clerks; instead, clients' phones have an application (app) that serves as their replacement. The artificial intelligence that powers this app consists of sensor fusion technology, deep learning algorithms, and computer vision. As items are picked up and as they leave the store, the system registers them. The app automatically matches clients and products. The system acquires information about inventory and workflow as well as client preferences and actions concerning products at any given time continuously. Amazon Go stores enhance the customer experience by removing the checkout lines. Customers can simply enter the store, grab the items they need, and walk out. The innovative "Just Walk Out" technology uses a combination of computer vision, sensor fusion, and deep learning algorithms to automatically detect items taken or returned to shelves. Amazon Go stores cater to customers' desire for convenience and speed. The elimination of traditional checkout processes saves customers time, allowing them to quickly grab what they need and leave the store. This is particularly beneficial for customers looking for a quick and efficient shopping experience. The Amazon Go app provides a personalized experience, allowing customers to view receipts, access virtual shopping carts, and receive personalized recommendations based on their purchase history. Amazon Go stores offer a wide variety of products, including fresh food, snacks, beverages, and grocery essentials. The selection is based on the needs and preferences of customers in the local area. The stores often include a mix of national brands and Amazon's private label products. This customer experience innovation framework helps in leveraging customer data from the Amazon Go app and provides personalized recommendations and offers. The app tracks customer preferences and purchasing history, enabling Amazon to offer tailored suggestions for future purchases. The store employees only focus on enhancing the overall shopping experience by answering questions, restocking shelves, and ensuring the store's cleanliness and organization. Amazon has expanded its Go stores to various locations, increasing accessibility for customers. This expansion allows a broader customer base to experience the convenience and innovation offered by the cashier-less shopping experience. Overall, Amazon Go stores exemplify a customer-centric approach by leveraging cutting-edge technology to provide a seamless, efficient, and personalized shopping experience. By eliminating friction points and leveraging customer data, Amazon can deliver a customer experience that is convenient, enjoyable, and tailored to individual preferences.

Lenskart

Lenskart is a large retail network for prescription glasses headquartered in Gurugram, India. Lenskart has more than 2,000 retail stores. To improve the customer experience, Lenskart has implemented Virtual Augmented Reality, an application that streamlines the process of purchasing sunglasses and eyeglasses online. This application enables you to scan and analyze your face, identify your face shape and temple size, and then receive recommendations for the ideal frames for you. The way people buy eyewear online has been revolutionized by technology and it is now much more easy and pleasant. Customers now find the process to be much more fun and convenient, and it has also helped to lower the likelihood of returns and exchanges.

CONCLUSION

Organizations looking to provide excellent customer experiences and achieving a competitive edge must implement a customer experience framework. It does have some difficulties though. Organizations must have a strategic and holistic mentality while implementing a customer experience framework to overcome these obstacles. Leadership commitment, clear communication, continual monitoring, and a readiness to change based on consumer feedback and data analysis are necessary for a successful deployment. It is an iterative process that calls for constant improvement and steadfast attention for designing and delivering exceptional client experiences. Organizations may develop solid customer relationships, encourage customer loyalty, and ultimately achieve sustainable business success in cutthroat economy by investing in a customer experience framework and solving the issues that come with it.

FUTURE RESEARCH DIRECTIONS

Although there has been a lot of research on customer experience frameworks, there are still many areas where research may be done in the future to improve our comprehension and use of these frameworks. Future studies on Omnichannel and multichannel experiences can look at the effects of feelings and sensory components on the client experience. Researchers may also concentrate on the adaptability and applicability of customer experience frameworks in various cultural contexts and marketplaces. An investigation regarding ethical aspects of the consumer experience such as privacy issues, data utilization, and transparency must be conducted. One can research how emerging technologies like augmented reality, virtual reality, blockchain, and the Internet of Things will influence customer experience frameworks in the future. These study fields can offer insightful information about enhancing and developing customer experience frameworks, assuring their efficacy and relevance in a constantly shifting corporate environment. Organizations can continue to improve consumer experiences and create competitive advantage by filling in these research gaps.

REFERENCES

Barbu, C. M., Florea, D. L., Dabija, D. C., & Barbu, M. C. R. (2021). Customer experience in fintech. *Journal of Theoretical and Applied Electronic Commerce Research*, *16*(5), 1415–1433. doi:10.3390/jtaer16050080

Botha, G. J., Kruger, P. S., & De Vries, M. (2012). Enhancing customer experience through business process improvement: An application of the Enhanced Customer Experience Framework (ECEF). *South African Journal of Industrial Engineering*, *23*(1), 39–56.

Botha, J., Kruger, P., & De Vries, M. (2010). *Enhancing customer experience through business process improvement*. Framework.

Bough, V., Breuer, R., Maechler, N., & Ungerman, K. (2020, October 27). *The three building blocks of successful customer-experience transformations.* McKinsey & Company. https://www.mckinsey.com/capabilities/growth-marketing-and-sales/our-insights/the-three-building-blocks-of-successful-customer-experience-transformations

Butterworth Collins. (2007). *Collins English dictionary*. Author.

De Keyser, A., Lemon, K. N., Klaus, P., & Keiningham, T. L. (2015). A framework for understanding and managing the customer experience. *Marketing Science Institute Working Paper Series, 85*(1), 15-121.

Delloite Digital. (2019, August). *How the right CX Operating Model can pave the way to future success.* Deloitte Touche Tohmatsu Limited. https://www2.deloitte.com/content/dam/Deloitte/de/Documents/technology/Deloitte_Digital_CX_Operating_Model_PoV.pdf

Drucker, P. F. (2001). Innovation and Management. *Wirtschaft und Politik, Düsseldorf, 1985*, 368.

Duan, W., Gu, B., & Whinston, A. B. (2008). Do online reviews matter?—An empirical investigation of panel data. *Decision Support Systems, 45*(4), 1007–1016. doi:10.1016/j.dss.2008.04.001

Garg, A. (2021, April 21). *Using Augmented reality to drive real business.* Lenskart Blogs. https://blog.lenskart.com/using-augmented-reality-to-drive-real-business-edd3b0244503

Gentile, C., Spiller, N., & Noci, G. (2007). How to sustain the customer experience: An overview of experience components that co-create value with the customer. *European Management Journal, 25*(5), 395–410. doi:10.1016/j.emj.2007.08.005

Havíř, D. (2017). A Comparison Of The Approaches To Customer Experience Analysis. *Economics & Business, 31*(1).

Horng, J. S., Hsu, H., & Tsai, C. Y. (2018). An assessment model of corporate social responsibility practice in the tourism industry. *Journal of Sustainable Tourism, 26*(7), 1085–1104. doi:10.1080/09669582.2017.1388384

Keiningham, T., Aksoy, L., Bruce, H. L., Cadet, F., Clennell, N., Hodgkinson, I. R., & Kearney, T. (2020). Customer experience driven business model innovation. *Journal of Business Research, 116*, 431–440. doi:10.1016/j.jbusres.2019.08.003

Mihardjo, L., Sasmoko, S., Alamsjah, F., & Elidjen, E. (2019). Digital leadership role in developing business model innovation and customer experience orientation in Industry 4.0. *Management Science Letters, 9*(11), 1749–1762. doi:10.5267/j.msl.2019.6.015

Nasution, R. A., Sembada, A. Y., Miliani, L., Resti, N. D., & Prawono, D. A. (2014). The customer experience framework as baseline for strategy and implementation in services marketing. *Procedia: Social and Behavioral Sciences, 148*, 254–261. doi:10.1016/j.sbspro.2014.07.041

Ngai, E. W. (2005). Customer relationship management research (1992-2002): An academic literature review and classification. *Marketing Intelligence & Planning, 23*(6), 582–605. doi:10.1108/02634500510624147

Nuseir, M., & Elrefae, G. (2022). The effects of facilitating conditions, customer experience, and brand loyalty on customer-based brand equity through social media marketing. *International Journal of Data and Network Science*, *6*(3), 875–884. doi:10.5267/j.ijdns.2022.2.009

Payne, A., & Frow, P. (2005). A strategic framework for customer relationship management. *Journal of Marketing*, *69*(4), 167–176. doi:10.1509/jmkg.2005.69.4.167

Sharma, S. (2021, August 11). *Lenskart plans to hire over 2,000 employees in India by next year.* Mint. https://www.livemint.com/companies/news/lenskart-plans-to-hire-over-2-000-employees-in-india-by-next-year-11628679429872.html

Singh, G., Slack, N., Sharma, S., Mudaliar, K., Narayan, S., Kaur, R., & Sharma, K. U. (2021). Antecedents involved in developing fast-food restaurant customer loyalty. *The TQM Journal*, *33*(8), 1753–1769. doi:10.1108/TQM-07-2020-0163

Sood, A., & Kumar, V. (2017). Analyzing client profitability across diffusion segments for a continuous innovation. *JMR, Journal of Marketing Research*, *54*(6), 932–951. doi:10.1509/jmr.16.0209

Swinyard, W. R. (1993). The effects of mood, involvement, and quality of store experience on shopping intentions. *The Journal of Consumer Research*, *20*(2), 271–280. doi:10.1086/209348

Tillman, M. (2020, February 25). *What is Amazon Go, where is it, and how does it work?* Pocket-lint. https://www.pocket-lint.com/phones/news/amazon/139650-what-is-amazongo-where-is-it-and-how-does-it-work

Trivedi, J. (2019). Examining the customer experience of using banking chatbots and its impact on brand love: The moderating role of perceived risk. *Journal of Internet Commerce*, *18*(1), 91–111. doi:10.1080/15332861.2019.1567188

Verhoef, P. C., Lemon, K. N., Parasuraman, A., Roggeveen, A., Tsiros, M., & Schlesinger, L. A. (2009). Customer experience creation: Determinants, dynamics and management strategies. *Journal of Retailing*, *85*(1), 31–41. doi:10.1016/j.jretai.2008.11.001

Vermeulen, I. E., & Seegers, D. (2009). Tried and tested: The impact of online hotel reviews on consumer consideration. *Tourism Management*, *30*(1), 123–127. doi:10.1016/j.tourman.2008.04.008

ADDITIONAL READING

Ban, H. J., & Kim, H. S. (2019). Understanding customer experience and satisfaction through airline passengers' online reviews. *Sustainability (Basel)*, *11*(15), 4066. doi:10.3390u11154066

Becker, L., & Jaakkola, E. (2020). Customer experience: Fundamental premises and implications for research. *Journal of the Academy of Marketing Science*, *48*(4), 630–648. doi:10.100711747-019-00718-x

Chen, J. S., Le, T. T. Y., & Florence, D. (2021). Usability and responsiveness of artificial intelligence chatbot on online customer experience in e-retailing. *International Journal of Retail & Distribution Management*, *49*(11), 1512–1531. doi:10.1108/IJRDM-08-2020-0312

Godovykh, M., & Tasci, A. D. (2020). Customer experience in tourism: A review of definitions, components, and measurements. *Tourism Management Perspectives, 35*, 100694. doi:10.1016/j.tmp.2020.100694

Khan, I., Hollebeek, L. D., Fatma, M., Islam, J. U., & Riivits-Arkonsuo, I. (2020). Customer experience and commitment in retailing: Does customer age matter? *Journal of Retailing and Consumer Services, 57*, 102219. doi:10.1016/j.jretconser.2020.102219

Kuppelwieser, V. G., & Klaus, P. (2021). Measuring customer experience quality: The EXQ scale revisited. *Journal of Business Research, 126*, 624–633. doi:10.1016/j.jbusres.2020.01.042

Lemon, K. N., & Verhoef, P. C. (2016). Understanding customer experience throughout the customer journey. *Journal of Marketing, 80*(6), 69–96. doi:10.1509/jm.15.0420

Pei, X. L., Guo, J. N., Wu, T. J., Zhou, W. X., & Yeh, S. P. (2020). Does the effect of customer experience on customer satisfaction create a sustainable competitive advantage? A comparative study of different shopping situations. *Sustainability (Basel), 12*(18), 7436. doi:10.3390u12187436

Rather, R. A. (2020). Customer experience and engagement in tourism destinations: The experiential marketing perspective. *Journal of Travel & Tourism Marketing, 37*(1), 15–32. doi:10.1080/10548408.2019.1686101

KEY TERMS AND DEFINITIONS

Artificial Intelligence (AI): AI is the branch of technology that develops intelligent machines for carrying out tasks that traditionally require human intelligence.

Business Innovation: It is the process of introducing novel concepts, approaches, solutions, or products that result in major advancements or changes inside an organization or its sector.

Customer: A customer is a person who receives a service, goods, or idea from a seller in exchange for money.

Customer Centricity: It is a company philosophy and practice that puts the customer at the center of all strategies, operations, and decision-making.

Customer Experience: It describes how consumers feel about a company or its products as a result of their interactions and involvement during the journey with the business.

Innovation: It is the dynamic process of developing new and valuable concepts, ideas, products, or solutions to problems or meet unmet requirements.

Modern Enterprises: It refers to those organizations that have adopted cutting-edge technologies, creative business models, and forward-thinking strategies to succeed in the fast-paced business environment.

Chapter 14
Innovation and ICT:
Key Factors of Successful Business

Ivana Domazet
https://orcid.org/0000-0002-3493-4616
Institute of Economic Sciences, Belgrade, Serbia

Darko Marjanović
Institute of Economic Sciences, Belgrade, Serbia

Deniz Ahmetagić
Faculty of Economics in Subotica, Serbia

Jadranka Stantić
Albert Engelman Consulting, Serbia

ABSTRACT

The research carried out in the chapter aims to analyze the importance of innovation and ICT as key factors of successful business, that is, to what extent innovation and ICT influence the competitiveness and development of the digital economy in Serbia compared to other countries of the Western Balkans. The research covered the period from 2020 to 2022, while the methodological concept is based on descriptive analysis of secondary data from the World Economic Forum. The results obtained through the research explicitly show that the countries of the Western Balkans do not invest enough funds in the ICT sector, which has a negative impact on their further development and growth of macro-competitiveness. Compared to other countries of the Western Balkans, Serbia is progressing significantly faster in the field of digital transformation. Despite this, it still lags behind the EU countries when it comes to the adoption of ICT, infrastructure, and innovation systems.

DOI: 10.4018/979-8-3693-0458-7.ch014

INTRODUCTION

Innovations have always been a significant element in the relative success of society, from the economic, intellectual and social aspects. Nowadays, when the world economy has moved from the model of independent, relatively loosely connected economies to a much deeper connection and global community, the phenomenon of innovation has gained additional importance. At the same time, the success of innovation depends on how much knowledge is integrated into the innovation process, whether it is product or service innovation. Innovation is the process by which entrepreneurs turn ideas into marketable opportunities, but also the way in which an entrepreneur exercises new wealth-creating resources or enriches existing resources with increased wealth-creating potential. In doing so, entrepreneurs can innovate in three ways (Domazet et al, 2023): by creating new information that will lead to the invention of new technologies, by using market inefficiencies to create their own advantage, or by creating innovations as their reaction to changes in the relations of relative costs and alternative benefits from the use of resources, which may be caused by changes of a demographic, political or legislative nature.

Information and communication technologies (ICT) are considered a significant factor in economic growth and development. In today's world, it is not possible to imagine the efficient functioning of an individual, the economy and the entire society without the use of ICT. The progress of ICT in recent years has caused significant structural changes when it comes to reorganizing the economy and expanding the level of trade. Likewise, the development of technology, especially ICT, has significant effects on the economy and other aspects of human life. In addition to ICTs playing a significant role in the development of the economic sector, they also affect the economic performance and success of many companies, especially when combined with investment in skills, organizational change and innovation. The transition to a post-industrial society enabled ICT to become one of the main components of the development of a knowledge-based digital economy. During the last decade, the great diffusion of ICT caused a dramatic transformation of the world into an information society.

The development and implementation of ICT has significantly improved the efficiency of resource allocation, considerably reduced production costs and promoted greater demand and investment in all economic sectors. While ICT progress in developing countries can serve as a tool for personal and economic development, policies and actions in developed countries should focus on other factors that can lead to higher levels of human development. Developing countries could more easily integrate into a more advanced economic environment if they made the most of the opportunities offered by new technologies. The dynamic growth of technical and economic characteristics of high-tech innovative products contributes to a significant increase in computing power and intellectual potential of products, as well as to the rapid change of outdated standards and technological platforms of information and communication systems and networks. ICT enables individuals to access information, enables social interaction, facilitates access to education (Stojanović, Domazet, 2020) and health care, and creates new business opportunities. The limited impact of ICT at the aggregate level in many OECD countries is not necessarily due to a lack of investment in ICT, but rather to a lack of complementary changes and investments that enable the full exploitation of ICT.

The digital economy represents an economy based on digital technologies and the predominant use of information technology, hardware, software, applications and telecommunications in all aspects of the economy. This includes internal activities of organizations and external activities between organizations, organizations and individuals, and individuals among themselves. It represents the knowledge economy because it is essentially based on professional and market knowledge, creativity and innovation of society. In a broader sense, the digital economy is a strategic determinant of modern society and the state in the 21st century. The digital economy implies a turn in the way of thinking, that is, a transition from the usual development methods characteristic of state economies to dynamic development models based on continuous improvement and perfection (Simović, Domazet, 2023). Countries that generate new technologies and encourage their adoption, as well as those that create innovations, grow faster than those countries that do not promote these activities.

This chapter aims to determine whether innovation and ICT influence the competitiveness and development of the digital economy in the Western Balkan country. Desk research is based on officially available secondary data published by the World Economic Forum. In this regard, the Network Readiness Index (NRI) has been used as one of the leading global indicators of the application and impact of ICT in economies worldwide and covers the period from 2020 to 2022. The research is focused on two interrelated segments: the economy's innovation capacity as a factor in improving the country's competitiveness and the impact of innovation and ICT on competitiveness and the development of the digital economy. To obtain adequate conclusions, in addition to Serbia, the analysis included other countries of the Western Balkans (Albania, Bosnia and Herzegovina, Montenegro and North Macedonia).

BACKGROUND

Innovation can be a source of competitive advantage for companies, either through the improvement of methods and techniques that will generate new products or services, or the improvement of existing ones (Marjanović et al., 2022). At the same time, innovations represent an interactive process that takes place on several different levels, between companies and scientific infrastructure in a national economy, between different functions within the company itself, and between producers and consumers, both within a company and at the market level. Innovations encourage competition among companies, but also represent a tool with which a company can create a "space for itself" in an extremely competitive market and thus acquire new consumers (Herrera, 2015; Ferauge, 2012). That is why the competitive environment affects the degree of innovativeness of the company, and it should be seen through the analysis of the demands, preferences, and value system of consumers, the characteristics of the product itself, such as its design, lifespan or branding, but also the characteristics of technology in a given branch of economy, which specifically refers to technological effectiveness and efficiency, and the life cycle of technology (Huse et al., 2005; Huang, 2011). The innovation process implies the adoption of new or significantly improved production methods. Innovations in the production process consist of a series of innovation events that have a functional nature and are applied in phases, according to a previously established order, and whose goal is to improve the production process (Chen & Guan, 2011; Bernstein & Singh, 2006).

Each national economy has its own specific characteristics that, to a greater or lesser extent, determine its innovative capabilities (Marjanović & Domazet, 2021a). The determinants that establish the structure of the innovation capacity of the economy include the innovation infrastructure of the economy, the innovation environment in national industrial clusters and the links between the common innovation infrastructure and specific clusters (Porter & Stern, 2004). When it comes to individual companies, the leadership style practiced by the top and middle layers of management, willingness to share knowledge and organizational support systems for innovation play a very important role as determinants of its innovation capacity (Le & Lei, 2019). Innovations are a necessary condition for economic and social development, new scientific knowledge is a necessary condition for innovation, scientific research is a necessary condition for the acquisition of new scientific knowledge, and for the above reasons, only a systemic approach to innovation in which universities, the economy and the state administration work synergistically can ensure sustainable and progressive socioeconomic development (Pejanovic et al., 2015).

The rapid progress of ICT around the world in the last three decades has attracted the increasing attention of many economists and researchers who have focused on studying the impact of the spread of ICT on the economic growth of developed and developing economies, while the results mostly speak in favor of the positive impact of ICT on economic growth (Shodiev et al., 2021; Adeleye & Eboagu, 2019; Barba-Sanchez et al., 2018; Savulescu, 2015). The ICT revolution has rapidly spread across countries, industries and socio-economic activities over the past few decades with profound transformational effects. As a result, ICT plays an increasingly important role in economic growth and structural changes (Savulescu (2015). In the last thirty years, there has been a significant transformation in the spread of ICT, the development of the venture capital industry and economic growth in European countries (Domazet et al., 2021). Fernández-Portillo et al. (2020) studied the relationship between ICT and economic growth in the countries of the European Union, and based on empirical results concluded that progress in the application and use of ICT drives the economic growth of countries that are part of developed European economies. Bilan et al. (2019) have dealt with the impact of ICT on economic growth at different hierarchical levels. Based on the global tendencies of ICT development and their use as a factor of competitive advantage, it has been proven that sustainable socioeconomic growth has acquired the characteristics of permanent digital development. Using panel data for the period 2000-2018, Shodiev et al. (2021) sought to determine whether there is a relationship between economic growth and ICT development in Central Asian countries. The results showed that inflation, trade openness, final consumption expenditure and unemployment significantly affect GDP per capita in Central Asian countries. Pradhan et al. (2019), have examined possible interrelationships between venture capital investment, ICT infrastructure and economic growth, based on annual data from 25 European countries between 1989 and 2016. The results showed that both economic growth and the development of ICT infrastructure affect all phases of venture capital investment in the long term. Higón et al. (2017) analyzed the impact of ICT on the environment and concluded that many developed countries have already reached the level of ICT development, whereby CO2 emissions decrease as the level of ICT development increases.

Stanley et al. (2018) investigated whether there is a relationship between ICT and national economic growth and concluded that ICT contributed positively to economic growth. Adeleye & Eboagu (2019) investigated the impact of ICT on economic growth in Africa on a sample of 54 countries in the period from 2005 to 2015 and concluded that ICT development has a statistically significant positive relationship with economic growth. Gërguri-Rashiti et al. (2017) examined the impact of ICT and innovation activities on company performance and concluded that the company will improve its performance if it undertakes appropriate innovation activities. Barba-Sanchez et al. (2018) analyzed the impact that the intensity of ICT adoption in the company and the attractiveness of the industry have on corporate performance, where the results showed that there is a significant positive relationship between the intensity of ICT use and corporate performance, emphasizing the importance of ICT in highly competitive environments.

The digital economy offers great opportunities for the development of a country's competitiveness system (Marjanović & Domazet, 2021). Modern technologies enable the use of a high-tech digital platform that minimizes the human factor and accompanying corruption and errors, automates the collection of statistical, tax and other reports and makes decisions based on the analysis of the real situation

(Selishcheva et al., 2020). Miethlich et al. (2020) in their research deal with national competitiveness, as well as the digital economy from a technological, industrial and social perspective. The advantages of the digital economy are the inclusion of innovations, the emergence of new markets, the growth of labor productivity, the reduction of production and sales costs, as well as the production of better-quality goods and services. Koch & Windsperger (2017) concluded through the conducted research that companies can achieve a competitive advantage by actively shaping the digital environment and creating the value of interconnected companies in the digital environment.

Despite the increasing use of digital technology in industrial production, it remains unclear how industrial digitalization affects the environmental performance of manufacturing activities. Wen et al. (2021) concluded that the environmental performance of manufacturing companies is significantly improved in the process of industrial digital transformation, whereby the structural effect is the main factor contributing to the positive environmental effects of the penetration of information and communication technologies. Innovation policy represents an increasingly important component of economic development management in most, and especially in economically leading countries in the world (Domazet et al., 2022a). In this regard, Pan et al. (2022) examined the effects of the innovation-driven digital economy on total factor productivity and concluded that the digital economy acts as an engine for extensive and sustainable development.

RESEARCH METHODOLOGY AND OBJECTIVES

The impact of innovation on the creation of competitive advantage is based on the ability of the company, which applies innovation, to meet the current needs of the market in a stable and sustainable way, better than the competition, by means of new ideas and knowledge, creating new value. The link between innovation and competitive advantages is determined by the company's strategic configuration, product and market choices that include factors for creating high values, gaining prestige based on the current advantages of a given industry, the total resources and capacities at the company's disposal, as well as the ability to sustainably improve them. Therefore, innovation capability is considered to be an important competitive advantage for companies (Domazet et al, 2022), given its importance for economic growth, wealth creation, business expansion and technological progress. In the modern era of competitive markets, globalization and dramatic changes in industries, companies have begun the search for a unique strategy and innovative tactics that will provide them with a sustainable competitive advantage. One of the new models that offer this is the business model of innovation, whose basic task is to act as the main engine for achieving competitiveness.

The main goal of this chapter is to determine whether innovation and ICT affect the competitiveness and development of the digital economy in the countries of the Western Balkans. Desk research is based on officially available secondary data published by the World Economic Forum. In this regard, the Network Readiness Index (NRI) was used as one of the leading global indicators of the application and impact of ICT in economies around the world. The research covered the period from 2020 to 2022.

After a clearly defined methodology and goals have been set, this chapter focuses on the state of the Serbian economy when it comes to investments and ICT. In order to be able to obtain adequate conclusions, the analysis included other countries of the Western Balkans (Albania, Bosnia and Herzegovina, Montenegro and North Macedonia).

The research is divided into two interconnected units:

1. Innovation capacity of the economy as a factor in improving the country's competitiveness.
2. The impact of innovation and ICT on competitiveness and the development of the digital economy.

Innovation Capacity of the Economy as a Factor in Improving the Country's Competitiveness

Innovation policy represents an increasingly important component of economic development management in most, especially in the world's economically leading countries. The concept of the national innovation system has a special place in the innovation policy of each country. Establishing such a concept is directly connected with the increase of innovation capacity at the national level. National innovation capacity represents the country's ability to produce and commercialize the flow of innovative technologies in the long term, the continuous transformation of knowledge and ideas into new products, processes and systems, to benefit the company. In practice, this means creating a driving force for the generation and research of new radical ideas and concepts, and their development into marketable and effective innovations, using internal and external resources and competencies. Since innovative capacity represents the ability to produce and commercialize the flow of innovative technologies in the long term and constitutes an essential factor affecting competitiveness, especially in developed, modern economies, it can be concluded that such economies are on the verge of exhausting the possibility for further growth based on capital investment and that investing in innovation represents a sustainable solution for those countries.

However, a well-functioning innovation infrastructure is a key, but not the only factor necessary for a country to ensure long-term stability in innovation development. Businesses invest in innovation to acquire new resources and explore the possibility of their own response to market demands. In doing so, they apply different strategies and react differently to changes in the environment. In addition, economic activities by themselves bring both a state of imbalance and dynamic processes of change, while the results of the application of new technologies cannot be fully predicted. At the same time, companies do not operate in isolation, but within a specific environment composed of a network of other entities, through which commercial and technical exchange is realized, as well as a large number of institutions that provide various types of services. Their results depend on the environment in which they operate, but also on the strategies of competing companies. In an increasingly competitive environment, businesses use their strategies in an effort to retain market share and increase profits. Only constant learning ensures the adaptation of companies to changing market conditions and enables them to respond to competitive challenges in the most efficient way. In situations where innovations occur as mutations of existing technologies, they can threaten the survival of those technologies. For this reason, the evolution of technology is linked to the selection process, because the market determines which innovations will result in success and rewards the efficiency of the company. At the same time, companies make decisions about investing in technology that are based on expected profits, where profit is important, not only for the evolution of technology, but also for economic growth, and in modern business conditions it can be generated through entrepreneurial initiative and innovation.

The inspiration and explanation for this claim is offered by the ability-based approach that has been increasingly present in the social sciences since the 1970s. This approach has a very wide application, above all in the explanation of the phenomenon of development studies and policy creation, where an abundance of social and economic indicators is used. One of the most commonly used indicators of development and well-being is the gross domestic product (GDP). Despite numerous limitations, it is widely accepted as an indicator that measures the total production of goods and the economic health of a country. The logic of using GDP as a measure of well-being is simple to apply, and based on it, a clear conclusion can be drawn that "if the economy grows, so does well-being", so the use of this indicator has been widely used since the 1960s.

When studies in the field of innovation, research and development are concerned, GDP is often used as an indicator of investment opportunities at the national level. This is done in order to gain insight into the possibilities of improving innovation and competitiveness both at the level of one country and at the level of several countries through their comparison. On the other hand, some authors who deal with comparative analyzes of developed and underdeveloped countries believe that the level of GDP in less developed countries is a limiting factor when it comes to investments in research and development (Krammer, 2009; Aghion et al., 2005). In this sense, the lack of financial resources is considered to be the main factor that prevents poorer countries from enjoying all the advantages that innovation, research and development can bring to a given national economy (Aghion et al., 2005). Innovations are an important factor in economic and social development. That is why developed countries pay a lot of attention to innovation culture, organization and the environment in which ideas should arise. This means that developed countries have a high-quality national innovation system that includes all structures of the economy and society for the creation of ideas and their implementation. The primary role of finance in the field of research and development is related to stimulating the creation and development of innovations. That is why the financial system of a country can play a very important role in mobilizing resources for the field of research and development, primarily through bank loans to the sector and the capitalization of companies listed on the domestic capital market (Fagerberg & Srholec, 2008). In the literature on finance and innovation, the fact that different types of businesses require different types of financing is often overlooked. Therefore, financing provided by public agencies or state investment banks is also necessary for innovation, and it is crucial that finance must go hand in hand with innovation-oriented policies and national industrial policy (Mazzucato, 2013). In addition, modern innovation financing flows include their financing from various types of donations and contributions, but also through the pooling of capital of two or more entities (Howell, 2017).

The basic indicator of the success degree of a particular state is its level of competitiveness. The level of competitiveness of a country depends on the ability of the economy to ensure production efficiency that will result in greater economic growth, guarantee the rate of return on invested funds in the economy and provide the population with a high level of income and consumption. In this sense, the concept of national productivity is the only meaningful concept of competitiveness at the national level, since states and companies should be viewed in the same way when it comes to productivity and competitiveness. That is why competitiveness at the national level can be described as the ability of the state to create, produce, distribute and service products in international trade, at the same time realizing increasing returns on its resources. In other words, competitiveness can be defined as the ability to achieve the main economic goals, including the growth of income and employment, without the appearance of a deficit in the balance of payments, and through increasing the level of real income and creating new jobs.

In the current context of globalization, competitiveness is the main economic goal that economic policymakers around the world often talk about, where competitiveness itself is most often associated with economic growth, prosperity and a high standard of living. During the past couple of decades, economic science has paid great attention to the phenomenon of competitiveness, treating it as one of the most important economic concepts, whose increase and measurement represent a difficult and complex process, and whose main driver can be identified as innovations (Kiselakova, et al., 2018).

Figure 1. The 12 pillars of competitiveness
Source: World Economic Forum (2011)

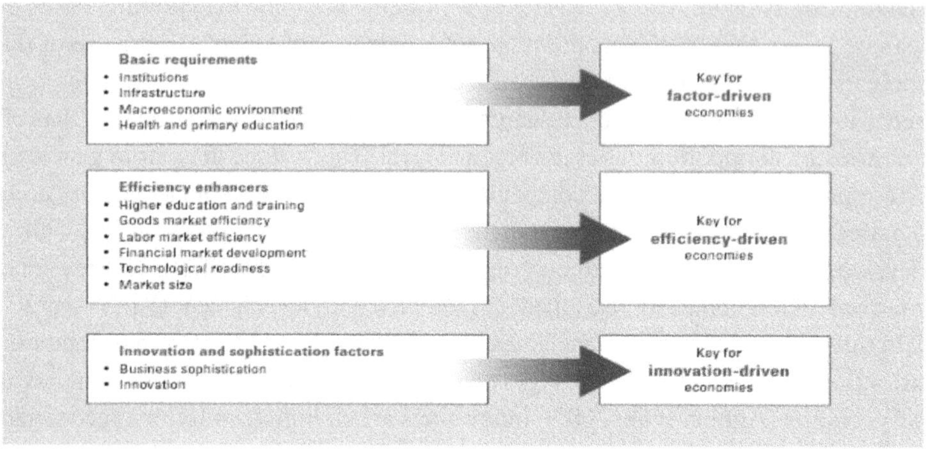

The competitiveness of a national economy itself is treated as a set of institutions, policies and factors that determine the country's productivity level, while the methodology of the Global Competitiveness Index (GCI) includes 12 pillars that aim to measure different aspects of competitiveness. The GCI uses an arithmetic mean, partially modulated by different weights, which are applied to individual pillars of competitiveness and enables the integration of each of the three established sub-indices. Conceptually, the World Economic Forum's Global Competitiveness Index aims to reveal the extent to which a country's institutions, its economic infrastructure, and the policies and practices that should support growth, serve to increase GDP per capita. (Bowen & Moesen, 2011).

Competitiveness is monitored based on 12 pillars. The first group includes four pillars, on the basis of which the sub-index – basic requirements are calculated. These are: institutions, infrastructure, macroeconomic environment and health and primary education. The second group includes six pillars that enable the calculation of sub-index – efficiency enhancers. These include: higher education and training, goods market efficiency, labor market efficiency, financial market development, technological readiness and market size. The third group consists of two pillars on the basis of which the sub-index – innovation and sophistication factors is calculated. These are business sophistication and innovation. All pillars of the Global Competitiveness Index are shown in Graph 1.

The twelfth pillar of the Global Competitiveness Index is dedicated to innovation. With the help of Innovations, sustainable economic development, increase in living standards, more efficient satisfaction of needs and improvement of overall competitiveness can be achieved. Less developed countries can increase productivity by adopting existing technologies or by various improvements in other areas. However, developed countries can achieve productivity and competitiveness only through innovation. Innovations are created and developed by the public and private sectors. This means that it is necessary to ensure investments in R&D, support quality scientific research institutions, establish cooperation in research between scientific research institutions and the economy, and ensure quality protection of intellectual property.

The Impact of Innovation and ICT on Competitiveness and the Development of the Digital Economy

Numerous empirical studies confirm the existence of a positive relationship between the level of economic development and investment in the ICT sector. In essence, developed countries have recognized the potential of investing in the ICT sector in the domain of further progress and growth of macro-competitiveness, and the investments of these countries in the ICT sector are more significant compared to the amounts of funds allocated by less developed countries for these purposes.

This part of the chapter presents the results of research based on secondary data, with the aim of determining the level of development of Serbia in comparison with other countries of the Western Balkans. In this regard, Network Readiness Index (NRI), was used as one of the leading global indices on the application and impact of ICT in economies around the world.

Table 1. NRI for Serbia, 2020-2022

	Rank 2020 (134 Countries)	**Result**	**Rank 2021 (130 Countries)**	**Result**	**Rank 2022 (131 Countries)**	**Result**
Global NRI	**52**	**52.96**	**57**	**53.60**	**55**	**53.52**
A. Technology	**53**	**44.89**	**71**	**42.68**	**77**	**42.26**
Accesibility	51	74.08	70	64.13	65	65.19
Content	42	41.63	44	44.88	46	42.46
Technology of the future	103	18.97	112	19.05	113	19.12
B. People	**52**	**51.53**	**56**	**51.35**	**57**	**47.42**
Individuals	65	55.95	65	62.71	53	51.45
Companies	48	50.79	57	43.57	65	42.84
Government	49	47.84	49	47.77	50	47.96
C. Management	**54**	**59.99**	**50**	**61.64**	**49**	**65.85**
Trust	57	46.12	51	51.62	53	54.98
Regulation	63	66.91	54	66.89	48	70.70
Inclusion	56	66.94	56	66.42	50	71.87
D. Influence	**54**	**55.41**	**50**	**58.73**	**48**	**58.57**
Economy	48	32.72	52	43.00	59	36.62
Living standard	55	68.35	56	71.51	43	75.11
Contribution of SDG	73	65.17	67	61.69	61	65.99

Source: Authors based on the World Economic Forum data

Based on the data shown in Table 1, the global NRI of Serbia has dropped by 5 positions in 2021 compared to 2020. The decline is even more pronounced considering that in 2020 this index covered 134 countries, while in 2021 it covered 130 countries. In 2022, a slight increase in global NRI by two positions is noticeable. Comparing the analyzed period (2020-2022), Serbia's greatest advantage is in the segment of management and influence, while, on the other hand, there is an evident decline when it comes to the other two analyzed pillars: technology and people. The biggest room for improvement is in the area of technology.

Table 2. Global NIR, 2020-2022

	Serbia			Bosnia and Herzegovina	
	'20	**'21**	**'22**	**'20**	**'21**
Goalni NRI	**52**	**57**	**55**	**87**	**86**
A Technology	**53**	**71**	**77**	**92**	**80**
Accesibility	51	70	65	91	61
Content	42	44	46	57	57
Technology of the future	103	112	113	129	125
B. People	**52**	**56**	**57**	**89**	**93**
Individuals	65	65	53	66	81
Companies	48	57	65	77	60
Government	49	49	50	125	123
C. Management	**54**	**50**	**49**	**77**	**81**
Trut	57	51	53	95	97
Regulation	63	54	48	57	68
Inclusion	56	56	50	79	78
D. nfluence	**54**	**50**	**48**	**89**	**86**
Ecoomy	48	52	59	90	78
Livng standard	55	56	43	57	64
Conribution of SDG*	73	67	61	102	103

*SDG - Sustainable Development Goals
Source: Authors based on the World Economic Forum data

Table 2 shows the global NIR in the countries of the Western Balkans for the period 2020-2022. During all three observed years, Serbia had the best result compared to other countries of the Western Balkans. Based on the presented data for the year 2022, which included 131 countries, Serbia is in 55th place, which is the best result compared to all other countries of the Western Balkans. This is followed by Montenegro (65th place), North Macedonia (69th place), Albania (80th place) and Bosnia and Herzegovina (90th place). Looking at each pillar individually, it is clear that in the domain of technology, Montenegro is in first place (39th place), while Serbia is significantly behind (77th place). However, despite the poor result in this pillar, the other countries of the Western Balkans are in a subordinate position. Serbia's progress is evident when it comes to pillars (c) management and (d) influence, where it is evident that the other countries of the Western Balkan's lag behind Serbia, which clearly indicates an inadequate methodological approach in treating these pillars.

When it comes to sub-pillars, Serbia's strongest indicators refer to living standard (43), content (46) and regulation (48). However, more could be done to improve the performance of the economy in accessibility, companies and the technology of the future. Regarding the result of NRI and GDP per capita, graph 2 shows the position of Serbia, where the trend line shows the expected result of NRI considering the level of income of the economy. As can be seen, Serbia is slightly above the trend line, suggesting that its network readiness is broadly in line with what would be expected given its income level.

Figure 2. NRI score and GDP per capita PPP (log)
Source: Network Readiness Index (2022)

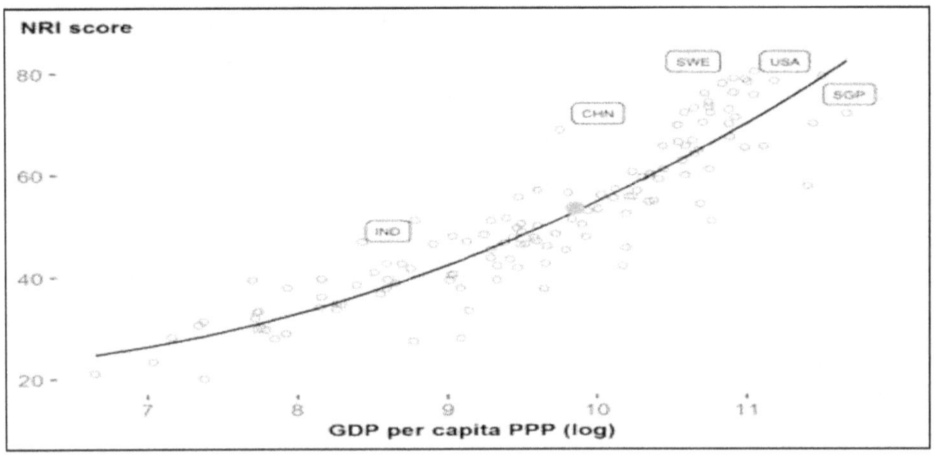

It should be noted that the best positions are held by the USA (Rank 1), Singapore (Rank 2) and Sweden (Rank 3), while Serbia belongs to the group of countries with higher middle incomes, lagging behind Sweden as the best country in Europe. Accordingly, Serbia is ranked 8th in the countries with upper-middle income group. In terms of pillar performance, it scores higher than the income group average in three of the four pillars: people, governance and influence. At the sub-pillar level, it outperforms upper-middle-income countries in eleven out of twelve sub-pillars: accessibility, content, individuals, companies, governments, trust, regulation, inclusion, economy, standard of living and contribution to the sustainable development goals (SDG).

In Serbia, there is a low level of ICT development of domestic companies in the segment of implementation of modern ERP and CRM systems, which is confirmed by the assessment of the World Economic Forum on the competitiveness of Serbia in the segment of business process sophistication and, consequently, innovation in business. One of the more significant challenges, which affects the low level of competitiveness of Serbian companies, is the insufficient implementation of the CRM system within the company's business processes. Namely, CRM represents the process of developing and managing customer relations. Adequate implementation of CRM contributes to a higher level of customer satisfaction, which is a prerequisite for their greater loyalty and, consequently, greater profitability of service companies. However, the use of the CRM concept requires the use of relatively sophisticated IT technologies, which include innovative models of modern IT architecture, databases, data management with modern software, statistical and information tools. Consequently, the repositioning of companies from this sector is also necessary, in order for Serbia to become a regional leader in attracting foreign direct investments, especially in the field of ICT, for which greater state assistance is needed. This is supported by the development of science and technology parks and the association of ICT companies into clusters, with the aim of increasing market power. When it comes to investments in the ICT sector, Serbian companies invest about 0.5% of total revenues, which is significantly below the amount invested by international companies, especially if we consider the amount of revenues of domestic companies in absolute terms. The situation is similar when it comes to the number of employees - Serbian companies employ four times less IT experts compared to IT companies operating in developed market economies.

Foreign direct investments are extremely important for developing countries, since they are expected to provide the country with access to new technologies and knowledge in addition to employment. Therefore, one of the main goals for Serbia is to attract as many FDIs as possible, whereby the result of such a policy is reflected in 4.4 billion euros of foreign direct investments during 2022, despite all global economic challenges. Foreign direct investments in the information technology sector are welcome, but they should be used wisely, for the benefit of the entire society, and not so that only companies that invest in a smaller number of employee's benefit. Foreign direct investments in the form of recapitalization of domestic companies are very important because in this way the foreign company would invest money in the joint development and improvement of the existing capacities and products of Serbian companies.

Thanks to the favorable business climate, the Serbian IT sector records y-o-y growth, which makes it the healthiest industrial branch in Serbia. Aware of the importance that IT has on the domestic economy, the Government of the Republic of Serbia implements a number of measures to support this sector, including tax incentives, subsidies and regulatory reforms. In the last few years, ICT exports have been constantly increasing. Income from the export of ICT services in 2020 reached 1.44 billion euros, which, despite the coronavirus pandemic, was more than the income from 2019. During 2021, exports amounted to 1.85 billion euros, which was a growth of 28 percent compared to 2020, while the value of this sector exceeded exports in the field of agriculture. Exports of the ICT sector in 2022 amounted to 2.692 billion euros, which is an increase of over 45 percent compared to 2021. Considering that in the same year, Serbia imported ICT services worth 732 million euros, there is an evident surplus in the exchange of ICT services of almost two billion euros, that is, the surplus has increased by 48.8 percent compared to 2021. The current situation is such that 20% of countries still have 80% of total investments in new technologies, which speaks in favor of the fact that there is still a big gap, which is especially present in smaller countries, including Serbia. If you look at the global technology map, Serbia is currently somewhere in the middle. In the following period, the focus should be on laying the foundations for stronger development and the chance to reduce the lag.

Economic competitiveness as well as society organization and transparency are best illustrated with the diagram of IT investment per capita according to economic strength (Graph 3). Huge differences are clearly visible among the European countries in IT investments per capita (Y-axis), GDP per capita (X-axis) and the size of the total IT market (circle size). After the analysis, 5 basic groups were formed (Tier levels), and each of them are country with a similar perspective, comparable by similar prospects for future technological development strategies (Matijević & Šolaja 2022).

Figure 3. IT investment according to economic strength (GDP)
Source: Matijević and Šolaja (2022)

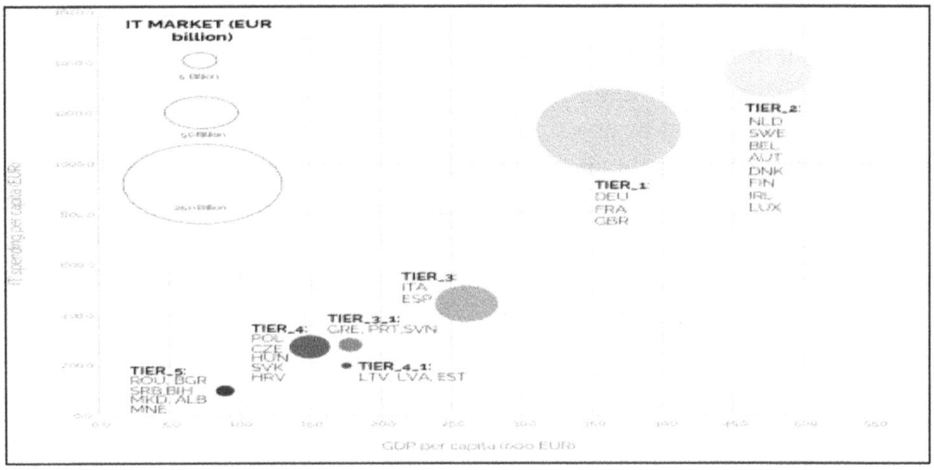

In the first group there are 7 Western European countries which are also the leaders in IT spending per capita (€1,350) and in GDP per capita (more than €45,000) (21% of the total EU IT market). Given the large population, they have the ability to strategically focus on the most important trends in global technological development. The second group comprises gigantic IT markets (DEU, FRA, GBR) with values of almost €250 billion in total, which is 60% total IT market of EU. The third group gathers sub-Mediterranean countries, which can be observed through two sub-groups: (1) comprises Italy and Spain, with large potential for IT market growth and for strong technological advancements. Both countries have large populations and economies and fall into the top five EU members, while (2) comprises Greece, Slovenia, and Portugal, that have smaller base, moderate capacity, and no high IT priority for now. Within the fourth group, on the one hand, there are Central European countries with a solid industrial tradition, but a high risk of technological lag and innovation, while, on the other hand, there are three Baltic countries (Lithuania, Latvia and Estonia) that can provide a very good basis for the implementation of joint strategic orientations. In the last, fifth group, there are the countries of the Western Balkans, which are characterized by weak economies (less than 10,000 euros GDP per capita), small capacities and very low levels of investment in IT (around 100 euros per capita).

Reducing the negative effects and thus reaching the European process of technological development is possible on the condition that these countries receive support at the EU level, through various forms and programs of financial assistance. Also, it is very likely that joint actions and strategic plans will be implemented more easily, given that the countries of the Western Balkans are geographically and culturally quite close. As long as total IT investments are below 2% of GDP, it is realistic to expect that there will be a global digital gap in Serbia. However, if investments in IT reach 3% of GDP by the end of 2025, we can talk about accelerated recovery and success of the Serbian economy. On the other hand, it is necessary to increase investments from 100 to 150 euros per capita, i.e. for the average annual growth rate of the IT market to be higher than 10% by the end of 2025, which would automatically be reflected in the reduction of the digital gap.

CONCLUSION

The national market represents one of the biggest potentials for IT companies operating in Serbia, but also in other countries of the Western Balkans. Considering that Serbia is still a country with a transitional economy, it is not surprising that domestic companies largely use outdated technology in their operations. However, further improvement of business creates awareness about the use of new, more modern IT solutions in further business. On the domestic IT market, there is a noticeable trend of creating science and technology parks and clusters, as special forms of cooperation between domestic IT companies. In addition to the development of science and technology parks, Serbian IT companies increase their visibility and attractiveness on the international market through the promotion and placement of their own original solutions in this area. On the other hand, the future modernization of governmental business represents another great potential and incentive for Serbian IT companies. The ICT sector in Serbia, although insufficiently developed for an intensive breakthrough in the digital economy, has significant potential. Considering that the domestic economy needs modern ICT solutions, but also that the ICT sector represents the engine of economic development, a more significant role of the state in assisting the domestic ICT sector in the coming period is a must. In this regard, better cooperation between the ICT sector, the education sector and the private sector would enable the creation of a synergistic effect that would benefit the entire society. Accordingly, our country is globally recognized as an extremely attractive alternative location for the development of sophisticated software, and domestic IT companies as entities that possess the necessary knowledge, experience, and resources to provide high-quality services.

In the coming period, the emphasis of development should be on the education of IT experts, modernization of the education system, as well as employment of graduates in IT companies operating in Serbia. The sources of growth can be either rapid productivity growth or labor imports, where productivity can be achieved through modern technologies, investment in equipment and the use of artificial intelligence. In Serbia, 2017 was a turning point when it came to the transformation of the economy towards an economy based on innovation and new technologies, which was also reflected in the results when it came to the growth of the gross domestic product, wages and pensions, as well as the growth of foreign direct investments. The main recommendations in order of actions to support the development of the domestic ICT sector are: (a) adapt the education system to the needs of the IT industry, (b) modernize the curriculum and increase enrollment quotas for IT studies, (c) introduce tax incentives that encourage investments in the IT sector, (d) support for domestic software exporters, (e) subsidies for beginners in the IT sector up to 25,000 euros and (f) subsidies for end users for the purchase of equipment and software.

Despite the importance of FDI on production, it is very important that Serbia also strengthens the attraction of foreign investments in services and ICT because, without a developed ICT sector, it is almost impossible to include Serbia in global flows. The ICT industry in Serbia has the potential that create a precondition for the faster development of all segments of the domestic economy. On the other hand, Serbian ICTs are competitive in the foreign market and can contribute to stabilizing the foreign trade balance by exporting. In reference to the insufficient use of modern ICT technologies in companies operating in Serbia, as well as the clear determination of the state regarding the intensive implementation of the electronic administration system and digitization of business, it can be concluded that the national market still represents one of the greatest growth potentials for domestic IT companies.

Finally, it should be noted that this chapter has several limitations: (a) research on the importance of innovation and ICT on competitiveness and the development of the digital economy was carried out on the example of only five countries; (b) the conducted research covered a shorter period (3 years) and (c) the analysis was performed exclusively based on secondary data from the World Economic Forum. In order for future research to be more detailed and meaningful, it is important to consider and implement the following guidelines: (a) include more countries in the analysis (eg EU countries, OECD countries, etc.); (b) do the analysis for a longer period of time (minimum 10 years) and (c) conduct the analysis based on primary data with the application of appropriate methodology adequate to the type of research to be conducted.

ACKNOWLEDGMENT

The research presented in this paper was funded by the Ministry of Science, Technological Development and Innovation of the Republic of Serbia under contract number 451-03-47/2023-01/200005.

REFERENCES

Adeleye, N., & Eboagu, C. (2019). Evaluation of ICT development and economic growth in Africa. *NETNOMICS: Economic Research and Electronic Networking*, *20*(1), 31–53. doi:10.100711066-019-09131-6

Aghion, P., Howitt, P., & Mayer-Foulkes, D. (2005). The effect of financial development on convergence: Theory and evidence. *The Quarterly Journal of Economics*, *120*(1), 173–222.

Barba-Sanchez, V., Calderón-Milán, M. J., & Atienza-Sahuquillo, C. (2018). A study of the value of ICT in improving corporate performance: A corporate competitiveness view. *Technological and Economic Development of Economy*, *24*(4), 1388–1407. doi:10.3846/tede.2018.3114

Bernstein, B., & Singh, P. J. (2006). An integrated innovation process model based on practices of Australian biotechnology firms. *Technovation*, *26*(5-6), 561–572. doi:10.1016/j.technovation.2004.11.006

Bilan, Y., Mishchuk, H., Samoliuk, N., & Grishnova, O. (2019). ICT and Economic Growth: Links and Possibilities of Engaging. *Intellectual Economics, 13*(1).

Bowen, H. P., & Moesen, W. (2011). Composite competitiveness indicators with endogenous versus predetermined weights: An application to the World Economic Forum's Global Competitiveness Index. *Competitiveness Review*, *21*(2), 129–151. doi:10.1108/10595421111117434

Chen, K., & Guan, J. (2011). Mapping the innovation production process from accumulative advantage to economic outcomes: A path modeling approach. *Technovation*, *31*(7), 336–346. doi:10.1016/j.technovation.2011.03.004

Domazet, I., Marjanović, D., & Ahmetagić, D. (2022). The Impact of High-Tech Products Exports on Economic Growth: The Case of Serbia, Bulgaria, Romania and Hungary. *Ekonomika preduzeća, 70*(3-4), 191-205.

Domazet, I., Marjanović, D., Ahmetagić, D., & Antonijević, M. (2022). Does the Increase in the Number of Registered Patents Affect Economic Growth? Evidence from Romania and Bulgaria. *Economic Analysis: Applied Research in Emerging Markets*, *55*(2), 49–65.

Domazet, I., Marjanović, D., Ahmetagić, D., & Bugarčić, M. (2021). The Impact of Innovation Indicators on Increasing Exports of High Technology Products. *Ekonomika preduzeća, 69*(1-2), 31-40.

Domazet, I., Marjanović, D., Ahmetagić, D., & Simović, V. (2023). The influence of the number of patents on the economic growth of the country – evidence from Serbia and Hungary. Strategic Management. *International Journal of Strategic Management and Decision Support Systems in Strategic Management, 28*(3). Advance online publication. doi:10.5937/StraMan2300048D

Fagerberg, J., & Srholec, M. (2008). National innovation systems, capabilities and economic development. *Research Policy, 37*(9), 1417–1435. doi:10.1016/j.respol.2008.06.003

Ferauge, P. (2012). A conceptual framework of corporate social responsibility and innovation. *Global Journal of Business Research, 6*(5), 85–96.

Fernández-Portillo, A., Almodóvar-González, M., & Hernández-Mogollón, R. (2020). Impact of ICT development on economic growth. A study of OECD European Union countries. *Technology in Society, 63*, 63. doi:10.1016/j.techsoc.2020.101420

Gërguri-Rashiti, S., Ramadani, V., Abazi-Alili, H., Dana, L. P., & Ratten, V. (2017). ICT, innovation and firm performance: The transition economies context. *Thunderbird International Business Review, 59*(1), 93–102. doi:10.1002/tie.21772

Herrera, M. E. B. (2015). Creating competitive advantage by institutionalizing corporate social innovation. *Journal of Business Research, 68*(7), 1468–1474. doi:10.1016/j.jbusres.2015.01.036

Higón, D. A., Gholami, R., & Shirazi, F. (2017). ICT and environmental sustainability: A global perspective. *Telematics and Informatics, 34*(4), 85–95. doi:10.1016/j.tele.2017.01.001

Howell, S. T. (2017). Financing innovation: Evidence from R&D grants. *The American Economic Review, 107*(4), 1136–1164. doi:10.1257/aer.20150808

Huang, K. (2011). Technology competencies in competitive environment. *Journal of Business Research, 64*(2), 172–179. doi:10.1016/j.jbusres.2010.02.003

Huse, M., Neubaum, D. O., & Gabrielsson, J. (2005). Corporate innovation and competitive environment. *The International Entrepreneurship and Management Journal, 1*(3), 313–333. doi:10.100711365-005-2596-2

Kiselakova, D., Sofrankova, B., Cabinova, V., Onuferova, E., & Soltesova, J. (2018). The impact of R&D expenditure on the development of global competitiveness within the CEE EU countries. *Journal of Competitiveness, 10*(3), 34–50. doi:10.7441/joc.2018.03.03

Koch, T., & Windsperger, J. (2017). Seeing through the network: Competitive advantage in the digital economy. *Journal of Organization Design, 6*(1), 1–30. doi:10.118641469-017-0016-z

Krammer, S. W. S. (2009). Drivers of national innovation in transition: Evidence from a panel of Eastern European countries. *Research Policy, 38*(5), 845–860. doi:10.1016/j.respol.2009.01.022

Le, P. B., & Lei, H. (2019). Determinants of innovation capability: The roles of transformational leadership, knowledge sharing and perceived organizational support. *Journal of Knowledge Management, 23*(3), 527–547. doi:10.1108/JKM-09-2018-0568

Marjanović, D., & Domazet, I. (2021). Foreign Direct Investments: A Key Factor for Business Globalization. In Y. Bayar (Ed.), *Institutional, Economic, and Social Impacts of Globalization and Liberalization* (pp. 96–116). IGI Global. doi:10.4018/978-1-7998-4459-4.ch006

Marjanović, D., & Domazet, I. (2021). Tax competitiveness as a significant factor in attracting foreign investment – the case of Serbia. *Argumenta Oeconomica, 2*(47), 63–80. doi:10.15611/aoe.2021.2.04

Marjanović, D., Domazet, I., & Vukmirović, I. (2022). Social Environment as a Factor of Capital Investment in Serbia. *Eastern European Economics, 60*(3), 247–264. Advance online publication. doi:10.1080/00128775.2022.2048181

Matijević, M., & Šolaja, M. (2022). *ICT in Serbia - At a Glance*. Vojvodina ICT Cluster.

Mazzucato, M. (2013). Financing innovation: Creative destruction vs. destructive creation. *Industrial and Corporate Change, 22*(4), 851–867. doi:10.1093/icc/dtt025

Miethlich, B., Belotserkovich, D., Abasova, S., Zatsarinnaya, E., & Veselitsky, O. (2020). Digital economy and its influence on the competitiveness of countries and regions. *Revista espacios, 41*(12).

Pan, W., Xie, T., Wang, Z., & Ma, L. (2022). Digital economy: An innovation driver for total factor productivity. *Journal of Business Research, 139*, 303–311. doi:10.1016/j.jbusres.2021.09.061

Pejanovic, R., Sedlak, O., & Kabok, J. (2015). Innovation and knowledge. In N. Zarkic Joksimovic & S. Benkovic (Eds.), *Finding the right path - higher education financing and social dimension in the Western-Balkan countries* (pp. 101–126). Faculty of Organizational Sciences, University of Belgrade.

Porter, M. E., & Stern, S. (2004). *Ranking national innovative capacity: findings from the National Innovative Capacity Index*. The Global Competitiveness Report 2003-2004.

Portulans Institute. (2022). *Network Readiness Index 2022 Serbia*. Available at: https://networkreadinessindex.org/country/serbia/

Pradhan, R. P., Arvin, M. B., Nair, M., Bennett, S. E., & Bahmani, S. (2019). Short-term and long-term dynamics of venture capital and economic growth in a digital economy: A study of European countries. *Technology in Society, 57*, 125–134. doi:10.1016/j.techsoc.2018.11.002

Savulescu, C. (2015). Dynamics of ICT development in the EU. *Procedia Economics and Finance, 23*, 513–520. doi:10.1016/S2212-5671(15)00552-3

Selishcheva, T. A., Sopina, N. V., Borkova, E. A., & Ilyina, O. P. (2020). Estimation of The Influence of Digital Economy on The Competitiveness of The World. *35th International Business Information Management Association Conference (IBIMA)*, 3757-3764.

Shodiev, T., Turayey, B., & Shodiyev, K. (2021). ICT and Economic Growth Nexus: Case of Central Asian Countries. *Procedia of Social Sciences and Humanities, 1*, 155–167. doi:10.21070/pssh.v1i.37

Simović, V., & Domazet, I. (2023). What Drives the Levels of Digital Entrepreneurial Competencies of University Students? A Research Roadmap and Preliminary Results. In A. D. Daniel & C. Fernandes (Eds.), *Female entrepreneurship as a driving force of economic growth and social change* (pp. 55–72). IGI Global. doi:10.4018/978-1-6684-7669-7.ch004

Stanley, T. D., Doucouliagos, H., & Steel, P. (2018). Does ICT generate economic growth? A meta-regression analysis. *Journal of Economic Surveys*, *32*(3), 705–726. doi:10.1111/joes.12211

Stojanović, D. & Domazet, I. (2020). Use of Information Technologies in Educational Purposes – Case from Serbia. *Economic Analysis: Journal of Emerging Economics, 53*(2), 68-78.

Wen, H., Lee, C. C., & Song, Z. (2021). Digitalization and environment: How does ICT affect enterprise environmental performance? *Environmental Science and Pollution Research International*, *28*(39), 54826–54841. doi:10.100711356-021-14474-5 PMID:34014481

World Economic Forum. (2011). *The Global Competitiveness Report 2011-2012*. Available at: https://www.weforum.org/reports/global-competitiveness-report-2011-2012/

ADDITIONAL READING

Afeltra, G., Alerasoul, S. A., & Strozzi, F. (2023). The evolution of sustainable innovation: From the past to the future. *European Journal of Innovation Management*, *26*(2), 386–421. doi:10.1108/EJIM-02-2021-0113

Ancillai, C., Sabatini, A., Gatti, M., & Perna, A. (2023). Digital technology and business model innovation: A systematic literature review and future research agenda. *Technological Forecasting and Social Change*, *188*, 188. doi:10.1016/j.techfore.2022.122307

Bigliardi, B., Ferraro, G., Filippelli, S., & Galati, F. (2021). The past, present and future of open innovation. *European Journal of Innovation Management*, *24*(4), 1130–1161. doi:10.1108/EJIM-10-2019-0296

Donges, A., Meier, J.-M., & Silva, R. C. (2023). The Impact of Institutions on Innovation. *Management Science*, *69*(4), 1951–1974. doi:10.1287/mnsc.2022.4403

Hund, A., Wagner, H.-T., Beimborn, D., & Weitzel, T. (2021). Digital innovation: Review and novel perspective. *The Journal of Strategic Information Systems*, *30*(4), 101695. doi:10.1016/j.jsis.2021.101695

Jabeen, F., Belas, J., Santoro, G., & Alam, G. M. (2023). The role of open innovation in fostering SMEs' business model innovation during the COVID-19 pandemic. *Journal of Knowledge Management*, *27*(6), 1562–1582. doi:10.1108/JKM-05-2022-0347

Li, S., Gao, L., Han, C., Gupta, B., Alhalabi, W., & Almakdi, S. (2023). Exploring the effect of digital transformation on Firms' innovation performance. *Journal of Innovation & Knowledge*, *8*(1), 100317. doi:10.1016/j.jik.2023.100317

Taques, F. H., López, M. G., Basso, L. F., & Areal, N. (2021). Indicators used to measure service innovation and manufacturing innovation. *Journal of Innovation & Knowledge*, *6*(1), 11–26. doi:10.1016/j.jik.2019.12.001

Yu, H., Ke, H., Ye, Y., & Fan, F. (2023). Agglomeration and flow of innovation elements and the impact on regional innovation efficiency. *International Journal of Technology Management*, *92*(3), 229–254. doi:10.1504/IJTM.2023.128840

Zheng, M., Feng, G.-F., Wang, Q.-J., & Chang, C.-P. (2023). Financial globalization and technological innovation: International evidence. *Economic Systems*, *47*(1), 101048. doi:10.1016/j.ecosys.2022.101048

KEY TERMS AND DEFINITIONS

Competitiveness: Competitiveness is the set of institutions, policies and factors determining a country's productivity level. Therefore, competitiveness is the characteristic or ability of any organization to achieve its mission, more successfully than competing organizations goods.

Digital Economy: The digital economy is the worldwide network of economic activities, commercial transactions and professional interactions enabled by information and communications technologies (ICT).

Economic Growth and Development: Economic growth and development are both important for the sustainability of a country's national economy. Economic growth means an increase in real national income/national output. Economic development means an improvement in the quality of life and living standards.

Information and Communications Technologies (ICT): Information and communication technologies is defined as a diverse set of technological tools and resources used to transmit, store, create, share or exchange information.

Innovation: Innovation is the multi-stage process whereby organizations transform ideas into new/improved products, service or processes, in order to advance, compete and differentiate themselves successfully in their marketplace.

Investment: Investments, that is, investing, is part of the global problem of development as a continuous process by which every society and every company ensures its future efficient operations.

Open Innovation: Open innovation is the practice of businesses and organizations sourcing ideas from external and internal sources. This means sharing knowledge and information about problems and looking to people outside the business for solutions and suggestions.

Chapter 15
Driving Social and Environmental Impact:
Exploring Sustainability and Corporate Social Responsibility Frameworks

Filiz Mızrak
https://orcid.org/0000-0002-3472-394X
Beykoz University, Turkey

ABSTRACT

The pursuit of sustainability and corporate social responsibility has become critical for businesses as they strive to create positive social and environmental impacts while ensuring long-term profitability. This chapter investigates the significance and implementation strategies of sustainability and corporate social responsibility in driving positive social and environmental impacts for businesses. By analyzing the origins, key principles, and practical applications of these frameworks, the research explores the evolving societal expectations and regulatory landscape that demand responsible and sustainable business practices. It examines the benefits and challenges associated with adopting sustainability and CSR, drawing on case studies of successful organizations that have integrated these principles into their core strategies. The findings contribute to the existing knowledge on sustainability and CSR, offering insights for practitioners, policymakers, and researchers, and encouraging businesses to embrace these frameworks to create long-term value for society and the environment.

INTRODUCTION

Corporate Social Responsibility (CSR) holds immense importance in today's business landscape. It refers to the responsibility of companies to contribute positively to society, beyond their economic goals. CSR encompasses a range of practices that involve environmental stewardship, social well-being, ethical conduct, and community engagement. The significance of CSR lies in its ability to create a sustainable and inclusive business environment (Fatima & Elbanna, 2023). By integrating social and environmental

DOI: 10.4018/979-8-3693-0458-7.ch015

considerations into their operations, companies can enhance their reputation, build trust with stakeholders, attract and retain top talent, mitigate risks, and foster long-term profitability. Moreover, CSR plays a crucial role in addressing societal challenges, such as poverty, inequality, and climate change. It enables businesses to be proactive agents of positive change, contributing to the well-being of communities and the preservation of the environment. In an era where stakeholders are increasingly conscious of corporate behavior, embracing CSR is not only a moral imperative but also a strategic necessity for businesses seeking to thrive in the long run (Cezarino et al., 2022).

The relationship between sustainability and Corporate Social Responsibility (CSR) is one of interconnectedness and mutual reinforcement. CSR serves as a framework and set of practices through which businesses can incorporate sustainability principles into their operations. It involves the integration of social, environmental, and ethical considerations into business strategies and decision-making processes (Madanaguli et al., 2022). By embracing CSR, companies can contribute to sustainable development by addressing social and environmental challenges, promoting responsible business practices, and creating value for both stakeholders and society at large. In turn, sustainability provides the overarching goal and vision that guides CSR efforts, ensuring that businesses operate in a manner that supports the well-being of people and the planet. Sustainability provides the context and purpose for CSR initiatives, driving businesses to go beyond compliance and embrace practices that foster long-term viability and positive impact (Al-Shammari et al., 2022). Ultimately, the relationship between sustainability and CSR is one of collaboration, where the principles and practices of CSR contribute to the broader goal of achieving sustainability and its associated benefits for society and the environment.

In recent years, the global business landscape has undergone a remarkable transformation, as companies increasingly recognize the profound impact they can have on society and the environment. As a result, the concepts of sustainability and Corporate Social Responsibility (CSR) have emerged as fundamental pillars of responsible business practices. Embracing these principles not only enables organizations to fulfill their moral obligations but also positions them as drivers of positive change in an ever-evolving world (Cezarino et al., 2022). This exploration delves into the frameworks that guide sustainability and CSR practices in businesses, examining their origins, key principles, and practical applications. By understanding the driving forces behind social and environmental impact, businesses can forge a path towards a more sustainable future, ensuring a harmonious balance between economic prosperity, social well-being, and ecological integrity.

The focus of this study is to explore sustainability and Corporate Social Responsibility (CSR) frameworks. The study aims to examine the frameworks that guide sustainability and CSR practices in businesses, including their origins, key principles, and practical applications. It seeks to understand how organizations integrate sustainability and CSR into their core business strategies, identify best practices, and analyze the challenges and effective implementation strategies associated with these frameworks. The study intends to provide insights into how businesses can drive social and environmental impact through the adoption of sustainability and CSR frameworks, ultimately contributing to long-term value creation for society and the environment.

BACKGROUND

Corporate Social Responsibility Frameworks

Sustainability and Corporate Social Responsibility (CSR) frameworks play a crucial role in guiding businesses towards responsible and sustainable practices. Firstly, understanding the origins of sustainability and CSR frameworks helps contextualize their development and evolution over time. These frameworks have emerged as a response to the growing recognition of the need for businesses to address social and environmental challenges. They have evolved from early concepts such as corporate philanthropy and ethical business practices to more comprehensive approaches that integrate sustainability into core business strategies (Shiri & Jafari-Sadeghi, 2023).

Key principles form the foundation of sustainability and CSR frameworks, guiding organizations towards responsible behavior. These principles typically include areas such as environmental stewardship, social equity, economic viability, and stakeholder engagement. By adhering to these principles, businesses can align their operations with the broader objectives of sustainable development, ensuring a positive impact on society and the environment (Le, 2022). Practical applications of sustainability and CSR frameworks encompass a range of strategies and initiatives that organizations can implement to effectively manage their social and environmental impacts while ensuring profitability. These applications are designed to align business practices with the principles and goals of sustainability and CSR (Fallah Shayan et al., 2022).

One key practical application is the adoption of sustainable supply chain practices. This involves evaluating and selecting suppliers based on their environmental and social performance, promoting fair labor practices, reducing waste generation, and optimizing transportation and logistics to minimize environmental impacts (Mirzaei & Shokouhyar, 2023). By integrating sustainability criteria into the supply chain, organizations can reduce their carbon footprint, enhance transparency, and mitigate risks associated with unethical or unsustainable practices.Another practical application is the reduction of greenhouse gas (GHG) emissions. Organizations can implement energy efficiency measures, transition to renewable energy sources, and invest in clean technologies to minimize their carbon emissions. This includes adopting energy-saving practices, optimizing manufacturing processes, and implementing emission reduction strategies such as carbon offset programs. By actively working to reduce GHG emissions, businesses contribute to combating climate change and demonstrate their commitment to environmental sustainability (Shekarian et al., 2022).

Promoting diversity and inclusion is another vital application of sustainability and CSR frameworks. Organizations can implement policies and practices that foster a diverse and inclusive workplace, ensuring equal opportunities and fair treatment for employees from different backgrounds. This includes initiatives to address gender and racial equality, promote workforce diversity, and provide training and development programs that support inclusivity. By prioritizing diversity and inclusion, businesses can enhance employee satisfaction, foster innovation, and contribute to social progress (Shah et al., 2022).

Engaging in community development projects is yet another practical application. Organizations can initiate and participate in projects that benefit local communities, such as education and skill-building programs, infrastructure development, or supporting social enterprises. These efforts can help address societal needs, create positive social impact, and enhance the reputation of the organization as a responsible corporate citizen (Shekarian et al., 2022). Integrating circular economy principles is also a practical application of sustainability and CSR frameworks. This involves designing products and services with a focus on minimizing waste, maximizing resource efficiency, and promoting recycling and reuse. Organizations can implement practices such as product life extension, materials recycling, and closed-loop supply chains to reduce resource consumption and minimize waste generation. By adopting circular economy principles, businesses can contribute to a more sustainable and resource-efficient economy (Salesa, León & Moneva, 2023).

Furthermore, sustainability and CSR frameworks often provide guidelines for reporting and measuring progress. Organizations may use various reporting standards and frameworks, such as the Global Reporting Initiative (GRI) or the Sustainability Accounting Standards Board (SASB), to communicate their sustainability performance and disclose relevant information to stakeholders. This transparency enhances accountability and allows for benchmarking against industry peers (Fatima & Elbanna, 2023). It is important to note that sustainability and CSR frameworks are not one-size-fits-all solutions. They can be tailored to the specific needs and context of each organization, considering factors such as industry, size, and geographical location. Implementing these frameworks requires a commitment from top management, as well as engagement from employees and stakeholders across the organization (Mizrak & Kizilcan, 2022).

Overall, exploring sustainability and CSR frameworks provides a deeper understanding of the principles and practices that guide responsible and sustainable behavior in businesses. By embracing these frameworks, organizations can create positive social and environmental impacts, build trust with stakeholders, and contribute to a more sustainable future.

Societal Expectations and Regulatory Landscape

Societal expectations regarding business behavior have evolved significantly in recent years. Stakeholders, including consumers, employees, investors, and communities, have become more conscious of the social and environmental impacts of businesses. There is an increasing expectation that companies not only generate profits but also act as responsible corporate citizens. This shift in societal expectations has led to a greater demand for businesses to demonstrate ethical practices, social engagement, and environmental stewardship (Patuelli, Carungu & Lattanzi, 2022).

The rise of social media and digital connectivity has amplified public scrutiny and made businesses more transparent than ever before. Misconduct or negligence in social and environmental matters can quickly tarnish a company's reputation and lead to significant financial consequences. As a result, businesses are under pressure to align their practices with societal values, meet stakeholder expectations, and proactively address social and environmental challenges (Fernando et al., 2022).

In parallel to evolving societal expectations, the regulatory landscape has also been adapting to address sustainability concerns. Governments and regulatory bodies are implementing new laws and regulations that impose stricter requirements on businesses regarding environmental impact, labor practices, human rights, and corporate governance. These regulations aim to ensure that companies operate in a responsible and sustainable manner, protect the interests of stakeholders, and contribute positively to society (Turk & Mizrak, 2021). The regulatory environment includes various initiatives and frameworks at the national, regional, and international levels. For example, governments may introduce carbon pricing mechanisms, renewable energy targets, or mandatory reporting requirements for sustainability metrics. International agreements like the United Nations Sustainable Development Goals (SDGs) further shape the expectations placed on businesses to contribute to global sustainability objectives.

Furthermore, investors are increasingly considering environmental, social, and governance (ESG) factors when making investment decisions. This has led to the rise of responsible investing and the integration of ESG criteria into investment strategies. As a result, businesses that demonstrate strong ESG performance often gain access to capital and investor support. In response to societal expectations and regulatory pressures, businesses are embracing sustainability and CSR frameworks as strategic imperatives. They recognize the importance of embedding responsible and sustainable practices throughout their operations and supply chains. By doing so, companies can not only meet compliance requirements but also gain a competitive advantage, enhance brand reputation, attract and retain talent, and foster long-term stakeholder trust (Whittingham et al., 2023).

Benefits and Challenges of Adopting Sustainability and CSR

Adopting sustainability and corporate social responsibility (CSR) practices offers several benefits for organizations, as well as society and the environment. However, it also comes with its share of challenges. Understanding the benefits and challenges is crucial for businesses considering the adoption of sustainability and CSR frameworks. One of the key benefits of adopting sustainability and CSR is the enhanced reputation and brand value that it brings. Embracing these practices can improve an organization's reputation and brand image. Consumers are increasingly drawn to companies that demonstrate a commitment to social and environmental responsibility, leading to increased customer loyalty and positive brand associations. This positive reputation can provide a competitive advantage and contribute to long-term success (Hristov et al., 2022).

Another benefit is the competitive advantage that sustainability and CSR practices can provide in the market. Businesses that integrate these practices into their core strategies differentiate themselves from competitors. They attract socially conscious consumers who prioritize sustainable and responsible products and services (Pai & Chandra, 2022). Moreover, adopting sustainability and CSR opens up new market opportunities by tapping into the growing demand for environmentally friendly and socially responsible solutions. Adopting sustainability and CSR practices also helps organizations mitigate risks associated with social and environmental factors. By addressing issues such as climate change, resource scarcity, and labor rights, companies reduce their vulnerability to regulatory fines, reputational damage, supply chain disruptions, and legal liabilities. Proactively managing these risks through sustainability and CSR measures can contribute to long-term business resilience (Winit, Kantabutra & Kantabutra, 2023).

Cost savings and improved operational efficiency are additional benefits of sustainability and CSR adoption. Many sustainability practices result in reduced resource consumption, waste generation, and energy usage. Energy-saving measures, waste reduction strategies, and resource optimization can lead to significant cost savings. By enhancing operational efficiency, businesses can allocate resources more effectively and increase their overall profitability. Embracing sustainability also fosters innovation and drives product differentiation (Chen et al., 2022). By incorporating sustainability considerations into research and development processes, businesses can develop new eco-friendly products, services, and technologies. This allows them to meet evolving consumer preferences, address societal challenges, and differentiate themselves from competitors. Sustainability-oriented innovation opens up opportunities for growth and positions organizations as leaders in their respective industries (Winit, Kantabutra & Kantabutra, 2023).

However, adopting sustainability and CSR practices is not without challenges. One common challenge is the need for significant cultural and organizational change. Incorporating sustainability and CSR into the core values and operations of an organization requires a shift in mindset and the development of new practices and processes. This cultural transformation can be complex and may require time, resources, and stakeholder engagement. Another challenge is the need for robust measurement and reporting mechanisms. To effectively implement sustainability and CSR practices, organizations must establish key performance indicators, track progress, and report their sustainability efforts transparently. This requires accurate data collection, analysis, and reporting systems, which can be resource-intensive and require investment in technology and expertise (Fernando et al., 2022).

Furthermore, businesses may face challenges in aligning sustainability and CSR goals with short-term financial objectives. Balancing economic viability with long-term sustainability goals can be a delicate task. Organizations need to find ways to integrate sustainability and CSR practices while ensuring profitability and demonstrating value to stakeholders (Patuelli, Carungu & Lattanzi, 2022).

In conclusion, adopting sustainability and CSR practices offers several benefits, including enhanced reputation, competitive advantage, risk mitigation, cost savings, and innovation opportunities. However, organizations must also navigate challenges related to cultural change, measurement and reporting, and balancing sustainability goals with financial objectives. By addressing these challenges and embracing sustainability and CSR, businesses can create long-term value for themselves and contribute positively to society and the environment.

CASE STUDIES OF SUCCESSFUL ORGANIZATIONS

This part focuses on real-world examples of organizations that have effectively integrated sustainability and corporate social responsibility (CSR) into their core business strategies. By analyzing these case studies, valuable insights can be gained regarding best practices, common challenges, and effective implementation strategies in the realm of sustainability and CSR. These case studies provide a wealth of information on organizations that have successfully aligned their business objectives with sustainable practices and social responsibility. They showcase how companies from various industries have embraced sustainability and CSR, creating positive impacts on the environment, society, and their own long-term success.

Patagonia

Patagonia, an esteemed outdoor clothing and gear company, stands as a notable case study in the realm of sustainability and corporate social responsibility (CSR). The company has exemplified a robust commitment to sustainability through various initiatives that align with its core values and have garnered widespread recognition. One of Patagonia's notable sustainability practices is its emphasis on using recycled materials. The company actively seeks to reduce its reliance on virgin resources by incorporating recycled materials into its products. This approach helps minimize the environmental impact associated with resource extraction, reduces waste, and promotes the circular economy (Soule & Sekhon, T. (2022).

Furthermore, Patagonia is dedicated to reducing water and energy consumption throughout its operations. The company implements innovative strategies and technologies to conserve water and minimize energy usage in its manufacturing processes, distribution centers, and retail stores. These efforts contribute to resource conservation and demonstrate Patagonia's commitment to minimizing its ecological footprint. In addition to environmental initiatives, Patagonia places a strong emphasis on fair labor practices. The company prioritizes the welfare and rights of workers in its supply chain, striving to ensure safe working conditions, fair wages, and ethical treatment for all employees involved in the production of its products. By championing fair labor practices, Patagonia promotes social responsibility and advocates for the well-being of workers throughout its global supply chain (Ferrell, Thorne & Ferrell, 2020).

Transparency is another key aspect of Patagonia's sustainability approach. The company provides detailed and comprehensive reporting on its environmental and social performance, allowing stakeholders to understand its progress and hold it accountable. By openly sharing information about its sustainability efforts, Patagonia fosters trust with its customers, partners, and the wider public. Patagonia's commitment to environmental and social responsibility has resulted in the creation of a loyal customer base that aligns with its values. The company has successfully cultivated a brand reputation as a leader in sustainable business practices. By prioritizing sustainability, Patagonia resonates with environmentally conscious consumers who value ethical and sustainable consumption. This alignment between the company's values and customer values strengthens its brand loyalty and supports long-term business success (Ócsai & Ócsai, 2021).

Moreover, Patagonia's sustainability initiatives have had a ripple effect within the industry, inspiring other companies to follow suit. The company actively shares its knowledge and best practices with the aim of promoting sustainability throughout the apparel industry and beyond. Patagonia's leadership in sustainable business practices serves as a powerful example and motivates other organizations to take similar steps (Soule & Sekhon, T. (2022).

In summary, Patagonia's case study highlights the company's strong commitment to sustainability and CSR. Through its initiatives focused on recycled materials, water and energy conservation, fair labor practices, and transparent reporting, Patagonia has established itself as a leader in sustainable business practices. Its dedication to environmental and social responsibility has attracted a loyal customer base and inspired other organizations to embrace sustainability. Patagonia serves as a shining example of how a company can successfully integrate sustainability into its core operations and make a positive impact on both the environment and society.

Unilever

Unilever, a multinational consumer goods company, stands out as another notable example of an organization that has successfully integrated sustainability and corporate social responsibility (CSR) into its operations. Unilever has gone beyond mere token gestures and has embedded sustainability and CSR principles throughout its entire value chain.One key aspect of Unilever's sustainability approach is its ambitious goals. The company has set targets to reduce its environmental footprint, particularly in areas such as greenhouse gas emissions, water usage, and waste generation. Unilever's goals are aligned with the United Nations' Sustainable Development Goals (SDGs) and reflect its commitment to addressing global sustainability challenges (Nisa et al., 2021).

Unilever's Sustainable Living Plan serves as a guiding framework for its sustainability and CSR efforts. This comprehensive plan focuses on three main areas: improving health and well-being, reducing environmental impact, and enhancing livelihoods. By integrating these objectives into its business strategies, Unilever demonstrates a holistic approach to sustainability and CSR. Sustainable sourcing is a critical component of Unilever's strategy. The company is committed to sourcing raw materials in an environmentally and socially responsible manner. It works closely with its suppliers to promote sustainable agricultural practices, reduce deforestation, and protect biodiversity. Unilever's efforts to ensure sustainable sourcing not only contribute to its environmental goals but also support the livelihoods of smallholder farmers and local communities (Iglesias et al., 2023).

Waste reduction is another significant aspect of Unilever's sustainability initiatives. The company strives to minimize waste generation throughout its value chain, from production to packaging and distribution. Unilever actively explores innovative solutions to reduce, reuse, and recycle materials. By adopting circular economy principles, the company aims to minimize waste and maximize resource efficiency. Unilever also recognizes the importance of social impact and community engagement. The company invests in various programs to enhance the livelihoods of individuals and communities around the world. These initiatives focus on areas such as hygiene and sanitation, women's empowerment, and fair trade practices. Unilever's commitment to social impact aligns with its belief that sustainable business growth should benefit society at large (Nisa et al., 2021).

The integration of sustainability and CSR into Unilever's business practices has not only driven positive change but has also contributed to its business growth and strengthened brand reputation. Consumers today are increasingly conscious of the social and environmental impact of the products they purchase. Unilever's sustainability initiatives resonate with these consumers, leading to increased brand loyalty and market share. Moreover, Unilever's sustainability efforts have garnered recognition and accolades from various stakeholders. The company has been included in sustainability indices and rankings, highlighting its leadership in sustainability performance and disclosure. Unilever's commitment to sustainability has become a distinguishing factor in its industry and has positioned the company as a role model for other organizations (Nisa et al., 2021).

Interface

Interface, a global leader in modular flooring, is a compelling case study of a company that has made sustainability a core component of its business strategy. Interface has been at the forefront of sustainable manufacturing practices, setting an example for the industry and showcasing the possibilities of aligning sustainability, innovation, and profitability. One of Interface's notable contributions to sustainability is its use of recycled materials. The company recognized the potential to reduce its environmental impact by incorporating recycled materials into its products. Interface developed innovative technologies and processes to transform discarded materials, such as fishing nets and post-consumer carpet, into new carpet tiles. By actively seeking out and utilizing recycled materials, Interface demonstrates its commitment to resource conservation and the circular economy (Zaman et al., 2022).

Interface's commitment to sustainability is further exemplified by its implementation of closed-loop production systems. The company aims to minimize waste and maximize resource efficiency by designing its products for recyclability and implementing processes that allow for the recycling and reprocessing of materials. This closed-loop approach reduces the company's reliance on virgin resources, decreases waste generation, and mitigates environmental impact. Interface's sustainable practices go beyond manufacturing (Süsi & Jaakson, 2020). The company has also adopted a holistic approach to sustainability by addressing social and environmental issues throughout its value chain. Interface engages with suppliers to ensure responsible sourcing practices and collaborates with customers to promote sustainable use and maintenance of its products. Additionally, the company invests in programs and initiatives that support community development and environmental conservation (Sarvaiya & Arrowsmith, 2023)

Importantly, Interface has demonstrated that sustainability and profitability can go hand in hand. By integrating sustainability into its business strategy, the company has not only achieved environmental stewardship but also financial success. Interface's commitment to sustainable practices has resonated with environmentally conscious consumers and has differentiated the company in the marketplace. Its sustainable products and initiatives have been well-received, contributing to increased market share and customer loyalty. Furthermore, Interface's sustainability efforts have garnered recognition and accolades from the industry and stakeholders. The company has been widely recognized for its commitment to sustainability, receiving certifications, awards, and inclusion in sustainability indices. This recognition reinforces Interface's leadership position in sustainable business practices and serves as a testament to the positive impact that sustainability can have on business performance (Sarvaiya & Arrowsmith, 2023).

Danone

Danone, founded in 1919, is a multinational food and beverage company that has embraced sustainability as a core component of its business strategy. Through its "One Planet. One Health" initiative, Danone aims to create a positive impact on both the planet and people's health. The company recognizes the interconnectedness of environmental sustainability and human well-being, and thus focuses on various key areas to drive sustainable practices (Kartikawangi, D. (2017). One of the primary areas of focus for Danone is sustainable agriculture. The company works closely with farmers and suppliers to promote regenerative farming practices, biodiversity conservation, and the responsible use of natural resources. Danone encourages sustainable sourcing of raw materials, including dairy, fruits, and grains, to ensure the long-term viability of the agricultural systems that support its operations. Water stewardship is another crucial aspect of Danone's sustainability strategy. The company recognizes the importance of water as a finite resource and strives to minimize water consumption throughout its value chain. Danone implements innovative water management practices, including water recycling and efficiency measures, to reduce its water footprint and preserve freshwater resources (Quairel-Lanoizelee, 2016).

Danone is also committed to carbon reduction and mitigating its impact on climate change. The company sets ambitious targets to reduce greenhouse gas emissions across its operations, from production to transportation and packaging. Danone actively invests in renewable energy sources and works to optimize energy efficiency to achieve its carbon reduction goals. In addition to its environmental efforts, Danone focuses on social responsibility and community engagement. The company promotes fair trade practices, supports local communities, and invests in social initiatives to address nutrition and health challenges globally. Danone's commitment to providing healthy and sustainable food products is reflected in its portfolio, which includes a range of brands offering nutritious options and addressing specific dietary needs (Zain, 2015).

Danone's sustainability initiatives align with its mission to bring health through food to as many people as possible while respecting the planet. The company's efforts demonstrate that integrating sustainability into business strategies is not only ethically responsible but also essential for long-term business success. Through its "One Planet. One Health" initiative, Danone serves as a role model for other food and beverage companies, showcasing the positive impact that can be achieved by prioritizing sustainability and social responsibility (Zain, 2015).

Starbucks

Starbucks, a global coffeehouse chain, has become a symbol of social responsibility and sustainability in the corporate world. The company's CSR initiatives reflect its commitment to ethical sourcing, community engagement, and environmental stewardship. One of Starbucks' key CSR initiatives is its commitment to ethically sourcing coffee beans. The company works directly with coffee farmers to ensure fair prices, promote sustainable farming practices, and improve the livelihoods of farmers and their communities. Through partnerships with organizations like Conservation International, Starbucks supports programs that focus on improving the resilience and productivity of coffee-growing regions while preserving biodiversity (Li, 2022).

Starbucks also promotes fair trade practices in the coffee industry. The company is a significant purchaser of Fairtrade-certified coffee, which ensures that farmers receive fair compensation for their crops. By supporting fair trade, Starbucks contributes to reducing poverty and supporting sustainable development in coffee-producing regions worldwide. Community engagement is another central aspect of Starbucks' CSR efforts. The Starbucks Foundation, established in 1997, supports initiatives aimed at enhancing education and economic development in underserved communities. The foundation provides grants and resources to organizations addressing critical community needs, such as access to quality education, youth development, and social entrepreneurship (Moon,Tang & Lee, 2022).

In terms of environmental sustainability, Starbucks has taken significant steps to reduce its ecological footprint. The company has set targets to minimize water usage, energy consumption, and waste generation in its stores and operations. Starbucks is committed to increasing recycling rates and has made efforts to develop and implement sustainable packaging solutions. Additionally, the company has committed to sourcing 100% ethically traded and sustainably grown coffee. Starbucks' commitment to CSR extends to its employees as well. The company provides comprehensive benefits, including healthcare, stock ownership, and educational opportunities, to its partners (employees). Starbucks strives to create a positive and inclusive work environment that values diversity and promotes social responsibility (Li, 2022).

Through its robust CSR initiatives, Starbucks demonstrates that businesses can make a meaningful impact on society and the environment. The company's commitment to ethically sourced coffee, fair trade practices, community engagement, and environmental sustainability showcases its dedication to responsible business practices. By aligning its core values with CSR principles, Starbucks has built a strong brand reputation and a loyal customer base, while also making a positive difference in the communities it serves.

The Body Shop

The Body Shop, a global beauty and cosmetics company, has gained recognition for its strong focus on ethical and sustainable practices. The company's commitment to Corporate Social Responsibility (CSR) is deeply rooted in its core values of animal welfare, fair trade, and environmental sustainability. One of The Body Shop's prominent CSR initiatives is its staunch stance against animal testing. Since its inception, the company has advocated for a global ban on animal testing for cosmetics and has actively campaigned for cruelty-free beauty. The Body Shop has been a pioneer in promoting alternatives to animal testing and has worked towards raising awareness and supporting legislative changes to eliminate animal testing in the beauty industry (Patsy et al., 2023).

The company also places significant emphasis on sourcing ingredients responsibly. The Body Shop works closely with community trade partners, particularly in developing countries, to source raw materials. By engaging in fair trade practices, the company ensures that its suppliers receive fair compensation, supporting the economic empowerment of communities and promoting sustainable development. Environmental sustainability is a key pillar of The Body Shop's CSR initiatives. The company has taken steps to reduce its carbon footprint by implementing energy-efficient practices, utilizing renewable energy sources, and investing in green technologies. The Body Shop has also made strides in sustainable packaging, exploring innovative solutions and reducing the use of plastic. The company actively promotes recycling and encourages customers to participate in its packaging return and refill programs (Lee & Jeong, 2022).

In addition to these initiatives, The Body Shop focuses on empowering women through its Community Trade program, which supports female entrepreneurs and provides them with fair income opportunities. The company also engages in various philanthropic activities through its foundation, addressing social and environmental issues such as education, human rights, and protecting endangered species. The Body Shop's ethical and sustainable approach has resonated with customers worldwide, earning the company a strong reputation as a socially responsible beauty brand. Through its CSR initiatives, The Body Shop demonstrates that businesses can be successful while actively promoting values of social and environmental responsibility. By advocating for animal welfare, practicing fair trade, reducing its environmental impact, and empowering communities, The Body Shop serves as an inspiration for the beauty industry and beyond, highlighting the potential for positive change through responsible business practices (Azzahra & Fachira, 2022).

These case studies highlight several best practices and effective implementation strategies that have contributed to the success of these organizations in integrating sustainability and CSR. They include (Morali & Searcy, 2013):

- Clear Vision and Leadership: Successful organizations exhibit strong leadership and a clear vision for sustainability and CSR. Top-level commitment and active involvement in driving sustainability initiatives are crucial for achieving long-term goals.
- Integration into Core Business Strategy: Sustainable practices are integrated into the core business strategy rather than treated as peripheral activities. This involves considering sustainability throughout the value chain, from product design and sourcing to manufacturing, distribution, and customer engagement.
- Setting Ambitious Goals: Successful organizations set ambitious goals and targets related to sustainability and CSR. These goals provide a clear roadmap and focus for action, and they inspire employees, customers, and stakeholders to actively contribute to the organization's sustainability agenda.
- Collaboration and Stakeholder Engagement: Engaging with stakeholders, including employees, customers, suppliers, and communities, is vital for successful sustainability and CSR implementation. Collaboration and dialogue help identify relevant issues, build trust, and create shared value.
- Measurement and Transparency: Effective measurement and transparent reporting of sustainability performance are essential. Organizations need to establish robust systems for collecting and analyzing data, tracking progress, and communicating their sustainability efforts to stakeholders.

- While these case studies showcase successful integration of sustainability and CSR, they also shed light on common challenges faced by organizations. These challenges may include resistance to change, resource constraints, complexity in supply chain management, and balancing sustainability objectives with short-term financial goals.

In conclusion, studying case studies of successful organizations that have integrated sustainability and CSR into their core business strategies provides valuable insights into best practices, effective implementation strategies, and common challenges. These case studies inspire and guide other organizations seeking to embark on their sustainability journey, demonstrating that sustainability and CSR can be catalysts for business success, innovation, and positive social and environmental impact.

ROLE OF TECHNOLOGY AND INNOVATION

The role of technology and innovation in driving sustainability efforts is a critical subtopic that highlights the potential of digital solutions in optimizing resource utilization, reducing emissions, and promoting responsible supply chain management. Technological advancements and innovative approaches have the power to significantly contribute to overall sustainability goals. One key aspect is the utilization of technology to improve resource efficiency. Digital solutions can enable organizations to monitor and analyze their resource consumption in real-time, identifying areas of waste and inefficiency. This allows for targeted interventions and optimization of resource utilization. For example, smart grid technologies can help manage and optimize energy consumption, while sensor-based systems can provide insights into water usage and identify opportunities for conservation. By leveraging technology, organizations can reduce their environmental footprint and improve operational efficiency (Nguyen, Pham & Tram, 2020).

Another important role of technology and innovation is in reducing emissions. Digital solutions can support the transition to clean energy sources, facilitate energy management systems, and optimize transportation and logistics networks. For instance, the adoption of renewable energy technologies such as solar panels and wind turbines can enable organizations to generate clean energy on-site. Advanced data analytics and machine learning algorithms can optimize transportation routes, leading to fuel savings and reduced emissions (Friedman & Ormiston, 2022). Additionally, the Internet of Things (IoT) devices can facilitate real-time monitoring and control of emissions from industrial processes, enabling proactive emission management and reduction (Rosário & Dias, 2022).

Responsible supply chain management is another area where technology and innovation play a crucial role in driving sustainability. Digital platforms and blockchain technology can enhance supply chain transparency, traceability, and accountability. These technologies enable organizations to track and verify the sustainability credentials of suppliers, ensuring adherence to social and environmental standards. By promoting responsible sourcing practices, organizations can minimize risks related to unethical labor practices, deforestation, and environmental degradation (Shekarian et al., 2022). Furthermore, technologies like artificial intelligence and data analytics can help organizations optimize inventory management, reduce waste, and improve product lifecycle assessment, thus contributing to a circular economy (Rosário & Dias, 2022).

Innovation also plays a pivotal role in advancing sustainability efforts. It involves the development of novel technologies, products, and business models that address environmental and social challenges. For example, the emergence of electric vehicles, renewable energy storage solutions, and sustainable materials reflects innovation in response to the need for decarbonization and resource conservation. Additionally, innovative business models such as sharing economies, circular economy initiatives, and collaborative platforms contribute to sustainable consumption and production patterns.However, it is important to acknowledge that the role of technology and innovation in driving sustainability is not without challenges. These challenges include the accessibility and affordability of technology, data privacy and security concerns, and the need for upskilling and capacity building to harness the full potential of digital solutions. Additionally, there is a risk of technological advancements perpetuating unsustainable consumption patterns or leading to unintended negative environmental and social consequences. Therefore, it is crucial to ensure that technology and innovation are guided by sustainability principles and a comprehensive understanding of their potential impacts (Nguyen, Pham & Tram, 2020).

CONCLUSION

As businesses navigate the complex challenges of the 21st century, the exploration of sustainability and CSR frameworks serves as a guiding light, illuminating the path towards responsible and impactful business practices. These frameworks provide organizations with a roadmap to effectively manage their social and environmental impacts, allowing them to embrace innovation, collaboration, and accountability. By incorporating sustainable supply chain practices, reducing greenhouse gas emissions, promoting diversity and inclusion, engaging in community development projects, and adopting circular economy principles, businesses can drive meaningful change at both the local and global levels.

The benefits of adopting sustainability and CSR frameworks extend beyond the immediate impact on society and the environment. Businesses that prioritize sustainability are more likely to attract and retain top talent, as employees seek purpose-driven organizations that align with their values. Moreover, stakeholders, including investors, customers, and communities, are increasingly demanding transparency, ethical behavior, and sustainability commitments from companies. By embracing sustainability and CSR, organizations can cultivate trust, strengthen relationships, and enhance their overall reputation.

However, it is important to acknowledge the challenges that come with adopting sustainability and CSR frameworks. Organizations may face resistance from internal stakeholders, encounter barriers in implementing sustainable practices, or struggle with balancing financial performance with social and environmental considerations. Overcoming these challenges requires strong leadership, collaboration across sectors, and a long-term perspective that prioritizes sustainable value creation over short-term gains.

As the world continues to grapple with pressing issues such as climate change, social inequality, and resource depletion, the role of sustainability and CSR frameworks becomes increasingly vital. The exploration and implementation of these frameworks not only drive positive impact but also contribute to the collective effort of creating a more just, equitable, and sustainable world. By embracing sustainability as a core business principle, organizations can become powerful agents of change, paving the way for a future where economic prosperity, social well-being, and environmental stewardship coexist harmoniously.

In conclusion, the exploration of sustainability and CSR frameworks is a call to action for businesses to drive social and environmental impact. By integrating these frameworks into their strategies, organizations can navigate the complexities of the modern business landscape while fostering positive change. The journey towards sustainability and CSR is a continuous one, requiring ongoing commitment, collaboration, and adaptation. As businesses embrace these frameworks, they not only contribute to a more sustainable future but also position themselves as leaders in their industries, creating value for both their stakeholders and the world at large.

In conclusion, this study has delved into the exploration of sustainability and Corporate Social Responsibility (CSR) frameworks, shedding light on their significance in driving social and environmental impact. By examining the origins, key principles, and practical applications of these frameworks, valuable insights have been gained into how organizations can integrate sustainability and CSR into their core business strategies. The study has showcased real-world case studies of successful organizations that have effectively implemented sustainability and CSR practices, identifying best practices, common challenges, and effective implementation strategies. The role of technology and innovation in driving sustainability efforts has been explored, highlighting their potential to optimize resource utilization, reduce emissions, and promote responsible supply chain management. The study also emphasizes the importance of contributing to knowledge and stakeholders, showcasing how research findings can inform and inspire businesses, policymakers, and researchers to embrace sustainability and CSR practices for long-term value creation. Overall, this study underscores the critical role of sustainability and CSR frameworks in driving positive social and environmental change, fostering responsible business practices, and contributing to a more sustainable and equitable future for all.

Future studies on sustainability and Corporate Social Responsibility (CSR) frameworks can focus on several key areas to enhance our understanding and drive meaningful progress. Firstly, conducting comparative analyses across industries and regions can provide valuable insights into the effectiveness and impact of different frameworks, helping identify best practices and contextual factors that influence implementation. Longitudinal studies are also important to assess the long-term effects and evolution of sustainability and CSR initiatives within organizations, allowing for a deeper understanding of their sustainability journeys. Additionally, exploring the integration of emerging technologies, such as artificial intelligence and blockchain, into sustainability and CSR practices can uncover innovative solutions and their potential to drive positive impact. Furthermore, investigating the role of collaboration and partnerships between businesses, governments, and civil society organizations can provide insights into effective multi-stakeholder approaches for addressing complex sustainability challenges. Finally, exploring the connection between financial performance and sustainability efforts can contribute to the business case for sustainability, demonstrating the potential for long-term value creation. These future studies can inform and guide businesses, policymakers, and researchers in advancing sustainability and CSR practices for a more sustainable and inclusive future.

REFERENCES

Al-Shammari, M. A., Banerjee, S. N., & Rasheed, A. A. (2022). Corporate social responsibility and firm performance: A theory of dual responsibility. *Management Decision*, *60*(6), 1513–1540. doi:10.1108/MD-12-2020-1584

Azzahra, S., & Fachira, I. (2022). The Influence of Bring Back Our Bottle Program on The Body Shop Indonesia Brand Image, Brand Trust, Brand Love and Brand Loyalty. *Asian Journal of Research in Business and Management*, *4*(3), 283–295.

Cezarino, L. O., Liboni, L. B., Hunter, T., Pacheco, L. M., & Martins, F. P. (2022). Corporate social responsibility in emerging markets: Opportunities and challenges for sustainability integration. *Journal of Cleaner Production*, *362*, 132224. doi:10.1016/j.jclepro.2022.132224

Chen, A. P. S., Huang, Y. F., & Do, M. H. (2022). Exploring the Challenges to Adopt Green Initiatives to Supply Chain Management for Manufacturing Industries. *Sustainability (Basel)*, *14*(20), 13516. doi:10.3390u142013516

Fallah Shayan, N., Mohabbati-Kalejahi, N., Alavi, S., & Zahed, M. A. (2022). Sustainable development goals (SDGs) as a framework for corporate social responsibility (CSR). *Sustainability (Basel)*, *14*(3), 1222. doi:10.3390u14031222

Fatima, T., & Elbanna, S. (2023). Corporate social responsibility (CSR) implementation: A review and a research agenda towards an integrative framework. *Journal of Business Ethics*, *183*(1), 105–121. doi:10.100710551-022-05047-8 PMID:35125567

Fernando, Y., Halili, M., Tseng, M. L., Tseng, J. W., & Lim, M. K. (2022). Sustainable social supply chain practices and firm social performance: Framework and empirical evidence. *Sustainable Production and Consumption*, *32*, 160–172. doi:10.1016/j.spc.2022.04.020

Ferrell, O. C., Thorne, D. M., & Ferrell, L. (2020). *Business & society: A strategic approach to social responsibility & ethics*. SAGE Publications.

Friedman, N., & Ormiston, J. (2022). Blockchain as a sustainability-oriented innovation?: Opportunities for and resistance to Blockchain technology as a driver of sustainability in global food supply chains. *Technological Forecasting and Social Change*, *175*, 121403. doi:10.1016/j.techfore.2021.121403

Hristov, I., Appolloni, A., Cheng, W., & Huisingh, D. (2022). Aligning corporate social responsibility practices with the environmental performance management systems: A critical review of the relevant literature. *Total Quality Management & Business Excellence*, •••, 1–25. doi:10.1080/14783363.2022.2048951

Iglesias, O., Mingione, M., Ind, N., & Markovic, S. (2023). How to build a conscientious corporate brand together with business partners: A case study of Unilever. *Industrial Marketing Management*, *109*, 1–13. doi:10.1016/j.indmarman.2022.12.008

Kartikawangi, D. (2017). Symbolic convergence of local wisdom in cross–cultural collaborative social responsibility: Indonesian case. *Public Relations Review*, *43*(1), 35–45. doi:10.1016/j.pubrev.2016.10.012

Le, T. T. (2022). How do corporate social responsibility and green innovation transform corporate green strategy into sustainable firm performance? *Journal of Cleaner Production*, *362*, 132228. doi:10.1016/j.jclepro.2022.132228

Lee, S. H., & Jeong, G. Y. (2022). The effect of corporate social responsibility compatibility and authenticity on brand trust and corporate sustainability management: For Korean cosmetics companies. *Frontiers in Psychology*, *13*, 895823. doi:10.3389/fpsyg.2022.895823 PMID:35645870

Li, X. (2022). The discursive construction of corporate identity in the corporate social responsibility reports: A case study of Starbucks. *Frontiers in Psychology*, *13*, 940541. doi:10.3389/fpsyg.2022.940541 PMID:36092082

Madanaguli, A., Srivastava, S., Ferraris, A., & Dhir, A. (2022). Corporate social responsibility and sustainability in the tourism sector: A systematic literature review and future outlook. *Sustainable Development (Bradford)*, *30*(3), 447–461. doi:10.1002d.2258

Mirzaei, S., & Shokouhyar, S. (2023). Applying a thematic analysis in identifying the role of circular economy in sustainable supply chain practices. *Environment, Development and Sustainability*, *25*(5), 4691–4722. doi:10.100710668-022-02217-6

Mizrak, K. C., & Kizilcan, S. (2022). Environmentally Sensitive Management Approach Within the Scope of Carbon-Free Airport: The Case of Sivas Nuri Demirağ Airport. *Cumhuriyet Üniversitesi İktisadi ve İdari Bilimler Dergisi*, *23*(3), 623–634. doi:10.37880/cumuiibf.1063147

Moon, J., Tang, R., & Lee, W. S. (2022). Antecedents and consequences of Starbucks' environmental, social and governance (ESG) implementation. *Journal of Quality Assurance in Hospitality & Tourism*, 1–23.

Morali, O., & Searcy, C. (2013). A review of sustainable supply chain management practices in Canada. *Journal of Business Ethics*, *117*(3), 635–658. doi:10.100710551-012-1539-4

Nguyen, T. T., Pham, T. A. T., & Tram, H. T. X. (2020). Role of information and communication technologies and innovation in driving carbon emissions and economic growth in selected G-20 countries. *Journal of Environmental Management*, *261*, 110162. doi:10.1016/j.jenvman.2020.110162 PMID:32148259

Nisa, D. K., Paksi, A. K., Hutami, A. N., & Fadilla, Q. Y. (2021). Unilever's contribution to achieving sustainable development goals 3 in Indonesia. In *E3S Web of Conferences* (Vol. 316, p. 01023). EDP Sciences. doi:10.1051/e3sconf/202131601023

Ócsai, A., & Ócsai, A. (2021). Ecologically Conscious Business Organizations and Their Value Orientations. *Ecologically Conscious Organizations: New Business Practices Based on Ecological Commitment*, 93-150.

Pai, V., & Chandra, S. (2022). Exploring factors influencing organizational adoption of artificial intelligence (AI) in corporate social responsibility (CSR) initiatives. *Pacific Asia Journal of the Association for Information Systems*, *14*(5), 4. doi:10.17705/1pais.14504

Patsy, E., Alfakihuddin, M. L. B., Butar, N. A. B., & Nethania, P. (2023). Corporate action on plastic pollution (the body shop case study). *Jurnal Ekonomi*, *12*(02), 1350–1355.

Patuelli, A., Carungu, J., & Lattanzi, N. (2022). Drivers and nuances of sustainable development goals: Transcending corporate social responsibility in family firms. *Journal of Cleaner Production*, *373*, 133723. doi:10.1016/j.jclepro.2022.133723

Quairel-Lanoizelee, F. (2016). Are competition and corporate social responsibility compatible? The myth of sustainable competitive advantage. *Society and Business Review*, *11*(2), 130–154. doi:10.1108/SBR-04-2016-0026

Rosário, A. T., & Dias, J. C. (2022). Sustainability and the digital transition: A literature review. *Sustainability (Basel), 14*(7), 4072. doi:10.3390u14074072

Salesa, A., León, R., & Moneva, J. M. (2023). Airlines practices to incorporate circular economy principles into the waste management system. *Corporate Social Responsibility and Environmental Management, 30*(1), 443–458. doi:10.1002/csr.2365

Sarvaiya, H., & Arrowsmith, J. (2023). Exploring the context and interface of corporate social responsibility and HRM. *Asia Pacific Journal of Human Resources, 61*(2), 300–323. doi:10.1111/1744-7941.12316

Shah, S. Q. A., Lai, F. W., Shad, M. K., & Jan, A. A. (2022). Developing a green governance framework for the performance enhancement of the oil and gas industry. *Sustainability (Basel), 14*(7), 3735. doi:10.3390u14073735

Shekarian, E., Ijadi, B., Zare, A., & Majava, J. (2022). Sustainable supply chain management: A comprehensive systematic review of industrial practices. *Sustainability (Basel), 14*(13), 7892. doi:10.3390u14137892

Shiri, N., & Jafari-Sadeghi, V. (2023). Corporate social responsibility and green behaviour: Towards sustainable food-business development. *Corporate Social Responsibility and Environmental Management, 30*(2), 605–620. doi:10.1002/csr.2377

Soule, C. A., & Sekhon, T. (2022). How Green Demarketing Brands Can Successfully Support Anti-Consumption. *Anti-Consumption: Exploring the Opposition to Consumer Culture.*

Süsi, V., & Jaakson, K. (2020). Corporate governance and corporate social responsibility interface: A case study of private equity. *Corporate Governance (Bradford), 20*(4), 703–717. doi:10.1108/CG-11-2019-0348

Türk, A., & Mızrak, K. C. (2021). Bibliometric analysis of research in the field of organizational communication in the web of science database. *Business & Management Studies: An International Journal, 9*(3), 1173–1185. doi:10.15295/bmij.v9i3.1832

Whittingham, K. L., Earle, A. G., Leyva-de la Hiz, D. I., & Argiolas, A. (2023). The impact of the United Nations Sustainable Development Goals on corporate sustainability reporting. *Business Research Quarterly, 26*(1), 45–61. doi:10.1177/23409444221085585

Winit, W., Kantabutra, S., & Kantabutra, S. (2023). Toward a Sustainability Brand Model: An Integrative Review. *Sustainability (Basel), 15*(6), 5212. doi:10.3390u15065212

Zain, Q. (2015). Collaboration Strategy dalam Implementasi Corporate Social Responsibility (CSR): Studi Kasus Aqua Danone Klaten. *Jurnal Hubungan Internasiona, 8*(2), 81–98.

Zaman, R., Jain, T., Samara, G., & Jamali, D. (2022). Corporate governance meets corporate social responsibility: Mapping the interface. *Business & Society, 61*(3), 690–752. doi:10.1177/0007650320973415

ADDITIONAL READING

Atrey, R. R. (2020). *Exploring Corporate Social Responsibility: Fundamentals and Implementation.* Studera Press.

Idowu, S. O., & Louche, C. (Eds.). (2011). *Theory and practice of corporate social responsibility.* Springer. doi:10.1007/978-3-642-16461-3

Ihlen, Ø., Bartlett, J., & May, S. (Eds.). (2011). *The handbook of communication and corporate social responsibility.* John Wiley & Sons. doi:10.1002/9781118083246

May, S. K., Cheney, G., & Roper, J. (Eds.). (2007). *The debate over corporate social responsibility.* Oxford University Press.

Schwartz, M. S. (2017). *Corporate social responsibility.* Routledge. doi:10.4324/9781315259222

Williams, O. F. (2013). *Corporate social responsibility: The role of business in sustainable development.* Routledge. doi:10.4324/9780203746752

KEY TERMS AND DEFINITIONS

Corporate Social Responsibility (CSR): Corporate social responsibility (CSR) is the concept through which businesses voluntarily take responsibility for their impact on society, beyond their economic and legal obligations. It involves ethical behavior, transparency, and engagement in activities that contribute positively to communities, the environment, and various stakeholders.

Implementation Strategies: Implementation strategies are structured plans and approaches designed to put ideas, policies, or initiatives into action effectively. These strategies outline the steps, resources, and timelines required to achieve specific objectives or goals.

Key Principles: Key principles are fundamental values, guidelines, or rules that underpin an approach or philosophy. They serve as foundational concepts that shape decision-making and behavior in alignment with a specific framework or ideology.

Long-Term Profitability: Long-term profitability refers to a business's ability to generate consistent and sustainable profits over an extended period. It emphasizes the importance of financial success that endures beyond short-term gains, taking into account factors such as strategic planning, innovation, and responsible resource management.

Positive Social and Environmental Impacts: Positive social and environmental impacts refer to the beneficial effects that a business's actions and practices have on society and the environment. These impacts may include improvements in community well-being, reduced environmental degradation, enhanced quality of life, and increased social equity.

Practical Applications: Practical applications refer to the tangible and actionable ways in which theories, concepts, or ideas are put into real-world use. They involve the translation of theoretical knowledge into practical solutions or approaches that yield tangible outcomes.

Regulatory Landscape: The regulatory landscape encompasses the complex network of laws, regulations, and policies that govern various aspects of business operations, often within a specific industry or geographical region. It outlines the legal framework within which businesses must operate.

Responsible Business Practices: Responsible business practices refer to ethical and sustainable behaviors that prioritize the well-being of stakeholders, society, and the environment. These practices go beyond mere legal compliance to encompass efforts that contribute positively to the greater good while minimizing negative impacts.

Societal Expectations: Societal expectations encompass the collective beliefs, norms, and standards that society holds regarding ethical behavior, responsibility, and conduct from individuals and organizations. These expectations influence how businesses are perceived and the behaviors that are deemed socially acceptable.

Sustainability: Sustainability refers to the practice of meeting current needs without compromising the ability of future generations to meet their own needs. It involves considering the social, economic, and environmental aspects of actions and decisions to ensure that they contribute to a balanced and lasting system that supports human well-being and the health of the planet.

Chapter 16
Agile and IoT Methodologies in Managing IoT Projects: A Comparative Study

Soukaina Merzouk
Polydisciplinary Faculty of Sidi Bennour, Chouaib Doukkali University, El Jadida, Morocco

Abdelaziz Marzak
Faculty of Sciences Ben M'sik, Hassan II University, Casablanca, Morocco

Nawal Sael
Faculty of Sciences Ben M'sik, Hassan II University, Casablanca, Morocco

ABSTRACT

The internet of things (IoT) is revolutionizing industries by connecting physical objects to the internet through technologies like RFID and short-range wireless communications. To develop IoT solutions, various software development approaches have been adapted, including Scrum, Kanban, Large-Scale Scrum, and Scaled Agile Framework. However, these methodologies often lack flexibility and struggle to handle the unique challenges of IoT projects. This study aims to analyze and evaluate existing agile and IoT methodologies such as DSDM, DAD, Less, and ELDAMeth, comparing their capabilities, characteristics, and behaviors. By providing this comprehensive comparison, the goal is to assist in selecting the most suitable methodology for IoT projects and identify their respective advantages and limitations of each approach to suggest a new, approved IoT management methodology.

INTRODUCTION

The development of IT can be categorized into three distinct waves. The first wave, which took place in the 1960s and 1970s, aimed to automate individual activities in the value chain and increase productivity by analysing large amounts of data. The second wave emerged in the 1980s and 1990s with the rise of the internet, allowing for coordination and integration across various activities, suppliers, customers, and

DOI: 10.4018/979-8-3693-0458-7.ch016

locations. The current third wave of IT involves the integration of technology into products themselves, with embedded sensors, processors, software, and connectivity, along with a cloud-based system for storing and analyzing product data. This has led to significant improvements in product functionality and performance (Sanchez, 2020).

Agile software development has come a long way since its inception in the 1990s. Early Agile methods, such as Extreme Programming, Scrum, and Crystal, focused on iterative and incremental development, frequent releases, and close collaboration between the development team and the customer. As Agile gained popularity, more organizations began adopting it, leading to the creation of new Agile frameworks such as Kanban and Lean Agile. However, as Agile adoption continued to grow, organizations faced challenges with scaling Agile to larger teams and complex projects. This led to the development of new frameworks such as Scaled Agile Framework (SAFe), LeSS, and Nexus, designed to help organizations scale Agile while maintaining its core principles (Cohn, 2005; Ebert & Paasivaara, 2017; Schwaber & Beedle, 2002).

The Internet of Things (IoT), also referred to as the Internet of Everything, is a disruptive computing concept that brings together various technologies such as Radio Frequency Identification (RFID), short-range wireless communication, and research disciplines to enable the connection of physical objects to the internet. This connection allows data to be collected and exchanged among these objects, which can then be analyzed to provide insights and inform decision-making processes. The IoT has the potential to revolutionize several industries, such as healthcare, transportation, and manufacturing, by facilitating the creation of novel applications and services that can enhance customer experiences, reduce costs, and improve efficiency (Elhadi et al., 2018; Feki et al., 2013).

Over the years, the IoT has evolved, and IoT project management has become a distinct field of study and practice. The management of IoT projects differs from the management of traditional IT projects that focus on hardware or software. IoT solutions are usually centered around cloud computing, which can introduce additional security and privacy challenges. Furthermore, hardware is crucial in IoT solutions, as it is responsible for collecting data and executing specific tasks. To keep up with the changing landscape, Agile and DevOps methodologies have been adapted for IoT projects, emphasizing collaboration, flexibility, and continuous improvement. Furthermore, many organizations developed IoT-specific project management methodologies and frameworks like Ignite and IoT Methodology to manage the complexity of IoT projects. Today, IoT project management continues to evolve rapidly, with a growing focus on security, data privacy, and interoperability. The integration of AI and machine learning into IoT projects is also becoming increasingly common, presenting new challenges and opportunities for project managers (Hurtoi & Avadanei, 2020; Moedt et al., 2023).

To assess the success of projects, it is common to evaluate four factors, namely project efficiency, customer impact, business success, and future preparedness (Moedt et al., 2023).

LITERATURE REVIEW

Agile Software Development

Agile software development methodologies are iterative and collaborative approaches to software development that prioritize flexibility, adaptability, and customer collaboration. Unlike traditional waterfall methods that follow a linear and sequential process, Agile methodologies embrace change and aim to deliver incremental value throughout the development process.

Agile methodologies, such as Scrum, Dynamic Systems Development Method (DSDM), and others, focus on small, self-organizing teams that work in short iterations to deliver working software. They emphasize close collaboration with customers and stakeholders, frequent feedback loops, and the ability to adapt to changing requirements.

On the other hand, scalable methodologies such as Disciplined Agile Delivery (DAD), Large-Scale Scrum (LeSS), etc. are designed to address the challenges of managing larger projects and organizations. These methodologies provide frameworks and guidelines for scaling Agile practices across multiple teams and ensuring alignment and coordination.

Scrum

Scrum, a widely known Agile methodology, divides the development process into short iterations called sprints, typically lasting two to four weeks. It emphasizes cross-functional teamwork and daily stand-up meetings (daily scrums) to synchronize progress and address obstacles. At the end of each sprint, a sprint review and retrospective are conducted to gather feedback and continuously improve the development process. Based on the Agile Manifesto, Scrum consists of roles (Product Owner, Scrum Master, and Development Team), events, artifacts, and rules that teams use to manage and control their work. It is designed to be flexible and adaptive, with a focus on delivering working software incrementally and iteratively (Merzouk et al., 2021; Schwaber & Sutherland, 2020).

Dynamic Systems Development Method

DSDM, a methodology and framework, focuses on delivering business value quickly while ensuring high-quality results. It incorporates principles such as frequent delivery, collaborative and empowered teams, active user involvement, timeboxing, and prioritizing requirements based on business value. Based on the Agile Manifesto, DSDM emphasizes collaboration between the business and development teams. It consists of a set of principles, roles, and practices designed to ensure projects are delivered on time, within budget, and to the required quality standards (DSDM, 1998).

Large-Scale Scrum

LeSS is a framework for scaling Scrum to large projects with multiple teams. It provides a set of principles and practices for coordinating and integrating the work of multiple Scrum teams. LeSS is designed to be flexible and adaptive, with a focus on delivering working software incrementally and iteratively (Larman et al., 2017).

Disciplined Agile Delivery

DAD is a process decision framework that provides guidance for applying agile and lean techniques to the delivery of software solutions. DAD is designed to be flexible and adaptive, with a focus on tailoring the approach to suit the needs of the project. DAD consists of a set of principles, practices, and roles that are designed to ensure that agile and lean techniques are applied effectively to the delivery of software solutions (Ambler & Lines, 2012).

These Agile methodologies, including Scrum, DSDM, SAFe, LeSS, and DAD, share common values such as customer collaboration, adaptability, and delivering value incrementally. They offer benefits such as increased customer satisfaction, faster time to market, and enhanced team collaboration. However, challenges can arise, including the need for effective communication, managing changing requirements, and ensuring alignment in larger organizations.

Internet of Things

The Internet of Things (IoT) is the interconnected network of physical devices, vehicles, appliances, and other objects that collect and exchange data through embedded sensors, software, and connectivity. This new disruptive computing paradigm encompasses technologies like RFID, short-range wireless communications, and research disciplines, enabling the connection of physical objects to the internet. To implement IoT solutions, software development approaches such as Scrum and Kanban are commonly used. However, the unique challenges posed by IoT projects have led to the emergence of adapted methodologies like the Scaled Agile Framework (SAFe). Additionally, IoT project teams have developed their own methodologies, such as Ignite I IoT Methodology and IoT Methodology, and others, based on their surveys and experiences. These methodologies provide structured approaches specifically designed to address the complexities and requirements of IoT projects, ensuring successful implementation and valuable outcomes.

The Ignite | IoT Methodology

This method focuses on identifying use cases and user requirements to design IoT solutions. It uses modeling tools to create IoT system architectures and deployment plans. This method is innovation-focused and geared towards creating new IoT products (Slama et al., 2016).

The IoT Methodology

The IoT Methodology adopts an iterative framework that draws inspiration from Lean startup and design thinking. Its primary aim is to encourage innovation in both companies and smart cities, through the establishment of a loosely structured ecosystem. The IoT methodology is characterized by several steps for iteration, including CoCreate, Ideate, Q&A, IoT OSI, Prototype, and Deploy (Collins, 2014).

IoT Application Development

This method focuses on developing IoT applications using development platforms such as Arduino and Raspberry Pi. It uses an agile approach to application development and emphasizes collaboration between developers and users. This method is geared towards rapid development of IoT prototypes and applications (Patel & Cassou, 2015).

ELDAMeth

ELDAMeth (Fortino et al., 2014, 2015; Fortino & Russo, 2012) is a methodology that is tailored for the simulation-based prototyping of distributed agent systems (DAS). It focuses on the ELDA (Event-driven Lightweight Distilled StateCharts Agent) agent model, along with relevant frameworks and tools. Additionally, it adopts an iterative development process that encompasses the modeling, simulation, and implementation phases of DAS. It is made up of three phases, namely The Modeling phase, The Simulation phase, and The Implementation & Deployment phase. In an IoT system, agents and the software components of things are very similar. These software components are called smart objects (SOs) because they share the autonomy feature that is also present in agents. As a result, SOs (which refer to the software component of things) are treated as the fundamental building blocks of IoT systems that operate in a distributed, networked environment.

RELATED WORK

This paper focuses on conducting a comparative study of nine different IoT system development methodologies. The main objective is to evaluate these methodologies based on a set of 14 criteria, which are derived from their characteristics. The study also includes an overview of various methodologies such as Ignite | IoT methodology, IoT methodology, and IoT Application Development.

The objective of Merzouk's (2017) article is to provide a comparative analysis of different agile methods, with a focus on developing a new model-based method. The study aims to evaluate and compare the existing agile methodologies to propose a novel approach. (Merzouk, 2017)

The study conducted by Saleh et al. (2019) compares the Scrum, XP, and Kanban methodologies. The main objective is to determine the essential variables to consider when evaluating these methods. The study presents an inspection strategy that focuses on the key features and characteristics of these agile approaches (Saleh et al., 2019).

Almeida and Espinheira (2021) conducted a comprehensive review of large-scale agile frameworks. Their study explored various frameworks, including SAFe, LeSS, Nexus, and Spotify model, and compared them in terms of scalability, collaboration, and alignment with organizational goals. The findings highlighted the strengths and limitations of each framework, providing valuable insights for organizations seeking to implement agile methodologies at a larger scale (Almeida & Espinheira, 2021).

The present paper is an extension of previous research on IoT methodologies (Merzouk et al., 2020). The paper includes a comparative study of different methods used for managing IoT projects. It aims to analyze and evaluate the advantages and disadvantages of each method. By building upon the previous work, this paper provides further insights and information on additional methodologies used in the field of IoT project management.

COMPARATIVE STUDY

Criteria

Before beginning development, every new project in a software firm requires research to establish its special needs, size, complexity, and so on. The team project then selects a management approach that gives workplace guidance to team members based on these criteria. However, there are various methods that share the same principles and values, but each has unique characteristics (e.g., process) and is not applicable in all cases. The outstanding choice of a certain technique is dependent on the method's understanding, i.e., the comprehension of practices, processes, roles, and so on. As a result, for this study, we established certain criteria that offer a basic overview of each selected approach.

- method creation information criterion
    - Methodologist: the person who developed this approach.
    - Organization: Where is this approach being developed?
    - Date: the date the approach was created.
- Approach: is a management technique that entails the team managing and controlling the processes that comprise their organizations, as well as managing these process interactions as a system.
- Team size: the number of development team members necessary to boost workplace efficiency using this strategy.
- Roles and responsibilities: defining and communicating "who does what" is essential for process performance.
- Artifacts: any type of information created, produced, changed, or used by a person in the creation of a computer "system."

Comparison

In this sub-section, we present a comparative analysis of the different agile methods discussed in the literature review. The aim is to identify and highlight the similarities, differences, and key findings across the studies.

Discussion

When comparing these methods, it is important to consider the specific needs of the IoT project, such as project scope, number of connected devices, user requirements, and available resources. Each method has its advantages and disadvantages (table 2), and the chosen method should be adapted to the specific needs of the project.

Table 1. Comparative study of methods used to manage IoT projects

	Ignite	IoT Methodology	Scrum	LeSS	DAD	ELDAMeth
Methodologist	Bosch software innovations team	Consultancy for Internet of Things team	Kent Scwaber and Jeff Sutherland		Scott Ambler & Mark Lines	Griancarlo Fortino & Wilma Russo
Organization	Bosch software innovations	Consultancy for Internet of Things (C4IOT)	Easel Corporation		-	Department of electronics, Informatics and systems university of Calabria, Italy
Date	2014-2015	2015	1995		2013	2012
Approach	No iterative	Iterative	Iterative			Iterative
Team size	Large	Large	Small			-
Roles and responsibilities	-	end user designer implementer project manager	Product owner Scrum master Cross-functional Team			Modeler Simulation Designer Developer Tester
Artifacts	IoT Project Dimensions IoT Architecture Blueprints IoT Technology Profiles	IoT Canvas IoT— Architecture Reference Model	Product Backlog Sprint Backlog Sprint Board Product increment/ release			Behavioral EldaMeth Design Model Structural EldaMeth Design Model Simulator program x Simulation results Testing Results Platform specific EldaMeth Code x
Meetings	budget planning business planning	kickoff sessions a blend of engineer meetings	Sprint planning Daily Scrum Sprint Review/Demo Sprint retrospective Backlog grooming			
Rhythm	-	-	2-4 weeks			
Change philosophy	No change	After an iteration	After a sprint			
Top priority	Security in IoT Solution Design phase	Creating a prototype of the solution	Items scheduled for the currents sprint			
Hardware	√	√	-	-	-	√
Software	√	√	√	√	√	√

√: Defined. -: Not defined

Table 2. Advantages and disadvantages of agile and IoT methods

	Advantages	Disadvantages
Scrum	- Provides a framework for delivering working software incrementally and iteratively - Encourages collaboration and communication between team members - Provides a structured approach to managing work and tracking progress - Can be easily adapted to suit the needs of the project	- Requires a high level of discipline and commitment from team members - Can be challenging to implement in organizations with a hierarchical culture - Can be difficult to scale to large projects with multiple teams
DSDM	- Provides a structured approach to delivering projects on time and within budget - Encourages collaboration between the business and development teams - Can be easily adapted to suit the needs of the project - Provides a framework for managing risk and ensuring quality	- Can be challenging to implement in organizations with a hierarchical culture - Requires a high level of discipline and commitment from team members - Can be less flexible than other methodologies, which can make it difficult to adapt to changing requirements
LeSS	- Provides a framework for scaling Scrum to large projects with multiple teams - Encourages collaboration and communication between teams - Provides a structured approach to managing dependencies and ensuring quality - Can be easily adapted to suit the needs of the project	- Can be difficult to implement in organizations with a hierarchical culture - Requires a high level of discipline and commitment from team members - Can be less flexible than other methodologies, which can make it difficult to adapt to changing requirements
DAD	- Provides a framework for applying agile and lean techniques to the delivery of software solutions - Encourages flexibility and adaptability in the approach to delivery - Provides a structured approach to managing dependencies and ensuring quality - Can be easily adapted to suit the needs of the project	- Can be complex and difficult to implement - Requires a high level of discipline and commitment from team members - Can be less structured than other methodologies, which can lead to confusion and uncertainty
Ignite	Facilitates rapid development and deployment of IoT applications, simplifies the development process through pre-built IoT modules, offers a user-friendly interface and intuitive development environment.	Limited flexibility in customization and adaptability for unique project requirements, potential dependency on Ignite platform and vendor lock-in, limited community support and documentation compared to other methodologies.
IoTMeth	Offers a holistic approach to IoT solution development, emphasizes addressing scalability and interoperability challenges, provides guidance for managing the entire IoT solution lifecycle.	Requires a comprehensive understanding of IoT technologies and ecosystems, may require significant investment in IoT infrastructure and tools, complexity in managing and integrating various IoT components.
EldaMeth	Provides a systematic approach for IoT application development, emphasizes effective data management and analysis, promotes collaboration and communication among team members.	Requires a learning curve for teams unfamiliar with the methodology, may require additional resources for implementation, potential resistance to change from existing development processes.
IoT Application Development	Tailored specifically for IoT applications, enables rapid prototyping and iterative development of IoT solutions, provides flexibility in adapting to changing requirements and technologies.	May require specialized knowledge and skills in IoT technologies, integration with existing systems and infrastructures may be complex, ensuring security and privacy in IoT applications can be challenging.

CONCLUSION

In conclusion, the evaluation of ELDAMeth, IoT Application Development, The IoT Methodology, and Ignite in the context of IoT application development underscores the significance of thoroughly assessing the specific advantages and disadvantages of each methodology. ELDAMeth offers a systematic approach that prioritizes effective data management and collaboration, while IoT Application Development facilitates rapid prototyping and adaptability. The IoT Methodology presents a comprehensive framework that addresses scalability and interoperability challenges and Ignite streamlines development through its pre-built modules. To ensure successful IoT solutions, organizations must carefully consider their project requirements, team capabilities, and integration needs when selecting the most suitable methodology. By leveraging the strengths and mitigating the limitations of these methodologies, organizations can enhance their ability to deliver optimal outcomes. Further research should explore hybrid approaches and empirically validate the effectiveness of these methodologies in real-world IoT projects.

REFERENCES

Almeida, F., & Espinheira, E. (2021). Large-scale agile frameworks: A comparative review. *Journal of Applied Sciences, Management and Engineering Technology*, *2*(1), 16–29.

Ambler, S. W., & Lines, M. (2012). *Disciplined Agile Delivery: A Practitioner's Guide to Agile Software Delivery in the Enterprise*. IBM Press.

Cohn, M. (2005). *Agile estimating and planning*. Pearson Education.

Collins, T. (2014). *A Methodology for Building the Internet of Things*. Academic Press.

DSDM. (1998). *Dynamic Systems Development Method*. https://docplayer.fr/5488317-Dynamic-systems-development-method.html

Ebert, C., & Paasivaara, M. (2017). ScalingAgile. *IEEE Software*, *34*(06), 98–103. doi:10.1109/MS.2017.4121226

Elhadi, S., Marzak, A., Sael, N., & Merzouk, S. (2018). Comparative Study of IoT Protocols. SSRN *Electronic Journal*. doi:10.2139/ssrn.3186315

Feki, M. A., Kawsar, F., Boussard, M., & Trappeniers, L. (2013). The Internet of Things: The Next Technological Revolution. *Computer*, *46*(2), 24–25. doi:10.1109/MC.2013.63

Fortino, G., Guerrieri, A., Russo, W., & Savaglio, C. (2015). Towards a Development Methodology for Smart Object-Oriented IoT Systems: A Metamodel Approach. *2015 IEEE International Conference on Systems, Man, and Cybernetics*, 1297–1302. 10.1109/SMC.2015.231

Fortino, G., Rango, F., & Russo, W. (2014). ELDAMeth Design Process. In M. Cossentino, V. Hilaire, A. Molesini, & V. Seidita (Eds.), *Handbook on Agent-Oriented Design Processes* (pp. 115–139). Springer Berlin Heidelberg. doi:10.1007/978-3-642-39975-6_5

Fortino, G., & Russo, W. (2012). ELDAMeth: An agent-oriented methodology for simulation-based prototyping of distributed agent systems. *Special Section: Engineering Complex Software Systems through Multi-Agent Systems and Simulation, 54*(6), 608–624. doi:10.1016/j.infsof.2011.08.006

Hurtoi, V., & Avadanei, D. (2020). IoT Project Management. *Informações Econômicas, 24*(3), 75–80. doi:10.24818/issn14531305/24.3.2020.07

Larman, C., Vodde, B., & Jensen, B. (2017). *Large-scale scrum*. Dpunkt.

Merzouk, S. (2017). A Comparative Study of Agile Methods. *Towards a New Model-based Method., 9*(4), 8.

Merzouk, S., Cherkaoui, A., Marzak, A., & Nawal, S. (2020). IoT methodologies: Comparative study. *Procedia Computer Science, 175*, 585–590. doi:10.1016/j.procs.2020.07.084

Merzouk, S., Cherkaoui, A., Marzak, A., Sael, N., & Guerss, F.-Z. (2021). The proposition of Process flow model for Scrum and eXtreme Programming. *Association for Computing Machinery, 6*, 1–6. Advance online publication. doi:10.1145/3454127.3457627

Moedt, W., Bernsteiner, R., Hall, M., & Fruhling, A. (2023). Enhancing IoT Project Success through Agile Best Practices. *ACM Transactions on Internet of Things, 4*(1), 5:1-5:31. doi:10.1145/3568170

Patel, P., & Cassou, D. (2015). Enabling high-level application development for the Internet of Things. *Journal of Systems and Software, 103*, 62–84. doi:10.1016/j.jss.2015.01.027

Saleh, S. M., Huq, S. M., & Rahman, M. A. (2019). Comparative Study within Scrum, Kanban, XP Focused on Their Practices. *2019 International Conference on Electrical, Computer and Communication Engineering (ECCE)*, 1–6. 10.1109/ECACE.2019.8679334

Sanchez, M. A. (2020). How Internet of Things Is Transforming Project Management. In Research Anthology on Digital Transformation, Organizational Change, and the Impact of Remote Work (pp. 463–484). IGI Global. doi:10.4018/978-1-7998-7297-9.ch024

Schwaber, K., & Beedle, M. (2002). *Agile Software Development with Scrum* (Vol. 1). Prentice Hall. https://books.google.co.ma/books?id=BpFYAAAAYAAJ

Schwaber, K., & Sutherland, J. (2020). *The Scrum Guide The Definitive Guide to Scrum: The Rules of the Game*. https://scrumguides.org/scrum-guide.html

Slama, D., Puhlmann, F., Morrish, J., & Bhatnagar, R. M. (Eds.). (2016). *Enterprise IoT: Enterprise IoT: strategies and best practices for connected products and services*. O'Reilly.

Compilation of References

(The) Standish Group. (2004). *Third quarter research report: Chaos demographics.* Author.

Wastes of Lean Manufacturing. (2020, September 4). TechSolve. Retrieved December 29, 2021, from https://www.techsolve.org/8-wastes-of-lean-manufacturing/

A Brief History of Lean. (n.d.). Lean Enterprise Institute. Retrieved December 29, 2021, from https://www.lean.org/explore-lean/a-brief-history-of-lean/

AccountAbility. (2018). *AA1000 Accountability Principles 2018.* AccountAbility. https://www.accountability.org/static/6b3863943105f2a5c4d5fc96affb750d/aa1000_accountability_principles_2018.pdf

Acharya, P. S., & Pandey, S. (2018). National spatial data infrastructure India (NSDI-India)-present status and the future strategies. Geospatial Infrastructure, Applications and Technologies: India Case Studies. doi:10.1007/978-981-13-2330-0_2

Ackerman, E. (2016). *Walmart and Five Elements Robotics Working on Robotic Shopping Cart.* IEEE. https://spectrum.ieee.org/automaton/robotics/industrial-robots/walmart-and-five-elementsrobotics-working-on-robotic-shopping-cart

Addeo, F., Delli Paoli, A., Esposito, M., & Ylenia Bolcato, M. (2019). Doing social research on online communities: The benefits of netnography. *Athens Journal of Social Sciences, 7*(1), 9–38. doi:10.30958/ajss.7-1-1

Adeleye, N., & Eboagu, C. (2019). Evaluation of ICT development and economic growth in Africa. *NETNOMICS: Economic Research and Electronic Networking, 20*(1), 31–53. doi:10.100711066-019-09131-6

Adeyelure, H. M. D. S., & Jokonya, O. (2019). Adoption of Business Intelligence in the South African public social sector Department. In *Proceedings of 4th International Conference on the* (*Vol. 12*, pp. 157-168). Academic Press.

Adhikari, R. (2017). *Robots May Become Go-To Customer Service Reps.* CRM Buyer. https://www.crmbuyer.com/story/84765.html

Afanasyev, I., Mazzara, M., Chakraborty, S., Zhuchkov, N., Maksatbek, A., Yesildirek, A., Kassab, M., & Distefano, S. (2019). Towards the Internet of robotic things: Analysis, architecture, components, and challenges. In *2019 12th International Conference on Developments in eSystems Engineering (DeSE)* (pp. 3-8). IEEE. 10.1109/DeSE.2019.00011

Afreen, S. (2023). *The Role of Big Data Analytics in Business Decision Making.* The Times of India. May 26, 2023. https://timesofindia.indiatimes.com/blogs/voices/the-role-of-big-data-analytics-in-business-decision-making/

Aghion, P., Howitt, P., & Mayer-Foulkes, D. (2005). The effect of financial development on convergence: Theory and evidence. *The Quarterly Journal of Economics, 120*(1), 173–222.

Agrawal, R., Majumdar, A., Majumdar, K., Raut, R. D., & Narkhede, B. E. (2022). Attaining sustainable development goals (SDGs) through supply chain practices and business strategies: A systematic review with bibliometric and network analyses [November.]. *Business Strategy and the Environment, Wiley Blackwell, 31*(7), 3669–3687.

Agyei-Ababio, N., Ansong, E., & Assa-Agyei, K. (2023). Digitalization of revenue mobilization in an emerging economy: The new Institutional Theory perspective. *International Journal of Information Systems and Project Management, 11*(2), 5–22. doi:10.12821/ijispm110201

Ahmad, M. F., Toh, L. Y., Chan, S. W., Ahmad, A. N. A., Raja Mohd Rasi, R. Z., Abdul Rahman, N. A., Muhd Nor, N. H., Hassan, M. F., & Hashim, F. A. (2017). Continuous improvement and its barriers in electrical and electronic industry. MATEC Web of Conferences 135, Langkawi, Malaysia. doi:10.1051/matecconf/201713500045

Ahmad, M., & Khiyal, M. S. H. (2023). Assessment of land administration in Pakistan and the potential role of volunteered geographic information. In Handbook of Research on Driving Socioeconomic Development With Big Data. doi:10.4018/978-1-6684-5959-1.ch014

Ahmad, M., Khayal, M. S. H., & Tahir, A. (2022). Analysis of Factors Affecting Adoption of Volunteered Geographic Information in the Context of National Spatial Data Infrastructure. *ISPRS International Journal of Geo-Information, 11*(2), 120. Advance online publication. doi:10.3390/ijgi11020120

Ahmed Soliman, M. H. (2013). Lean transformation guidance: Why organizations fail to achieve and sustain excellence through lean improvement. *International Journal of Lean Thinking, 4*(1), 31–40.

AIM Change Management Methodology. (n.d.). IMA | Change Management. Retrieved September 3, 2023, from https://www.imaworldwide.com/aim-change-management-methodology

Ako-Nai, A., & Singh, A. M. (2019). Information technology governance framework for improving organisational performance. *South African Journal of Information Management, 21*(1), 1–11. doi:10.4102ajim.v21i1.1010

Al Najem, M., Dhakal, H., & Bennett, N. (2012). The role of culture and leadership in lean transformation: A review and assessment model. *International Journal of Lean Thinking, 3*(1), 119–138.

Al Omari, L., Barnes, P., & Pitman, G. (2012). Optimising COBIT 5 for IT governance: examples from the public sector. In *Proceedings of the ATISR 2012: 2nd International Conference on Applied and Theoretical Information Systems Research* (pp. 1-13). Academy of Taiwan Information Systems Research (ATISR).

Aladwani, A. M. (2001). Change management strategies for successful ERP implementation. *Business Process Management Journal, 7*(3), 266–275. doi:10.1108/14637150110392764

Albert, M. (1993). *Capitalism Against Capitalism.* Wiley.

AlDajani, I. M. (2020). Phronetic Netnography Research Design. In *Internet Communication Technology (ICT) for Reconciliation* (pp. 155–201). Springer. doi:10.1007/978-3-030-41203-6_7

Alhawari, O., Awan, U., Bhutta, M. K. S., & Ülkü, M. A. (2021). Insights from circular economy literature: A review of extant definitions and unravelling paths to future research. *Sustainability, 13*(2), 859.

Ali, A., & Ahmad, M. (2012). Is SDI Development, Waste of Time and Money for Pakistan? In *Global geospatial conference 2012 - Spatially enabling government, industry and citizens* (p. 13). Academic Press.

Ali, A., & Imran, M. (2021). National Spatial Data Infrastructure vs. Cadastre System for Economic Development: Evidence from Pakistan. *Land (Basel), 10*(2), 188. doi:10.3390/land10020188

Ali, A., Imran, M., Jabeen, M., Ali, Z., & Mahmood, S. A. (2021). Factors influencing integrated information management: Spatial data infrastructure in Pakistan. *Information Development.* Advance online publication. doi:10.1177/02666669211048483

Alla, L., Hmioui, A., & Bentalha, B. (2020). La netnographie dans les recherches marketing: La communauté virtuelle comme consom'acteur vecteur d'efficacité marketing. *Alternatives Managériales Economiques*, *2*(4), 631–652. doi:10.48374/IMIST.PRSM/ame-v2i4.23559

Almeida, F., & Espinheira, E. (2021). Large-scale agile frameworks: A comparative review. *Journal of Applied Sciences, Management and Engineering Technology*, *2*(1), 16–29.

Almeida, J. A., Almeida, A. T., & Costa, A. P. C. S. (2014). Portfolio selection of information systems projects using PROMETHEE V with c-optimal concept. *Pesquisa Operacional*, *34*(02), 275–299. doi:10.1590/0101-7438.2014.034.02.0275

Aloini, D., Martini, A., & Pellegrini, L. (2011). A structural equation model for continuous improvement: A test for capabilities, tools and performance. *Production Planning and Control*, *22*(7), 628–648. doi:10.1080/09537287.2010.508759

Al-Shammari, M. A., Banerjee, S. N., & Rasheed, A. A. (2022). Corporate social responsibility and firm performance: A theory of dual responsibility. *Management Decision*, *60*(6), 1513–1540. doi:10.1108/MD-12-2020-1584

Alukal, G. (2006, October). 2006). Keeping lean alive. *Quality Progress*, *39*(10), 67–69. https://asq.org/quality-progress/articles/lean-lessons-keeping-lean-alive?id=b90de437aa374da689bba4c848cb6ef1

Ambler, S. W., & Lines, M. (2012). *Disciplined Agile Delivery: A Practitioner's Guide to Agile Software Delivery in the Enterprise*. IBM Press.

American Educational Research Association, American Psychological Association, & National Council on Measurement in Education. (2014). Standards for educational and psychological testing. American Education Research Association.

Anderson, M., Schulze, K., Cassini, A., Plachouras, D., & Mossialos, E. (2019). A governance framework for development and assessment of national action plans on antimicrobial resistance. In The Lancet Infectious Diseases (Vol. 19, Issue 11). doi:10.1016/S1473-3099(19)30415-3

Anyieni, A. G., Bcom, M., & Campus, N. (2013). Effect of strategic planning on the performance of small and medium enterprises in Kenya: A summary review of the literature. *The International Journal of Professional Management*, *8*(6), 1–10.

Ardana, I. M. S., & Suharjito. (2017). Software development evaluation process using CMMI-Dev on limited resources company. In *2017 3rd International Conference on Science in Information Technology (ICSITech)* (pp. 319-324). . doi:10.1109/ICSITech.2017.8257132

Arjaliès. Diane-Laure & Mundy, Julia. (2013). The Use of Management Control Systems to Manage CSR Strategy: A Levers of Control Perspective. *Management Accounting Research.* 24. http://dx.doi.org/10.1016/j.mar.2013.06.003

Arnheiter, E. D., & Maleyeff, J. (2005). The integration of lean management and Six Sigma. *The TQM Magazine*, *17*(1), 5–18. doi:10.1108/09544780510573020

Aron, R., Shantanu, D., Ramkumar, J., & Praveen, A. P. (2011). The Impact of Automation of Systems on Medical Errors: Evidence from Field Research. *Information Systems Research*, *22*(3), 429–446. doi:10.1287/isre.1110.0350

Asana. (2022). *Waterfall vs. Agile vs. Kanban vs. Scrum: What's the difference?* Retrieved from https://asana.com/resources/waterfall-agile-kanban-scrum

Ashrafi, R., & Mueller, J. (2015). Delineating IT resources and capabilities to obtain competitive advantage and improve firm performance. *Information Systems Management*, *32*(1), 15–38. doi:10.1080/10580530.2015.983016

Association for Manufacturing Excellence. (2009). Sustaining lean: Case studies in transforming culture. CRC Press.

Association for Project Management. (2022). *What is agile project management?* Retrieved from https://www.apm.org.uk/resources/find-a-resource/agile-project-management/

Auditor General South Africa (AGSA). (2019). *12 information technology controls.* Available online at https://www.agsa.co.za/Portals/0/Reports/PFMA/201617/GR/12%20information%20technology%20controls.pdf

Auditor-General of South Africa (AGSA). (2019). *Consolidated General Report on the audit outcomes of local government 2017-2018.* Government Printer.

Aulbur, W., & Singh, H.V. (2014). *Next Generation Manufacturing: Industry 4.0: A Look at the Changing Landscapes in Manufacturing.* CII and Roland Berger.

Awan, U., Sroufe, R., & Shahbaz, M. (2021). Industry 4.0 and the circular economy: A literature review and recommendations for future research. *Business Strategy and the Environment, 30*(4), 2038–2060.

AXELOS Limited. (2017). Managing Successful Projects with PRINCE2 (6th ed.). Norwich: The Stationery Office.

Ayala-Orozco, B., Rosell, J. A., Merçon, J., Bueno, I., Alatorre-Frenk, G., Langle-Flores, A., & Lobato, A. (2018). Challenges and strategies in place-based multi-stakeholder collaboration for sustainability: Learning from experiences in the Global South. *Sustainability, 10*(9), 3217.

Ayanlade, A., Orimoogunje, I. O. O., & Borisade, P. B. (2008). Geospatial data infrastructure for sustainable development in sub-Saharan countries. *International Journal of Digital Earth, 1*(3), 247–258. doi:10.1080/17538940802149940

Azzahra, S., & Fachira, I. (2022). The Influence of Bring Back Our Bottle Program on The Body Shop Indonesia Brand Image, Brand Trust, Brand Love and Brand Loyalty. *Asian Journal of Research in Business and Management, 4*(3), 283–295.

Azzi, R., Chamoun, R. K., & Sokhn, M. (2019). The power of a blockchain-based supply chain. *Computers & Industrial Engineering, 135*, 582–592. doi:10.1016/j.cie.2019.06.042

Back, A. (2017, Nov 6). Using Blockchain for Supply Chain Transparency and Traceability. Medium. https://medium.com/blockchain-review/the-visible-supply-chain-ab73a80863fd

Bajpai, N., & Biberman, J. (2019). *The Future Work in India: Adopting to the Fourth Industrial Revolution.* ICT Working Paper No. 11.

Bana e Costa, C. A., & Vansnick, J. C. (1994). MACBETH - An interactive path towards the construction of cardinal value functions. *International Transactions in Operational Research, 1*(4), 489–500. doi:10.1016/0969-6016(94)90010-8

Banalieva, E., & Dhanaraj, C. (2019). Internalization theory for the digital economy. *Journal of International Business Studies, 50*(8), 1372–1387. doi:10.105741267-019-00243-7

Barba-Sanchez, V., Calderón-Milán, M. J., & Atienza-Sahuquillo, C. (2018). A study of the value of ICT in improving corporate performance: A corporate competitiveness view. *Technological and Economic Development of Economy, 24*(4), 1388–1407. doi:10.3846/tede.2018.3114

Barbu, C. M., Florea, D. L., Dabija, D. C., & Barbu, M. C. R. (2021). Customer experience in fintech. *Journal of Theoretical and Applied Electronic Commerce Research, 16*(5), 1415–1433. doi:10.3390/jtaer16050080

Bardin, L. (2011). Análise de Conteúdo (1° ed, Vol. 1). Edições 70.

Barenji, A. V., Li, Z., Wang, W. M., Huang, G. Q., & Guerra-Zubiaga, D. A. (2020). Blockchain-based ubiquitous manufacturing: A secure and reliable cyber-physical system. *International Journal of Production Research, 58*(7), 2200–2221. doi:10.1080/00207543.2019.1680899

Barlow, G. L. (2002). Auditing hospital queuing. *Managerial Auditing Journal, 17*(7), 397–403. doi:10.1108/02686900210437507

Bartl, M., Kannan, V. K., & Stockinger, H. (2016). A review and analysis of literature on netnographie research. *International Journal of Technology Marketing, 11*(2), 165–196. doi:10.1504/IJTMKT.2016.075687

Basl, J., & Kopp, J. (2017). Study of the Readiness of Czech Companies to the Industry 4.0. *Journal of Systems Integration, 8*, 40–45.

Batth, R. S., Nayyar, A., & Nagpal, A. (2018). Internet of robotic things: driving intelligent robotics of future-concept, architecture, applications and technologies. In *2018 4th International Conference on Computing Sciences (ICCS)* (pp. 151-160). IEEE. 10.1109/ICCS.2018.00033

Battini, D., Calzavara, M., Persona, A., & Sgarbossa, F. (2017). Additional effort estimation due to ergonomic conditions in order picking systems. *International Journal of Production Research, 55*(10), 2764–2774. doi:10.1080/00207543.2016.1190879

Baturina, O. (2019, May 2). *40 Stats and Real-Life Examples of How Companies Use Big Data.* ScienceSoft. https://www.scnsoft.com/blog/big-data-use-cases-stats-and-examples#1

Bauer, H., Brandl, F., Lock, C., & Reinhart, G. (2018). Integration of Industrie 4.0 in Lean Manufacturing Learning Factories. *Procedia Manufacturing, 23*, 147–152. doi:10.1016/j.promfg.2018.04.008

Baumgartner, R. J. (2009). Organizational Culture and Leadership: Preconditions for the Development of a Sustainable Corporation. *Sustainable Development, 17*, 102–113.

Bell, K., Lamb, A., Lipej, B., Evtimov, V., Hilton, A., Galic, Z., Hunter, G., Shreesh, R., Dhakal, S., & Rawal, N. (2020). *Technical Assistance to Develop the Land Administration and Geospatial Information Systems of Nepal.* doi:10.13140/RG.2.2.13525.78564

Beltramello, A., Haie-Fayle, L., & Pilat, D. (2013). Why New Business Models Matter for Green Growth (No. 2013/1). OECD Publishing.

Benchmarking Definition. (n.d.). iSixSigma. Retrieved December 29, 2021, from https://www.isixsigma.com/dictionary/benchmarking/

Benkarim, A., & Imbeau, D. (2021). Organizational commitment and lean sustainability: Literature review and directions for future research. *Sustainability (Basel), 13*(6), 3357. doi:10.3390u13063357

Benner, M. J., & Tushman, M. L. (2003). Exploitation, exploration, and process management: The productivity dilemma revisited. *Academy of Management Review, 28*(2), 238–256. doi:10.2307/30040711

Benn, S., Edwards, M., & Williams, T. (2014). *Organizational Change for Corporate Sustainability* (4th ed.). Routledge.

Bentalha, B. (2023). A Framework for Exploring the Global Performance of Service Supply Chain Management: A Qualitative Study. *Government Impact on Sustainable and Responsible Supply Chain Management*, 106-129.

Bentalha, B., Hmioui, A., & Alla, L. (2023). Green Transportation Balanced Scorecard: A VIKOR Fuzzy Method for Evaluating Green Logistics Initiatives. In *International Conference on Digital Technologies and Applications* (pp. 916-925). Cham: Springer Nature Switzerland. 10.1007/978-3-031-29857-8_91

Bentalha, B. (2020). Big-Data et Service Supply Chain Management: Challenges et Opportunités. *IJBTSR International Journal of Business And Technology Studies and Research, 1*(3). Advance online publication. doi:10.5281/zenodo.3607357

Bentalha, B. (2022). Green transportation Balanced scorecard model: a fuzzy-delphi approach during COVID-19. In *Computational Intelligence Techniques for Green Smart Cities* (pp. 107–127). Springer International Publishing. doi:10.1007/978-3-030-96429-0_5

Bentalha, B., & Hmioui, A. (2021). Smart Service Supply Chain and Just Walk Out Technology: A Netnographic Approach. In *The Proceedings of the International Conference on Smart City Applications* (223-236). Springer.

Bentalha, B., Hmioui, A., & Alla, L. (2019). The digitalization of the supply chain management of service companies: a prospective approach. In *Proceedings of the 4th International Conference on Smart City Applications* (pp. 1-8). 10.1145/3368756.3369005

Bentalha, B., Hmioui, A., & Alla, L. (2020). The global performance of a service supply chain: a simulation-optimization under arena. In *The Proceedings of the Third International Conference on Smart City Applications* (pp. 489-502). Cham: Springer International Publishing.

Ben-Tovim, D. I., Bassham, J. E., Bolch, D., Martin, M. A., Dougherty, M., & Szwarcbord, M. (2007). Lean thinking across a hospital: Redesigning care at the Flinders Medical Centre. *Australian Health Review, 31*(1), 10. doi:10.1071/AH070010 PMID:17266483

Bernarda, G., Pigneur, Y., Osterwalder, A., & Smith, A. (2014). *Value Proposition Design: How to Create Products and Services Customers Want.* Wiley.

Bernstein, B., & Singh, P. J. (2006). An integrated innovation process model based on practices of Australian biotechnology firms. *Technovation, 26*(5-6), 561–572. doi:10.1016/j.technovation.2004.11.006

Bertelli, A. M. (2008). Credible governance? Transparency, political control, the personal vote and British quangos. *Political Studies, 56*(4), 807–829. doi:10.1111/j.1467-9248.2007.00713.x

Bhatta, G. P., Dangol, S., & Sapkota, R. K. (2016). Role of Land Professionals and Spatial Data Infrastructure in Disaster Risk Reduction: In the Context of Post 2015 Nepal Earthquake: General Review. *Nepalese Journal on Geoinformatics, 15*, 59–65. doi:10.3126/njg.v15i1.51187

Bielen, F., & Demoulin, N. (2007). Waiting time influence on the satisfaction-loyalty relationship in services. *Managing Service Quality, 17*(2), 174–193. doi:10.1108/09604520710735182

Bilan, Y., Mishchuk, H., Samoliuk, N., & Grishnova, O. (2019). ICT and Economic Growth: Links and Possibilities of Engaging. *Intellectual Economics, 13*(1).

Bilir, C., & Yafez, E. (2021). Project success/failure rates in Turkey. *International Journal of Information Systems and Project Management, 9*(4), 24–40. doi:10.12821/ijispm090402

Bin Che Ani, M. N., & Bin Shafei, M. S. S. (2013). The Effectiveness of the Single Minute Exchange of Die (SMED) Technique for the Productivity Improvement. *Applied Mechanics and Materials, 465–466*, 1144–1148. . doi:10.4028/www.scientific.net/AMM.465-466.1144

Binder Maitra, J. (2015). National Spatial Data Infrastructure (NSDI). In S. Shekhar, H. Xiong, & X. Zhou (Eds.), *Encyclopedia of GIS* (pp. 1–7). Springer International Publishing. doi:10.1007/978-3-319-23519-6_860-2

Bjorkdahl, J. (2020). Strategies for digitalisation in manufacturing firms. *California Management Review, 62*(4), 17–36. doi:10.1177/0008125620920349

Blackman, D. A., Buick, F., O'Donnell, M. E., & Ilahee, N. (2022). Changing the conversation to create organizational change. *Journal of Change Management, 22*(3), 252–272. doi:10.1080/14697017.2022.2040570

Bleicher, J., & Stanley, H. (2016). Digitization as a catalyst for business model innovation a three-step approach to facilitating economic success. *Journal of Business and Management*, *8*, 62–71.

Boateng, G. O., Neilands, T. B., Frongillo, E. A., Melgar-Quiñonez, H. R., & Young, S. L. (2018). Best practices for developing and validating scales for health, social, and behavioral research: A primer. *Frontiers in Public Health*, *6*(149), 1–18. doi:10.3389/fpubh.2018.00149 PMID:29942800

Bogue, R. (2016). Growth in e-commerce boosts innovation in the warehouse robot market. *The Industrial Robot*, *43*(6), 583–587. doi:10.1108/IR-07-2016-0194

Böhle, F., Heidling, E., & Schoper, Y. (2016). A new orientation to deal with uncertainty in projects. *International Journal of Project Management*, *34*(07), 1384–1392. doi:10.1016/j.ijproman.2015.11.002

Bonamigo, A., Bernardes, P. M. M., Conrado, L. F., Torres, L. F., & Calado, R. D. (2022). Patient Flow Optimization: SMED adoption in Emergency Care Units. *IFAC-PapersOnLine*, *55*(10), 204–209. doi:10.1016/j.ifacol.2022.09.391

Boszormenyi-Nagy, I., & Spark, G. (1973). *Invisible loyalties: Reciprocity in intergenerational family therapy*. Harper & Row.

Botha, G. J., Kruger, P. S., & De Vries, M. (2012). Enhancing customer experience through business process improvement: An application of the Enhanced Customer Experience Framework (ECEF). *South African Journal of Industrial Engineering*, *23*(1), 39–56.

Botha, J., Kruger, P., & De Vries, M. (2010). *Enhancing customer experience through business process improvement*. Framework.

Bough, V., Breuer, R., Maechler, N., & Ungerman, K. (2020, October 27). *The three building blocks of successful customer-experience transformations*. McKinsey & Company. https://www.mckinsey.com/capabilities/growth-marketing-and-sales/our-insights/the-three-building-blocks-of-successful-customer-experience-transformations

Bowen, P. L., Cheung, M. Y. D., & Rohde, F. H. (2007). Enhancing IT governance practices: A model and case study of an organization's efforts. *International Journal of Accounting Information Systems, 8*(3), 191-221.

Bowen, H. P., & Moesen, W. (2011). Composite competitiveness indicators with endogenous versus predetermined weights: An application to the World Economic Forum's Global Competitiveness Index. *Competitiveness Review*, *21*(2), 129–151. doi:10.1108/10595421111117434

Boxall, N. (2023, April 20). Circular economy roadmap for plastics, glass, paper and tyres - Circular Economy. Circular Economy. https://research.csiro.au/circulareconomy/circular-economy-roadmap-for-plastics-glass-paper-and-tyres/

Boysen, N., Briskorn, D., & Emde, S. (2017). Parts-to-picker based order processing in a rack-moving mobile robots environment. *European Journal of Operational Research*, *262*(2), 550–562. doi:10.1016/j.ejor.2017.03.053

Bresciani, S., Ferraris, A., & Del Giudice, M. (2018). The management of organisational ambidexterity through alliances in a new context of analysis: Internet of Things (IoT) smart city projects. *Technological Forecasting and Social Change*, *136*, 331–338. doi:10.1016/j.techfore.2017.03.002

Bressanelli, G., Adrodegari, F., Perona, M., & Saccani, N. (2018). Exploring how usage-focused business models enable circular economy through digital technologies. *Sustainability*, *10*(3), 639.

Broccardo, L., Zicari, A., Jabeen, F., & Bhatti, Z. A. (2023). How digitalization supports a sustainable business model: A literature review. *Technological Forecasting and Social Change*, *187*, 122146.

Brunet, M. (2021). Making sense of a governance framework for megaprojects: The challenge of finding equilibrium. *International Journal of Project Management, 39*(4), 406–416. Advance online publication. doi:10.1016/j.ijproman.2020.09.001

Brunet, M., & Aubry, M. (2016). The three dimensions of a governance framework for major public projects. *International Journal of Project Management, 34*(8), 1596–1607. Advance online publication. doi:10.1016/j.ijproman.2016.09.004

Buchanan, D., Fitzgerald, L., Ketley, D., Gollop, R., Jones, J. L., Lamont, S. S., & Whitby, E. (2005). No going back: A review of the literature on sustaining organizational change. *International Journal of Management Reviews, 7*(3), 189–205. doi:10.1111/j.1468-2370.2005.00111.x

Bulbulia, T. (2022, May 5). *De Beers Introduces Pioneer Blockchain-backed Diamond Source Platform at Scale.* Mining Weekly. https://www.miningweekly.com/article/de-beers-introduces-pioneer-blockchain-backed-diamond-source-platform-at-scale-2022-05-05

Burch, M. K. (2008). *Lean longevity: Kaizen events and determinants of sustainable improvement.* University of Massachusetts Amherst.

Burke, C., Fraser, J., & Handler, J. (2020, October 16). *Lean Governance: Just Enough Structure to Secure Great Outcomes from Multiple Agile Teams.* VMware Tanzu. Retrieved December 30, 2021, from https://tanzu.vmware.com/content/blog/lean-governance-just-enough-structure-great-outcomes-multiple-agile-teams

Burnes, B. (2019). The Origins of Lewin's Three-Step Model of Change. *The Journal of Applied Behavioral Science.* https://journals.sagepub.com/doi/full/10.1177/0021886319892685

Burnes, B. (2017). *Managing change* (7th ed.). Pearson Education Ltd.

Busert, T., & Fay, A. (2019). Extended Value Stream Mapping Method for Information Based Improvement of Production Logistics Processes. *IEEE Engineering Management Review, 47*(4), 119–127. doi:10.1109/EMR.2019.2934953

Butterworth Collins. (2007). *Collins English dictionary.* Author.

Byrne, B. M. (2016). Structural equation modeling with AMOS: Basic concepts, applications, and programming (3rd ed.). Routledge, Taylor & Francis Group.

Cal, P., & Galindo, M. (2021, January 26). *Work motivation: the value behind the task.* BetterUp. Retrieved December 29, 2021, from https://www.betterup.com/blog/work-motivation-the-value-behind-the-task

Calfas, J. (2019). *Robots Are Coming to Walmart and Making Employees Scared for Their Jobs' Money.* https://money.com/money/5641542/walmart-jobs-robot-union

Cambridge dictionary. (2021, December 22). *Strategic Advantage | Meaning in the Cambridge English Dictionary.* Cambridge Dictionary. Retrieved December 28, 2021, from https://dictionary.cambridge.org/dictionary/english/strategic-advantage

Campbell, J., McDonald, C., & Sethibe, T. (2010). Public and private sector IT governance: Identifying contextual differences. *AJIS. Australasian Journal of Information Systems, 16*(2). Advance online publication. doi:10.3127/ajis.v16i2.538

Cane, S. (1996). *Kaizen Strategies for Winning Through People: How to Create a Human Resources Program for Competitiveness & Profitability.* Pitman Pub.

Cao, X., Li, T., & Wang, Q. (2018). RFID-based multi-attribute logistics information processing and anomaly mining in production logistics. *International Journal of Production Research, 57*(17), 5453–5466. doi:10.1080/00207543.2018.1526421

Carpenter, S. (2018). Ten steps in scale development and reporting: A guide for researchers. *Communication Methods and Measures*, *12*(1), 25–44. doi:10.1080/19312458.2017.1396583

Carvalho, M. M., & Rabechini, R. Jr. (2006). *Construindo competências para gerenciar projetos: teoria e casos [Building competeences to manage projects: theory and cases]*. Atlas.

Castelein, W. T., Bregt, A. K., & Grus, L. (2013). The role of collaboration in spatial data infrastructures. *URISA Journal*, *25*(2).

Castelo-Branco, I., Cruz-Jesus, F., & Oliveira, T. (2019). Assessing Industry 4.0 readiness in manufacturing: Evidence for the European Union. *Computers in Industry*, *107*, 22–32. doi:10.1016/j.compind.2019.01.007

Castro, H. F., Carvalho, A. R. F., Leal, F., & Gouveia, H. (2019). Assessing Industry 4.0 Readiness of Portuguese Companies. In H. Almeida & J. Vasco (Eds.), Progress in Digital and Physical Manufacturing, ProDPM 2019. Academic Press.

Cerdeira, A. K. (2020). *SisperaH: Sistema Inteligente de Gestão de Lista de Espera Hospitalar: regulação de leitos, lista de espera, gestão e inovação em saúde*. Universidade Federal do Rio Grande do Norte. https://repositorio.ufrn.br/handle/123456789/31857

Cerpa, N., & Verner, J. (2009). Why Did Your Project Fail? *Communications of the ACM*, *52*(12), 130–134. doi:10.1145/1610252.1610286

Ceulemans, K., Scarff Seatter, C., Molderez, I., Van Liedekerke, L., & Lozano, R. (2020). Unfolding the complexities of the sustainability reporting process in higher education: a case study in the university of British Columbia. *International business, trade and institutional sustainability*, 1043-1070.

Cezarino, L. O., Liboni, L. B., Hunter, T., Pacheco, L. M., & Martins, F. P. (2022). Corporate social responsibility in emerging markets: Opportunities and challenges for sustainability integration. *Journal of Cleaner Production*, *362*, 132224. doi:10.1016/j.jclepro.2022.132224

Chaiyan, P., AnuKul, T., & Ployravee, K. (2017). Standard interpret: ISO/IEC TR 29110 management and engineering guide: basic profile (1st ed.). Ministry of Information and Communication Technology, Bangkok, Thailand.

Chan, K. W., & Li, S. Y. (2010). Understanding consumer-to-consumer interactions in virtual communities: The salience of reciprocity. *Journal of Business Research*, *63*(9-10), 1033–1040. doi:10.1016/j.jbusres.2008.08.009

Chaouch, S., Mejri, A., & Ghannouchi, S. A. (2019). A framework for risk management in Scrum development process. *Procedia Computer Science*, *164*, 187–192. doi:10.1016/j.procs.2019.12.171

Charron, R., Harrington, H. J., Voehl, F., & Wiggin, H. (2014). *The Lean Management Systems Handbook*. Productivity Press., doi:10.1201/b17201

Chaturvedi, K., Matheus, A., Nguyen, S. H., & Kolbe, T. H. (2019). Securing Spatial Data Infrastructures for Distributed Smart City applications and services. *Future Generation Computer Systems*, *101*, 723–736. Advance online publication. doi:10.1016/j.future.2019.07.002

Cheah, J.-H., Sarstedt, M., Ringle, C. M., Ramayah, T., & Ting, H. (2018). Convergent validity assessment of formatively measured constructs in PLS-SEM. *International Journal of Contemporary Hospitality Management*, *30*(11), 3192–3210. doi:10.1108/IJCHM-10-2017-0649

Chen, A. P. S., Huang, Y. F., & Do, M. H. (2022). Exploring the Challenges to Adopt Green Initiatives to Supply Chain Management for Manufacturing Industries. *Sustainability (Basel)*, *14*(20), 13516. doi:10.3390u142013516

Chen, K., & Guan, J. (2011). Mapping the innovation production process from accumulative advantage to economic outcomes: A path modeling approach. *Technovation, 31*(7), 336–346. doi:10.1016/j.technovation.2011.03.004

Chesbrough, H. W. (2006). *Open Innovation: The New Imperative for Creating and Profiting from Technology*. Harvard Business Press.

Chiarini, A., & Baccarani, C. (2016). TQM and lean strategy deployment in Italian hospitals. *Leadership in Health Services, 29*(4), 377–391. doi:10.1108/LHS-07-2015-0019 PMID:27707152

Chin, W. W. (1998). The partial least squares approach for structural equation modeling. In *Modern Methods for Business Research* (pp. 295–336). Lawrence Erlbaum Associates Publishers.

Chladek, N. 2019. Why you Need Sustainability in your Business Strategy. [online] Harvard Business School. *Business Insights*. https://online.hbs.edu/blog/post/business-sustainability-strategies

Chong, J. Y., Puvanasvaran, A. P., & Feng, C. J. (2020). Exploring critical success factors for the implementation of lean manufacturing in machinery and equipment SMEs. *Engineering Management in Production and Services, 12*(4).

Chouaibi, S., Festa, G., Quaglia, R., & Rossi, M. (2022). The risky impact of digital transformation on organizational performance – evidence from Tunisia. *Technological Forecasting and Social Change, 178*, 121571. doi:10.1016/j.techfore.2022.121571

Choudhury, S. R. (2016). *SoftBank's Pepper Robot Gets a Job Waiting Tables at Pizza Hut*. CNBC. https://www.cnbc.com/2016/05/24/mastercardteamedupwithpizzahutrestaurantsasiatobringrobotsint

Choudhury, T. T., Paul, S. K., Rahman, H. F., Jia, Z., & Shukla, N. (2020). A systematic literature review on the service supply chain: Research agenda and future research directions. *Production Planning and Control, 31*(16), 1363–1384. doi:10.1080/09537287.2019.1709132

Ciccullo, F., Fabbri, M., Abdelkafi, N., & Pero, M. (2022). Exploring the potential of business models for sustainability and big data for food waste reduction. *Journal of Cleaner Production*. Vol. 340, 130673, ISSN 0959-6526. https://doi.org/10.1016/j.jclepro.2022.130673

CIO vs CTO: What's the Difference? – BMC Software | Blogs. (2021, November 5). BMC Software. Retrieved December 30, 2021, from https://www.bmc.com/blogs/cio-vs-cto-whats-the-difference/

Claro, D. P., & Ramos, C. (2018). Sales intrafirm networks and the performance impact of sales cross-functional collaboration with marketing and customer service. *Journal of Personal Selling & Sales Management, 38*(2), 172–190. doi:10.1080/08853134.2018.1437353

Cloete, F. (2012). E-government lessons from South Africa 2001-2011: institutions, state of progress and measurement: Section II: Country perspectives on e-government emergence. *The African Journal of Information and Communication, 2012*(12), 128-142.

Cohn, M. (2005). *Agile estimating and planning*. Pearson Education.

Collins, T. (2014). *A Methodology for Building the Internet of Things*. Academic Press.

Corti, P., Bartoli, F., Fabiani, A., Giovando, C., Kralidis, A. T., & Tzotsos, A. (2019). GeoNode: An open source framework to build spatial data infrastructures. *PeerJ*, 7.

Costa, F., Lispi, L., Staudacher, A. P., Rossini, M., Kundu, K., & Cifone, F. D. (2019). How to foster sustainable continuous improvement: A cause-effect relations map of lean soft practices. *Operations Research Perspectives, 6*, 100091. doi:10.1016/j.orp.2018.100091

Costa, H. G., da Silva, M. H. T., Santos, G. N., Bonamigo, A., & Callado, R. D. (2022). Clustering Brazilian Public Emergency Healthcare Units. *IFAC-PapersOnLine*, *55*(10), 566–571. doi:10.1016/j.ifacol.2022.09.454

Costantino, F., Di Gravio, G., & Nonino, F. (2015). Project selection in project portfolio management: An artificial neural network model based on critical success factors. *International Journal of Project Management*, *33*(08), 1744–1754. doi:10.1016/j.ijproman.2015.07.003

Covey, S. R. (2004). *The Seven Habits of Highly Effective People*. Audio-Tech Business Book Summaries.

Cox, J., & Goldratt, E. M. (1986). *The goal: a process of ongoing improvement*. North River Press.

Craglia, M., & Johnston, A. (2004). Assessing the impacts of spatial data infrastructures: methods and gaps. *7th AGILE Conference on Geographic Information Science*.

Crema, M., & Verbano, C. (2021). Simulation modelling and lean management in healthcare: First evidences and research agenda. *Total Quality Management & Business Excellence*, *32*(3–4), 448–466. doi:10.1080/14783363.2019.1572504

Crompvoets, J., Vancauwenberghe, G., Ho, S., Masser, I., & Vries, W. T. (2018). Governance of national spatial data infrastructures in Europe. *International Journal of Spatial Data Infrastructures Research Citation, 13*.

Crompvoets, J., Bregt, A., Rajabifard, A., & Williamson, I. (2004). Assessing the worldwide developments of national spatial data clearinghouses. *International Journal of Geographical Information Science*, *18*(7), 665–689. doi:10.1080/13658810410001702030

Crosby, P. (1989). Let's Talk Quality: 96 Questions You Always Wanted to Ask (1° ed, Vol. 1). McGraw-Hill.

Csikszentmihalyi, M. (2008). *Flow: The Psychology of Optimal Experience*. HarperCollins.

Culture Investments. (2019, March 28). Grant Thornton. Retrieved December 30, 2021, from https://www.grantthornton.com/library/articles/advisory/2019/return-on-culture/looking-ROI-in-all-right-places.aspx

D'Andrea, R., & Wurman, P. (2008). Future challenges of coordinating hundreds of autonomous vehicles in distribution facilities. In *Proceedings of 2008 IEEE International Conference on Technologies for Practical Robot Applications* (pp. 80-83). IEEE. 10.1109/TEPRA.2008.4686677

Dale, B. G. (1996). Sustaining a process of continuous improvement: Definition and key factors. *The TQM Magazine*, *8*(2), 49–51. doi:10.1108/09544789610114867

Davies, P. (1992). Holding the gains. *The TQM Magazine*, *4*(3). Advance online publication. doi:10.1108/09544789210034347

Davis, B. M. (2010). Applying Lean to the Perioperative Environment. *AORN Journal*, *92*(S6). Advance online publication. doi:10.1016/j.aorn.2010.09.012

Davis, F. D. (1989). Perceived Usefulness, Perceived Ease of Use, and User Acceptance of Information Technology. *Management Information Systems Quarterly*, *13*(3), 319–340. doi:10.2307/249008

Davis, L. L. (1992). Instrument review: Getting the most from a panel of experts. *Applied Nursing Research*, *5*(4), 194–197. doi:10.1016/S0897-1897(05)80008-4

de Amaral, L., Calado, R., Teixeira, A., da Silva, M. H., Bourguignon, S., & Costa, H. (2021). *Systematic review and meta-analysis of the use of lean methods and tools in healthcare services: an alternative to improve care during the pandemic*. Research Square.

De Haes, S., & Van Grembergen, W. (2008). Practices in IT governance and business/IT alignment. *Information Systems Control Journal*, *2*, 1–5.

De Keyser, A., Lemon, K. N., Klaus, P., & Keiningham, T. L. (2015). A framework for understanding and managing the customer experience. *Marketing Science Institute Working Paper Series, 85*(1), 15-121.

De Kleijn, M., van Manen, N., Kolen, J., & Scholten, H. (2014). Towards a User-centric SDI Framework for Historical and Heritage European Landscape Research. *International Journal of Spatial Data Infrastructures Research*, 9.

De Lange, J., Von Solms, R., & Gerber, M. (2015, May). *Better information security management in municipalities. In 2015 IST-Africa Conference*. IEEE.

De Prins, P., Letens, G., & Verweire, K. (2017). *Six batteries of change: laad je bedrijf op voor verandering*. LannooCampus.

De Smet, A., & Schaninger, B. (2021). *From the great attrition to the great adaptation*. McKinsey & Company. https://www.mckinsey.com/business-functions/people-and-organizational-performance/our-insights/from-the-great-attrition-to-the-great-adaptation?cid=app

de Souza, L. B., & Pidd, M. (2011). Exploring the barriers to lean health care implementation. *Public Money & Management, 31*(1), 59–66. doi:10.1080/09540962.2011.545548

de Souza, W., Buss, L., Candido, D., Carrera, J.-P., Li, S., Zarebski, A., Pereira, R. H., Prete, C., Santos, A., Parag, K., Belotti, M. C., Vincenti-Gonzalez, M., Messina, J., da Silva Sales, F. C., Andrade, P., Nascimento, V., Ghilardi, F., Abade, L., Gutierrez, B., ... Faria, N. (2020). Epidemiological and clinical characteristics of the COVID-19 epidemic in Brazil. *Nature Human Behaviour, 4*(8), 856–865. doi:10.103841562-020-0928-4 PMID:32737472

Delloite Digital. (2019, August). *How the right CX Operating Model can pave the way to future success*. Deloitte Touche Tohmatsu Limited. https://www2.deloitte.com/content/dam/Deloitte/de/Documents/technology/Deloitte_Digital_CX_Operating_Model_PoV.pdf

Deloitte. (2018). *Managing risk in digital transformation*. Deloitte.

Deloitte. (2023). *Using blockchain to drive supply chain transparency*. Deloitte. Pp. 4-5. https://www2.deloitte.com/content/dam/Deloitte/us/Documents/us-ent-supply-chain-pov.pdf

Dennis, A., Wixom, B. H., & Tegarden, D. (2009). *System Analysis Design UML Version 2.0: An Object-Oriented Approach*. John Wiley & Sons.

Dery, K., Sebastian, I. M., & van der Meulen, N. (2017). The digital workplace is key to digital innovation. *MIS Quarterly Executive, 16*, 135–152.

Dess, G. G., Lumpkin, G. T., & Eisner, A. B. (2010). Strategic management: Creating competitive advantages. 5 Hill Irwin.

Devadoss, P. R., Pan, S. L., & Huang, J. C. (2002). Structurational Analysis of eGovernment Initiatives: A Case Study of SCO. *Decision Support Systems, 34*(3), 253–269. doi:10.1016/S0167-9236(02)00120-3

Diamantopoulos, A., & Siguaw, J. A. (2006). Formative versus reflective indicators in organizational measure development: A comparison and empirical illustration. *British Journal of Management, 17*(4), 263–282. doi:10.1111/j.1467-8551.2006.00500.x

Dienes, D., Sassen, R., & Fischer, J. (2016). What are the drivers of sustainability reporting? A systematic review. *Sustainability Accounting. Management and Policy Journal, 7*(2), 154–189.

Difrancesco, R. M., Meena, P., & Kumar, G. (2023). How blockchain technology improves sustainable supply chain processes: a practical guide. Oper Manag Res 16, 620–641 https://doi.org/10.1007/s12063-022-00343-y

DiMaggio, P., & Powell, W. (1983). The Iron Cage Revisited: Institutional Isomorphism and Collective Rationality in Organizational Fields. *American Sociological Review, 48*(2), 147–160. doi:10.2307/2095101

Ding, K., & Jiang, P. Y. (2018). RFID-based production data analysis in an IoT-enabled smart job-shop. *IEEE/CAA Journal of Automatica Sinica*, *5*(1), 128 – 138. doi:10.1109/JAS.2017.7510418

Dobele, A. R., Westberg, K., Steel, M., & Flowers, K. (2014). An examination of corporate social responsibility implementation and stakeholder engagement: A case study in the Australian mining industry. [Crossref.]. *Business Strategy and the Environment*, *23*(3), 145–159.

Doleski, O. D. (2015). *Integrated Business Model: applying the St. Gallen Management concept to business models.* Springer.

Domazet, I., Marjanović, D., & Ahmetagić, D. (2022). The Impact of High-Tech Products Exports on Economic Growth: The Case of Serbia, Bulgaria, Romania and Hungary. *Ekonomika preduzeća, 70*(3-4), 191-205.

Domazet, I., Marjanović, D., Ahmetagić, D., & Bugarčić, M. (2021). The Impact of Innovation Indicators on Increasing Exports of High Technology Products. *Ekonomika preduzeća, 69*(1-2), 31-40.

Domazet, I., Marjanović, D., Ahmetagić, D., & Antonijević, M. (2022). Does the Increase in the Number of Registered Patents Affect Economic Growth? Evidence from Romania and Bulgaria. *Economic Analysis: Applied Research in Emerging Markets*, *55*(2), 49–65.

Domazet, I., Marjanović, D., Ahmetagić, D., & Simović, V. (2023). The influence of the number of patents on the economic growth of the country – evidence from Serbia and Hungary. Strategic Management. *International Journal of Strategic Management and Decision Support Systems in Strategic Management*, *28*(3). Advance online publication. doi:10.5937/StraMan2300048D

Dong-yuan, Ga-oan, & Zhong-shun (2018). Exploration of Key Technologies of Smart Logistics Based on Big Data. *Proceedings of 2nd International Conference on Education Science and Economic Management (ICESEM 2018)*, 1256-1259.

Doorn, J. V., Mende, M., Noble, S. M., Hulland, J., Ostrom, A. L., Grewal, D., & Petersen, J. A. (2017). Domo Arigato Mr. Roboto: Emergence of Automated Social Presence in Organizational Frontlines and Customers' Service Experiences. *Journal of Service Research*, *20*(1), 43–58. doi:10.1177/1094670516679272

Dou. (2016). Based on the background of smart logistics Kiva warehouse robot Application analysis and prospect. *Global Journal of Engineering, Design, and Technology, 5*(3), 1-4.

DPSA. (2012). e-Government policy. Department of Public Administration (DPSA).

Drucker, P. F. (1963). Managing for business effectiveness. *Harvard Business Review*, *41*(3).

Drucker, P. F. (2001). Innovation and Management. *Wirtschaft und Politik, Düsseldorf, 1985*, 368.

DSDM. (1998). *Dynamic Systems Development Method*. https://docplayer.fr/5488317-Dynamic-systems-development-method.html

Duan, W., Gu, B., & Whinston, A. B. (2008). Do online reviews matter?—An empirical investigation of panel data. *Decision Support Systems*, *45*(4), 1007–1016. doi:10.1016/j.dss.2008.04.001

Dutta, P., Choi, T., Somani, S., & Butala, R. (2020) Blockchain technology in supply chain operations : Applications, challenges and research opportunities. Transp Res Part E 142:102067. https://doi.org/10.1016/j.tre.2020.102067

Dutta, P., Choi, T. M., Somani, S., & Butala, R. (2020). Blockchain technology in supply chain operations: Applications, challenges and research opportunities. *Transportation Research Part E, Logistics and Transportation Review*, *142*, 102067. doi:10.1016/j.tre.2020.102067 PMID:33013183

Dye, L. D., & Pennypacker, J. S. (1999). *Project portfolio management: selecting and prioritizing projects for competitive advantage*. Center for Business Practices.

Eastern Cape Spending Reviews. (2021). *Presented by D Makoni. EC SPENDING REVIEWS 2021 Improving the efficiency and effectiveness of spending on ICT in the Eastern Cape*. Available online at https://www.gtac.gov.za/wp-content/uploads/2022/05/EC_ICT_WebinarSeries.pdf

Ebert, C., & Paasivaara, M. (2017). ScalingAgile. *IEEE Software*, *34*(06), 98–103. doi:10.1109/MS.2017.4121226

Ehsan, N., Perwaiz, A., Arif, J., Mirza, E., & Ishaque, A. (2010). CMMI / SPICE based process improvement. In *2010 IEEE International Conference on Management of Innovation & Technology* (pp. 859-862). IEEE. 10.1109/ICMIT.2010.5492803

EIU. (2014). *Networked manufacturing: The digital future*. Economist Intelligence Unit.

El Massah, S., & Mohieldin, M. (2020). Digital transformation and localizing the sustainable development goals (SDGs). *Ecological Economics*, *169*, 106490. doi:10.1016/j.ecolecon.2019.106490

Elhadi, S., Marzak, A., Sael, N., & Merzouk, S. (2018). Comparative Study of IoT Protocols. SSRN *Electronic Journal*. doi:10.2139/ssrn.3186315

Elkington, J. (1994). Towards the sustainable corporation: Win-win-win business strategies for sustainable development. *California Management Review*, *36*(2), 90–100.

Elkington, J. (1998). Partnerships from cannibals with forks: The triple bottom line of 21st-century business. *Environmental Quality Management*, *8*(1), 37–51.

Enduring Ideas: The 7-S Framework. (2008, March 1). McKinsey. Retrieved September 3, 2023, from https://www.mckinsey.com/capabilities/strategy-and-corporate-finance/our-insights/enduring-ideas-the-7-s-framework

Enright, J. J., & Wurman, P. R. (2011). Optimization and coordinated autonomy in mobile fulfillment systems. *Proceedings of the 25th AAAI Conference on Artificial Intelligence*.

Epstein, M. J., Buhovac, A. R., & Yuthas, K. (2015). Managing social, environmental and financial performance simultaneously. *Long Range Planning*, *48*(1), 35–45.

Erthal, A., Frangeskou, M., & Marques, L. (2021). Cultural tensions in lean healthcare implementation: A paradox theory lens. *International Journal of Production Economics*, *233*, 107968. doi:10.1016/j.ijpe.2020.107968

Fagerberg, J., & Srholec, M. (2008). National innovation systems, capabilities and economic development. *Research Policy*, *37*(9), 1417–1435. doi:10.1016/j.respol.2008.06.003

Fallah Shayan, N., Mohabbati-Kalejahi, N., Alavi, S., & Zahed, M. A. (2022). Sustainable development goals (SDGs) as a framework for corporate social responsibility (CSR). *Sustainability (Basel)*, *14*(3), 1222. doi:10.3390u14031222

Fatima, T., & Elbanna, S. (2023). Corporate social responsibility (CSR) implementation: A review and a research agenda towards an integrative framework. *Journal of Business Ethics*, *183*(1), 105–121. doi:10.100710551-022-05047-8 PMID:35125567

Feeney, M., Rajabifard, A., & Williamson, I. P. (2001). Spatial data infrastructure frameworks to support decision-making for sustainable development. *5th Global Spatial Data Infrastructure Conference*.

Feki, M. A., Kawsar, F., Boussard, M., & Trappeniers, L. (2013). The Internet of Things: The Next Technological Revolution. *Computer*, *46*(2), 24–25. doi:10.1109/MC.2013.63

Ferauge, P. (2012). A conceptual framework of corporate social responsibility and innovation. *Global Journal of Business Research*, *6*(5), 85–96.

Ferenhof, H. A., Da Cunha, A. H., Bonamigo, A., & Forcellini, F. A. (2018). Toyota Kata as a KM solution to the inhibitors of implementing lean service in service companies. *VINE Journal of Information and Knowledge Management Systems*, *48*(3), 404–426. doi:10.1108/VJIKMS-11-2017-0083

Fernández-Portillo, A., Almodóvar-González, M., & Hernández-Mogollón, R. (2020). Impact of ICT development on economic growth. A study of OECD European Union countries. *Technology in Society*, *63*, 63. doi:10.1016/j.techsoc.2020.101420

Fernando, Y., Halili, M., Tseng, M. L., Tseng, J. W., & Lim, M. K. (2022). Sustainable social supply chain practices and firm social performance: Framework and empirical evidence. *Sustainable Production and Consumption*, *32*, 160–172. doi:10.1016/j.spc.2022.04.020

Ferrell, O. C., Thorne, D. M., & Ferrell, L. (2020). *Business & society: A strategic approach to social responsibility & ethics*. SAGE Publications.

Figueredo, K. (2021, March 10). *Product Management Implications of AI for IoT.* IoT For All. https://www.iotforall.com/product-management-implications-of-ai-for-iot

Filchev, L., Pashova, L., Kolev, V., & Frye, S. (2020). Surveys, Catalogues, Databases/Archives, and State-of-the-Art Methods for Geoscience Data Processing. In P. Škoda & F. Adam (Eds.), *Knowledge Discovery in Big Data from Astronomy and Earth Observation* (pp. 103–136). Elsevier. doi:10.1016/B978-0-12-819154-5.00016-3

Fillingham, D. (2007). Can lean save lives? *Leadership in Health Services*, *20*(4), 231–241. doi:10.1108/17511870710829346 PMID:20698096

Fisher, S. (2020). *7 Ways to pretest your survey before you send it*. Qualtrics. Retrieved July 17th from https://www.qualtrics.com/blog/6-ways-to-pretest-your-survey-before-you-send-it/?fbclid=IwAR0BVDBgLceDDBqhRDoHNtDVHxsiUg-IMt416h_TUTLS52gW39Qszbyo8v0

Flora, H. K., & Chande, S. V. (2014). A Systematic Study on Agile Software Development Methodologies and Practices. *International Journal of Computer Science and Information Technologies*, *5*(3), 3626–3637. http://www.ijcsit.com/docs/Volume 5/vol5issue03/ijcsit20140503214.pdf

Fluss, D. (2017). The AI Revolution in Customer Service, Customer Relationship Management. *January, 38*. https://www.destinationcrm.com/Articles/Columns-Departments/Scouting-Report/The-AI-Revolution-in-Customer-Service-115528.aspx

Fobbe, L. (2020). Analysing organisational collaboration practices for sustainability. *Sustainability*, *12*(6), 2466.

Forbes. (2018, February 8). *13 Reasons Google Deserves Its 'Best Company Culture' Award.* Forbes. https://www.forbes.com/sites/forbestechcouncil/2018/02/08/13-reasons-google-deserves-its-best-company-culture-award/?sh=72a26b534828

Fornell, C., & Larcker, D. F. (1981). Evaluating Structural Equation Models with unobservable variables and measurement error. *JMR, Journal of Marketing Research*, *18*(1), 39–50. doi:10.1177/002224378101800104

Forth, P., Reichert, T., de Laubier, R., & Saibal, C. (2020). *Flipping the Odds of Digital Transformation Success.* Retrieved from https://www.bcg.com/publications/2020/increasing-odds-of-success-in-digital-transformation

Fortino, G., & Russo, W. (2012). ELDAMeth: An agent-oriented methodology for simulation-based prototyping of distributed agent systems. *Special Section: Engineering Complex Software Systems through Multi-Agent Systems and Simulation, 54*(6), 608–624. doi:10.1016/j.infsof.2011.08.006

Fortino, G., Guerrieri, A., Russo, W., & Savaglio, C. (2015). Towards a Development Methodology for Smart Object-Oriented IoT Systems: A Metamodel Approach. *2015 IEEE International Conference on Systems, Man, and Cybernetics*, 1297–1302. 10.1109/SMC.2015.231

Fortino, G., Rango, F., & Russo, W. (2014). ELDAMeth Design Process. In M. Cossentino, V. Hilaire, A. Molesini, & V. Seidita (Eds.), *Handbook on Agent-Oriented Design Processes* (pp. 115–139). Springer Berlin Heidelberg. doi:10.1007/978-3-642-39975-6_5

Fraenkel, J. R., Wallen, N. E., & Hyun, H. H. (2012). *How to design and evaluate research in education* (8th ed.). McGraw-Hill Companies, Inc.

Freudenreich, B., Lüdeke-Freund, F., & Schaltegger, S. (2020). A stakeholder theory perspective on business models: Value creation for sustainability. *Journal of Business Ethics*, *166*, 3–18.

Friedman, N., & Ormiston, J. (2022). Blockchain as a sustainability-oriented innovation?: Opportunities for and resistance to Blockchain technology as a driver of sustainability in global food supply chains. *Technological Forecasting and Social Change*, *175*, 121403. doi:10.1016/j.techfore.2021.121403

Fullerton, R. R., Kennedy, F. A., & Widener, S. K. (2014). Lean manufacturing and firm performance: The incremental contribution of lean management accounting practices. *Journal of Operations Management*, *32*(7), 414–428. doi:10.1016/j.jom.2014.09.002

Fu, X. M., Bao, Q., Xie, H., & Fu, X. (2021). Diffusion of industrial robotics and inclusive growth: Labour market evidence from cross country data. *Journal of Business Research*, *122*(1), 670–684. doi:10.1016/j.jbusres.2020.05.051

Gaiardelli, P., Resta, B., & Dotti, S. (2019). Exploring the role of human factors in lean management. *International Journal of Lean Six Sigma*, *10*(1), 339–366. doi:10.1108/IJLSS-08-2017-0094

Galani, A., Koutsouris, N., Poulios, G., Tsagkaris, K., & Demestichas, P. (2013). Designing the governance framework for network and service management in Future Networks. *2013 Future Network & Mobile Summit*, 1–8.

Galeazzo, A. (2019). Degree of leanness and lean maturity: Exploring the effects on financial performance. *Total Quality Management & Business Excellence*, 1–19. doi:10.1080/14783363.2019.1634469

Galeazzo, A., Furlan, A., & Vinelli, A. (2017). The organizational infrastructure of continuous improvement – an empirical analysis. *Operations Management Research : Advancing Practice Through Research*, *10*(1), 33–46. doi:10.100712063-016-0112-1

Gallis, C. (2013). ncreasing productivity and controlling of work fatigue in forest operations by using prescribed active pauses: A selective review. *Croatian Journal of Forest Engineering: Journal for Theory and Application of Forestry Engineering*, *34*(1), 103–112.

Garg, A. (2021, April 21). *Using Augmented reality to drive real business.* Lenskart Blogs. https://blog.lenskart.com/using-augmented-reality-to-drive-real-business-edd3b0244503

Garvey, J. (2019, May 16). *Total quality management methods to drive team performance.* PeopleGoal. Retrieved December 29, 2021, from https://www.peoplegoal.com/blog/quality-management-techniques-to-drive-team-performance

Gefen, D., Straub, D., & Boudreau, M.-C. (2000). Structural Equation Modeling and Regression: Guidelines for research practice. *Communications of the Association for Information Systems*, *4*, 7. doi:10.17705/1CAIS.00407

Geissdoerfer, M., Savaget, P., Bocken, N. M., & Hultink, E. J. (2017). The Circular Economy–A new sustainability paradigm? *Journal of Cleaner Production*, *143*, 757–768.

Gentile, C., Spiller, N., & Noci, G. (2007). How to sustain the customer experience: An overview of experience components that co-create value with the customer. *European Management Journal, 25*(5), 395–410. doi:10.1016/j.emj.2007.08.005

Gërguri-Rashiti, S., Ramadani, V., Abazi-Alili, H., Dana, L. P., & Ratten, V. (2017). ICT, innovation and firm performance: The transition economies context. *Thunderbird International Business Review, 59*(1), 93–102. doi:10.1002/tie.21772

Gershon, P. (2009). *Review of the Australian Government's Use of Information and Communication Technology*. Department of Finance and Deregulation, The Australian Government Information Management Office.

Ghapanchi, A. H., Tavana, M., Khakbaz, M. H., & Low, G. (2012). A methodology for selecting portfolios of projects with interactions and under uncertainty. *International Journal of Project Management, 30*(07), 791–803. doi:10.1016/j.ijproman.2012.01.012

Giovanni, P. D. (2020). Blockchain and smart contracts in supply chain management: A game theoretic model. *International Journal of Production Economics, 228*(107855), 1–18. doi:10.1016/j.ijpe.2020.107855

Giuliani, G., Lacroix, P., Guigoz, Y., Roncella, R., Bigagli, L., Santoro, M., Mazzetti, P., Nativi, S., Ray, N., & Lehmann, A. (2017). Bringing GEOSS Services into Practice: A Capacity Building Resource on Spatial Data Infrastructures (SDI). *Transactions in GIS, 21*(4), 811–824. Advance online publication. doi:10.1111/tgis.12209

GOI. (2006). *Resolution on "Constitution of National Spatial Data Infrastructure (NSDI)*. GOI.

GOI. (2011). *NSDI working Groups Report*. GOI.

GOI. (2012). *National Data Sharing and Accessibility Policy*. Ministry of Science and Technology, Government of India.

GOI. (2018). *Internet of Things (IoT)*. IoT India Magazine.

Goldratt, E. M. (2004). *The Goal: A Process of Ongoing Improvement*. Academic Press.

Gomes, S. B., Santoro, F. M., Da Silva, M. M., & Iacob, M. E. (2019, October). A reference model for digital transformation and innovation. In *2019 IEEE 23rd International Enterprise Distributed Object Computing Conference (EDOC)* (pp. 21-30). IEEE.

Gomes, J. G. C., Okano, M. T., Guerra, R. S., Cordeiro, D. D. S., Santos, H. C. L. D., & Fernandes, M. E. (2022). Analysis of Sustainable Business Models: Exploratory Study in Two Brazilian Logistics Companies. *Sustainability, 14*(2), 694.

Gomez-Trujillo, A. M., & Gonzalez-Perez, M. A. (2021). Digital transformation as a strategy to reach sustainability. Smart Sustain. Built Environ. (2021). https://doi.org/10.1108/sasbe-01-2021-0011

Governance institute Australia. (n.d.). *What is governance?* Governance Institute of Australia. Retrieved December 28, 2021, from https://www.governanceinstitute.com.au/resources/what-is-governance/

Govindarajan, V., Srivastava, A., & Enache, L. (2019). How India Plans to Protect Consumer Data. *Harvard Business Review*.

Graban, M., & Toussaint, J. (2018). *Lean Hospitals*. Productivity Press. doi:10.4324/9781315380827

Graetz, F., & Smith, A. C. (2010). Managing organizational change: A philosophies of change approach. *Journal of Change Management, 10*(2), 135–154. doi:10.1080/14697011003795602

Graham, J. R., Harvey, C. R., & Rajgopal, S. (2005). The economic implications of corporate financial reporting. *Journal of Accounting and Economics, 40*(1-3), 3–73.

Graham, J., & Dennis, C. (2019). Digital transformation: OKRs as a governance mechanism. *The Journal of Business Strategy, 40*(1), 36–42.

Grainger-Brown, J., & Malekpour, S. (2019). Implementing the sustainable development goals: A review of strategic tools and frameworks available to organisations. *Sustainability, 11*(5), 1381.

Grant, R. M. (1996). Toward a knowledge-based theory of the firm. *Strategic Management Journal, 17*(S2), 109–122. doi:10.1002mj.4250171110

GRI. (2013). *G4 Sustainability Reporting Guidelines.* Global Reporting Initiative. https://respect.international/wp-content/uploads/2017/10/G4-Sustainability-Reporting-Guidelines-Implementation-Manual-GRI-2013.pdf

GRI. (2016). *Global Sustainability Standards Board.* Global Reporting Initiative. https://www.globalreporting.org/standards/global-sustainability-standards-board/

Grigg, N. P., Goodyer, J. E., & Frater, T. G. (2018). Sustaining lean in SMEs: Key findings from a 10-year study involving New Zealand manufacturers. *Total Quality Management & Business Excellence, 31*(5-6), 609–622. doi:10.1080/14783363.2018.1436964

Groot, R., & McLaughlin, J. (2000). Geospatial data infrastructure : concepts, cases and good practice. In R. Groot & J. McLaughlin (Eds.), *GeoSpatial Data Infrastructure: Concepts, Cases and Good Practice.* Oxford University Press. https://research.utwente.nl/en/publications/geospatial-data-infrastructure-concepts-cases-and-good-practice

Groth, A., Bognar, S., & Reichert, J. (2018, October 9). *What is holacracy? The management approach tested by Google and Zappos. — Quartz at Work.* Quartz. Retrieved December 30, 2021, from https://qz.com/work/1397516/is-holacracy-the-future-of-work-or-a-management-cult/

Grover, V., & Kohli, R. (2013). Revealing your hand: Caveats in implementing digital business strategy. *Management Information Systems Quarterly, 37*, 655–663.

GSDI. (2004). Developing Spatial Data Infrastructures: The SDI Cookbook. GSDI/Nebert.

GTZ – Gesellschaft für Technische Zusammenarbeit. (2006). *ZOPP – Ziel-Orientierte Projekt Planung.* German Government. Available in: https://pmkb.com.br/uploads/2013/08/cartilha-zopp-portugues.pdf

Gusmerotti, N. M., Testa, F., Corsini, F., Pretner, G., & Iraldo, F. (2019). Drivers and approaches to the circular economy in manufacturing firms. Journal of Cleaner Production, Volume 230, Pages 314-327, ISSN 0959-6526. https://doi.org/10.1016/j.jclepro.2019.05.044

Habidin, N. F., Mohd Zubir, A. F., Mohd Fuzi, N., & Salleh, M. I. (2020). The relationship between sustainable manufacturing practices, lean improvement and performance. *World Review of Entrepreneurship, Management and Sustainable Development, 16*(1), 92–107. doi:10.1504/WREMSD.2020.105529

Haessler, P. (2020). Strategic decisions between short-term profit and sustainability. *Administrative Sciences, 10*(3), 63.

Haidar, H. (2021). Historical Perspectives and the Emergence of the Sustainability Concept in Organizations. *Open Journal of Business and Management, 9*, 2277–2298. doi:10.4236/ojbm.2021.95123

Hair, J. F., Black, W. C., Babin, B. J., & Anderson, R. E. (2019). *Multivariate data analysis* (8th ed.). Cengage Learning.

Hair, J. F., Hult, G. T. M., Ringle, C. M., & Sarstedt, M. (2022). *A primer on partial least squares structural equation modeling (PLS-SEM)* (3rd ed.). SAGE Publications Inc.

Hair, J. F., Risher, J. J., Sarstedt, M., & Ringle, C. M. (2019). When to use and how to report the results of PLS-SEM. *European Business Review, 31*(1), 2–24. doi:10.1108/EBR-11-2018-0203

Hallam, C. R. A., & Contreras, C. (2018). Lean healthcare: Scale, scope and sustainability. *International Journal of Health Care Quality Assurance, 31*(7), 684–696. doi:10.1108/IJHCQA-02-2017-0023 PMID:30354875

Handy, C. B. (1995). *The Empty Raincoat: Making Sense of the Future*. Arrow Business Books.

Hanson, R., Medbo, L., & Johansson, M. I. (2018). Performance characteristics of robotic mobile fulfilment systems in order picking applications. *IFAC-PapersOnLine*, *51*(11), 1493–1498. doi:10.1016/j.ifacol.2018.08.290

Hardcopf, R., Liu, G., & Shah, R. (2021). Lean production and operational performance: The influence of organizational culture. *International Journal of Production Economics, 108060*. Advance online publication. doi:10.1016/j.ijpe.2021.108060

Harry, M. J., & Schroeder, R. R. (2000). *Six sigma: the breakthrough management strategy revolutionising the world's top corporations*. Currency.

Hasan, M. Z. (2021). *Relationship between lean manufacturing practices and sustainability in manufacturing organisations: Mediating effect of manufacturing performance and moderating effect of ethical climate*. Universiti Utara Malaysia.

Havíř, D. (2017). A Comparison Of The Approaches To Customer Experience Analysis. *Economics & Business, 31*(1).

Heinonen, K., & Medberg, G. (2018). Netnography as a tool for understanding customers: Implications for service research and practice. *Journal of Services Marketing*, *32*(1), 657–679. doi:10.1108/JSM-08-2017-0294

Helo, P., & Hao, Y. (2019). Blockchains in operation and supply chains: A model and reference implementation. *Computers & Industrial Engineering*, *136*, 242–251. doi:10.1016/j.cie.2019.07.023

Hennart, J. F. (2019). Digitalized service multinationals and international business theory. *Journal of International Business Studies*, *50*(8), 1388–1400. doi:10.105741267-019-00256-2

Hernandez-Matias, J. C., Ocampo, J. R., Hidalgo, A., & Vizan, A. (2020). Lean manufacturing and operational performance: Interrelationships between human-related lean practices. *Journal of Manufacturing Technology Management*, *31*(2), 217–235. doi:10.1108/JMTM-04-2019-0140

Herrera, M. E. B. (2015). Creating competitive advantage by institutionalizing corporate social innovation. *Journal of Business Research*, *68*(7), 1468–1474. doi:10.1016/j.jbusres.2015.01.036

Herrmann, P. N., & Dennis, O. (2015). Beating Irrationality: Does Delegating to IT Alleviate the Sunk Cost Effect? *Management Science*, *61*(4), 831–850. doi:10.1287/mnsc.2014.1955

He, Z., Aggarwal, V., & Nof, S. Y. (2018). Differentiated service policy in smart warehouse automation. *International Journal of Production Research*, *56*(22), 6956–6970. doi:10.1080/00207543.2017.1421789

Higón, D. A., Gholami, R., & Shirazi, F. (2017). ICT and environmental sustainability: A global perspective. *Telematics and Informatics*, *34*(4), 85–95. doi:10.1016/j.tele.2017.01.001

Hines, P., Found, P. A., Griffiths, G., & Harrison, R. (2011). *Staying lean: Thriving, not just surviving* (2nd ed.). Lean Enterprise Research Centre, Cardiff University., https://orca.cf.ac.uk/52764/1/stayinglean.pdf

Hmioui, A., & Bentalha, B. (2021). Service supply chain management: A literature review. *International Journal of Logistics Systems and Management*, *40*(3), 332–353. doi:10.1504/IJLSM.2021.120253

Hoffman, D. L., & Novak, T. P. (2018). Consumer and Object Experience in the Internet of Things: An Assemblage Theory Approach. *The Journal of Consumer Research*, *44*(6), 1178–1204. doi:10.1093/jcr/ucx105

Hofmann, E., & Ru¨sch, M. (2017). Industry 4.0 and the current status as well as future prospects on logistics. *Computers in Industry*, *89*, 23–34. doi:10.1016/j.compind.2017.04.002

Hogan, B. J. (2009, December 1). Sustaining a lean culture. *Manufacturing Engineering Magazine, 143*(5), 71-76. http://advancedmanufacturing.org/sustaining-lean-culture/

Horng, J. S., Hsu, H., & Tsai, C. Y. (2018). An assessment model of corporate social responsibility practice in the tourism industry. *Journal of Sustainable Tourism, 26*(7), 1085–1104. doi:10.1080/09669582.2017.1388384

Hou, Y., Khokhar, M., Sharma, A., Sarkar, J. B., & Hossain, M. A. (2023). Converging concepts of sustainability and supply chain networks: a systematic literature review approach. Environ Sci Pollut Res 30, 46120–46130 https://doi.org/10.1007/s11356-023-25412-y

Hourneaux, F. Jr, Gabriel, M. L. D. S., & Gallardo-Vázquez, D. A. (2018). Triple bottom line and sustainable performance measurement in industrial companies. *Revista de Gestão*, *25*(4), 413–429.

Howell, S. T. (2017). Financing innovation: Evidence from R&D grants. *The American Economic Review*, *107*(4), 1136–1164. doi:10.1257/aer.20150808

Hristov, I., Appolloni, A., Cheng, W., & Huisingh, D. (2022). Aligning corporate social responsibility practices with the environmental performance management systems: A critical review of the relevant literature. *Total Quality Management & Business Excellence*, •••, 1–25. doi:10.1080/14783363.2022.2048951

Huang, K. (2011). Technology competencies in competitive environment. *Journal of Business Research*, *64*(2), 172–179. doi:10.1016/j.jbusres.2010.02.003

Huang, M. H., & Rust, R. T. (2021). A strategic framework for artificial intelligence in marketing. *Journal of the Academy of Marketing Science*, *49*(1), 30–50. doi:10.100711747-020-00749-9

Huang, Z., Kim, J., Sadri, A., Dowey, S., & Dargusch, M. S. (2019). Industry 4.0: Development of a multi-agent system for dynamic value stream mapping in SMEs. *Journal of Manufacturing Systems*, *52*, 1–12. doi:10.1016/j.jmsy.2019.05.001

Hurst, J. (2000). Challenges for health systems in member countries of the Organisation for Economic Co-operation and Development. *Bulletin of the World Health Organization*, *78*(6), 751–760. PMID:10916912

Hurtoi, V., & Avadanei, D. (2020). IoT Project Management. *Informações Econômicas*, *24*(3), 75–80. doi:10.24818/issn14531305/24.3.2020.07

Huse, M., Neubaum, D. O., & Gabrielsson, J. (2005). Corporate innovation and competitive environment. *The International Entrepreneurship and Management Journal*, *1*(3), 313–333. doi:10.100711365-005-2596-2

Hussain, F. (2016). Digital contradictions in Bangladesh: Encouragement and deterrence of citizen engagement via ICTs. *Information Technologies and International Development*, *12*(2).

Iakovaki, A., Srai, J. S., & Harrington, T. (2009), *Service supply chain integration in multiorganisation networks. Applying integration enablers and aligning process capabilities.* 14th Cambridge International Manufacturing Symposium. Configuring manufacturing value chains. Responding to an uncertain world, The Moller Center, Cambridge.

IEEE. (1998). *IEEE Guide for Software Requirements Specification (ANSI/IEEE Std. 830-1998).* Institute of Electrical and Electronics Engineers, Inc.

IEEE. (2006). *ANSI/IEEE Standard for Developing a Software Project Life Cycle Process (IEEE Std. 1074-2006).* Institute of Electrical and Electronics Engineers, Inc.

IEEE. (2008). *ANSI/IEEE Standard Information Technology-Software Life Cycle Process, IEEE/EIA Std.* Institute of Electrical and Electronics Engineers, Inc.

Ienca, M., Fins, J. J., Jox, R. J., Jotterand, F., Voeneky, S., Andorno, R., Ball, T., Castelluccia, C., Chavarriaga, R., Chneiweiss, H., Ferretti, A., Friedrich, O., Hurst, S., Merkel, G., Molnár-Gábor, F., Rickli, J. M., Scheibner, J., Vayena, E., Yuste, R., & Kellmeyer, P. (2022). Towards a Governance Framework for Brain Data. *Neuroethics*, *15*(2), 20. Advance online publication. doi:10.100712152-022-09498-8

Iglesias, O., Mingione, M., Ind, N., & Markovic, S. (2023). How to build a conscientious corporate brand together with business partners: A case study of Unilever. *Industrial Marketing Management*, *109*, 1–13. doi:10.1016/j.indmarman.2022.12.008

Improta, G., Romano, M., Di Cicco, M. V., Ferraro, A., Borrelli, A., Verdoliva, C., Triassi, M., & Cesarelli, M. (2018). Lean thinking to improve emergency department throughput at AORN Cardarelli hospital. *BMC Health Services Research*, *18*(1), 914. doi:10.118612913-018-3654-0 PMID:30509286

Indeed Editorial Team. (2023, March 11). Strategic Management: Definition, Purpose and Example. Indeed. https://www.indeed.com/career-advice/career-development/what-is-strategic-management

Industrial Revolution: Definitions, Causes & Inventions - History. (n.d.). History.com. Retrieved December 29, 2021, from https://www.history.com/topics/industrial-revolution/industrial-revolution

Ingemarsdotter, E., Jamsin, E., Kortuem, G., & Balkenende, R. (2019). Circular strategies enabled by the Internet of Things—A framework and analysis of current practice. *Sustainability (Switzerland)*, 11(20), 5689. https://doi.org/10.3390/su11205689

International Organization for Standardization. (2011). ISO Technical report for Systems and software engineering — Lifecycle profiles for Very Small Entities (VSEs) — Part 4-1: Profile specifications: Generic profile group (ISO/IEC 29110-4-1) (1st ed.).

International Organization for Standardization. (2016). *ISO/IEC TR 29110-1*. Systems and Software Engineering - Lifecycle profiles for Very Small Entities (VSEs) - Part 1: Overview.

Iqbal, M. (2020). *The Standard of Project Management and PMBOK 7*. Retrieved from https://mudassiriqbal.net/the-standard-of-project-management-and-pmbok-7/

Iranmanesh, M., Zailani, S., Hyun, S. S., Ali, M. H., & Kim, K. (2019). Impact of lean manufacturing practices on firms' sustainable performance: Lean culture as a moderator. *Sustainability (Basel)*, *11*(4), 1112. doi:10.3390u11041112

Iriarte, C., & Bayona, S. (2020). It projects success factors: A literature review. *International Journal of Information Systems and Project Management*, *8*(2), 49–78. doi:10.12821/ijispm080203

Ishwarappa, K., & Anuradha, J. (2015). A Brief Introduction on Big Data 5Vs Characteristics and Hadoop Technology. Procedia Computer Science 48 (2015) 319 – 324. https://doi.org/10.1016/j.procs.2015.04.188

Islam, S., & Evans, N. (2020). Key Success Factors of PRINCE2 Project Management Method in Software Development Project. *International Journal of Engineering Materials and Manufacture*, *5*(3), 76–84. doi:10.26776/ijemm.05.03.2020.02

ISO38500. (2008). *Corporate governance of information technology*. International Standards Organization.

ISO-International Organization for Standardization. (2017). *ISO 10006:2017(en) Quality management — Guidelines for quality management in projects*.

ISO-International Organization for Standardization. (2021). *ISO 21500:2021 Project, programme and portfolio management — Context and concepts*.

Iteng, R. (2013). *The relationship between lean production, operational performance and business performance in Malaysian manufacturing industry*. Universiti Kebangsaan Malaysia.

ITGI. (2009). *IT Governance Institute*. www.itgi.org

ITIL. (2009). *What is ITIL?* Available at: http://www.itilofficalsite.com/AboutITIL/WhatisITL.asp

Jacoby, S., Smith, J., Ting, L., & Williamson, I. (2002). Developing a common spatial data infrastructure between state and local government - An Australian case study. *International Journal of Geographical Information Science*, *16*(4), 305–322. Advance online publication. doi:10.1080/13658810110096001

Jadhav, J. R., Mantha, S., & Rane, S. B. (2014). Development of framework for sustainable lean implementation: An ISM approach. *Journal of Industrial Engineering International*, *10*(3), 72. doi:10.100740092-014-0072-8

Jafari-Sadeghi, V., Garcia-Perez, A., Candelo, A., & Couturier, J. (2021). Exploring the impact of digital transformation on technology entrepreneurship and technological market expansion: The role of technology readiness, exploration and exploitation. *Journal of Business Research*, *124*, 100–111. doi:10.1016/j.jbusres.2020.11.020

Jain, D., & Sharma, Y. (2017). Adoption of next generation robotics: A case study on Amazon. *PERSPECTIVA A Case Research Journal*, *3*(1), 9–23.

Jamali, G., & Oveisi, M. (2016). A Study on Project Management Based on PMBOK and PRINCE2. *Modern Applied Science*, *10*(6), 142. doi:10.5539/mas.v10n6p142

Janahi, L., Griffiths, M., & Al-Ammal, H. (2015, July). A conceptual model for IT governance in public sectors. In *2015 Fourth International Conference on Future Generation Communication Technology (FGCT)* (pp. 1-9). IEEE. 10.1109/FGCT.2015.7300242

Javaid, M., Haleem, A., Singh, R. P., Khan, S., & Suman, R. (2021). Blockchain technology applications for Industry 4.0: A literature-based review. *Blockchain: Research and Applications*, *2*(4), 1-11. doi:10.1016/j.bcra.2021.100027

Javaid, M., Haleem, A., Vaishya, R., Bahl, S., Suman, R., & Vaish, A. (2020). Industry 4.0 technologies and their applications in fighting COVID-19 pandemic. *Diabetes & Metabolic Syndrome*, *14*(4), 419–422. doi:10.1016/j.dsx.2020.04.032 PMID:32344370

Javelosa, J. (2017). *Major Firm Announces It's Replacing Its Employees with A.I.* Futurism. http://advice.careerbuilder.com/posts/6softskillseveryprofessionalneeds

Jayaraman, K., Teo, L. K., & Keng, L. S. (2012). The perceptions and perspectives of Lean Six Sigma (LSS) practitioners: An empirical study in Malaysia. *The TQM Journal*, *24*(5), 433–446. doi:10.1108/17542731211261584

Jerry, T. (2021, December 27). What Makes Patagonia A World Leader In Sustainability. *Medium*. https://medium.com/climate-conscious/what-makes-patagonia-a-world-leader-in-sustainability-486073f0daa

Jia, F., Yin, S., Chen, L., & Chen, X. (2020). The circular economy in the textile and apparel industry: A systematic literature review. Journal of Cleaner Production, Volume 259, 120728,ISSN 0959-6526. https://doi.org/10.1016/j.jclepro.2020.120728

Joembunthanaphong, P., & Sriharee, G. (2022). The Improvement Process for The Software Development and Requirements Management to Achieve Capability Level 3 of CMMI. In *2022 26th International Computer Science and Engineering Conference (ICSEC)* (pp. 296-301). 10.1109/ICSEC56337.2022.10049356

Johnny. (2003). *Longitudinal Qualitative Research: Analyzing Change through time.* Altamira Press a Division of Rowman & Littlefield Publishers Inc.

Johnson, T. (2020). *Lean Methodology Mastery Collection: 8 Books in 1: Lean Six Sigma, Startup, Enterprise, Analytics, Agile Project Management, Kanban, Scrum and Kaizen*. Amazon Digital Services LLC - KDP Print US.

Johnston, M. (2006). *Good governance: Rule of law, transparency, and accountability*. United Nations Public Administration Network.

Jørgensen, F., Matthiesen, R., Nielsen, J., & Johansen, J. (2007). Lean maturity, lean sustainability. In J. Olhager & F. Persson (Eds.), *Advances in Production Management Systems* (pp. 371–378). IFIP International Federation for Information Processing. doi:10.1007/978-0-387-74157-4_44

Joshi, P. P. K. (2023, April). *Geospatial Technology for Sustainable Development*. Geospatial World. https://www.geospatialworld.net/prime/prime-opinion/geospatial-technology-for-sustainable-development/

Jouët, J., & Le Caroff, C. (2016). L'observation ethographique en ligne. *Future Generation Computer Systems*, *76*(1), 159–162.

Jovanovic, M., Kostic, N., Sebastian, I. M., & Sedej, T. (2022). Managing a blockchain-based platform ecosystem for industry-wide adoption: The case of TradeLens. *Technological Forecasting and Social Change*, *184*(121981), 1–15. doi:10.1016/j.techfore.2022.121981

Juran, J. M., & Defeo, J. A. (2016). *Juran's Quality Handbook: The Complete Guide to Performance Excellence* (J. A. Defeo, Ed.; 7th ed.). McGraw-Hill Education.

Kagermann, H., Wahlster, W., & Helbig, J. (2013). *Recommendations for Implementing the Strategic Initiative Industrie 4.0, Final Report of the Industrie 4.0 Working Group*. Forschungs Union and Acatech.

Kam, A. W., Collins, S., Park, T., Mihail, M., Stanaway, F. F., Lewis, N. L., Polya, D., Fraser-Bell, S., Roberts, T. V., & Smith, J. E. (2021). Using Lean Six Sigma techniques to improve efficiency in outpatient ophthalmology clinics. *BMC Health Services Research*, *21*(1), 1–9. doi:10.118612913-020-06034-3 PMID:33413381

Kamal Najjar, S., & Al-Sarayreh, K. T. (2015). Capability Maturity Model of Software Requirements Process and Integration (SRPCMMI). ACM.

Kanbanize. (n.d.). *What Is Continuous Improvement? Definition and Tools*. Kanbanize. Retrieved December 29, 2021, from https://kanbanize.com/lean-management/improvement/what-is-continuous-improvement

Kano, L. (2018). Global value chain governance: A relational perspective. *Journal of International Business Studies*, *49*(6), 684–705. doi:10.105741267-017-0086-8

Kanter, R. M., Stein, B. A., & Jick, T. D. (1992). *The Challenge of Organisational Change*. The Free Press.

Kaplan, R. S., & Norton, D. P. (1998). Putting the Balanced Scorecard to Work. In T. Siesfeld, J. Cefola, & D. Neef (Eds.), *The Economic Impact of Knowledge*. Butterworth Heinemann.

Kaplan, R., & Norton, D. (1992). The Balanced Scorecard—Measures That Drive Performance. *Harvard Business Review*, •••, 79. PMID:10119714

Karam, A.-A., Liviu, M., Cristina, V., & Radu, H. (2018). The contribution of lean manufacturing tools to changeover time decrease in the pharmaceutical industry. A SMED project. *Procedia Manufacturing*, *22*, 886–892. doi:10.1016/j.promfg.2018.03.125

Kartikawangi, D. (2017). Symbolic convergence of local wisdom in cross–cultural collaborative social responsibility: Indonesian case. *Public Relations Review*, *43*(1), 35–45. doi:10.1016/j.pubrev.2016.10.012

Kasten, J. E. (2020). Engineering and Manufacturing on the Blockchain: A Systematic Review. *IEEE Engineering Management Review*, *48*(1), 31–47. doi:10.1109/EMR.2020.2964224

Keiningham, T., Aksoy, L., Bruce, H. L., Cadet, F., Clennell, N., Hodgkinson, I. R., & Kearney, T. (2020). Customer experience driven business model innovation. *Journal of Business Research*, *116*, 431–440. doi:10.1016/j.jbusres.2019.08.003

Ken Lee, K. H., Matthew Austin, J., & Pronovost, P. J. (2016). Developing a Measure of Value in Health Care. *Value in Health*, *19*(4), 323–325. doi:10.1016/j.jval.2014.12.009 PMID:27325323

Kennerley, M., & Neely, A. (2002). Performance measurement frameworks: A review. *Business performance measurement. Theory into Practice*, *2*(3), 145–155.

Kevin, D. (2023a). *Future of Project Management: Future Trends and Skills*. Retrieved from https://www.knowledgehut.com/blog/project-management/future-of-project-management

Kevin, D. (2023b). *Project management Demand: Career Opportunities*. Retrieved from https://www.knowledgehut.com/blog/project-management/project-management-demand

Khan, S., Yu, Z., & Farooq, K. (2022). Green capabilities, green purchasing, and triple bottom line performance: Leading toward environmental sustainability. *Business Strategy and the Environment*. Advance online publication. doi:10.1002/bse.3234

Khusaini, N. S., Jaffar, A., & Yusoff, N. (2014). *A survey on lean manufacturing tools implementation in Malaysian food and beverages industry using rasch model*. Advanced Materials Research, Johor Bahru, MY.

Kim, H. Y., & Cho, J. S. (2018). Data governance framework for big data implementation with NPS Case Analysis in Korea. *The Journal of Business and Retail Management Research*, *12*(3), 36–46. doi:10.24052/JBRMR/V12IS03/ART-04

Kiselakova, D., Sofrankova, B., Cabinova, V., Onuferova, E., & Soltesova, J. (2018). The impact of R&D expenditure on the development of global competitiveness within the CEE EU countries. *Journal of Competitiveness*, *10*(3), 34–50. doi:10.7441/joc.2018.03.03

Kissflow. (2022). *What is a Project in Project Management?* Retrieved from https://kissflow.com/project/what-is-a-project/

Kline, R. B. (2015). *Principles and practice of structural equation modeling* (4th ed.). The Guilford Press.

Knoll, D., Reinhart, G., & Prüglmeier, M. (2019). Enabling value stream mapping for internal logistics using multidimensional process mining. *Expert Systems with Applications*, *124*, 130–142. doi:10.1016/j.eswa.2019.01.026

Knowledgehut. (2023). *ITIL Certification vs PRINCE2 – Understanding the Differences*. Retrieved from https://www.knowledgehut.com/blog/it-service-management/itil-vs-prince2

Koch, T., & Windsperger, J. (2017). Seeing through the network: Competitive advantage in the digital economy. *Journal of Organization Design*, *6*(1), 1–30. doi:10.118641469-017-0016-z

Kolk, A. (2003). Trends in sustainability reporting by the Fortune Global 250¢. *Business Strategy and the Environment*, *12*(5), 279–291.

Kolk, A. (2004). A decade of sustainability reporting: Developments and significance. *International Journal of Environment and Sustainable Development*, *3*(1), 51–64.

Korhonen, J. (2004). Industrial ecology in the strategic sustainable development model: strategic applications of industrial ecology. Journal of Cleaner Production, Volume 12, Issues 8–10, Pages 809-823. ISSN 0959-6526. https://doi.org/10.1016/j.jclepro.2004.02.026

Koteen, J. (1989). *Strategic Management in Public and Nonprofit Organizations: Thinking and Acting Strategically on Public Concerns*. Praeger.

Kotter, J. P. (2012). *Leading Change*. Harvard Business Review Press.

Kotter, J. P. (2014). *Accelerate: Building Strategic Agility for a Faster-moving World*. Harvard Business Review Press.

Kozinets, R. V. (2010). *Netnography. Doing Ethnographic Research Online*. Sage Publications.

Kozinets, R. V. (2015). Netnography: Redefined. *Sage (Atlanta, Ga.)*.

KPMG. (2014). *The essentials of materiality assessment*. KPMG Sustainable Insight. p. 32-33. https://assets.kpmg.com/content/dam/kpmg/pdf/2014/10/materiality-assessment.pdf

Kraaijenbrink, J. (2018, December 19). *What Does VUCA Really Mean?* Forbes. https://www.forbes.com/sites/jeroen-kraaijenbrink/2018/12/19/what-does-vuca-really-mean/?sh=6cfcaab17d62

Krammer, S. W. S. (2009). Drivers of national innovation in transition: Evidence from a panel of Eastern European countries. *Research Policy*, *38*(5), 845–860. doi:10.1016/j.respol.2009.01.022

Kraus, S., Schiavone, F., Pluzhnikova, A., & Invernizzi, A. (2021). Digital transformation in health care: Analyzing the current state-of-research. *Journal of Business Research*, *123*, 557–567. doi:10.1016/j.jbusres.2020.10.030

Kruger, W., & Rudman, R. (2013). Strategic Alignment Of Application Software Packages And Business Processes Using PRINCE2. *The International Business & Economics Research Journal*, *12*(10), 1239. doi:10.19030/iber.v12i10.8134

Kshetri, N. (2005). Pattern of global cyber war and crime: A conceptual framework. *Journal of International Management*, *11*(4), 541–562. doi:10.1016/j.intman.2005.09.009

Kübler-Ross, E. (2014). *On Death and Dying: What the Dying Have to Teach Doctors, Nurses, Clergy and Their Own Families*. Scribner.

Kujala, J., Aaltonen, K., Gotcheva, N., & Lahdenperä, P. (2021). Dimensions of governance in interorganizational project networks. *International Journal of Managing Projects in Business*, *14*(3), 625–651. Advance online publication. doi:10.1108/IJMPB-12-2019-0312

Kun, L. A., Eng, T. S., Wei, H., Xuecheng, D., & Seeram, R. (2021). Sustainability framework for pharmaceutical manufacturing (PM): A review of research landscape and implementation barriers for circular economy transition, Journal of Cleaner Production, Volume 280, Part 2, 124264, ISSN 0959-6526. https://doi.org/10.1016/j.jclepro.2020.124264

Kyle, W. (2022, May). *Not Just Who, But Where: The need for geospatial data to achieve the Sustainable Development Goals*. International Institute for Sustainable Development. https://www.iisd.org/articles/insight/not-just-who-where-need-geospatial-data-achieve-sustainable-development-goals

La Londe, B. J., & Masters, J. M. (1994). Emerging Logistics Strategies. *International Journal of Physical Distribution & Logistics Management*, *24*(7), 35–47. doi:10.1108/09600039410070975

Lacy, P., Cooper, T., Hayward, R., & Neuberger, L. (2010). *A new era of sustainability. UN Global Compact*. Accenture.

Lai, E. (n.d.). *Lean Governance - Oxymoron or Essential Strategy?* Cprime. Retrieved December 30, 2021, from https://www.cprime.com/resources/blog/lean-governance-an-oxymoron-or-essential-strategy/

Lamballais, T., Roy, D., & De Koster, M. B. M. (2017). Estimating performance in a robotic mobile fulfillment system. *European Journal of Operational Research*, *256*(3), 976–990. doi:10.1016/j.ejor.2016.06.063

Lamsiah, A., Benabderrazik, Y., & Bentalha, B. (2021). The Economic and political components of diplomatic discourse: State actors in Morocco-UK Free Trade Agreement as a case study. *Alternatives Managériales Economiques*, *3*(4), 496–517.

Larman, C., Vodde, B., & Jensen, B. (2017). *Large-scale scrum*. Dpunkt.

Latapí Agudelo, M. A., Jóhannsdóttir, L., & Davídsdóttir, B. A literature review of the history and evolution of corporate social responsibility. Int J Corporate Soc Responsibility 4, 1 (2019). https://doi.org/10.1186/s40991-018-0039-y

Lawal, A. K., Rotter, T., Kinsman, L., Sari, N., Harrison, L., Jeffery, C., Kutz, M., Khan, M. F., & Flynn, R. (2014). Lean management in health care: Definition, concepts, methodology and effects reported (systematic review protocol). *Systematic Reviews*, *3*(1), 103. doi:10.1186/2046-4053-3-103 PMID:25238974

Lazarus, R. J. (2004). *The Making of Environmental Law*. University of Chicago Press.

Lee, J., Bagheri, B., & Kao, H. (2015). A Cyber-Physical Systems Architecture for Industry 4.0.-based on manufacturing systems. *Manufacturing Letters*, *3*, 18–23. doi:10.1016/j.mfglet.2014.12.001

Lee, S. H. (2019). An analysis on the changes of logistics industry using internet of things. *Journal of Advanced Information Technology and Convergence*, *9*(1), 57–66. doi:10.14801/JAITC.2019.9.1.57

Lee, S. H., & Jeong, G. Y. (2022). The effect of corporate social responsibility compatibility and authenticity on brand trust and corporate sustainability management: For Korean cosmetics companies. *Frontiers in Psychology*, *13*, 895823. doi:10.3389/fpsyg.2022.895823 PMID:35645870

Leibowitz, G. (2017, March 28). *How to Build a Great Company Culture Like Google, According to an Ex-Googler*. Inc. Magazine. Retrieved December 30, 2021, from https://www.inc.com/glenn-leibowitz/how-one-startup-founder-borrowed-the-best-bits-of-googles-culture-for-his-own-co.html

Leite, H., Bateman, N., & Radnor, Z. (2020). Beyond the ostensible: An exploration of barriers to lean implementation and sustainability in healthcare. *Production Planning and Control*, *31*(1), 1–18. doi:10.1080/09537287.2019.1623426

Lencioni, P. M. (2012). *The advantage: Why organisational health trumps everything else in business*. Jossey-Bass.

Leng, J., Yan, D., Liu, Q., Xu, K., Zhao, J. L., Shi, R., Wei, L., Zhang, D., & Chen, X. (2020). ManuChain: Combining Permissioned Blockchain with a Holistic Optimization Model as Bi-Level Intelligence for Smart Manufacturing. *IEEE Transactions on Systems, Man, and Cybernetics. Systems*, *50*(1), 182–192. doi:10.1109/TSMC.2019.2930418

Leng, J., Ye, S., Zhou, M., Zhao, J. L., Liu, Q., Guo, W., Cao, W., & Fu, L. (2021). Blockchain-Secured Smart Manufacturing in Industry 4.0: A Survey. *IEEE Transactions on Systems, Man, and Cybernetics. Systems*, *51*(1), 237–252. doi:10.1109/TSMC.2020.3040789

Le, P. B., & Lei, H. (2019). Determinants of innovation capability: The roles of transformational leadership, knowledge sharing and perceived organizational support. *Journal of Knowledge Management*, *23*(3), 527–547. doi:10.1108/JKM-09-2018-0568

Le, T. T. (2022). How do corporate social responsibility and green innovation transform corporate green strategy into sustainable firm performance? *Journal of Cleaner Production*, *362*, 132228. doi:10.1016/j.jclepro.2022.132228

Letsoalo, K., Brown, I., & Njenga, K. N. (2006). An investigation of enablers and inhibitors of IT governance implementation: A case study of a South African enterprise. In *Proceedings of the ITG International Conference* (pp. 27-35). Academic Press.

Levinson, W., & Shojania, K. G. (2011). Bad experiences in the hospital: The stories keep coming. *BMJ Quality & Safety*, *20*(11), 911–913. doi:10.1136/bmjqs-2011-000474 PMID:21964611

Lieder, M., & Rashid, A. (2016). Towards circular economy implementation: a comprehensive review in context of manufacturing industry. Journal of Cleaner Production, Volume 115, Pages 36-51. ISSN 0959-6526. https://doi.org/10.1016/j.jclepro.2015.12.042

Li, J. T., & Liu, H. J. (2016). Design optimization of amazon robotics. *Automation, Control and Intelligent Systems*, *4*(2), 48–52. doi:10.11648/j.acis.20160402.17

Liker, J. (2004). The Toyota Way: 14 Management Principles from the World's Greatest Manufacturer (1° ed). McGraw Hill.

Liker, J. K. (2004). *The Toyota way*. McGraw-Hill Education.

Liker, J. K. (2004). *The Toyota way: 14 management principles from the world's greatest manufacturer* (1st ed.). McGraw-Hill Education.

Likert, R. (1932). A Technique for the Measurement of Attitudes. *Archives de Psychologie*, *140*, 1–55.

Likert, R. A. (1961). *New Patterns of Management*. McGraw-Hill Book Company, Inc.

Lim, M. K., Li, Y., Wang, C., & Tseng, M. L. (2021). A literature review of blockchain technology applications in supply chains: A comprehensive analysis of themes, methodologies and industries. *Computers & Industrial Engineering*, *154*(107133), 1–14. doi:10.1016/j.cie.2021.107133

Lina, Z., & Dan, S. (2012). Research on Combining Scrum with CMMI in Small and Medium Organizations. In *2012 International Conference on Computer Science and Electronics Engineering* (pp. 554-557). 10.1109/ICCSEE.2012.477

Linnenluecke, M. K., & Griffiths, A. (2010). Corporate Sustainability and Organizational Culture. *Journal of World Business, 45,* pp. 357-366. https://doi.org/10.1016/j.jwb.2009.08.006

Liu, Y., Zhang, W., Pan, S., Li, Y., & Chen, Y. (2020). Analyzing the robotic behavior in a smart city with deep enforcement and imitation learning using IoRT. *Computer Communications*, *150*(1), 346–356. doi:10.1016/j.comcom.2019.11.031

Liu, Z., & Li, Z. (2020). A blockchain-based framework of cross-border e-commerce supply chain. *International Journal of Information Management*, *52*(102059), 1–18. doi:10.1016/j.ijinfomgt.2019.102059

Li, X. (2022). The discursive construction of corporate identity in the corporate social responsibility reports: A case study of Starbucks. *Frontiers in Psychology*, *13*, 940541. doi:10.3389/fpsyg.2022.940541 PMID:36092082

Lohmer, J., & Lasch, R. (2020). Blockchain in operations management and manufacturing: Potential and barriers. *Computers & Industrial Engineering*, *149*(106789), 1–15. doi:10.1016/j.cie.2020.106789

Longo, F., Nicoletti, L., Padovano, A., D'Atri, G., & Forte, M. (2019). Blockchain-enabled supply chain: An experimental study. *Computers & Industrial Engineering*, *136*, 57–69. doi:10.1016/j.cie.2019.07.026

Losonci, D., & Demeter, K. (2013). Lean production and business performance: International empirical results. *Competitiveness Review*, *23*(3), 218–233. doi:10.1108/10595421311319816

Lozano, R., & Carpenter, A., & Sammalisto, K. (2020). Analysing Organisational Change Management in Seaports: Stakeholder Perception, Communication, Drivers for, and Barriers to Sustainability at the Port of Gävle. (In book: European Port Cities in Transition) DOI: . doi:10.1007/978-3-030-36464-9_12

Lozano, R., Barreiro-Gen, M., & Zafar, A. (2021). Collaboration for organizational sustainability limits to growth: Developing a factors, benefits, and challenges framework. *Sustainable Development*, *29*(4), 728–737.

Lucey, J., Bateman, N., & Hines, P. (2005). Why major lean transitions have not been sustained. *Management Services*, *49*(2), 9–13.

Luo, Y. (2021). A general framework of digitalization risks in international business. *Journal of International Business Studies*.

Lynn, M. R. (1986). Determination and quantification of content validity. *Nursing Research*, *35*(6), 382–385. doi:10.1097/00006199-198611000-00017 PMID:3640358

Madanaguli, A., Srivastava, S., Ferraris, A., & Dhir, A. (2022). Corporate social responsibility and sustainability in the tourism sector: A systematic literature review and future outlook. *Sustainable Development (Bradford)*, *30*(3), 447–461. doi:10.1002d.2258

Madsen, D. Ø., Berg, T., Stenheim, T., Moum, J. V., Bordewich, I. O., & Storsveen, M. (2019). The long-term sustainability of lean as a management practice: Survey evidence on diffusion and use of the concept in Norway in the period 2015–2017. *Sustainability (Basel)*, *11*(11), 3120. doi:10.3390u11113120

Magnusson, J., Koutsikouri, D., & Päivärinta, T. (2020). Efficiency creep and shadow innovation: Enacting ambidextrous IT Governance in the public sector. *European Journal of Information Systems*, *29*(4), 329–349. doi:10.1080/0960085X.2020.1740617

Maione, E., Bruno, G., & Lombardi, F. (2020). *Lean healthcare application for patient flow analysis in Cardiology department*. Politecnico di Torino, Corso di Laurea Magistrale in Ingegneria Gestionale. https://webthesis.biblio.polito.it/id/eprint/14000

Managing Successful Projects with PRINCE2. (2017). TSO.

Mann, D. W. (2015). *Creating a lean culture: Tools to sustain lean conversions* (3rd ed.). CRC Press.

Manyika, J., Lund, S., Bughin, J., Woetzel, J., Stamenov, K., & Dhringra, D. (2016). *Digital globalization: The new era of global flows*. McKinsey Global Institute.

Mao, Z., Wu, J., Qiao, Y., & Yao, H. (2022). Government data governance framework based on a data middle platform. *Aslib Journal of Information Management*, *74*(2), 289–310. Advance online publication. doi:10.1108/AJIM-03-2021-0068

March, J. G. (1991). Exploration and exploitation in organizational learning. *Organization Science*, *2*(1), 71–87. doi:10.1287/orsc.2.1.71

Marchwinski, C. (2014). *Sustain your lean business system with a "Golden Triangle"*. Lean Enterprise Institute. Retrieved Dec 1st from https://www.lean.org/common/display/?o=2592

Marjanović, D., & Domazet, I. (2021). Foreign Direct Investments: A Key Factor for Business Globalization. In Y. Bayar (Ed.), *Institutional, Economic, and Social Impacts of Globalization and Liberalization* (pp. 96–116). IGI Global. doi:10.4018/978-1-7998-4459-4.ch006

Marjanović, D., & Domazet, I. (2021). Tax competitiveness as a significant factor in attracting foreign investment – the case of Serbia. *Argumenta Oeconomica*, *2*(47), 63–80. doi:10.15611/aoe.2021.2.04

Marjanović, D., Domazet, I., & Vukmirović, I. (2022). Social Environment as a Factor of Capital Investment in Serbia. *Eastern European Economics*, *60*(3), 247–264. Advance online publication. doi:10.1080/00128775.2022.2048181

Markos, S., & Sridevi, M. S. (2010). Employee Engagement: The Key to Improving Performance. *International Journal of Business and Management*, *2*(12), 89–96.

Marshak, R. J., & Bushe, G. R. (2018). Planned and generative change in organization development. *OD Practitioner*, *50*(4), 9–15.

Marshall, D. A. (2014). *Lean transformation: Overcoming the challenges, managing performance, and sustaining success*. University of Kentucky.

Martin, A., & Martin, A. (2023). Introduction to an agile framework a for the management of technology transfer projects. *Procedia Computer Science, 219*(2022), 1963–1968. doi:10.1016/j.procs.2023.01.496

Martino, F., Perfilieva, I., & Sessa, S. (2021). *A Summary of F-Transform Techniques in Data Analysis*. Available in: https://www.researchgate.net/publication/353461547

Martinus, W., Wahab, M. S., Yudi, & Ham, H. (2021). Data Transmission Using RFID System on Smart Shopping Carts for Checkout Process Efficiency in Supermarket at Indonesia. *Procedia Computer Science, 179*, 902–912. doi:10.1016/j.procs.2021.01.080

Masilela, L., & Nel, D. (2021). The role of data and information security governance in protecting public sector data and information assets in national government in South Africa. *Africa's Public Service Delivery and Performance Review, 9*(1), 385. doi:10.4102/apsdpr.v9i1.385

Masser, I. (2005). GIS worlds: creating spatial data infrastructures (Vol. 338). ESRI Press.

Masser, I. (1999). All shapes and sizes: The first generation of national spatial data infrastructures. *International Journal of Geographical Information Science, 13*(1), 67–84. doi:10.1080/136588199241463

Masuti, P. M., & Dabade, U. A. (2019). Lean manufacturing implementation using value stream mapping at excavator manufacturing company. *Materials Today: Proceedings, 19*, 606–610. doi:10.1016/j.matpr.2019.07.740

Matheus, R., & Janssen, M. (2016, June). Towards an ambidextrous government: Strategies for balancing exploration and exploitation in open government. In *Proceedings of the 17th International Digital Government Research Conference on Digital Government Research* (pp. 334-341). 10.1145/2912160.2912192

Matijević, M., & Šolaja, M. (2022). *ICT in Serbia - At a Glance*. Vojvodina ICT Cluster.

Mausner, B., Herzberg, F., & Snyderman, B. B. (1966). *The motivation to work*. Transaction Publishers.

Mazzucato, M. (2013). Financing innovation: Creative destruction vs. destructive creation. *Industrial and Corporate Change, 22*(4), 851–867. doi:10.1093/icc/dtt025

McDonough, W., & Braungart, M. (2002). Design for the triple top line: New tools for sustainable commerce. *Corporate Environmental Strategy, 9*(3), 251–258.

McGoldrick, M., Gerson, R., & Shellenberger, S. (1999). *Genograms: Assessment and Intervention*. W.W. Norton & Company.

McGrath, K. M., Bennett, D. M., Ben-Tovim, D. I., Boyages, S. C., Lyons, N. J., & O'Connell, T. J. (2008). Implementing and sustaining transformational change in health care: Lessons learnt about clinical process redesign. *The Medical Journal of Australia, 188*(7, S6), 422. Advance online publication. doi:10.5694/j.1326-5377.2008.tb01692.x PMID:18341474

McKinley, W., & Mone, M. A. (2003). Micro and macro perspectives in organization theory: a tale of incommensurability. In W. McKinley, M. Mone, H. Tsoukas, & C. Knudsen (Eds.), *The Oxford Handbook of Organization Theory* (pp. 345–372). Sage.

McKinsey. (2020). *Risk, resilience, and rebalancing in global value chains*. McKinsey Global Institute.

McLaughlin, J. D. (1991). Towards national spatial data infrastructure. *Proceedings of the Canadian Conference on GIS*, 1–5.

McLaughlin, J., & Nichols, S. (1994). Developing a national spatial data infrastructure. *Journal of Surveying Engineering, 120*(2), 62–76. doi:10.1061/(ASCE)0733-9453(1994)120:2(62)

Meehan, P. (2020). Objectives and key results (OKRs): Driving focus, alignment, and engagement in governance. *Corporate Governance Review, 28*(2), 16–21.

Melo, V. (2018). Collaborative Efforts for Sustainable Development: Surveying the Literature on Multi-Stakeholder Initiatives to Realize the Sustainable Development Goals. *Task Team on CSO Development Effectiveness and Enabling Environment, 10.*

Memon, M. A., Ting, H., Cheah, J. H., Ramayah, T., Chuah, F., & Cham, T. H. (2020). Sample size for survey research: Review and recommendations. *Journal of Applied Structural Equation Modelling, 4*(2), 1–20. doi:10.47263/JASEM.4(2)01

Mende, M., Maura, L. S., Van Doorn, J., Grewal, D., & Shanks, I. (2019). Service Robots Rising: How Humanoid Robots Influence Service Experiences and Elicit Compensatory Consumer Responses. *JMR, Journal of Marketing Research, 56*(4), 535–556. doi:10.1177/0022243718822827

Merschformann, M., Lamballais, T., De Koster, M. B. M., & Suhl, L. (2019). Decision rules for robotic mobile fulfillment systems. *Operations Research Perspectives, 6*(1), 100128. Advance online publication. doi:10.1016/j.orp.2019.100128

Merzouk, S. (2017). A Comparative Study of Agile Methods. *Towards a New Model-based Method., 9*(4), 8.

Merzouk, S., Cherkaoui, A., Marzak, A., & Nawal, S. (2020). IoT methodologies: Comparative study. *Procedia Computer Science, 175*, 585–590. doi:10.1016/j.procs.2020.07.084

Merzouk, S., Cherkaoui, A., Marzak, A., Sael, N., & Guerss, F.-Z. (2021). The proposition of Process flow model for Scrum and eXtreme Programming. *Association for Computing Machinery, 6*, 1–6. Advance online publication. doi:10.1145/3454127.3457627

Miethlich, B., Belotserkovich, D., Abasova, S., Zatsarinnaya, E., & Veselitsky, O. (2020). Digital economy and its influence on the competitiveness of countries and regions. *Revista espacios, 41*(12).

Mihardjo, L., Sasmoko, S., Alamsjah, F., & Elidjen, E. (2019). Digital leadership role in developing business model innovation and customer experience orientation in Industry 4.0. *Management Science Letters, 9*(11), 1749–1762. doi:10.5267/j.msl.2019.6.015

Millar, C., Hind, P., & Magala, S. (2012). Sustainability and the need for change: Organizational change and transformational vision. *Journal of Organizational Change Management, 25*(4), 489–500.

Mirzaei, S., & Shokouhyar, S. (2023). Applying a thematic analysis in identifying the role of circular economy in sustainable supply chain practices. *Environment, Development and Sustainability, 25*(5), 4691–4722. doi:10.100710668-022-02217-6

Mithas, S., Tafti, A., & Mitchell, W. (2013). How a firm's competitive environment and digital strategy posture influence digital business strategy. *Management Information Systems Quarterly, 37*(2), 511–536. doi:10.25300/MISQ/2013/37.2.09

Mizrak, K. C., & Kizilcan, S. (2022). Environmentally Sensitive Management Approach Within the Scope of Carbon-Free Airport: The Case of Sivas Nuri Demirağ Airport. *Cumhuriyet Üniversitesi İktisadi ve İdari Bilimler Dergisi, 23*(3), 623–634. doi:10.37880/cumuiibf.1063147

Moedt, W., Bernsteiner, R., Hall, M., & Fruhling, A. (2023). Enhancing IoT Project Success through Agile Best Practices. *ACM Transactions on Internet of Things, 4*(1), 5:1-5:31. doi:10.1145/3568170

Moeuf, A., Pellerin, R., Lamouri, S., Tamayo-Giraldo, S., & Barbaray, R. (2017). The industrial management of SMEs in the era of Industry 4.0. *International Journal of Production Research, 7543*, 1–19.

Mohamed Ismail, R. (2014). *Mediation impact of manufacturing strategies on external environmental factors and manufacturing performance*. Universiti Utara Malaysia.

Mohammadi, H. (2008). *The Integration of multi-source spatial datasets in the context of SDI initiatives* [PhD thesis]. Department of Geomatics, The University of Melbourne.

Mohd Rose, A. N., Md Deros, B., & Ab Rahman, M. N. (2013). *Lean manufacturing practices implementation in Malaysian's SME automotive component industry*. Applied Mechanics and Materials.

Mohd Yusof, S., & Aoki, K. (2016, March 8-10). *Proposed lean sustained factors*. The 6th International Conference on Industrial Engineering and Operations Management (IEOM 2016), Kuala Lumpur, Malaysia.

Molesky, J., O'Reilly, B., & Humble, J. (2020). *Lean Enterprise: How High Performance Organizations Innovate at Scale*. O'Reilly Media, Incorporated.

Momanyi, C. (2020). Influence of Sustainable Strategic Management Practices on the Performance of Technical and Vocational Education and Training: A Literature Based Review. *Journal of Strategic Management*, *4*(3), 10–29.

Moon, J., Tang, R., & Lee, W. S. (2022). Antecedents and consequences of Starbucks' environmental, social and governance (ESG) implementation. *Journal of Quality Assurance in Hospitality & Tourism*, 1–23.

Moraes, A. J. M. (1985). *Alocação de Recursos em Projetos de Processamento de Dados - Fatores Determinantes* [Resource Allocation in Data Processing Projects - Determinant Factors]. MMFV/1a. Versão. VII Congresso Regional e IV Feira Nacional da SUCESU / BR - Sociedade dos Usuários de Computadores e Equipamentos Subsidiários, Sao Paulo/State of Sao Paulo/Brazil.

Moraes, A. J. M. (1989). *Alocação de Recursos em Projetos de Processamento de Dados - Fatores Determinantes* [Resource Allocation in Data Processing Projects - Determinant Factors]. MMFV/2a. Versão). XXII Congresso Nacional e IX Feira Internacional da SUCESU / BR - Sociedade dos Usuários de Computadores e Equipamentos Subsidiários., Sao Paulo/State of Sao Paulo/Brazil.

Moraes, A. J. M. (2011). *Proposta do M2A3-GovTI – Modelo de Maturidade para Análise do Alinhamento das Atividades relacionadas à Governança da TI em conformidade com as expectativas de resultado planejadas pela Organização* [2M3A-GovIT Proposal – Maturity Model for Analysis of the Alignment of Activities related to IT Governance in accordance with the expectations of results planned by the Organization]. Production Engineering Doctorate Thesis. PPGEP - Programa de Pós-Graduação *Stricto-Sensu* em Engenharia de Produção. Universidade Paulista (UNIP). 406 p. São Paulo; Brazil.

Moraes, A. J. M. (2015). *Worksheet of Exogenous Variables that Impact the Success of Validation Stage of Product Delivery of a Project*. 6th International Multi-Conference on Complexity, Informatics and Cybernetics: IMCIC 2015. Available in https://www.iiisci.org/Journal/SCI/Abstract.asp?var=&id=ZA646OI15

Moraes, A. J. M. (2017). *Interpretation of the results of a Case Study about Impacts and Influences of Exogenous Variables in the planning of Chronogram and Budget in Software Projects*. 21st World Multi-Conference on Systemics, Cybernetics and Informatics: WMSCI 2017. Available in https://www.iiisci.org/Journal/SCI/Abstract.asp?var=&id=SA820QW17

Morais, G. M., Santos, V. F., & Gonçalves, C. A. (2020). Netnography: Origins, Foundations, Evolution and Axiological and Methodological Developments and Trends. *Qualitative Report*, *25*(1), 441–455. doi:10.46743/2160-3715/2020.4227

Morali, O., & Searcy, C. (2013). A review of sustainable supply chain management practices in Canada. *Journal of Business Ethics*, *117*(3), 635–658. doi:10.100710551-012-1539-4

Morjane, W., Bannari, R., & Gharib, J. (2022). Overview of Project Management Methodologies: Traditional Versus Agile Approach. *European International Conference on Industrial Engineering and Operations Management, 5*, 783–794. 10.46254/EU05.20220157

Munim, Z. H., Balasubramaniyan, S., Kouhizadeh, M., & Hossain, N. U. I. (2022). Assessing blockchain technology adoption in the Norwegian oil and gas industry using Bayesian Best Worst Method. *Journal of Industrial Information Integration*, *28*(100346), 1–14. doi:10.1016/j.jii.2022.100346

Munir, A., Asmat, A., Donald, G., Walter, T. D. V., Giles, F. D., & Muhammad, I. (2023). *2nd Workshop on Feasibility Study for Establishment of National Spatial Data Infrastructure (NSDI) for Pakistan.* Researchgate. https://www.researchgate.net/publication/369021769_2nd_WORKSHOP_ON_FEASIBILITY_STUDY_FOR_ESTABLISHMENT_OF_NATIONAL_SPATIAL_DATA_INFRASTRUCTURE_NSDI_FOR_PAKISTAN

Murphy, S. A. (2019). The power of objectives and key results (OKRs) in corporate governance. *International Journal of Business, Humanities, and Technology*, *9*(5), 63–68.

Murti, Y. (2009). *Sustaining lean in New Zealand manufacturing organisations.* Massey University.

Nambisan, S., Lyytinen, K. J., Majchrzak, A., & Song, M. (2017). Digital innovation management: Reinventing innovation management research in a digital world. *Management Information Systems Quarterly*, *4*(1), 223–238. doi:10.25300/MISQ/2017/41:1.03

Nasution, R. A., Sembada, A. Y., Miliani, L., Resti, N. D., & Prawono, D. A. (2014). The customer experience framework as baseline for strategy and implementation in services marketing. *Procedia: Social and Behavioral Sciences*, *148*, 254–261. doi:10.1016/j.sbspro.2014.07.041

nationalgeoportal.gov.np . (2023). *National Spatial Data Center.* https://nationalgeoportal.gov.np/

Nawanir, G., Lim, K. T., & Othman, S. N. (2016). Lean manufacturing practices in Indonesian manufacturing firms. *International Journal of Lean Six Sigma*, *7*(2), 149–170. doi:10.1108/IJLSS-06-2014-0013

Neely, A. D., Adams, C., & Kennerley, M. (2002). *The performance prism: The scorecard for measuring and managing business success* (pp. 159-160). London: Prentice Hall Financial Times.

Neely, A., Adams, C., & Crowe, P. (2001). The performance prism in practice. *Measuring Business Excellence*, *5*(2), 6–13.

Neri, A., Cagno, E., Lepri, M., & Trianni, A. (2021). A triple bottom line balanced set of key performance indicators to measure the sustainability performance of industrial supply chains. *Sustainable Production and Consumption.* Vol 26. pp. 648-691,ISSN 2352-5509. https://doi.org/10.1016/j.spc.2020.12.018

Netland, T. H., Powell, D. J., & Hines, P. (2020). Demystifying lean leadership. *International Journal of Lean Six Sigma*, *11*(3), 543–554. doi:10.1108/IJLSS-07-2019-0076

Ngai, E. W. (2005). Customer relationship management research (1992-2002): An academic literature review and classification. *Marketing Intelligence & Planning*, *23*(6), 582–605. doi:10.1108/02634500510624147

Nguyen, T. T., Pham, T. A. T., & Tram, H. T. X. (2020). Role of information and communication technologies and innovation in driving carbon emissions and economic growth in selected G-20 countries. *Journal of Environmental Management*, *261*, 110162. doi:10.1016/j.jenvman.2020.110162 PMID:32148259

Nick, G., Szaller, A., Bergmann, J., & Va'rgedő, T. (2019). Industry 4.0 readiness in Hungary: Model, and the first results in connection to data application. *IFAC-PapersOnLine*, *52*(13), 289–294. doi:10.1016/j.ifacol.2019.11.185

Nickolas, B. (2006). *Essentials of Change.* Thousands Oak.

Nidumolu, R., Prahalad, C. K., & Rangaswami, M. R. (2009). Why sustainability is now the key driverof innovation? *Harvard Business Review*, (September), 56–64.

Nisa, D. K., Paksi, A. K., Hutami, A. N., & Fadilla, Q. Y. (2021). Unilever's contribution to achieving sustainable development goals 3 in Indonesia. In *E3S Web of Conferences* (Vol. 316, p. 01023). EDP Sciences. doi:10.1051/e3sconf/202131601023

Nishimura, T. (2018). *Big Data Analytics Market – Future Scope in India.* Silicon India.

Nonaka, I., & Takeuchi, H. (1995). The knowledge-creating company. *Harvard Business Review, 73*(4), 96–104.

Nonaka, I., & von Krogh, G. (2009). Tacit knowledge and knowledge conversion: Controversy and advancement in organisational knowledge creation theory. *Organization Science, 20*(3), 635–652. doi:10.1287/orsc.1080.0412

nsdi.gov.lk. (2023a). *Governance Structure.* https://nsdi.gov.lk/governance-structure

nsdi.gov.lk. (2023b). *NSDI.* https://nsdi.gov.lk/nsdi

nsdi.gov.lk. (2023c). *Outreach Plan.* https://www.nsdi.gov.lk/outreach-plan

Nuseir, M., & Elrefae, G. (2022). The effects of facilitating conditions, customer experience, and brand loyalty on customer-based brand equity through social media marketing. *International Journal of Data and Network Science, 6*(3), 875–884. doi:10.5267/j.ijdns.2022.2.009

Nussbaum, R. (2015). *Changing the tooth-to-tail ratio using robotics and automation to beat sequestration. Air And Space Power,* Journal Maxwell Afb Al. Technical Report.

Nxozi, M., & Flowerday, S. (2021). IT Governance Adoption and Use by State-owned Entities in South Africa: A Public Administration Perspective. In Interdisciplinary Research in Technology and Management (pp. 181-187). CRC Press. doi:10.1201/9781003202240-29

Occhiuzzi, C., Amendola, S., Nappi, S., D'Uva, N., & Marrocco, G. (2019). RFID Technology for Industry 4.0: Architectures and Challenges. *IEEE International Conference on RFID Technology and Applications (RFID-TA)*, 181 – 186. 10.1109/RFID-TA.2019.8892049

Ócsai, A., & Ócsai, A. (2021). Ecologically Conscious Business Organizations and Their Value Orientations. *Ecologically Conscious Organizations: New Business Practices Based on Ecological Commitment*, 93-150.

OECD. (1999). *OECD Principles of Corporate Governance.* OECD.

OECD. (2004). The OECD principles of corporate governance. *Contaduría y Administración*, 216.

OECD. (2021). Key future uncertainties in digital transformation and potential implications for Latvia. In *Going Digital in Latvia*. OECD Publishing.

OGC – Office of Government Commerce. (2018). *PRINCE2® – Project In a Controlled Environment.* Available in: https://www.leansixsigma.com.br/acervo/26181926.pdf

Okano, M. T., Antunes, S., Langhi, C., & Simões, E. (2019). Digital Transformation: News Technologies and Business Model. *Ijsrm.Human,* 2019; Vol. 13 (3): 81-100. https://ijsrm.humanjournals.com/wp-content/uploads/2019/10/6.Marcelo-T-Okano-Samira-Antunes-Celi-Langhi-Eliane-Sim%C3%B5es.pdf

Ole, J. K., Terry, M. W., Terry, W., & Ole, M. M. (2009). *Governance Frameworks for Public Project Development and Estimation.* Project Management Institute.

Onofrei, G., Prester, J., Fynes, B., Humphreys, P., & Wiengarten, F. (2019). The relationship between investments in lean practices and operational performance: Exploring the moderating effects of operational intellectual capital. *International Journal of Operations &amp. International Journal of Operations & Production Management, 39*(3), 406–428. doi:10.1108/IJOPM-04-2018-0201

Origin of holacracy. (n.d.). Holacracy I Reflect. Retrieved December 30, 2021, from https://www.reflect-beratung.de/en/holacracy/

OstadabbasH.MerzH.WeippertH. (2021). Integration of urban spatial data management and visualization with enterprise applications using open-source software. *International Archives of the Photogrammetry, Remote Sensing and Spatial Information Sciences - ISPRS Archives, 43*(B4-2021). doi:10.5194/isprs-archives-XLIII-B4-2021-307-2021

Osterrieder, P., Budde, L., & Friedli, T. (2020). The smart factory as a key construct of industry 4.0: A systematic literature review. *International Journal of Production Economics, 2020*(221), 107476. doi:10.1016/j.ijpe.2019.08.011

Our Philosophy to Modern Change Management. (n.d.). Lean Change Management. Retrieved September 3, 2023, from https://leanchange.org/philosophy

Oxley, J., & Yeung, B. (2001). E-commerce readiness: Institutional environment and international competitiveness. *Journal of International Business Studies, 32*(4), 705–723. doi:10.1057/palgrave.jibs.8490991

Padayachee, V. (2013). Corporate governance in South Africa: from 'Old Boys Club' to 'Ubuntu'? *Transformation: Critical Perspectives on Southern Africa, 81*(1), 260–290.

Pai, V., & Chandra, S. (2022). Exploring factors influencing organizational adoption of artificial intelligence (AI) in corporate social responsibility (CSR) initiatives. *Pacific Asia Journal of the Association for Information Systems, 14*(5), 4. doi:10.17705/1pais.14504

Pankratz, O., & Basten, D. (2014). Ladder to success – Eliciting project managers' perceptions of IS project success criteria. *International Journal of Information Systems and Project Management, 2*(2), 5–24. doi:10.12821/ijispm020201

Pan, W., Xie, T., Wang, Z., & Ma, L. (2022). Digital economy: An innovation driver for total factor productivity. *Journal of Business Research, 139*, 303–311. doi:10.1016/j.jbusres.2021.09.061

Patagonia. (2022). The Activist Company. Retrieved from https://www.patagonia.com/the-activist-company.html

Patel, P., & Cassou, D. (2015). Enabling high-level application development for the Internet of Things. *Journal of Systems and Software, 103*, 62–84. doi:10.1016/j.jss.2015.01.027

Patra, A. (2023). *12 Project Management Trends Emerging in 2023.* Retrieved from https://www.replicon.com/blog/project-management-trends/

Patsy, E., Alfakihuddin, M. L. B., Butar, N. A. B., & Nethania, P. (2023). Corporate action on plastic pollution (the body shop case study). *Jurnal Ekonomi, 12*(02), 1350–1355.

Patuelli, A., Carungu, J., & Lattanzi, N. (2022). Drivers and nuances of sustainable development goals: Transcending corporate social responsibility in family firms. *Journal of Cleaner Production, 373*, 133723. doi:10.1016/j.jclepro.2022.133723

Păun, T., & Pinzaru, F. (2021). Advancing strategic management through sustainable finance. *Management Dynamics in the Knowledge Economy, 9*(2), 279–291.

Payne, A., & Frow, P. (2005). A strategic framework for customer relationship management. *Journal of Marketing, 69*(4), 167–176. doi:10.1509/jmkg.2005.69.4.167

Pearce, A., & Pons, D. (2019). Advancing lean management: The missing quantitative approach. *Operations Research Perspectives*, *6*, 100114. doi:10.1016/j.orp.2019.100114

Peimbert-García, R. E., Gutiérrez-Mendoza, L. M., & García-Reyes, H. (2021). Applying Lean Healthcare to Improve the Discharge Process in a Mexican Academic Medical Center. *Sustainability (Basel)*, *13*(19), 10911. doi:10.3390u131910911

Pejanovic, R., Sedlak, O., & Kabok, J. (2015). Innovation and knowledge. In N. Zarkic Joksimovic & S. Benkovic (Eds.), *Finding the right path - higher education financing and social dimension in the Western-Balkan countries* (pp. 101–126). Faculty of Organizational Sciences, University of Belgrade.

Pentlicki, J. H. (2014). *Barriers and success strategies for sustainable lean manufacturing implementation: A qualitative case study*. University of Phoenix.

Peterson, R. R. (2003). Information strategies and tactics for information technology governance. In Strategies for information technology governance. Idea Group Publishing.

Pettersen, J. (2009). Defining lean production: Some conceptual and practical issues. *The TQM Journal*, *21*(2), 127–142. doi:10.1108/17542730910938137

Phillips, J. B. (2021). *Change happens: Practitioner use of change management strategies*. The Florida State University.

Piller, F., Ihl, C., & Vossen, A. (2011). Customer co-creation: Open innovation with customers. New forms of collaboration and Innovation in Internet, 31-63.

Pink, D. H. (2009). *Drive: The Surprising Truth About What Motivates Us*. Penguin Publishing Group.

Plenert, G. J. (2011). *Lean Management Principles for Information Technology*. CRC Press. doi:10.1201/b11549

PMI. (2006). *The Standard for Portfolio Management*. Project Management Institute.

PMI. (2022). *PMBoK© – A Guide to Project Management Body of Knowledge* (7th ed.). PMI – Project Management Institute.

Poister, T. H., & Streib, G. D. (1999). Strategic management in the public sector: Concepts, models, and processes. *Public Productivity & Management Review*, •••, 308–325.

Poksinska, B., & Swartling, D. (2018). From successful to sustainable lean production: The case of a Lean Prize Award Winner. *Total Quality Management & Business Excellence*, *29*(9-10), 996–1011. doi:10.1080/14783363.2018.1486539

Polanyi, M. (1966). *The Tacit Dimension*. Routledge & Kegan Paul.

Polit, D. F., & Beck, C. T. (2006). The content validity index: Are you sure you know what's being reported? Critique and recommendations. *Research in Nursing & Health*, *29*(5), 489–497. doi:10.1002/nur.20147 PMID:16977646

Popoola, O. A. (2000). Developmeny of a methodology for the rapid implementation of a sustainable lean manufacturing system. Massachusetts Institute of Technology (MIT).

Porter, M. E., & Stern, S. (2004). *Ranking national innovative capacity: findings from the National Innovative Capacity Index*. The Global Competitiveness Report 2003-2004.

Portulans Institute. (2022). *Network Readiness Index 2022 Serbia*. Available at: https://networkreadinessindex.org/country/serbia/

Pradhan, R. P., Arvin, M. B., Nair, M., Bennett, S. E., & Bahmani, S. (2019). Short-term and long-term dynamics of venture capital and economic growth in a digital economy: A study of European countries. *Technology in Society*, *57*, 125–134. doi:10.1016/j.techsoc.2018.11.002

Praharaj, S., & Bandyopadhyay, S. (2019). Understanding the open data challenge for building smart cities in India. In *Open Cities | Open Data*. Collaborative Cities in the Information Era. doi:10.1007/978-981-13-6605-5_16

Prakash, A. (2017). Robots in Retail: Amazon Go Heralds New Customer Service Era. *Robotics Business Review*. https://www.roboticsbusinessreview.com/retail-hospitality/robots-retail-amazon-go-heralds-new-customer-service-era

Pratt, M. K. (2021). *Why IT projects still fail*. Retrieved from https://www.cio.com/article/230427/why-it-projects-still-fail.html

Pressman, R. S. (2010). *Software Engineering: A Practitioner's Approach* (7th ed.). McGraw-Hill, Inc.

PRINCE2. (2023). Retrieved from https://www.prince2.com/eur

Priori, F. R., & Saurin, T. A. (2020). Solução de problemas em uma emergência hospitalar: Avaliação dos métodos A3 e análise de causa raiz. *Revista Produção Online*, *20*(1), 63–94. doi:10.14488/1676-1901.v20i1.3258

Procter, H. G., & Dalgety, R. (2004). Professional development for culturally competent practice. *Journal of Family Social Work*, *8*(3), 13–27.

Project Management Institute. (2004). A Guide to the Project Management Body of Knowledge (3rd ed.). Project Management Inst).

Project Management Institute. (2017a). *A Guide to the Project Management Body of Knowledge* (7th ed.). Project Management Institute.

Project Management Institute. (2017b). *Job Growth and Talent Gap 2017-2027*. Retrieved from https://www.pmi.org/-/media/pmi/documents/public/pdf/learning/job-growth-report.pdf?sc_lang_temp=en

Prosci Methodology Overview. (n.d.-a). Prosci. Retrieved September 3, 2023, from https://www.prosci.com/methodology-overview

Prosci. (n.d.-b). *Primary Sponsor's Role and Importance*. Prosci. Retrieved December 28, 2021, from https://www.prosci.com/resources/articles/primary-sponsors-role-and-importance

Prosci. (n.d.-c). *Prosci Methodology*. Prosci. https://www.prosci.com/resources/articles/prosci-methodology

Puvanasvaran, A. P., Tan, B. H., Megat Ahmad, M. H., Tang, S. H., Muhamad, M. R., & Hamouda, A. M. (2008). Degree of leanness and managerial commitment in an aerospace company. *Journal of Statistics and Management Systems*, *11*(4), 653–673. doi:10.1080/09720510.2008.10701336

PWC & FICCI. (2019). *Fast Forward: Relevant Skill for a Buoyant Indian Economy*. Author.

PwC. (n.d.). Sustainable Development Goals (SDG) - Impact on business. https://pwc.to/3as3Vid

Quairel-Lanoizelee, F. (2016). Are competition and corporate social responsibility compatible? The myth of sustainable competitive advantage. *Society and Business Review*, *11*(2), 130–154. doi:10.1108/SBR-04-2016-0026

Rabahi, N. (2020). De l'éthnographie à la netnographie: « Les communautés virtuelles » un nouveau terrain de recherche. *Journal of Social and Human Science Studies*, *9*(2).

RADAR DE PROJETOS. (2015). *Matriz RAB - Rapidez, Autonomia e Benefício* [RAB Matrix - Rapidity, Autonomy and Benefit]. Available in: http://www.radardeprojetos.com.br/2015/04/matriz-de-priorizacao-rab-rapidez.html

Rahman, M., & Szabó, G. (2023). Assessing the Status of National Spatial Data Infrastructure (NSDI) of Bangladesh. *ISPRS International Journal of Geo-Information*, *12*(6), 236. Advance online publication. doi:10.3390/ijgi12060236

Rajabifard, A., Binns, A., Masser, I., & Williamson, I. (2006). The role of sub-national government and the private sector in future spatial data infrastructures. *International Journal of Geographical Information Science, 20*(7), 727–741. Advance online publication. doi:10.1080/13658810500432224

Rajabifard, A., Feeney, M. E. F., & Williamson, I. P. (2002). Future directions for SDI development. *International Journal of Applied Earth Observation and Geoinformation, 4*(1), 11–22. doi:10.1016/S0303-2434(02)00002-8

Rao, M. (2007). NSDI – then, now and whenever. *Coordinates: A Resource on Positioning, Navigation and Beyond.* https://mycoordinates.org/nsdi-%E2%80%93-then-now-and-whenever/all/1/

Rasolofo-Distler, F., & Distler, F. (2018). Using the balanced scorecard to manage service supply chain uncertainty: Case studies in French real estate services. *Knowledge and Process Management, 25*(3), 129–142. doi:10.1002/kpm.1572

Rathi, R., Vakharia, A., & Shadab, M. (2022). Lean six sigma in the healthcare sector: A systematic literature review. *Materials Today: Proceedings, 50*, 773–781. doi:10.1016/j.matpr.2021.05.534 PMID:35155129

Ray, P. P. (2016). Internet of robotic things: Concept, technologies, and challenges. *IEEE Access : Practical Innovations, Open Solutions, 4*(1), 9489–9500. doi:10.1109/ACCESS.2017.2647747

Reed, M. (2003). Open doors and brick walls: the agency/structure dilemma in organization theory. In H. Tsoukas & C. Knudsen (Eds.), *The Oxford Handbook of Organization Theory* (pp. 289–309). Sage.

Régis, T. K. O., Santos, L. C., & Gohr, C. F. (2019). A case-based methodology for lean implementation in hospital operations. *Journal of Health Organization and Management, 33*(6), 656–676. doi:10.1108/JHOM-09-2018-0267 PMID:31625821

Rentes, A. F., Araujo, C. A. C., & Rentes, V. C. (2009). Best practice examples in sustaining improvements from Lean implementation. *Proceedings of the 2009 Industrial Engineering Research Conference.*

ReportLinker. (2019). *Europe Digital Transformation Market to 2025 - Regional Analysis and Forecasts by Components; Deployment Type; and End-User.* The Insight Partners.

Reyck, B., Grushka-Cockayne, Y., Lockett, M., Calderini, S. R., Moura, M., & Sloper, A. (2005). The impact of project portfolio management on information technology projects. *International Journal of Project Management, 23*(7), 524–537. doi:10.1016/j.ijproman.2005.02.003

Reyes, C. (2021). *What is Digital Strategy?* Liferay.

Rezaei, J. (2016). Best-worst multi-criteria decision-making method: Some properties and a linear model. *Omega, 64*, 126–130. doi:10.1016/j.omega.2015.12.001

Ricci, F., Scafarto, V., Ferri, S., & Tron, A.,(2020). Value relevance of digitalisation: the moderating role of corporate sustainability. An empirical study of Italian listed companies. *Journal of Cleaner Production, 276*, 123–282. https://doi.org/.jclepro.2020.123282 doi:10.1016/j

Ringle, C. M., Wende, S., & Becker, J.-M. (2022). *SmartPLS 4.* SmartPLS. http://www.smartpls.com

Riquetta, A. C. B. (2018). *Aplicativo para dispositivo móvel direcionado aos usuários das Unidades de Pronto Atendimento (UPA) 24 horas de Curitiba.* Universidade Tecnológica Federal do Paraná. http://repositorio.utfpr.edu.br/jspui/handle/1/3932

Robin, K., (2016). Robotics in the Real World. *Juvenile Nonfiction*, 48-56.

Romero, L. F., & Arce, A. (2017). Applying Value Stream Mapping in Manufacturing: A Systematic Literature Review. *IFAC-PapersOnLine, 50-1*(1), 1075–1086. doi:10.1016/j.ifacol.2017.08.385

Rosa, C., Silva, F. J. G., Ferreira, L. P., & Campilho, R. (2017). SMED methodology: The reduction of setup times for Steel Wire-Rope assembly lines in the automotive industry. *Procedia Manufacturing*, *13*, 1034–1042. doi:10.1016/j.promfg.2017.09.110

Rosário, A. T., & Dias, J. C. (2022). Sustainability and the digital transition: A literature review. *Sustainability (Basel)*, *14*(7), 4072. doi:10.3390u14074072

Ross, J. W., Beath, C. M., & Sebastian, I. M. (2017). How to develop a great digital strategy. *MIT Sloan Management Review*, *58*(2), 7.

Rother, M. (2009). The Toyota Kata: Managing People for Improvement. Adaptiveness and Superior Results (1° ed, Vol. 1). McGraw Hill.

Roth, G. (2011). Sustaining lean transformation through growth and positive organizational change. *Journal of Enterprise Transformation*, *1*(2), 119–146. doi:10.1080/19488289.2011.579228

Rotter, T., Plishka, C., Lawal, A., Harrison, L., Sari, N., Goodridge, D., Flynn, R., Chan, J., Fiander, M., Poksinska, B., Willoughby, K., & Kinsman, L. (2019). What Is Lean Management in Health Care? Development of an Operational Definition for a Cochrane Systematic Review. *Evaluation & the Health Professions*, *42*(3), 366–390. doi:10.1177/0163278718756992 PMID:29635950

Rouse, M. (2011). *Software Development Life Cycle Model*. Retrieved from https://www.techopedia.com/definition/25976/software-development-life-cycle-model-sdlc

Roy, B. (1968). Classement et choix en présence de points de vue multiples (la méthode ÉLECTRE). *La Revue d'Informatique et de Recherche Opérationelle*, (8), 57–75.

Rožman, N., Diaci, J., & Corn, M. (2021). Scalable framework for blockchain-based shared manufacturing. *Robotics and Computer-integrated Manufacturing*, *71*(102139), 1–14. doi:10.1016/j.rcim.2021.102139

Rubio, D. M., Berg-Weger, M., Tebb, S. S., Lee, E. S., & Rauch, S. (2003). Objectifying content validity: Conducting a content validity study in social work research. *Social Work Research*, *27*(2), 94–104. doi:10.1093wr/27.2.94

Ruffa, S. A. (2011). Going lean fieldbook - A practical guide to lean transformation and sustainable success. American Management Association (AMACOM).

Saastamoinen, I., & Tukiainen, M. (2004). Software Process Improvement in Small and Medium Sized Software Enterprises in Eastern Finland: A State-of-the-Practice Study. In T. Dingsøyr (Ed.), *EuroSPI 2004* (pp. 69–78). Springer-Verlag Berlin Heidelberg. doi:10.1007/978-3-540-30181-3_7

Saaty, T. L. (1980). *The Analytic Hierarchy Process: Planning, Priority Setting, Resource Allocation*. McGraw-Hill.

Sahwan, M. A., Ab Rahman, M. N., & Md Deros, B. (2012). Barriers to implement lean manufacturing in malaysian automotive industry. *Jurnal Teknologi*, *59*(2), 107–110. doi:10.11113/jt.v59.2571

Saleh, S. M., Huq, S. M., & Rahman, M. A. (2019). Comparative Study within Scrum, Kanban, XP Focused on Their Practices. *2019 International Conference on Electrical, Computer and Communication Engineering (ECCE)*, 1–6. 10.1109/ECACE.2019.8679334

Salesa, A., León, R., & Moneva, J. M. (2023). Airlines practices to incorporate circular economy principles into the waste management system. *Corporate Social Responsibility and Environmental Management*, *30*(1), 443–458. doi:10.1002/csr.2365

Sampson, S. E., & Spring, M. (2012). Customer roles in service supply chains and opportunities for innovation. *The Journal of Supply Chain Management*, *48*(4), 30–50. doi:10.1111/j.1745-493X.2012.03282.x

Sanchez, M. A. (2020). How Internet of Things Is Transforming Project Management. In Research Anthology on Digital Transformation, Organizational Change, and the Impact of Remote Work (pp. 463–484). IGI Global. doi:10.4018/978-1-7998-7297-9.ch024

Santos, M. Y., Oliveira, J., Andrade, C., Lima, F. V., Costa, E., & Costa, C. (2017). A big data system supporting Bosch Braga industry 4.0 strategy. *International Journal of Information Management*, *37*(6), 750–760. doi:10.1016/j.ijinfomgt.2017.07.012

Sarstedt, M., Hair, J. F. Jr, Cheah, J. H., Becker, J.-M., & Ringle, C. M. (2019). How to specify, estimate, and validate higher-order constructs in PLS-SEM. *Australasian Marketing Journal*, *27*(3), 197–211. doi:10.1016/j.ausmj.2019.05.003

Sarvaiya, H., & Arrowsmith, J. (2023). Exploring the context and interface of corporate social responsibility and HRM. *Asia Pacific Journal of Human Resources*, *61*(2), 300–323. doi:10.1111/1744-7941.12316

Savolainen, P., Ahonen, J. J., & Richardson, I. (2015). When did your project start? - The software supplier's perspective. *Journal of Systems and Software*, *104*, 32–40. doi:10.1016/j.jss.2015.02.041

Savulescu, C. (2015). Dynamics of ICT development in the EU. *Procedia Economics and Finance*, *23*, 513–520. doi:10.1016/S2212-5671(15)00552-3

Schiopu, R. (2020). *Business Digitalization in the European Union*. Sciendo.

Schlichting, C. (2009). *Sustaining lean improvements*. Worcester Polytechnic Institute.

Schmidt, C. G., & Wagner, S. M. (2019). Blockchain and supply chain relations: A transaction cost theory perspective. *Journal of Purchasing and Supply Management*, *25*(100552), 1–13. doi:10.1016/j.pursup.2019.100552

Schragenheim, E., & H. (2000). *Simplified Drum-Buffer-Rope: A Whole System Approach to High Velocity Manufacturing*. William Dettmer.

Schroedel, J. (2019, December 10). *Radical vs incremental change: what is the difference?* CitizenLab. Retrieved December 28, 2021, from https://www.citizenlab.co/blog/e-government/whats-the-difference-radical-vs-incremental-change/

Schwaber, K., & Beedle, M. (2002). *Agile Software Development with Scrum* (Vol. 1). Prentice Hall. https://books.google.co.ma/books?id=BpFYAAAAYAAJ

Schwaber, K., & Sutherland, J. (2020). *The Scrum Guide The Definitive Guide to Scrum: The Rules of the Game*. https://scrumguides.org/scrum-guide.html

Scott, W. R. (2005). Institutional theory: Contributing to a theoretical research program. *Great minds in management: The process of theory development, 37*(2), 460-484.

SEI. (2011). Method Definition Document of Standard CMMI Appraisal Method for Process Improvement. SCAMPIsm. Software Engineering Institute, Carnegie Mellon University.

SEI. (2018). *Capability Maturity Model Integration. CMMI® V2.0 for Development, Version 2.3*. Software Engineering Institute.

Selishcheva, T. A., Sopina, N. V., Borkova, E. A., & Ilyina, O. P. (2020). Estimation of The Influence of Digital Economy on The Competitiveness of The World. *35th International Business Information Management Association Conference (IBIMA),* 3757-3764.

Shad, M. K., Lai, F. W., Fatt, C. L., Klemeš, J. J., & Bokhari, A. (2019). Integrating sustainability reporting into enterprise risk management and its relationship with business performance: A conceptual framework. *Journal of Cleaner Production*, *208*, 415–425.

Shah, S. Q. A., Lai, F. W., Shad, M. K., & Jan, A. A. (2022). Developing a green governance framework for the performance enhancement of the oil and gas industry. *Sustainability (Basel)*, *14*(7), 3735. doi:10.3390u14073735

Sharma, S. (2021, August 11). *Lenskart plans to hire over 2,000 employees in India by next year.* Mint. https://www.livemint.com/companies/news/lenskart-plans-to-hire-over-2-000-employees-in-india-by-next-year-11628679429872.html

Sharma, P., Jain, K., Kingshott, R. P., & Ueno, A. (2020). Customer engagement and relationships in multi-actor service ecosystems. *Journal of Business Research*, *121*(1), 487–494. doi:10.1016/j.jbusres.2020.07.031

Sharma, P., Sivakumaran, B., & Marshall, R. (2014). Exploring impulse buying in services: Toward an integrative framework. *Journal of the Academy of Marketing Science*, *42*(2), 154–170. doi:10.100711747-013-0346-5

Shekarian, E., Ijadi, B., Zare, A., & Majava, J. (2022). Sustainable supply chain management: A comprehensive systematic review of industrial practices. *Sustainability (Basel)*, *14*(13), 7892. doi:10.3390u14137892

Shen, M., Tang, C. S., Wu, D., Yuan, R., & Zhou, W. (2020). Jd. com: Transaction-level data for the 2020 msom data driven research challenge. *Manufacturing & Service Operations Management*, msom.2020.0900. doi:10.1287/msom.2020.0900

Shingo, S. (2019). *A Revolution in Manufacturing: The SMED System.* Routledge. doi:10.4324/9781315136479

Shiri, N., & Jafari-Sadeghi, V. (2023). Corporate social responsibility and green behaviour: Towards sustainable food-business development. *Corporate Social Responsibility and Environmental Management*, *30*(2), 605–620. doi:10.1002/csr.2377

Shodiev, T., Turayey, B., & Shodiyev, K. (2021). ICT and Economic Growth Nexus: Case of Central Asian Countries. *Procedia of Social Sciences and Humanities*, *1*, 155–167. doi:10.21070/pssh.v1i.37

Shortell, S. M., Blodgett, J. C., Rundall, T. G., & Kralovec, P. (2018). Use of Lean and Related Transformational Performance Improvement Systems in Hospitals in the United States: Results From a National Survey. *Joint Commission Journal on Quality and Patient Safety*, *44*(10), 574–582. doi:10.1016/j.jcjq.2018.03.002 PMID:30243359

Sibanda, M., & von Solms, R. (2019). Devising a strategy for IT governance implementation in municipalities. A case study of South Africa. *The Electronic Journal on Information Systems in Developing Countries*, *85*(2), e12067. doi:10.1002/isd2.12067

Sigma, S. (2019). *Solution Selection Matrix*. Available in: https://goleansixsigma.com/solution-selection-matrix/

Simmons, S. (2018). Metadata and Spatial Data Infrastructure. In B. Huang (Ed.), *Comprehensive Geographic Information Systems* (pp. 110–124). Elsevier. doi:10.1016/B978-0-12-409548-9.09611-1

Simović, V., & Domazet, I. (2023). What Drives the Levels of Digital Entrepreneurial Competencies of University Students? A Research Roadmap and Preliminary Results. In A. D. Daniel & C. Fernandes (Eds.), *Female entrepreneurship as a driving force of economic growth and social change* (pp. 55–72). IGI Global. doi:10.4018/978-1-6684-7669-7.ch004

Singh, B., & Pandey, S. (2018). Geospatial policies in India and their implementation in good governance. In Geospatial Infrastructure, Applications and Technologies: India Case Studies. doi:10.1007/978-981-13-2330-0_1

Singh, G., Slack, N., Sharma, S., Mudaliar, K., Narayan, S., Kaur, R., & Sharma, K. U. (2021). Antecedents involved in developing fast-food restaurant customer loyalty. *The TQM Journal*, *33*(8), 1753–1769. doi:10.1108/TQM-07-2020-0163

Singh, P. K. (2009). Spatial Data Infrastructure in India : Status, Governance Challenges, and Strategies for Effective Functioning. *International Journal of Spatial Data Infrastructures Research*, 4.

Singh, S., Verma, R., & Koul, S. (2022). A collaborative method for simultaneous operations: Case of an eye clinic. *OPSEARCH*, *59*(2), 711–731. doi:10.100712597-021-00513-9

Sisson, J. A., & Elshennawy, A. (2015). Achieving success with lean. *International Journal of Lean Six Sigma*, *6*(3), 263–280. doi:10.1108/IJLSS-07-2014-0024

Sjoukema, J. W., Samia, J., Bregt, A. K., & Crompvoets, J. (2021). Governance interactions of spatial data infrastructures: An agent-based modelling approach. *International Journal of Digital Earth*, *14*(6), 696–713. Advance online publication. doi:10.1080/17538947.2020.1868585

Sjoukema, J., Bregt, A. K., & Crompvoets, J. (2020). Understanding governance dynamics: The governing system of spatial data infrastructures. *International Journal of Spatial Data Infrastructures Research*, 15.

Slama, D., Puhlmann, F., Morrish, J., & Bhatnagar, R. M. (Eds.). (2016). *Enterprise IoT: Enterprise IoT: strategies and best practices for connected products and services*. O'Reilly.

Sommerville, I., & Sawyer, P. (1997). *Requirements Engineering: A Good Practice Guide* (1st ed.). John Wiley & Sons Ltd.

Song, J. M., Sung, J., & Park, T. (2019). Applications of Blockchain to Improve Supply Chain Traceability. *Procedia Computer Science*, *162*, 119–122. doi:10.1016/j.procs.2019.11.266

Sood, A., & Kumar, V. (2017). Analyzing client profitability across diffusion segments for a continuous innovation. *JMR, Journal of Marketing Research*, *54*(6), 932–951. doi:10.1509/jmr.16.0209

Soule, C. A., & Sekhon, T. (2022). How Green Demarketing Brands Can Successfully Support Anti-Consumption. *Anti-Consumption: Exploring the Opposition to Consumer Culture*.

Souls, E. (2019). *Industry 4.0: Importance and Necessity in India Fabian Wanke (2021). EU Digital Transformation Challenges*. ARC Advisory Group.

Sousa, M. J., & Rocha, A. (2019). Skills for disruptive digital business. *Journal of Business Research*, *94*(1), 257–263. doi:10.1016/j.jbusres.2017.12.051

Spindler, R. A. (2019). *Evolution of German corporate governance*. https://eprints.whiterose.ac.uk/141762/1/Evolution%20of%20German%20corporate%20governance.pdf

Stadnicka, D., & Litwin, P. (2019). Value stream mapping and system dynamics integration for manufacturing line modelling and analysis. *International Journal of Production Economics*, *208*, 400–411. doi:10.1016/j.ijpe.2018.12.011

Stanley, T. D., Doucouliagos, H., & Steel, P. (2018). Does ICT generate economic growth? A meta-regression analysis. *Journal of Economic Surveys*, *32*(3), 705–726. doi:10.1111/joes.12211

Steffen, W., Richardson, K., Rockström, J., Cornell, S. E., Fetzer, I., Bennett, E. M., Biggs, R., Carpenter, S. R., De Vries, W., De Wit, C. A., Folke, C., Gerten, D., Heinke, J., Mace, G. M., Persson, L. M., Ramanathan, V., Reyers, B., & Sörlin, S. (2015). Planetary Boundaries: Guiding Human Development on a Changing Planet: https://science.sciencemag.org/content/347/6223/1259855

Stickdorn, M., Hormess, M., Schneider, J., & Lawrence, A. (2018). *This is Service Design Doing: Applying Service Design Thinking in the Real World: a Practitioner's Handbook*. Academic Press.

Stock, K., & Guesgen, H. (2016). Geospatial Reasoning With Open Data. In R. Layton & P. A. Watters (Eds.), *Automating Open Source Intelligence* (pp. 171–204). Syngress. doi:10.1016/B978-0-12-802916-9.00010-5

Stojanović, D. & Domazet, I. (2020). Use of Information Technologies in Educational Purposes – Case from Serbia. *Economic Analysis: Journal of Emerging Economics, 53*(2), 68-78.

Stone, V., Führ, M., Feindt, P. H., Bouwmeester, H., Linkov, I., Sabella, S., Murphy, F., Bizer, K., Tran, L., Ågerstrand, M., Fito, C., Andersen, T., Anderson, D., Bergamaschi, E., Cherrie, J. W., Cowan, S., Dalemcourt, J. F., Faure, M., Gabbert, S., ... Poortvliet, P. M. (2018). The Essential Elements of a Risk Governance Framework for Current and Future Nanotechnologies. *Risk Analysis*, *38*(7), 1321–1331. Advance online publication. doi:10.1111/risa.12954 PMID:29240986

Strategic Policy Forum on Digital Entrepreneurship. (2016). Accelerating the digital transformation of European industry and enterprises. *European Union.*

Strategy Market Research Consulting. (2020). *Internet of Robotic Things- Global Market Outlook 2017-2023.* https://www.strategymrc.com/report/internet-of-robotic-thingsmarket-2017

Streamline. (2019, May 21). *Which should you use – ISO 9001, Six Sigma or Lean?* Streamline. https://streamline.business/which-should-you-use-iso-9001-six-sigma-or-lean

Su, D., Zhang, L., Peng, H., Saeidi, P., & Tirkolaee, E. B. (2023). Technical challenges of blockchain technology for sustainable manufacturing paradigm in Industry 4.0 era using a fuzzy decision support system. *Technological Forecasting and Social Change*, *188*(122275), 1–15. doi:10.1016/j.techfore.2022.122275

Sultan, F. A., Routroy, S., & Thakur, M. (2021). A simulation-based performance investigation of downstream operations in the Indian Surimi Supply Chain using environmental value stream mapping. *Journal of Cleaner Production*, *286*(125389), 1–15. doi:10.1016/j.jclepro.2020.125389

Surveying and Mapping Act (2014).

Susanty, A., Sumiyati, L. S., Syaiful, S., & Nihlah, Z. (2021). The impact of lean manufacturing practices on operational and business performances at SMES in the wooden furniture industry. *International Journal of Lean Six Sigma*. doi:10.1108/IJLSS-08-2020-0124

Süsi, V., & Jaakson, K. (2020). Corporate governance and corporate social responsibility interface: A case study of private equity. *Corporate Governance (Bradford)*, *20*(4), 703–717. doi:10.1108/CG-11-2019-0348

Sustainability/UNEP. (1998). *The non-reporting report.*

Swinyard, W. R. (1993). The effects of mood, involvement, and quality of store experience on shopping intentions. *The Journal of Consumer Research*, *20*(2), 271–280. doi:10.1086/209348

Szabo, R., Vuksanović, I., Herceg Hana'k, R., Hortovanyi, L., Romanova´, A., Mocan, M., & ... . (2020). Industry 4.0 Implementation in B2B Companies: Cross-Country Empirical Evidence on Digital Transformation in the CEE Region. *Sustainability (Basel)*, *19*(22), 9538. doi:10.3390u12229538

Tachanunachanun, K., Apinporn, M., & Chayakorn, P. (2012). Technical Challenges of CMMI-based Assessment Team. *International Journal of Digital Content Technology and its Applications*, *6*(21), 101-110. doi:10.4156/jdcta.vol6.issue21.10

Taherdoost, H., & Madanchian, M. (2023). *Multi-Criteria Decision Making (MCDM) Methods and Concepts*. Available in: https://www.mdpi.com/2673-8392/3/1/6#

Tallman, S., Luo, Y., & Buckley, P. (2018). Business models in global competition. *Global Strategy Journal*, *8*(4), 517–535. doi:10.1002/gsj.1165

Tan, Y. T., Shen, L. Y., Langston, C., & Liu, Y. (2010). Construction project selection using fuzzy TOPSIS approach. *Journal of Modelling in Management*, *5*(3), 302–315. doi:10.1108/17465661011092669

Tao, F., Zhang, Y., Cheng, Y., Ren, J., Wang, D., Qi, Q., & Li, P. (2021). Digital twin and blockchain enhanced smart manufacturing service collaboration and management. *Journal of Manufacturing Systems*, *62*, 903–914. doi:10.1016/j.jmsy.2020.11.008

Tariq, A., Khan, S. A., & Iftikhar, S. (2014). Remapping of CMMI level-2 KPA's for development process improvement of Software-as-a-Service (SaaS) cloud environment. In *2014 International Conference on Open Source Systems & Technologies* (pp. 43-51). 10.1109/ICOSST.2014.7029318

Tawfik, D. (2022). *Traditional project management vs. Agile: How to choose*. Retrieved from https://monday.com/blog/project-management/traditional-project-management/

Taylor, A., Taylor, M., & McSweeney, A. (2013). Towards greater understanding of success and survival of lean systems. *International Journal of Production Research*, *51*(22), 6607–6630. doi:10.1080/00207543.2013.825382

Taylor, F. W. (1998). *The Principles of Scientific Management*. Dover Publications.

Teczke, M., Sansyzbayevna Bespayeva, R., & Olzhabayevna Bugubayeva, R. (2017). Approaches and models for change management. *Jagiellonian Journal of Management, 3*(3).

Tekin, M., Arslandere, M., Etlioğlu, M., Koyuncuoğlu, Ö., & Tekin, E. (2019). An Application of SMED and Jidoka in Lean Production. In *Proceedings of the International Symposium for Production Research 2018* (p. 530–545). Springer International Publishing. 10.1007/978-3-319-92267-6_45

Teng, Y., Li, L., Song, L., Yu, F. R., & Leung, V. C. M. (2021). Profit Maximizing Smart Manufacturing over AI Enabled Configurable Blockchains. *IEEE Internet of Things Journal*, *9*(1), 346–358. doi:10.1109/JIOT.2021.3098917

The 8-Step Process for Leading Change | Dr. John Kotter. (n.d.). Kotter International. Retrieved September 3, 2023, from https://www.kotterinc.com/methodology/8-steps/

The Britannica Dictionary. (2023). *Project*. Retrieved from https://www.britannica.com/dictionary/project

The Knowledge Academy. (2023). *What sectors use PRINCE2?* Retrieved from https://www.theknowledgeacademy.com/courses/prince2-training/what-sectors-use-prince2/

Tillman, M. (2020, February 25). *What is Amazon Go, where is it, and how does it work?* Pocket-lint. https://www.pocket-lint.com/phones/news/amazon/139650-what-is-amazongo-where-is-it-and-how-does-it-work

Tlapa, D., Zepeda-Lugo, C. A., Tortorella, G. L., Baez-Lopez, Y. A., Limon-Romero, J., Alvarado-Iniesta, A., & Rodriguez-Borbon, M. I. (2020). Effects of Lean Healthcare on Patient Flow: A Systematic Review. *Value in Health*, *23*(2), 260–273. doi:10.1016/j.jval.2019.11.002 PMID:32113632

Tonelli, A. O., de Souza Bermejo, P. H., Aparecida dos Santos, P., Zuppo, L., & Zambalde, A. L. (2017). IT governance in the public sector: A conceptual model. *Information Systems Frontiers*, *19*(3), 593–610. doi:10.100710796-015-9614-x

Tong J. (2015). Wisdom logistics development present situation and countermeasure research in China. *Journal of Lanzhou Institute of Education, 31*(9), 50-51.

Tracey, M. W., & Flinchbaugh, J. (2009). How human resource department can help lean transformation. In Sustaining lean: Case studies in transforming culture (pp. 119-128). CRC Press.

Trakulsunti, Y., Antony, J., Edgeman, R., Cudney, B., Dempsey, M., & Brennan, A. (2022). Reducing pharmacy medication errors using Lean Six Sigma: A Thai hospital case study. *Total Quality Management & Business Excellence*, *33*(5-6), 664–682. doi:10.1080/14783363.2021.1885292

Tricker, B. (2021). *The Evolution of Corporate Governance*. Cambridge University Press.

Trivedi, J. (2019). Examining the customer experience of using banking chatbots and its impact on brand love: The moderating role of perceived risk. *Journal of Internet Commerce, 18*(1), 91–111. doi:10.1080/15332861.2019.1567188

Tseng, F. M., Liang, C. W., & Nguyen, N. B. (2023). Blockchain technology adoption and business performance in large enterprises: A *comparison* of the United States and China. *Technology in Society, 73*(102230), 1–9. doi:10.1016/j.techsoc.2023.102230

Tsoukas, H. (2003). Do we really understand tacit knowledge? In E. Chelladurai & R. A. Berger (Eds.), *Strategy and Organization: Realising Strategic Management* (pp. 197–218). Palgrave Macmillan.

Turesky, E. F., & Connell, P. (2010). Off the rails: Understanding the derailment of a lean manufacturing initiative. *Organizational Management Journal, 7*(2), 110–132. doi:10.1057/omj.2010.14

Türk, A., & Mızrak, K. C. (2021). Bibliometric analysis of research in the field of organizational communication in the web of science database. *Business & Management Studies: An International Journal, 9*(3), 1173–1185. doi:10.15295/bmij.v9i3.1832

Udagepola, K. P. (2016). A Framework for Spatial Data Visualization: Sri Lanka Globe (S-Globe). *37th Asian Conference on Remote Sensing,* 17–21.

UNCTAD. (2015). Information economy report: Unlocking the potential of E-commerce for developing countries. UNCTAD.

UNDP. (1997). *Governance for sustainable human development - A UNDP policy document.* United Nations Development Programme.

UNGGIM. (2012). *Country Report - Nepal.* https://ggim.un.org/country-reports/documents/Nepal-2012-country-report.pdf

UNGGIM. (2019). *Country Report - Sri Lanka.* http://ggim.un.org/docs/meetings/GGIM5/GGIM5 Report Draft 14Aug.pdf

UNGGIM. (2022). *Country Report - India.* https://ggim.un.org/country-reports/documents/India_Country_Report-2022.pdf

Val IT. (2009). *Val IT Overview.* Author.

Val, I. T. (2008). *Enterprise Value: Governance of IT Investments – The Val IT Framework 2.0.* IT Governance Institute.

van Assen, M. F. (2020). Training, employee involvement and continuous improvement – the moderating effect of a common improvement method. *Production Planning and Control,* 1–13. doi:10.1080/09537287.2020.1716405

van der Merwe, K. R. (2016). Leadership behaviours and lean culture attainment in automotive component manufacturers. *Journal for New Generation Sciences, 14*(3), 259–278.

Van Grembergen, W. (2003). Introduction to the minitrack "IT governance and its mechanisms." HICSS 2003. System Sciences, 242.

Van Landeghem, H., Bauters, K., & Limère, V. (2013). A management system for sustainable lean implementation. *IIE Annual Conference. Proceedings,* 941-950. http://eserv.uum.edu.my/scholarly-journals/management-system-sustainable-lean-implementation/docview/1471958596/se-2?accountid=42599

Vancauwenberghe, G., & van Loenen, B. (2018). *Exploring the Emergence of Open Spatial Data Infrastructures: Analysis of Recent Developments and Trends in Europe.* doi:10.1007/978-3-319-59442-2_2

Varajão, J., & Trigo, A. (2016). Evaluation of IS project success in InfSysmakers: An exploratory case study. *2016 International Conference on Information Systems, ICIS 2016,* 1–10.

Vats, A., Goin, K. H., & Fortenberry, J. D. (2011). Lean analysis of a pediatric intensive care unit physician group rounding process to identify inefficiencies and opportunities for improvement. *Pediatric Critical Care Medicine*, *12*(4), 415–421. doi:10.1097/PCC.0b013e3181fe2e3c PMID:20975612

Venkatesh, V., & Bala, H. (2008). Technology Acceptance Model 3 and a Research Agenda on Interventions. *Decision Sciences*, *39*(2), 273–315. doi:10.1111/j.1540-5915.2008.00192.x

Verhoef, P. C., Lemon, K. N., Parasuraman, A., Roggeveen, A., Tsiros, M., & Schlesinger, L. A. (2009). Customer experience creation: Determinants, dynamics and management strategies. *Journal of Retailing*, *85*(1), 31–41. doi:10.1016/j.jretai.2008.11.001

Vermeulen, I. E., & Seegers, D. (2009). Tried and tested: The impact of online hotel reviews on consumer consideration. *Tourism Management*, *30*(1), 123–127. doi:10.1016/j.tourman.2008.04.008

Vinten, G. (2002). The corporate governance lessons of Enron. *Corporate Governance (Bradford)*, *2*(4), 4–9. doi:10.1108/14720700210447632

Vivek, C. M., Ramkumar, P., & Srividhya, P. K. (2022). Sustainability and the Industrial Revolution. In *The Palgrave Handbook of Global Sustainability*. Palgrave Macmillan., .https://doi.org/10.1007/978-3-030-38948-2_147-1

Vodonick, J. (2018). The key to Organizational Sustainability. Nurturing a Culture of Change. *Systems Research and Behavioral Science*, *35*(4), 458–468.

von Rosing, M., Scheer, A., & von Scheel, H. (2020, January 9). *What is Six Sigma? Definition, Methodology and Tools*. Six Sigma Daily. Retrieved December 29, 2021, from https://www.sixsigmadaily.com/what-is-six-sigma/

Wang, B., Wang, P., & Tu, Y. (2021). Customer satisfaction service match and service quality-based blockchain cloud manufacturing. *International Journal of Production Economics*, *240*(108220), 1–13. doi:10.1016/j.ijpe.2021.108220

Wang, S., Wan, J., Zhang, D., Li, D., & Zhang, C. (2016). Towards smart factory for industry 4.0: A self-organized multiagent system with big data based feedback and coordination. *Computer Networks*, *101*, 158–168. doi:10.1016/j.comnet.2015.12.017

Wang, Y., & Zhang, W. (2018). Development Strategy of Intelligent Thinking System Based on Big Data. *Logistic Engineering and Management*, *40*(12), 14–16.

Wang, Z., Wang, T., Hu, H., Gong, J., Ren, X., & Xiao, Q. (2020). Blockchain-based framework for improving supply chain traceability and information sharing in precast construction. *Automation in Construction*, *111*(103063), 1–13. doi:10.1016/j.autcon.2019.103063

Watanabe, C., Naveed, N., & Neittaanmäki, P. (2018). Digital solutions transform the forest-based bioeconomy into a digital platform industry-A suggestion for a disruptive business model in the digital economy. *Technology in Society*, *54*, 168–188.

Weidinger, F., Boysen, N., & Briskorn, D. (2018). Storage assignment with rack-moving mobile robots in KIVA warehouses. *Transportation Science*, *52*(6), 1479–1495. doi:10.1287/trsc.2018.0826

Wenger, E. (1998). *Communities of Practice: Learning, Meaning, and Identity*. Cambridge University Press. doi:10.1017/CBO9780511803932

Wen, H., Lee, C. C., & Song, Z. (2021). Digitalization and environment: How does ICT affect enterprise environmental performance? *Environmental Science and Pollution Research International*, *28*(39), 54826–54841. doi:10.100711356-021-14474-5 PMID:34014481

Wessels, E., & Loggerenberg, J. V. (2006, September). *IT governance: theory and practice*. In *Conference on Information Technology in Tertiary Education*, Pretoria, South Africa.

Westerkamp, M., Victor, F., & Küpper, A. (2020). Tracing manufacturing processes using blockchain-based token compositions. *Digital Communications and Networks*, *6*(2), 167–176. doi:10.1016/j.dcan.2019.01.007

Wetzel, R., & Van Gorp, L. (2014). Eighteen shades of grey? An explorative literature review into the theoretical flavours of organizational change research. *Journal of Organizational Change Management*, *27*(1), 115–146. doi:10.1108/JOCM-01-2013-0007

Whittingham, K. L., Earle, A. G., Leyva-de la Hiz, D. I., & Argiolas, A. (2023). The impact of the United Nations Sustainable Development Goals on corporate sustainability reporting. *Business Research Quarterly*, *26*(1), 45–61. doi:10.1177/23409444221085585

Wilkin, C. L., & Campbell, J. (2010). *Corporate governance of IT: A case study in an Australian government department*. Academic Press.

Wilkin, C. L., Couchman, P. K., Sohal, A., & Zutshi, A. (2016). Exploring differences between smaller and large organizations' corporate governance of information technology. *International Journal of Accounting Information Systems*, *22*, 6–25. doi:10.1016/j.accinf.2016.07.002

Williams, R. T. (2023). Software project management. Thesis Commons *Vbax2, Center for Open Science.* Retrieved from https://ideas.repec.org/p/osf/thesis/vbax2.html

Wingfield, N. (2017). As amazon pushes forward with robots, workers find new roles. *The New York Times*. https://nyti.ms/2xUhVgM

Winit, W., Kantabutra, S., & Kantabutra, S. (2023). Toward a Sustainability Brand Model: An Integrative Review. *Sustainability (Basel)*, *15*(6), 5212. doi:10.3390u15065212

Womack, J. P., & Jones, D. T. (1996). *Lean thinking: Banish waste and create wealth in your organisation* (Vol. 397). Simon & Schuster.

Womack, J. P., & Jones, D. T. (1997). Lean Thinking: Banish Waste and Create Wealth in your Corporation. *The Journal of the Operational Research Society*, *48*(11), 1148–1148. doi:10.1057/palgrave.jors.2600967

Wong, Y. C., Wong, K. Y., & Ali, A. (2009). A study on lean manufacturing implementation in the Malaysian electrical and electronics industry. *European Journal of Scientific Research*, *38*(4), 521–535.

World - Leadership Skills & Strategies. (n.d.). Retrieved December 28, 2021, from https://www.vuca-world.org/

World Bank. (2016). World Development Report 2016: Digital dividends. Author.

World Bank. (2018). *Poverty and shared prosperity 2018: Piecing together the poverty puzzle*. Author.

World Economic Forum. (2011). *The Global Competitiveness Report 2011-2012*. Available at: https://www.weforum.org/reports/global-competitiveness-report-2011-2012/

World Economic Forum. (2020). Unlocking Technology for the Global Goals. https://www3.weforum.org/docs/Unlocking_Technology_for_the_Global_Goals.pdf

World Economic Forum. (2023). Guidelines for Improving Blockchain's Environmental, Social and Economic Impact. p. 9. https://www3.weforum.org/docs/WEF_Guidelines_for_Improving_Blockchain%E2%80%99s_Environmental_Social_and_Economic_Impact_2023.pdf

World, V. U. C. A. (n.d.). *Best practice was yesterday. Best thinking is in demand today and tomorrow*. VUCA.

Wozniak, K. (n.d.). Strategic management system. CEOpedia. https://ceopedia.org/index.php/Strategic_management_system#:~:text=A%20strategic%20management%20system%20is,the%20success%20of%20the%20business

Wu, S. P. J., Straub, D. W., & Liang, T. P. (2015). How information technology governance mechanisms and strategic alignment influence organizational performance. *Management Information Systems Quarterly*, *39*(2), 497–518. doi:10.25300/MISQ/2015/39.2.10

Wu, Y., & Ge, D. (2019). Key technologies of warehousing robot for intelligent logistics. *1st Int. Symp. Manage. Social Sci. (ISMSS)*, 13-14. 10.2991/ismss-19.2019.16

Wynstra, F., Spring, M., & Schoenherr, T. (2015). Service triads: A research agenda for buyer–supplier–customer triads in business services. *Journal of Operations Management*, *35*(1), 1–20. doi:10.1016/j.jom.2014.10.002

Xiao, L., & Kumar, V. (2021). Robotics for customer service: A useful complement or an ultimate substitute? *Journal of Service Research*, *24*(1), 9–29. doi:10.1177/1094670519878881

Xu, L., Peng, X., & Prybutok, V. (2019). Formative measurements in operations management research: Using partial least squares. *The Quality Management Journal*, *26*(1), 18–31. doi:10.1080/10686967.2018.1542287

Yang, A., Li, Y., Liu, C., Li, J., Zhang, Y., & Wang, J. (2019). Research on logistics supply chain of iron and steel enterprises based on block chain technology. *Future Generation Computer Systems*, *101*, 635–645. doi:10.1016/j.future.2019.07.008

Yang, X., Hua, G., Hu, L., Cheng, T. C. E., & Huang, A. (2021). Joint optimization of order sequencing and rack scheduling in the robotic mobile fulfilment system. *Computers & Operations Research*, *135*(1).

Yu¨ksel, H. (2021). An empirical evaluation of industry 4.0 applications of companies in Turkey: The case of a developing country. *Technology in Society*, *63*, 101364. doi:10.1016/j.techsoc.2020.101364

Yuan, Z., & Gong, Y. (2017). Bot-In-Time Delivery for Robotic Mobile Fulfillment Systems. *IEEE Transactions on Engineering Management*, *64*(1), 83–93. doi:10.1109/TEM.2016.2634540

Yu, C., Jiang, X., Yu, S., & Yang, C. (2020). Blockchain-based shared manufacturing in support of cyber physical systems: Concept, framework, and operation. *Robotics and Computer-integrated Manufacturing*, *64*(101931), 1–15. doi:10.1016/j.rcim.2019.101931

Yudiansyah, A., Keke, Y., & Veronica, V. (2020). Can the mobile robot be a future order-picking solution?: A case study at Amazon fulfillment center. *Advances in Transportation and Logistics Research*, *3*(1), 800–806.

Zain, Q. (2015). Collaboration Strategy dalam Implementasi Corporate Social Responsibility (CSR): Studi Kasus Aqua Danone Klaten. *Jurnal Hubungan Internasiona*, *8*(2), 81–98.

Zamanifard, H., Alizadeh, T., & Bosman, C. (2018). Towards a framework of public space governance. *Cities (London, England)*, *78*, 155–165. Advance online publication. doi:10.1016/j.cities.2018.02.010

Zaman, R., Jain, T., Samara, G., & Jamali, D. (2022). Corporate governance meets corporate social responsibility: Mapping the interface. *Business & Society*, *61*(3), 690–752. doi:10.1177/0007650320973415

Zhang, C., Zhou, G., Li, H., & Cao, Y. (2020). Manufacturing Blockchain of Things for the Configuration of a Data- and Knowledge-Driven Digital Twin Manufacturing Cell. *IEEE Internet of Things Journal*, *7*(12), 11884–11894. doi:10.1109/JIOT.2020.3005729

Zhang, L. H., Li, T., & Fan, T. J. (2018). Inventory misplacement and demand forecast error in the supply chain: Profitable RFID strategies under wholesale and buy-back contracts. *International Journal of Production Research*, *56*(15), 5188–5205. doi:10.1080/00207543.2018.1463110

Zhang, Y., & Wang, Z. (2019). Optimal RFID Deployment in a Multiple-Stage Production System Under Inventory Inaccuracy and Robust Control Policy. *IEEE Transactions on Industrial Informatics*, *15*(6), 3230–3242. doi:10.1109/TII.2018.2878638

Zhang, Y., Xu, X., Liu, A., Lu, Q., Xu, L., & Tao, F. (2019). Blockchain-Based Trust Mechanism for IoT-Based Smart Manufacturing System. *IEEE Transactions on Computational Social Systems*, *6*(6), 1386–1394. doi:10.1109/TCSS.2019.2918467

Zhang, Z., Wang, Z., Li, A., Ye, X., Usery, E. L., & Li, D. (2021). An al-based spatial knowledge graph for enhancing spatial data and knowledge search and discovery. *Proceedings of the 1st ACM SIGSPATIAL International Workshop on Searching and Mining Large Collections of Geospatial Data, GeoSearch 2021*. 10.1145/3486640.3491393

About the Contributors

Anacleto Correia (M) is an Associate Professor and lecturer of Management and Information Systems subjects at the Portuguese Navy Academy. He holds a Ph.D. in Computer Science, an M.Sc. in Statistics and Information Management, a B.Sc. degree in Management, and also a B.Sc. at Portuguese Naval Academy. His research interests are focused on requirements engineering, software engineering, process modeling, data mining, machine learning, and business engineering. He has also more than 20 years of experience in industry-leading projects and architecting large software development projects and is the author of several scientific papers in journals and conference proceedings.

Pedro B. Agua has his PhD, MBA, CENG. He holds Senior leadership and management positions in Naval Defence, ICT companies and Tier 1 Subsea Oil & Gas engineering companies. He is a Technology manager experienced in identifying business opportunities, with a proven track record of technical innovation, systems engineering leadership, project management (PMP®/PMI certified), project governance, PMO and organizational development. He has been Senior Manager within the Subsea Oil & Gas industry in UK, with cumulative responsibilities for project engineering, systems engineering and analysis teams´ leadership, planning & business development support. He is also a PON Research Center & Council board member. Lecturer. He also serves as a Deputy Director at the PRT NRC.

* * *

Munir Ahmad is a Ph.D. in Computer Science. over 24 years of extensive experience in spatial data development, management, processing, visualization, and quality control. He is dedicated expertise in open data, crowdsourced data, volunteered geographic information and spatial data infrastructure. A seasoned professional with extensive knowledge in the field, having served as a trainer for the latest spatial technologies. With a passion for research and over 30 publications in the same field. In 2022, he got PhD degree in Computer Science from Preston University Rawalpindi, Pakistan. He is dedicated to advancing the industry and spreading knowledge through my expertise and experience.

Deniz Ahmetagić works at the Faculty of Economics in Subotica, in the position of an Expert associate in science. He is enrolled in a doctoral Study at the Faculty of Economics in Subotica study program Management and Business. He has participated in the development of project proposals and project management activity for projects funded by the programs of the European Commission, TEMPUS, SEE IPA and others. He also participated in the management of national projects funded by the Provincial Secretariat for Science and Technological Development, the Republic of Serbia, the Ministry of Education Science and Technological Development, and others. Deniz has published as an author or co-author of more than 30 articles in management and finance. He is a member of the Scientific Society of Economists of Serbia.

Asmat Ali is PhD in Remote Sensing & GIS. He is Director of Cartography and GIS at Survey of Pakistan. In, 1998 he earned Professional Master Degree in Geoinformatics with specialization in Cartography from Faculty of Geo-Information Science and Earth Observation (ITC), University of Twente, Enschede The Netherlands. Later on, he got MSc Degree in Geo-information Science and Earth Observation, with specialization in Geo-Information Management from the same university. In 2022, he got PhD degree in Remote Sensing and GIS from PMAS-Arid Agriculture University Rawalpindi, Pakistan. He has 35 years of experience in geospatial information production and management discipline as practitioner, trainer and educator. He has served on a number of operational, administrative and instructional appointments. He was in-charge of the team which started GIS mapping and digital Cartography at Survey of Pakistan in 1999. His more than 25 research papers including three book chapters and articles on Spatial Data Infrastructure (SDI), GIS, Remote Sensing, E-governance, as well as Land Administration have been published in various international conferences and renowned journals. In 2008, SDI Asia-Pacific identified him as focal point for SDI development in Pakistan. GSDI in 2016, acknowledged and awarded him as SDI implementer from Pakistan. He is on the visiting faculty of Bahria University Islamabad and PMAS- Arid Agriculture University Rawalpindi, Pakistan.

Chukwuemeka U. Azinge is a Nigerian social entrepreneur, academic, and consultant. He has a first degree in Law from Cardiff University, United Kingdom, a Masters degree in Commercial and Financial law from the prestigious King's College London, United Kingdom, and a Doctor of Business Administration degree from the University of Liverpool, United Kingdom, specializing in Strategy Formulation and Execution. Dr. Azinge is an expert in enterprise strategy and management and is a member of faculty at the Lagos Business School, one of the leading business schools in Africa. Dr. Azinge has over 15 years of experience in enterprise strategy development, execution and management and has consulted for a range of organizations, including non-profits, government agencies, and private sector companies.

Badr Bentalha received his PhD in Service Logistics and performance at Sidi Mohammed Ben Abdellah University, Fez, Morocco. He is a Professor in Economics and Management. He has written several articles and participated in various international conferences. He is a member of numerous scientific committees of international journals and conferences. Since 2009, Mr. Bentalha has helped sundry companies implement an audit system, resolve issues and improve performance. Disciplines Managerial Economics Business Administration Supply chain management Qualitative Social Research Skills and expertise Management Marketing Management Management studies AuditSupply Chain Supply Chain Management Green Supply Chain Account Management Operations Research Organization and Administration Service Service Operations Management Service Supply Chain Languages English French

Patricia Bernardes is a master's student in Industrial Engineering with emphasis on Decision Support Systems - Universidade Federal Fluminense. Graduated in Industrial Engineering - Universidade Federal Fluminense (2022). Technical degree in Business - FAETEC (2016). Researcher at LabDGE (Laboratory of Design Thinking, Management, and Industrial Engineering), conducting research in the Lean Healthcare area. Former Researcher at the Study and Research Group in Service Engineering - GEPES/UFF, where conducted research in the area of Knowledge Management applied to Engineering and Service Economics. Interested in Lean Thinking in service management, Quality Management in process optimization and waste reduction, Innovation in industrial services, Decision support systems, and Computational Simulation.

Robisom Calado is an Adjunct Professor at the Department of Production Engineering, Universidade Federal Fluminense (UFF), Brazil. He has a postdoctoral degree in Lean Six Sigma and coordinates the LabDGE – Laboratory of Design Thinking, Management and Industrial Engineering at UFF. His current professional activity focuses on teaching and/or research in Industrial Engineering and Management Systems. He currently coordinates the Lean Healthcare Research Project and implementation in 100 Health Emergency Departments, with funding from the Brazilian Ministry of Health. He has over 150 publications and has had over 150 mentors. He has IFIP-APMS publications; IFAC Proceedings, International Journal of Lean Six Sigma and International Journal of Productivity and Performance Management.

Luiz Conrado is a master's student in Production/Industrial Engineering at Fluminense Federal University - UFF(2022) and has a Technician in Industrial Automation - IFRJ (2015). He is a researcher at LabDGE (Laboratory of Design Thinking, Management and Industrial Engineering), currently working as a researcher in a project at the Ministry of Agriculture and Livestock (MAPA).

Ivana Domazet is a Principal Research Fellow at the Institute of Economic Sciences and Professor at the Faculty for Banking, Insurance and Finance, Union University. She teaches courses on Marketing Management, Market Research and Competitiveness Enhancement (postgraduate studies). Her scientific interest refers to: Improving Competitiveness, National Branding, Marketing Research and Strategy, CRM and Strategic Management. She published a numerous papers related to foregoing topics. She is President of Scientific Council at the Institute of Economic Sciences, Vice-president of Board member of the Institute of Economics Sciences, Board member of the Institute of Social Science, member of Serbian Scientific Association of Economists and Serbian Marketing Association.

Pitiphat Joembunthanaphong is an instructor in the field of Software Engineering at the Faculty of Information Technology and Digital Innovation at North Bangkok University. With a solid academic background and a deep understanding of industry standards, Pitiphat specializes in ISO/IEC 29110 and ISO/IEC 15504 (33000) standards. He offers a comprehensive range of services, including consultation, auditing, and training, to assist organizations in improving their processes and ensuring compliance with these standards. In addition to his role as an instructor and standards expert, Pitiphat proudly holds the title of Digital Transformation Consultant (DTD), specializing in digital industry standards like ISO 29110 and ISO/IEC 15504 (33000). His dedication is focused on supporting organizations in their journey towards process improvement and adherence to international standards. Pitiphat is committed to bridging the gap between academia and industry, helping organizations thrive in the ever-evolving digital landscape.

Anitha Kumari is an Assistant Professor in the Department of Business Analytics at GITAM School of Business, GITAM University, Bengaluru. She completed her Ph.D. in Information Systems at the Department of Business Administration, Hindustan Institute of Technology and Science, India. Her Bachelor's degree was in Computer Applications, while she obtained a Master's in Business Administration with a specialisation in finance and systems. Her current research focuses on information systems, blockchain, Fintech, business analytics, and technological innovation. She has 6 years of teaching and research experience.

Darko Marjanović is Senior Research Associate at the Institute of Economic Sciences. He completed his graduate, master, and doctoral studies at the Faculty of Economics in Subotica, University of Novi Sad. He served as a financial director (CFO) in a large trading company BB Trade ad from 2015 to 2018. His current areas of professional interest are competitiveness, FDI and public finance. He has published, as author or co-author, more than 60 scientific papers. He has participated in a few international projects, as well as several research and scientific projects, financed by the Ministry of Education, Science, and Technological Development of the Republic of Serbia and Provincial Secretariat for Science and Technological Development of the Autonomous Province of Vojvodina. He is a member of the Scientific Board at the Institute of Economic Sciences and associate member of the Scientific Society of Economists of Serbia. He was a Vice President of the Scientific Board at the Institute of Economic Sciences, head of the Center for Strategic Cooperation, coordinator of the Macroeconomics Department and editor-in-chief of the international publication SEE-6 Economic Outlook.

Abdelaziz Marzak received his Ph.D. in Computer Science from Mohammed V University - Rabat, National School of Computer Science and Systems Analysis, Rabat, Morocco, 2000. Currently, he is a professor of Computer Science and director of the Information Technology and Modeling Laboratory at Faculty of Science Ben M'sik, Casablanca, Morocco. His research interests include agile software development, metamodeling, the applications of artificial intelligence, software engineering, data mining, educational data mining, machine learning, and the Internet of things.

Soukaina Merzouk received the Master's degree in Information Science and Engineering from Hassan II University - Casablanca Faculty of Science Ben M'sik, Casablanca, Morocco, in 2016 and the Ph.D. degree in Computer Science from Hassan II University - Casablanca Faculty of Science Ben M'sik, Casablanca, Morocco, in 2022. Her research interests include agile software development, metamodeling, Internet of Things, artificial intelligence applications, data mining techniques, Big Data, and machine learning.

Filiz Mizrak is an Assistant Professor holding a Doctorate degree in Management and Strategy from Istanbul Medipol University. She was born on May 12, 1986. She completed her undergraduate studies in American Culture and Literature at Istanbul University in 2009. Later, she pursued her Master's degree in Executive MBA at Bahçeşehir University in 2015. Filiz MIZRAK's passion for research and academia led her to obtain her doctoral degree in Management and Strategy from Istanbul Medipol University in 2021. Currently, she is working as an Assistant Professor at Istanbul Medipol University. Her research interests include strategic management, organizational behavior, and business strategy.

Hop Nguyen currently works at the School of Industrial Engineering and Management, Ho Chi Minh City International University. Nguyen does research in Fuzzy Stochastic Optimization, Optimization for Manufacturing and Supply Chain Systems. His website is: https://iem.hcmiu.edu.vn/nvhop.aaf2162d-9930-4413-879b-959be578c14e

Lam Nguyen was an undergraduate student at the School of Industrial Engineering and Management, Ho Chi Minh City International University, Vietnam.

Ahmad Nazif Noor Kamar is a lecturer for Industrial Technology Management Program at Faculty of Industrial Management, Universiti Malaysia Pahang (UMP). He holds a Master of Science in Industrial Management and Technology from Universiti Kebangsaan Malaysia, Bachelor Degree in Industrial Chemistry from Universiti Sains Malaysia and Diploma in Science from Institut Teknologi MARA. Prior to joining UMP, he had enjoyed a flourishing career, spanning 10 years in the manufacturing industries with key positions as a Production Manager. As production personnel in producing automotive component, he had involved in projects related to process improvement such as Kaizen, Line Balancing, SMED, TPM, FMEA, etc. Since joining UMP in 2010, he has lectured Operations Management, Quality Management, Lean Manufacturing, Manufacturing System, Statistical Process Control, Production Planning and Control courses. Currently he pursues his study in PhD level specializing in production process improvement using computer simulation modeling.

Azim Osman is a senior lecturer in the Industrial Technology Management program at the Faculty of Industrial Management, Universiti Malaysia Pahang (UMP). He holds a diploma and Bachelor's Degree in Engineering (Manufacturing) with Honours, an MBA specializing in engineering management from University Malaysia Perlis (UniMAP), and a Ph.D. in Operations Management from Universiti Utara Malaysia (UUM). His teaching expertise lies in business research methodology, operations management, production planning and control, and industrial quality management. Prior to joining UMP, he worked as a research assistant at UUM. Azim's research interests encompass Lean Management, Quality Management, Change Management, survey methodology, and scale development. His commitment to advancing knowledge is evident through his involvement in over 10 research grants, including university grants, Fundamental Research Grant Scheme (FRGS), Transdisciplinary Research Grant Scheme (TRGS), and external agency grants.

Mampilo Phahlane is a senior lecturer in the school of computing in the information systems department, her research interests include e-goverment, e-health, management sciences and education.

Syed Radzi currently serves as a Lecturer at the Faculty of Industrial Management in the Business Engineering program at Universiti Malaysia Pahang. With extensive management experience in renowned GLC (Government-Linked Companies) organizations, he brings a unique perspective to his academic role. Prior to joining academia, Mr. Syed Radzi held positions such as Service Manager at Sime Darby Auto Hyundai and Planning Engineer in the R&D department of Perusahaan Otomobil Nasional Berhad. Having spent nearly a decade in the corporate sector, he transitioned to the academic arena in 2014. Mr. Syed Radzi holds a PhD in Manufacturing Systems, which he recently completed in 2023. His research interests primarily revolve around lean digital and smart manufacturing, with a focus on leveraging advanced technologies to enhance manufacturing processes. Additionally, he is an active member of the Malaysian Board of Technologies (MBOT) and holds the designation of Professional Technologist, demonstrating his commitment to the field of Manufacturing Technologies and staying updated with industry advancements.

Nawal Sael received her Ph.D. in Computer Science from Hassan II University - Casablanca Faculty of Science Ben M'sik, Casablanca, Morocco, 2013, and her engineer degree in software engineering from ENSIAS, Morocco, in 2002. Currently, she is a professor of Computer Science and a member of the Information Technology and Modeling Laboratory at Faculty of Science Ben M'sik, Casablanca, Morocco. Her research interests include software engineering, data mining, educational data mining, machine learning, the Internet of things, and artificial intelligence.

Deepa Sharma has done Ph.D., MBA in Human Resource Management, currently working as Assistant Professor at MMIM, Maharishi Markandeshwar (Deemed to be University), NAAC Accredited Grade 'A++' University, Mullana, Ambala (Haryana). She has more than 7 years of experience in academics. She has written 45+ research papers for various Scopus and UGC listed referred National & International Journals. And has published two book chapters out of which 1 book chapter is published in Taylor & Francis and has earned 45 citations and an h-index of 4 credentials that may be verified on various research platforms like Google Scholar, SSRN, LinkedIn, and Research gate and 5 papers appear in the Scopus preview. She has actively participated in national and international conferences.

Jadranka Stantić works at Albert Engelma consulting doo, in the position of company director. She completed her doctoral studies at the Josip Juraj Strossmayer University in Osijek, study program European doctoral study. Her scientific interests are related to competitiveness, innovation, EU regional policy, the research and development sector, and programming EU strategic policy. She published a book in the field of public finance, as well as numerous works related to the aforementioned topics. She participated in the development of project proposals and project management activities for projects financed by the programs of the European Commission, TEMPUS, SEE IPA and others. She also participated in the management of national projects financed by the Provincial Secretariat for Economy and Tourism of Serbia, Ministry of Education, Science and Technological Development, i.e. the other one, more than 30 international projects. She is the founder and member of the board of the Innovative Network, the Subotica-Palić Microregion Tourism Cluster Fund, the Agro-Industry Cluster, and the Association of Professional Societies of Subotica.

Index

F

G

H

I

K

L

M

N

O

P

R

S

T

U

V

W

www.ingramcontent.com/pod-product-compliance
Lightning Source LLC
La Vergne TN
LVHW062111300926
849161LV00010B/2427